American Casebook Series
Hornbook Series and Basic Legal Texts
Black Letter Series and Nutshell Series

of

WEST PUBLISHING COMPANY
P.O. Box 64526
St. Paul, Minnesota 55164–0526

Accounting

FARIS' ACCOUNTING AND LAW IN A NUTSHELL, 377 pages, 1984. Softcover. (Text)

FIFLIS, KRIPKE AND FOSTER'S TEACHING MATERIALS ON ACCOUNTING FOR BUSINESS LAWYERS, Third Edition, 838 pages, 1984. (Casebook)

SIEGEL AND SIEGEL'S ACCOUNTING AND FINANCIAL DISCLOSURE: A GUIDE TO BASIC CONCEPTS, 259 pages, 1983. Softcover. (Text)

Administrative Law

BONFIELD AND ASIMOW'S STATE AND FEDERAL ADMINISTRATIVE LAW, 826 pages, 1989. Teacher's Manual available. (Casebook)

GELLHORN AND LEVIN'S ADMINISTRATIVE LAW AND PROCESS IN A NUTSHELL, Third Edition, approximately 420 pages, 1990. Softcover. (Text)

MASHAW AND MERRILL'S CASES AND MATERIALS ON ADMINISTRATIVE LAW—THE AMERICAN PUBLIC LAW SYSTEM, Second Edition, 976 pages, 1985. (Casebook) 1989 Supplement.

ROBINSON, GELLHORN AND BRUFF'S THE ADMINISTRATIVE PROCESS, Third Edition, 978 pages, 1986. (Casebook)

Admiralty

HEALY AND SHARPE'S CASES AND MATERIALS ON ADMIRALTY, Second Edition, 876 pages, 1986. (Casebook)

MARAIST'S ADMIRALTY IN A NUTSHELL, Second Edition, 379 pages, 1988. Softcover. (Text)

SCHOENBAUM'S HORNBOOK ON ADMIRALTY AND MARITIME LAW, Student Edition, 692 pages, 1987 with 1989 pocket part. (Text)

Agency—Partnership

FESSLER'S ALTERNATIVES TO INCORPORATION FOR PERSONS IN QUEST OF PROFIT, Second Edition, 326 pages, 1986. Softcover. Teacher's Manual available. (Casebook)

HENN'S CASES AND MATERIALS ON AGENCY, PARTNERSHIP AND OTHER UNINCORPORATED BUSINESS ENTERPRISES, Second Edition, 733 pages, 1985. Teacher's Manual available. (Casebook)

REUSCHLEIN AND GREGORY'S HORNBOOK ON THE LAW OF AGENCY AND PARTNERSHIP, Second Edition, 683 pages, 1990. (Text)

SELECTED CORPORATION AND PARTNERSHIP STATUTES, RULES AND FORMS. Softcover. 727 pages, 1989.

STEFFEN AND KERR'S CASES ON AGENCY-PARTNERSHIP, Fourth Edition, 859 pages, 1980. (Casebook)

STEFFEN'S AGENCY-PARTNERSHIP IN A NUTSHELL, 364 pages, 1977. Softcover. (Text)

Agricultural Law

MEYER, PEDERSEN, THORSON AND DAVIDSON'S AGRICULTURAL LAW: CASES AND MATERIALS, 931 pages, 1985. Teacher's Manual available. (Casebook)

Alternative Dispute Resolution

KANOWITZ' CASES AND MATERIALS ON ALTERNATIVE DISPUTE RESOLUTION, 1024 pages,

LAW SCHOOL PUBLICATIONS—Continued

Alternative Dispute Resolution—Cont'd
1986. Teacher's Manual available. (Casebook) 1990 Supplement.

RISKIN AND WESTBROOK'S DISPUTE RESOLUTION AND LAWYERS, 468 pages, 1987. Teacher's Manual available. (Casebook)

RISKIN AND WESTBROOK'S DISPUTE RESOLUTION AND LAWYERS, Abridged Edition, 223 pages, 1987. Softcover. Teacher's Manual available. (Casebook)

American Indian Law

CANBY'S AMERICAN INDIAN LAW IN A NUTSHELL, Second Edition, 336 pages, 1988. Softcover. (Text)

GETCHES AND WILKINSON'S CASES AND MATERIALS ON FEDERAL INDIAN LAW, Second Edition, 880 pages, 1986. (Casebook)

Antitrust—see also Regulated Industries, Trade Regulation

FOX AND SULLIVAN'S CASES AND MATERIALS ON ANTITRUST, 935 pages, 1989. Teacher's Manual available. (Casebook)

GELLHORN'S ANTITRUST LAW AND ECONOMICS IN A NUTSHELL, Third Edition, 472 pages, 1986. Softcover. (Text)

HOVENKAMP'S BLACK LETTER ON ANTITRUST, 323 pages, 1986. Softcover. (Review)

HOVENKAMP'S HORNBOOK ON ECONOMICS AND FEDERAL ANTITRUST LAW, Student Edition, 414 pages, 1985. (Text)

OPPENHEIM, WESTON AND MCCARTHY'S CASES AND COMMENTS ON FEDERAL ANTITRUST LAWS, Fourth Edition, 1168 pages, 1981. (Casebook) 1985 Supplement.

POSNER AND EASTERBROOK'S CASES AND ECONOMIC NOTES ON ANTITRUST, Second Edition, 1077 pages, 1981. (Casebook) 1984–85 Supplement.

SULLIVAN'S HORNBOOK OF THE LAW OF ANTITRUST, 886 pages, 1977. (Text)

Appellate Advocacy—see Trial and Appellate Advocacy

Architecture and Engineering Law

SWEET'S LEGAL ASPECTS OF ARCHITECTURE, ENGINEERING AND THE CONSTRUCTION PROCESS, Fourth Edition, 889 pages, 1989. Teacher's Manual available. (Casebook)

Art Law

DUBOFF'S ART LAW IN A NUTSHELL, 335 pages, 1984. Softcover. (Text)

Banking Law

LOVETT'S BANKING AND FINANCIAL INSTITUTIONS LAW IN A NUTSHELL, Second Edition, 464 pages, 1988. Softcover. (Text)

SYMONS AND WHITE'S TEACHING MATERIALS ON BANKING LAW, Second Edition, 993 pages, 1984. Teacher's Manual available. (Casebook) 1987 Supplement.

Business Planning—see also Corporate Finance

PAINTER'S PROBLEMS AND MATERIALS IN BUSINESS PLANNING, Second Edition, 1008 pages, 1984. (Casebook) 1990 Supplement.

Statutory Supplement. *See Selected Corporation and Partnership*

SELECTED CORPORATION AND PARTNERSHIP STATUTES, RULES AND FORMS. 727 pages, 1989. Softcover.

Civil Procedure—see also Federal Jurisdiction and Procedure

AMERICAN BAR ASSOCIATION SECTION OF LITIGATION—READINGS ON ADVERSARIAL JUSTICE: THE AMERICAN APPROACH TO ADJUDICATION, 217 pages, 1988. Softcover. (Coursebook)

CLERMONT'S BLACK LETTER ON CIVIL PROCEDURE, Second Edition, 332 pages, 1988. Softcover. (Review)

COUND, FRIEDENTHAL, MILLER AND SEXTON'S CASES AND MATERIALS ON CIVIL PROCEDURE, Fifth Edition, 1284 pages, 1989. Teacher's Manual available. (Casebook)

COUND, FRIEDENTHAL, MILLER AND SEXTON'S CIVIL PROCEDURE SUPPLEMENT. Approximately 450 pages, 1990. Softcover. (Casebook Supplement)

FEDERAL RULES OF CIVIL PROCEDURE—EDUCATIONAL EDITION. Softcover. Approximately 635 pages, 1990.

FRIEDENTHAL, KANE AND MILLER'S HORNBOOK ON CIVIL PROCEDURE, 876 pages, 1985. (Text)

KANE AND LEVINE'S CIVIL PROCEDURE IN CALIFORNIA: STATE AND FEDERAL 498 pages, 1989. Softcover. (Casebook Supplement)

Civil Procedure—Cont'd

KANE'S CIVIL PROCEDURE IN A NUTSHELL, Second Edition, 306 pages, 1986. Softcover. (Text)

KOFFLER AND REPPY'S HORNBOOK ON COMMON LAW PLEADING, 663 pages, 1969. (Text)

MARCUS, REDISH AND SHERMAN'S CIVIL PROCEDURE: A MODERN APPROACH, 1027 pages, 1989. Teacher's Manual available. (Casebook)

MARCUS AND SHERMAN'S COMPLEX LITIGATION–CASES AND MATERIALS ON ADVANCED CIVIL PROCEDURE, 846 pages, 1985. Teacher's Manual available. (Casebook) 1989 Supplement.

PARK'S COMPUTER-AIDED EXERCISES ON CIVIL PROCEDURE, Second Edition, 167 pages, 1983. Softcover. (Coursebook)

SIEGEL'S HORNBOOK ON NEW YORK PRACTICE, 1011 pages, 1978, with 1987 pocket part. (Text)

Commercial Law

BAILEY AND HAGEDORN'S SECURED TRANSACTIONS IN A NUTSHELL, Third Edition, 390 pages, 1988. Softcover. (Text)

EPSTEIN, MARTIN, HENNING AND NICKLES' BASIC UNIFORM COMMERCIAL CODE TEACHING MATERIALS, Third Edition, 704 pages, 1988. Teacher's Manual available. (Casebook)

HENSON'S HORNBOOK ON SECURED TRANSACTIONS UNDER THE U.C.C., Second Edition, 504 pages, 1979, with 1979 pocket part. (Text)

MURRAY'S COMMERCIAL LAW, PROBLEMS AND MATERIALS, 366 pages, 1975. Teacher's Manual available. Softcover. (Coursebook)

NICKLES' BLACK LETTER ON COMMERCIAL PAPER, 450 pages, 1988. Softcover. (Review)

NICKLES, MATHESON AND DOLAN'S MATERIALS FOR UNDERSTANDING CREDIT AND PAYMENT SYSTEMS, 923 pages, 1987. Teacher's Manual available. (Casebook)

NORDSTROM, MURRAY AND CLOVIS' PROBLEMS AND MATERIALS ON SALES, 515 pages, 1982. (Casebook)

NORDSTROM, MURRAY AND CLOVIS' PROBLEMS AND MATERIALS ON SECURED TRANSACTIONS, 594 pages, 1987. (Casebook)

RUBIN AND COOTER'S THE PAYMENT SYSTEM: CASES, MATERIALS AND ISSUES, 885 pages, 1989. (Casebook)

SELECTED COMMERCIAL STATUTES. Softcover. Approximately 1650 pages, 1990.

SPEIDEL'S BLACK LETTER ON SALES AND SALES FINANCING, 363 pages, 1984. Softcover. (Review)

SPEIDEL, SUMMERS AND WHITE'S COMMERCIAL LAW: TEACHING MATERIALS, Fourth Edition, 1448 pages, 1987. Teacher's Manual available. (Casebook)

SPEIDEL, SUMMERS AND WHITE'S COMMERCIAL PAPER: TEACHING MATERIALS, Fourth Edition, 578 pages, 1987. Reprint from Speidel et al., Commercial Law, Fourth Edition. Teacher's Manual available. (Casebook)

SPEIDEL, SUMMERS AND WHITE'S SALES: TEACHING MATERIALS, Fourth Edition, 804 pages, 1987. Reprint from Speidel et al., Commercial Law, Fourth Edition. Teacher's Manual available. (Casebook)

SPEIDEL, SUMMERS AND WHITE'S SECURED TRANSACTIONS: TEACHING MATERIALS, Fourth Edition, 485 pages, 1987. Reprint from Speidel et al., Commercial Law, Fourth Edition. Teacher's Manual available. (Casebook)

STOCKTON'S SALES IN A NUTSHELL, Second Edition, 370 pages, 1981. Softcover. (Text)

STONE'S UNIFORM COMMERCIAL CODE IN A NUTSHELL, Third Edition, 580 pages, 1989. Softcover. (Text)

WEBER AND SPEIDEL'S COMMERCIAL PAPER IN A NUTSHELL, Third Edition, 404 pages, 1982. Softcover. (Text)

WHITE AND SUMMERS' HORNBOOK ON THE UNIFORM COMMERCIAL CODE, Third Edition, Student Edition, 1386 pages, 1988. (Text)

Community Property

MENNELL AND BOYKOFF'S COMMUNITY PROPERTY IN A NUTSHELL, Second Edition, 432 pages, 1988. Softcover. (Text)

VERRALL AND BIRD'S CASES AND MATERIALS

Community Property—Cont'd

ON CALIFORNIA COMMUNITY PROPERTY, Fifth Edition, 604 pages, 1988. (Casebook)

Comparative Law

BARTON, GIBBS, LI AND MERRYMAN'S LAW IN RADICALLY DIFFERENT CULTURES, 960 pages, 1983. (Casebook)

GLENDON, GORDON AND OSAKWE'S COMPARATIVE LEGAL TRADITIONS: TEXT, MATERIALS AND CASES ON THE CIVIL LAW, COMMON LAW AND SOCIALIST LAW TRADITIONS, 1091 pages, 1985. (Casebook)

GLENDON, GORDON AND OSAKWE'S COMPARATIVE LEGAL TRADITIONS IN A NUTSHELL. 402 pages, 1982. Softcover. (Text)

LANGBEIN'S COMPARATIVE CRIMINAL PROCEDURE: GERMANY, 172 pages, 1977. Softcover. (Casebook)

Computers and Law

MAGGS AND SPROWL'S COMPUTER APPLICATIONS IN THE LAW, 316 pages, 1987. (Coursebook)

MASON'S USING COMPUTERS IN THE LAW: AN INTRODUCTION AND PRACTICAL GUIDE, Second Edition, 288 pages, 1988. Softcover. (Coursebook)

Conflict of Laws

CRAMTON, CURRIE AND KAY'S CASES–COMMENTS–QUESTIONS ON CONFLICT OF LAWS, Fourth Edition, 876 pages, 1987. (Casebook)

HAY'S BLACK LETTER ON CONFLICT OF LAWS, 330 pages, 1989. Softcover. (Review)

SCOLES AND HAY'S HORNBOOK ON CONFLICT OF LAWS, Student Edition, 1085 pages, 1982, with 1988–89 pocket part. (Text)

SEIGEL'S CONFLICTS IN A NUTSHELL, 470 pages, 1982. Softcover. (Text)

Constitutional Law—Civil Rights—see also Foreign Relations and National Security Law

ABERNATHY'S CASES AND MATERIALS ON CIVIL RIGHTS, 660 pages, 1980. (Casebook)

BARRON AND DIENES' BLACK LETTER ON CONSTITUTIONAL LAW, Second Edition, 310 pages, 1987. Softcover. (Review)

BARRON AND DIENES' CONSTITUTIONAL LAW IN A NUTSHELL, 389 pages, 1986. Softcover. (Text)

ENGDAHL'S CONSTITUTIONAL FEDERALISM IN A NUTSHELL, Second Edition, 411 pages, 1987. Softcover. (Text)

FARBER AND SHERRY'S HISTORY OF THE AMERICAN CONSTITUTION, 458 pages, 1990. Softcover. Teacher's Manual available. (Text)

GARVEY AND ALEINIKOFF'S MODERN CONSTITUTIONAL THEORY: A READER, 494 pages, 1989. Softcover. (Reader)

LOCKHART, KAMISAR, CHOPER AND SHIFFRIN'S CONSTITUTIONAL LAW: CASES–COMMENTS–QUESTIONS, Sixth Edition, 1601 pages, 1986. (Casebook) 1990 Supplement.

LOCKHART, KAMISAR, CHOPER AND SHIFFRIN'S THE AMERICAN CONSTITUTION: CASES AND MATERIALS, Sixth Edition, 1260 pages, 1986. Abridged version of Lockhart, et al., Constitutional Law: Cases–Comments–Questions, Sixth Edition. (Casebook) 1990 Supplement.

LOCKHART, KAMISAR, CHOPER AND SHIFFRIN'S CONSTITUTIONAL RIGHTS AND LIBERTIES: CASES AND MATERIALS, Sixth Edition, 1266 pages, 1986. Reprint from Lockhart, et al., Constitutional Law: Cases–Comments–Questions, Sixth Edition. (Casebook) 1990 Supplement.

MARKS AND COOPER'S STATE CONSTITUTIONAL LAW IN A NUTSHELL, 329 pages, 1988. Softcover. (Text)

NOWAK, ROTUNDA AND YOUNG'S HORNBOOK ON CONSTITUTIONAL LAW, Third Edition, 1191 pages, 1986 with 1988 pocket part. (Text)

ROTUNDA'S MODERN CONSTITUTIONAL LAW: CASES AND NOTES, Third Edition, 1085 pages, 1989. (Casebook) 1990 Supplement.

VIEIRA'S CONSTITUTIONAL CIVIL RIGHTS IN A NUTSHELL, Second Edition, 322 pages, 1990. Softcover. (Text)

WILLIAMS' CONSTITUTIONAL ANALYSIS IN A NUTSHELL, 388 pages, 1979. Softcover. (Text)

Consumer Law—see also Commercial Law

EPSTEIN AND NICKLES' CONSUMER LAW IN A NUTSHELL, Second Edition, 418 pages,

Consumer Law—Cont'd
1981. Softcover. (Text)

SELECTED COMMERCIAL STATUTES. Softcover. Approximately 1650 pages, 1990.

SPANOGLE AND ROHNER'S CASES AND MATERIALS ON CONSUMER LAW, 693 pages, 1979. Teacher's Manual available. (Casebook) 1982 Supplement.

Contracts

CALAMARI AND PERILLO'S BLACK LETTER ON CONTRACTS, Second Edition, approximately 450 pages, 1990. Softcover. (Review)

CALAMARI AND PERILLO'S HORNBOOK ON CONTRACTS, Third Edition, 1049 pages, 1987. (Text)

CALAMARI, PERILLO AND BENDER'S CASES AND PROBLEMS ON CONTRACTS, Second Edition, 905 pages, 1989. Teacher's Manual Available. (Casebook)

CORBIN'S TEXT ON CONTRACTS, One Volume Student Edition, 1224 pages, 1952. (Text)

FESSLER AND LOISEAUX'S CASES AND MATERIALS ON CONTRACTS—MORALITY, ECONOMICS AND THE MARKET PLACE, 837 pages, 1982. Teacher's Manual available. (Casebook)

FRIEDMAN'S CONTRACT REMEDIES IN A NUTSHELL, 323 pages, 1981. Softcover. (Text)

FULLER AND EISENBERG'S CASES ON BASIC CONTRACT LAW, Fifth Edition, approximately 1100 pages, 1990. (Casebook)

HAMILTON, RAU AND WEINTRAUB'S CASES AND MATERIALS ON CONTRACTS, 830 pages, 1984. (Casebook)

JACKSON AND BOLLINGER'S CASES ON CONTRACT LAW IN MODERN SOCIETY, Second Edition, 1329 pages, 1980. Teacher's Manual available. (Casebook)

KEYES' GOVERNMENT CONTRACTS IN A NUTSHELL, Second Edition, approximately 530 pages, 1990. Softcover. (Text)

SCHABER AND ROHWER'S CONTRACTS IN A NUTSHELL, Third Edition, approximately 438 pages, 1990. Softcover. (Text)

SUMMERS AND HILLMAN'S CONTRACT AND RELATED OBLIGATION: THEORY, DOCTRINE AND PRACTICE, 1074 pages, 1987. Teacher's Manual available. (Casebook)

Copyright—see Patent and Copyright Law

Corporate Finance

HAMILTON'S CASES AND MATERIALS ON CORPORATION FINANCE, Second Edition, 1221 pages, 1989. (Casebook)

Corporations

HAMILTON'S BLACK LETTER ON CORPORATIONS, Second Edition, 513 pages, 1986. Softcover. (Review)

HAMILTON'S CASES AND MATERIALS ON CORPORATIONS—INCLUDING PARTNERSHIPS AND LIMITED PARTNERSHIPS, Fourth Edition, approximately 1250 pages, 1990. (Casebook) 1990 Statutory Supplement.

HAMILTON'S THE LAW OF CORPORATIONS IN A NUTSHELL, Second Edition, 515 pages, 1987. Softcover. (Text)

HENN'S TEACHING MATERIALS ON THE LAW OF CORPORATIONS, Second Edition, 1204 pages, 1986. Teacher's Manual available. (Casebook)

Statutory Supplement. *See Selected Corporation and Partnership*

HENN AND ALEXANDER'S HORNBOOK ON LAWS OF CORPORATIONS, Third Edition, Student Edition, 1371 pages, 1983, with 1986 pocket part. (Text)

SELECTED CORPORATION AND PARTNERSHIP STATUTES, RULES AND FORMS. Softcover. 727 pages, 1989.

SOLOMON, SCHWARTZ AND BAUMAN'S MATERIALS AND PROBLEMS ON CORPORATIONS: LAW AND POLICY, Second Edition, 1391 pages, 1988. Teacher's Manual available. (Casebook) 1990 Supplement.

Statutory Supplement. *See Selected Corporation and Partnership*

Corrections

KRANTZ' CASES AND MATERIALS ON THE LAW OF CORRECTIONS AND PRISONERS' RIGHTS, Third Edition, 855 pages, 1986. (Casebook) 1988 Supplement.

KRANTZ' THE LAW OF CORRECTIONS AND PRISONERS' RIGHTS IN A NUTSHELL, Third Edition, 407 pages, 1988. Softcover. (Text)

ROBBINS' CASES AND MATERIALS ON POST-CONVICTION REMEDIES, 506 pages, 1982. (Casebook)

Creditors' Rights

BANKRUPTCY CODE, RULES AND OFFICIAL FORMS, LAW SCHOOL EDITION. Approximately 875 pages, 1990. Softcover.

EPSTEIN'S DEBTOR-CREDITOR RELATIONS IN A NUTSHELL, Third Edition, 383 pages, 1986. Softcover. (Text)

EPSTEIN, LANDERS AND NICKLES' CASES AND MATERIALS ON DEBTORS AND CREDITORS, Third Edition, 1059 pages, 1987. Teacher's Manual available. (Casebook)

LOPUCKI'S PLAYER'S MANUAL FOR THE DEBTOR-CREDITOR GAME, 123 pages, 1985. Softcover. (Coursebook)

NICKLES AND EPSTEIN'S BLACK LETTER ON CREDITORS' RIGHTS AND BANKRUPTCY, 576 pages, 1989. (Review)

RIESENFELD'S CASES AND MATERIALS ON CREDITORS' REMEDIES AND DEBTORS' PROTECTION, Fourth Edition, 914 pages, 1987. (Casebook) 1990 Supplement.

WHITE'S CASES AND MATERIALS ON BANKRUPTCY AND CREDITORS' RIGHTS, 812 pages, 1985. Teacher's Manual available. (Casebook) 1987 Supplement.

Criminal Law and Criminal Procedure—see also Corrections, Juvenile Justice

ABRAMS' FEDERAL CRIMINAL LAW AND ITS ENFORCEMENT, 866 pages, 1986. (Casebook) 1988 Supplement.

AMERICAN CRIMINAL JUSTICE PROCESS: SELECTED RULES, STATUTES AND GUIDELINES. 723 pages, 1989. Softcover.

CARLSON'S ADJUDICATION OF CRIMINAL JUSTICE: PROBLEMS AND REFERENCES, 130 pages, 1986. Softcover. (Casebook)

DIX AND SHARLOT'S CASES AND MATERIALS ON CRIMINAL LAW, Third Edition, 846 pages, 1987. (Casebook)

GRANO'S PROBLEMS IN CRIMINAL PROCEDURE, Second Edition, 176 pages, 1981. Teacher's Manual available. Softcover. (Coursebook)

HEYMANN AND KENETY'S THE MURDER TRIAL OF WILBUR JACKSON: A HOMICIDE IN THE FAMILY, Second Edition, 347 pages, 1985. (Coursebook)

ISRAEL, KAMISAR AND LAFAVE'S CRIMINAL PROCEDURE AND THE CONSTITUTION: LEADING SUPREME COURT CASES AND INTRODUCTORY TEXT. Approximately 725 pages, 1990 Edition. Softcover. (Casebook)

ISRAEL AND LAFAVE'S CRIMINAL PROCEDURE—CONSTITUTIONAL LIMITATIONS IN A NUTSHELL, Fourth Edition, 461 pages, 1988. Softcover. (Text)

JOHNSON'S CASES, MATERIALS AND TEXT ON CRIMINAL LAW, Fourth Edition, approximately 790 pages, 1990. Teacher's Manual available. (Casebook)

JOHNSON'S CASES AND MATERIALS ON CRIMINAL PROCEDURE, 859 pages, 1988. (Casebook) 1990 Supplement.

KAMISAR, LAFAVE AND ISRAEL'S MODERN CRIMINAL PROCEDURE: CASES, COMMENTS AND QUESTIONS, Seventh Edition, 1593 pages, 1990. (Casebook) 1990 Supplement.

KAMISAR, LAFAVE AND ISRAEL'S BASIC CRIMINAL PROCEDURE: CASES, COMMENTS AND QUESTIONS, Seventh Edition, 792 pages, 1990. Softcover reprint from Kamisar, et al., Modern Criminal Procedure: Cases, Comments and Questions, Seventh Edition. (Casebook) 1990 Supplement.

LAFAVE'S MODERN CRIMINAL LAW: CASES, COMMENTS AND QUESTIONS, Second Edition, 903 pages, 1988. (Casebook)

LAFAVE AND ISRAEL'S HORNBOOK ON CRIMINAL PROCEDURE, Student Edition, 1142 pages, 1985, with 1989 pocket part. (Text)

LAFAVE AND SCOTT'S HORNBOOK ON CRIMINAL LAW, Second Edition, 918 pages, 1986. (Text)

LANGBEIN'S COMPARATIVE CRIMINAL PROCEDURE: GERMANY, 172 pages, 1977. Softcover. (Casebook)

LOEWY'S CRIMINAL LAW IN A NUTSHELL, Second Edition, 321 pages, 1987. Softcover. (Text)

LOW'S BLACK LETTER ON CRIMINAL LAW, Revised First Edition, approximately 430 pages, 1990. Softcover. (Review)

SALTZBURG'S CASES AND COMMENTARY ON AMERICAN CRIMINAL PROCEDURE, Third Edition, 1302 pages, 1988. Teacher's Manual available. (Casebook) 1990 Supplement.

LAW SCHOOL PUBLICATIONS—Continued

Criminal Law and Criminal Procedure—Cont'd

UVILLER'S THE PROCESSES OF CRIMINAL JUSTICE: INVESTIGATION AND ADJUDICATION, Second Edition, 1384 pages, 1979. (Casebook) 1979 Statutory Supplement. 1986 Update.

VORENBERG'S CASES ON CRIMINAL LAW AND PROCEDURE, Second Edition, 1088 pages, 1981. Teacher's Manual available. (Casebook) 1990 Supplement.

Decedents' Estates—see Trusts and Estates

Domestic Relations

CLARK'S HORNBOOK ON DOMESTIC RELATIONS, Second Edition, Student Edition, 1050 pages, 1988. (Text)

CLARK AND GLOWINSKY'S CASES AND PROBLEMS ON DOMESTIC RELATIONS, Fourth Edition. Approximately 1125 pages, 1990. Teacher's Manual available. (Casebook)

KRAUSE'S BLACK LETTER ON FAMILY LAW, 314 pages, 1988. Softcover. (Review)

KRAUSE'S CASES, COMMENTS AND QUESTIONS ON FAMILY LAW, Third Edition, 1433 pages, 1990. (Casebook)

KRAUSE'S FAMILY LAW IN A NUTSHELL, Second Edition, 444 pages, 1986. Softcover. (Text)

KRAUSKOPF'S CASES ON PROPERTY DIVISION AT MARRIAGE DISSOLUTION, 250 pages, 1984. Softcover. (Casebook)

Economics, Law and—see also Antitrust, Regulated Industries

GOETZ' CASES AND MATERIALS ON LAW AND ECONOMICS, 547 pages, 1984. (Casebook)

MALLOY'S LAW AND ECONOMICS: A COMPARATIVE APPROACH TO THEORY AND PRACTICE, Approximately 152 pages, 1990. Softcover. (Text)

Education Law

ALEXANDER AND ALEXANDER'S THE LAW OF SCHOOLS, STUDENTS AND TEACHERS IN A NUTSHELL, 409 pages, 1984. Softcover. (Text)

Employment Discrimination—see also Women and the Law

ESTREICHER AND HARPER'S CASES AND MATERIALS ON THE LAW GOVERNING THE EMPLOYMENT RELATIONSHIP, 962 pages, 1990. Teacher's Manual available. (Casebook) Statutory Supplement.

JONES, MURPHY AND BELTON'S CASES AND MATERIALS ON DISCRIMINATION IN EMPLOYMENT, (The Labor Law Group). Fifth Edition, 1116 pages, 1987. (Casebook) 1990 Supplement.

PLAYER'S FEDERAL LAW OF EMPLOYMENT DISCRIMINATION IN A NUTSHELL, Second Edition, 402 pages, 1981. Softcover. (Text)

PLAYER'S HORNBOOK ON EMPLOYMENT DISCRIMINATION LAW, Student Edition, 708 pages, 1988. (Text)

PLAYER, SHOBEN AND LIEBERWITZ' CASES AND MATERIALS ON EMPLOYMENT DISCRIMINATION LAW, Approximately 810 pages, 1990. (Casebook)

Energy and Natural Resources Law—see also Oil and Gas

LAITOS' CASES AND MATERIALS ON NATURAL RESOURCES LAW, 938 pages, 1985. Teacher's Manual available. (Casebook)

SELECTED ENVIRONMENTAL LAW STATUTES—EDUCATIONAL EDITION. Softcover. Approximately 1040 pages, 1990.

Environmental Law—see also Energy and Natural Resources Law; Sea, Law of

BONINE AND MCGARITY'S THE LAW OF ENVIRONMENTAL PROTECTION: CASES—LEGISLATION—POLICIES, 1076 pages, 1984. Teacher's Manual available. (Casebook)

FINDLEY AND FARBER'S CASES AND MATERIALS ON ENVIRONMENTAL LAW, Second Edition, 813 pages, 1985. (Casebook) 1988 Supplement.

FINDLEY AND FARBER'S ENVIRONMENTAL LAW IN A NUTSHELL, Second Edition, 367 pages, 1988. Softcover. (Text)

RODGERS' HORNBOOK ON ENVIRONMENTAL LAW, 956 pages, 1977, with 1984 pocket part. (Text)

SELECTED ENVIRONMENTAL LAW STATUTES—EDUCATIONAL EDITION. Softcover. Approximately 1040 pages, 1990.

Equity—see Remedies

Estate Planning—see also Trusts and Estates; Taxation—Estate and Gift

LYNN'S AN INTRODUCTION TO ESTATE PLANNING IN A NUTSHELL, Third Edition, 370 pages, 1983. Softcover. (Text)

Evidence

BROUN AND BLAKEY'S BLACK LETTER ON EVIDENCE, 269 pages, 1984. Softcover. (Review)

BROUN, MEISENHOLDER, STRONG AND MOSTELLER'S PROBLEMS IN EVIDENCE, Third Edition, 238 pages, 1988. Teacher's Manual available. Softcover. (Coursebook)

CLEARY, STRONG, BROUN AND MOSTELLER'S CASES AND MATERIALS ON EVIDENCE, Fourth Edition, 1060 pages, 1988. (Casebook)

FEDERAL RULES OF EVIDENCE FOR UNITED STATES COURTS AND MAGISTRATES. Softcover. Approximately 380 pages, 1990.

GRAHAM'S FEDERAL RULES OF EVIDENCE IN A NUTSHELL, Second Edition, 473 pages, 1987. Softcover. (Text)

LEMPERT AND SALTZBURG'S A MODERN APPROACH TO EVIDENCE: TEXT, PROBLEMS, TRANSCRIPTS AND CASES, Second Edition, 1232 pages, 1983. Teacher's Manual available. (Casebook)

LILLY'S AN INTRODUCTION TO THE LAW OF EVIDENCE, Second Edition, 585 pages, 1987. (Text)

MCCORMICK, SUTTON AND WELLBORN'S CASES AND MATERIALS ON EVIDENCE, Sixth Edition, 1067 pages, 1987. (Casebook)

MCCORMICK'S HORNBOOK ON EVIDENCE, Third Edition, Student Edition, 1156 pages, 1984, with 1987 pocket part. (Text)

ROTHSTEIN'S EVIDENCE IN A NUTSHELL: STATE AND FEDERAL RULES, Second Edition, 514 pages, 1981. Softcover. (Text)

Federal Jurisdiction and Procedure

CURRIE'S CASES AND MATERIALS ON FEDERAL COURTS, Fourth Edition, approximately 1125 pages, 1990. (Casebook)

CURRIE'S FEDERAL JURISDICTION IN A NUTSHELL, Third Edition, approximately 260 pages, 1990. Softcover. (Text)

FEDERAL RULES OF CIVIL PROCEDURE—EDUCATIONAL EDITION. Softcover. Approximately 635 pages, 1990.

REDISH'S BLACK LETTER ON FEDERAL JURISDICTION, 219 pages, 1985. Softcover. (Review)

REDISH'S CASES, COMMENTS AND QUESTIONS ON FEDERAL COURTS, Second Edition, 1122 pages, 1989. (Casebook) 1990 Supplement.

VETRI AND MERRILL'S FEDERAL COURTS PROBLEMS AND MATERIALS, Second Edition, 232 pages, 1984. Softcover. (Coursebook)

WRIGHT'S HORNBOOK ON FEDERAL COURTS, Fourth Edition, Student Edition, 870 pages, 1983. (Text)

Foreign Relations and National Security Law

FRANCK AND GLENNON'S FOREIGN RELATIONS AND NATIONAL SECURITY LAW, 941 pages, 1987. (Casebook)

Future Interests—see Trusts and Estates

Health Law—see Medicine, Law and

Human Rights—see International Law

Immigration Law

ALEINIKOFF AND MARTIN'S IMMIGRATION PROCESS AND POLICY, Second Edition, approximately 1100 pages, October, 1990 (Casebook)

Statutory Supplement. *See Immigration and Nationality Laws*

IMMIGRATION AND NATIONALITY LAWS OF THE UNITED STATES: SELECTED STATUTES, REGULATIONS AND FORMS. Softcover. Approximately 400 pages, 1990.

WEISSBRODT'S IMMIGRATION LAW AND PROCEDURE IN A NUTSHELL, Second Edition, 438 pages, 1989, Softcover. (Text)

Indian Law—see American Indian Law

Insurance Law

DEVINE AND TERRY'S PROBLEMS IN INSURANCE LAW, 240 pages, 1989. Softcover. Teacher's Manual available. (Course book)

DOBBYN'S INSURANCE LAW IN A NUTSHELL, Second Edition, 316 pages, 1989. Softcover. (Text)

KEETON'S CASES ON BASIC INSURANCE LAW,

Insurance Law—Cont'd

Second Edition, 1086 pages, 1977. Teacher's Manual available. (Casebook)

KEETON'S COMPUTER-AIDED AND WORKBOOK EXERCISES ON INSURANCE LAW, 255 pages, 1990. Softcover. (Coursebook)

KEETON AND WIDISS' INSURANCE LAW, Student Edition, 1359 pages, 1988. (Text)

WIDISS AND KEETON'S COURSE SUPPLEMENT TO KEETON AND WIDISS' INSURANCE LAW, 502 pages, 1988. Softcover. (Casebook)

WIDISS' INSURANCE: MATERIALS ON FUNDAMENTAL PRINCIPLES, LEGAL DOCTRINES AND REGULATORY ACTS, 1186 pages, 1989. (Casebook)

YORK AND WHELAN'S CASES, MATERIALS AND PROBLEMS ON GENERAL PRACTICE INSURANCE LAW, Second Edition, 787 pages, 1988. Teacher's Manual available. (Casebook)

International Law—see also Sea, Law of

BUERGENTHAL'S INTERNATIONAL HUMAN RIGHTS IN A NUTSHELL, 283 pages, 1988. Softcover. (Text)

BUERGENTHAL AND MAIER'S PUBLIC INTERNATIONAL LAW IN A NUTSHELL, Second Edition, 275 pages, 1990. Softcover. (Text)

FOLSOM, GORDON AND SPANOGLE'S INTERNATIONAL BUSINESS TRANSACTIONS—A PROBLEM-ORIENTED COURSEBOOK, 1160 pages, 1986. Teacher's Manual available. (Casebook) 1989 Documents Supplement.

FOLSOM, GORDON AND SPANOGLE'S INTERNATIONAL BUSINESS TRANSACTIONS IN A NUTSHELL, Third Edition, 509 pages, 1988. Softcover. (Text)

HENKIN, PUGH, SCHACHTER AND SMIT'S CASES AND MATERIALS ON INTERNATIONAL LAW, Second Edition, 1517 pages, 1987. (Casebook) Documents Supplement.

JACKSON AND DAVEY'S CASES, MATERIALS AND TEXT ON LEGAL PROBLEMS OF INTERNATIONAL ECONOMIC RELATIONS, Second Edition, 1269 pages, 1986. (Casebook) 1989 Documents Supplement.

KIRGIS' INTERNATIONAL ORGANIZATIONS IN THEIR LEGAL SETTING, 1016 pages, 1977. Teacher's Manual available. (Casebook) 1981 Supplement.

WESTON, FALK AND D'AMATO'S INTERNATIONAL LAW AND WORLD ORDER—A PROBLEM-ORIENTED COURSEBOOK, Second Edition, approximately 1305 pages, 1990. Teacher's Manual available. (Casebook) Documents Supplement.

Interviewing and Counseling

BINDER AND PRICE'S LEGAL INTERVIEWING AND COUNSELING, 232 pages, 1977. Teacher's Manual available. Softcover. (Coursebook)

BINDER, BERGMAN AND PRICE'S LAWYERS AS COUNSELORS: A CLIENT CENTERED APPROACH, Approximately 400 pages, October, 1990 Pub. Softcover. (Coursebook)

SHAFFER AND ELKINS' LEGAL INTERVIEWING AND COUNSELING IN A NUTSHELL, Second Edition, 487 pages, 1987. Softcover. (Text)

Introduction to Law—see Legal Method and Legal System

Introduction to Law Study

HEGLAND'S INTRODUCTION TO THE STUDY AND PRACTICE OF LAW IN A NUTSHELL, 418 pages, 1983. Softcover. (Text)

KINYON'S INTRODUCTION TO LAW STUDY AND LAW EXAMINATIONS IN A NUTSHELL, 389 pages, 1971. Softcover. (Text)

Judicial Process—see Legal Method and Legal System

Jurisprudence

CHRISTIE'S JURISPRUDENCE—TEXT AND READINGS ON THE PHILOSOPHY OF LAW, 1056 pages, 1973. (Casebook)

Juvenile Justice

FOX'S CASES AND MATERIALS ON MODERN JUVENILE JUSTICE, Second Edition, 960 pages, 1981. (Casebook)

FOX'S JUVENILE COURTS IN A NUTSHELL, Third Edition, 291 pages, 1984. Softcover. (Text)

Labor and Employment Law—see also Employment Discrimination, Social Legislation

FINKIN, GOLDMAN AND SUMMERS' LEGAL PROTECTION OF INDIVIDUAL EMPLOYEES, (The La-

Labor and Employment Law—Cont'd
bor Law Group). 1164 pages, 1989. (Casebook)

GORMAN'S BASIC TEXT ON LABOR LAW—UNIONIZATION AND COLLECTIVE BARGAINING, 914 pages, 1976. (Text)

LESLIE'S LABOR LAW IN A NUTSHELL, Second Edition, 397 pages, 1986. Softcover. (Text)

NOLAN'S LABOR ARBITRATION LAW AND PRACTICE IN A NUTSHELL, 358 pages, 1979. Softcover. (Text)

OBERER, HANSLOWE, ANDERSEN AND HEINSZ' CASES AND MATERIALS ON LABOR LAW—COLLECTIVE BARGAINING IN A FREE SOCIETY, Third Edition, 1163 pages, 1986. (Casebook) Statutory Supplement.

RABIN, SILVERSTEIN AND SCHATZKI'S LABOR AND EMPLOYMENT LAW: PROBLEMS, CASES AND MATERIALS IN THE LAW OF WORK, (The Labor Law Group). 1014 pages, 1988. Teacher's Manual available. (Casebook) 1988 Statutory Supplement.

Land Finance—Property Security—see Real Estate Transactions

Land Use

CALLIES AND FREILICH'S CASES AND MATERIALS ON LAND USE, 1233 pages, 1986. (Casebook) 1988 Supplement.

HAGMAN AND JUERGENSMEYER'S HORNBOOK ON URBAN PLANNING AND LAND DEVELOPMENT CONTROL LAW, Second Edition, Student Edition, 680 pages, 1986. (Text)

WRIGHT AND GITELMAN'S CASES AND MATERIALS ON LAND USE, Third Edition, 1300 pages, 1982. Teacher's Manual available. (Casebook) 1987 Supplement.

WRIGHT AND WRIGHT'S LAND USE IN A NUTSHELL, Second Edition, 356 pages, 1985. Softcover. (Text)

Legal History—see also Legal Method and Legal System

PRESSER AND ZAINALDIN'S CASES AND MATERIALS ON LAW AND JURISPRUDENCE IN AMERICAN HISTORY, Second Edition, 1092 pages, 1989. Teacher's Manual available. (Casebook)

Legal Method and Legal System—see also Legal Research, Legal Writing

ALDISERT'S READINGS, MATERIALS AND CASES IN THE JUDICIAL PROCESS, 948 pages, 1976. (Casebook)

BERCH AND BERCH'S INTRODUCTION TO LEGAL METHOD AND PROCESS, 550 pages, 1985. Teacher's Manual available. (Casebook)

BODENHEIMER, OAKLEY AND LOVE'S READINGS AND CASES ON AN INTRODUCTION TO THE ANGLO-AMERICAN LEGAL SYSTEM, Second Edition, 166 pages, 1988. Softcover. (Casebook)

DAVIES AND LAWRY'S INSTITUTIONS AND METHODS OF THE LAW—INTRODUCTORY TEACHING MATERIALS, 547 pages, 1982. Teacher's Manual available. (Casebook)

DVORKIN, HIMMELSTEIN AND LESNICK'S BECOMING A LAWYER: A HUMANISTIC PERSPECTIVE ON LEGAL EDUCATION AND PROFESSIONALISM, 211 pages, 1981. Softcover. (Text)

KEETON'S JUDGING, 842 pages, 1990. Softcover. (Coursebook)

KELSO AND KELSO'S STUDYING LAW: AN INTRODUCTION, 587 pages, 1984. (Coursebook)

KEMPIN'S HISTORICAL INTRODUCTION TO ANGLO-AMERICAN LAW IN A NUTSHELL, Third Edition, approximately 302 pages, 1990. Softcover. (Text)

REYNOLDS' JUDICIAL PROCESS IN A NUTSHELL, 292 pages, 1980. Softcover. (Text)

Legal Research

COHEN'S LEGAL RESEARCH IN A NUTSHELL, Fourth Edition, 452 pages, 1985. Softcover. (Text)

COHEN, BERRING AND OLSON'S HOW TO FIND THE LAW, Ninth Edition, 716 pages, 1989. (Text)

COHEN, BERRING AND OLSON'S FINDING THE LAW, 570 pages, 1989. Softcover reprint from Cohen, Berring and Olson's How to Find the Law, Ninth Edition. (Coursebook)

Legal Research Exercises, 3rd Ed., for use with Cohen, Berring and Olson, 229 pages, 1989. Teacher's Manual available.

ROMBAUER'S LEGAL PROBLEM SOLVING—

LAW SCHOOL PUBLICATIONS—Continued

Legal Research—Cont'd

ANALYSIS, RESEARCH AND WRITING, Fourth Edition, 424 pages, 1983. Teacher's Manual with problems available. (Coursebook)

STATSKY'S LEGAL RESEARCH AND WRITING, Third Edition, 257 pages, 1986. Softcover. (Coursebook)

TEPLY'S LEGAL RESEARCH AND CITATION, Third Edition, 472 pages, 1989. Softcover. (Coursebook)

   Student Library Exercises, 3rd ed., 391 pages, 1989. Answer Key available.

Legal Writing

CHILD'S DRAFTING LEGAL DOCUMENTS: MATERIALS AND PROBLEMS, 286 pages, 1988. Softcover. Teacher's Manual available. (Coursebook)

DICKERSON'S MATERIALS ON LEGAL DRAFTING, 425 pages, 1981. Teacher's Manual available. (Coursebook)

FELSENFELD AND SIEGEL'S WRITING CONTRACTS IN PLAIN ENGLISH, 290 pages, 1981. Softcover. (Text)

GOPEN'S WRITING FROM A LEGAL PERSPECTIVE, 225 pages, 1981. (Text)

MELLINKOFF'S LEGAL WRITING—SENSE AND NONSENSE, 242 pages, 1982. Softcover. Teacher's Manual available. (Text)

PRATT'S LEGAL WRITING: A SYSTEMATIC APPROACH, 422 pages, 1989. Teacher's Manual available. (Coursebook)

RAY AND RAMSFIELD'S LEGAL WRITING: GETTING IT RIGHT AND GETTING IT WRITTEN, 250 pages, 1987. Softcover. (Text)

SQUIRES AND ROMBAUER'S LEGAL WRITING IN A NUTSHELL, 294 pages, 1982. Softcover. (Text)

STATSKY AND WERNET'S CASE ANALYSIS AND FUNDAMENTALS OF LEGAL WRITING, Third Edition, 424 pages, 1989. Teacher's Manual available. (Text)

TEPLY'S LEGAL WRITING, ANALYSIS AND ORAL ARGUMENT, 576 pages, 1990. Softcover. Teacher's Manual available. (Coursebook)

WEIHOFEN'S LEGAL WRITING STYLE, Second Edition, 332 pages, 1980. (Text)

Legislation

DAVIES' LEGISLATIVE LAW AND PROCESS IN A NUTSHELL, Second Edition, 346 pages, 1986. Softcover. (Text)

ESKRIDGE AND FRICKEY'S CASES AND MATERIALS ON LEGISLATION: STATUTES AND THE CREATION OF PUBLIC POLICY, 937 pages, 1988. Teacher's Manual available. (Casebook) 1990 Supplement.

NUTTING AND DICKERSON'S CASES AND MATERIALS ON LEGISLATION, Fifth Edition, 744 pages, 1978. (Casebook)

STATSKY'S LEGISLATIVE ANALYSIS AND DRAFTING, Second Edition, 217 pages, 1984. Teacher's Manual available. (Text)

Local Government

FRUG'S CASES AND MATERIALS ON LOCAL GOVERNMENT LAW, 1005 pages, 1988. (Casebook)

MCCARTHY'S LOCAL GOVERNMENT LAW IN A NUTSHELL, Third Edition, approximately 400 pages, 1990. Softcover. (Text)

REYNOLDS' HORNBOOK ON LOCAL GOVERNMENT LAW, 860 pages, 1982, with 1990 pocket part. (Text)

VALENTE'S CASES AND MATERIALS ON LOCAL GOVERNMENT LAW, Third Edition, 1010 pages, 1987. Teacher's Manual available. (Casebook) 1989 Supplement.

Mass Communication Law

GILLMOR, BARRON, SIMON AND TERRY'S CASES AND COMMENT ON MASS COMMUNICATION LAW, Fifth Edition, 947 pages, 1990. (Casebook)

GINSBURG'S REGULATION OF BROADCASTING: LAW AND POLICY TOWARDS RADIO, TELEVISION AND CABLE COMMUNICATIONS, 741 pages, 1979 (Casebook) 1983 Supplement.

ZUCKMAN, GAYNES, CARTER AND DEE'S MASS COMMUNICATIONS LAW IN A NUTSHELL, Third Edition, 538 pages, 1988. Softcover. (Text)

Medicine, Law and

FURROW, JOHNSON, JOST AND SCHWARTZ' HEALTH LAW: CASES, MATERIALS AND PROBLEMS, 1005 pages, 1987. Teacher's Manual available. (Casebook) 1989 Supplement.

HALL AND ELLMAN'S HEALTH CARE LAW AND

Medicine, Law and—Cont'd

Ethics in a Nutshell, 401 pages, 1990. Softcover (Text)

King's The Law of Medical Malpractice in a Nutshell, Second Edition, 342 pages, 1986. Softcover. (Text)

Shapiro and Spece's Cases, Materials and Problems on Bioethics and Law, 892 pages, 1981. (Casebook)

Sharpe, Boumil, Fiscina and Head's Cases and Materials on Medical Liability, Approximately 500 pages, September, 1990 Pub. (Casebook)

Military Law

Shanor and Terrell's Military Law in a Nutshell, 378 pages, 1980. Softcover. (Text)

Mortgages—see Real Estate Transactions

Natural Resources Law—see Energy and Natural Resources Law, Environmental Law

Negotiation

Gifford's Legal Negotiation: Theory and Applications, 225 pages, 1989. Softcover. (Text)

Williams' Legal Negotiation and Settlement, 207 pages, 1983. Softcover. Teacher's Manual available. (Coursebook)

Office Practice—see also Computers and Law, Interviewing and Counseling, Negotiation

Hegland's Trial and Practice Skills in a Nutshell, 346 pages, 1978. Softcover (Text)

Strong and Clark's Law Office Management, 424 pages, 1974. (Casebook)

Oil and Gas—see also Energy and Natural Resources Law

Hemingway's Hornbook on Oil and Gas, Second Edition, Student Edition, 543 pages, 1983, with 1989 pocket part. (Text)

Kuntz, Lowe, Anderson and Smith's Cases and Materials on Oil and Gas Law, 857 pages, 1986. Teacher's Manual available. (Casebook) Forms Manual. Revised.

Lowe's Oil and Gas Law in a Nutshell, Second Edition, 465 pages, 1988. Softcover. (Text)

Partnership—see Agency—Partnership

Patent and Copyright Law

Choate, Francis and Collins' Cases and Materials on Patent Law, Including Trade Secrets, Copyrights, Trademarks, Third Edition, 1009 pages, 1987. (Casebook)

Miller and Davis' Intellectual Property—Patents, Trademarks and Copyright in a Nutshell, Second Edition, approximately 440 pages, 1990. Softcover. (Text)

Nimmer's Cases and Materials on Copyright and Other Aspects of Entertainment Litigation Illustrated—Including Unfair Competition, Defamation and Privacy, Third Edition, 1025 pages, 1985. (Casebook) 1989 Supplement.

Products Liability

Fischer and Powers' Cases and Materials on Products Liability, 685 pages, 1988. Teacher's Manual available. (Casebook)

Noel and Phillips' Cases on Products Liability, Second Edition, 821 pages, 1982. (Casebook)

Phillips' Products Liability in a Nutshell, Third Edition, 307 pages, 1988. Softcover. (Text)

Professional Responsibility

Aronson, Devine and Fisch's Problems, Cases and Materials in Professional Responsibility, 745 pages, 1985. Teacher's Manual available. (Casebook)

Aronson and Weckstein's Professional Responsibility in a Nutshell, 399 pages, 1980. Softcover. (Text)

Mellinkoff's The Conscience of a Lawyer, 304 pages, 1973. (Text)

Pirsig and Kirwin's Cases and Materials on Professional Responsibility, Fourth Edition, 603 pages, 1984. Teacher's Manual available. (Casebook)

Rotunda's Black Letter on Professional Responsibility, Second Edition, 414 pages, 1988. Softcover. (Review)

Schwartz and Wydick's Problems in Le-

LAW SCHOOL PUBLICATIONS—Continued

Professional Responsibility—Cont'd

GAL ETHICS, Second Edition, 341 pages, 1988. (Coursebook)

SELECTED STATUTES, RULES AND STANDARDS ON THE LEGAL PROFESSION. Softcover. Approximately 600 pages, 1990.

SMITH AND MALLEN'S PREVENTING LEGAL MALPRACTICE, 264 pages, 1989. Reprint from Mallen and Smith's Legal Malpractice, Third Edition. (Text)

SUTTON AND DZIENKOWSKI'S CASES AND MATERIALS ON THE PROFESSIONAL RESPONSIBILITY FOR LAWYERS, 839 pages, 1989. Teacher's Manual available. (Casebook)

WOLFRAM'S HORNBOOK ON MODERN LEGAL ETHICS, Student Edition, 1120 pages, 1986. (Text)

Property—see also Real Estate Transactions, Land Use, Trusts and Estates

BERNHARDT'S BLACK LETTER ON PROPERTY, 318 pages, 1983. Softcover. (Review)

BERNHARDT'S REAL PROPERTY IN A NUTSHELL, Second Edition, 448 pages, 1981. Softcover. (Text)

BOYER'S SURVEY OF THE LAW OF PROPERTY, Third Edition, 766 pages, 1981. (Text)

BROWDER, CUNNINGHAM, NELSON, STOEBUCK AND WHITMAN'S CASES ON BASIC PROPERTY LAW, Fifth Edition, 1386 pages, 1989. Teacher's Manual available. (Casebook)

BRUCE, ELY AND BOSTICK'S CASES AND MATERIALS ON MODERN PROPERTY LAW, Second Edition, 953 pages, 1989. Teacher's Manual available. (Casebook)

BURKE'S PERSONAL PROPERTY IN A NUTSHELL, 322 pages, 1983. Softcover. (Text)

CUNNINGHAM, STOEBUCK AND WHITMAN'S HORNBOOK ON THE LAW OF PROPERTY, Student Edition, 916 pages, 1984, with 1987 pocket part. (Text)

DONAHUE, KAUPER AND MARTIN'S CASES ON PROPERTY, Second Edition, 1362 pages, 1983. Teacher's Manual available. (Casebook)

HILL'S LANDLORD AND TENANT LAW IN A NUTSHELL, Second Edition, 311 pages, 1986. Softcover. (Text)

KURTZ AND HOVENKAMP'S CASES AND MATERIALS ON AMERICAN PROPERTY LAW, 1296 pages, 1987. Teacher's Manual available. (Casebook) 1988 Supplement.

MOYNIHAN'S INTRODUCTION TO REAL PROPERTY, Second Edition, 239 pages, 1988. (Text)

Psychiatry, Law and

REISNER AND SLOBOGIN'S LAW AND THE MENTAL HEALTH SYSTEM, CIVIL AND CRIMINAL ASPECTS, Second Edition, approximately 1127 pages, 1990. (Casebook)

Real Estate Transactions

BRUCE'S REAL ESTATE FINANCE IN A NUTSHELL, Second Edition, 262 pages, 1985. Softcover. (Text)

MAXWELL, RIESENFELD, HETLAND AND WARREN'S CASES ON CALIFORNIA SECURITY TRANSACTIONS IN LAND, Third Edition, 728 pages, 1984. (Casebook)

NELSON AND WHITMAN'S BLACK LETTER ON LAND TRANSACTIONS AND FINANCE, Second Edition, 466 pages, 1988. Softcover. (Review)

NELSON AND WHITMAN'S CASES ON REAL ESTATE TRANSFER, FINANCE AND DEVELOPMENT, Third Edition, 1184 pages, 1987. (Casebook)

NELSON AND WHITMAN'S HORNBOOK ON REAL ESTATE FINANCE LAW, Second Edition, 941 pages, 1985 with 1989 pocket part. (Text)

Regulated Industries—see also Mass Communication Law, Banking Law

GELLHORN AND PIERCE'S REGULATED INDUSTRIES IN A NUTSHELL, Second Edition, 389 pages, 1987. Softcover. (Text)

MORGAN, HARRISON AND VERKUIL'S CASES AND MATERIALS ON ECONOMIC REGULATION OF BUSINESS, Second Edition, 666 pages, 1985. (Casebook)

Remedies

DOBBS' HORNBOOK ON REMEDIES, 1067 pages, 1973. (Text)

DOBBS' PROBLEMS IN REMEDIES. 137 pages, 1974. Teacher's Manual available. Softcover. (Coursebook)

DOBBYN'S INJUNCTIONS IN A NUTSHELL, 264 pages, 1974. Softcover. (Text)

Remedies—Cont'd

FRIEDMAN'S CONTRACT REMEDIES IN A NUTSHELL, 323 pages, 1981. Softcover. (Text)

LEAVELL, LOVE AND NELSON'S CASES AND MATERIALS ON EQUITABLE REMEDIES, RESTITUTION AND DAMAGES, Fourth Edition, 1111 pages, 1986. Teacher's Manual available. (Casebook)

McCORMICK'S HORNBOOK ON DAMAGES, 811 pages, 1935. (Text)

O'CONNELL'S REMEDIES IN A NUTSHELL, Second Edition, 320 pages, 1985. Softcover. (Text)

SCHOENBROD, MACBETH, LEVINE AND JUNG'S CASES AND MATERIALS ON REMEDIES: PUBLIC AND PRIVATE, Approximately 807 pages, 1990. Teacher's Manual available. (Casebook)

YORK, BAUMAN AND RENDLEMAN'S CASES AND MATERIALS ON REMEDIES, Fourth Edition, 1029 pages, 1985. Teacher's Manual available. (Casebook)

Sea, Law of

SOHN AND GUSTAFSON'S THE LAW OF THE SEA IN A NUTSHELL, 264 pages, 1984. Softcover. (Text)

Securities Regulation

HAZEN'S HORNBOOK ON THE LAW OF SECURITIES REGULATION, Second Edition, Student Edition, approximately 1000 pages, 1990. (Text)

RATNER'S MATERIALS ON SECURITIES REGULATION, Third Edition, 1000 pages, 1986. Teacher's Manual available. (Casebook) 1989 Supplement.

Statutory Supplement. *See Selected Securities Regulation*

RATNER'S SECURITIES REGULATION IN A NUTSHELL, Third Edition, 316 pages, 1988. Softcover. (Text)

SELECTED STATUTES, REGULATIONS, RULES, DOCUMENTS AND FORMS ON SECURITIES REGULATION. Softcover. 1272 pages, 1990.

Social Legislation

HOOD, HARDY AND LEWIS' WORKERS' COMPENSATION AND EMPLOYEE PROTECTION LAWS IN A NUTSHELL, Second Edition, 361 pages, 1990. Softcover. (Text)

LAFRANCE'S WELFARE LAW: STRUCTURE AND ENTITLEMENT IN A NUTSHELL, 455 pages, 1979. Softcover. (Text)

MALONE, PLANT AND LITTLE'S CASES ON WORKERS' COMPENSATION AND EMPLOYMENT RIGHTS, Second Edition, 951 pages, 1980. Teacher's Manual available. (Casebook)

Sports Law

SCHUBERT, SMITH AND TRENTADUE'S SPORTS LAW, 395 pages, 1986. (Text)

Tax Practice and Procedure

GARBIS, STRUNTZ AND RUBIN'S CASES AND MATERIALS ON TAX PROCEDURE AND TAX FRAUD, Second Edition, 687 pages, 1987. (Casebook)

MORGAN'S TAX PROCEDURE AND TAX FRAUD IN A NUTSHELL, Approximately 382 pages, 1990. Softcover. (Text)

Taxation—Corporate

KAHN AND GANN'S CORPORATE TAXATION, Third Edition, 980 pages, 1989. Teacher's Manual available. (Casebook)

WEIDENBRUCH AND BURKE'S FEDERAL INCOME TAXATION OF CORPORATIONS AND STOCKHOLDERS IN A NUTSHELL, Third Edition, 309 pages, 1989. Softcover. (Text)

Taxation—Estate & Gift—see also Estate Planning, Trusts and Estates

McNULTY'S FEDERAL ESTATE AND GIFT TAXATION IN A NUTSHELL, Fourth Edition, 496 pages, 1989. Softcover. (Text)

PENNELL'S CASES AND MATERIALS ON INCOME TAXATION OF TRUSTS, ESTATES, GRANTORS AND BENEFICIARIES, 460 pages, 1987. Teacher's Manual available. (Casebook)

Taxation—Individual

DODGE'S THE LOGIC OF TAX, 343 pages, 1989. Softcover. (Text)

GUNN AND WARD'S CASES, TEXT AND PROBLEMS ON FEDERAL INCOME TAXATION, Second Edition, 835 pages, 1988. Teacher's Manual available. (Casebook) 1990 Supplement.

HUDSON AND LIND'S BLACK LETTER ON FEDERAL INCOME TAXATION, Third Edition, approximately 390 pages, 1990. Softcover. (Review)

LAW SCHOOL PUBLICATIONS—Continued

Taxation—Individual—Cont'd

KRAGEN AND MCNULTY'S CASES AND MATERIALS ON FEDERAL INCOME TAXATION—INDIVIDUALS, CORPORATIONS, PARTNERSHIPS, Fourth Edition, 1287 pages, 1985. (Casebook)

MCNULTY'S FEDERAL INCOME TAXATION OF INDIVIDUALS IN A NUTSHELL, Fourth Edition, 503 pages, 1988. Softcover. (Text)

POSIN'S HORNBOOK ON FEDERAL INCOME TAXATION, Student Edition, 491 pages, 1983, with 1989 pocket part. (Text)

ROSE AND CHOMMIE'S HORNBOOK ON FEDERAL INCOME TAXATION, Third Edition, 923 pages, 1988, with 1989 pocket part. (Text)

SELECTED FEDERAL TAXATION STATUTES AND REGULATIONS. Softcover. Approximately 1650 pages, 1991.

SOLOMON AND HESCH'S PROBLEMS, CASES AND MATERIALS ON FEDERAL INCOME TAXATION OF INDIVIDUALS, 1068 pages, 1987. Teacher's Manual available. (Casebook)

Taxation—International

DOERNBERG'S INTERNATIONAL TAXATION IN A NUTSHELL, 325 pages, 1989. Softcover. (Text)

KAPLAN'S FEDERAL TAXATION OF INTERNATIONAL TRANSACTIONS: PRINCIPLES, PLANNING AND POLICY, 635 pages, 1988. (Casebook)

Taxation—Partnership

BERGER AND WIEDENBECK'S CASES AND MATERIALS ON PARTNERSHIP TAXATION, 788 pages, 1989. Teacher's Manual available. (Casebook)

Taxation—State & Local

GELFAND AND SALSICH'S STATE AND LOCAL TAXATION AND FINANCE IN A NUTSHELL, 309 pages, 1986. Softcover. (Text)

HELLERSTEIN AND HELLERSTEIN'S CASES AND MATERIALS ON STATE AND LOCAL TAXATION, Fifth Edition, 1071 pages, 1988. (Casebook)

Torts—see also Products Liability

CHRISTIE AND MEEKS' CASES AND MATERIALS ON THE LAW OF TORTS, Second Edition, 1264 pages, 1990. (Casebook)

DOBBS' TORTS AND COMPENSATION—PERSONAL ACCOUNTABILITY AND SOCIAL RESPONSIBILITY FOR INJURY, 955 pages, 1985. Teacher's Manual available. (Casebook) 1990 Supplement.

KEETON, KEETON, SARGENTICH AND STEINER'S CASES AND MATERIALS ON TORT AND ACCIDENT LAW, Second Edition, 1318 pages, 1989. (Casebook)

KIONKA'S BLACK LETTER ON TORTS, 339 pages, 1988. Softcover. (Review)

KIONKA'S TORTS IN A NUTSHELL: INJURIES TO PERSONS AND PROPERTY, 434 pages, 1977. Softcover. (Text)

MALONE'S TORTS IN A NUTSHELL: INJURIES TO FAMILY, SOCIAL AND TRADE RELATIONS, 358 pages, 1979. Softcover. (Text)

PROSSER AND KEETON'S HORNBOOK ON TORTS, Fifth Edition, Student Edition, 1286 pages, 1984 with 1988 pocket part. (Text)

ROBERTSON, POWERS AND ANDERSON'S CASES AND MATERIALS ON TORTS, 932 pages, 1989. Teacher's Manual available. (Casebook)

Trade Regulation—see also Antitrust, Regulated Industries

MCMANIS' UNFAIR TRADE PRACTICES IN A NUTSHELL, Second Edition, 464 pages, 1988. Softcover. (Text)

OPPENHEIM, WESTON, MAGGS AND SCHECHTER'S CASES AND MATERIALS ON UNFAIR TRADE PRACTICES AND CONSUMER PROTECTION, Fourth Edition, 1038 pages, 1983. Teacher's Manual available. (Casebook) 1986 Supplement.

SCHECHTER'S BLACK LETTER ON UNFAIR TRADE PRACTICES, 272 pages, 1986. Softcover. (Review)

Trial and Appellate Advocacy—see also Civil Procedure

APPELLATE ADVOCACY, HANDBOOK OF, Second Edition, 182 pages, 1986. Softcover. (Text)

BERGMAN'S TRIAL ADVOCACY IN A NUTSHELL, Second Edition, 354 pages, 1989. Softcover. (Text)

BINDER AND BERGMAN'S FACT INVESTIGATION: FROM HYPOTHESIS TO PROOF, 354 pages, 1984. Teacher's Manual available. (Coursebook)

Trial and Appellate Advocacy—Cont'd

CARLSON AND IMWINKELRIED'S DYNAMICS OF TRIAL PRACTICE: PROBLEMS AND MATERIALS, 414 pages, 1989. Teacher's Manual available. (Coursebook)

GOLDBERG'S THE FIRST TRIAL (WHERE DO I SIT? WHAT DO I SAY?) IN A NUTSHELL, 396 pages, 1982. Softcover. (Text)

HAYDOCK, HERR, AND STEMPEL'S FUNDAMENTALS OF PRE-TRIAL LITIGATION, 768 pages, 1985. Softcover. Teacher's Manual available. (Coursebook)

HEGLAND'S TRIAL AND PRACTICE SKILLS IN A NUTSHELL, 346 pages, 1978. Softcover. (Text)

HORNSTEIN'S APPELLATE ADVOCACY IN A NUTSHELL, 325 pages, 1984. Softcover. (Text)

JEANS' HANDBOOK ON TRIAL ADVOCACY, Student Edition, 473 pages, 1975. Softcover. (Text)

LISNEK AND KAUFMAN'S DEPOSITIONS: PROCEDURE, STRATEGY AND TECHNIQUE, Law School and CLE Edition. 250 pages, 1990. Softcover. (Text)

MARTINEAU'S CASES AND MATERIALS ON APPELLATE PRACTICE AND PROCEDURE, 565 pages, 1987. (Casebook)

NOLAN'S CASES AND MATERIALS ON TRIAL PRACTICE, 518 pages, 1981. (Casebook)

SONSTENG AND HAYDOCK'S TRIAL: THEORIES, TACTICS, TECHNIQUE, Approximately 650 pages, 1990. Softcover. (Text)

SONSTENG, HAYDOCK AND BOYD'S THE TRIALBOOK: A TOTAL SYSTEM FOR PREPARATION AND PRESENTATION OF A CASE, 404 pages, 1984. Softcover. (Coursebook)

WHARTON, HAYDOCK AND SONSTENG'S CALIFORNIA CIVIL TRIALBOOK, Law School and CLE Edition. Approximately 300 pages, 1990. Softcover. (Text)

Trusts and Estates

ATKINSON'S HORNBOOK ON WILLS, Second Edition, 975 pages, 1953. (Text)

AVERILL'S UNIFORM PROBATE CODE IN A NUTSHELL, Second Edition, 454 pages, 1987. Softcover. (Text)

BOGERT'S HORNBOOK ON TRUSTS, Sixth Edition, Student Edition, 794 pages, 1987. (Text)

CLARK, LUSKY AND MURPHY'S CASES AND MATERIALS ON GRATUITOUS TRANSFERS, Third Edition, 970 pages, 1985. (Casebook)

DODGE'S WILLS, TRUSTS AND ESTATE PLANNING–LAW AND TAXATION, CASES AND MATERIALS, 665 pages, 1988. (Casebook)

KURTZ' PROBLEMS, CASES AND OTHER MATERIALS ON FAMILY ESTATE PLANNING, 853 pages, 1983. Teacher's Manual available. (Casebook)

MCGOVERN'S CASES AND MATERIALS ON WILLS, TRUSTS AND FUTURE INTERESTS: AN INTRODUCTION TO ESTATE PLANNING, 750 pages, 1983. (Casebook)

MCGOVERN, KURTZ AND REIN'S HORNBOOK ON WILLS, TRUSTS AND ESTATES–INCLUDING TAXATION AND FUTURE INTERESTS, 996 pages, 1988. (Text)

MENNELL'S WILLS AND TRUSTS IN A NUTSHELL, 392 pages, 1979. Softcover. (Text)

SIMES' HORNBOOK ON FUTURE INTERESTS, Second Edition, 355 pages, 1966. (Text)

TURANO AND RADIGAN'S HORNBOOK ON NEW YORK ESTATE ADMINISTRATION, 676 pages, 1986. (Text)

UNIFORM PROBATE CODE, OFFICIAL TEXT WITH COMMENTS. 615 pages, 1989. Softcover.

WAGGONER'S FUTURE INTERESTS IN A NUTSHELL, 361 pages, 1981. Softcover. (Text)

WATERBURY'S MATERIALS ON TRUSTS AND ESTATES, 1039 pages, 1986. Teacher's Manual available. (Casebook)

Water Law—see also Energy and Natural Resources Law, Environmental Law

GETCHES' WATER LAW IN A NUTSHELL, Second Edition, approximately 441 pages, 1990. Softcover. (Text)

SAX AND ABRAMS' LEGAL CONTROL OF WATER RESOURCES: CASES AND MATERIALS, 941 pages, 1986. (Casebook)

TRELEASE AND GOULD'S CASES AND MATERIALS ON WATER LAW, Fourth Edition, 816 pages, 1986. (Casebook)

Wills—see Trusts and Estates

Women and the Law—see also Employment Discrimination

Kay's Text, Cases and Materials on Sex-Based Discrimination, Third Edition, 1001 pages, 1988. (Casebook) 1990 Supplement.

Thomas' Sex Discrimination in a Nutshell, 399 pages, 1982. Softcover. (Text)

Workers' Compensation—see Social Legislation

WEST'S LAW SCHOOL
ADVISORY BOARD

JOHN A. BAUMAN
Professor of Law, University of California, Los Angeles

CURTIS J. BERGER
Professor of Law, Columbia University

JESSE H. CHOPER
Dean and Professor of Law,
University of California, Berkeley

DAVID P. CURRIE
Professor of Law, University of Chicago

YALE KAMISAR
Professor of Law, University of Michigan

MARY KAY KANE
Professor of Law, University of California,
Hastings College of the Law

WAYNE R. LaFAVE
Professor of Law, University of Illinois

RICHARD C. MAXWELL
Professor of Law, Duke University

ARTHUR R. MILLER
Professor of Law, Harvard University

ROBERT A. STEIN
Dean and Professor of Law, University of Minnesota

JAMES J. WHITE
Professor of Law, University of Michigan

CHARLES ALAN WRIGHT
Professor of Law, University of Texas

MEDICAL LIABILITY

By

Sal Fiscina, M.D., J.D.
Professorial Lecturer in Law
The George Washington University

Marcia Mobilia Boumil, M.S., J.D., LL.M.
Visiting Assistant Professor of Law
Suffolk University

David J. Sharpe, LL.B., S.J.D.
Professor of Law
The George Washington University

Murdock Head, D.D.S., M.D., J.D.
Airlie Professor Emeritus
The George Washington University

AMERICAN CASEBOOK SERIES®

WEST PUBLISHING CO.
ST. PAUL, MINN., 1991

American Casebook Series, the key number appearing on the front cover and the WP symbol are registered trademarks of West Publishing Co. Registered in U.S. Patent and Trademark Office.

COPYRIGHT © 1991 By WEST PUBLISHING CO.
50 West Kellogg Boulevard
P.O. Box 64526
St. Paul, MN 55164–0526
All rights reserved
Printed in the United States of America

Library of Congress Cataloging-in-Publication Data

Medical liability / by Salvatore F. Fiscina ... [et al.].
    p.   cm. — (American casebook series)
  Includes index.
  ISBN 0–314–75264–1
  1. Physicians—Malpractice—United States—Cases. I. Fiscina, Salvatore Francis, 1941– . II. Series.
KF2905.3.A7 1991
346.7303'32—dc20
[347.306332]
                                                                   90–37048
                                                                       CIP

ISBN 0–314–75264–1

(F., B., S. & H.) Medical Liability ACB

*To members of our families
for their patience and understanding*

———

*Jo-Ann, Chris, Lynne, Rick,
Margy,
Syl, Jim, Gregory,
and Mark*

Preface

During the last 30 years, "law-and-" courses in medico-legal areas have achieved legitimacy with law school curriculum committees and popularity with students, and general-purpose law school casebooks on law and medicine have proliferated. The general casebooks have grown in size as they have sought to include materials on bioethics, health care delivery, and behavioral science, and now specialized casebooks deal at length with the topics. Three of the present editors in 1978 joined with the publisher in presenting a general casebook on law and medicine, but in considering an updated version, they and their new partner concluded that it would be more useful to create a new, short, specialized casebook focused on medical liability, and designed to support a Medical Liability course along the same lines, taught by specialists.

Medical Liability will be what the teacher makes it. Obviously, as a bread-and-butter course, it can introduce a lively legal subspecialty of personal injury litigation. Alternatively, as legal process, Medical Liability can show the expansion of doctrine and the efforts to restrain it, the interactions of courts and legislatures and lobbies, the complex arrangements of law and procedure that respond to the presence of multiple parties, and the conflicts of professional ethics.

While Medical Liability is a course worthy of the attention of full-time teachers, the editors anticipate that many people who teach Medial Liability will do so part-time, that is, full-time lawyers in the medical liability field who teach law students a two-credit course once a year. Practitioner-teachers can and will adapt teaching methods to their own experience—some lecture, some discussion, some simulation—with photoduplicated supplemental materials. Many teachers will use physicians as guest speakers or collaborators, but the editors do not assume that courses will be co-taught fully by physicians as well as lawyers.

As for the materials selected for the casebook, a person has only to read the newspapers and advance sheets to know that medical liability is an important field of law practice, but illustrating the field required selection criteria. One inclusion criterion was a recent date: of the cases included here, 51 were decided after 1984, and the median date is 1985. Another inclusion criterion was broad geographic scope, because medical liability is not peculiar to any area of the United States. Then, because the facts are so important as well as so interesting in medical liability litigation, the editors tried to select cases with thorough statements of facts as well as intelligible discussions of law. Finally, a good many cases illustrate commonplace situations in medical practice that lawyers have to discuss with doctors over and over. The principal exclusion criterion was to avoid medical and legal horror stories as such, though not every case included is suitable for dinnertable conversation.

The medical practitioner orientation of the book arises from its structure, which looks at medical liability through the eyes of litigators and clients rather than administrators and planners. The editors are not plaintiff-oriented or defendant-oriented; they are trying to show the interplay of the primary contenders in many roles as the United States law of medical liability has evolved since the Second World War.

The editors, intending to make a casebook for classroom use, have taken liberties with the published texts of reports that other editors may regard as excessive. Omissions have been indicated, though contiguous omissions have not. In several reports, with warning footnotes, the parties' names have supplanted the court's use of equivalents such as "petitioner" and "respondent." The editors warn users not to quote the casebook in place of the law reports; they would not do so themselves.

A few minor changes have not been flagged. For example, where captions and omitted passages reveal the first names of parties, the names have been supplied without bracketing. Likewise short-form citations have been expanded where prior omissions included the full forms. Obvious errors have been corrected without advertising them by "[sic]." Punctuation has been made uniform, and so has citation form, particularly in matters of dates, abbreviations, and pinpoint cites. A few commas have been added and one or two were subtracted. The editors acknowledge that unadvertised changes in the work of courts violates Bluebook rules. They plead that they have used restraint, and that they have tried to enhance readability without changing meaning.

The medical liability case in the Appendix presents the usual elements of liability, causation, and damages, but each element arises in an unusually difficult setting. Teachers and students can simply read the case in order to see how a complex medical malpractice trial can be organized and put forward. The materials can also be the cornerstone for simulating portions of a simulated medical malpractice case, especially depositions, interrogatories, and the examination and cross-examination of medical expert witnesses.

The editors acknowledge with gratitude the assistance of many unnamed persons and organizations, but they take particular note of Paul J. Connors, M.D., J.D.; Jane C. Corrigan, R.N.; the George Washington University's Airlie Center and Department of Biomedical Communications; Kathy Hale, R.N.; the International Academy of

Preventive Medicine; Barbara McGraw of Education in Legal Medicine, Inc.; Nicholas J. Phillips, J.D.; Prof. Maximilian A. Pock; and Janet B. Seifert, J.D.

> SAL FISCINA
> Chevy Chase, Maryland
> MARCIA MOBILIA BOUMIL
> Lowell, Massachusetts
> DAVID J. SHARPE
> Washington, D.C.
> MURDOCK HEAD
> Airlie, Virginia

Summer, 1990

Introduction

This casebook is composed of materials on medical liability. "Medical liability" is the phrase presently used to describe the legal claims and defenses that arise from medical injuries. Medical negligence is the most important claim within medical liability, but the claim for lack of informed consent originated in the medical context, and several other tort and contract claim theories may also be applied in the medical context. Medical liability is a problem in health care, and so in addition to claims and defenses, the casebook addresses many of the medical liability solutions that are being tested, especially statutes that try to reshape the litigation system and inevitably stimulate constitutional litigation.

While a book or course on Medical Liability thus possesses the circumstantial coherence that an industrial setting imposes upon mixed legal questions, medical liability also has a core of intellectual coherence that can be addressed through the question, "Is there a medical liability crisis?"

A crisis is a turning-point, an event followed by a reaction, but it is more than a point along a trend. For example, the United States is in an upward trend in national expenditures on health care—lately they are said to be 11% of the gross national product—and with the increase in the cost and quantity of medical treatment, one might expect medical liability claims to rise also; but of itself, the increase in claims would not be a crisis.

Malpractice insurance is another example. Insurance premiums have risen dramatically in the past three decades; insurance has not always been readily available to practicing physicians; and premium costs are a substantial component of the rising cost of health care. These developments have called forth new combinations of care, compensation, and cost within changing patterns of medical service delivery. Do these changes constitute reactions that evidence a now-past crisis, or are they part of a long evolutionary trend having occasional episodes of national attention?

Since 1970, two waves of national attention have produced reports by the United States government indicating that the trends had reached levels of serious difficulty,[1] but Congress, having no constitutional power to make private law in the area, has only enacted a few

---

1. E.g., Report of the Secretary's Commission on Medical Malpractice (U.S. Dep't of Health, Education & Welfare 1973); Report of the Task Force on Medical Liability and Malpractice (U.S. Dep't of Health & Human Services 1987). For a recent bibliography, see Macchiaroli, Medical Malpractice Screening Panels; Proposed Model Legislation to Cure Judicial Ills, 58 Geo.Wash.L.Rev. 181 (1990).

remedial measures, mostly appended to funding legislation, that do not indicate a preceding crisis.

It has been at the state level that medical societies and insurance companies have persuaded legislatures that a medical liability crisis existed.[2] In the mid-1970's state legislatures responded with remedial statutes. Some of the statutes were free-standing laws, and others were comprehensive packages. For example, the Governor of California included this statement in the proclamation that summoned the California legislature to an extraordinary session that enacted a well-known and much-tested package, the Medical Injury Compensation Reform Act of 1975 (MICRA):[3]

> The cost of medical malpractice insurance has risen to levels which many physicians and surgeons find intolerable. The inability of doctors to obtain such insurance at reasonable rates is endangering the health of the people of this State, and threatens the closing of many hospitals. The longer term consequences of such closings could seriously limit the health care provided to hundreds of thousands of our citizens. * * *

By contrast, the Idaho Supreme Court declined to take judicial notice that there was a crisis supporting legislation that otherwise would be unconstitutional:

> It is argued that the 1975 Hospital-Medical Liability Act is a necessary legislative response to a "crisis in medical malpractice insurance" in Idaho, but the record does not demonstrate any such "crisis."[4]

State by state, legislation has gone foreward, as though a crisis existed and as though the new laws could produce beneficial changes.

The latest and in many respects the best evidence to support arguments over the existence of a medical liability crisis appeared in early 1990 as the first results of the Harvard Medical Practice Study, an empirical survey of medical accidents in New York State done under contract by a team of Harvard University law and medical school researchers.[5] The Harvard Medical Practice Study indicated that medical negligence affected about 1% of all hospitalized persons, but that "[a]bout 16 times as many patients suffered an injury from negligence

---

2. See California Med. Ass'n & California Hosp. Ass'n, Medical Insurance Feasibility Study (Don Harper Mills ed. 1977), which focused on measuring the incidence of "potentially compensable events" in California in 1974, looking to a no-fault compensation system.

3. 1975 Cal.Stat. ch. 1–2 (Second Ex. Sess. 1975–1976), quoted in American Bank & Trust Co. v. Community Hosp., 326 Cal.3d 359, 204 Cal.Rptr. 671, 683 P.2d 670, 672 n. 1 (1984). The court accepted the crisis as justification for changing the mode of payment of malpractice damages from a lump sum to periodic payments.

4. Jones v. State Board of Medicine, 97 Idaho 859, 555 P.2d 399, cert. denied, 431 U.S. 914, 97 S.Ct. 2173, 53 L.Ed.2d 223 (1977) (extensive and skeptical survey of assertion of crisis; judgment of unconstitutionality reversed and remanded for further findings of fact).

5. Patients, Doctors, and Lawyers: Medical Injury, Malpractice Litigation, and Patient Compensation in New York.

as received compensation from the tort liability system."[6] It looks as if the medical liability problem is larger than had been supposed, and that it is different from excessive verdicts and malpractice insurance premiums; yet the threat to availability of medical services is not necessarily of "crisis" proportions and nature, because insurance premiums have levelled off.

Once a crisis has been asserted, a predictable reaction by the public and its representatives is the search for scapegoats, such as contingent-fee-hungry plaintiffs' lawyers or profit-rich insurance companies. Some of the would-be scapegoats have produced public benefit. For example, while patients' lawsuits are not a desirable outcome of health care, the litigation-driven rise of informed consent forms and risk management and quality assurance practices seem to be producing safer hospitals and more competent staffs. But scapegoating does not reduce tensions or improve situations.

Improving the medical liability situation calls for education, sympathy, patience, and the toning-down of caricatures and scapegoating among the professions most concerned. The law—claims, defenses, procedures, and lawyers—is a substantial aspect of the problems of medical liability, but discarding the law will not make the problems go away, because the law is also essential to the solutions—statutes, rules, contracts, arbitrators, negotiators, and legislators. The more sensitive the doctors and lawyers are to one another's legitimate concerns about performance, ethics, economics, and dignity, the more confidently they can use the legal system to advance their common objectives and to compromise their differences. Consequently the academic study of Medical Liability has the potential to facilitate speedier and more satisfactory solutions to the legal problems of health care, whether medical liability is in a crisis or not.

6. Id., executive summary at 6.

Summary of Contents

	Page
PREFACE	xxiii
INTRODUCTION	xxvii
TABLE OF CASES	xli

PART I. MEDICAL LIABILITY CLAIMS

Chapter 1. The Medical Professional Relationship 2
Section
- A. Commencement of the Professional Relationship 3
- B. Allocation of Liabilities Among Providers 6
- C. Professional Services That Harm Non–Patients 15

Chapter 2. Negligence of the Health Care Provider 22
- A. Defining Medical Due Care 23
- B. Failure to Use Due Care 35
- C. Third Parties and Medical Negligence 43

Chapter 3. Claims Against Multiple Medical Defendants 54
- A. Physician Liability Under Respondeat Superior 56
- B. Medical Liability of Institutions 60
- C. Multiple Health Care Providers' Liabilities 67

Chapter 4. Evidence of Medical Negligence 78
- A. Medical Evidence 79
- B. Expert Medical Testimony 90
- C. Proof of Medical Negligence Without Experts 105
- D. Medical Evidence and Jury Verdicts 113

Chapter 5. Causation, Harms and Damages 118
- A. Causation of Harm by Medical Negligence 120
- B. Harms 124
- C. Damage Dollar Amounts 138

Chapter 6. Defending the Medical Negligence Case 155
- A. Immunities 156
- B. Affirmative Defenses 175
- C. Countersuits 189

Chapter 7. Treatment Consent, Information and Refusal 193
- A. Treatment Without Consent 195
- B. Informed Consent 204
- C. Consent to Research 211
- D. Refused Services 219

xxxi

	Page
Chapter 8. Product-Related Medical Liability	234
Chapter 9. Non-Medical Acts	254
A. Promises and Damages	255
B. Misrepresentations	267
C. Tortious Conduct	272

PART II. TREATING THE MEDICAL LIABILITY CRISIS

Chapter 10. Insurance and Medical Liability	294
A. Availability and Coverage	295
B. Defense of Claims	305
C. Settlement	309
Chapter 11. Changing the Litigation System	321
A. The Mechanisms of Change	321
B. Forestalling Claims	327
C. Litigation Alternatives and Hurdles	329
D. Actions	338
E. Recoveries	340
Chapter 12. Access to High-Quality Health Services	348
A. Access to Services	350
B. Utilization Review	354
C. Peer Review	364
D. Extra-Professional Forces	381
Appendix. Case Record in Remington v. Avery	386
A. Introduction	388
B. Pre-Surgery Documents	395
C. First Hospitalization: Subcutaneous Mastectomy and Insertion of Implants	397
D. Documentation of Medical Care Between Hospitalizations	414
E. Second Hospitalization: Removal of Implants	415
F. Third Hospitalization Documents: Submuscular Insertion of Implants	419
G. Pre-Filing Documents	423
H. The Complaint	431
I. Discovery Documents	433
J. Pretrial Hearing Preparation	473
K. Glossary	477
Index	479

Table of Contents

	Page
PREFACE	xxiii
INTRODUCTION	xxvii
TABLE OF CASES	xli

PART I. MEDICAL LIABILITY CLAIMS

Chapter 1. The Medical Professional Relationship ... 2
    Introductory Note ... 2

Section
- A. Commencement of the Professional Relationship ... 3
  - *Hiser v. Randolph* (Ariz.App.1980) ... 3
- B. Allocation of Liabilities Among Providers ... 6
  - *Largess v. Tatem* (Vt.1972) ... 6
  - *Jackson v. Power* (Alaska 1987) ... 10
- C. Professional Services That Harm Non-Patients ... 15
  - *Keene v. Wiggins* (Cal.App.1977) ... 15
  - *Chatman v. Millis* (Ark.1975) ... 17

Chapter 2. Negligence of the Health Care Provider ... 22
    Introductory Note ... 22
- A. Defining Medical Due Care ... 23
  - *Pike v. Honsinger* (N.Y.1898) ... 23
  - *Shilkret v. Annapolis Emergency Hosp. Ass'n* (Md.1975) ... 25
  - *Helling v. Carey* (Wash.1974) ... 30
  - Note on the Aftermath of Helling v. Carey ... 33
- B. Failure to Use Due Care ... 35
  - *McCord v. Maguire* (9th Cir.1989) ... 35
  - *Toth v. Community Hosp.* (N.Y.1968) ... 37
  - *DiFilippo v. Preston* (Del.1961) ... 40
- C. Third Parties and Medical Negligence ... 43
  - Note on Unusual Duties to Patients ... 43
  - *Clarke v. Hoek* (Cal.App.1985) ... 44
  - *Bardoni v. Kim* (Mich.App.1986) ... 48
  - *Shepard v. Redford Commun. Hosp.* (Mich.App.1986) ... 53

Chapter 3. Claims Against Multiple Medical Defendants ... 54
    Introductory Note ... 54
- A. Physician Liability Under Respondeat Superior ... 56
  - *Sparger v. Worley Hosp., Inc.* (Tex.1977) ... 56
- B. Medical Liability of Institutions ... 60
  - *Sloan v. Metropolitan Health Council* (Ind.App.1987) ... 60
  - *Pedroza v. Bryant* (Wash.1984) ... 62
  - *Schoening v. Grays Harbor Commun. Hosp.* (Wash.App.1985) ... 65

Section	Page
C. Multiple Health Care Providers' Liabilities	67
Gilson v. Mitchell (Ga.App.1974)	67
Foote v. United States v. Michael Reese Hosp. (N.D.Ill.1986)	70
Lum v. Stinnett (Nev.1971)	72
Note on Mary Carter Agreements	76

Chapter 4. Evidence of Medical Negligence — 78

Introductory Note	78
A. Medical Evidence	79
Wilson v. Bodian (N.Y.App.Div.1987)	79
Hill v. Springer (N.Y.Sup.Ct.1986)	84
Bond v. District Court (Colo.1984)	85
B. Expert Medical Testimony	90
Lee v. Miles (N.D.Tex.1970)	90
Trower v. Jones (Ill.1988)	92
Meyer v. McDonnell (Md.Spec.App.1978)	96
Johns Hopkins Hosp. v. Genda (Md.1969)	99
McDermott v. Manhattan Eye, Ear & Throat Hosp. (N.Y.1964)	101
Note on the Aftermath of the McDermott Case	104
C. Proof of Medical Negligence Without Experts	105
Ravi v. Williams (Ala.1988)	105
Ward v. Levy & Unger (Mass.App.1989)	107
Horner v. Northern Pac. Beneficial Ass'n Hosps., Inc. (Wash.1963)	108
Anderson v. Somberg (N.J.1975) (cross-ref.)	113
D. Medical Evidence and Jury Verdicts	113
Nicastro v. Park (N.Y.App.Div.1985)	113

Chapter 5. Causation, Harms and Damages — 118

Introductory Note	118
A. Causation of Harm by Medical Negligence	120
Willey v. Ketterer (1st Cir. 1989)	120
Alfonso v. Lund (10th Cir. 1986)	122
B. Harms	124
Ferrara v. Galluchio (N.Y.1958)	124
Siemieniec v. Lutheran Gen. Hosp. (Ill.1987)	127
C.S. v. Nielson (Utah 1988)	133
C. Damage Dollar Amounts	138
Herman v. Milwaukee Children's Hosp. (Wis.App.1984)	138
Boody v. United States (D.Kan.1989)	143
Ostrowski v. Azzara (N.J.1988)	150

Chapter 6. Defending the Medical Negligence Case — 155

Introductory Note	155
A. Immunities	156
Lilly v. Fieldstone (10th Cir. 1989)	156
Note on the Medical Liability of the United States and Its Employees	159
Bing v. Thunig (N.Y.1957)	160

Section	Page
A. Immunities—Continued	
Panaro v. Electrolux Corp. (Conn.1988)	164
McCain v. Batson (Mont.1988)	167
Kearns v. Superior Court (Cal.App.1988)	172
B. Affirmative Defenses	175
Weil v. Seltzer (D.C.Cir. 1989)	175
Ray v. Wagner (Minn.1970)	179
United States v. Kubrick (U.S.1979)	180
Morgan v. Cohen (Md.1987)	184
C. Countersuits	189
Morowitz v. Marvel (D.C.1980)	189

Chapter 7. Treatment Consent, Information and Refusal — 193

Introductory Note	193
A. Treatment Without Consent	195
Mattocks v. Bell (D.C.1963)	195
Mohr v. Williams (Minn.1905)	196
Kennedy v. Parrott (N.C.1956)	198
Perna v. Pirozzi (N.J.1983)	201
B. Informed Consent	204
Logan v. Greenwich Hosp. Ass'n (Conn.1983)	204
Hook v. Rothstein (S.C.App.1984)	210
C. Consent to Research	211
Estrada v. Jaques (N.C.App.1984)	211
Note on Institutional Review Boards	215
D. Refused Services	219
Truman v. Thomas (Cal.1980)	219
Public Health Trust v. Wons (Fla.1989)	225
Leach v. Shapiro (Ohio App.1984)	229

Chapter 8. Product–Related Medical Liability — 234

Introductory Note	234
Note on Medical Product Manufacturers' Liability	235
Thompson v. Carter (Miss.1987)	236
Tresemer v. Barke (Cal.App.1978)	241
Ashman v. SK & F Lab Co. (N.D.Ill.1988)	243
Anderson v. Somberg (N.J.1975)	245
Samson v. Greenville Hosp. System (S.C.1988)	249

Chapter 9. Non–Medical Acts — 254

Introductory Note	254
A. Promises and Damages	255
Sullivan v. O'Connor (Mass.1973)	255
Murray v. University of Pa. Hosp. (Pa.Super.1985)	259
Stewart v. Rudner (Mich.1957)	262
Chew v. Paul D. Meyer, M.D., P.A. (Md.Spec.App.1987)	264
B. Misrepresentations	267
Simcuski v. Saeli (N.Y.1978)	267

Section	Page
C. Tortious Conduct	272
Millsaps v. Bankers Life Co. (Ill.App.1976)	272
Bundren v. Superior Court (Cal.App.1983)	273
Humphers v. First Interstate Bank (Or.1985)	275
Ascher v. Gutierrez (D.C.Cir.1976)	282
Strachan v. John F. Kennedy Hosp. (N.J.1988)	284
Burgess v. Perdue (Kan.1986)	290

PART II. TREATING THE MEDICAL LIABILITY CRISIS

Chapter 10. Insurance and Medical Liability — 294
Introductory Note — 294
A. Availability and Coverage — 295
    Note on Medical Liability Insurance — 295
    Langley v. Mutual Fire, Marine & Inland Ins. Co. (Ala.1987) — 300
    Note on Problems of Policy Construction — 304
B. Defense of Claims — 305
    Rea v. Pardo (N.Y.App.Div.1987) — 305
    Note on the Insurer's Duty to Defend — 307
C. Settlement — 309
    Feliberty v. Damon (N.Y.1988) — 309
    Arana v. Koerner (Mo.App.1987) — 312
    Insurance Co. of North Amer. v. Medical Protective Co. (10th Cir. 1985) — 313

Chapter 11. Changing the Litigation System — 321
Introductory Note — 321
A. The Mechanisms of Change — 321
    Note on the Mechanisms of Change — 321
B. Forestalling Claims — 327
    Tatham v. Hoke (W.D.N.C.1979) — 327
    Emory Univ. v. Porubiansky (Ga.1981) — 328
C. Litigation Alternatives and Hurdles — 329
    Note on Agreements to Arbitrate Future Disputes — 329
    Keyes v. Humana Hosp. Alaska, Inc. (Alaska 1988) — 331
    Note on Certificate of Merit Legislation — 337
D. Actions — 338
    Note on Limitation of Medical Liability Actions — 338
E. Recoveries — 340
    Etheridge v. Medical Center Hosps. (Va.1989) — 340
    Note on Collateral Sources — 344
    Jackson v. United States (9th Cir. 1989) — 346

Chapter 12. Access to High-Quality Health Services — 348
Introductory Note — 348

Section	Page
A. Access to Services	350
Ritter v. Wayne County Gen. Hosp. (Mich.App.1988)	350
Reid v. Indianapolis Osteopathic Medical Hosp., Inc. (S.D.Ind.1989)	352
B. Utilization Review	354
Cassim v. Bowen (9th Cir. 1987)	354
Wickline v. State (Cal.App.1986)	358
C. Peer Review	364
De Leon v. St. Joseph Hosp., Inc. (4th Cir. 1989)	364
Humana Hosp. v. Superior Ct. (Ariz.App.1987)	369
Salaymeh v. St. Vincent Memorial Hosp. Corp. (C.D.Ill.1989)	374
Patrick v. Burget (U.S.1988)	377
D. Extra–Professional Forces	381
Gilbert v. Medical Economics Co. (10th Cir. 1981)	381
United States v. Zwick (N.D.Ohio 1976)	384

APPENDIX. CASE RECORD IN REMINGTON v. AVERY

		Page
A.	Introduction	388
	Introductory Note	388
	Factual Summary of Remington v. Avery	391
	Initial Interview with Susan Remington	392
B.	Pre–Surgery Documents	395
	Exhibit A. Office Records of Dr. Avery	395
	Exhibit B. Office Records of Dr. Marshall	396
	Exhibit C. Breasts before Surgery	396
C.	First Hospitalization: Subcutaneous Mastectomy and Insertion of Implants	397
	Exhibit D. Admission Summary	397
	Exhibit E. Physician's Orders	398
	Exhibit F. Operative Consent Form	399
	Exhibit G. Operative Notes	400
	Exhibit H. Anatomy of the Normal Breast	401
	Exhibit I. Subcutaneous Implantation	402
	Exhibit J. Prosthesis of the Type Implanted in Susan Remington's Breasts	403
	Exhibit K. Anesthesia Record	404
	Exhibit L. Recovery Room Record	405
	Exhibit M. Physician Progress Record	406
	Exhibit N. Nursing Progress Record	407
	Exhibit O. Computerized Medication Record Summary	410
	Exhibit P. Laboratory Reports: Fluid Intake & Output, Hematology	411
	Exhibit Q. Breast Hematoma	412
	Exhibit R. Pathology Report	413
	Exhibit S. Discharge Summary	413
D.	Documentation of Medical Care Between Hospitalizations	414
	Exhibit T. Office Records of Dr. Reeves	414

TABLE OF CONTENTS

Section			Page
E.	Second Hospitalization: Removal of Implants		415
	Exhibit U.	Admission Summary	415
	Exhibit V.	Mrs. Remington with Breast Skin Necrosis	416
	Exhibit W.	Operative Notes	417
	Exhibit X.	Pathology Report	418
	Exhibit Y.	Discharge Summary	418
F.	Third Hospitalization Documents: Submuscular Insertion of Implants		419
	Exhibit Z.	Admission Summary	419
	Exhibit AA.	Breasts before Submuscular Insertion of Implants	420
	Exhibit BB.	Operative Notes	421
	Exhibit CC.	Submuscular Implantation	422
G.	Pre-Filing Documents		423
	Exhibit DD.	Breasts after Submuscular Insertion of Implants	423
	Exhibit EE.	Dr. Avery's Letter to Plaintiff's Lawyer	424
	Exhibit FF.	Report of Dr. Bergan to Mr. Brown	425
	Exhibit GG.	Report of Dr. Sears to Mr. Brown	426
	Exhibit HH.	Report of Dr. Shumacher to Mr. Brown	427
	Exhibit II.	Report of Dr. Burns to Mr. Brown	429
	Exhibit JJ.	Report of Dr. Hickman to Mr. Brown	430
H.	The Complaint		431
I.	Discovery Documents		433
	Document 1.	Dr. Avery's Interrogatories to Mrs. Remington	433
	Document 2.	Dr. Avery's Deposition of Mrs. Remington	439
	Document 3.	Mrs. Remington's Deposition of Dr. Avery	446
	Document 4.	Mrs. Remington's Deposition of Dr. Reeves	453
	Document 5.	Dr. Avery's Deposition of Dr. Sears	455
	Document 6.	Dr. Avery's Deposition of Dr. Shumacher	461
	Document 7.	Dr. Avery's Deposition of Dr. Bryant	465
	Document 8.	Dr. Avery's Deposition of Claire Garvey	468
	Document 9.	Dr. Avery's Deposition of Sheila Elliott	469
	Document 10.	Dr. Avery's Supplemental Interrogatories to Mrs. Remington	470
	Document 11.	Mrs. Remington's Request for Admissions to Dr. Avery	471
J.	Pretrial Hearing Preparation		473
	Document 12.	Pretrial Stipulation Rules	473
	Document 13.	Concise Statement of Fact	473
	Document 14.	Plaintiff's Proposed Pretrial Stipulations of Issues of Law for Determination at Trial	474
	Document 15.	Plaintiff's Proposed Pretrial Stipulations of Issues of Fact for Determination at Trial	475

Section	Page
K. Glossary	477
Glossary of Medical Terms Relating to Breast Surgery	477
INDEX	479

Table of Cases

The names and pages of principal cases are printed in italic type, and those of cases cited or discussed are shown in roman type. All references are to pages.

Adamski v. Tacoma Gen. Hosp., 11, 64
Aetna Cas. & Sur. Co. v. Price, 307
Aetna Cas. & Sur. Co. v. Yeatts, 308
Affett v. Milwaukee & Sub. Transp. Corp., 142–143
Agnew v. Parks, 96
Ahern v. Veterans Admin., 215
Alden v. Providence Hosp., 11
Alderman v. Ford, 291
Alfonso v. Lund, 122
American Bank & Trust Co v. Community Hosp., 326
American Fidelity Ins. Co. v. Employers Mut. Cas. Co., 319
Ammerman v. Newman, 190
Anderson v. Somberg, 113, 245
Anderson v. Wagner, 340
Application of (see name of party)
Arana v. Koerner, 312
Ascher v. Gutierrez, 282
Ashman v. SK & F Lab Co., 243
Associated Metals & Minerals Corp. v. Dixon Chem. & Research, Inc., 153

"B," In re, 90
Backlund v. Board of Comm'rs, 297
Baker v. Sadick, 331
Baker v. Vanderbilt Univ., 345
Ball v. Mudge, 136
Bardoni v. Kim, 48
Barnett v. Bachrach, 200
Becker v. Schwartz, 129
Bennan v. Parsonnet, 200
Berlin v. Nathan, 192
Berman v. Allan, 289
Bernstein v. Alameda-Contra Costa Med. Ass'n, 96
Bing v. Thunig, 160
Blair v. Eblen, 28, 29
Blake v. Cruz, 131
Blancato v. Feldspar Corp., 166
Bollinger v. Nuss, 318
Bond v. District Court, 85
Boody v. United States, 143
Booth v. Mary Carter Paint Co., 56, 76, 77
Borysewicz v. Dineen, 108
Boucher v. Riner, 367
Boyd v. Bulala, 344
Brown, In re, 228

Brown v. Guaranty Ins. Co., 318
Brown v. Superior Court, 235
Brune v. Belinkoff, 27, 29
Bulloch County Hosp. Auth. v. Fowler, 68, 69
Bundren v. Superior Court, 273
Burciaga v. St. John's Hosp., 174
Burgess v. Perdue, 290
Burton v. Leftwich, 195
Byrd v. Wesley Medical Center, 135–136
Byrne v. Boadle, 110–113

C.S. v. Nielson, 133
Caesar v. Mountanos, 90
California Retail Liquor Dealers Ass'n v. Midcal Aluminum, Inc., 379
Canterbury v. Spence, 207–208
Carson v. Maurer, 322
Cassim v. Bowen, 354
Chatman v. Millis, 17
Chew v. Paul D. Meyer, M.D., P.A., 264
Christensen v. Thornby, 136
City of Delta Junction v. Mack Trucks, 12
City of New Orleans v. Dukes, 252
Clark v. District Court, 88
Clarke v. Hoek, 44
Clayman v. Bernstein, 277
Cobbs v. Grant, 207, 221–222, 224–225
Cockrum v. Baumgartner, 131
Cohen v. Hallmark Cards, 115
Coira v. Florida Med. Ass'n, Inc., 298
Colby v. Schwartz, 173
Comisky v. Arlen, 332
Cooper v. Sisters of Charity of Cincinnati, Inc., 147
Crowder v. Conlan, 352

Darling v. Charleston Commun. Mem. Hosp., 63
Davis v. Lhim, 50
De Leon v. St. Joseph Hosp., Inc., 364
Delgado v. Board of Educ., 115
Delta Junction, City of v. Mack Trucks, 12
DeLuna v. St. Elizabeth's Hosp., 338
DiFilippo v. Preston, 40
Doe v. Roe, 277
Donoghue v. Stevenson, 277
Doran v. Priddy, 345

Douglas v. Hugh A. Stallings, M.D., Inc., 340
Drago v. Buonagurio, 192
Duprey v. Shane, 165

Eichner, In re, 230
Eisbrenner v. Stanley, 131
Elam v. College Park Hosp., 47
Ellis v. Hoelzel, 115
Emory Univ. v. Porubiansky, 328
Estrada v. Jaques, 211
Etheridge v. Medical Center Hosps., 340

Farmers Union Fed. Coop. Shipping Ass'n v. McChesney, 142
Farris v. United States Fidelity & Guar. Co., 277
Fein v. Permanente Med. Group, 326
Feinstein v. Massachusetts Gen. Hosp., 324
Feliberty v. Damon, 309
Feres v. United States, 157, 159
Ferrara v. Galluchio, 124
Flagiello v. Pennsylvania Hosp., 57
Fogo v. Cutter Laboratories, Inc., 242
Foote v. United States v. Michael Reese Hosp., 70
Fosgate v. Corona, 152
Frazier v. Boccardo, 46
Frazor v. Osborne, 339
Fruit v. Schreiner, 11
Furniss v. Fitchett, 277

Gaines v. Preterm-Cleveland, Inc., 340
Garger v. New Jersey, see Quinlan
Gary Concrete Prods, Inc. v. Riley, 252
Gates v. Jensen, 33-34
Gault v. Sideman, 256
Georgetown College Inc., Application of, 228
Gilbert v. Medical Economics Co., 381
Gilson v. Mitchell, 67
Goodman v. Kennedy, 191-192
Govar v. Chicago Ins. Co., 300
Gray v. Zurich Ins. Co., 307
Gross v. James A. Recabaren, M.D., Inc., 331
Guerrero v. Copper Queen Hosp., 5
Guilmet v. Campbell, 256
Guy v. Thomas Co., 165

Hackman v. Dandamudi, 77
Hall v. Hollywood Credit Clothing Co., 190
Hall v. May Dep't Stores Co., 276, 278
Hamilton v. Individual Mausoleum Co., 291
Hammonds v. Aetna Casualty & Sur. Co., 277
Harbeson v. Parke-Davis, Inc., 130
Hardy v. VerMeulen, 340
Harris v. Groth, 34-35
Hartford Cas. Ins. Co. v. Shehata, 308
Hasler v. United States, 160
Hawkins v. McGee, 257
Heller v. State, 84

Helling v. Carey, 30, 33
Henderson v. Bluemink, 160
Herman v. Milwaukee Children's Hosp., 138
Hill v. Springer, 84
Hiser v. Randolph, 3
Hoem v. State, 337
Hoffman v. United States, 326
Hook v. Rothstein, 210
Hooper, The T.J., 32
Horne v. Patton, 277
Horner v. Northern Pac. Beneficial Ass'n Hosp., Inc., 108
Howle v. Camp Amon Carter, 57
Hull v. Plume, 103
Humana Hosp. Desert Valley v. Superior Ct., 369
Humphers v. First Interstate Bank, 275
Hyman v. Jewish Chronic Disease Hosp., 216
Hymowitz v. Eli Lilly & Co., 235

In re (see name of party)
Insurance Co. of N. Am. v. Medical Protective Co., 313
Iterman v. Baker, 61, 62

J.A. Robinson Sons, Inc. v. Wigart, 56-57
Jackovach v. Yocom, 200
Jackson v. Bumgardner, 134
Jackson v. Power, 10
Jackson v. United States, 346
Jaffe v. Cranford Ins. Co., 308
James & Hackworth v. Continental Cas. Co., 302
Jett v. Dunlap, 166
Jezowski v. Beach, 81
Johns Hopkins Hosp. v. Genda, 99
Johnson, United States v., 159
Johnston v. Elkins, 134-135

Kansas Malpractice Victims Coalition v. Bell, 326
Karp v. Cooley, 215
Kearns v. Superior Court, 172
Keene v. Wiggins, 15
Kemeny v. Skorch, 94
Kennedy v. Parrott, 198
Keyes v. Humana Hosp. Alaska, Inc., 331
Kirk v. Michael Reese Hosp. & Med. Center, 244
Klucken v. Levi, 108
Konrad v. DeLong, 96
Kraushaar Bros. & Co., People ex rel., v. Thorpe, 104
Kubrick, United States v., 180

Langis v. Danforth, 108
Langley v. Mutual Fire, Marine & Inland Ins. Co., 300, 308
Largess v. Tatem, 6
Lather v. Beadle County, 159
Lawless v. Calaway, 103
Leach v. Akron Gen. Med. Ctr., 229

TABLE OF CASES

Leach v. Shapiro, 229
Lee v. Miles, 90
Lewis v. Equitable Life Ins. Soc., 368
Lifschutz, In re, 90
Lilly v. Fieldstone, 156, 159
Lipari v. Sears, Roebuck & Co., 50
Lipman v. Lustig, 108
Logan v. Greenwich Hosp. Ass'n, 204
Logue v. United States, 157
L'Orange v. Medical Protective Co., 96
Lum v. Stinnett, 72
Lupton v. Torbey, 314
Lurch v. United States, 157

MacDonald v. Clinger, 306
MacDonald v. Ortho Pharmaceutical Corp., 235
Malone v. Bianchi, 108
Mann v. Hunt, 116
Marchesi v. Franchino, 369
Martin v. Trevino, 190
Mary Carter Pain Co., Booth v., 56, 76–77
Mattocks v. Bell, 195
Mazza v. Huffaker, 43, 304
Mazza v. Medical Mut. Ins. Co., 304, 309
McCain v. Batson, 167
McConnell v. Williams, 57
McCord v. Maguire, 35
McDaniel v. Sage, 165
McDermott v. Manhattan Eye, Ear & Throat Hosp., 101, 104
McDonald v. Massachusetts Gen. Hosp., 161
McDonnell v. Commission on Medical Discipline, 98
McGee v. United States Fidelity & Guar. Co., 257
McKenna v. Cedars of Lebanon Hosp., 174
McKinstry v. Valley Obstetrics–Gynecology Clinic, P.C., 330
McMahon v. Chicago City Ry. Co., 94, 96
McQuaid v. Michou, 257
Mehlman v. Powell, 12
Meyer v. McDonnell, 96
Milks v. McIver, 125
Miller v. Marrocco, 298
Miller v. Peterson, 35
Mills v. Atlantic City Dep't of Vital Statistics, 278
Millsaps v. Bankers Life Co., 272
Mingachos v. CBS, Inc., 166
Mohr v. Williams, 196
Mominee v. Scherbarth, 340
Monroe v. Harper, 215
Moore v. City of Detroit, 352
Morgan v. Cohen, 184
Morgan v. Kirk Bros., Inc., 71
Morowitz v. Marvel, 189
Morris v. Francisco, 149
Morris v. Sanchez, 134
Morrison v. Acton, 271
Morrison v. McNamara, 176–177
Muhl v. Magan, 297

Muniz v. United Hosps. Med. Center Presbyterian Hosp., 289
Murray v. University of Pa. Hosp., 259

National Savings Bank v. Ward, 191
New Orleans, City of, v. Dukes, 252
New York Times Co. v. Sullivan, 369
Newhouse v. Board of Osteopathic Exam'rs, 173
Newsome v. Vanderbilt Univ., 351–352
Nicastro v. Park, 113
Nichols v. Wilson, 196, 265
Nixdorf v. Hicken, 135
Nolan v. Allstate Home Equip. Co., 190
NOPCO Chem. Div. v. Blaw-Knox Co., 247
Norton v. Murphy, 157

Omer v. Edgren, 43
Osborne v. Frazor, 339
Osborne v. Hartford Acc. & Indem. Co., 339
Ostrowski v. Azzara, 150

Pacific Indem. Co. v. Interstate Fire & Cas. Co., 304
Panaro v. Electrolux Corp., 164
Pantone v. Demos, 192
Parikh v. Cunningham, 213
Parker v. Brown, 379
Patrick v. Burget, 377
Paugh v. Hanks, 233
Pedroza v. Bryant, 62, 66
Pennsylvania Cas. Co. v. Chris Simopoulos, M.D., Ltd., 298
People ex rel. Kraushaar Bros. & Co. v. Thorpe, 104
Perna v. Pirozzi, 201
Phillips v. United States, 132
Piehl v. Dalles Gen. Hosp., 56
Pike v. Honsinger, 23
Portee v. Jaffee, 289
Powell v. Mullins, 106
Powers v. Allstate Ins. Co., 140
President & Directors of Georgetown College, Inc., Application of, 228
Procanik v. Cillo, 130
Public Health Trust v. Wons, 225
Public Service Mut. Ins. Co. v. Levy, 308

Quarles v. Sutherland, 277
Quilico v. Kaplan, 157
Quinlan, In re, 229, 231, 288
Quintal v. Laurel Grove Hosp., 247

Railroad Telegraphers v. Railway Express Agency, 181–182
Raitt v. Johns Hopkins Hosp., 26, 27
Ravi v. Williams, 105
Ray v. Wagner, 179
Rea v. Pardo, 305
Reid v. Indianapolis Osteopathic Medical Hosp., Inc., 352
Renslow v. Mennonite Hosp., 129
Reynolds v. Porter, 339
Rhoads v. Service Mach. Co., 20

TABLE OF CASES

Richardson v. Richardson-Merrell, Inc., 235
Richardson-Merrell, Inc., In re, 235
Rickey v. Chicago Transit Auth., 132–133
Ritter v. Wayne County Gen. Hosp., 350
Roa v. Lodi Medical Group, Inc., 346
Robak v. United States, 131
Roberson v. Counselman, 146–147, 150
Robins v. Finestone, 258
Rockhill v. Pollard, 278
Rowe v. Bennett, 44

Safian v. Aetna Life Ins. Co., 299
Saikewicz, Sup't of Belchertown State School v., 230
St. Paul Fire & Marine Ins. Co. v. House, 305, 309
St. Paul Fire & Marine Ins. Co. v. Insurance Comm'r, 297
St. Paul Ins. Co. v. Armas, 308
Salaymeh v. St. Vincent Memorial Hosp. Corp., 374
Samson v. Greenville Hosp. System, 249
Sard v. Hardy, 256
Satz v. Perlmutter, 226–229
Schack v. Holland, 339
Schloendorff v. Society of N.Y. Hosp., 161–163
Schoening v. Grays Harbor Commun. Hosp., 65
Sears v. Rutishauser, 94–95
Semerjian v. Stetson, 108
Senn v. Merrell-Dow Pharmaceuticals, Inc., 235
Shepard v. Redford Commun. Hosp., 53
Sherlock v. Stillwater Clinic, 136
Shilkret v. Annapolis Emergency Hosp. Ass'n, 25
Siemieniec v. Lutheran Gen. Hosp., 127
Simcuski v. Saeli, 267
Simonsen v. Swenson, 281
Simpson v. Dickson, 213
Sloan v. Metropolitan Health Council, 60
Small v. Howard, 27
Smith v. Smith, 250
Sparger v. Worley Hosp., Inc., 56
Speck v. Finegold, 131
Spring v. Constantino, 167
Stager v. Schneider, 177
State v. Williams, 61
Steiginga v. Thron, 96
Stewart v. Rudner, 262
Storar, In re, 230
Strachan v. John F. Kennedy Hosp., 284
Strahler v. St. Luke's Hosp., 340
Striegel v. Tofano, 84
Sullivan v. Commonwealth Ins. Dep't, 298
Sullivan v. O'Connor, 255

Superintendent of Belchertown State School v. Saikewicz, 230

T.J. Hooper, The, 32
Tarasoff v. Regents of the Univ. of Cal., 51
Tarpley, In re, 325
Tatham v. Hoke, 327
Tatrai v. Presbyterian Univ. Hosp., 165
Texas & P. Ry. v. Behymer, 31
Thomas v. Hutchinson, 57
Thompson v. Carter, 236
Thompson v. County of Alameda, 50
Thompson v. Sun City Commun. Hosp., 148
Thorpe, People ex rel. Kraushaar Bros. & Co., 104
Tiller v. Atlantic Coast Line R.R., 57
Toth v. Community Hosp., 37
Toy v. Mackintosh, 108
Tresemer v. Barke, 241
Trieschman v. Eaton, 185
Trower v. Jones, 92
Truman v. Thomas, 219
Turpin v. Sortini, 130

United States v. Johnson, 159
United States v. Kubrick, 180
United States v. Zwick, 384
United States v. Young, 121
University of Ariz. v. Superior Ct., 136–137

Ward v. Levy & Unger, 107
Ward v. Ochoa, 77
Waterson v. General Motors Corp., 153
Weil v. Seltzer, 175
Weirum v. RKO General, Inc., 46
Wentling v. Medical Anesthesia Services, P.A., 345–346
Wheeler v. St. Joseph Hosp., 329
Wickline v. State, 358
Wilkinson v. Vesey, 207
Willey v. Ketterer, 120
Williams, State v., 61
Williams v. State, 47
Wilson v. Bodian, 79
Wilson v. Clark, 94
Wilson v. Scott, 215
Wood v. Carpenter, 181
Woods v. Lancet, 163
Wooten v. Johnson & Johnson Prods., Inc., 244
Wright v. Central DuPage Hosp. Ass'n, 322

Ybarra v. Spangard, 55
Young, United States v., 121
Young v. St. Elizabeth Hosp., 165

Zichichi v. Middlesex Mem. Hosp., 251
Zwick, United States v., 384

MEDICAL LIABILITY

Part I
MEDICAL LIABILITY CLAIMS

Chapter 1

THE MEDICAL PROFESSIONAL RELATIONSHIP

INTRODUCTORY NOTE

Cases about the medical professional relationship show that patients and physicians often have different viewpoints about the existence and scope of physicians' professional duties. The courts allocate legal duties by deciding whether a medical professional relationship existed in law, and if it did, how breach of the relationship can be pleaded by the victim.

When a physician promises to use best efforts to perform medical services, and when a patient promises to pay for the services, the parties have created a medical professional relationship. When the physician performs services badly and the patient sues, usually the theory of claim is not breach of contract but tort, for "malpractice," where "mal" means "bad," and "practice" means "work." Ordinarily the damages for breach of a personal service contract do not include non-pecuniary elements, such as pain and suffering and loss of enjoyment, but malpractice as a tort permits the plaintiff to recover for a long list of non-pecuniary damages. In either the tort or the contract theory of claim, if there was no relationship, there is no claim.

The sections of this chapter deal with (a) whether and when the professional relationship commenced, (b) displacement of the defendant physicians' legal duties by another provider, and (c) medical services that never created a professional relationship with the plaintiff.

SECTION A. COMMENCEMENT OF THE PROFESSIONAL RELATIONSHIP

HISER v. RANDOLPH
Court of Appeals of Arizona, 1980.
126 Ariz. 608, 617 P.2d 774, review denied.

JACOBSON, JUDGE.

In this medical malpractice case, two issues are presented for resolution: (1) Whether a physician paid by a hospital to render emergency room services has a duty to render care to anyone presenting themselves to the hospital for emergency care; and (2) under the facts presented here, whether plaintiff has raised a factual issue that proximate cause exists between the failure to render care and the subsequent death of the patient.

These issues were resolved by summary judgment in favor of the defendant physician, Dr. W. Alan Randolph, and the decedent's spouse has appealed.

* * *

Mohave County General Hospital is the only hospital serving the community of Kingman, Arizona. It maintains an emergency room for the treatment of people in need of immediate medical service. Dr. Randolph and seven other doctors, comprising the medical profession in the Kingman area with admitting privileges at the hospital, established a program with the hospital by which each would take turns in manning the emergency room as the "on call physician" for a 12-hour period.

The on call physician was paid by the hospital at a basic rate of $100 for each day or shift served. Emergency patients and resident patients presenting themselves to the emergency room in need of immediate attention were referred to the on call physician.

From the record it appears that plaintiff's wife, Bonita Hiser, went with her husband to the emergency room at the hospital at approximately 11:45 p.m. on June 12, 1973. She was in a semi-comatose condition and the nurse in charge of the emergency room evaluated her as appearing to be very ill. Mrs. Hiser had an acute diabetic condition described as juvenile onset diabetes of the "brittle" variety. She had been treated in the emergency room at the hospital on the preceding day by Dr. Arnold of Kingman, her regular physician.

The emergency room nurse, after viewing Mrs. Hiser, immediately contacted Dr. Randolph, the "on call physician" at that time. Upon being advised as to who the patient was, Dr. Randolph stated to the nurse, at 11:50 p.m., that he would not attend or treat Mrs. Hiser, and that the nurse should call Dr. Arnold. When the nurse called Dr. Arnold he responded by stating that he would not come to the hospital at that time and that the on call physician should attend Mrs. Hiser.

The nurse relayed this information to Dr. Randolph who again refused to attend to or see Mrs. Hiser. The nurse then called Dr. Lingenfelter, Chief of Staff of the hospital. After a subsequent telephone conversation between Dr. Lingenfelter and Dr. Randolph in which Dr. Randolph reiterated that he would not treat Mrs. Hiser, Dr. Lingenfelter came to the hospital and attended Mrs. Hiser, arriving at approximately 12:30 a.m. Dr. Lingenfelter immediately commenced tests and treatment for Mrs. Hiser, whom he regarded as being very ill at the time. Dr. Lingenfelter stayed at the hospital throughout the night until Dr. Arnold arrived in the morning. Mrs. Hiser died at 11:00 a.m. on June 13.

As to the reason for Dr. Randolph's refusal to attend to Mrs. Hiser, a factual dispute exists. Dr. Randolph testified by deposition that the refusal was based upon his inability to adequately treat diabetes. From the evidence presented, however, a trier of fact could conclude that the refusal was based upon a personal animosity between Dr. Randolph and Mrs. Hiser or the fact that Mrs. Hiser's husband was a lawyer. Because the fact that Dr. Randolph refused to treat is undisputed and because of the posture in which this matter reaches us, we assume the refusal was medically unjustified.

The expert testimony indicates that Mrs. Hiser was suffering from acute hyperglycemia according to tests which were run by Dr. Lingenfelter immediately after he arrived at the hospital at 12:30 a.m. on June 13. On the issue of causation, Dr. Bryant I. Pickering, a Phoenix doctor specializing in internal medicine with whom Mrs. Hiser had consulted on previous occasions, testified in his deposition that given the circumstances surrounding Mrs. Hiser's condition upon her admission to the emergency room, the patient was in need of immediate care by a physician. He was further of the opinion based upon his review of the admission records that Mrs. Hiser had a substantial chance for survival if hospital emergency room procedures had been instituted immediately, and that if those procedures were withheld for an hour, the chance of survival would be reduced. In particular, the doctor testified that delay in treating Mrs. Hiser's chemical imbalance "would substantially increase the risk of death."

* * * Dr. Randolph contends that medical malpractice can only arise where the relationship of physician-patient is established; that this relationship is a consensual one; and that in the absence of special circumstances not present here, no physician can be required to treat a particular patient or incur liability for failure to do so. The plaintiff, while conceding the validity of this basic rule, contends that because of the contractual relationship between Dr. Randolph and Mohave General Hospital and the bylaws of the staff of that hospital, the doctor has obligated himself to treat all emergency patients.

In examining this issue we start with the general rule, with which we agree, that a medical practitioner is free to contract for his services as he sees fit and in the absence of prior contractual obligations, he can refuse to treat a patient, even under emergency situations.[1] * * *

The question remains whether Dr. Randolph has contracted away this right, while being the doctor "on call" in charge of the emergency room at Mohave General Hospital and being paid the sum of $100 a day to perform those services.

It is now clear, in Arizona, that a hospital which provides emergency room services is obligated to provide those services to everyone who is in need of them. Guerrero v. Copper Queen Hosp., 112 Ariz. 104, 537 P.2d 1329 (1975). Possibly in prerecognition of the hospital's obligation to undertake these services, bylaws were adopted by Mohave General Hospital to which Dr. Randolph was a party and bound. These bylaws in pertinent part provided:

> Article II: Purposes. The purposes of this organization shall be:
>
> 1. To insure that all patients admitted to this hospital or treated in the Emergency Room receive the best possible care.

The rules and regulations promulgated as a part of the bylaws provided as follows:

> 9. Except in emergency, no patient shall be admitted to the hospital until after a provisional diagnosis has been stated and the consent of the administrator or his delegate secured. In case of emergency the provisional diagnosis shall be stated as soon after admission as possible.
>
> * * *
>
> 11. The hospital shall admit patients suffering from all types of diseases. * * *

In our opinion, Dr. Randolph, by assenting to these bylaws, and rules and regulations, and accepting payment from the hospital to act as the emergency room doctor "on call," personally became bound "to insure that all patients * * * treated in the Emergency Room receive the best possible care," and agreed to insure "in the case of emergency the provisional diagnosis shall be started as soon after admission as possible." Moreover, these services were to be performed for all persons whom the "hospital shall admit * * * suffering from all types of disease."

While the various doctors in this case indicated that they were of the belief they had the right to refuse to treat an individual under varying circumstances, the obviously intended effect of the bylaws and rules and regulations was to obligate the emergency room doctor "on call" to provide emergency treatment to the best of the doctor's ability to any emergency patient of the hospital. Under these circumstances, the lack of a consensual physician-patient relationship before a duty to treat can arise has been waived by the signatory doctors.

---

1. We speak here only of legal obligations. As to ethical obligations, see § 5, Code of Ethics of the American Medical Association, which in part provides: A physician may choose whom he shall serve. In an emergency, however, he *should* render service to the best of his ability. (Emphasis added.)

Dr. Randolph cites rules 4 and 7 of the hospital rules and regulations, set forth in the margin,[2] in support of his position, but we do not think they qualify the duty to attend under the facts as thus far developed. Dr. Arnold, Mrs. Hiser's attending physician, effectively designated Dr. Randolph to attend Bonita Hiser on the night in question.

Viewing the evidence as we must on a motion for summary judgment, * * * Mrs. Hiser was in obvious need of emergency treatment. If there were other reasons possibly tending to excuse Dr. Randolph from attending to Mrs. Hiser, arising out of their previous relationship or otherwise, they have been stated by the doctor's counsel to be irrelevant to this appeal. We hold on the basis of the record and the issues presented to us that Dr. Randolph was obligated by contract to treat Mrs. Hiser to the best of his ability.

Our holding, as such, is not in any sense based upon Section 5 of the Code of Ethics previously quoted in footnote 1, supra. Our holding would be the same even without the incorporation of the Code of Ethics into the bylaws. The provision in the Code of Ethics in regard to emergency treatment is confirmatory, however, of an overall intent that emergency patients be treated as quickly as possible.

* * *

The judgment is reversed and the cause is remanded for further proceedings consistent herewith.

SECTION B. ALLOCATION OF LIABILITIES AMONG PROVIDERS

LARGESS v. TATEM
Supreme Court of Vermont, 1972.
130 Vt. 271, 291 A.2d 398.

DALEY, JUSTICE.

* * * The plaintiff, a 77-year-old woman, weighing 85 pounds, fell in her kitchen, in Bellows Falls, Vermont, and fractured her left hip on or about November 14, 1966. The defendant, William Tatem, a doctor of medicine, engaged in the general practice of medicine in Walpole, New Hampshire, and the general vicinity of Bellows Falls, Vermont, was called and caused her to be admitted to the Rockingham Memorial Hospital for treatment. X-rays were taken, and the injury was diagnosed as a comminuted intertrochanteric fracture of the left

---

2. * * *

4. Private patients shall be attended by their own private physicians. Private patients applying for admission who have no attending physician shall be referred to the physician on call.

* * *

7. Each member of medical staff not resident in the city or immediately available shall name a member of the medical staff who is resident in the city, who may be called to attend patients in emergency. In case of failure to name such associate, the administrator of the hospital shall have authority to call any member of the staff should he consider it necessary.

hip. Dr. Tatem concluded that the reduction of such fracture was beyond his training and experience and called Dr. William Chard into the case. Dr. Chard is an acknowledged specialist in orthopedic surgery with unquestioned qualifications in the field and extensive experience in intertrochanteric hip fractures. Dr. Chard recommended open reduction and internal fixation of the fracture fragments by an internal fixation device known as the "Jewett nail." With Dr. Tatem's concurrence and with Dr. Tatem assisting, Dr. Chard performed this procedure on November 15, 1966. The installation of the Jewett nail and the operating procedures connected therewith were skillfully and successfully performed with good result.

* * *

The fixation device, the Jewett nail, was not designed to permit full early weight bearing nor was it so recommended; it was in fact packaged with a printed admonition to the effect that "no implant can be expected to withstand the unsupported stresses of full weight bearing." Dr. Chard was generally familiar with this admonition, but Dr. Tatem was not. This admonition was also accompanied by a printed instruction as follows:

> 4. POST OPERATIVE CARE IS IMPORTANT. The patient should be instructed in the limitations of his metallic implant and should be cautioned regarding weight bearing and body stresses on the appliance prior to secure bone healing.

The court found that Dr. Chard was familiar with the limitations as to weight bearing. There is no evidence that such knowledge was within Dr. Tatem's field of general practice.

Dr. Chard for some time following the operation directed the course of plaintiff's treatment. All post-operative orders were written on the doctor's order sheet on the plaintiff's hospital chart. On November 22, Dr. Chard wrote the following order on the doctor's order sheet: "To P.T. [Physical Therapy] for ambulation with no wt. [weight] bearing. J. Chard."

On November 23, Dr. Chard entered the following on the plaintiff's progress notes: "23 Nov. Doing well. Will give P.T. a chance to ambulate her on non-wt. bearing * * *. J. Chard." He later made an entry on the progress notes on November 28: "Doing fairly well with walker * * *. J. Chard."

The last entry made by Dr. Chard on the plaintiff's progress notes was as follows:

> 1 Dec. Ambulating very well. Check x-rays look good. Wound healing well—not red or tender. Cause of temp. on 27 and 30 Nov. is not clear. May go home if Dr. Tatem feels general condition permits. J. Chard.

After the above entry, Dr. Chard took no further action in plaintiff's behalf except to call upon her once while visiting another patient. Plaintiff remained in the hospital until December 23, 1966, when she was discharged by Dr. Tatem. At the time of her discharge, she walked out of the hospital unassisted by any person or weight supporting device. On January 18, 1967, plaintiff was readmitted to the hospital. X-rays revealed that the Jewett nail had fractured along with the bone at the fracture site, necessitating a second operation to remove the broken appliance and insert a new one.

In Finding 18, the court found:

> [T]he failure would not have occurred without the prolonged and frequent course of full weight bearing to which it was subjected by the plaintiff, so that the failure of the device was proximately caused by the negligence of the defendant Tatem as found in Findings 15, supra. The second fracture of the hip was also so caused.

* * * The specific finding of negligence objected to by the defendant is contained in Finding 15:

> Dr. Tatem knew of the instructions given by Dr. Chard. He was aware that they had not been revised or countermanded. He made no attempt to advise or consult with Dr. Chard as to the advisability of the full weight bearing which he knew was occurring. In light of his admitted unfamiliarity with the type of fixation device here employed, and his admitted reliance upon Dr. Chard as an expert in the field, we find that permitting such weight bearing without Dr. Chard's advice or consent, and his failure to so consult with Dr. Chard, was negligence on his part.

* * *

At the time the plaintiff was recuperating in the hospital following the initial hip fracture, the defendant's knowledge concerning the treatment of fractures, in particular the one sustained by the plaintiff, was of a general nature, as was his knowledge concerning the healing of fractured bones and due limitations on weight bearing during healing. His experience was limited to non-complicated fractures in which the healing period for a bone such as the femur is from two to three months, during which period it is very essential to avoid motion. The bone must be kept quiet to obtain proper healing and X-rays are usually taken to check the healing prior to the allowance of weight bearing. The defendant admitted that the bone in question had not healed with full bony union at the time he discharged the plaintiff from the hospital, 38 days after her admission.

The treatment of intertrochanteric fractures was not within his field of expertise; he had never attempted to personally handle such type of fracture.

He knew by his assistance in the surgical process that the Jewett nail had been inserted, a device with which he was not professionally familiar; the defendant admitted that at the time he had not had any occasion or opportunity for specialized knowledge as to the limitation of such device or other internal fixation devices. He merely assumed, without inquiry, the strength and effect of an implanted device, the limitations of which were unknown to him.

At the time the defendant made such assumption, the plaintiff was in his general charge and supervision. The defendant, based upon the entry made by Dr. Chard on December 1, 1966, inferred that Dr. Chard was withdrawing from the case, was no longer going to write any orders or give any instructions, and the defendant was to use his own judgment from then on. In spite of his lack of training in the field of orthopedic practice, his lack of knowledge of the implanted device, the lack of any order or instruction permitting weight bearing, the defendant nevertheless by his own admission condoned full weight bearing without consulting or attempting to consult Dr. Chard, the expert upon whom he relied; the defendant alone made judgment that it was safe for the plaintiff to bear weight which resulted in injury to the plaintiff.

The defendant and the plaintiff occupied the status of physician and patient; the defendant was under a duty of at least employing due ordinary care for the safety of his patient; reasonable care. * * * Actions inconsistent with due care are within the ambit of negligence; an error in judgment inconsistent with due care under the circumstances then and there existing is condemnable as negligence if injurious consequences follow. * * *

In our view, the following definition expresses the duties and obligations of the defendant under the circumstances attending his postoperative supervision and treatment:

> [One] may * * * be engaged in an activity or stand in relationship to others which imposes upon him an obligation to investigate and find out so that he becomes liable not so much for being ignorant as for remaining ignorant; and this obligation may require him to know at least enough to conduct an intelligent inquiry as to what he does not know. W. Prosser, Torts § 32 at 160 (4th ed. 1971).

In the light of the defendant's admitted unfamiliarity with fixation devices, the hospital order which he had read relative to weight bearing, an obligation to investigate arose and became part of his duty when he took over plaintiff's care and supervision. Such duty under the circumstances found by the court preceded the making of any judgment concerning weight bearing on the part of the plaintiff. The defendant Tatem's admitted reliance upon Dr. Chard as an expert in a field (intertrochanteric fractures) in which the defendant possessed little, if any, training and experience imposed upon the defendant the duty of consultation prior to allowing full weight bearing upon plaintiff's injured limb, which as the court found, she did with the defendant's full knowledge and consent and with no instructions to the contrary from him.

The actions of the defendant when viewed in the light of his failure to inquire resulting in judgments formed by him are inconsistent with due care, and as the trial court found, constitute negligence.

* * *

Under the circumstances of this case, the evidence presented to the trier of fact clearly indicated the failure of the defendant to inquire prior to making a judgment concerning the weight bearing of the plaintiff was a gross violation of the due care owed by a physician to a patient. This violation of that due care being so apparent to be comprehensible to the lay trier of fact, expert medical testimony is not needed to substantiate the violation which is already apparent.

* * *

Judgment affirmed.

JACKSON v. POWER
Supreme Court of Alaska, 1987.
743 P.2d 1376.

BURKE, JUSTICE. * * *

On the evening of May 22, 1981, 16-year old Brett Jackson was seriously injured when he fell from a cliff. Jackson was airlifted to Fairbanks Memorial Hospital (FMH). Shortly after midnight, he was received in the hospital's emergency room.

Jackson was examined by respondent John Power, M.D., one of two emergency room physicians on duty at the time. Dr. Power's examination revealed multiple lacerations and abrasions of the patient's face and scalp, multiple contusions and lacerations of the lumbar area, several broken vertebrae and gastric distension, suggesting possible internal injuries. Dr. Power ordered several tests, but did not order certain procedures that could have been used to ascertain whether there had been damage to the patient's kidneys. Jackson had, in fact, suffered damage to the renal arteries and veins which supply blood to and remove blood from the kidneys. This damage, undetected for approximately nine to ten hours after Jackson's arrival at FMH, ultimately caused Jackson to lose both of his kidneys.

Jackson and his mother, Linda Estrada (hereinafter referred to collectively as Jackson), filed suit. In their complaint they alleged negligence in the diagnosis, care and treatment Jackson received at FMH. Jackson moved for partial summary judgment seeking to hold FMH vicariously liable as a matter of law for the care rendered by Dr. Power. In support of his motion, Jackson advanced three separate theories: (1) enterprise liability; (2) apparent authority; and (3) nondelegable duty.

After briefing and argument, the superior court held, as a matter of law, that FMH could not be held liable under an enterprise liability theory, and that genuine issues of material fact precluded summary judgment on the two remaining theories. We subsequently granted Jackson's petition for review of the court's ruling.

Initially, it is important to clarify the exact issue that we have been asked to resolve. Jackson has conceded, for purposes of this appeal, that Dr. Power was not an employee of FMH, but an independent contractor employed by respondent Emergency Room, Inc. (ERI), and that ERI and FMH are separate legal entities. Traditional rules of respondeat superior are, therefore, inapposite. Jackson also makes no claim that FMH was itself negligent in its selection, retention, or supervision of Dr. Power. * * *

Jackson argues that our decision in Fruit v. Schreiner, 502 P.2d 133 (Alaska 1972), establishes that the law of "vicarious legal responsibility" in Alaska is "enterprise liability." Thus, he contends, if the enterprise impacts society and the negligent act occurred during an activity performed for the benefit or in the interest of the enterprise, the enterprise is liable.

Jackson's argument proves unpersuasive. First, Jackson's interpretation of *Fruit* is flawed. A close reading of that case shows that we did not view "enterprise liability" as a separate theory of liability or a distinct cause of action. Rather, enterprise liability was seen as one of two widely accepted theories used by courts to justify imposition of vicarious liability in an established employer/employee context. * * *

* * * Moreover, although at least two courts appear to have implicitly indicated a willingness to recognize a theory of enterprise liability, see Alden v. Providence Hosp., 382 F.2d 163, 166 (D.C.Cir. 1967); Adamski v. Tacoma Gen. Hosp., 20 Wash.App. 98, 579 P.2d 970, 977 & n. 5 (1978), to date, no court has explicitly embraced that concept.

* * *

Jackson next argues that the trial court erred in holding that genuine issues of material fact prevented it from granting summary judgment on his theory of apparent authority.

* * *

Cases from other jurisdictions show a strong trend toward liability against hospitals that permit or encourage patients to believe that independent contractor/physicians are, in fact, authorized agents of the hospitals. These courts have held hospitals vicariously liable under a doctrine labeled either "ostensible" or "apparent" agency or "agency by estoppel." * * * Although courts and commentators often use these terms interchangeably, they are not theoretically identical.

The "ostensible" or "apparent" agency theory is based on § 429 of the Restatement (Second) of Torts (1965), which provides:

> One who employs an independent contractor to perform services for another which are accepted in the reasonable belief that the services are being rendered by the employer or by his servants, is subject to liability for physical harm caused by the negligence of the contractor in supplying such services, to the same extent as though the employer were supplying them himself or by his servants.

Two factors are relevant to a finding of ostensible agency: (1) whether the patient looks to the institution, rather than the individual physician, for care; and (2) whether the hospital "holds out" the physician as its employee. * * *

"Agency by estoppel," in contrast, is predicated on the arguably stricter standard of the Restatement (Second) of Agency § 267 (1958). Section 267 provides:

> One who represents that another is his servant or agent and thereby causes a third person justifiably to rely upon the care or skill of such apparent agent is subject to liability to the third person for harm caused by the lack of care or skill of the one appearing to be a servant or other agent as if he were such.

Under this theory, there must be actual reliance upon the representations of the principal by the person injured. Mehlman v. Powell, 281 Md. 269, 378 A.2d 1121, 1123 (1977). * * *

* * * We believe that traditional rules of apparent authority provide sufficient guidelines.

In City of Delta Junction v. Mack Trucks, 670 P.2d 1128 (Alaska 1983), we defined the doctrine of apparent authority in Alaska as follows:

> Apparent authority to do an act is created as to third persons by written or spoken word or any other conduct of the principal which, reasonably interpreted, causes the third person to believe that the principal consents to have the act done on his behalf by the person purporting to act for him. 670 P.2d at 1130 (quoting Restatement (Second) of Agency § 27 at 103 (1958)).

We went on to emphasize that it is the principal's conduct that gives rise to his liability and not the conduct of the alleged agent:

> [O]ne dealing with an alleged agent must prove that the principal was responsible for the appearance of authority, by doing something or permitting the alleged agent to do something that led others, including the plaintiff, to believe that the agent had the authority he purported to have. Id. (quoting W. Seavey, Handbook of the Law of Agency § 8 at 13 (1964)).

Relying on *City of Delta Junction,* the trial court held that existing factual disputes required Jackson to submit his apparent authority theory to the jury. * * *

Drawing all reasonable inferences in the light most favorable to FMH, the record shows the following: at the time of Jackson's accident, FMH was the only civilian hospital north of Anchorage providing emergency room services in Alaska. Two road signs in Fairbanks note the location of the hospital. However, neither of these signs specifically refer to the existence of emergency room services. The signs were not constructed or situated by FMH. In fact, FMH does no advertising at all.

From the time of its establishment in 1972, FMH has never staffed its emergency room with its own physician employees, but has always relied upon local physicians to provide that service. Prior to the formation of ERI in 1977, FMH's emergency room was serviced by three local clinics, each providing one physician on a nightly basis. After

1977, ERI provided one physician on a nightly basis who worked a 14-hour graveyard shift (6:00 p.m. to 8:00 a.m.). While on duty in the emergency room, the ERI physician was "in charge" and no FMH personnel were responsible for either scheduling or monitoring the emergency room physicians. No contractual arrangement existed between FMH and ERI for the provision of emergency room physicians.

In apparent non-life threatening situations the first person an incoming patient sees at the emergency room is the admissions clerk. Immediately adjacent to the clerk's desk is a sign which indicated that physicians from ERI were working in the emergency room. Although the exact state of Jackson's awareness is not entirely clear, there is evidence suggesting that he was admitted in a conscious state.[3] Neither Jackson nor his mother selected FMH as the place of treatment nor Dr. Power as Jackson's physician.

From the above, a jury could conclude that FMH held itself out as providing emergency care services to the public. A jury could also find that Jackson reasonably believed that Dr. Power was employed by the hospital to deliver emergency room service. It is also possible, however, that a jury could find to the contrary.[4]

Unless the evidence allows but one inference, the question of apparent authority is one of fact for the jury. * * * Thus, the trial court properly denied summary judgment on this issue.

Jackson's final point is that the trial court erred in refusing to rule, as a matter of law, that FMH, as a general acute care hospital, has a non-delegable duty to provide non-negligent physician care in its emergency room. In essence, Jackson's position is that when a hospital undertakes to operate an emergency room as an integral part of its health care enterprise, public policy dictates that it not be allowed to insulate itself from liability by shunting that responsibility onto another.

FMH, on the other hand, argues that a hospital does not have a non-delegable duty to guarantee safe treatment in its emergency room. Physicians, not hospitals, FMH asserts, have a duty to practice medicine non-negligently. Thus, according to FMH, a hospital cannot be held to have delegated away a duty it never had.

---

3. Jackson testified at his deposition that he recalled being placed in the helicopter but had no recollection of being removed from it, being taken to FMH, or of meeting the doctor who treated him. On the other hand, the medical records indicate that Jackson appeared to be neurologically stable, completely oriented, and gave no indication that he was unconscious or in distress. Moreover, at his deposition, Dr. Power testified that "Jackson was talking" and "completely oriented."

4. In this regard, we agree with the weight of authority that application of apparent authority in the hospital/emergency room physician situation does not require an express representation to the patient that the treating physician is an employee of the hospital. Nor is direct testimony as to reliance required, absent evidence that the patient knew or should have known that the treating physician was not a hospital employee when the treatment was rendered. * * *

[T]he threshold question is whether FMH had a duty to provide emergency room care. Only if it did, is it necessary to determine what that duty entailed.

FMH is licensed as a "general acute care hospital." As such, it is required to comply with state regulations designed to promote "safe and adequate treatment of individuals in hospitals in the interest of public health, safety and welfare." Alaska Stat. § 18.20.060. These regulations provided, at the time of Jackson's accident, that an acute care hospital shall "insure that a physician is available to respond to an emergency at all times." Former 7 Alaska Admin. Code § 12.110(c)(2).[5] Thus, at a minimum, the law imposed a duty on FMH to provide emergency care physicians on a 24–hour basis.

FMH, however, voluntarily assumed a much broader duty. At the time of Jackson's accident, FMH was accredited by the Joint Committee on the Accreditation of Hospitals (JCAH). In order to receive and maintain accreditation, FMH had to comply with the JCAH's standards promulgated in the Accreditations Manual for Hospitals, Emergency Services. Standard I mandates that all accredited hospitals implement a well defined plan for emergency care based on community need and the capability of the hospital. The JCAH standards also mandate, among other things, that: (1) FMH's emergency room be directed by a physician member of the active medical staff (Standard II); (2) FMH's emergency room be integrated with other units and departments of the hospital (Standard III); (3) that emergency care be guided by written policies and procedures; and (4) that the quality of care be continually reviewed, evaluated and assured through establishment of quality control mechanisms (Standard V).

Additionally, FMH's own bylaws provided for the establishment and maintenance of an emergency room. * * *

Based upon the above, it cannot seriously be questioned that FMH had a duty to provide emergency room services and that part of that duty was to provide physician care in its emergency room. Having so determined, we must next ascertain whether FMH's duty to provide physician care in the emergency room is non-delegable. That is, we must determine whether, having assumed the duty to staff an emergency room, FMH should be allowed to avoid responsibility for the care rendered therein by claiming that the physicians it provides are not its employees. We conclude that it cannot.

A non-delegable duty is an established exception to the rule that an employer is not liable for the negligence of an independent contractor. * * *

* * * It is the hospital that is required to ensure compliance with the regulations and thus, relevant to the instant case, it is the hospital that bears final accountability for the provision of physicians for

---

5. In 1983, this regulation was amended to provide that "[a] general acute care hospital *must* provide * * * [among other services not relevant here] emergency care services." 7 Alaska Admin. Code § 12.105. (Emphasis added.)

emergency room care. We, therefore, hold that a general acute care hospital's duty to provide physicians for emergency room care is non-delegable. Thus, a hospital such as FMH may not shield itself from liability by claiming that it is not responsible for the results of negligently performed health care when the law imposes a duty on the hospital to provide that health care.

* * *

In the instant case, Jackson came to FMH as an institution seeking emergency room services. Dr. Power was a physician FMH had a non-delegable duty to provide. FMH is, therefore, vicariously liable as a matter of law for any negligence or malpractice that Dr. Power may have committed. Accordingly, the trial court's ruling on this issue must be reversed. Jackson is entitled to partial summary judgment on the issue of FMH's vicarious liability.

* * *

SECTION C. PROFESSIONAL SERVICES THAT HARM NON-PATIENTS

KEENE v. WIGGINS

California Court of Appeal, 1977, hearing denied.
69 Cal.App.3d 308, 138 Cal.Rptr. 3.

COLOGNE, ASSOCIATE JUSTICE.

Charles I. Keene filed a complaint charging Howell E. Wiggins, M.D., and others, with medical malpractice. * * *

On November 22, 1972, Keene received injuries admittedly compensable by his employer under workers' compensation. He was later admitted to Palomar Memorial Hospital and treated by Rollin E. Weber, M.D., for "old operative adhesions and arachnoiditis" and released. In January 1973 he was readmitted to the hospital, where he underwent * * * a laminectomy. Following surgery he had chills, fever, nausea, and experienced low back pain radiating into his right leg. The condition persisted, and at the request of Industrial Indemnity, the employer's workers' compensation carrier, various medical consultants were called in to verify the need for further surgery. * * *

Industrial Indemnity wrote Dr. Wiggins and asked him to examine Keene and review the entire record, giving Industrial Indemnity his opinion as to what the permanent disability was at that time and what it might be should Keene undergo surgery.

Dr. Wiggins wrote Industrial Indemnity that Keene had arachnoiditis not amenable to surgery and recommended no further medical treatment or surgery. Keene received a copy of that report and asserts he relied on it to his detriment.

* * *

It is well established by authorities in other states that the physician is liable for malpractice or negligence only where there is a relationship of physician-patient as a result of a contract, express or implied, that the doctor will treat the patient with proper professional skill, and there is a breach of professional duty to the patient.[6] [W]here no physician-patient relationship exists, the doctor's only duty is to conduct the examination in a manner not to cause harm to the person being examined. The physician acts as an agent of the person requesting the examination * * *, and absent special circumstances, his duty to observe good standards of professional skill in reporting the results of the examination runs only to the person employing him. * * *

Measured against any standard of foreseeability, the physician, as here, hired solely to conduct an examination for purposes of rating disability compensation benefits, could not reasonably expect the claimant to rely on his opinion. Such a report is initiated by, arranged for and forwarded directly to Industrial Indemnity for the carrier's own best interests. The person under examination is seeking benefits from the employer's carrier and is pursuing a claim adverse to the interests of the employer.

While the law expects the physician to be objective in these matters, and there is nothing to suggest that Dr. Wiggins is anything other than objective in this case, it is common knowledge there are claimant's doctors and insurance company doctors, and the claimant cannot assume the insurance company's physician will be as generous as his own physician when assessing the injury to be rated. If it is a matter of opinion, the claimant should not expect the most advantageous conclusions. That expectation would be altered, of course, if the carrier's physician treats the claimant or otherwise seeks to provide a benefit; that situation is not presented here.

The physician who engages in any substantial amount of workers' compensation rating work may be aware of the fact the carrier must furnish the claimant with a copy of all medical reports, see Cal. Lab. Code § 4055, but in that event he must also reasonably expect from the adversary nature of the proceedings the claimant would not rely on it.
* * *

In the absence of special factors justifying reliance, it is not foreseeable a claimant in a workers' compensation case would, without question, accept and rely upon medical reports of the employer's insurance carrier. This is at least true where the examining physician is not the treating physician approved by the patient and is used by the carrier solely to assess the value of the claim where the parties will be dealing at arm's length. Reliance is even less likely where the employee has expressed dissatisfaction with the benefits then being offered by the employer's carrier. In view of the adverse relationship with the

---

6. Editors' Note: See Annot., Physician's Duties and Liabilities to Person Examined Pursuant to Physician's Contract with Such Person's Prospective or Actual Employer or Insurer, 10 A.L.R.3d 1071–1077 (1966). See also Annot., Master's Liability for Failure to Inform Servant of Disease or Physical Condition Disclosed by Medical Examination, 69 A.L.R.2d 1206–1221 (1960).

person being examined, the doctor's conduct is not morally blameworthy.

* * *

Here we find no physician-patient relationship, express or implied, of the sort giving rise to a duty of care owed to Keene in connection with the report. The uncontradicted declarations assert Keene went to Dr. Wiggins' office at the request of the carrier for "examination." Keene was present because he was required to submit to examination as a claimant. There is no assertion Dr. Wiggins did anything more than examine Keene and make his report to Industrial Indemnity as he was hired to do. The carrier requested this examination to verify the opinions of the other consulting doctors who had stated no operation or treatment was called for and to rate the disability. The Wiggins opinion was needed to properly rate the case for settlement of Keene's claim, see Cal.Lab.Code § 4600; as such the opinion was solely for the carrier's benefit in the adversary workers' compensation proceedings. None of the declarations suggest Wiggins's examination was part of Keene's care or treatment; nor do they suggest Wiggins voluntarily offered Keene any advice and counsel or otherwise intended to benefit Keene personally.[7]

* * * Dr. Wiggins's alleged failure to advise Keene of some medical condition did not give rise to a cause of action under the circumstances of this case. * * *

Judgment affirmed.

CHATMAN v. MILLIS

Supreme Court of Arkansas, 1975.
257 Ark. 451, 517 S.W.2d 504.

HARRIS, CHIEF JUSTICE.

* * * Mrs. Robbie Chatman was divorced from her husband Jerry Chatman, appellant herein. Chatman had visitation privileges with the couple's 2½ year old son. Mrs. Chatman, partly because of actions of the child, became concerned that Chatman had subjected the child to homosexual conduct, and, as a matter of terminating his visiting privileges, sought the aid of appellee, Willard Millis, Jr., Ph.D., in evaluating Chatman's conduct.[8] After talking with Mrs. Chatman and the child, Dr. Millis wrote her attorney a letter advising that Mrs. Chatman and her child had been referred to him by Dr. Ben Lowery for the purpose of his providing assistance in determining whether or not the child (Christopher) had been sexually molested by his father, and if so, the future implications for Christopher's psychosexual development.

---

7. Had Dr. Wiggins volunteered care or treatment or otherwise attempted to serve or benefit Keene in a direct manner, we would undoubtedly find a duty running to Keene. See Restatement (Second) of Torts § 323 (1965). Wiggins's declaration specially negated any such service or benefit and that fact was not controverted by Keene.

8. Editors' Note: "Chatman" has been substituted for "appellant," and "Dr. Millis" for "appellee," throughout.

In this letter, Dr. Millis went into detail as to comment made to him by Christopher and concluded his letter by stating:

> While it will be the Court's decision, and not mine, I feel that it would not be a good idea to allow Chris to continue to visit his father at all. If it is necessary that visitation rights be continued, I would strongly urge that the presence of a third person, preferably a relative, be in their presence at all times.
>
> As I mentioned in our telephone conversation of April 10, 1973 I would be willing to testify in Court about my interview or the statements made in the letter above.

Thereafter, Chatman instituted suit in the circuit court of White County, home of Chatman, alleging both defamation of character and malpractice against Dr. Millis. * * *

On hearing, the court held that no action for malpractice exists in this state against a psychologist; that even if such an action were permitted in this jurisdiction, there would have to be a doctor-patient relationship or some similar relationship between the parties, and that the complaint in the instant litigation alleged, and counsel had admitted, that Chatman had never been examined by Dr. Millis, and in fact, was not even known to the doctor; accordingly, there could be no action for malpractice. * * *

It is not necessary, in determining this litigation, to pass on the question of whether there is a cause of action in Arkansas for malpractice available against a psychological examiner or psychologist, since we are of the view that, even though such a cause of action exists, the allegations of Chatman's complaint do not state a cause of action.

We do not flatly state that a cause for malpractice must be predicated upon a contractual agreement between a doctor (psychologist) and patient, but we do say that a doctor-patient relationship must exist, i.e., there must be a duty, as a doctor, owed from the practitioner to the patient. Under the allegations before us, Dr. Millis made no examination of Chatman; in fact, he did not even know Chatman, and had never seen him. Chatman was not a patient of Dr. Millis, and the diagnosis reached was not for the benefit of Chatman. Even if the findings of the psychologist were negligently made, Chatman did not rely upon this diagnosis to his detriment.

Of course, all persons owe a duty to refrain from defaming others, but this is simply a duty that all citizens have toward each other, and has nothing to do with a doctor-patient relationship. After all, Chatman was not damaged by the allegedly negligent diagnosis—he was damaged by the alleged defamation. An example given by Dr. Millis appears pertinent to illustrate the point. Let us assume that a physician is engaged in lighthearted pleasure at a large cocktail party. Assume further that this physician openly refers to a non-patient individual, and by name refers to him as a homosexual. Certainly, under these circumstances, the physician might be found to have slandered that person's character, and, if so found, held to be answerable to that person for damages sustained. However, the fact that the speaker happened to be a physician does not mean that what was said constituted malpractice.

Concisely stated, we simply reiterate that under the facts alleged, Dr. Millis owed no duty, as a doctor, to Chatman, and this duty must be in existence before Chatman can recover because of negligence constituting malpractice.

Since we agree that, under the allegations, no action for malpractice exists, and it being admitted that the complaint was correctly dismissed because of improper venue on the defamation count, the judgment quashing the service is affirmed.

JONES, J., concurs.

FOGLEMAN, JUSTICE, dissenting.

The peculiar manner in which the issues presented reach this court puts them in an odd perspective for proper treatment on appellate review. * * *

This complaint was not tested by demurrer. Dr. Millis entered a special appearance and moved the summons be quashed because venue was not properly laid in White County. The grounds stated were that the complaint alleged a cause of action based upon defamation * * *. Dr. Millis did not then allege and has never contended he could not be liable for malpractice. * * * If an action for malpractice was stated, then the motion to quash was not well taken, because the venue was proper. * * *

I see no way we can approach this problem except by determining whether a malpractice action was brought in this case. * * *

Malpractice has been defined as "Any professional misconduct, unreasonable lack of skill or fidelity in professional or fiduciary duties, evil practice, or illegal or immoral conduct." Black's Law Dictionary 1111 (4th ed. 1951). In Arkansas, malpractice has been recognized as negligence in the practice of various professions, among which are law, medicine, and dentistry. [T]he rules governing duties and liabilities of physicians and surgeons * * * [apply] to practice of kindred branches of the healing arts. Our statutes make the practice of psychology a profession of the healing arts. Arkansas Stat.Ann. §§ 72-1501—72-1518 (1957) deal with this profession. They provide for licensing of psychological examiners and psychologists and for suspension and revocation of licenses, for privileged communication between such a licensee and his client, and for a code of ethics governing practice and behavior. It seems so clear such a malpractice action can lie against such a practitioner as to be beyond argument. This should end this court's inquiry and serve as a basis for reversal of the order granting the motion to quash, because it is clear the pleader was asserting such a cause of action separate and distinct from the cause of action for defamation. Any defect could easily be cured by amendment when and if a demurrer or motion to make more definite and certain was filed.

* * * I thoroughly disagree with the view that a doctor-patient relationship—as it is described by the majority—is a necessary prerequisite to a recovery for malpractice by Chatman. I submit that the attempt to analogize this case and this issue to cocktail party chatter is illustrative of the majority's approach to the issue and the faulty basis for its result. The dissimilarity of this example to this case should be obvious. It does not involve the professional relationship in any aspect or even remotely approach an involvement of the practice of a profession. I agree with the premise of the majority's result only in the respect that, in order for a presumably skilled professional to be liable, he must have owed a duty to the person who claims to have been injured and he must have violated that duty. Thereafter, I agree only with the conclusion that the physician at the cocktail party might be held answerable for his chatter in defamation, but not in a malpractice action. The majority's result has imported a rule of privity into malpractice actions. I consider this not only undesirable but improper.

A malpractice action, however it may be necessary to define it in order to give recognition to factors peculiar to the practice of a profession, should be considered nothing more or less than a tort action to recover damages for either willful, ignorant or negligent misconduct of a practitioner in the practice of his profession. * * *

[T]here can be no actionable negligence unless the actor has violated a duty he owed the victim of his act or omission. Prosser, Law of Torts § 42 at 244 (4th ed. 1971). The question then becomes, "To whom does the practitioner owe a duty?" Actionable negligence must arise from violation of a duty imposed upon the actor by common law, by statute or by contract. * * * Judge Cardozo said that negligence was a matter of relationship between the parties which must be founded upon the foreseeability of harm to the person in fact injured. * * * "Duty" is determined by answering the question whether the defendant is under any obligation for the benefit of the other party. * * * Arkansas cases hold that a duty to use care arises when it is reasonably foreseeable that injury will probably result to another if care is not used, and that it depends upon the foreseeability of injury or damage, not upon privity of contract. Rhoads v. Service Mach. Co., 329 F.Supp. 367 (E.D.Ark.1971).

* * * It seems to me that the public policy of Arkansas is clearly opposed to the privity requirement where one person suffers as a result of the failure of another to use reasonable care. We should not resurrect the "privity" doctrine by imposing it where we have never imposed it before.

The allegations in this case are that Chatman was damaged by Dr. Millis's failure to exercise the requisite degree of skill in making a psychological diagnosis of Chatman. Such diagnoses are certainly within the scope of Dr. Millis's practice. Assuming the allegations of the complaint to be true, as we must, it would border on absurdity to say that Dr. Millis could not reasonably have foreseen that a misdiagnosis of homosexuality would harm Chatman. The fact that the diagnosis was made without Dr. Millis's having known, seen or interviewed Chatman or having administered any tests to him would seem, in and of itself, to be malpractice, but whether it is or not is a matter of evidence when the case is tried on its merits. It certainly is a sufficient allegation to state a cause of action. As a matter of fact, the only flaw the majority perceives in the complaint is the fact that Chatman was not a patient of Dr. Millis. I submit that reason and logic do not support the majority opinion. I would remand this case for further proceedings.

I am authorized to state that MR. JUSTICE BROWN joins in this dissent.

Chapter 2

NEGLIGENCE OF THE HEALTH CARE PROVIDER

INTRODUCTORY NOTE

Negligence is the failure to use due care under the circumstances. This definition needs no citation, but how does it apply to medical negligence today?

In a bygone fatalistic age, when a trip to the doctor was an intimation of mortality, and when most people left the hospital feet first, a medical "bad result" was usually accepted by patients and next of kin without litigation. Today, patients and next of kin expect health care providers to make people well, and "bad result," to these lay persons, is a euphemism for medical negligence. Physicians are aware of the irony, that they are the legal victims of scientific medicine's successes.

While medical attendance is a contract for personal services, a bad result accomplished through the physician's "best efforts" is not good enough; the tort theory of claim, demanding due care under the circumstances, has displaced breach of contract.

Standards of "due care" involves two components: defining the forms of words in which the standards are expressed, and defining the eligibility of persons to apply the definitions. The courts (and lately the legislatures), necessarily assisted by medical experts, but not necessarily governed by them, set the form of words, and this chapter deals with the process of formulation. Chapter four treats the need for and the eligibility of experts to apply the definitions in particular cases.

The practical outcome of due care standards is to sort medical negligence cases into three groups, so that the victims of plain medical negligence will be compensated, bad results that happen in spite of due care will not be called medical negligence, and juries will decide doubtful cases with minimum precedential effect.

This chapter's first section deals with establishing due care standards—personal, primary care, specialty, local, regional or national— and adjusting due care to medical progress. The second section looks at unusual cases alleging that a health care provider's lack of due care toward one person caused harmful consequences to the plaintiff, a different person.

SECTION A. DEFINING MEDICAL DUE CARE

PIKE v. HONSINGER

Court of Appeals of New York, 1898.
155 N.Y. 201, 49 N.E. 760.

By this action the plaintiff, George W. Pike, sought to recover damages from the defendant, Willis T. Honsinger, a physician and surgeon, for negligence in treating his knee, which had been injured by an accident. * * * At the close of all the evidence the court directed a verdict in favor of the defendant. After an affirmance by the general term, without an opinion, 32 N.Y.S. 1149 (1895), the plaintiff came here. * * *

VANN, J. * * *

On the second of May 1888, the plaintiff, then 44 years of age, with good health and sound limbs, had the patella or kneepan of his right leg broken by the kick of a horse. When the accident happened he was five miles from home and two and one-half miles from the village where the defendant, a physician and surgeon, resided. He drove to the office of the defendant * * *.

[The court summarized the evidence at length. Dr. Honsinger was attentive and active in treating Pike, but Pike's expert witnesses testified that Dr. Honsinger failed to diagnose the fractured patella and did not adequately immobilize the knee and leg.]

While there was much conflict in the evidence, both in relation to the treatment actually pursued, and as to the treatment that should have been pursued, it was within the province of the jury to settle the conflict by finding the facts as thus stated. Could they, from those facts, have drawn the inference of negligence, resulting injury, and liability therefor?

The law relating to malpractice is simple and well settled, although not always easy of application. A physician and surgeon, by taking charge of a case, impliedly represents that he possesses, and the law places upon him the duty of possessing, that reasonable degree of learning and skill that is ordinarily possessed by physicians and surgeons in the locality where he practices, and which is ordinarily regarded by those conversant with the employment as necessary to qualify him to engage in the business of practicing medicine and surgery. Upon consenting to treat a patient, it becomes his duty to use reasonable care and diligence in the exercise of his skill and the application of his learning to accomplish the purpose for which he was employed. He is under the further obligation to use his best judgment in exercising his skill and applying his knowledge. The law holds him liable for an injury to his patient resulting from want of the requisite knowledge and skill, or the omission to exercise reasonable care, or the failure to use his best judgment.

The rule in relation to learning and skill does not require the surgeon to possess that extraordinary learning and skill which belong only to a few men of rare endowments, but such as is possessed by the average member of the medical profession in good standing. Still, he is bound to keep abreast of the times, and a departure from approved methods in general use, if it injures the patient, will render him liable, however good his intentions may have been.

The rule of reasonable care and diligence does not require the exercise of the highest possible degree of care, and, to render a physician and surgeon liable, it is not enough that there has been a less degree of care than some other medical man might have shown, or less than even he himself might have bestowed, but there must be a want of ordinary and reasonable care, leading to a bad result. This includes not only the diagnosis and treatment, but also the giving of proper instructions to his patient in relation to conduct, exercise, and the use of an injured limb.

The rule requiring him to use his best judgment does not hold him liable for a mere error of judgment, provided he does what he thinks is best after careful examination. His implied engagement with his patient does not guaranty a good result, but he promises by implication to use the skill and learning of the average physician, to exercise reasonable care, and to exert his best judgment in the effort to bring about a good result. * * *

Having thus stated the nature of the injury and the condition of the plaintiff when the defendant took charge of him, the treatment actually pursued and the treatment that should have been pursued, as the jury might have found, as well as the general principles of law applicable to such cases, we think it follows that the learned trial judge should have submitted the case to the jury. While they might have found for the defendant if they believed him and his witnesses, if, on the other hand, they believed the plaintiff and his witnesses, they might have found that the defendant was guilty of negligence in omitting to reduce the swelling so that a safe diagnosis could be made; in failing to discover that the real nature of the injury was a broken patella instead of a rupture of the ligaments; in omitting to place the broken parts in apposition, and to keep them there with proper appliances, and by taking proper precautions as to quiet for a sufficient length of time to bring about the best result; in dressing and flexing the leg without adequate care to keep the broken bones together, and in telling the plaintiff to flex it, without proper instructions to that end; in permitting the plaintiff to use his leg too soon and in a hazardous manner; and in assuring him that his knee was getting along all right, and that he would have a good leg, and thereby preventing him from securing other medical treatment. They might also have found that such negligence injured the plaintiff by preventing a better recovery, which would lead to an assessment of damages.

We think there were questions of fact for the determination of the jury, and that, for the error in directing a verdict, the judgment should be reversed, and a new trial granted * * *.

[BARTLETT, J., dissented.]

SHILKRET v. ANNAPOLIS EMERGENCY HOSP. ASS'N

Court of Appeals of Maryland, 1975.
276 Md. 187, 349 A.2d 245, 99 A.L.R.3d 1119.[1]

LEVINE, JUDGE. * * *

[T]he infant plaintiff, Mark Alan Shilkret, was born at the Anne Arundel General Hospital (Anne Arundel) on December 22, 1968, and has been continuously institutionalized since that date because of brain damage that appellants allege resulted from intracranial bleeding caused by negligence at delivery. This was allegedly complicated by subsequent treatment rendered by appellees, the various attending physicians and the hospital. The several physicians who are appellees here include two obstetricians who treated the mother throughout the prenatal stage and then delivered the infant, an anesthesiologist in attendance at birth, and a pediatrician at the hospital who allegedly examined the infant the day after his birth.

At the trial, after excerpts from the depositions of the four defendant-physicians had been admitted in evidence, argument ensued over the applicable standard of care. When the court indicated that it would apply "the strict locality rule," [plaintiff-]appellants conceded that they could not prove their case against appellees under that standard and requested leave to make a proffer of expert medical testimony which "could meet any other rule in medical negligence cases." They were afforded this opportunity and proceeded with extensive statements of what their two experts, an obstetrician-gynecologist and a neurosurgeon, would say if called as witnesses. Each expert had an impressive curriculum vitae.

The proffered testimony of the obstetrician-gynecologist established that Anne Arundel belongs to the American Hospital Association, one of several members of the accrediting body known as the Joint Commission on Accreditation of Hospitals. It was his opinion that all hospitals belonging to this group meet a national standard in caring for obstetrical patients. At the time of the infant's birth, the witness had been chief of the obstetrical-gynecological services at the U.S. Army Hospital at Aberdeen Proving Ground. He believed that in this branch of medicine, the standards at Anne Arundel were the same as those observed at Aberdeen and at all other accredited hospitals in the

---

1. Annot., Modern Status of "Locality Rule" in Malpractice Action against Physician Who Is Not a Specialist, 99 A.L.R.3d 1133–1178 (1980).

United States. Similarly, as a member of the American College of Gynecologists and Obstetricians, and being board certified, he believed that a national standard of care applied to those with the same qualifications. He then detailed how the failure of the four physicians and the hospital to meet the national standards of care applicable to them resulted in the injury to the plaintiff.

The other expert witness whose testimony was proffered would have stated in some detail that he was employed as a neurosurgeon at the National Institutes of Health at Bethesda, Maryland, that a national standard of care is observed in the diagnosis and treatment of neurological diseases, the knowledge of which is also possessed by general practitioners, and that each of the defendants had violated what he believed to be a national standard regarding the care of newborn infants.

Following these proffers, the trial judge granted each appellee's motion for a directed verdict. He adhered to his previously pronounced belief that the "strict locality" standard applies in Maryland, rather than the "national" (in which the standard of care is not tied to a particular geographic locality) or "similar locality" (the standard of care observed by physicians of ordinary skill and care in either the defendant-physician's locality or in a similar community) tests urged by appellants, and therefore ruled that the latter had failed to present a sufficient case for the jury. The Court of Special Appeals affirmed, holding that its own prior cases—and the decisions of this Court—compelled this result. * * *

Recently, in Raitt v. Johns Hopkins Hospital, 274 Md. 489, 336 A.2d 90, 96 (1975), where we held that an expert medical witness need not necessarily reside or practice in the defendant's community to testify as to the applicable standard of care in a medical malpractice case, we intimated that despite the plethora of reported medical malpractice decisions in Maryland, this court actually had never been confronted with the need to adopt a standard of care from among the three we have mentioned.

* * *

The earliest traces of the strict locality rule appeared a century ago. * * * The rule was unquestionably developed to protect the rural and small town practitioner, who was presumed to be less adequately informed and equipped than his big city brother. * * *

Ultimately, the rule came under sharp attack on two grounds. First,

> It effectively immunized from malpractice liability any doctor who happened to be the sole practitioner in his community. He could be treating bone fractures by the application of wet grape leaves and yet remain beyond the criticism of more enlightened practitioners from other communities. Waltz, The Rise and Gradual Fall of the Locality Rule in Medical Malpractice Litigation, 18 DePaul L.Rev. 408, 411 (1969).

Secondly, a "conspiracy of silence" in the plaintiff's locality could effectively preclude any possibility of obtaining expert medical testimony. * * *[2]

Whatever may have justified the strict locality rule fifty or a hundred years ago, it cannot be reconciled with the realities of medical practice today.[3] * * *

A distinct minority of states, however, cling to the strict locality rule. * * * Nevertheless, recognizing the significant developments which have occurred in the training and practice of medicine, and the population shifts which have marked the increased urbanization of our society, a majority of American courts have now abandoned the strict locality rule as being too narrow. We, too, conclude that it can be sustained no longer given the current state of medical science.

A plurality, if not a majority, of states apply the similar locality rule. * * *

The similar locality rule answers some of the criticism aimed at the strict locality standard by enabling the plaintiff to obtain expert witnesses from different communities, thus reducing the likelihood of their acquaintance with the defendant. It does not, however, effectively alleviate the other potential problem, a low standard of care in some of the smaller communities, because the standard in similar communities is apt to be the same. Another criticism leveled at the similar locality rule is the difficulty which arises in defining a "similar" locality.[4] For these reasons, the similar locality rule is regarded as no more than a slight improvement over the stricter standard.

These deficiencies in the locality rules and the increasing emphasis on the availability of medical facilities have led some courts to dilute the rules by extending geographical boundaries to include those centers

---

2. This problem, of course, has been obviated in Maryland by our decision in *Raitt.*

3. The absurdity of coupling the standard of care with the doctor's community is aptly illustrated in Brune v. Belinkoff, 354 Mass. 102, 235 N.E.2d 793 (1968), in which the Supreme Judicial Court of Massachusetts overruled its earlier decision in Small v. Howard, 128 Mass. 131, 35 Am. Rep. 363 (1880), containing one of the first enunciations of the similar locality rule. In *Brune,* which involved an act of alleged malpractice in the city of New Bedford, slightly more than 50 miles from Boston, the trial judge had instructed the jury:

> If, in a given case, it were determined by a jury that the ability and skill of the physician in New Bedford were 50% inferior to that which existed in Boston, a defendant in New Bedford would be required to measure up to the standard of skill and competence and ability that is ordinarily found by physicians in New Bedford. 235 N.E.2d at 795.

4. One standard which has been applied is geographic proximity between communities, which retains much of the "same" locality flavor. Other courts have considered socioeconomic factors such as population, type of economy, size of city, and income of inhabitants. Most courts applying this standard, however, have adopted the view that "similar" locality should be defined in terms of medical factors such as the existence of research and laboratory facilities, medical schools, teaching hospitals and modern equipment in the localities to be compared. The commentators agree that this is the most logical application of the rule when measured against a major reason for its adoption—the availability of resources which will enable the physician to maintain the standard of his practice. * * *

that are readily accessible for appropriate treatment. * * * This expanded rule, expressed in terms of "medical neighborhood" or "medical locality," has paved the way for the national standard. In any event, the trend continues away from standards which rest solely on geographic considerations.

Ever-increasing emphasis on medical specialization has accelerated the erosion of the locality rules and the concomitant emergence of the so-called national standard. Even within the framework of the locality rules, it has been generally accepted that where a physician holds himself out as a specialist, he is held to a higher standard of knowledge and skill than a general practitioner. Some courts, therefore, have abandoned the locality rules for a national standard only as to specialists. * * * This is consistent with the position of the American Law Institute, which otherwise adopts the similar locality rule.

Were we to adopt a standard tied to locality for specialists, we would clearly be ignoring the realities of medical life. As we have indicated, the various specialties have established uniform requirements for certification. The national boards dictate the length of residency training, subjects to be covered, and the examinations given to the candidates for certification. Since the medical profession itself recognizes national standards for specialists that are not determined by geography, the law should follow suit.

The courts in another group of cases, however, have gone further, and have adopted this same standard of care—one which is not governed by the locality of the defendant—for all physicians regardless of whether they are specialists or not. Blair v. Eblen, 461 S.W.2d 370, 372–73 (Ky.1970) ("that degree of care and skill which is expected of a reasonably competent practitioner in the same class to which he belongs, acting in the same or similar circumstances") * * *.

We agree with these courts that justification for the locality rules no longer exists. The modern physician bears little resemblance to his predecessors. As we have indicated at length, the medical schools of yesterday could not possibly compare with the accredited institutions of today, many of which are associated with teaching hospitals. But the contrast merely begins at that point in the medical career: vastly superior postgraduate training, the dynamic impact of modern communications and transportation, the proliferation of medical literature, frequent seminars and conferences on a variety of professional subjects, and the growing availability of modern clinical facilities are but some of the developments in the medical profession which combine to produce contemporary standards that are not only much higher than they were just a few short years ago, but also are national in scope.

* * *

Moreover, while a specialist may be held to greater skill and knowledge in his particular field than would be required of a general practitioner under the same or similar circumstances, one standard can be fashioned for all physicians * * *. To that extent, there is no valid basis for distinguishing between general practitioners and specialists in applying standards of care. Although national board certification in the specialties has contributed significantly to standardization on a nationwide scale, all of the other reasons which justify a national standard of care apply with equal validity to general practitioners.

Nevertheless, in one important respect there is even a difference of opinion among * * * [the courts of Kentucky, Washington, and Wisconsin] and the Massachusetts court. As we noted earlier, the Massachusetts court articulated two standards, one for the "*average* qualified practitioner" and the other for the "*average* member of the profession practising [a] specialty." Brune v. Belinkoff, 354 Mass. 102, 235 N.E.2d 793, 798 (1968). (Emphasis added.) * * * The Kentucky Court of Appeals, however, substituted "the term 'reasonably competent' for the term 'average' * * *." Blair v. Eblen, 461 S.W.2d 370, 373 (1970).

In eschewing the term "average," the Kentucky court sided with the American Law Institute, which, in comment e to Restatement (Second) of Torts § 299A (1965), states:

> [The standard] is not that of the most highly skilled, nor is it that of the average member of the profession * * *, since those who have less than median or average skill may still be competent and qualified. Half of the physicians of America do not automatically become negligent in practicing medicine at all, merely because their skill is less than the professional average. On the other hand, the standard is not that of the charlatan, the quack, the unqualified or incompetent individual who has succeeded in entering the profession * * *.

We align ourselves with the Kentucky court and hold that a physician is under a duty to use that degree of care and skill which is expected of a reasonably competent practitioner in the same class to which he belongs, acting in the same or similar circumstances. Under this standard, advances in the profession, availability of facilities, specialization or general practice, proximity of specialists and special facilities, together with all other relevant considerations, are to be taken into account. * * *

We hold * * * [also] that a hospital is required to use that degree of care and skill which is expected of a reasonably competent hospital in the same or similar circumstances. As in cases brought against physicians, advances in the profession, availability of special facilities and specialists, together with all other relevant considerations, are to be taken into account.

Here, there was evidence that there is a national standard of care for accredited hospitals in the prenatal, intrapartum and perinatal periods of pregnancy. Similarly, the evidence proffered by appellants showed national standards of care for child delivery, infant care, and the treatment of neurological problems generally, and the measure of vital functions specifically, that are observed by specialists and general practitioners alike. Under our holdings here, this evidence was sufficient to take the standard of care issue to the jury as to all of the appellees. * * *

Judgment of the Court of Special Appeals reversed; remanded to that court with instructions to remand the case as against all appellees to the Circuit Court for Anne Arundel County for a new trial; appellees to pay costs.

HELLING v. CAREY

Supreme Court of Washington, 1974.
83 Wash.2d 514, 519 P.2d 981, 67 A.L.R.3d 175.[5]

HUNTER, ASSOCIATE JUSTICE. * * *

The plaintiff, Barbara Helling, suffers from primary open-angle glaucoma. Primary open-angle glaucoma is essentially a condition of the eye in which there is an interference in the ease with which the nourishing fluids can flow out of the eye. Such a condition results in pressure gradually rising above the normal level to such an extent that damage is produced to the optic nerve and its fibers with resultant loss in vision. The first loss usually occurs in the periphery of the field of vision. The disease usually has few symptoms and, in the absence of a pressure test, is often undetected until the damage has become extensive and irreversible.

The defendants (respondents), Dr. Thomas F. Carey and Dr. Robert C. Laughlin, are partners who practice the medical specialty of ophthalmology. Ophthalmology involves the diagnosis and treatment of defects and diseases of the eye.

The plaintiff first consulted the defendants for myopia, nearsightedness, in 1959. At that time she was fitted with contact lenses. She next consulted the defendants in September 1963 concerning irritation caused by the contact lenses. Additional consultations occurred in October 1963, February 1967, September 1967, October 1967, May 1968, July 1968, August 1968, September 1968, and October 1968. Until the October 1968 consultation, the defendants considered the plaintiff's visual problems to be related solely to complications associated with her contact lenses. On that occasion, the defendant, Dr. Carey, tested the plaintiff's eye pressure and field of vision for the first time. This test indicated that the plaintiff had glaucoma. The plaintiff, who was then 32 years of age, had essentially lost her peripheral vision, and her central vision was reduced to approximately 5 degrees vertical by 10 degrees horizontal.

Thereafter, in August of 1969, after consulting other physicians, the plaintiff filed a complaint against the defendants alleging, among other things, that she sustained severe and permanent damage to her eyes as a proximate result of the defendants' negligence. During trial,

---

5. Annot., Failure to Administer Glaucoma Test as Malpractice, 67 A.L.R.3d 183 (1975).

the testimony of the medical experts for both the plaintiff and the defendants established that the standards of the profession for that specialty in the same or similar circumstances do not require routine pressure tests for glaucoma upon patients under 40 years of age. The reason the pressure test for glaucoma is not given as a regular practice to patients under the age of 40 is that the disease rarely occurs in this age group. Testimony indicated, however, that the standards of the profession do require pressure tests if the patient's complaints and symptoms reveal to the physician that glaucoma should be suspected.

The trial court entered judgment for the defendants following a defense verdict. * * * [The Court of Appeals affirmed without a reported opinion.]

[T]he plaintiff contends, in effect, that she was unable to argue her theory of the case to the jury: that the standard of care for the specialty of ophthalmology was inadequate to protect the plaintiff from the incidence of glaucoma; and that the defendants, by reason of their special ability, knowledge and information, were negligent in failing to give the pressure test to the plaintiff at an earlier point in time which, if given, would have detected her condition and enabled the defendants to have averted the resulting substantial loss in her vision.

We find this to be a unique case. The testimony of the medical experts is undisputed concerning the standards of the profession for the specialty of ophthalmology. * * * The issue is whether the defendants' compliance with the standard of the profession of ophthalmology, which does not require the giving of a routine pressure test to persons under 40 years of age, should insulate them from liability under the facts in this case, where the plaintiff has lost a substantial amount of her vision due to the failure of the defendants to timely give the pressure test to the plaintiff.

* * *

The incidence of glaucoma in one out of 25,000 persons under the age of 40 may appear quite minimal. However, that one person, the plaintiff in this instance, is entitled to the same protection as afforded persons over 40, essential for timely detection of the evidence of glaucoma when it can be arrested to avoid the grave and devastating result of this disease. The test is a simple pressure test, relatively inexpensive. There is no judgment factor involved, and there is no doubt that by giving the test the evidence of glaucoma can be detected. The giving of the test is harmless if the physical condition of the eye permits. The testimony indicates that although the condition of the plaintiff's eyes might have at times prevented the defendants from administering the pressure test, there is an absence of evidence in the record that the test could not have been timely given.

Justice Holmes stated in Texas & P. Ry. v. Behymer, 189 U.S. 468, 470, 23 S.Ct. 622, 47 L.Ed. 905 (1903), "What usually is done may be evidence of what ought to be done, but what ought to be done is fixed by a standard of reasonable prudence, whether it usually is complied with or not."

In The T.J. Hooper, 60 F.2d 737, 740 (2d Cir.1932), Judge Hand stated:

> [I]n most cases reasonable prudence is in fact common prudence; but strictly it is never its measure; a whole calling may have unduly lagged in the adoption of new and available devices. It never may set its own tests, however persuasive be its usages. *Courts must in the end say what is required; there are precautions so imperative that even their universal disregard will not excuse their omission.* (Italics ours.)

Under the facts of this case reasonable prudence required the timely giving of the pressure test to this plaintiff. The precaution of giving this test to detect the incidence of glaucoma to patients under 40 years of age is so imperative that irrespective of its disregard by the standards of the ophthalmology profession, it is the duty of the courts to say what is required to protect patients under 40 from the damaging results of glaucoma.

We therefore hold, as a matter of law, that the reasonable standard that should have been followed under the undisputed facts of this case was the timely giving of this simple, harmless pressure test to this plaintiff, and that, in failing to do so, the defendants were negligent, which proximately resulted in the blindness sustained by the plaintiff for which the defendants are liable.

There are no disputed facts to submit to the jury on the issue of the defendants' liability. Hence, a discussion of the plaintiff's proposed instructions would be inconsequential in view of our disposition of the case.

The judgment of the trial court and the decision of the court of appeals is reversed, and the case is remanded for a new trial on the issue of damages only.

* * *

UTTER, ASSOCIATE JUSTICE, concurring.

I concur in the result reached by the majority. I believe a greater duty of care could be imposed on the defendants than was established by their profession. * * *

The difficulty with this approach is that we as judges, by using a negligence analysis, seem to be imposing a stigma of moral blame upon the doctors who, in this case, used all the precautions commonly prescribed by their profession in diagnosis and treatment. Lacking their training in this highly sophisticated profession, it seems illogical for this court to say they failed to exercise a reasonable standard of care. It seems to me we are, in reality, imposing liability, because, in choosing between an innocent plaintiff and a doctor, who acted reasonably according to his specialty but who could have prevented the full effects of this disease by administering a simple, harmless test and treatment, the plaintiff should not have to bear the risk of loss. As such, imposition of liability approaches that of strict liability.

[S]trict liability serves a compensatory function in situations where the defendant is, through the use of insurance, the financially more responsible person. * * *

If the standard of a reasonably prudent specialist is, in fact, inadequate to offer reasonable protection to the plaintiff, then liability can be imposed without fault. To do so under the narrow facts of this case does not offend my sense of justice. The pressure test to measure intraocular pressure with the Schiotz tonometer and the Goldman applanometer takes a short time, involves no damage to the patient, and consists of placing the instrument against the eyeball. An abnormally high pressure requires other tests which would either confirm or deny the existence of glaucoma. It is generally believed that from 5 to 10 years of detectable increased pressure must exist before there is permanent damage to the optic nerves.

* * *

FINLEY and HAMILTON, JJ., concurred.

Note on the Aftermath of Helling v. Carey

Probably the outcome of Helling v. Carey[6] could have been explained as well by the physicians' negligent failure to rule out a specific (if unlikely) cause of Mrs. Helling's eye complaints, rather than by their negligent failure to use a test designed for screening large populations for glaucoma. However that may be, the court's strong rule on its capacity to set the standard of medical care threatened the structure of lawmaking. While no reported opinion followed the remand, *Helling* did not fade into the legal literature; the repercussions of the court's declaration of lawmaking freedom were felt throughout the United States.[7]

One might expect the physicians to seek relief from the legislature, and sure enough, the Washington state legislature at its first extraordinary session in 1975 enacted this statute:

> In any civil action for damages based on professional negligence against * * * a member of the healing arts * * *, the plaintiff in order to prevail shall be required to prove by a preponderance of the evidence that the defendant or defendants failed to exercise that degree of skill, care, and learning possessed by other persons in the same profession * * *. Wash.Rev.Code § 4.24.290.

In 1979 Gates v. Jensen, another glaucoma case[8] reached the Washington supreme court. A woman 54 years old had tested borderline for glaucoma, but she was not given then either of two further tests, dilation of the pupils for better view of the optic nerve discs, or a visual field examination—tests that, she later alleged, would have showed that she suffered from the disease. The trial judge let the jury have the case

---

6. 83 Wash.2d 514, 519 P.2d 981 (1974).

7. See Schwartz & Komesar, Doctors, Damages and Deterrence; An Economic View of Medical Malpractice, 298 N.E.J. Med. 1282 (June 1978).

8. 92 Wash.2d 246, 595 P.2d 919 (1979).

without the *Helling* instruction, and the jury found for defendant ophthalmologists. The court of appeals affirmed, holding that § 4.24.290 had overruled *Helling*.⁹ The supreme court reversed, holding that *Helling* was still in effect:

> The original house bill would have established the standard of care as that skill and care *practiced* by others in the same profession and specialty. H.B. 246, 44th Regular Sess. (1975). Respondent contends the clear intent of this bill was to abrogate the *Helling* rule. The original bill was amended, though. The statute as passed requires physicians to exercise the skill, care and learning *possessed* by others in the same profession. This standard is much broader than the one embodied in the original bill, and allows ample scope for the application of the limited *Helling* rule. It is not argued that respondent and other ophthalmologists did not possess the skill, care and learning required to choose and administer the two alternative, simple and risk-free tests. We therefore find no bar to the requested instruction under Wash.Rev.Code § 4.24.290. 595 P.2d at 924.

Wrote a dissenting justice,

> The *Helling* decision represented a deviation from the "standard of the profession" test used in medical malpractice actions. It rested on the "reasonably prudent person" standard which is applied in ordinary tort cases. * * *
>
> * * * I do not believe that the change of the word "practiced" to "possessed" frustrated the legislature's purpose in enacting Wash.Rev. Code § 4.24.290. * * *
>
> * * * Plaintiff's proposed supplemental instruction No. 3 says that even if the defendants met "the applicable standard of care followed by practicing ophthalmologists in the diagnosis of glaucoma" the jury could still find defendants negligent. This is absolutely contrary to the mandate of the legislature. 595 P.2d at 925.

In 1983 came Harris v. Groth,¹⁰ yet another glaucoma case. The trial judge kept the plaintiff's sole expert (who was not a physician) from testifying on the standard of care, and he refused to give the *Helling* instruction, and so the jury found for the defendant. After summarizing the evolution of Washington law and citing law review comment, the court noted that in 1975 the legislature had enacted a second standard-setting statute, West's Rev.Code Wash.Ann. § 7.70.040, applicable only to actions arising after June 25, 1976—which was too late for *Gates*. Section 7.70.040 called for a "reasonably prudent health care provider," while the pre-*Helling* case-law standard had said "average medical or dental practitioner." Affirming the trial court's rejection of the plaintiff's proffered instruction,¹¹ the court wrote,

> The instruction should have been framed in the language of * * * [the two statutes], i.e., whether a reasonably prudent ophthal-

---

9. Gates v. Jensen, 20 Wash.App. 81, 579 P.2d 374 (1978).

10. 99 Wash.2d 438, 663 P.2d 113 (1983).

11. 663 P.2d at 115.

mologist, possessing the degree of skill, care, and learning possessed by other ophthalmologists in the state of Washington, and acting in the same or similar circumstances as the defendant, would have performed an intraocular pressure test. 663 P.2d at 118.

Judgment for the defendant was affirmed.

Apparently the model jury instructions have settled down in the format of the passage quoted from *Harris*.[12] As of mid–1989, the Washington legislature had not tried to draw together the two code sections, and the muscle that the supreme court showed in *Helling* had not been flexed again.

SECTION B. FAILURE TO USE DUE CARE

McCORD v. MAGUIRE

United States Court of Appeals for the Ninth Circuit, 1989.
873 F.2d 1271.

KOZINSKI, CIRCUIT JUDGE. * * *

On February 6, 1985, Dr. John Maguire performed elective surgery to remove Dorothy R. McCord's gallbladder. During the course of the surgery, Maguire performed an x-ray procedure called a cholangiogram to determine whether there were any stones in the common bile duct. In this procedure, dye is injected via a catheter into the common bile duct and x-ray pictures are taken. Maguire inserted the catheter in the wrong place, and thus was unable to obtain a useful x-ray. He retracted the catheter and injected 25 cc. of dye into the bile duct. Maguire then took a second x-ray, saw what he thought was a gallstone, and proceeded to surgically explore the duct. This surgical procedure is not routinely performed because it greatly increases the patient's risks. Maguire found no stones. Five days after the surgery McCord was discharged from the hospital.

A month later, on March 12, McCord was taken to the emergency room with abdominal pain and gastrointestinal bleeding; she was vomiting blood. Maguire's examination showed that McCord's common bile duct was completely obstructed and that there was hemobilia, or bleeding into the biliary passages. Although hemobilia may be treated by embolization, i.e., by injecting a substance which blocks the sources of bleeding into the blood stream, Maguire did not use this technique. Instead, he performed exploratory surgery three days later, on March 15.

The surgical exploration revealed that the bleeding into the bile duct had obstructed the hepatic artery, which supplies blood to the liver. Further exploration resulted in the destruction of the common bile duct, but also revealed that the source of the bleeding was a fistula or hole between the common bile duct and gastroduodenal artery. Maguire tied off the gastroduodenal artery to stop the bleeding, but was

---

12. See Miller v. Peterson, 42 Wash. App. 822, 714 P.2d 695 (1986).

unable to reconstruct the common bile duct. Throughout the six-hour surgery, Maguire gave McCord heparin, a blood-thinning medication which worsened her bleeding problem.

The next day McCord began bleeding profusely and was sent by helicopter to Portland Adventist Medical Center Hospital. When she arrived at the hospital, she was found to have adult respiratory distress syndrome, congestive heart failure and kidney failure; she also lacked a pathway for drainage of the bile to the small intestine, which is essential for life. Because of the obstruction of the hepatic blood supply (the blood supply to her liver), all of the left lobe and much of the right lobe of her liver were destroyed. McCord's life expectancy is now limited.

In her amended complaint, * * * McCord supported her claim that Maguire failed "to use that degree of care, skill, and diligence which is used by ordinarily careful general surgeons in the same or similar circumstances in his or similar community" by alleging thirteen acts of negligence. During the trial, five of the thirteen specifications were withdrawn. The district court submitted the remaining eight specifications of negligence to the jury [13] * * *. The jury found that Maguire had been negligent in one or more of the respects claimed by McCord, and that the negligence had injured or damaged her.

Maguire now claims that the evidence presented at trial was insufficient to support four of the specifications of negligence submitted to the jury: that Maguire negligently injected too much contrast dye during McCord's first surgery; that he was negligent in causing a fistula; that he negligently failed to treat the fistula with embolization; and that he negligently destroyed McCord's hepatic blood supply. Relying on cases holding that a general verdict cannot stand when one or more alternative theories of liability were improperly submitted to the jury * * *, Maguire claims he is entitled to a new trial.

---

13. The court stated:

The plaintiffs charge the defendant, Dr. Maguire, with the following specifications of negligence:

First, in causing during his treatment of Mrs. McCord on February 6, 1985, a fistula to be created between the biliary tract and the vascular structure;

Second, failing to interpret properly the intraoperative cholangiogram films that demonstrate an improper placement of the tip of the cholangiogram catheter;

Third, injected an abnormally high amount, 25 cc., of contrast [medium] after pulling the catheter back while conducting the intraoperative cholangiogram;

Four, in interpreting the intraoperative cholangiogram as showing the filling defect, resulting in unnecessary exploration of the common duct;

Fifth, in failing to order angiogram tests at the time of the third hospitalization that would have assisted in the diagnosis and treatment of her complication;

Sixth, in failing to treat the fistula between the biliary tract and the vascular structure with embolism rather than surgical techniques;

Seventh, in destroying the common bile duct, Mrs. McCord's hepatic blood supply during the March 15, * * * '85 surgery.

[E]ighth, administering the drug, heparin, to Mrs. McCord which was contraindicated and which increased her excessive bleeding.

The cases cited by Maguire deal with a situation where the jury may have based its conclusions on a legal theory unsupported by substantial evidence. However, this case involves a claim that one or more factual theories were unsupported by sufficient evidence. When a general verdict may have rested on factual allegations unsupported by substantial evidence, we will uphold the verdict if the evidence is sufficient with respect to any of the allegations. * * *.

In this case, plaintiff made a single claim of medical negligence and advanced eight factual theories as possible bases for finding liability. Even if one or more of the alleged acts of negligence were unsubstantiated, we must uphold the general verdict so long as it was sufficiently supported by at least one negligent act. As it is undisputed that four of the alleged acts of negligence were supported by the evidence, the general verdict for the plaintiff must be upheld.

Maguire nevertheless contends that the jury may have based its verdict solely on the four allegedly unsubstantiated factual theories. This is a legitimate concern. However, Maguire's failure to request a special verdict [14] as to each factual theory in the case prevents him from pressing this argument on appeal. "Federal Rule of Civil Procedure 49(a) gives district courts wide discretion in the use of special verdicts; refusal of a special verdict form is therefore reviewed only for gross abuse. * * * Litigants like Maguire who wish to challenge the sufficiency of the evidence as to some, but not all, specifications of negligence must present an appropriate record for review by asking the jury to make separate factual determinations as to each specification. Any other rule would unnecessarily jeopardize jury verdicts that are otherwise fully supported by the record on the mere theoretical possibility that the jury based its decision on unsupported specifications. We will not allow litigants to play procedural brinkmanship with the jury system and take advantage of uncertainties they could well have avoided.

* * *

Affirmed.

TOTH v. COMMUNITY HOSP.

Court of Appeals of New York, 1968.
22 N.Y.2d 255, 292 N.Y.S.2d 440, 239 N.E.2d 368.

KEATING, JUDGE.

Stephanie and Jane Toth were born prematurely on the night of June 16, 1953, at the Community Hospital at Glen Cove, New York. From the moment of their birth they were dangerously ill. Their pediatrician, Dr. Charles H. Hellmann, fearful for their lives, immediately ordered that they be placed in an isolette, a type of incubator, and

---

14. See Fed.R.Civ.P. 49(a). Under this rule, a judge may require a jury to return written findings upon each issue of fact necessary to a verdict. The special verdict makes clear the grounds on which the jury reached its conclusion and enables the court of appeals to review the sufficiency of the evidence supporting the jury's findings.

that oxygen be administered to them. His written orders were to the effect that the infants should receive oxygen at the rate of 6 liters per minute for the first 12 hours, and thereafter at the rate of 4 liters per minute.

The theory behind this oxygen treatment was that maintenance of premature babies in an oxygen environment would sustain life and prevent brain damage. Shortly after the birth of the twins, a Cooperative Study of Retrolental Fibroplasia and the Use of Oxygen, conducted for the National Institute for Neurological Diseases and Blindness, indisputably established that the course of treatment was tragically mistaken. The study showed that, while the use of oxygen might mitigate brain damage, it did not reduce the mortality rate at all, and did cause retrolental fibroplasia (RLF), resulting in blindness in many infants. This was the result here. The twins were given oxygen for over 30 days—Stephanie, the elder, until July 20 and Jane until July 27. Stephanie lost all useful vision in her left eye, while Jane developed RLF in both eyes and lost her sight completely.

Steve Toth, the children's father, as guardian ad litem, has brought this action against the pediatrician and the hospital * * *.

The claim against the pediatrician has two aspects. Mr. Toth contends, first, that the administration of oxygen was contrary to good medical practice in June 1953. His second contention, which is also the basis of the claim against the hospital, is that the nurses failed to follow the pediatrician's orders concerning the amount of oxygen to be given the babies, and that, in fact, 6 liters per minute of oxygen were constantly administered to the children for some four weeks after their birth, rather than the prescribed 4 liters per minute. It is contended the nurses were negligent in not adhering to the pediatrician's orders, and the doctor was negligent in not discovering promptly that the oxygen dosage had not been reduced by the nurses as he had directed.

* * *

The case against the doctors was submitted to the jury. A reading of the trial court's charge, however, establishes that the only question the jury was asked to decide was whether the doctors had conformed to acceptable medical practice in their respective specialties.[15] The jury

---

15. Editors' Note: The dissenting opinion gives the judge's sole charge, which asked for a general verdict:

It is claimed here that the defendant, Dr. Hellmann, by his carelessness in departing from the approved medical practice of pediatrics in the area where he practiced, caused injuries to the plaintiffs. The fact that the oxygen caused the injury which is readily conceded, does not make Dr. Hellmann liable. Before you can hold Dr. Hellmann liable for these injuries, you would first have to decide whether Dr. Hellmann, as a specialist in the field of pediatrics, consider-ing all of the circumstances of the premature birth and their health at the time of the delivery, did what a physician practicing his specialty in June of 1953, possessed of the skill and knowledge of other pediatricians in the area, other men practicing that specialty in this area at that time, whether he did what they would have done under like circumstances.

You may take into consideration whether or not such a physician, having the knowledge of men practicing the specialty in the area and following accepted medical procedures, would have foreseen

returned a verdict in favor of the doctors. On appeal, the appellate division affirmed, one justice dissenting * * *. 28 A.D.2d 923, 282 N.Y.S.2d 945 (1967) (mem.).

On the issue whether the oxygen treatment was correct, the evidence was conflicting and the issue strenuously contested. The record supports the conclusion that while it was well recognized by June 1953 that there was a risk of RLF in the oxygen therapy, and many physicians and institutions were already convinced that the oxygen therapy was either useless or not worth the risk of RLF involved, there were many reputable institutions holding the opinion that the oxygen treatment was necessary or at least a worthwhile risk. There was, therefore, ample evidence to support the jury's finding that the defendant pediatrician, who viewed the oxygen treatment as a necessary calculated risk, had acted in accordance with acceptable medical practice. Consequently, on this question the jury's verdict must be deemed conclusive, and the issue of acceptable medical practice may not be submitted to the jury on a new trial.

* * * [But] there was sufficient evidence to establish every element of plaintiffs' second theory of liability as reflected in their fifth request to charge. To summarize, a jury could find, although under the facts here, it certainly would not be compelled to do so: (a) that 6 liters of oxygen per minute were given the children continuously; (b) that, had the pediatrician's orders been followed strictly, the RLF would not have occurred or the consequences would not have been as severe; (c) that the doctor had opportunity to discover the deviation, but did not do so; (d) that there was general knowledge that there was a danger in the excessive use of oxygen and that the doctor was aware of this knowledge; and (e) that his written orders were made with a view toward minimizing that risk. If the jury so found, it could properly find that the doctor's failure to assure that his orders were carried out was negligence.

* * *

The order of the appellate division should be modified so as to order a new trial against the defendants, Community Hospital at Glen Cove and Hellmann, with costs to abide the event * * *.

BERGAN, JUDGE, dissenting. * * *

The majority opinion finds as the sole ground for reversal error in a failure to submit to the jury a "second theory," whether this defendant could be found guilty of malpractice "for not noticing that his orders were not being followed by the hospital nursing staff."

the probability of injury as a result of the use of oxygen. You would also consider whether or not such a physician would have taken into account the possibility fatality, the possible death of the infants, or other injury, if he had not followed the procedure. And if he were confronted with the choice of more than one procedure, whether a pediatrician, possessing the average skills of accepted medical practice in the area, would have done what Dr. Hellmann did in order to sustain the life of the children.

There was no such "second theory" of liability in the sense it could be deemed a separable entity apart from the general charge of negligence and malpractice against Dr. Hellmann under the pleadings, the bill of particulars, or the argument of the plaintiffs' counsel to the jury.

* * *

The hospital's procedures, as well as those of the physicians, followed accepted standards of medical care in June and July of 1953. The proof was that the administration of supplementary oxygen was followed in many of the leading hospitals at that time.

That later scientific discovery showed some other procedure should have been followed ought not to bring home a retroactive liability either to physician or hospital. The prime purpose of the procedure was to save the lives of the children; that later knowledge showed the serious side effects might have been avoided ought not spell out a liability under this record.

The order should be affirmed. * * * FULD, C.J., and SCILEPPI, J., concur.

DI FILIPPO v. PRESTON

Supreme Court of Delaware, 1961.
53 Del. (3 Storey) 539, 173 A.2d 333.

WOLCOTT, JUSTICE.

This is an appeal from a judgment entered on a directed verdict for the defendant in an action for personal injuries and medical expenses resulting from alleged malpractice of the defendant * * *.

Anne C. DiFilippo * * * is a 43-year old housewife. In April of 1957 she consulted her family physician, Dr. Russo, complaining of a visible lump in her throat causing some pressure symptoms. Dr. Russo diagnosed her condition as an enlarged thyroid gland, i.e., a goiter, and recommended that she consult a surgeon. Of two suggested surgeons, Mrs. DiFilippo selected Dr. Daniel J. Preston, the defendant.

Dr. Preston examined Mrs. DiFilippo and confirmed the diagnosis of Dr. Russo. He considered further tests but determined against them as inadvisable, and recommended that because of the pressure on her windpipe and because of the possibility that a goiter, i.e., a diseased thyroid, might become malignant, the thyroid be removed by surgery. This operation is called a thyroidectomy.

* * *

Dr. Preston operated on Mrs. DiFilippo in May 1957. The operation was uneventful. In the course of the operation, Dr. Preston was able to find no undiseased tissue in the thyroid gland and, consequently, removed 95% of the gland, leaving 5% of tissue in the posterior area to enable the gland to function partially, and also as a protection against damage to the recurrent laryngeal nerves.

* * *

Since the operation Mrs. DiFilippo has been unable to speak above a hoarse whisper, the cause of which has been diagnosed as injury to the recurrent laryngeal nerves resulting in a paralysis of the vocal cords. As a result of the paralysis of the vocal cords, in the fall of 1957, Mrs. DiFilippo was forced to submit to a tracheotomy, an operation consisting of making an opening through the patient's neck into the windpipe and the insertion of a four-inch metal tube through which the patient breathes. Since the performance of this operation, Mrs. DiFilippo has worn constantly a tracheal tube and presumably will be forced to wear it for the balance of her life.

The theory of the action is that Dr. Preston was negligent and thus guilty of malpractice in performing the thyroidectomy as he did, and that he should have followed the so-called Lahey technique to expose to view the recurrent laryngeal nerves and thus avoid injury to them.

Dr. Preston does not deny the possibility that Mrs. DiFilippo's recurrent laryngeal nerves were damaged as a direct result of the operation performed by him. * * *

[T]he case presents one fundamental question[:] * * * whether or not the selection by Dr. Preston of the surgical technique followed in this thyroidectomy was, of itself, negligent. If it was then a verdict against him would be justified. If, however, the selection of this technique was not a negligent act, then it follows that Dr. Preston has been exonerated of negligence. We say this because there is no evidence in this record that Dr. Preston failed to perform the operation by the technique selected by him in accordance with due care and the standards of competence demanded of surgeons employing the particular technique.

* * *

The defendant called three surgeons as experts, two of whom were practicing surgeons in the Wilmington area, and the third of whom was an admittedly qualified if not leading surgeon of the Philadelphia area, whose testimony indicates a familiarity with the standards of competence required in the Wilmington area. These three experts are in general agreement as to the recognized and accepted techniques for the surgical treatment of infected thyroids, i.e., goiters, and the performance of thyroidectomies. Their testimony may be summarized as follows.

Surgeons generally recognize that in the performance of thyroidectomies there is a risk of resultant injury to the recurrent laryngeal nerves because of the intimate relationship of those nerves to the thyroid gland, and because of variations in individuals of the course of those nerves around or, in some cases, even through the thyroid gland. The possibility of resultant injury to these nerves is heightened because of their structure, which means that it is not necessary to cut the nerve to injure it. Injury may result by a mere squeezing or stretching. One of the main problems in a thyroidectomy is, therefore, to perform the operation in a manner to avoid resulting injury to the nerves or, at least, minimize the possibility of such injury.

One recognized method or technique to accomplish this is to remove a major part of the thyroid gland by dissection, leaving a small residue of tissue in the area where the nerves would normally be located as a shield or a buffer against the dissection. In this technique, no attempt is made by the surgeon to see, identify, and separate the nerves from the thyroid in order to avoid injury to them. The surgeon following this technique relies on his knowledge of the area of the gland adjacent to the nerves and, by avoiding dissection of that area, attempts to protect the nerves from injury. This technique is referred to in the record as the standard technique and was the one followed by Dr. Preston in operating upon Mrs. DiFilippo.

The second or alternative method or technique is named for its originator, Dr. Lahey, who proposed that in a thyroidectomy the recurrent laryngeal nerves be visualized by the surgeon. This is done by cutting into the area in which the nerves normally lie, identifying the nerves, and putting them aside from the area in which the dissection is to take place. The Lahey technique is of more recent origin and is gradually receiving wider acceptance among surgeons, but among qualified surgeons there still exists a difference of opinion as to which technique is preferable.

Neither technique for the performance of thyroidectomies wholly eliminates the possibility of resulting damage to the recurrent laryngeal nerves. Such possibility exists in the so-called standard technique because the nerves may not be in their normal location and position. Such possibility exists in the Lahey technique because the mere handling of the nerves and the difficulty of identifying them may inadvertently be sufficient to cause damage to them, either through cutting, stretching or squeezing. Particularly is this so in the Lahey technique in the case of a diseased thyroid because such a gland is more likely to be tightly adherent to the surrounding tissue and to parts of the nerves, a circumstance which thus increases the hazard of exposing them.

Either of the two above described techniques for the performance of thyroidectomies is recognized by surgeons generally as acceptable and as conformable to the standards required of surgeons, not only in the Wilmington area, but probably throughout the country. In the use of either technique, even though the surgeon uses meticulous care in the operation, statistics show an incidence of permanent damage to the recurrent laryngeal nerves of about 2%.

Plaintiffs insist that Dr. Graubard took a diametrically opposed view to that of the three surgeons called as experts by the defendant, thus creating an issue of fact to be resolved by the jury. Plaintiffs contend that Dr. Graubard, whom, for this purpose, we assume to be qualified to testify with respect to standards required of surgeons in the Wilmington area, testified that the only acceptable standard for the performance of thyroidectomies was the Lahey technique. We think, however, a careful reading of his testimony demonstrates that it is more accurate to say that he recognized the existence of the two techniques; that there was a division of opinion among qualified surgeons as to which was the better, but that he personally thought the Lahey technique was the only proper one to be used.

While Dr. Graubard might well prefer the Lahey technique, at least an equal number of his fellow surgeons throughout the country apparently prefer the so-called standard technique. Since both are recognized as acceptable, it follows that the choice by Dr. Preston of one of two acceptable techniques was not a negligent act on his part.

* * *

We think, therefore, that the plaintiffs failed to make a submissible issue of negligence for the jury and that, consequently, on this phase of the case the direction of a verdict for the defendant was proper.

* * *

[T]he judgment below is affirmed.

SECTION C. THIRD PARTIES AND MEDICAL NEGLIGENCE

Note on Unusual Duties to Patients

A number of medical malpractice cases have arisen from sexual relations between treating physicians and patients,[16] but patients can also be harmed by relations between the medical care provider and the patient's significant others.

In Mazza v. Huffaker,[17] a psychiatrist was held to have a duty to his patient not to have a sexual affair with the patient's estranged wife:

> Psychiatrists are physicians. The first duty of a physician to a patient is to do no harm; the second is to maintain the patient's trust and confidence in the physician. These basic duties apply and are even more stringent with psychiatrists, since a psychiatrist's patient reveals his innermost thoughts, feelings, worries, and concerns. Psychiatrists, therefore, have a strict duty not to breach the trusting relationship and must be very careful about what they say and how they influence patients. * * * Special duties exist in the practice of medicine not to ruin a doctor and patient relationship, and those duties are more critical in psychiatry than in other areas of medicine. If the relationships are not terminated properly, but too abruptly, great harm can result to a patient. * * * Covert sexual relations between a psychiatrist and a patient's wife, if discovered by the patient, would make it extremely difficult for the patient to establish ever again a necessary trusting relationship with any psychiatrist, would render previous treatment useless, and would do harm to the mental well-

---

16. E.g., Omer v. Edgren, 38 Wash.App. 376, 685 P.2d 635 (1984). See Annot., Civil Liability of Doctor or Psychologist for Having Sexual Relationship with Patient, 33 A.L.R.3d 1393 (1970).

17. 61 N.C.App. 170, 300 S.E.2d 833 (1983).

being of the patient. A psychiatrist who becomes sexually involved with a relative of a patient is not exercising the requisite amount of skill, learning, and ability that a psychiatrist in any community in the United States ought to exercise.

The court went on to uphold punitive damages:

> The evidence tends to show a wilful act by defendant Huffaker of having sex with his patient's wife, and an awareness, although disregarded, of the risks such an act posed towards his patient * * *. This evidence was sufficient to support an inference by the jury that defendant * * * acted with conscious disregard of the mental well-being of * * * [the plaintiff], the very mental well-being with which defendant * * * had been entrusted.

In Rowe v. Bennett,[18] a social worker, in counseling the plaintiff about problems with the plaintiff's lesbian companion, met the companion. The counselor then developed a social relationship with the companion, and later she lied to the plaintiff about why she had stopped counseling the plaintiff individually. It was the opinion of a subsequent treating psychiatrist that because of the social relationship between the social worker and the plaintiff's companion, "the plaintiff felt abandoned and humiliated, suffered intense emotional turmoil and anguish manifested by disturbed sleep, loss of weight, poor concentration, crying spells and intermittent thoughts of suicide." [19]

In reversing summary judgment for the social worker and her employer, the Maine supreme court held that a genuine issue of fact existed as to whether the social worker breached her professional duty as a counselor, and that "because of the unique nature of a psychotherapist-patient relationship," the negligent infliction of serious emotional distress upon plaintiff was sufficient damage without either physical impact or an underlying tort.

CLARKE v. HOEK
California Court of Appeal, 1985.
174 Cal.App.3d 208, 219 Cal.Rptr. 845.

SCOTT, ASSOCIATE JUSTICE. * * *

* * * At all relevant times, respondent Kenneth J. Hoek, M.D. (Dr. Hoek) was a physician and surgeon licensed since 1968 to practice in California, and certified since 1976 by the American Board of Orthopedic Surgery. Dr. Hoek acted as proctor during two separate orthopedic surgeries performed on appellant Frances M. Clarke (Mrs. Clarke) by Drs. Frank LoBianco (Dr. LoBianco) and William Mason (Dr. Mason), during the course of which Mrs. Clarke was allegedly injured as a result of the negligence of the two surgeons.[20]

---

18. 514 A.2d 802 (Me.1986).

19. Id. at 804.

20. Editors' Note: The parties' names have been substituted throughout for "appellant" and "respondent."

Dr. Hoek was an active medical staff member of both the Ukiah Adventist Hospital and the Mendocino Community Hospital.[21] On or about October 19, 1979, Dr. Hoek was appointed by the joint credentials committee of Ukiah General and Ukiah Adventist Hospitals to be a proctor for Dr. LoBianco, who was an applicant for medical staff privileges at Ukiah Adventist Hospital. * * * In accordance with the by-laws of the Ukiah Adventist Hospital, Dr. Hoek was asked to observe ten surgeries performed by Dr. LoBianco and then to submit a written report to the credentials committee. On February 8, 1980, Dr. Hoek was present at and observed an operation performed on Mrs. Clarke by Drs. LoBianco and Mason at Ukiah Adventist Hospital.

Sometime thereafter, Dr. Hoek was again asked to proctor Dr. LoBianco, this time at Mendocino Community Hospital. The by-laws of the Mendocino Community Hospital, like those of the Ukiah Adventist Hospital, provided that proctors were to prepare written reports after observing and evaluating all aspects of an applicant's management of a case. Dr. Phranklin Apfel, Chief of Staff at Mendocino Community Hospital, asked Dr. Hoek to observe ten surgeries performed by Dr. LoBianco and to submit a report. On May 21, 1980, Dr. Hoek was present at and observed surgery performed on Mrs. Clarke by Drs. LoBianco and Mason at Mendocino Community Hospital.

Prior to each of the two operations, Dr. Hoek reviewed Mrs. Clarke's X-rays and discussed the operative plan with Dr. LoBianco. Otherwise, Dr. Hoek did not take any part in the care and treatment of Mrs. Clarke. During the actual operations, he did not participate in the surgeries; nor was he ever asked to do so by Mrs. Clarke, any medical personnel, or any hospital official. Dr. Hoek did not believe that such intervention was warranted. He did not "scrub in" for the surgeries; rather, he simply observed them from a position outside "the sterile field."

As of the times of the subject surgeries, Dr. Hoek had never met Mrs. Clarke; neither had he entered into any contractual relationship with her. He did not request, receive or expect any payment from any source for proctoring the two operations. * * *

[The trial judge entered summary judgment for Dr. Hoek, and Mrs. Clarke appealed.]

The question of the existence of a legal duty of care in a given factual situation presents a question of law which is to be determined by the courts alone. * * * Since the existence of a duty of care is an essential element in any assessment of liability for negligence * * *, entry of summary judgment in favor of the defendant in a negligence action is proper where the plaintiff is unable to show that the defendant owed such a duty of care. * * *

21. A "staff physician" is one who has been accorded "staff privileges" at a hospital, ordinarily for a period of not more than two years. A physician must be a member of a hospital's medical staff to admit patients to that hospital. * * *

In this case, if Dr. Hoek's declarations in support of the motion for summary judgment demonstrate an absence of an essential element of Mrs. Clarke's case, and Mrs. Clarke's declarations submitted in reply do not show that a triable issue of fact exists with respect to that essential element, "no amount of factual conflicts upon other aspects of the case will affect the result and the motion for summary judgment should be granted." Frazier v. Boccardo, 70 Cal.App.3d 331, 138 Cal.Rptr. 670, 673 (1977).

Despite Mrs. Clarke's assertions on appeal, there were no triable issues of material fact which would bar its grant of summary judgment. The alleged "conflicts" in the evidence before the court at the time of the hearing on the motion were actually divergent opinions on whether or not Dr. Hoek owed a duty of care to Mrs. Clarke in his role as a medical proctor. The fact that Mrs. Clarke's doctor experts opined that Dr. Hoek had a duty to "ensure that the patient receives proper surgical treatment within the standard of care" and that failure to intervene falls below the standard of care, does not create a triable issue of fact. The doctor's opinion as to Dr. Hoek's duty is erroneous as a matter of law. There can be no issue of fact as to whether Dr. Hoek discharged such "duty."

Mrs. Clarke seeks to inject the issue of foreseeability into that of duty, and argues that since foreseeability is a question of fact for the jury, the trial court's granting of summary judgment was improper. Although the element of foreseeability of unreasonable risk is a factor determining the existence of a duty of care, Weirum v. RKO General, Inc., 15 Cal.3d 40, 123 Cal.Rptr. 468, 539 P.2d 36, 39 (1975), this does not make the determination of duty a question of fact. While it is the province of the jury, as trier of fact, to determine whether an unreasonable risk of harm was foreseeable under the particular facts of a given case, the trial court must still decide as a matter of law whether there was a duty in the first place, even if that determination includes a consideration of foreseeability. * * * The fact that harm to a plaintiff may have been foreseeable does not automatically impose a duty. A court may find that no duty exists, despite foreseeability of harm, because of other factors and considerations of public policy. * * *

Moreover, the rule that conduct is negligent where some unreasonable risk of danger to others would have been foreseen by a reasonable person is applicable only to cases of misfeasance. Absent a special relationship giving rise to a duty to act, a person is under no duty to take affirmative action to assist or protect another, no matter how great the danger in which the other is placed, or how easily he could be rescued. * * *[22] A corollary of this principle is that an individual is under no duty to control the conduct of third parties unless a special

---

22. Section 314 of the Restatement (Second) of Torts (1965) states:

The fact that the actor realizes or should realize that action on his part is necessary for another's aid or protection does not of itself impose upon him a duty to take such action.

relationship exists between the individual and either the third parties or the persons affected by their conduct. Restatement (Second) of Torts § 315 (1965) * * *. Conversely, if a person not required to perform services for another nevertheless undertakes to do so, he or she is under a duty to exercise due care in performance of those services. Restatement (Second) of Torts §§ 323–324 (1965) * * *.[23]

The instant case is one of allegedly tortious nonfeasance to which the issue of foreseeability, as it relates to duty, is inapplicable. Liability here is not predicated upon Dr. Hoek's allegedly active creation of an unreasonable risk of harm to Mrs. Clarke, but rather on Dr. Hoek's failure to intervene for the benefit of Mrs. Clarke in the course of the proctored surgery.

Thus, the question of law for the trial court to decide in this case was whether there was some "special relationship" between Dr. Hoek and either Mrs. Clarke or the surgeons performing the operation, which could give rise to a duty on Dr. Hoek's part to intervene in the surgery. The trial court concluded that there was no such special relationship here, and that considerations of public policy weighed heavily against imposing a duty under the undisputed facts of this case. We agree with this conclusion.

* * *

Mrs. Clarke argues that Dr. Hoek's proctoring of her operations "constituted a voluntary undertaking from which a duty arose." This contention is singularly without merit.

* * *

Mrs. Clarke asserts that Dr. Hoek's duty to her was "commensurate" with that of the hospital. We disagree.

Although a hospital clearly has a duty to its patients to review and maintain the competency of its staff members, and a corresponding liability for the malpractice of a physician who is employed by or otherwise an agent of the hospital, Elam v. College Park Hosp., 132 Cal. App.3d 332, 183 Cal.Rptr. 156, 161 (1982) * * *, no court in this or any other state has ever held that an individual proctor owes a duty of due care to the patient in a proctored surgery, much less an affirmative obligation to intervene in the operation to prevent malpractice on the part of the physicians performing the surgery. * * *

Moreover, the duty imposed on hospitals by the decision in Elam v. College Park Hospital is simply to review and screen the competency of medical staff members, not to supervise them. To the extent a proctor

---

23. As a rule, one has no duty to come to the aid of another. A person who has not created a peril is not liable in tort merely for failure to take affirmative action to assist or protect another unless there is some relationship between them which gives rise to a duty to act. * * * Also pertinent to our discussion is the role of the volunteer who, having no initial duty to do so, undertakes to come to the aid of another—the "Good Samaritan." He is under a duty to exercise due care in performance and is liable if (a) his failure to exercise such care increases the risk of such harm, or (b) the harm is suffered because of the other's reliance upon the undertaking. Williams v. State, 34 Cal.3d 18, 192 Cal.Rptr. 233, 664 P.2d 137, 139 (1983).

is an agent of the hospital—an issue we need not address—he or she would have no more duty to supervise and intervene in a proctored surgery than would the hospital itself. Like the hospital, the proctor's only duty is to observe and evaluate the competence of medical staff members in the course of the actual discharge of their professional responsibilities.

Finally, we agree with the trial court that important considerations of public policy weigh heavily against the imposition of a duty of care on medical proctors under the circumstances presented by this case. * * *

There is a strong public interest in supporting, encouraging and protecting effective medical peer review programs and activities. * * * The fear of potential malpractice liability would not only discourage participation by medical professionals in these volunteer review committees, but would stifle candor and impair objectivity in staff evaluations.

The legislature has made unmistakably clear its recognition of the importance of medical peer review by enacting various statutes providing protection for activities aimed at maintaining professional standards on hospital medical staffs. * * *[24]

We conclude that imposition on Dr. Hoek of the duty to Mrs. Clarke would violate the spirit and intent of these statutes, contradict the intention of the legislature, and disserve significant public policy interests.

The judgment is affirmed.

BARDONI v. KIM
Court of Appeals of Michigan, 1986.
151 Mich.App. 169, 390 N.W.2d 218, leave to appeal denied.

PER CURIAM. * * *

On February 24, 1978, Richard Bardoni (Bardoni) came under the care and supervision of Dr. Soon K. Kim, a psychiatrist. Bardoni had been psychotic for at least ten years and was previously under psychiatric care. From his initial evaluation, Dr. Kim classified Bardoni as a paranoid schizophrenic. Because paranoid schizophrenics can become dangerous to themselves or others, Dr. Kim told his patient's wife, Evelyn Bardoni, to contact him immediately if her husband showed any signs of violence or if she thought he could no longer control himself. The major treatment at this point was psychotropic drugs.

Between March 10, 1978, and October 25, 1978, Dr. Kim saw Bardoni on a total of about nine occasions. The sessions lasted between

---

24. [T]he fact that a surgery is proctored and the identity of the proctor are generally not subject to discovery and therefore not known by or available to a patient at all. In this case, Dr. Hoek's identity and role in the operation were known to Mrs. Clarke only because Dr. LoBianco happened to mention to Mrs. Clarke's husband the fact that the operation would be proctored.

30 and 60 minutes and Dr. Kim recorded his impressions after each session. Dr. Kim's notes indicated that his patient was highly nervous, anxious, unable to function properly, and delusional, with the delusions centering primarily on his former employer. Bardoni had been fired as a school teacher and he believed that the school system had "attacked his character." He also believed that the school administrator had mental problems. Evelyn Bardoni also informed Dr. Kim that her husband thought someone was out to get him.

During the course of treatment under Dr. Kim, Bardoni often refused to take medication prescribed, and in the summer of 1978 broke off treatment altogether. Evelyn Bardoni indicated that her husband stopped seeing Dr. Kim during the summer because, in her opinion, his condition had improved significantly.

On September 15, 1978, Bardoni left home and traveled to Ohio. He was taken into custody by Ohio police and transported to a local hospital after he repeatedly told the officers he wanted to commit suicide. The Toledo Mental Health Center records indicated that Bardoni was brought in there in a psychotic state. During his four-day stay at the Center, the staff's notes recorded its impression that Bardoni was potentially dangerous and showed signs of aggressive behavior. The records also indicated that Bardoni told the staff that he had recently found out that his wife had been poisoning him and that she had been dating his older brother, Robert Bardoni. A progress note on September 18, 1978, indicated that Bardoni stated that his family was not safe and that somebody was going to hurt them, and that he had a great deal of guilt towards the things he had done to his family and others. The Center classified Bardoni as a possible threat to himself or others. Dr. Kim did not recall whether or not he received a copy of these Ohio records, but recalled that he had spoken with someone at the Center regarding his patient. The Toledo Health Center records indicated that Dr. Kim had been contacted, and that Bardoni had been put on a waiting list for an available bed in a private hospital.

After Bardoni was discharged from the Toledo Mental Health Center, Dr. Kim attempted to have him placed in a hospital in Michigan, but Bardoni refused to go voluntarily, and his wife refused to sign commitment papers because she did not feel that he was dangerous. Upon Bardoni's return from Ohio, Dr. Kim noted that Bardoni was having somatic delusions and that he believed his blood was being poisoned. Dr. Kim testified that, upon inquiry into who Bardoni thought was poisoning him, Bardoni indicated it might be the school system where he had been employed or air pollution. After the Ohio incident, Dr. Kim saw Bardoni only two more times, the last meeting being on October 25, 1978. Bardoni failed to show up for any further appointments.

At no time during his sessions with Bardoni did Dr. Kim ever note any signs of violent behavior. Evelyn Bardoni informed Dr. Kim that she did not think that her husband was dangerous. Evelyn Bardoni did indicate in her deposition that her husband had expressed a desire to kill his brother on several occasions. Although Dr. Kim had requested that she inform him if she felt her husband was dangerous, she had never passed this information on to Dr. Kim, nor did she think Dr. Kim was aware of this fact.

On January 14, 1979, Richard Bardoni assaulted his wife, and murdered his brother, Robert Bardoni, and his mother, Catherine Bardoni, before being captured by police.

Separate suits arising from the deaths of Robert and Catherine Bardoni were commenced in Wayne County Circuit Court. The complaints alleged that Dr. Kim failed to properly diagnose Richard Bardoni and failed to warn members of the Bardoni family who were foreseeable victims of Richard Bardoni's violence.

In both suits Dr. Kim filed motions for summary judgment after discovery. Dr. Kim asserted that Richard Bardoni showed no signs of violent behavior and that plaintiffs' decedents could not be considered readily identifiable victims to whom Dr. Kim owed any duty to warn.

Plaintiffs responded with the affidavits of psychiatrist Dr. Bruce Danto, which stated that Dr. Kim had failed to exercise the appropriate standard of care of a psychiatrist and that, if he had done so, plaintiffs' decedents would have been readily identifiable as persons endangered by Richard Bardoni.

The trial court ruled as a matter of law in both cases that plaintiffs' decedents were not readily identifiable victims as required by Davis v. Lhim, 124 Mich.App. 291, 335 N.W.2d 481 (1983), * * * and granted defendant Dr. Kim's motions for summary judgment * * *.

When a psychiatrist determines or, pursuant to the standard of care of his profession, should determine that his patient poses a serious danger of violence to a readily identifiable third person,[25] the psychiatrist has a duty to use reasonable care to protect that individual against such danger.[26] *Davis*, 335 N.W.2d at 489, citing Thompson v. County of Alameda, 27 Cal.3d 741, 167 Cal.Rptr. 70, 614 P.2d 728 (1980), with approval. Absent the existence of material issues of fact pertinent to these determinations, the existence of the psychiatrist's duty to the third person is a question of law for the court. * * *

25. Other jurisdictions have rejected the readily identifiable limitation and couch their determinations of duty in terms of reasonable foreseeability. See e.g., Lipari v. Sears, Roebuck & Co., 497 F.Supp. 185, 194 (D.Neb.1980) (construing Nebraska law).

26. The discharge of the duty owed by a psychiatrist to a person endangered by his patient does not necessarily require warnings to that person. Rather, the psychiatrist must take reasonable steps to protect the endangered person. *Davis*, 335 N.W.2d at 489. These steps can involve warnings to that person, warnings to the custodian of the patient, commitment of the patient, etc. In the instant case, however, plaintiffs specifically claimed that Dr. Kim breached his alleged duty to decedents by failing to warn them of the threat of danger posed by his patient.

In maintaining a claim such as the one at bar, plaintiff must be able to establish a duty on the part of the defendant psychiatrist running to the injured third party. To do so plaintiff must be able to show not only that (1) the defendant psychiatrist knew or, according to the standards of his profession, should have known that his patient posed a serious threat of danger to others, but also that (2) the psychiatrist knew or should have known that his patient was dangerous specifically to the injured third party.

* * *

This is the first time that our court has considered whether the existence of a psychiatrist's duty to third persons can be based on an allegation that the psychiatrist should have known of the target of his patient's violence. Our review of the case law of other jurisdictions reveals that those cases establishing a psychiatrist's duty to protect third persons endangered by his patient involved situations where the existence of a target of the patient's violence was actually known by the psychiatrist and the target was identified or readily identifiable by the psychiatrist. See, e.g., Tarasoff v. Regents of the Univ. of Cal., 17 Cal. 3d 425, 131 Cal.Rptr. 14, 551 P.2d 334, 343 (1976) * * *. The question in this case, however, is whether defendant psychiatrist, in accordance with the standards of his profession, *should have been aware* of the existence of a particular target of his patient's aggression and the identity of the target.

The existence of a psychiatrist's duty to protect an endangered person is easily determined when there is an awareness on the part of the psychiatrist that the patient is focusing his aggression on a particular person. The question is then simply whether the target was identified or readily identifiable by the psychiatrist. However, if a duty to take reasonable steps to protect a third person is limited only to those victims which are actually known to the psychiatrist, * * * an extremely negligent psychiatrist may not ascertain that the patient is even dangerous or that the patient is dangerous to anyone in particular. * * * The relevant determination then becomes whether the psychiatrist should have ascertained, by acting in accordance with the standards of his profession, e.g., by reading the hospital records, that there existed a target of his patient's aggression and the identity of the target. Thus, whether the treating psychiatrist actually knows of a target and whether that target is actually identified or readily identifiable by the psychiatrist is not always the appropriate focus in determining the extent of a psychiatrist's duty to persons endangered by his patient.[27]

---

27. For example, what if, even before addressing the readily identifiable person issue, plaintiff asserts that defendant psychiatrist breached the standards of his profession by failing to ascertain that his patient posed a serious threat of danger to others? How can the psychiatrist know of a specific target of his patient's violence if he has failed to even diagnose his patient as dangerous to others? Since our court, as well as other jurisdictions, has extended a duty to protect or warn to situations where the psychiatrist knows or should have known of the danger posed by his patient, we must also extend the duty to specific persons whom the psychiatrist

We therefore find that, when a plaintiff claims that a defendant psychiatrist *should have known* of the existence and identity of the target of his patient's violence, the plaintiff must be able to establish (a) that the target of the patient's violence was, at least extrinsically, identified or readily identifiable, *and* (b) that the defendant psychiatrist, according to the standards of his profession, should have known that that specific person was the target of his patient's serious threat of violence. * * *

After considering the record before us, we find that the trial court correctly found as a matter of law that Richard Bardoni's mother, Catherine Bardoni, was not a readily identifiable victim. However, the court erred in finding as a matter of law that Richard Bardoni's brother, Robert Bardoni, was not a readily identifiable victim and, consequently, that Dr. Kim had no duty to take reasonable care to protect him from Richard Bardoni's violence.

[T]he next question is whether plaintiff established or could have established that Dr. Kim, according to the standards of his profession, should have known that his patient was dangerous specifically to his brother, Robert Bardoni. Dr. Kim stated in his affidavit and deposition that his patient's paranoia was directed at the school system, that his patient never exhibited any hostility toward or threatened decedents, and that he was never informed of any such hostility or threats. Based on these facts, Dr. Kim's position was that he was under no duty to protect the decedents (i.e., he should not have known that decedents were targets of his patient's violence). However, plaintiff's psychiatric expert stated in a second affidavit that, had Dr. Kim performed in accordance with the standard of care of his profession, he would have determined that Robert Bardoni was a specific individual who was in danger from Richard Bardoni. The expert supported this conclusion by stating that Dr. Kim, although recognizing the danger posed by his patient, improperly relied on Evelyn Bardoni's statements that she felt her husband was not dangerous and so failed to specifically inquire into the nature of his patient's delusions. According to plaintiff's expert, Dr. Kim, who diagnosed Richard Bardoni as a paranoid schizophrenic, failed to more specifically inquire as to the nature of his patient's paranoia and, had he done so, his inquiry would have revealed who the patient thought was attacking him (i.e., his brother), and that the patient was laying the groundwork to attack those persons. Plaintiff's expert further stated that Dr. Kim should have known that his patient's refusal of treatment and medication would render him a prime prospect for another psychotic break that very possibly would have resulted in an attack on those who he thought were attacking him.

* * * This showing, although recognizably slim, was sufficient to at least survive defendant Dr. Kim's motion for summary judgment. * * *

---

knows or should have known were endangered.

Although the question of duty is generally one of law, disputed issues which ultimately bear on the question of duty, such as, in this case, what the defendant psychiatrist, according to the standards of his profession, should have known, are questions for the fact finder. Furthermore, even if the underlying evidentiary facts are not, as in the instant case, in dispute, when the inferences to be drawn from these facts (i.e., what a defendant should have known) are such that reasonable persons could differ, there exists a material and ultimate question of fact which must be resolved by the fact finder.

Thus, we find that summary judgment for defendant Dr. Kim on the suit brought on behalf of Robert Bardoni's estate should not have been granted on the basis that Dr. Kim, as a matter of law, owed no duty to Robert Bardoni.

Affirmed in part and reversed in part.

SHEPARD v. REDFORD COMMUN. HOSP., 151 Mich.App. 242, 390 N.W.2d 239 (1986). Mrs. Karen Shepard went to defendant Hospital's emergency room on April 4, 1981, complaining of high fever, leg pain, congestion, headaches, and weakness. A physician diagnosed an upper respiratory infection and prescribed an antibiotic, and Mrs. Shepard went home. Feeling unable to take care of her five-year-old son Eric, she took Eric to a grandmother. Although Mrs. Shepard's fever subsided, she got sicker with nausea, stiff neck, and headache, but she did not return to the Hospital.

On April 6, the grandmother noticed that Eric was quiet, feverish, and nauseated. She gave him aspirin on the advice of a telephone call to another hospital. The next day Eric had a chest and face rash, which a hospital told the grandmother was a typical response to high fever. When Eric became unresponsive, the grandmother took him in a taxi to Mt. Carmel Hospital, where he died half an hour later from spinal meningitis. Mrs. Shepard was then admitted to Mt. Carmel Hospital and diagnosed as having spinal meningitis.

Mrs. Shepard brought a wrongful death action against Redford Community Hospital, alleging that its negligent diagnosis and treatment of her resulted in the death of Eric. The trial court dismissed the action for failure to state a claim, on the ground that the Hospital owed no duty to Eric in the absence of a physician-patient relationship with him.

The Court of Appeals reversed and remanded. It found that the physician-patient relationship between Mrs. Shepard and the Hospital was a "special relationship" that could establish a Hospital duty of reasonable care to Eric, though he was never a Hospital patient himself; indeed, the court declined to characterize the action for his wrongful death as an action for medical malpractice.

Chapter 3

CLAIMS AGAINST MULTIPLE MEDICAL DEFENDANTS

INTRODUCTORY NOTE

The law has ways of allocating medical liability between defendants who are physicians and defendants who are lay persons.

Making physicians liable for the medical negligence of their allied health care helpers (lay persons in this usage) is no longer an issue. Suppose that a physician employs a nurse, who has assets inadequate to pay a large medical malpractice judgment. If the nurse negligently injures a patient without any involvement of the physician except the employment relation, the patient can recover against the physician under respondeat superior—let the higher-up pay. Legal complications arise when the negligent nurse was employed by one master, such as a hospital, but at the time of the harm was directed by an independent master, such as a surgeon. The first section summarizes these developments.

Making hospitals and other institutional health care providers liable for physicians' negligence is a more recent development. Fifty years ago a hospital was regarded as a hotel where physicians practiced medicine, and because a lay organization could not "control" the medical acts of a physician, respondeat superior could not make the innocent employer liable for the employed physician's negligence. Today the issue is whether a hospital can be liable for the medical negligence of a non-employee physician who has the privilege of practicing within the hospital. The second section brings these matters up to date.

The third section takes up situations in which a plaintiff has a medical liability claim against two or more medical defendants, a situation that today is more the rule than the exception. The plaintiff also may have two or more theories of claim that run against fewer than all the defendants. Some of the problems arise from procedure, others from substantive law.

In a perfect world of logic in litigation, all of the claims and defendants would be sorted out before the summons and complaint were served, and common law pleading had that objective. But for 50 years now, the Federal Rules of Civil Procedure, and the large number of state pleading systems based on the Federal Rules, have turned to a different logic, the logic of getting everybody involved into court first, and sorting out thereafter who is alleged to be liable to whom for what:

> Rule 20. Permissive Joinder of Parties. (a) * * * All persons * * * may be joined in one action as defendants if there is asserted against them jointly, severally, or in the alternative, any right to relief in respect of or arising out of the same transaction, occurrence, or series of transactions or occurrences and if any question of law or fact common to all defendants will arise in the action.

But what if the plaintiff joins health care defendants who cannot all be liable, yet the plaintiff cannot produce the evidence to show which is which? It occurred to defendants that if they hung together, they could tie up the evidence so that they could not hang separately, but the courts shrewdly made too great the risk that all would be found liable:

> [Otherwise] a patient who received permanent injuries of a serious character, obviously the result of some one's negligence, would be entirely unable to recover unless the doctors and nurses in attendance voluntarily chose to disclose the identity of the negligent person and the facts establishing liability. * * * If this were the state of the law of negligence, the courts, to avoid gross injustice, would be forced to invoke the principles of absolute liability, irrespective of negligence, in actions by persons suffering injuries during the course of treatment under anesthesia. Ybarra v. Spangard, 25 Cal.2d 486, 154 P.2d 687, 689 (1944).

Today the plaintiff's lawyer expects multiple defendants to whipsaw one another, furnishing evidence to the plaintiff that exonerates some and thereby implicates others.

Another aspect of joinder of defendants troubles physicians: why not wait to join them until the plaintiff has done enough discovery to indicate whether they are truly involved? The answer is lawyer-logic. While adding a defendant looks easy under Fed.R. 21, to do so after the proceedings are well under way requires the judge's permission, Fed.R. 15(a), and it can be altogether impossible, Fed.R. 15(c). The opposite practice is quite simple: if as the pre-trial proceedings move along, a previously joined defendant turns out not to be involved, the defendant is "dropped" under Fed.R. 21 or its state-court equivalent.

After it has been established that all the remaining defendants are or may be liable to the plaintiff, substantive liability law, not procedure, governs the ways of sharing and spreading the plaintiff's damages among the defendants. One provider can sue another provider for indemnification (passing all the liability along), and under the laws of most states today, one provider can sue another provider for contribution (sharing the liability equally or in proportion to fault).

This leads to a particularly troublesome legal problem. The plaintiff has the capacity to let some of the defendants out of the case by settling with them, leaving only one or two defendants actively engaged at trial. On the one hand, the law encourages settlements; on the other hand, if a jury doesn't know the contractual arrangements in a "Mary Carter" agreement between the plaintiff and settling defendants for sharing a plaintiff's judgment among parties who are only nominally in the case, the jury verdict may be seriously skewed against the remaining parties. Whether to permit Mary Carter agreements seems to be a dead issue, but how to handle them before juries is a very lively issue.

SECTION A. PHYSICIAN LIABILITY UNDER RESPONDEAT SUPERIOR

SPARGER v. WORLEY HOSP., INC.
Supreme Court of Texas, 1977.
547 S.W.2d 582.

POPE, JUSTICE.

* * * The plaintiff Sylvia Caldwell sued Worley Hospital, Inc., and Dr. C.F. Sparger for injuries resulting from the failure to remove a sponge [1] from Mrs. Caldwell's abdominal cavity after an operation. The trial court rendered judgment on a jury verdict for plaintiff against Worley Hospital only. * * *

The plaintiff did not sue the [Worley Hospital] nurses * * *. The jury answers exonerated Dr. Sparger from every act of negligence for which he was charged and found instead that the nurses were negligent. Dr. Sparger is therefore before us with an application for writ of error in which he insists that the court of civil appeals should not have held him vicariously liable as a matter of law for the negligence of the nurses under the so-called captain of the ship doctrine. 529 S.W.2d 639 (1975). Worley Hospital's application contends that Dr. Sparger must bear the sole liability, since the captain of the ship doctrine made the nurses his exclusive employees. * * *

If this was anything but a malpractice case, the question before us would be resolved by the jury's refusal to find that Dr. Sparger had borrowed the Worley Hospital's nurses so as to make them his employees. * * *

Texas has long recognized that a general employee of one employer may become the borrowed servant of another. J.A. Robinson Sons, Inc. v. Wigart, 431 S.W.2d 327 (Tex.1968); * * * Restatement (Second) of

---

1. Editors' Note: The surgery was a "laparotomy" (the opening of the abdomen), and the "sponge" was a 16-inch square of 5 or 6 thicknesses of gauze. For details of what a "lap sponge" looks like and how people can overlook it, see Piehl v. Dalles Gen. Hosp., 280 Or. 613, 571 P.2d 149 (1977).

Agency § 227 (1958). Under the borrowed servant doctrine the essential inquiry would be whether or not the surgeon had the right to control the assisting nurses in the details "of the specific act raising the issue of liability." J.A. Robinson Sons, Inc. v. Wigart, 431 S.W.2d at 330. The right of control is ordinarily a question of fact. * * *

The principle of borrowed servant cuts across the entire law of principal and agent and employer and employee, and is therefore also applicable to the legal relationships between a physician or surgeon and a nurse. Physicians and surgeons are and should be subject to the usual rules applicable to borrowed servants. In some jurisdictions, however, there has been imposed upon the medical profession, a special and more onerous form of vicarious liability. * * *

The phrase "captain of the ship" was first employed in the medical malpractice context in the case of McConnell v. Williams, 361 Pa. 355, 65 A.2d 243 (1959). It was used in that case as an apt analogy, but in some jurisdictions the phrase has grown into a separate and independent concept of agency which specially applies to medical malpractice cases. * * *

Similes sometimes help to explain a factual situation, but in legal writing, phrases have a way of being canonized and of growing until they can stand and walk independently of the usual general rules. Mr. Justice Frankfurter once wrote concerning such phrase-making in judicial opinions:

> The phrase * * * is an excellent illustration of the extent to which uncritical use of words bedevils the law. A phrase begins life as a literary expression; its felicity leads to its lazy repetition; and repetition soon establishes it as a legal formula, undiscriminatingly used to express different and sometimes contradictory ideas. Tiller v. Atlantic Coast Line R.R., 318 U.S. 54, 68, 63 S.Ct. 444, 87 L.Ed. 610 (1942).

The result in the use of captain of the ship is that a surgeon or physician may be held liable, not as others upon the basis of the general rule of borrowed servant, but as captain of the ship.

The jurisdiction which first employed the metaphor has now retreated from the concept, so that occurrences in the operating room might be brought back to the confines of the more general borrowed servant concept. The court in Thomas v. Hutchinson, 442 Pa. 118, 275 A.2d 23 (1971), said that the captain of the ship example was intended as an adaptation of the familiar borrowed servant principle that applies generally in the law of agency.[2] See Note, Malpractice—Vicarious Liability of an Operating Surgeon, 10 Duq.L.Rev. 117 (1971). Hence, where there are inconsistent factual inferences concerning the ser-

---

2. Editors' Note: As the Pennsylvania Supreme Court acknowledged in the *Thomas* case, it had abolished the defense of charitable immunity in 1965, Flagiello v. Pennsylvania Hosp., 417 Pa. 486, 208 A.2d 193, making the charitable hospital fully responsible for the medical negligence of its employees. The Texas Supreme Court abolished charitable immunity in 1971 as to claims arising after 1966. Howle v. Camp Amon Carter, 470 S.W.2d 629.

vant's employer which can be reasonably drawn from evidence, the issue should be resolved factually as any other borrowed servant issue.

* * *

* * * We disapprove the captain of the ship doctrine and hold that it is a false special rule of agency. Operating surgeons and hospitals are subject to the principles of agency law which apply to others. * * * The state of the facts may in some cases be such as to make one a surgeon's employee or borrowed servant as a matter of law, but that is not the factual situation before us in this case.

The question remains whether the facts show that, as a matter of law, the nurses were the borrowed servants of Dr. Sparger. Three nurses had assignments in the operating room during the operation. They were hired by and were the general employees of the hospital and were assigned by the hospital for the operation. Dr. Sparger did not participate in their selection. Marjie Holland was the "circulating nurse." As such, she served in that part of the operating room that was designated as the non-sterile field. Wanda Ensey was the "scrub nurse" who was required to remain in the sterile field so that she could assist the surgeon throughout the operation. Geneva Finney was positioned at the foot of the operating table, but she had no responsibilities concerning the sponges.

The duties of the circulating and scrub nurses were detailed in the hospital's Policy & Procedure Manual. There were general instructions which applied to both nurses. There were specific duties assigned to the circulating nurse and specific duties assigned to the scrub nurse. The procedures for the sponge counts were intended for use regardless of the surgeon who was performing an operation in the Worley Hospital.

The mistake in leaving the sponge in plaintiff's abdomen was explained in this way. The circulating nurse had prepared the operating room by laying out the necessary supplies and equipment. She remained in the non-sterile area of the operating room during the operation. The scrub nurse stood within the sterile field and assisted the surgeon by handing him instruments, clamps, and sponges. Before surgery began, the scrub nurse in front of the circulating nurse counted the sponges which had been laid out. The circulating nurse recorded that count. When Dr. Sparger was ready to close the inner layer of tissue, the scrub nurse counted the unused sponges, and the circulating nurse counted the used ones. The total was reported by the scrub nurse as tallying with the record.

Wanda Ensey, the scrub nurse, testified that Dr. Sparger did not direct her and Mrs. Holland to make the sponge count. Mrs. Ensey stated that the two nurses knew how to perform the sponge count, because it was part of the manual regulations which they followed. Reasonable minds might differ as to the facts which presented the borrowed servant issue.

We conclude, therefore, as did the trial court, that plaintiff should have judgment against Worley Hospital, since the jury made a finding that it was hospital's employees who were negligent. Since the captain of the ship idea is a false issue and the jury found as a fact that the nurses were not the borrowed servants of Dr. Sparger, plaintiff was not entitled to a judgment against Dr. Sparger.

* * *

SAM D. JOHNSON, JUSTICE, dissenting.

[A] surgeon may be liable for the negligence occurring in the operating room. * * * The special relationship that exists between the surgeon and the patient in the operating room justifies the imposition of such liability.

This special relationship arises from the conscious selection by the patient of a particular surgeon, the reliance by the patient on the skill and judgment of the surgeon, the inability of the patient to control any of the actions occurring during surgery, the expectation that the surgeon selected will control the operation, the patient's expectation that the surgeon will require the operating room personnel to follow proper medical procedures, the expectation that the surgeon will protect the patient from the negligence of the operating room personnel, and the responsibility accepted by the surgeon to require the application of proper medical procedures and to exclude unqualified personnel from the operating room. This special relationship is not the only justification for the imposition of liability on the surgeon for negligence in the operating room. The knowledge of such potential liability will prompt the surgeon to initiate every possible safeguard to prevent negligence in the operating room.

Whether the doctrine is known as "captain of the ship" or by some other label, this writer would hold that a surgeon may be liable for any negligence occurring in the operating theater. Liability may be imposed on the theory that the surgeon had the right to control the negligent individual or, if there was no right to control, on the theory that the surgeon was negligent in failing to insist on the right to control.

Even applying the standard adopted by the majority, an examination of the evidence in the instant case leads inevitably to the conclusion that the operating surgeon, Dr. Sparger, as a matter of law had the right to control the actions of the nurses with respect to the sponge counts during the course of the operation. Indeed, in the opinion of this writer, such evidence is overwhelming.

* * *

[Editors' Note: On motion for rehearing, the supreme court remanded the case to the court of civil appeals, asking it to decide whether the jury's special finding, that the nurses were not the borrowed servants of Dr. Sparger, was "against the great and overwhelming weight of the evidence." The court of civil appeals accepted the

SECTION B. MEDICAL LIABILITY OF INSTITUTIONS

SLOAN v. METROPOLITAN HEALTH COUNCIL
Court of Appeals of Indiana, 1987.
516 N.E.2d 1104.

NEAL, JUDGE. * * *

* * * Metro [The Metropolitan Health Council of Indianapolis, Inc., doing business as Metro–Health Plan] is a not-for-profit corporation organized to provide a prepaid health care delivery plan, or, as it terms itself, a health maintenance organization, and it is regulated under Ind.Code § 27–8–7–1 to –21. Metro's members pay a monthly charge, plus certain specified fees listed in a schedule; in return, they are entitled to specifically enumerated medical services. Metro advertises one complete system which delivers its members health care in return for prepaid payment. The member selects one of Metro's staff physicians, who then treats the member, orders tests, prescribes medicine, or arranges for other professional care or hospitalization. It boasts of simplicity: one medical office, one phone number, and one medical record for each member. Metro physicians are on call 24 hours a day, every day, for emergencies involving members. All complaints are made to Metro, not to physicians. Enrollment in the plan is with Metro, not the physician. Billing is made by Metro, not the physician, and Metro has the right of subrogation.

The physicians who treat members are engaged by Metro by a written contract denominated as an "employment contract," wherein Metro is labeled the "Employer" and the physician is called the "Physician." The Physician is paid an annual salary, increased yearly and paid in biweekly installments, in addition to which he receives such fringe benefits as sick leave, life, health, and malpractice insurance, a tax-sheltered annuity, vacation pay, and professional leave. The Physician cannot engage in outside work without Metro's consent.

* * * Metro is a federally qualified health maintenance organization under Title XIII of the Public Health Service Act, 42 U.S.C. § 300e.

The Sloans, members of Metro since 1978, brought suit alleging a negligent failure to diagnose. In its affidavit filed in support of its motion for summary judgment, Metro claims that the physicians it employs are independent in their practice of medicine, and Metro does not control their judgment in diagnosis or treatment decisions. Physicians are reviewed periodically as a matter of quality assurance, they are not overseen for the purpose of questioning their conclusions, and Metro does not enjoy veto power over tests, diagnoses, prescriptions, or treatment.

The trial court granted summary judgment to Metro on the basis that a corporation cannot be vicariously liable for the malpractice of a physician in its employment. The sole question here is the correctness of that ruling.

* * * Metro supports the trial court's ruling with reliance upon the case of Iterman v. Baker, 214 Ind. 308, 15 N.E.2d 365 (1938), and its progeny * * *.

Iterman was a malpractice case against the New Castle Clinic, a corporation owned by physicians who were the directors, officers, and employees. The corporation owned the building and equipment, collected the fees, and paid the physicians a salary. Baker consulted Dr. Iterman who, with the consultation of two other employee-physicians, diagnosed and treated him. There was no reference in the doctor-patient relationship to a contract with the corporation. The court denied recovery as a matter of law. Its rationale is stated as follows:

> The complaint is upon the theory that the corporation was engaged in practicing medicine and surgery, and that it contracted to diagnose and treat the appellee's injury. The right to practice medicine is, in this state, controlled by statute. It is held in some jurisdictions that corporations may legally engage in the practice of medicine and surgery. *The question involves the consideration and construction of local statutes. Under the statutes of this state it has never been doubted that it is unlawful for a corporation to practice medicine, and any contract made in the name of a corporation, binding it to diagnose or treat ailments or diseases, is not only ultra vires, but unlawful and against public policy.* The right to practice medicine and surgery under a license by the state is a personal privilege. It cannot be delegated, and a corporation, or other unlicensed person may not engage in the practice of medicine by employing one who is licensed to do the things which constitute practicing the profession. State v. Williams, 211 Ind. 186, 5 N.E.2d 961 (1937). If a licensed physician employs assistants, who work under his direction as assistants, in the practice of medicine or surgery, the respondeat superior rule applies. But a licensed physician may not accept directions and instructions in diagnosing and treating ailments from a corporation or an individual who is not a licensed practitioner. 15 N.E.2d at 369–70. (Emphasis added.)

The court stated that if a contract for medical services was made with a corporation, the contract would be complied with by using reasonable and ordinary care to employ qualified, reputable, and licensed physicians. In such cases the physicians or surgeons are independent contractors. The corporation is not estopped to assert the defense because all persons are presumed to know the law, that a corporation cannot practice medicine.

* * *

The entire rationale for the holding in *Iterman* is based upon the conclusion reached by the court that, since no Indiana statute existed at that time which permitted a corporation to practice medicine, a public policy existed prohibiting a corporation to practice medicine; thus, the doctrine of respondeat superior was inapplicable. We believe that the Professional Corporation Act of 1983, Ind.Code § 23–1.5–1–1 to –5–2, totally abolished such a public policy if, indeed, it ever existed. We acknowledge that Metro is not incorporated under the Professional Corporation Act, but the Act stands as a pronouncement of public policy concerning a corporation's vicarious liability for the acts of its employee-physician. We are mindful that no statute existed at the time of *Iterman* which expressly forbade a corporation to practice medicine, but the pronouncement in *Iterman* was a court-created rule based upon legislative silence.

* * *

As shown by the statement of facts, there is evidence that Metro's staff physicians were under the control of its medical director, a physician, who policed medical services and established policy. His judgment was final. The circumstances establish an employment relationship where the employee performed acts within the scope of his employment. The employee-physician was supervised by a physician, not a layperson, an objection voiced in *Iterman*. We are of the opinion that, upon the advent of the Professional Corporation Act, a public policy no longer exists in Indiana shielding medical corporations from malpractice liability of their employee physicians. * * * No statutory scheme exists to abolish the doctrine of respondeat superior for medical corporations regardless of whether the corporation is a professional corporation or not. *Iterman* is no longer applicable. The practice of medicine by Metro is, according to the facts, exactly the same as the practice of medicine by a professional corporation. We see no reason why Metro should be exempt from the doctrine of respondeat superior while professional corporations are not. Metro cannot escape the operation of the doctrine by the simple expedience of not incorporating under the Professional Corporation Act. Should we succumb to Metro's argument that it is not incorporated under the Professional Corporation Act, and therefore, the rules governing that entity are not applicable, we would be required to take the next step and hold that the entire operation was illegal. We hold that where the usual requisites of agency or an employer-employee relationship exist, a corporation may be held vicariously liable for malpractice for the acts of its employee-physicians.

For the above reasons this cause is reversed, and the trial court is directed to overrule Metro's motion for summary judgment.

PEDROZA v. BRYANT
Supreme Court of Washington, 1984.
101 Wash.2d 226, 677 P.2d 166.

PEARSON, JUSTICE.

The issue before us is whether a hospital may be held liable under a theory of corporate negligence for its action in granting privileges to a nonemployee doctor who allegedly commits malpractice while in private practice off the hospital premises.

* * *

It should be noted at the outset that plaintiff is not claiming that defendant hospital is vicariously liable for the negligence of Dr. Bryant under the theory of respondeat superior. Dr. Bryant is an independent contractor, not an employee of defendant hospital. Plaintiff is instead relying solely on the doctrine of corporate negligence, which differs from respondeat superior in that it imposes on the hospital a nondelegable duty owed directly to the patient, regardless of the details of the doctor-hospital relationship. Plaintiff contends that defendant hospital owed a duty to Maria Pedroza of carefully selecting and reviewing the competency of its staff physicians. ("Staff physicians" are those doctors who have been given "staff privileges" at the hospital. A physician must be a member of the hospital's medical staff in order to regularly admit patients to the hospital.) Plaintiff alleges that defendant hospital breached this duty by allowing Dr. Bryant to possess staff privileges at the hospital, and that this breach was the proximate cause of Mrs. Pedroza's death.

* * * The doctrine of corporate negligence appears to have been introduced in Darling v. Charleston Commun. Mem. Hosp., 33 Ill.2d 326, 211 N.E.2d 253 (1965), where the Illinois Supreme Court found defendant hospital liable for its failure to review the plaintiff-patient's treatment and require consultation with appropriate medical staff members as needed. This established the concept that a hospital had an independent responsibility to patients to supervise the medical treatment provided by members of its medical staff. Liability for failure to do so was not founded on respondeat superior, which had been the traditional mode of recovery; rather, the court found the hospital liable for its own negligence and not that of the physician.

The doctrine of corporate negligence has since been utilized by courts to require hospitals to exercise reasonable care to insure that the physicians selected as members of hospital medical staffs are competent. * * * Jurisdictions adopting corporate negligence have also held that hospitals have a continuing duty to review and delineate staff privileges so that incompetent staff physicians are not retained.

* * *

Before the emergence of corporate negligence, hospital liability for the negligence of a staff physician was based on the theory of respondeat superior. Plaintiffs found it difficult to recover, however, as courts tended to classify physicians as independent contractors for whose acts the hospital was not liable. Some states, Washington among them, have attempted to avoid the somewhat artificial distinctions associated with the independent contractor defense (e.g., classifying an independent private physician with staff privileges who is retained by the patient as an "independent contractor" while a physician whose salary is paid by the hospital is a "servant," even though both are on the same medical staff, performing the same tasks.) They have tried to avoid these distinctions by affixing vicarious liability upon the hospital when the individual is performing an "inherent function" of the hospital, or acting as an "ostensible agent." See Adamski v. Tacoma Gen. Hosp., 20 Wash.App. 98, 579 P.2d 970 (1978). Such an analysis does not, however, address the question of the hospital's direct negligence in its selection or retention of an incompetent doctor on the hospital's medical staff.

The doctrine of corporate negligence reflects the public's perception of the modern hospital as a multifaceted health care facility responsible for the quality of medical care and treatment rendered. The community hospital has evolved into a corporate institution, assuming "the role of a comprehensive health center ultimately responsible for arranging and co-ordinating total health care." Southwick, The Hospital as an Institution—Expanding Responsibilities Change Its Relationship with the Staff Physician, 9 Cal.W.L.Rev. 429 (1973). The patient treated in such a facility receives care from a number of individuals of varying capacities and is not merely treated by a physician acting in isolation. * * * This increased public reliance upon hospitals favors adoption of corporate negligence.

Hospitals are also in a superior position to monitor and control physician performance. * * *

Forcing hospitals to assume responsibility for their corporate negligence may also provide those hospitals a financial incentive to insure the competency of their medical staffs. The most effective way to cut liability insurance costs is to avoid corporate negligence.

* * *

We hereby expressly adopt the theory of corporate negligence. * * * Nearly every jurisdiction that has addressed the issue in the last 15 years has adopted corporate negligence. In addition, the doctrine is justified by the policy reasons already discussed.

* * * The alleged acts of malpractice committed by Dr. Bryant occurred entirely outside the hospital. Mrs. Pedroza was not a patient of the hospital at the time. For plaintiff to prevail, we must decide that the duty of care owed by hospitals under the corporate negligence doctrine extends not only to hospital patients, but also to patients treated by hospital staff members in those staff members' private office practices, where the hospital is not involved. No other jurisdiction appears to have done this; all the cases involve acts of malpractice committed at the hospital.

* * * The hospital holds itself out to the community as a competent provider of medical care. The hospital does not hold itself out as an inspector or insurer of the private office practices of its staff members. The delineation of staff privileges by the hospital can only affect the procedures used by staff members while they are inside hospital walls. The public cannot reasonably expect anything more.

* * *

Accordingly, we hold that a hospital's duty of care under the doctrine of corporate negligence extends only to those who are patients within the hospital. Defendant Skagit Valley Hospital owed no duty to Maria Pedroza under the doctrine because she was not a hospital patient when the harm occurred. The fact that she had been a patient at defendant hospital in years past does not make her a patient for purposes of this case. Each of those prior hospital-patient relationships ended upon her discharge from the hospital; they did not continue indefinitely.

Since there are no allegations of negligence after Mrs. Pedroza was admitted to the hospital, we affirm the trial court's order of summary judgment.

SCHOENING v. GRAYS HARBOR COMMUN. HOSP.
Court of Appeals of Washington, 1985.
40 Wash.App. 331, 698 P.2d 593.

ALEXANDER, JUDGE. * * *

Alison and Larry * * * Schoenings' first child was born on September 22, 1980 at the Grays Harbor Community Hospital. The child and mother were released from the hospital two days later. That night Mrs. Schoening returned to the hospital's emergency room complaining of breast engorgement and perineal tenderness. Unable to reach her physician, Dr. Charles Ward, emergency room personnel summoned Dr. Thomas Wu, who was taking Dr. Ward's calls. Dr. Wu prescribed antibiotics and sent Mrs. Schoening home. In the early morning hours of the next day, September 25, 1980, she returned to the emergency room. She said the pain was worse, and she was feeling faint. Dr. Ward admitted her to the hospital and suggested that surgery might be required. The Schoenings said they would like a second opinion on surgery and, thereafter, Dr. Ward ceased treating her. At the request of Dr. Ward and Mrs. Schoening's family, Dr. Wu then assumed responsibility for the care of Mrs. Schoening. Alison Schoening remained at Grays Harbor Community Hospital for seven days. During this time Dr. Wu consulted with Dr. Alan Failor, an internal medicine specialist employed at the United States Public Health Service, and the two doctors treated Mrs. Schoening with antibiotics. However, her condition continued to deteriorate, and by October 2, 1980, it was deemed "life threatening." Dr. Wu then consulted specialists at the University of Washington, performed exploratory surgery and transferred Mrs. Schoening to the University of Washington Medical Center. She remained there until October 27, 1980, undergoing a colostomy and other surgery.

This suit was commenced by the Schoenings in September 1981 against the Grays Harbor Community Hospital and the three doctors who treated Mrs. Schoening there. The hospital moved for summary judgment and presented argument. The trial judge filed a memorandum decision in which he indicated the hospital's motion would be granted. * * *

The Schoenings argued that the hospital could be liable for the negligent acts of the doctors under theories of respondeat superior and corporate negligence. Recovery under the first theory has been precluded by a settlement with the doctors.[3] If the doctors were agents of the hospital, the hospital was released from liability by their satisfaction of the claim. * * * This point was conceded by plaintiffs at the hearing before this court.

The second theory, that the hospital has independent liability, is not disposed of by the settlement, however. It is based on the proposition that a hospital owes an independent duty of care to its patients. This duty was recognized in Pedroza v. Bryant, 101 Wash.2d 226, 677 P.2d 166 (1984), which expressly applied the theory of corporate negligence to hospitals. * * *

Furthermore, Wash.Rev.Code § 4.24.290 provides that the applicable standard of care for a hospital is "to exercise that degree of skill, care, and learning possessed at that time by other persons in the same profession * * *."

The question then is: Did the hospital violate this standard of care by its failure to intervene in the treatment of Mrs. Schoening? The trial court determined as a matter of law that it had not. That decision was proper only if there is no genuine issue as to any material facts * * *.

[W]e conclude that a fact question exists concerning whether the Grays Harbor Community Hospital met its duty of care to its patients. [T]he hospital clearly has a duty to monitor the treatment of its patients and intervene if there is obvious negligence. According to Dr. Miller's affidavit, that standard of care was not met. * * *

Hospital personnel were certainly aware of Mrs. Schoening's deteriorating condition. It is not clear, however, whether that deterioration, itself, was enough to indicate that the attending physicians' treatment was such that the hospital should act independently of the attending physician. Dr. Miller apparently feels the hospital should have intervened. Whether they should have or not is a question for the trier of fact. It is not a question resolvable on summary judgment.

[W]e reverse and remand the matter to the Grays Harbor County Superior Court for trial.

3. The three doctors, Wu, Ward and Koeniger, are associated in the practice of medicine at the Hoquiam Obstetrical and Gynecological Clinic, P.S., and that professional services corporation is a named defendant. The Schoenings subsequently reached a settlement with these doctors. * * *

SECTION C. MULTIPLE HEALTH CARE PROVIDERS' LIABILITIES

GILSON v. MITCHELL
Court of Appeals of Georgia, 1974.
131 Ga.App. 321, 205 S.E.2d 421.

HALL, PRESIDING JUDGE.

* * * The suit grew out of the alleged negligence of the defendants in connection with the use of a central venous pressure catheter (CVP catheter) in Mr. Irving Gilson's right external jugular vein throughout a period of several days of hospitalization, during which time he underwent stomach surgery. Such a CVP catheter is a flexible tube normally several inches long, designed to reach from the neck through a vein into the heart area, and the insertion of the one in question was done by Dr. Raul Soria. The removal was accomplished by Dr. W.E. Mitchell, Jr., who found the catheter so short upon pulling it out of the vein that he, in conjunction with Dr. W.E. Mitchell, Sr., concluded that the missing length was adrift somewhere in Mr. Gilson's circulatory system where it could produce quick death. Mr. Gilson was inconclusively x-rayed to locate the missing part and then flown to Texas for treatment by a heart specialist whose tests were also inconclusive. Apparently, the fate of the missing length has never been medically determined.

Mr. Gilson's negligence suit against the three doctors sought recovery for his unnecessary subjection to mental distress and to surgical procedures, on the theory that the alleged missing length never existed but was in fact cut off by Dr. Soria prior to insertion. * * * The Gilsons alleged independent but concurring acts of negligence by the doctors, and sought a joint recovery against them. The rewritten and modified complaint advanced the claim that the doctors were joint tortfeasors and that their acts of negligence were as follows: Dr. Soria, without informing the Drs. Mitchell, and without telling plaintiffs of the experimental nature of his proceeding, inserted an abnormally short catheter and subsequently did not follow the patient's progress through removal of the catheter; the Drs. Mitchell, upon discovering the strangely short catheter, did not inquire of Dr. Soria the length he used, but jumped to the conclusion that a piece was lost and immediately subjected the patient to expensive and painful procedures to "locate" the missing part. Thus the various acts of the Drs. Mitchell and Dr. Soria together produced the single injury to plaintiff of needless subjection to medical procedures and mental distress.

* * * The doctors argued successfully below that they were not joint tortfeasors because they were not alleged to have acted in concert. The trial judge agreed with the doctors and ruled that they were not joint tortfeasors but were merely defendants in two separate negligence

actions—one against the Drs. Mitchell as medical partners [4] and one against Dr. Soria * * *.

[The jury verdict was in favor of all the defendants, and the plaintiffs appealed.]

* * *

Let it be emphasized here that this discussion is concerned with the joint tortfeasor concept as a matter of substantive law, and not merely as a procedural concept affected by recent joinder rules.

It has always been true that where concert of action appears, a joint tortfeasor relation is presented, and all joint tortfeasors are jointly and severally liable for the full amount of plaintiff's damage. However, American law has expanded over the years from this beginning point, and presently textwriters and most Georgia cases are agreed that concert of action is not required—concurrent and independent wrongdoers are joint tortfeasors *if* their actions produce a single indivisible result and a rational apportionment of damages cannot be made. Examples of such an indivisible result could be death, a broken leg, any single wound, the total burning of a house, or sinking of a barge. W. Prosser, Torts § 52 at 315 (4th ed. 1971). * * *

This test for determining joint tortfeasors, namely, whether the injury is divisible or indivisible, is that proposed in the Restatement (Second) of Torts which, summing up an entire chapter on "Contributing Tortfeasors" in the prior Restatement, set forth this criterion:

(1) Damages for harm are to be apportioned among two or more causes where

(a) there are distinct harms, or

(b) there is a reasonable basis for determining the contribution of each cause to a single harm.

(2) Damages for any other harm cannot be apportioned among two or more causes. Restatement (Second) of Torts § 433A (1965).

Thus, those tortfeasors among whom damages cannot be apportioned under these rules are properly regarded as joint tortfeasors. This is a refinement of the first Restatement * * *.

The weight of authority in Georgia is entirely consistent with this view. * * *

Against the weight of Georgia authority * * *, however, stand certain cases creating or appearing to create a conflict by adopting the opposite view, namely, that concert of action is required. One such case is our own recent decision in Bulloch County Hosp. Auth. v. Fowler, 124 Ga.App. 242, 183 S.E.2d 586 (1971). There, plaintiff's husband suffered a heart attack and was taken to the hospital. His doctor was called to come immediately, but dawdled on the way for an hour, chatting with a friend. Knowing that he had been summoned,

---

4. Editors' Note: See Annot., Liability of One Physician or Surgeon for Malpractice of Another, 85 A.L.R.2d 872 (1962).

the hospital refused plaintiff's urgent request to call for other help. The husband died. In plaintiff's suit against the doctor and the hospital, seeking damages against them jointly on the basis for their concurring acts of negligence, this court held

> There was no concert of action. The actions of the doctor and of the hospital were mutually independent. They were not joint tortfeasors. Separate verdicts will be required. 183 S.E.2d at 589.

This conclusion was in error, and we hold today that so much of the opinion * * * as held that the defendants were not joint tortfeasors and that separate verdicts were required was incorrect, and we expressly overrule it. * * *

* * * The rule henceforth will be that even though voluntary, intentional concert is lacking, if the separate and independent acts of negligence of several persons combine naturally and directly to produce a single indivisible injury, and a rational basis does not exist for an apportionment of damages, the actors are joint tortfeasors. * * *

* * * Drs. Mitchell and Dr. Soria may correctly be sued as joint tortfeasors. Though their alleged acts of negligence did not occur at the same time, they combined naturally and directly to create an urgent situation in which the missing portion of the catheter was thought to be in Gilson's blood stream, which required that he be subjected to further medical procedures. On these facts his subjection to medical procedures is not capable of apportionment, that is, so much for the negligence of Dr. Soria initially and so much for the negligence of the Drs. Mitchell. Under plaintiff's theory of his case, the entire course of the procedures was required by the combined acts of the doctors, and he is entitled to sue them as joint tortfeasors.

[W]e cannot say that the Drs. Mitchell were found not negligent on the merits at a proper trial. * * *. We rule that this verdict is entire and inseparable and our reversal runs to all defendants. A further inequity of an opposite holding would be that should the judgment for the Mitchells stand and should Dr. Soria lose upon retrial, he would have no right of contribution from the Mitchells, and the question of their negligence on the merits will not have been determined in a properly tried case.

[O]ur ruling that the defendants were joint tortfeasors leads to the further conclusion that the trial judge erred in disallowing a joint verdict and in instructing the jury that if they found for plaintiffs, separate verdicts against the doctors would be required. * * *

Judgment reversed.

EVANS, J., concurred specially. * * *

[I]n Georgia, where suit is brought against joint defendants for * * * injury to the person, each defendant is liable for the whole or entire damage, even though one defendant may have committed only simple negligence, while the other defendant committed wilful and wanton misconduct, and thus contributed in a greater degree to the injury. Each is liable for the whole damage, and if one of the wrongdoers is not sued, the one who is sued shall be liable for all of the damage.

* * *

[Editors' Note: The Supreme Court of Georgia granted certiorari. Its opinion said, "We conclude that the opinion of the Court of Appeals correctly states the law of Georgia on this subject, and we adopt this opinion and affirm the judgment of the Court of Appeals." 233 Ga. 453, 211 S.E.2d 744, 745 (1975).]

FOOTE v. UNITED STATES v. MICHAEL REESE HOSP.

United States District Court for the Northern District of Illinois, 1986.
648 F.Supp. 735.

ASPEN, DISTRICT JUDGE.

Abraham Foote brought this action under the Federal Tort Claims Act, 28 U.S.C.A. § 1346(b), against the United States of America ("the government") for injuries allegedly incurred as a result of the failure of medical personnel at a government hospital to diagnose and properly treat a ruptured quadriceps mechanism which Foote had suffered. The government then filed a third-party complaint under Fed.R.Civ.P. 14(a) against Michael Reese Hospital & Medical Center ("Reese") seeking contribution * * * with respect to treatment rendered by Reese to Foote prior to his visit to the government facility. * * *

On January 15, 1981, Foote first went to Reese for treatment of an injury to his right leg. He was seen in the emergency room and released. Ten days later Foote went to Naval Regional Medical Center at Great Lakes ("Naval Regional") complaining of pain, stiffness, and weakness in the knees. He was seen in the emergency room and released, but returned to Naval Regional later during the same year for treatment. * * *

In its third-party complaint, the government alleges that it is entitled to contribution from Reese regarding any liability to Foote which the government might have, because Reese first failed to diagnose the problem in Foote's leg. Reese asserts that the government fails to state a claim because Reese's treatment of Foote predated that of the government, and Reese therefore cannot be the cause or a contributing cause of the alleged injury claimed in Foote's lawsuit.

* * *

State law governs liability, including the right to indemnity or contribution, under the Federal Tort Claims Act * * *. Reese and Naval Regional, the only places where Foote sought medical treatment for his leg, are both located in Illinois. Thus, the basis for the government's third-party complaint against Reese is the Illinois Contribution Act, Ill.Rev.Stat. ch. 70, § 302(a), which states:

[W]here two or more persons are subject to liability in tort arising out of the same injury to person or property * * * there is a right of contribution among them, even though judgment has not been entered against any or all of them.

* * *

Reese contends that the "same injury" requirement has not been satisfied, pointing out that the earlier care rendered at Reese and that care rendered at Naval Regional are distinct and unrelated activities. From this Reese concludes that "any misfeasance or malfeasance that the government alleges may have occurred at Michael Reese could not possibly be the same injury of which plaintiff complains from the care rendered by the Government." We disagree.

[I]f damage to the leg has resulted in part from the failure to diagnose and promptly treat Foote's ruptured quadriceps mechanism, then it is quite possible that Reese's alleged failure to diagnose the problem on January 15 contributed to or aggravated Foote's injury, notwithstanding the government's later treatment. Indeed, under some circumstances, the first negligent treating party might even be liable to the injured plaintiff for all foreseeable injuries resulting from the later negligent medical treatment of a second party. * * *

Although no Illinois case appears to have addressed the question of whether two different physicians who fail to make a proper diagnosis on successive occasions are co-tortfeasors within the meaning of the Contribution Act, there is language in other cases which indicates that Reese would fall into the co-tortfeasor category. In Morgan v. Kirk Bros., Inc., 111 Ill.App.3d 914, 67 Ill.Dec. 268, 444 N.E.2d 504, 507 (1983), the court observed that

> [N]either § 302(a) nor the published legislative history requires that the tortfeasors be joint in the strict sense that their tortious acts be simultaneous, or that they act in concert, before contribution will lie,

adding that

> The currently accepted definition of the term "joint tortfeasors" includes all cases where there is joint liability for a tort, whether the acts of those liable were concerted, merely concurrent, or even successive in time * * *. 444 N.E.2d at 507 n. 2.

Under this analysis, if Reese's failure to diagnose the ruptured quadriceps was responsible in part for causing the injury, Reese may be liable to the government for contribution under the Illinois Contribution Act, notwithstanding the separation in time between its treatment and the government's treatment. Thus, Reese may ultimately be liable to the government for all or part of Foote's claim against the government and is a proper third-party defendant. * * *

* * * [Reese's] motion to dismiss the government's third-party complaint is denied. * * *

LUM v. STINNETT
Supreme Court of Nevada, 1971.
87 Nev. 402, 488 P.2d 347.

GUNDERSON, JUSTICE.

This appeal arises from a malpractice action commenced by respondent William Stinnett against three physicians: Dr. Greene, who attended Stinnett at a hospital emergency room; Dr. Romeo, Stinnett's "family doctor," who consulted with Dr. Greene by telephone, directed that Stinnett be X-rayed, and thereafter attended him; and appellant Dr. James Lum, who "read" the X-rays.[5] Stinnett's theory was that defendants negligently failed to detect and treat a compression fracture in Stinnett's spine. * * *

All parties announced ready for trial on October 29, 1969, and jury selection continued through the morning of October 30; counsel for Drs. Greene and Romeo took a major part in choosing the jury, jurors being selected whom Dr. Lum's counsel might well have rejected had he known his apparent allies were then negotiating a "settlement" with Stinnett. By a letter hand-delivered to counsel for Drs. Greene and Romeo on October 29, Stinnett's counsel, with some self-serving recitals, proposed: (1) if the jury awarded nothing or less than $20,000, the insurance carriers for Drs. Greene and Romeo were to pay the sum necessary to bring recovery to $20,000; (2) if the verdict exceeded $20,000, Stinnett would not execute against Drs. Greene and Romeo; and (3) Stinnett would not oppose a motion for directed verdict in favor of Drs. Greene and Romeo.[6] On October 30, when jury selection was completed, counsel for Drs. Greene and Romeo told Dr. Lum's counsel something of this proposal, and that they had decided to accept it. By letter of October 31, counsel for Drs. Greene and Romeo did advise Stinnett's counsel they accepted the proposal, if Stinnett's counsel agreed not to "oppose a motion made pursuant to Nev.R.Civ.P. 41(b) or 50(a) at the close of plaintiff's case"; to "press forth actively against Dr. Lum"; not to settle with him for less than $20,000 without their written consent; and to urge a jury verdict in excess of $20,000. Stinnett's counsel approved and signed this counter-proposal.

On November 3, when court reconvened to begin trial, Dr. Lum's counsel moved to withdraw and asked a continuance because he could not agree with Dr. Lum's insurance carrier on how to meet problems

---

5. Editors' Note: "Stinnett" has been substituted for "respondent," and "Dr. Lum" for "appellant," throughout.

6. Melded into the proposal were at least these self-serving recitals: (a) Lum's insurance carrier had taken an "irresponsible position"; (b) this was why Stinnett would deal separately concerning Greene and Romeo; (c) Stinnett's counsel believed Greene and Romeo negligent; (d) nonetheless, they "recognize[d] that the greater share of responsibility is upon Dr. Lum," and believed him 80% to blame; (e) Stinnett's damages were approximately $100,000; (f) accordingly, Stinnett was willing to settle concerning Greene and Romeo for $20,000; (g) a smaller verdict was no more than a "remote possibility."

the "settlement" posed to his defense. The motion being denied, a trial ensued, noteworthy aspects of which were as follows.

First, while Dr. Romeo seemed the prime target of Stinnett's complaint, Stinnett's counsel focused on Dr. Lum in his opening statement to the jury, displaying apparent candor regarding Drs. Greene and Romeo. Dr. Greene's counsel then announced he would reserve his opening statement; thus, Dr. Lum's counsel could do the same, or hazard being left no way to meet opening statements made later by counsel for the "co-defendants."

Thereafter, though now furthering the interests of Drs. Greene, Romeo, and their insurance carriers, Stinnett's counsel called Dr. Greene as an "adverse party," and then opposed full cross-examination by Dr. Lum's counsel on the ground his own interrogation was "cross-examination"; he defeated an objection that he was leading Dr. Romeo by contending Dr. Romeo was an "adverse witness," and led him at will. When Stinnett's counsel omitted to ask Stinnett's former employer if Stinnett had received "tips" as well as wages, Dr. Greene's counsel went into this item of special damage on "cross-examination," in a notable departure from his usual nonchalance. In contrast to the placid role played by counsel for Dr. Lum's "co-defendants," his own counsel's efforts must have suggested only Dr. Lum had cause for concern. This inference can only have been strengthened when, at the close of Stinnett's case, the court granted Rule 41(b) motions for dismissal of Drs. Greene and Romeo, without opposition by Stinnett's counsel, but over Dr. Lum's objection that he would be prejudiced if not similarly dismissed. Dr. Lum's Rule 41(b) motion for dismissal was denied.

Dr. Lum's counsel then moved for a mistrial, on grounds that the dismissal of Drs. Greene and Romeo would "prejudice defendant Lum in the eyes of the jury," that the jury would infer they were free from negligence while he was not, and that "the overall prejudicial effect of these circumstances cannot be overcome by any instructions or admonitions to the jury." Stinnett's counsel countered, saying: "If this court desires and if he desires to put the agreement in before the jury, I think that that would probably be all right. * * * " After further colloquy, the court required copies of the agreement for the court and Dr. Lum's counsel; then it denied the motion for mistrial, without determining whether or how the jury might be informed of the agreement.

By this time, having already called Drs. Greene and Romeo as "adverse witnesses," Stinnett had the benefit of their testimony without being bound by it. By logical extension of the trial court's rulings, if Dr. Lum recalled them now, they would be his witnesses, particularly since they now were not parties. Dr. Lum's counsel tried another approach.

Uncontroverted testimony supporting Dr. Lum's motion for a new trial shows that before closing his case, Dr. Lum's counsel asked that counsel approach the bench. He was, he told the court, prepared to call a witness to prove the terms of the agreement, and inquired how the problem was to be handled. (Perhaps recognizing dangers inherent in calling Drs. Greene or Romeo, he testified he had decided to call Stinnett's counsel, or counsel for Drs. Greene or Romeo.) The court told him "the matter would be handled by jury instructions," and it does not appear that Stinnett's counsel manifested opposition to this.

However, the record reflects that when Dr. Lum's counsel submitted an instruction on the subject, and reminded the court it had said the matter would be handled by instructions, Stinnett's counsel said, "It is our position that if he desired to show that there was an agreement in existence that the best evidence would be the agreement itself." Without indicating what instruction it had intended to give, the court refused the one offered by Dr. Lum, saying that Drs. Greene and Romeo were dismissed by the court pursuant to Rule 41(b). Naturally, since Drs. Greene and Romeo had been thus dismissed, no verdict forms regarding them were provided the jury, nor could any special instructions regarding their possible liability be expected. The jury was, in effect, asked to decide if Dr. Lum was negligent or no one was.

On final argument to the jury, Stinnett's counsel did not suggest that Drs. Greene or Romeo were in the least negligent, although counsel's letter of October 29 recited the belief this was so. Nor did counsel suggest the verdict be diminished 20%, or any amount, so Dr. Lum would not have to pay for the negligence of Drs. Greene and Romeo. Of them he said, "They both are no longer in the case," and proceeded to rely on their testimony. He even suggested Dr. Romeo's apparent respect for one of Stinnett's other witnesses was reason to credit the latter.

The jury returned a verdict for $50,000; judgment was entered for the amount of the verdict plus costs * * *.

First, we perceive that strangers to the action, insurance carriers for Drs. Greene and Romeo (themselves strangers to claims against Dr. Lum), promised to pay $20,000 if Stinnett would prosecute his action against Dr. Lum, and not settle without consent for less than $20,000. Such an agreement is the very definition of the common law offense of maintenance. "Maintenance exists when a person without interest in a suit officiously intermeddles therein by assisting either party with money or otherwise to prosecute or defend it." 14 C.J.S., Champerty and Maintenance § 1b. In addition, the insurance carriers were to profit from any recovery against Dr. Lum; for while they "settled" their liability at $20,000, any verdict against Dr. Lum was to reduce their obligation. "Champerty is maintenance with the additional feature of an agreement for the payment of compensation or personal profit from the subject matter of the suit." Id. § 2.

* * * If insurance companies may contend, and they do, that they have so little relationship to actions against their insureds that the policies they issue are not discoverable even by vitally concerned plaintiffs * * *, then surely no one will contend a carrier has such

relationship to a plaintiff's action as justifies fostering it, for profit, against defendants with whom the carrier and its insureds have no relationship whatever.

Next, we perceive the insurance companies were to become the parties truly interested in the action, to the extent of $20,000, with right to refuse its being settled for less. * * *

We deem agreements whereby insurance carriers agree to pay any consideration to foster litigation in which they are not interested, in order to avoid their own liabilities, contrary to law and public policy.

Considering the propriety of certain "settlement agreements" calling for defense counsel to participate in litigation when they were actually interested in furthering the plaintiff's cause, the Arizona State Bar Committee on Rules of Professional Conduct concluded * * * [that settlement agreements] contravened policy of Canons of Professional Conduct concerned with representing conflicting interests, candor and fairness, taking technical advantage of opposing counsel, and unjustifiable litigation. * * * Op. No. 70–18, Ariz. State Bar Comm. on Rules of Prof. Conduct (1970).

Manifestly * * * the champertous agreement between Stinnett and the insurance carriers for Drs. Greene and Romeo called for improper conduct on the part of all attorneys concerned; and while we recognize they became involved only out of devotion to their clients, the agreement nonetheless contravened policy expressed in the Rules of Professional Conduct, Sup.Ct.R. 163 et seq.

Stinnett's counsel contend everything they did was "open and aboveboard," and we are sure they did not perceive the essential impropriety of the agreement. Yet they cannot, we think, suggest they did not bargain for and utilize its inherent advantages, which we find inimical to true adversary process. If they wanted no more than a fair trial against Dr. Lum, why was the agreement framed to retain Drs. Greene and Romeo as sham "adverse parties" in the case? It is no answer to say Dr. Lum was not stabbed in the back. If his hands were tied, it matters little that he could see the blow coming.

Stinnett suggests Dr. Lum was free to bring the agreement into the open, e.g., through examination of Drs. Greene and Romeo. On interrogation by this court during oral argument, Stinnett's counsel acknowledged the agreement itself might prejudice the jury, since it contains references to Stinnett's damages, and to Dr. Lum's liability, his insurance, and his insurance carrier's "irresponsible position." Counsel met this dilemma by telling us Dr. Lum might have asked the trial court to excise these prejudicial portions of the agreement; yet counsel conceded this request would have been met by an objection based on the "best evidence rule," as was Dr. Lum's attempt to obtain an instruction on the subject. Back to his dilemma, counsel suggested to us a "best evidence" objection to use of an edited copy of such an agreement probably is unsound. Thus, we think, the sum of counsel's argument is that nimbler opposing counsel and an alert trial judge might have defeated his plan.

With this we are not concerned; nor are we at all sure it is so. If Dr. Lum's counsel had undertaken to examine Drs. Greene and Romeo on an edited text of the agreement, could he be sure its prejudicial aspects would not be revealed to the jury by their answers? Further, had its bare terms been laid before the jury, how would this have affected their treatment of Dr. Lum? Might they not then be more casual about awarding at least some recovery against Dr. Lum, knowing Drs. Greene and Romeo must pay the difference up to $20,000? Might they not infer, even from the agreement's bare terms, that the others considered Dr. Lum the intransigent wrongdoer, and let this affect their verdict against him? Might knowledge a minimum value of $20,000 had been placed on Stinnett's injuries affect their deliberations? We do not know; we know only that Dr. Lum had the right to litigate his case without hazarding the prospect that such considerations might affect the jury's verdict.

Stinnett contends no prejudice is shown because the "codefendants" testified substantially as in their depositions; Dr. Lum suggests there were material differences. If Stinnett be correct, we still could not determine the trial testimony would not have been different absent the agreement, or its impact different if not supposedly elicited from "adverse parties." Further, if we could make these determinations, this still would not meet Dr. Lum's basic contention that, by other irregularities proceeding from the agreement, the trial was deprived its proper adversary character.

It is sufficient to see from the record, as we do, that such irregularities so warped presentation of the case as to deny a fair trial, that the record contains nothing amounting to a waiver, and that the question has been preserved for our review. As mentioned, Dr. Lum's counsel repeatedly sought the trial court's protection, showing no disposition to gamble on the verdict and later complain. Most of these attempts are involved in Dr. Lum's assignments of error, but we need not consider the specifics of all of them. We see no waiver; the gravamen of the problem was lucidly presented by Dr. Lum's motion for new trial; the court erred in denying that motion.

* * * Because Stinnett's agreement with the carriers for Drs. Greene and Romeo is void, in order to place all parties in their original position as nearly as may be, we order that on remand the action shall stand reinstated against Drs. Greene and Romeo, as well as Dr. Lum.

* * *

Note on Mary Carter Agreements

The contract in Lum v. Stinnett is known among personal injury specialists as a "Mary Carter" agreement, after Booth v. Mary Carter Paint

Co.[7] *Lum* shows in detail the mechanics and bad features of Mary Carter agreements, but Nevada is the only state that clearly invalidates them today. As of 1986, seven other states had considered Mary Carter agreements and, perhaps reluctantly, declared them valid subject to disclosure to the jury.

In the medical malpractice context, only one later case has considered a Mary Carter agreement, Hackman v. Dandamudi.[8] The court there had this to say, accepting a case-by-case approach:

> [C]ourts allow the agreements in circumstances and under conditions which are designed to prevent prejudice. The agreements can be edited in order to remove prejudicial phraseology and then allowed into evidence; or the agreements themselves can be excluded, and the courts can admit evidence of the existence of such an agreement where that is necessary to prevent possible prejudice.
>
> Of course, it is fundamentally unfair for the settling defendant to feign cooperation with the nonsettling defendant, while keeping the agreement secret. Once such an agreement has been entered into the settling defendant must not hide his position as an adversary party of the nonsettling defendant. * * *
>
> There is a strong public policy against allowing secret agreements to work a fraud on either the nonsettling defendant(s), the jury, or the trial court. However, there are also strong public policy considerations in favor of allowing plaintiffs to control their own cases and settle with defendants as they choose. This court finds no reason that these policies cannot coexist, even in the presence of a Mary Carter Agreement, so long as the other defendant is not deceived.

---

7. 202 So.2d 8 (Fla.App.1967). *Mary Carter* itself was a motor vehicle case; it was overruled on other grounds in Ward v. Ochoa, 284 So.2d 385 (Fla.1973). Florida now partially regulates the subject by statute, Fla.L.1967, ch. 67–254, § 45, codified as West's Fla.Stat.Ann. § 768.041. See Annot., Validity and Effect of Agreement with One Cotortfeasor Setting His Maximum Liability and Providing for Reduction or Extinguishment Thereof Relative to Recovery Against Nonagreeing Cotortfeasor, 65 A.L.R.3d 602 (1975).

8. 733 S.W.2d 452 (Mo.App.1986).

Chapter 4

EVIDENCE OF MEDICAL NEGLIGENCE

INTRODUCTORY NOTE

Evidence of medical negligence comes in three kinds: materials (chiefly medical records) that tell what *treatment* was administered before, during, and after the allegedly negligent event; materials external to the particular case that set the *standard of care;* and materials generated after the patient became a plaintiff, for *trial preparation.* Most of these records, like treatment records, are documents, which can either be introduced or used as the foundation for oral testimony; other testimony will be reduced to documentary form (affidavits, answers to interrogatories, and depositions); and items of tangible property may be used as exhibits at trial, whether they were actually involved in the case or whether they merely illustrate what happened.

Another way of looking at medical evidence is to match up hurdles to discovery against the types and times of evidence. Inadmissibility is not an obstacle in federal courts, because modern rules of procedure let the parties engage in fishing expeditions.[1] Privileged communications rules are obstacles, however, because the matter fished for must not be privileged, nor may it consist of "trial preparation materials," that is, the work product of the lawyers, not the doctors. Privileges can be waived, and they usually are waived by putting the plaintiff's condition in controversy. The minuet sketched in Federal Rule 35(b) shows how trial preparation materials can be obtained from an adversary, quite apart from showing substantial need and undue hardship under Federal Rule 26(b)(3). Throughout the chapter, as throughout medical liability practice, lawyers keep asking a pair of questions about each item of medical evidence of negligence: (1) What is it? (2) Can we get it?

Assuming that medical evidence is available for presentation in litigation, another type of hurdle presents itself: How can technical

---

1. Federal R.Civ.P. 26(b)(1): "It is not ground for objection that the information sought will be inadmissible at the trial if the information sought appears reasonably calculated to lead to the discovery of admissible evidence."

evidence be turned into information that the trier of fact (whether jury or judge) can assimilate? Medical scientific evidence comes in three classes:

Data: Outputs such as symbols, lines, columns of figures, and electrical impulses, that can be observed and recorded but intrinsically have no communicative value;

Fact: Data expressed within theoretical frameworks to produce linguistic formulations by which experts convey meaning among themselves ("narrowing" shown in an x-ray; "P-wave" in an electrocardiogram); and

Opinion: Interpretations of facts imparting a sense of perspective that can be explained and communicated to intelligent lay persons ("within normal limits"; "unusual electrical activity").

Theoretically, an infinite number of scientists given the same *data* would express the data as the same *facts;* but the scientists' *opinions* on the same facts could legitimately range from agreement to disagreement.

The key to using scientific medical evidence in the courtroom is expert medical opinion, even though using it leads to battles of experts. Most medical liability cases use medical experts, whether they are required or not. Occasionally the medical negligence in a case will be so obvious that the plaintiff need not produce expert opinion testimony on the violation of the standard of care, but expert opinion testimony is still likely to be needed on causation and damages.

As litigation proceeds, the evidence can be tested by motions asserting that the evidence is insufficient to justify going forward with the proceedings: motions for summary judgment (before trial), directed verdict (during trial), and judgment notwithstanding the verdict (after judgment on the verdict); and, likewise after judgment, the weight of the evidence can be challenged, by motion for new trial on the ground that the verdict was against the clear weight of the evidence.

SECTION A. MEDICAL EVIDENCE

WILSON v. BODIAN

New York Supreme Court, Appellate Division, 1987.
130 A.D.2d 221, 519 N.Y.S.2d 126.

SPATT, JUSTICE. * * *

The plaintiff, Helen Wilson, consulted a Dr. Hyman, an ophthalmologist, in late 1979 and early 1980 with complaints concerning a growth on her left eyelid. This growth had existed for approximately three years prior to that time and had grown larger. Dr. Hyman saw the plaintiff a number of times before referring her to * * * the defendant Dr. Martin Bodian, an ophthalmological plastic surgeon.[2]

---

2. Editors' Note: "Mrs. Wilson" has been substituted for "plaintiff," and "Dr. Bodian" has been used consistently, throughout the opinion.

* * * She first saw Dr. Bodian in April 1980, and he diagnosed the growth on the Mrs. Wilson's eyelid to be either cancerous or precancerous and recommended that it be surgically removed. According to Dr. Bodian, he did not consider taking a biopsy of the growth because it was his opinion, from his visual inspection, that it would have to be surgically removed regardless of the results of the biopsy, and he did not wish to subject this patient of advanced years to the trauma of the biopsy procedure. He did concede, however, that if the growth was not malignant, the surgery would have been less radical.

The surgery to remove the growth was performed by Dr. Bodian at the Brookdale Hospital Medical Center on June 6, 1980. After the initial operation, three additional corrective surgical procedures were performed on Mrs. Wilson's left eyelid, two by Dr. Bodian and one by a Dr. Hornblass. Following the surgical procedures and after Dr. Bodian's involvement ceased, Mrs. Wilson continued to see Dr. Hyman, the original treating ophthalmologist.

In this medical malpractice action against Dr. Bodian and the Brookdale Hospital Medical Center, Mrs. Wilson alleged, essentially, that Dr. Bodian was negligent in failing to perform certain presurgical diagnostic procedures which would have avoided what Mrs. Wilson contended was unnecessary surgery. She maintained that as a result of the medical malpractice * * * she suffered needless mutilation, has constant tearing in her left eye, and is unable to completely close the eye. * * *

[T]wo key issues of fact presented were (1) whether a biopsy should have been performed on the growth on Mrs. Wilson's eyelid prior to the initial surgery, and (2) whether Mrs. Wilson suffered from tearing in the affected eye prior to the surgery. Dr. Hyman was a material witness with regard to both issues and did not testify.

* * * Since Dr. Bodian conceded that he did not seek to have the growth biopsied, a significant issue arose during the trial as to whether a biopsy had previously been performed at Dr. Hyman's request. Mrs. Wilson also contended that if Dr. Bodian had consulted with Dr. Hyman, he would have learned that a biopsy had indeed been performed and that a diagnosis of actinic keratosis had been made. Mrs. Wilson's case was, therefore, enlarged to include the theory that a biopsy had been taken which revealed the condition to be actinic keratosis, and that, therefore, conservative treatment rather than surgery would have been the accepted standard.

* * *

The jury returned a verdict against Dr. Bodian in the sum of $100,000. On this appeal, Dr. Bodian seeks reversal on two grounds. First, he contends that the office records of Dr. Hyman * * * were erroneously admitted. In particular, he objects to three notations in the office records of Dr. Hyman, namely, (1) "Bx nose lesion—keratosis"; (2) "Had large area removed [with] flap—poor result"; and (3) "2° [second] repair unsuccessful." Second, Dr. Bodian contends that the refusal of the trial court to give a "missing witness" charge with respect to Dr. Hyman * * * was prejudicial error.

We begin with the premise that as out-of-court declarations offered for their truth, Dr. Hyman's office records are hearsay documents and inadmissible unless they fall within an exception to the hearsay rule. In this case, we are concerned with whether Dr. Hyman's records qualify under the "business records" exception to the hearsay rule. See N.Y.Civ.Prac.L. & R. 4518(a).

* * * Since it is the business of a hospital's staff "to diagnose and treat its patients' ailments," * * * entries made in a hospital record relevant to diagnosis and treatment qualify for admission as prima facie evidence of the facts contained in the record under the statutory business records rule * * * and special statutory provisions. N.Y. Civ.Prac.L. & R. 4518(c), 2306.

Hospital records * * * must be distinguished from physicians' office records. A further distinction must be drawn between physicians' office records and physicians' *reports*.

Doctors' reports are often prepared at the request of counsel on behalf of the parties. Such reports are generally material prepared for litigation and are not the systematic, routine, day-by-day type of record envisioned by the business-records exception * * *. Therefore, physicans' reports prepared for litigation are generally inadmissible in evidence under the business records exception to the hearsay rule. * * *

Cases specifically addressing the admissibility of physicans' office records, unlike those dealing with hospital records, are few and are inconsistent. Some courts have held office records to be admissible. Jezowski v. Beach, 59 Misc.2d 224, 298 N.Y.S.2d 360 (Sup.Ct.1968), involved the admissibility of handwritten "office cards" of a deceased doctor in a negligence case. The doctor's widow identified the office cards which were written in the doctor's handwriting each time he saw the patient. * * *

Other cases, however, have held physicians' office records to be inadmissible, because they contain medical opinions. In fact, the courts have exhibited marked reluctance to allow such medical opinions into evidence. * * *

While this court at one time expressed a contrary view, we have recently held * * * and now reaffirm that a physician's office records, supported by the statutory foundations set forth in N.Y.Civ.Prac.L. & R. 4518(a), are admissible in evidence as business records. Similar to hospital records, it is the business and duty of a physician to diagnose and treat a patient's illness. Therefore, entries in the office records germane to diagnosis and treatment are admissible, including medical opinions and conclusions. In this regard, the entries in Dr. Hyman's office records "Had large area removed [with] flap—poor result" and

"2° [second] repair unsuccessful" were both opinions germane to treatment and diagnosis and were properly admitted.

We now turn to the third specific notation at issue, namely, "Bx nose lesion—keratosis." Generally, business records need not take any particular form to be admissible and can consist of marks, figures or symbols. * * * In this case, Dr. Hyman's records consisted almost exclusively of short notations, some of which were illegible, and sketches. Where records are illegible or, as here, comprehensible only to the creator, the probative value is minimal or nonexistent. * * * A tape recording that is so inaudible and indistinct that a jury must speculate as to its contents is inadmissible. * * * Similarly, a notation in a physician's office record which is illegible is not admissible. * * *

[T]he "Bx" entry * * * is a symbol or abbreviation which is not comprehensible to a jury on its face and which must be interpreted. Unlike hospital records, which contain generally accepted and standard medical abbreviations, a physician's office records may contain purely personal abbreviations known only to the physician. In order to admit a medical abbreviation or symbol written by a doctor in his office record, which abbreviation is not within the ken of the jury, in the absence of the physician author, there must be a foundation laid that such an abbreviation has a well-known and accepted meaning in the medical profession. An abbreviation of this kind that is not interpretable as having a definite and accepted meaning is not admissible. * * *

* * * Despite the pivotal importance of this symbol "Bx," in the absence of the author there was no underlying proof of its generally accepted meaning in the medical profession. There was no proof that this abbreviation was "well known and usual" in the medical community. Indeed, the two physicians who testified as to the meaning of "Bx" differed as to its interpretation. Dr. Bodian initially testified that he was not familiar with the abbreviation and later, after hearing counsel state that "Bx means biopsy," changed his initial interpretation. However, there was no evidence adduced that the abbreviation "Bx" was an accepted medical term; and, in this regard, we note that Mrs. Wilson called her own medical expert but did not question her on this subject.

There are other evidentiary obstacles to the admissibility of the "Bx" notation. Even assuming that the term "Bx" does mean biopsy, the source of this notation was undisclosed. * * * There was no evidence as to who performed the test, when the test was performed, or the results of such a test. Perhaps the biopsy data was related to Dr. Hyman by Mrs. Wilson. In addition, if the "Bx" notation actually meant that a biopsy had been performed, since Dr. Hyman is an ophthalmologist, it probably constituted a test performed by an unnamed third party. In that event, the procedures that individual used to perform the test and make the diagnosis were unknown, and the scientific reliability of the alleged biopsy could not be explored by the appellant. * * * All of this critical information could, of course, have been furnished by the purported author of the notation, the missing Dr. Hyman.

In view of the infirmities in the "Bx" notation as heretofore stated, any probative value of this notation was greatly outweighed by the appellant's lack of opportunity to test Mrs. Wilson's factual assumption by cross-examination. * * * Therefore, even under the increasing enlargement of the scope of the "business records" rule, the notation as to the "Bx nose lesion—keratosis" was inadmissible hearsay.

* * *

The trial court declined Dr. Bodian's request to give a "missing witness" charge with regard to Dr. Hyman * * *. It is well established that the missing witness charge with respect to a treating physician should be given where the witness is under Mrs. Wilson's control and is in a position to give substantial, not merely cumulative, evidence. * * * Dr. Hyman's testimony was of vital importance on the issues of liability and damages. As Mrs. Wilson's treating physician prior to the surgery, Dr. Hyman not only could have interpreted the "Bx" entry in his office records, but he could have furnished material, relevant and noncumulative testimony including whether a biopsy was performed and its result. In addition, he was the only treating physician who had knowledge as to whether Mrs. Wilson suffered from the tearing condition prior to the surgery.

* * *

Dr. Hyman treated Mrs. Wilson prior to Dr. Bodian's surgery and continued to treat her for more than three years after Dr. Bodian's involvement ceased. There is no indication of any hostility between Mrs. Wilson and Dr. Hyman, whose office assistant testified and produced Mrs. Wilson's records. Mrs. Wilson had the burden of proof to show that Dr. Hyman was not available or under her "control." * * * Despite this burden, Mrs. Wilson made no attempt to show the unavailability of Dr. Hyman or his unwillingness to testify, other than counsel's unsubstantiated assertion that Dr. Hyman was subpoenaed but failed to appear. No testimony by any process server was ever offered, nor was an affidavit of service produced. Moreover, Dr. Hyman's employee testified for Mrs. Wilson, and her counsel never inquired as to Dr. Hyman's unwillingness to appear or his unavailability. Under the circumstances of this case, Dr. Hyman was a witness who would naturally be expected to give testimony favorable to Mrs. Wilson. * * * In light of Mrs. Wilson's failure to demonstrate that Dr. Hyman was unavailable, * * * no longer under her control, or in any way hostile to her, * * * and especially in view of the blanket admission of Dr. Hyman's office records, the trial court should have given a missing witness charge as to Dr. Hyman.

[T]he judgment insofar as it is in favor of Mrs. Wilson should be reversed, and a new trial should be granted of Mrs. Wilson's action insofar as it is against * * * [Dr. Bodian].

* * *

HILL v. SPRINGER
Supreme Court, New York County, 1986.
132 Misc.2d 1012, 506 N.Y.S.2d 255.

STANLEY L. SKLAR, JUSTICE. * * *

Terrance Hill was operated on in November 1983. The operation was performed by Dr. Stuart Springer, one of a small number of physicians who perform that type of operation. Since the operation was not of a garden variety nature, he had it videotaped for use in connection with his teaching of other physicians.

Hill has consulted counsel, who want to obtain a copy of the videotape for a review by a medical expert to determine whether Hill has a medical malpractice claim. Hill claims to be entitled to the videotape on two grounds: (1) as pre-litigation discovery pursuant to N.Y.Civ.Prac.L. & R. 3102(c), and (2) as a medical record.

Rule 3102(c) authorizes pre-litigation disclosure in aid of bringing an action.[3] However, the rule is well settled that the statute only authorizes disclosure "to aid in the framing of a claim for a known cause of action, but * * * may not be used by a potential claimant to determine whether he has a cause of action." Heller v. State, 57 Misc. 2d 976, 293 N.Y.S.2d 869, 871 (Ct.Cl.1968) * * *. Mr. Hill's assertion that the decision in Striegel v. Tofano, 92 Misc.2d 113, 399 N.Y.S.2d 584 (Sup.Ct.1977), states a different rule with respect to medical malpractice claims is incorrect. The *Striegel* court, rather, held that the patient in that case had made a sufficient showing for pre-litigation discovery of her medical records. In other words, "[s]tated another way, the supporting papers demonstrate[d]" a probability of a good cause of action, and not that the patient was merely taking a stab in the dark. *Striegel,* 399 N.Y.S.2d at 585. The papers on this application are totally different. They make no showing whatever of the existence of any cause of action or even of any injury allegedly suffered. * * *

Mr. Hill asserts, in conclusory fashion, that the videotape constitutes a "medical record," and that he is entitled to examine his own medical record. He errs. The videotape is not a medical record that is required to be released to him. His reliance on Pub.Health L. § 17 is misplaced. That statute states that, upon written request, a "physician or hospital must release and deliver, exclusive of personal notes of the said physician or hospital, copies of all X-rays, medical records * * * regarding that patient to any other designated physician or hospital * * *." The statute clearly requires a turnover only to another doctor or hospital.

Mr. Hill also relies on Title 8, § 29, 2(a)(6) N.Y.Comp.Codes R. & R. (Rules of the Board of Regents). That rule, clearly expanding on the statute, declares that it shall be unprofessional conduct to fail to make

---

3. Editors' Note: "§ 3102(c). Before an action is commenced, disclosure to aid in bringing an action, to preserve information or to aid in arbitration, may be obtained, but only by court order. * * *"

available to a patient, upon written request, "copies of the record required by ¶ (3) of this subdivision." Paragraph (3) requires the maintenance of "a record for each patient which accurately reflects the evaluation and treatment of the patient."

The videotape of the operation falls outside the ambit of Pub. Health L. § 17 and the regulation. It was not required to be made by the hospital and it was not stored at the hospital. It was not required to be made by Dr. Springer. The videotape was not made in any respect for the care or treatment of Mr. Hill, but solely as a personal record for Dr. Springer's use in his teaching of physicians. Accordingly, the videotape is not a medical record and Dr. Springer does not have to make it available to Mr. Hill pursuant to the statute or the rule.

This decision is of course limited to the requested disclosure of the videotape at this time, before the commencement of any action, and is without prejudice to any application for discovery of the videotape in the event a malpractice action is ultimately instituted. * * *

The petition is dismissed.

BOND v. DISTRICT COURT

Supreme Court of Colorado, 1984.
682 P.2d 33.

NEIGHBORS, JUSTICE.

In this original proceeding instituted under Colo.App.R. 21, the petitioners, who are the plaintiffs in a personal injury action filed in the Denver District Court against YMCA of the Rockies (YMCA), seek reversal of the respondent judge's order denying their request for a protective order regarding discovery * * * by YMCA of notes and records kept by their mental health therapists concerning psychological evaluations and treatments.[4] * * *

On August 20, 1982, Erin Bond, then four years old, was severely injured when she fell off a truck in which she and her family were riding and was run over by one of its wheels. The truck was owned and operated by YMCA. As a result of the incident, the child and members of her family filed suit against YMCA for negligence. In their complaint the plaintiffs seek recovery of damages for physical pain and suffering, mental pain and suffering, past and future medical and psychiatric expenses, loss of enjoyment of life, and loss of earnings.[5]

---

4. Editors' Note: "Plaintiff" has been substituted for "petitioner," and "judge" for "respondent" and "court" throughout.

5. Editors' Note: The entire Bond family—father, mother, Ryan (age 6), Erin (age 4), and Sydney (age 2)—were riding on the back of a flatbed truck, taking a Rocky Mountain YMCA camp "hayride." Erin stood up and fell off, and a truck wheel passed over her abdomen, causing hip damage and serious bleeding. With the whole family watching helplessly, Erin nearly died before a weather-impeded air rescue could get her to a Denver hospital. She survived and seemed to be making a good recovery when the lawsuit was settled late in the 1980s.

The accident struck a family that already had mental health problems, most of which were not relevant to Erin's injuries: the mother and father did not have a stable marriage, and the accident apparently

During discovery proceedings, YMCA sought to obtain copies of all written notes and records made by the plaintiffs' therapists during psychological evaluations and psychiatric care and treatment of the plaintiffs at the Foothills Clinic. YMCA specifically requested

> Any and all medical bills, statements, narrative medical reports, hospital records, medical test results, receipts for prescriptions, and any and all other written document or material concerning the Plaintiffs' alleged personal injuries and damages as a result of the incident which is the subject matter of this suit.

Plaintiffs provided YMCA with an evaluation report prepared by Dr. Marshall Vary and Dr. Julie Brody of the Foothills Clinic. However, no notes or other records were made available. * * *

YMCA filed a motion for an order compelling discovery and the plaintiffs filed a motion for a protective order. A hearing on the motions was held on September 1, 1983. The judge ruled:

> The Court is going to deny the Motion for Protective Orders; order that the records requested be furnished with the proviso they be kept confidential with the defendant. The Court in ruling this way is aware of the fact that the plaintiffs are the ones who are seeking recovery in this matter and they're asking for a substantial amount, and in order for the defendant to know what to defend against, it is necessary they not be limited to the information the plaintiff wants to reveal.
>
> I think they have the right to look at the records and they themselves determine what is something they can use or not use.

The plaintiffs then filed this original proceeding and we issued a rule to show cause.

We recognize at the outset that, as a general rule, orders pertaining to pretrial discovery are interlocutory in nature and not reviewable in an original proceeding. However, we have made exceptions to the general rule when a pretrial discovery order causes unwarranted damage to a litigant that cannot be cured on appeal. * * *

We begin our analysis with a consideration of the discovery rules which are set forth in the Colorado Rules of Civil Procedure. Rule 26(b)(1) defines what information is discoverable:

> Scope of Discovery. Unless otherwise limited by order of the court in accordance with these rules, the scope of discovery is as follows:
>
> (1) In General. Parties may obtain discovery regarding any matter, *not privileged,* which is relevant to the subject matter involved in the pending action, whether it relates to the claim or defense of the party seeking discovery or to the claim or defense of any other party, including the existence, description, nature, custody, condition, and location of any books, documents, or other tangible things and the

---

precipitated their divorce; the mother was hospitalized for anxiety brought on by the accident; and Sydney (whose mother actually held the child in her lap) had a guilt fantasy that she had pushed Erin off the truck. The trial judge ultimately viewed the plaintiff family's psychotherapeutic records in camera and released a sanitized version to the defense.

identity and location of persons having knowledge of any discoverable matter. It is not ground for objection that the information sought will be inadmissible at the trial if the information sought appears reasonably calculated to lead to the discovery of admissible evidence. (Emphasis added.)

Rule 26(c) provides that a court may issue a protective order under certain circumstances:

> Protective Orders. Upon motion by a party or by the person from whom discovery is sought, and for good cause shown, the court in which the action is pending or alternatively, on matters relating to a deposition, the court in the district where the deposition is to be taken may make any order which justice requires to protect a party or person from annoyance, embarrassment, oppression, or undue burden or expense, including one or more of the following: (1) That the discovery not be had; (2) that the discovery may be had only on specified terms and conditions, including a designation of the time or place; (3) that the discovery may be had only by a method of discovery other than that selected by the party seeking discovery; (4) that certain matters not be inquired into, or that the scope of the discovery be limited to certain matters; (5) that discovery be conducted with no one present except persons designated by the court; (6) that a deposition after being sealed be opened only by order of the court; (7) that a trade secret or other confidential research, development, or commercial information not be disclosed or be disclosed only in a designated way; (8) that the parties simultaneously file specified documents or information enclosed in sealed envelopes to be opened as directed by the court.

In the circumstances of this case, there are two arguments why the therapists' notes and records are not discoverable under Rule 26. First, the information is privileged and thus not discoverable under Rule 26(b)(1). Second, good cause has been shown under Rule 26(c), and thus a protective order should issue to protect the plaintiffs from embarrassment and oppression.

The information sought by YMCA is privileged under the physician-patient or psychologist-patient privileges if these privileges have not been waived. Section 13–90–107(1), Colo.Rev.Stat.1973, provides that there are

> [P]articular relations in which it is the policy of the law to encourage confidence and to preserve it inviolate; therefore, a person shall not be examined as a witness in the following cases.

Physicians and certified psychologists are included as persons who may not testify without the consent of their patient or client. Section 13–90–107(1)(d) (1983 Supp.) provides in part:

> A physician, surgeon, or registered professional nurse duly authorized to practice his profession pursuant to the laws of this state or any other state shall not be examined *without the consent* of his patient as to any information acquired in attending the patient which was necessary to enable him to prescribe or act for the patient * * *. (Emphasis added.)

A psychiatrist comes within the purview of this section. * * * Section 13–90–107(1)(g) provides in part:

> A licensed psychologist shall not be examined *without the consent* of his client as to any communication made by the client to him or his advice given thereon in the course of professional employment * * *. (Emphasis added.)

The mental health therapists who evaluated and are treating the plaintiffs are persons within the meaning of these statutory provisions. The privilege, once it attaches, prohibits pretrial discovery as to privileged information as well as any testimonial disclosure in court. Clark v. District Court, 668 P.2d 3 (Colo.1983).

The judge contends, however, that the plaintiffs waived the privilege by placing their mental condition in issue by bringing the personal injury lawsuit in which they have requested damages for mental suffering and expenses for psychiatric counseling. The privilege statute provides that a physician or certified psychologist may not testify *without* the patient's *consent.* This provision impliedly permits a waiver of the privilege. A waiver is a form of "consent" to disclosure which may be express or implied. *Clark,* 668 P.2d at 8. Waiver is established by a showing that the privilege holder has expressly or impliedly "forsaken his claim of confidentiality with respect to the information in question." Id. * * * In *Clark,* we held that the proper test for determining whether a patient has waived the privilege is "whether the privilege holder has injected his * * * mental condition into the case as the basis of a claim or an affirmative defense." 668 P.2d at 10. The rationale for waiver in the context of a lawsuit is that it is inconsistent for the patient-litigant to base a claim upon his/her mental condition and then use the physician or psychologist privilege to prevent the opposing party from obtaining and presenting any conflicting evidence pertaining to that condition. See * * * Annot., Privilege, in Judicial or Quasi–Judicial Proceedings, Arising from Relationship Between Psychiatrist or Psychologist and Patient, 44 A.L.R.3d 24, 51 (1972) * * *. The plaintiffs concede they have injected their mental condition into the case as the basis of a claim. Therefore, we hold that the plaintiffs have waived their privilege by requesting an award of damages for mental suffering and expenses for psychiatric care. * * *

The public policy consideration which underlies the physician-patient and psychologist-patient privileges is to

> [E]nhance the effective diagnosis and treatment of illness by protecting the patient from the embarrassment and humiliation that might be caused by the physician's disclosure of information imparted to him by the patient during the course of a consultation for purposes of medical treatment. Clark v. District Court, 668 P.2d 3, 8 (Colo.1983).

The privilege encourages and protects the person seeking treatment. * * * This policy consideration is even more compelling in the therapist-patient relationship than in the physician-patient relationship. A physical ailment may be treated by a doctor whom the patient does not trust, but if a psychologist or psychiatrist does not have the patient's trust, the therapist cannot treat the patient. * * * The mental health therapist's ability to help his patient is completely dependent upon the patient's willingness and ability to talk freely. See Proposed Fed.R.Evid. 504 advisory committee note. * * *

The plaintiffs provided YMCA with a "Report of Psychological Evaluation and Projected Costs for Psychiatric Care" which was prepared by Drs. Vary and Brody of the Foothills Clinic. The report includes the evaluation and diagnosis of the mental condition of each plaintiff and detailed recommendations for the psychiatric treatment needed by each person, including the length of the proposed treatment and the projected costs. In order to prepare this report, Drs. Vary and Brody personally examined and evaluated the parents and Erin.

When it considered the plaintiffs' motion for a protective order, the judge had before him the affidavit of Dr. Vary, who is the Director of the Foothills Clinic where the plaintiffs were evaluated and continue to receive treatment. Dr. Vary believes that the treatment of the Bonds would be seriously undermined if their sense of trust in the psychotherapy process were to be eroded. Dr. Vary stated in his affidavit:

> [T]o further provide detailed notes and records of patient visits as requested by the Defendant would, in my expert opinion, cause serious and irreparable harm to Erin, Wendell and Eileen Bond for the following reasons:
>
> a. The Bonds are in a high degree of turmoil and confusion. The clarity and stability in their lives at the present time is in their psychiatric treatment. If notes or other records in connection with this treatment were used against them in an adversary proceeding, it could destroy a major portion of that clarity which would be highly detrimental to their emotional health and further treatment.
>
> * * *
>
> c. Very significant is the fact that the issues relating to the injury to Erin are complicated and involve distortions. If details of distorted perceptions become part of a legal proceeding, for example, Erin could become seriously and unnecessarily laden with guilt to her severe detriment.

* * *

The policy considerations and the plaintiffs' evidentiary foundation lead us to conclude that there are compelling public policy reasons for keeping confidential any communications revealed during the mental health treatment of the plaintiffs in order to preserve the effectiveness of that care. On the other hand, there are equally compelling policy considerations which encourage full disclosure during discovery. The purposes of pretrial discovery include: the elimination of surprise at trial, the discovery of relevant evidence, the simplification of the issues, and the promotion of expeditious settlement of cases. * * * In order to accomplish these purposes, the discovery rules are construed liberally. * * * However, in adopting the rules of discovery this court recognized the need for a procedure to limit discovery in certain cases. * * *

Under Rule 26(c) a trial court, for good cause shown, may grant a protective order to protect a party from annoyance, embarrassment, oppression, or undue burden or expense. The party who seeks to prevent discovery has the burden to show annoyance, embarrassment, or oppression. * * * What constitutes good cause depends upon the facts of each particular case. * * * Discovery rulings are ordinarily within the discretion of the trial court. * * *

In view of these competing interests, the judge should have balanced the plaintiffs' interest in protecting the confidentiality of their communications with their treating therapists against YMCA's interest in obtaining sufficient evidence to contest the damage claims for mental suffering and emotional distress.[6] * * *

The judge's order does not reflect that it took into account the plaintiffs' interests in arriving at its decision. * * * Without evaluating the appropriateness of the conclusion reached by the judge in his ruling, we make the rule absolute and remand the case to permit the judge to reconsider his ruling, applying the correct balancing standard.

SECTION B. EXPERT MEDICAL TESTIMONY

LEE v. MILES

United States District Court for the Northern District of Texas, 1970.
317 F.Supp. 1404.

BREWSTER, DISTRICT JUDGE.

This malpractice action against an osteopathic physician seeks damages for personal injuries alleged to have been suffered by the plaintiff, Patricia Lee, as a result of negligence of the defendant, Dr. J.H. Miles, in performing an operation on her. A jury has returned a verdict awarding the plaintiffs the sum of $22,500 plus medical and hospital expense totalling $1846.75. * * *

It is the settled law in Texas that there can be no recovery in a malpractice action against a physician unless it is proved by a medical expert of the same school of practice [7] as the defendant that plaintiff

---

6. Some courts have constitutionalized communications by a patient to a psychiatrist or psychologist during treatment under the right of privacy rationale. See, e.g., Caesar v. Mountanos, 542 F.2d 1064 (9th Cir.1976), cert. denied, 430 U.S. 954, 97 S.Ct. 1598, 51 L.Ed.2d 804 (1977); In re Lifschutz, 2 Cal.3d 415, 85 Cal.Rptr. 829, 467 P.2d 557 (1970); In re "B", 482 Pa. 471, 394 A.2d 419 (1978). We leave that issue for another day * * *.

Editors' Note: The *Bond* case was not a medical malpractice case. The issue that the court wisely left to another day is whether the privilege not to testify belongs to the psychiatrist, so that it is not waivable by the patient in other litigation. So far, no court has so held, even though psychiatrists have been held in contempt of court to test their strongly held views on confidentiality. Where the plaintiff sues a physician for medical malpractice, it seems unlikely that the physician could claim that communications with the patient-plaintiff were privileged, though the protective orders issue might arise.

7. [See] Annots., Necessity of Expert Evidence to Support an Action for Mal-

suffered personal injuries as a proximate result of the defendant's professional negligence. * * *

This rule contemplates a bona fide, not a phony expert witness. It would be meaningless otherwise.

Apparently, the plaintiffs could not find a medical expert witness in the whole state of Texas who would support their case. They attempted to meet their obligation under this rule by importing from Pueblo, Colorado, an itinerant jack-of-all-trades. There is no more resemblance between this witness and the type of expert contemplated by the above cited authorities than there is between a tiger lily and a tiger.

This witness, Lewis Guenther, was licensed in 1959 to practice in Texas as an osteopathic physician. In 1969 he moved to Pueblo, Colorado, where he now resides.

During the ten years he was in Texas, the witness never stayed in any place or with any business or profession very long. He was constantly jumping from pillar to post both as to occupation and location. In that period, he tried his hand not only at osteopathy, but at the practice of law,[8] accounting, fitting of eye glasses, management of a local dispensing office for Lee Optical Co., lecturing at a chiropractic school, preparation of income tax returns, and stenotype reporting. He is now studying to be a coroner. On occasions, he was working at several of such occupations at the same time, usually in an "office" in the residential quarters he then happened to be occupying. He was not a success at any of them. He devoted his efforts to those occupations in cities and towns from one end of Texas to the other. Some of those places where he stopped long enough to set up a residential office were Houston, El Paso, Corpus Christi, Baytown, Mesquite, Galveston, Haltom City, Bellaire, Big Spring, Galena Park, Rockport and Lipan. His stays in most of them were usually short, and he moved in and out of some of the towns more than one time. He wound up his ten years in Texas with his osteopathic table in a room in his residential quarters in Lipan, Texas, a rural community of about 300 people.

After being unable to make a success in Texas of any of his many occupations, or of any combination of them, he moved to Pueblo, Colorado, where he is examining eyes for glasses [9] while studying to be a coroner. The sign on the outside of the building where he does eye

practice Against a Physician or Surgeon, 81 A.L.R.2d 597 (1962); Competency of Physician or Surgeon of School of Practice Other Than That to Which Defendant Belongs to Testify in Malpractice Case, 85 A.L.R.2d 1022 (1962) * * *.

8. He studied law at night school after he got his license as an osteopath. He practiced law for only a few months and quit it because he could not make any money at it. It was during his stint at law practice that he met counsel for the plaintiffs. He was officing with some lawyers in the same building where they were located.

9. The skill required for the kind of work the witness does in this connection is indicated by the fact that he said he had been doing it since he was a sophomore in osteopathic college at Kirksville, Mo.

examinations says, "Eyes Examined, Lewis Guenther, D.O.," even though he has never been licensed to practice osteopathy in Colorado.

The witness has never been a member of the staff of any hospital, osteopathic or otherwise. He has never had an office for practice of osteopathy outside a room in his living quarters, wherever he happened to be at the time. The type of his practice of osteopathy appears to have been very limited. He admitted that on the few occasions when sick people happened to come to him as late as the short period he was practicing in Lipan, he sent them twenty miles away to an osteopath in Granbury, Texas, for treatment. Even though he gave testimony as an expert on the type of operation involved in this case, he had never performed or seen one. Except for one operation [10] he had witnessed recently during his study to become a coroner, he had not even seen an operation of any kind in seven years. If he had ever done anything more than give rubdowns during the time of his so-called practice, he did not mention it.

The growth of malpractice litigation has opened a new possibility to this transient man of many occupations. His smattering of knowledge of osteopathy and law gives him a conception of how to criticize and second guess the work of a practicing physician, and how to tell it so that it will be significant. He comes to advocate from the witness stand. This is the second time in recent months that he has interrupted his study in Colorado to become a coroner to travel to distant places in Texas for the purpose of testifying as an expert witness for the plaintiff in a medical malpractice action. The lawyers for the plaintiff in each of those cases are the same. It would be a miscarriage of justice to permit an award of damages based upon his testimony to stand.

The court is of the opinion that a recovery of $7,500, plus the doctor, hospital and medical expenses found by the jury in answer to Question No. 9, can be justified on legitimate testimony. * * * Unless the plaintiffs file a remittitur, on or before September 8, 1970, of all amounts over and above the sums just specified and agree to the conditions herein set out, a new trial will be granted as to the portion of their suit against the defendant, Dr. Miles. * * *

TROWER v. JONES
Supreme Court of Illinois, 1988.
121 Ill.2d 211, 117 Ill.Dec. 136, 520 N.E.2d 297.

JUSTICE CUNNINGHAM delivered the opinion of the court.

[P]laintiffs, Cindy R. Connour (now Cindy R. Trower) and Donald E. Connour, filed a two-count complaint against defendant, Grant A. Jones, M.D. * * * The jury returned verdicts in favor of defendant, and the court entered judgment on the verdicts. Finding that the

---

10. The evidence fails to show whether or not this was just an autopsy.

circuit court had erroneously permitted defendant to impeach plaintiffs' expert * * *, the appellate court reversed the judgment of the circuit court and remanded for a new trial. 149 Ill.App.3d 705, 103 Ill. Dec. 63, 500 N.E.2d 1134 (1986). * * *

* * * Plaintiffs called Dr. James K. Martins as their expert witness. His testimony during direct examination included a discussion of his education, his experience as a physician, and other credentials. He also explained how he became involved in this case. He stated that he was a "fellow" of the American Board of Medical Legal Consultants (Board) and that the Board had asked him to review the case. He described the Board as "a group of medical legal consultants that attempt to determine whether lack of standard of care, injuries, or malpractice has occurred in a variety of cases." He explained that when the Board sends him a medical file to review, the file comes with a check, the amount of which depends upon how voluminous the file is.

On cross-examination, Dr. Martins acknowledged that the Board is a for-profit organization and that its purpose is to review cases involving suspected malpractice and to furnish expert testimony. Dr. Martins further acknowledged that most of the Board's cases are obtained through attorneys. He further stated that 80% of his professional time is devoted to work for the Board. He stated that since 1983, when he began working for the Board, he had reviewed over 700 cases for the Board, had given depositions in approximately 60 of those cases, and had given expert trial testimony in approximately 30 of those cases. He acknowledged that these trials had encompassed over a dozen states throughout the country, and had involved matters as diverse as alleged inadequate neurological examination, osteomyelitis (an infection in bone), septicemia following a cortisone injection, and alleged failure to diagnose a brain tumor.

Over objection, he was asked the following question regarding the approximately 30 trials in which he has given expert testimony: "All of these cases have been for plaintiffs, or that is people suing doctors?" Dr. Martins responded, "Of the majority, yes."

Also over objection, Dr. Martins was asked the following question regarding his work for the Board: "In [1983] your income from this type of work was $29,000 approximately?"

Dr. Martins answered affirmatively. On further questioning he also acknowledged (over objection) that in 1984 his income from such work was $44,000.

Defendant and amicus curiae Illinois Association of Defense Trial Counsel contend that it was within the discretion of the circuit court to permit inquiry into both the frequency with which Dr. Martins testifies for a particular class of party, i.e., plaintiffs, and the amount of annual income derived from testifying as an expert witness. They argue that the appellate court failed to recognize the discretion vested in the circuit court. They note that the appellate court apparently found the questions per se inadmissible. Plaintiffs and amicus curiae Illinois

Trial Lawyers Association do not refute that the appellate court found the questions per se inadmissible. However, they contend that the appellate court's decision is fully supported both by precedent and sound policy considerations.

Many years ago this court indicated, in McMahon v. Chicago City Ry. Co., 239 Ill. 334, 88 N.E. 223 (1909), that an expert witness should not be questioned with regard to the number of occasions on which he has previously testified for a given category of party (such as plaintiffs or defendants). * * * Several early decisions of this court also arguably indicate that an expert should not be questioned regarding compensation received for testifying in cases unrelated to the parties or their attorneys. * * *

Since these cited Illinois cases were decided, many years ago, both the difficulty and paramount importance of thorough, comprehensive cross-examination of experts have increased markedly. Cross-examination has been made more difficult in part by the increased latitude given experts when rendering their opinions. For example, in Wilson v. Clark, 84 Ill.2d 186, 49 Ill.Dec. 308, 417 N.E.2d 1322 (1981), this court adopted Rules 703 and 705 of the Federal Rules of Evidence with respect to expert testimony. Accordingly, experts can now render opinions without prior disclosure of the underlying facts or data upon which those opinions are based. Further, experts can now render opinions based upon certain inadmissible evidence (if such evidence is reasonably relied upon by experts in the field in forming opinions upon the subject). Although we view this expansion as prudent, we do recognize the added burden which these changes place upon a party during cross-examination in attempting to discredit his opponent's expert, and we also recognize that these changes heighten the importance of such cross-examination.

Adding to the importance of effective cross-examination is the proliferation of expert "locator" services which, as a practical matter, can help the litigants of either side of most any case find an expert who will help advocate the desired position. As this case helps illustrate, many experts today spend so much of their time testifying throughout the country that they might be deemed not only experts in their field but also experts in the art of being a persuasive witness and in the art of handling cross-examination. As was stated in Kemeny v. Skorch, 22 Ill.App.2d 160, 159 N.E.2d 489, 494 (1959), little has the nonlitigating public (including the jury) realized "the true rhetorical masterpieces that came from the lips of medical experts."

* * *

We have long recognized that the principal safeguard against errant expert testimony is the opportunity of opposing counsel to cross-examine, which includes the opportunity to probe bias, partisanship or financial interest. Sears v. Rutishauser, 102 Ill.2d 402, 80 Ill.Dec. 758, 466 N.E.2d 210 (1984) * * *.

* * * Plaintiffs argue that evidence of an expert's financial interest in the case should be limited to the remuneration received for testifying (1) in a particular case, (2) for a particular party, or (3) for a particular party's attorney. * * *

We believe that the questions regarding Dr. Martins' income which are at issue here were permissible, and we do not base our conclusion on the strict analogy to the facts in *Sears* suggested by defendant. Rather, we reach our decision based on an appreciation of the fact that the financial advantage which accrues to an expert witness in a particular case can extend beyond the remuneration he receives for testifying in that case. A favorable verdict may well help him establish a "track record" which, to a professional witness, can be all-important in determining not only the frequency with which he is asked to testify but also the price which he can demand for such testimony.[11] * * *

We recognize that when evidence of a particular matter is introduced, and a party will be unfairly prejudiced if not given the opportunity to respond to such testimony, generally a response must be permitted. * * * However, we are not convinced that testimony regarding an expert witness' income from serving as an expert witness will necessitate a lengthy and detailed "rehabilitation." Evidence that a witness makes substantial income from testifying does not necessarily imply that his fees are unreasonable, but such evidence does illuminate the financial interest the expert has in giving such testimony. We think that an explanation by the witness as to how he determines his fees (such as with regard to fees charged by his colleagues for rendering testimony in similar matters) should be sufficient in most situations to avoid unfair prejudice. An evaluation of the extent to which such rehabilitation testimony should be permitted must be left largely to the circuit court to decide on a case-by-case basis, weighing both the need to explain the reasonableness of the fees as well as the need to avoid confusion of issues and undue delay of the trial. * * *

We also find that the circuit court properly permitted counsel to inquire, on cross-examination, as to the frequency with which Dr. Martins testifies for plaintiffs. Such information clearly has some relevance in determining whether an expert witness is biased or his opinion skewed. Attorneys, judges and many trial experts themselves are well aware that certain expert witnesses appear particularly willing to testify that medical negligence has occurred, while others appear particularly inclined to testify that there was no deviation from the appropriate standard of care.

[W]e are confident in the jury's ability to recognize that the fact that a witness has typically testified for a category of party does not mean that his testimony in the previous cases was ill-founded. An explanation by the witness (the extent of which is properly left to the

---

11. Editors' Note: The court quoted from Annot., Propriety of Cross-Examining Expert Witness Regarding His Status as "Professional Witness," 39 A.L.R.4th 742 (1985).

circuit court's discretion) regarding why he has an apparent tendency to testify for one category of party should allow the jury to view his tendency in the proper perspective. Of course, absent any explanation by the witness, a jury is likely to conclude, and not without justification, that the witness may have some favoritism toward a particular category of party.

* * * To the extent that McMahon v. Chicago City Ry., 239 Ill. 334, 88 N.E. 223 (1909), * * * [and other cases cited] are inconsistent with this holding, those cases are overruled.

The judgment of the appellate court is reversed, and the judgment of the circuit court is affirmed.

MEYER v. McDONNELL
Court of Special Appeals of Maryland, 1978.
40 Md.App. 524, 392 A.2d 1129, 4 A.L.R.4th 819.[12]

THOMPSON, JUDGE.

Alvin Meyer, hereinafter called appellant, filed suit against Edmond J. McDonnell, M.D., the appellee,[13] in Baltimore City Court, alleging that as the result of an orthopedic operation upon his back, he suffered sexual impotency and a lack of bowel and bladder control. * * * [The jury's verdict was for Dr. McDonnell.] Although the trial judge was mild in his characterization of Dr. McDonnell's conduct during the trial, in our view that conduct was outrageous.[14]

The record shows that on Friday, May 13, 1977, the fourth day of trial, Dr. McDonnell directed his secretary to call Dr. Robert P. Keyser, of Miami, Florida, an acquaintance and a fellow member of the American Scoliosis Society, and tell him that Dr. Robert B. Nystrom was scheduled to testify against Dr. McDonnell, and that his testimony would be transcribed and disseminated to Dr. Nystrom's local medical society in Miami and to the American Academy of Orthopedic Surgeons. The secretary immediately carried out such a call, and Dr. Keyser replied that he wanted to relay this information to Dr. Nystrom. This reaction was what Dr. McDonnell had expected and intended. Dr. McDonnell's secretary then requested that Dr. Keyser do so before Dr. Nystrom testified, and gave him the phone numbers of both trial counsels and the trial judge. Just before noon on that same day, Dr. Keyser telephoned Dr. Nystrom, who was in the [Baltimore] City Bar Library awaiting commencement of his testimony. Dr. Keyser, who

---

12. Annot., Admissibility and Effect, on Issue of Party's Credibility or Merits of His Case, of Evidence of Attempts to Intimidate or Influence Witness in Civil Action, 4 A.L.R.4th 829 (1981).

13. Editors' Note: "Appellant" has been changed to "Mr. Meyer," and "appellee" has been changed to "Dr. McDonnell," throughout.

14. Our view of such conduct is shared by others. See L'Orange v. Medical Protective Co., 394 F.2d 57 (6th Cir.1968); Konrad v. DeLong, 57 F.R.D. 123 (N.D.Ill. 1972); Agnew v. Parks, 172 Cal.App.2d 756, 343 P.2d 118 (1959); Bernstein v. Alameda–Contra Costa Med. Ass'n, 139 Cal.App.2d 241, 293 P.2d 862 (1956); Steiginga v. Thron, 30 N.J.Super. 423, 105 A.2d 10 (1954).

was a mentor of Dr. Nystrom and a man whom Dr. Nystrom admired and respected, related the information about dissemination of testimony, and, with the preface that "this is not a threat, but," admonished him to tread lightly. In retrospect, Dr. Keyser considers his involvement inadvisable.

Dr. Nystrom was intimidated by the communication and felt that he would be unable to testify with a normal degree of candor. The trial judge, in ruling that testimony of the transaction was admissible * * *, found specifically that the message was clearly intimidating and intended by Dr. McDonnell to be so.

On Thursday, May 12, 1977, Dr. McDonnell telephoned his friend and colleague, Dr. William H.M. Finney, a Baltimore neurosurgeon. He asked Dr. Finney to call Dr. Thomas H. Langfitt, former Chief of Neurosurgery at the University of Pennsylvania, and a long-time friend of Dr. Finney, and advise him that Dr. Francis J. Pizzi was scheduled to testify against Dr. McDonnell, and that his testimony would be transcribed and disseminated to his local medical society in Trenton, New Jersey. Dr. Finney made such a call that same evening, advising Dr. Langfitt that Dr. Pizzi was in the process of testifying against Dr. McDonnell, that the testimony would be disseminated, and that it might not be a particularly good thing for Dr. Pizzi to testify in an out of state medical malpractice trial with an impending appearance before the American Board of Neurological Surgery for the oral portion of his certification examinations.

Dr. Langfitt attempted to call Dr. Pizzi at the outset of his testimony on May 12 or 13, but was unsuccessful. On Saturday morning, May 14, he reached Dr. Pizzi by telephone at his home and relayed the information conveyed by Dr. Finney, including the admonition as to the impending oral Board examinations. Dr. Langfitt was the person responsible for bringing Dr. Pizzi into neurosurgery. He also trained Dr. Pizzi who characterized him as "very important to me," and a person whom he admired and respected. Dr. Pizzi expressed to Dr. Langfitt that he was fearful that he might now be blackballed by the Board as a result of false information which may have been spread about him as a "violator of the conspiracy of silence," but that his evaluation of the case was objectively correct and that he felt committed to give an honest opinion in testimony. Dr. Langfitt told him to let his conscience be his guide with regard to continuing his testimony, but that they would have to "sit down and talk about a few things afterward." This communication had the calculated effect on Dr. Pizzi. He testified that as a result of his conversation with Dr. Langfitt he was so upset that he was forced to cancel his plans to attend the commemoration of his father's 50 years in the practice of medicine.

With respect to the evidence adduced concerning Dr. McDonnell's tampering with the witnesses, the trial judge included in his instructions the following:

Now, if you find that either the plaintiff or the defendant or both tried to intimidate any of the other witnesses, an inference would arise that the testimony of such witness would be unfavorable to the case of the one who so tried to intimidate. However, such inference, if indeed you do find one to exist, does not amount to substantive proof and it can't take the place of proof of a fact necessary to the other party's case.

* * *

[T]he conduct of Dr. McDonnell in attempting to intimidate Doctors Nystrom and Pizzi is admissible as tending to show his consciousness of the weakness of his case, and a belief that his defense would not prevail without the aid of such improper and unfair tactics as those in which he engaged. This, in conjunction with the other evidence in the case, may lead to the further inference that Dr. McDonnell considers his case to be weak because he, in fact, is guilty of the negligence which Mr. Meyer asserts he committed. Such inferences are, of course, merely permissible, and the jury is free to either accept or reject them as it sees fit.

In light of the foregoing discussion it is clear that the trial court's instruction in the instant case was too confining. Under that instruction the jury properly could not have considered the corroborative effect of the evidence of attempted intimidation. Such evidence may not be sufficient to establish a prima facie case, but that is not an issue which we need to decide here. Rather, our holding is that the evidence in question had probative value insofar as it related to the Dr. McDonnell's consciousness of the weakness of his case, and it could have been considered by the jury for that purpose. There was evidence that the operation caused Mr. Meyer's complaints. There was also evidence that Mr. Meyer's complaints were not true and that in any event they were not caused by the operation. We cannot say that the evidence of the doctor's misconduct in attempting to influence witnesses for the opposition would not have turned the scales of justice in the jury's mind if they had been properly instructed on the question. We therefore reverse [and remand for a new trial].[15]

* * *

---

15. Editors' Note: The Maryland Commission on Medical Discipline found that Dr. McDonnell had engaged in "immoral conduct of a physician in his practice as a physician," in violation of Md. Code art. 43, § 130(h)(8), and reprimanded him. The reprimand was reversed by a trial court; the reversal was vacated and remanded, McDonnell v. Commission on Medical Discipline, 56 Md.App. 391, 467 A.2d 1072 (1983); and ultimately the Commission was directed to dismiss the disciplinary petition, 301 Md. 426, 483 A.2d 76, 80 (1984):

Although we agree that Dr. McDonnell's conduct was improper and not to be condoned, we hold that it is not censurable under § 130(h)(8). We think that "immoral conduct" under that provision must occur while in the performance of a physician's practice * * *.

JOHNS HOPKINS HOSP. v. GENDA
Court of Appeals of Maryland, 1969.
255 Md. 616, 258 A.2d 595.

FINAN, JUDGE. * * *

Robert J. Genda, Jr., son of appellees, had been afflicted with a congenital heart disorder since his birth in 1951. He had made annual trips to the Johns Hopkins Hospital from his home in Pittsburgh, Pennsylvania. Finally, in 1960 it was decided that open heart surgery would be necessary to remove an obstruction that was causing eight times the normal pressure to the right ventricle of the heart. Dr. Frank Spencer, operating surgeon, and Dr. R. Robinson Baker,[16] who acted as first assistant, performed the operation.

While suturing the incision, the needle which Dr. Baker was using broke. After initially attempting to remove the fragment, a decision was made to leave it as the time factor created additional risks. There was no contention by appellees that this decision was improper. Dr. Baker did not reveal the fact that the needle had broken to the parents since he believed it could cause the child no physical harm and would only upset the parents. Only in 1962 did the child and appellees learn of the needle fragment when an X-ray was taken incident to plastic surgery to excise a keloid scar remaining after heart surgery. Subsequent to learning of it, the child started complaining of chest pains and became frightened to participate in normal, youthful activities.

At the trial the primary issue was whether the breaking of the needle constituted an act of negligence on the part of Dr. Baker, who was an admitted agent of the defendant-appellant. The major evidence introduced by appellees was the following dialogue between Dr. Baker and appellees' counsel at a pretrial deposition.

> Q. Could you express any opinion as to why this needle may have broken at this particular time?
>
> A. Obviously, if it broke, it was put in at the wrong angle.
>
> Q. If it was put in at the wrong angle, you put it in at the wrong angle. Is that right?
>
> A. That is correct.

This was the only expert testimony appellees were able to introduce on the issue of negligence. * * * On direct examination, in defendant's case at trial, Dr. Baker gave the following explanation of his deposition testimony:

16. Dr. R. Robinson Baker, Johns Hopkins University School of Medicine, M.D. 1954; Surgical Intern Johns Hopkins Hospital 1954–1955; Senior Assistant Surgeon National Heart Institute, Bethesda, Maryland, 1955–1957; Assistant Resident in Surgery Johns Hopkins Hospital 1957–1962; Chief Resident in Surgery Johns Hopkins Hospital 1962; presently Associate Professor of Surgery John Hopkins Hospital; member of the American College of Surgeons.

Q. * * * Now in using that movement, that which you've demonstrated, you stated in answer to Mr. Engelman's question when he deposed you, Dr. Baker, that it was the wrong angle. You remember that?

A. Yes.

Q. Why did you say it was the wrong angle? What do you mean by that?

A. I said it was the wrong angle because after the needle had broken, after the fact, really, I decided that I must have put it in at the wrong angle, but I have no way of knowing what that wrong angle is. I said I put it at the wrong angle because it broke after I put it in there.

Q. Was it, would you use the same angle today as you used then?

[A.] * * * Yes, I would use the same angle. I literally put thousands, tens of thousands of these sutures in before and since this particular incident, and occasionally the needle breaks. I really don't know why it breaks. Yesterday I tried to break this needle to demonstrate the angle, but I can't break it on purpose.

At the close of the case, appellant renewed its motion for a directed verdict on the ground that there was insufficient evidence produced to allow a finding of negligence. [The motion was denied, and the jury verdict awarded plaintiff $50,000.] * * *

The plaintiff predicated his entire case on two things: first, that the needle broke, and second, that Dr. Baker when being deposed stated that the needle broke because, "it was put in at the wrong angle."

The plaintiffs vigorously contend that they are not relying on the doctrine of res ipsa loquitur and that they have produced expert testimony, in the nature of Dr. Baker's own statement that, "he put it [the needle] in at the wrong angle." The plaintiffs would in effect have the court and jury adduce from this statement of Dr. Baker's, that at one and the same time a standard was established (a proper angle vis a vis a wrong or improper angle) and a violation of the same. The plaintiffs place a self-serving and artificial construction on Dr. Baker's statement, for the simple reason that they have taken his statement out of context and with complete disregard for his explanation as to what he meant when he stated the needle "was put in at the wrong angle."

His testimony, wherein he explains this statement, shows that there was no way by which he could tell ahead of time whether he was inserting the needle at the wrong angle, rather than the right angle, other than from the after-the-fact knowledge that it broke. In other words he could not tell prior to making the stitch whether the needle was inserted correctly or not, other than by the successful or unsuccessful carry through of the suture. His statement certainly cannot, without distortion, be said to be an admission of the lack of that skill ordinarily applied. He stated that he used the same motion and angle that he would use were he to perform the same specific act again, and that he had successfully put in the needle in the same manner in similar operations tens of thousands of times.

* * *

The plaintiffs vigorously contend that Dr. Baker's act in putting in the needle at the wrong angle was an isolated and singular act of negligence; and they further analogize it with the act of carelessly dropping a scalpel or a knife on the patient causing him to be cut or dropping some fluid on the patient causing him to be burned. However, we think the analogy fails for the simple reason that the dropping of a scalpel or a knife or acid carelessly on a patient is, fortunately, not a part of any operative technique, whereas the evidence in this case is uncontroverted that the accepted technique to suture the fascia (the gristly rectus muscle below the chest cavity) which Dr. Baker was closing, was to use the same motion and angle which he was using at the time that the needle broke.

In spite of the plaintiffs' protestations to the contrary, their argument is scarcely discernible from the doctrine of res ipsa loquitur, which this Court has not as yet applied in a malpractice case. * * *

The record in this case being devoid of any evidence that Dr. Baker sutured the abdominal cavity in any manner other than with that reasonable degree of care and skill which a surgeon would ordinarily employ, we are of the opinion that the lower court erred in failing to direct a verdict for the defendant.

Judgment reversed, appellees to pay costs.

McDERMOTT v. MANHATTAN EYE, EAR & THROAT HOSP.

Court of Appeals of New York, 1964.
15 N.Y.2d 20, 255 N.Y.S.2d 65, 203 N.E.2d 469.

FULD, JUDGE. * * *

The plaintiff, Kathleen McDermott, was for many years aware that she was suffering in both eyes from some corneal disease and had, on a number of occasions, consulted with various physicians with reference to her condition and been advised of the possible merits of a corneal transplant. In August of 1957, she visited Dr. Walter S. Schachat, an ophthalmologist, who * * * referred her to Dr. Richard Townley Paton, the physician in charge of the corneal clinic at the Manhattan Eye, Ear and Throat Hospital and, admittedly, one of the leading ophthalmologists in the world.

* * * Dr. Paton, called as a witness by the plaintiff, testified that he diagnosed the condition of the plaintiff's eyes as "Fuch's dystrophy," a rare ailment marked by progressive clouding of the cornea, that the disease "extended pretty well to the periphery" of the cornea in each eye, and that the plaintiff's vision without glasses was 5/200 in each

eye, her best corrected vision being 20/200. He recommended a "curettement of the endothelium," which is a scraping of the back layer of the cornea, to be followed by a corneal transplant, both operations to be performed, in the first instance, on the plaintiff's left, and worse, eye. * * * There is no dispute but that the operations were unsuccessful and the plaintiff rendered virtually blind in her left eye. At the same time, Dr. Paton's testimony indicated that, contrary to any dire predictions, the plaintiff's right eye, upon which no surgery was performed, showed a natural, marked improvement in visual acuity.

The plaintiff thereupon brought this action against the several doctors and the hospital * * *.

It is not Miss McDermott's plaint that the operations were in any respect negligently performed but, rather, that the two-step surgical procedure, the scraping and the actual transplant, should never have been recommended or undertaken. * * *

* * * At the trial, the plaintiff testified on her own behalf and called but two other witnesses, the defendants Dr. Paton and Dr. Kleinhandler. She did not call an expert witness of her own nor did she introduce any other medical proof to establish her claim of malpractice. Instead, the plaintiff, after eliciting responses from Dr. Paton as to his examination, diagnosis and treatment in her case, and after establishing that he had written a book on the subject of corneal transplants, Keratoplasty (1955), sought to further question him—and, later, Dr. Kleinhandler—as to (1) the general background and risks of such operations; (2) the favorable conditions which, typically, must be present in a patient's diseased eyes before transplanting is deemed suitable; and (3) the usual significance of a diagnosis of Fuch's dystrophy extending to the periphery of the cornea and uncorrected vision of less than 20/200 on a patient's chances for a successful transplant. In short, the plaintiff attempted to prove her malpractice case by questioning the defendants, Paton and Kleinhandler, as to the established medical practice in the field of keratoplasty and their knowledge of it.

The trial court, by sustaining objections to all such questions and, later, rejecting her offer of proof, prevented the plaintiff from eliciting such expert opinion evidence from the two defendants. As a result, the plaintiff's case was barren of expert testimony tending to establish a deviation by the defendants from proper and approved medical practice, and the trial court had no choice, at that point, but to dismiss her complaint. The Appellate Division agreed that the plaintiff had placed "mistaken reliance upon the expertise" of the defendants and * * * modified the judgment of the trial court solely in light of "the possibility that the plaintiff may be able to supply the necessary expert medical evidence" in a new action. 16 A.D.2d 374, 228 N.Y.S.2d 143, 149 (1962).

* * *

It has long been recognized in this state that a party in a civil suit may be called as a witness by his adversary and, as a general proposition, questioned as to matters relevant to the issues in dispute. * * *

Statutes in virtually every other jurisdiction reflect such a rule insofar as they provide, for example, that a party may call his adversary for interrogation * * *. Modern rules of evidence have thus removed the common-law disability of parties to testify as witnesses * * *.

While recognizing the right of a plaintiff in a malpractice action to call as a witness the defendant doctor, the courts of several states have sought to limit the type of questions which the plaintiff may put to him. Specifically, it has been held that a defendant physician may be required to testify to "facts within his knowledge" that is, "what [he] actually saw and did," but not as to whether his actions deviated from the accepted standard of medical practice in the community, a matter deemed to call for "expert opinion." Hull v. Plume, 131 N.J.L. 511, 37 A.2d 53, 56 (1944) * * *. Other courts, however, permit the plaintiff to examine his doctor-opponent as freely and fully as he could any other qualified witness. See Lawless v. Calaway, 24 Cal.2d 81, 147 P.2d 604, 608 (1944) * * *.

The latter decisions strike us as the more enlightened. * * *

The importance of enabling the plaintiff to take the testimony of the defendant doctor as to both "fact" and "opinion" is accentuated by recognition of the difficulty inherent in securing "independent" expert witnesses. It is not always a simple matter to have one expert, a doctor in this case, condemn in open court the practice of another, particularly if the latter is a leader in his field. In consequence, the plaintiff's only recourse in many cases may be to question the defendant doctor as an expert, in the hope that he will thereby be able to establish his malpractice claim.

There is nothing unfair about such a practice. Unlike his counterpart in a criminal prosecution, the defendant in a civil suit has no inherent right to remain silent or, once on the stand, to answer only those inquiries which will have no adverse effect on his case. Rather, he must, if called as a witness, respond to virtually all questions aimed at eliciting information he may possess relevant to the issues, even though his testimony on such matters might further the plaintiff's case. We cannot agree with the suggestion that it is somehow neither sporting nor consistent with the adversary system to allow a party to prove his case through his opponent's own testimony * * *, but, whatever the merits of this view, we prefer to believe that, in a situation such as the present, "[t]he ultimate requirement that judicial decisions be based on the * * * facts overcomes any detriment which might be suffered by the adversary system." Friedenthal, Discovery and Use of an Adverse Party's Expert Information, 14 Stan.L.Rev. 455, 487 (1962) * * *.

In this case, the plaintiff insists that she hoped to prove by the testimony of Dr. Paton himself that he was guilty of malpractice by questioning him as to the propriety of a corneal transplant in view of the condition of her eyes and, then, if necessary, by attempting to induce him to give testimony favorable to her case by use of his authoritative text on the subject. We perceive nothing wrong in such a technique or tactic, nor any reason for denying the plaintiff the opportunity so to proceed. Courts are intent upon arriving at just decisions and upon employing properly expedient means to attain such an end. If a defendant in a malpractice action may truthfully testify that his conduct conformed to the standard required, his case is, of course, substantially strengthened and, if he cannot so testify, the plaintiff's chances or recovery are unquestionably increased. In either case, the objective of the court in doing justice is achieved.

It is true that, in People ex rel. Kraushaar Bros. & Co. v. Thorpe, 296 N.Y. 223, 72 N.E.2d 165 (1947), upon which the courts below and the defendants rely, this court explicitly held that a person may not be compelled to testify and give his opinion as an expert against his will. Our holding in *Kraushaar,* however, is not dispositive of the issue now before us. In that case, the witness (a real estate appraiser) called to testify as an expert was not a party to the action. Such an independent, disinterested witness, we held, could not be required to testify as an expert. * * *

In short, then, a plaintiff in a malpractice action is entitled to call the defendant doctor to the stand and question him both as to his factual knowledge of the case (that is, as to his examination, diagnosis, treatment and the like) and, if he be so qualified, as an expert for the purpose of establishing the generally accepted medical practice in the community.[17] While it may be the height of optimism to expect that such a plaintiff will gain anything by being able to call and question (as an expert) the very doctor he is suing, the decision whether or not to do so is one which rests with the plaintiff alone.

* * *

The judgment appealed from should be modified to the extent of granting a new trial as to defendants Paton, Kleinhandler, and the hospital * * *.

Note on the Aftermath of the McDermott Case

The case was re-tried, and the jury brought in its verdict for Miss McDermott in an undisclosed amount. The Appellate Division reversed as to all defendants except Dr. Paton. 26 A.D.2d 519, 270 N.Y.S.2d 955 (1966). Miss McDermott questioned the defendant doctors on whether the operation was contraindicated "but obviously failed to satisfy the jury," which could not reach a verdict on this theory of claim. Said the Appellate Division:

> [W]e believe the attempt did not even raise an issue for submission to them.

---

17. It is, of course, assumed that a plaintiff, in naming a doctor as a defendant, has done so in good faith, on the basis of his relationship with the case, and not as a device or subterfuge in order to afford the plaintiff an opportunity to call him as an expert witness.

> [T]he particular disease from which plaintiff was suffering has been the subject of intensive research in the past decade, and certain beliefs professionally held and expressed in texts have been subjected to radical correction. No one testified that in the light of current information the operation would be doomed to failure; in fact, the contrary was stoutly maintained. Support for plaintiff's contention rests solely on the argument made by her counsel from his interpretation of the medical texts. In view of the situation in the field, that is not a sufficient basis on which to raise an issue. Id.

Justice McNally dissented; he would have ordered a new trial on the contraindication issue.

The Court of Appeals affirmed without opinion, 18 N.Y.2d 970, 278 N.Y.S.2d 209, 224 N.E.2d 717 (1966), and the Appellate Division later extended its opinion to Dr. Paton. 28 A.D.2d 1108, 284 N.Y.S.2d 1001 (1967).

SECTION C. PROOF OF MEDICAL NEGLIGENCE WITHOUT EXPERTS

RAVI v. WILLIAMS
Supreme Court of Alabama, 1988.
536 So.2d 1374.

SHORES, JUSTICE. * * *

On April 1, 1985, Carolyn Sue Williams went to Dr. C.H. Paine's medical clinic, complaining of vaginal bleeding and back and pelvic pain. Dr. Paine recommended a hysterectomy. * * *

On April 3, 1985, Dr. P.B. Ravi performed the surgery, with Dr. Paine assisting. The scrub nurse and circulating nurse were supposed to keep a correct count of the sponges used during the operation. One of the attending nurses informed Dr. Ravi that all of the sponges had been accounted for, and the operation was completed.

On April 12, Williams was experiencing abdominal pain and emergency surgery was performed. One of the surgical sponges [18] had been left in the plaintiff's abdomen during the previous operation.

Williams brought this action against Drs. Paine and Ravi and the D.E. Jackson Memorial Hospital, alleging negligence in leaving the sponge inside her abdomen * * *. The complaint alleged that the defendants failed to exercise the degree of care required by law of physicians and hospitals in administering medical care.

The court entered summary judgment for Dr. Paine, and a pro tanto settlement was reached between Williams and D.E. Jackson Memorial Hospital. The case against Dr. Ravi proceeded to trial, and

---

18. Editors' Note: According to plaintiff's counsel, it was a laparotomy or "lap" sponge, an object the size of a dishtowel and perhaps an eighth of an inch thick—quite different from the common "surgical sponge" that is about three inches square and composed of a few folds of gauze.

the jury returned a verdict for Williams in the amount of $20,000. The court entered a judgment in that amount.

On appeal Dr. Ravi first contends that the trial court improperly charged the jury on the law to be applied when a foreign object is left in a patient's body by a physician. He argues that the trial court incorrectly charged the jury (1) that the failure to remove from a patient's body sponges placed there during an operation is negligence per se, and (2) that such conduct falls beneath the standard of care as a matter of law.

* * *

Considering the entirety of the court's charge to the jury, we hold that it was not so incorrect or confusing as to constitute reversible error. * * *

In arguing that the trial court's statement in charging the jury that "there is no issue [about his fault]" was erroneous, Dr. Ravi asserts that there was expert testimony that the failure to remove all sponges after a search and after receiving information from a nurse that the sponge count was correct does not fall below the standard of care. * * *

The physician bears the responsibility for removing sponges from the patient's body and cannot, by delegating the task of counting, relieve himself from liability for injury to a patient caused by leaving a sponge in the body. The fact that all physicians engaged in practice within the defendant's same general neighborhood routinely delegate the task of accounting for surgical sponges and rely on counts given them by nurses or other assistants does not relieve them of liability when a sponge is left inside a patient's body.

The reason for this rule is stated in Powell v. Mullins, 479 So.2d 1119, 1126 (Ala.1985), as follows:

> * * * The responsibility to remove the sponges was that of the doctor and not that of the nurses assisting him. He exercised exclusive control over the sponges from the time he placed them inside the plaintiff until he removed them. The mere fact that the defendant delegated the task of *counting* the sponges, once *he* had *removed* them from the patient, does not, in any way, relieve the defendant of his responsibility to remove them in the first instance. He had the duty and responsibility of removing all the sponges. The nurses' responsibility of counting them afterward amounts to only an added *precaution* taken by the defendant to help insure that he had properly performed his duty.

* * *

Affirmed.

WARD v. LEVY & UNGER
Appeals Court of Massachusetts, 1989.
27 Mass.App.Ct. 1101, 534 N.E.2d 308.

Before ARMSTRONG, KASS and WARNER, JJ. * * *

* * * The only question presented by the plaintiff's appeal is whether the plaintiff made a sufficient showing that the defendant William Unger negligently caused physical injury to the plaintiff in the course of extracting his tooth. At the heart of the issue is the failure of the plaintiff to offer any expert opinion that Unger's conduct did not conform to good dental practice.

The plaintiff's offer of proof comprised of his own affidavit, a photograph of part of the plaintiff's face, the defendants' patient records concerning the plaintiff, and a letter and related documents from a surgeon who treated the plaintiff for a facial injury. We summarize the offered evidence in the light most favorable to the plaintiff.

On January 7, 1986, the plaintiff visited the offices of the defendants, with whom he had had no prior contact, complaining of a toothache which had begun at work. After consultation, the defendant Unger anesthetized the plaintiff's mouth with what the plaintiff believed was novocaine. The mouth numbed, and Unger extracted a lower left rear tooth. During the process, Unger was "pulling" on the left side of the plaintiff's mouth where he was injured. After the extraction, Unger told the plaintiff that his lips were chapped and bleeding and that he should put Vaseline on them. When the plaintiff returned to the car of a coworker who had driven the plaintiff to the defendants' offices, the coworker said: "What happened to you, there is blood running all over your cheek." The plaintiff looked in the car mirror and thought the blood was from chapped lips. On the plaintiff's return to his place of work, he wiped away the blood and noticed he had a wound which is fairly represented by a color photograph taken on the next day. The photograph shows what was later described by a surgeon as an abrasive type lesion, extending from the left lower lip to the cheek, about three centimeters in length. About a week and one-half after the incident, the injury was treated with antibiotics and rinses and, after a month, the wound healed. A prominent scar was left, however, and surgery was recommended to ameliorate this condition. The scar resulted partially because of the type of wound but also because Black people have a propensity to form keloid tissue.

* * *

The evidence would warrant an inference that the plaintiff's injury had been incurred during the course of extraction of his tooth. There is, however, insufficient evidence to support an inference that the harm was caused by the negligence of Unger. There is no evidence of the condition of the tooth, the degree of difficulty of the extraction, or of the effects of use of the dental tool or tools necessary or proper for the purpose. There is no evidence of the possible relationship between chapped lips (which the photograph suggests that the plaintiff had and which he seems to acknowledge) and the occurrence or the extent of the injury the plaintiff suffered. As to these matters, in the posture of the case which the plaintiff presented by his offer of proof, a jury would not be sufficiently instructed by common knowledge or experience but would be left to conjecture. * * * In these circumstances, it was incumbent on the plaintiff to offer expert opinion on the appropriate dental practice in treating the plaintiff in the condition which he presented on the date of the injury.[19]

Judgment [dismissing plaintiff's action] affirmed.

HORNER v. NORTHERN PAC. BENEFICIAL ASS'N HOSPS., INC.

Supreme Court of Washington, 1963.
62 Wash.2d 351, 382 P.2d 518.

HALE, JUDGE. * * *

Respondent, Mrs. Pauline Horner, an x-ray technician, was a member of a prepaid medical insurance plan and entitled to medical and hospital care from the appellant, which operates a hospital in Tacoma.[20] On June 17, 1957, she entered the Hospital as a patient to have a hysterectomy, an abdominal operation involving removal of the uterus.

Mrs. Horner was given a preoperative sedative, taken to surgery by cart, and placed on her back on an adjustable operating table. Her

---

19. Editors' Note: The opinion presents the following cases and parentheticals in a slightly different format.

See and compare: Semerjian v. Stetson, 284 Mass. 510, 187 N.E. 829 (1933): The mere fact that pain, inflammation and an ulcer followed the placing of an unidentified liquid in the plaintiff's eye did not warrant an inference of negligence without expert testimony.

Klucken v. Levi, 293 Mass. 545, 200 N.E. 566 (1936): Evidence that ether entered the plaintiff's eye during operation would not support an inference of negligence of the anesthetist without expert testimony.

Borysewicz v. Dineen, 302 Mass. 461, 19 N.E.2d 540 (1939): A finding of negligence was not warranted in the absence of expert testimony that anything the dentist did or did not do following the breaking of a tooth in an attempted extraction caused the plaintiff's injuries.

Langis v. Danforth, 308 Mass. 508, 33 N.E.2d 287 (1941): Expert testimony on the proper care of a patient to whom nitrous oxide had been administered would have been necessary but for the fact that the dentist by his own testimony provided the evidence.

With: Toy v. Mackintosh, 222 Mass. 430, 110 N.E. 1034 (1916): Jury were competent to determine, without the aid of expert testimony, whether a dentist was negligent in allowing an unconscious plaintiff to inhale a tooth during an operation for the extraction of several teeth.

Malone v. Bianchi, 318 Mass. 179, 61 N.E.2d 1 (1945): A jury, on the basis of common knowledge and experience, could determine whether a dentist was negligent in allowing the plaintiff's tooth to become lodged in her bronchus during the course of multiple extractions under anesthesia.

Lipman v. Lustig, 346 Mass. 182, 190 N.E.2d 675 (1963): Unaided by expert testimony, a jury were warranted in finding negligence on the part of a dentist who dropped in the plaintiff's throat a reamer which was later surgically removed from her stomach.

20. Editors' Note: "Mrs. Horner" has been substituted for "respondent," and "the Hospital" for "appellant," throughout.

right arm was extended to the side on what is called an "arm board" for injection of sodium pentothal and curare, a muscle relaxant, while her left arm was kept at her side and a blood pressure cuff applied to it. Across the top of the left shoulder a padded, metal, crescent-shaped brace, which projects upward from the operating table, was securely fixed to prevent the patient from sliding. Her feet were lowered, by means of lowering the end of the table, and were wrapped in cloth which was then tied beneath the table to prevent sliding in that direction. The patient was placed in what the medical profession calls the Trendelenburg position, that is, feet lowered, head and shoulders slightly lowered, and the abdominal area slightly elevated. Placing the abdominal area on a higher plane than that of the remainder of the body is recognized medically as the approved position for the performance of the type of abdominal surgery called for in this operation.

After placing Mrs. Horner in the Trendelenburg position, a general anesthetic was administered to her, and the hysterectomy was successfully performed.

When Mrs. Horner regained consciousness in her hospital room, she became aware of an itching sensation in her shoulder and back. She attempted to move her right arm but found that it was paralyzed. This paralysis of Mrs. Horner's right arm was described by one doctor as a severe traction brachioplexus neuropathy, and by other doctors as due to an injury of the brachial plexus, probably resulting from trauma or traction or pressure. "Plexus," as used here, means a network of interlacing nerves located in the neck, shoulder and armpit, and composed of the front or anterior branches of the first thoracic and lower four cervical nerves running through the forward aspect of the shoulder to the armpits.

Paralysis of the right arm persisted in Mrs. Horner for a period of over four years in slowly diminishing degrees through courses of medical treatment and series of physical therapy treatments, until the time of trial, October 1961, by which time most of the symptoms had disappeared. The Hospital gave no explanation as to the cause of the injury other than to show that this type of paralysis may be produced by some form of trauma, pressure or traction while a patient is under anesthesia. Mrs. Horner's action against the hospital corporation, which operates the Hospital and employed all of the medical and nonmedical personnel connected with her surgery, resulted in a verdict of $25,000.

The Hospital appeals * * *.

The instruction upon which this appeal depends reads:

> Evidence is of two kinds—direct and circumstantial. In giving direct evidence, a witness testifies directly of his own knowledge concerning facts to be proved. Circumstantial evidence is proof of certain facts and circumstances from which may be inferred other and connected facts which usually and reasonably follow according to the common experience of mankind.

The value and weight of circumstantial evidence are to be determined from its character and nature and from its relation to all of the other facts otherwise established by the other evidence in the case. Nothing in the nature of circumstantial evidence renders it less valuable than other evidence.

In connection with the foregoing, you are instructed that it is for you to determine whether the manner of the occurrence of the injury sustained by Mrs. Horner, and the attendant circumstances connected therewith are of such character as would, in your judgment, warrant an inference that the injury would not have occurred had due diligence and care been exercised by defendant's employees.

The rule is that when an agency or instrumentality which produces injury is under the control of a defendant or its employees, and the injury which occurred would ordinarily not have resulted if those in control had used proper care, then, in the absence of satisfactory explanation, you are at liberty to infer (though you are not required to so infer) that the defendant, or its employees, were at some point negligent, and that such negligence produced the injury complained of by the plaintiff.[21]

The Hospital forcibly argues that the foregoing instruction was error; that this is no case for res ipsa loquitur; that a finding of negligence here was pure speculation; and that there was neither proof of negligence in performing the surgery nor evidence that the hospital in any way departed from the standards of care within the community.

We must first ascertain from the facts in the case, rather than from the common experience of mankind, whether Mrs. Horner's paralysis was of such a nature, or was produced in so unusual a way or under such strange circumstances, as to permit the inference of negligence in its causation without further evidence.

[W]e must ascertain whether the case is a proper one for res ipsa loquitur. The myriad of cases and the accumulation of text material following the first overt application of the doctrine in 1863 have tended to enshroud what seems to be a simple, straightforward assertion of a principle of law in an obscuring mist. A return to the font may dispel the vapor and permit us to see the rule clearly. If the rule was a good one when first declared, and meets the requirements of our day, why not apply it in its pristine context? Byrne v. Boadle, 2 H. & C. 722, 159 Eng.Rep. 299 (Ex. 1863).

The essential simplicity of the rule as originally declared has been clouded through failure to understand that the case when argued evoked comment among the judges and counsel because of differences between the allegations in the declaration and the proof submitted at trial. In this landmark case of Byrne v. Boadle, plaintiff alleged that defendant, by his servants, negligently and unskillfully lowered certain

---

21. No error was assigned to the form or language of this instruction. We point out, though, that the use of parentheses around the phrase "though you are not required to so infer" tends to deemphasize and subordinate the thought expressed. The parentheses should be omitted in the future and different punctuation used.

barrels of flour by means of a jigger-hoist and machinery attached to defendant's shop; that plaintiff was passing along the highway upon which the shop was situated; and that, because of the negligence of defendant's servants, one of the barrels of flour fell upon the plaintiff causing him injuries. * * *

The plaintiff had no knowledge of what had happened, as he felt no blow. He was knocked unconscious. Only one other witness described the accident; he simply saw a barrel falling upon the plaintiff. It was admitted at the trial that the defendant was a dealer in flour. Thus, there was no evidence whatever of causation—only of the ultimate event—and on the basis that there was no evidence of negligence, the trial court nonsuited the plaintiff.

The coining of the phrase which expresses the rule came about during colloquy between court and counsel concerning the failure of plaintiff's proof to meet the allegation of his declaration. The colloquy is as follows:

* * *

Counsel: [T]hese facts do not disclose any evidence for the jury of negligence. The plaintiff was bound to give affirmative proof of negligence. But there was not a scintilla of evidence, unless the occurrence is of itself evidence of negligence. There was not even evidence that the barrel was being lowered by a jigger-hoist as alleged in the declaration.

Pollock, C.B.: There are certain cases of which it may be said *res ipsa loquitur,* and this seems one of them.

* * *

Distilled from the straightforward opinion of Byrne v. Boadle, we find the following rule:

Further proof of negligence is not essential to take a case to the jury or to overcome challenges to the sufficiency of the evidence where (1) the accident or occurrence producing the injury is of a kind which ordinarily does not happen in the absence of someone's negligence, (2) the injuries are caused by an agency or instrumentality within the exclusive control of the defendant, and (3) the injury-causing accident or occurrence is not due to any voluntary action or contribution on the part of the plaintiff. W. Prosser, Torts § 42 at 199, 201 (2d ed. 1955) * * *.

That Mrs. Horner, all of the surgical and hospital equipment, the drugs administered to her, and the personnel having to do with her surgery, were under the exclusive control of the Hospital is self-evident. Likewise, that her injuries were not due to any voluntary action or contributing factor on her part, considered in light of the fact that before, during and following surgery, Mrs. Horner was under general anesthesia, is too clear for argument. The principal problem remaining then is whether the injury was so extraordinary as to warrant an inference that it would not occur under these circumstances but for someone's negligence. * * *

Granting exclusive control of the instrumentality, and eliminating voluntary participation or contribution by Mrs. Horner to the acts producing the injury, we feel that negligence may then be inferred in three situations without affirmative proof thereof: (1) When the act causing the injury is so palpably negligent that it may be inferred as a matter of law, i.e., leaving foreign objects, sponges, scissors, etc., in the body, or amputation of a wrong member; (2) when the general experience and observation of mankind teaches that the result would not be expected without negligence; and (3) when proof by experts in an esoteric field creates an inference that negligence caused the injuries.

We are of the opinion that the case at bar falls within both the second and third situations. The Hospital produced no evidence to show what happened to Mrs. Horner or to give evidence of causation, but limited its proof to explanation of the many ways in which such paralysis might be induced during general anesthesia. Thus, the Hospital gave no explanation of the accident.

Surely, to emerge from abdominal surgery with a paralyzed arm is so extraordinary an occurrence within the general observations of mankind as to raise an inference of negligence that requires both an explanation and proof of non-negligence to meet. It may well be that surgery to or manipulation of a part of the human anatomy will normally produce drastic symptoms in other parts of the body not related to the situs of such surgery or manipulation, but, if so, we may be sure that this could readily be proved.

Secondly, the medical evidence itself—once the conclusions, which are properly the province of the jury and not of the witness, are eliminated—leaves inference of negligence. Highly competent medical experts testified that injury to the brachioplexus was of traumatic origin under anesthesia, and that this injury was caused in numerous ways: by faulty posturing and positioning of the patient, by rotating the arm while abducted, by movement of the patient while the table was tilted, or perhaps by the application of traction and pressure to the arm or shoulder or both. That this paralysis is extraordinary is shown by proof that a nurse-anesthetist, practicing her profession in this very surgery for over 20 years, had never encountered a case of this kind, and a physician, specializing in treatment of injuries to and disorders of the nervous system, sees only 3 to 6 cases of this type in a year. Another witness, a nurse-anesthetist, who had participated in at least 5500 operations, testified that she had never heard of this result nor had she seen such paralysis resulting from surgery before. Finally, there is the evidence given by a neurosurgeon that, in the last analysis, this was an uncommon occurrence and could have happened while transferring the patient under deep anesthesia from the operating table to the surgical cart to the bed. Considering the medical evidence alone, and divorcing it from the common experiences of mankind, we find that it likewise creates an inference that this type of injury would not have been produced but for the negligent acts or overt omissions of someone acting for the Hospital in the performance of this operation. Thus, all of these considerations impel us to conclude that the case is within the doctrine announced by Byrne v. Boadle in 1863.

Accordingly, under this rule, there was evidence from which the jury could infer negligence, and the verdict is held to be supported by the evidence.

The judgment is, therefore, affirmed.

ANDERSON v. SOMBERG
Supreme Court of New Jersey, 1975.

Editors' Note: The opinion appears in Chapter 8.

SECTION D. MEDICAL EVIDENCE AND JURY VERDICTS

NICASTRO v. PARK
New York Supreme Court, Appellate Division, 1985.
113 A.D.2d 129, 495 N.Y.S.2d 184.

LAZER, JUSTICE PRESIDING.[22]

Alexander Nicastro died on July 10, 1977 as a result of a coronary thrombosis due to occlusive coronary atherosclerosis. Nicastro, then a 35–year-old welder who owned a small welding company, had previously been hospitalized twice due to chest pains indicative of a coronary problem. On both occasions Dr. Fred Eugene Park, his family physician, was his attending physician. During the first hospitalization, in May of 1976, Dr. Richard H. Mermelstein was called in for consultation because Dr. Park's limited privileges at the hospital required him to obtain consultation for treatment of cardiac failure. Although the evidence at trial indicated that Nicastro was suffering from a developing myocardial infarction, which is a result of arteriosclerosis, Dr. Mermelstein misdiagnosed the problem as a virally induced pleurodynia on the basis of test results which even appellants' experts admitted were inconclusive at best, and in the absence of numerous symptoms normally associated with virally induced pleurodynia. Moreover, after making this diagnosis, Dr. Mermelstein withdrew from the case and did not follow up on those test results which were inconsistent with his diagnosis.

As to Dr. Park, the record indicates no attempt to follow up electrocardiograms and other test reports which suggested a developing infarction both before and after Dr. Mermelstein's withdrawal. Moreover, the record indicates that Nicastro, a heavy smoker and coffee drinker whose work involved physical labor, was released to normal activity. There is no indication that he was given any treatment or

---

22. Editors' Note: The statement of facts has been moved forward from its original location. Citations to New York authorities have been deleted freely; the essential distinctions apply in federal practice.

even advised to change his lifestyle to avoid coronary risk factors, despite Dr. Park's belief, as indicated by his testimony at an examination before trial, that Nicastro was disabled and unable to work from May 1976 to the date of his death because he suffered from a coronary insufficiency.

Similarly, during the second hospitalization in February of 1977, Dr. Park failed to order appropriate tests and appears to have discharged Nicastro without adequate treatment. Indeed, in June of 1977, Dr. Park filled out a Social Services form in connection with Nicastro's application for disability, in which he stated that Nicastro, a welder, suffered only from a "coronary neurosis," could work full time without limitation, and was receiving no treatment.

Although appellants' experts testified that Drs. Park and Mermelstein had acted in accordance with accepted medical standards in the community, they also agreed that the test results were inconclusive at best, that further testing would have been helpful, and that the records were barren of any indication of treatment for a coronary problem.

* * *

* * * Since Dr. Mermelstein died prior to the commencement of the action, and Dr. Park died subsequent to its commencement but before the trial, none of the principal participants in the events underlying the action survived to testify at the trial. As a result, all parties relied heavily on relevant medical records and other documentary evidence, as well as upon portions of an examination before trial of Dr. Park. There was also, of course, testimony by numerous medical experts.

At the conclusion of the lengthy trial, the jury rendered a special verdict in favor of appellants. The first question relating to each appellant in the special verdict form was whether the defendant was negligent, and, as to each, the jury's answer was "no." * * *

Upon hearing the jury's verdict, plaintiff moved to set it aside and for a new trial * * *. The court granted the motion * * *.

[I]t was well settled by Blackstone's day that a jury verdict could be set aside and a new trial ordered if the verdict was contrary to the evidence, or if for some other reason it appeared that substantial justice had not been done. This was deemed to be an intrinsic part of a viable judicial system, for it was believed that the acceptance of clearly erroneous verdicts would cause the courts to fall into disrepute. See 3 W. Blackstone, Commentaries on the Laws of England *387–393. Thus the doctrine that permits judicial interference with jury verdicts had its origin in the idea that for a judicial system to function properly, it must be perceived by the public as normally reaching the correct result. While this certainly remains true, current concepts may have shifted the focus to the desire to provide every litigant with substantial justice.

[W]hether a jury verdict is against the weight of the evidence is essentially a discretionary and factual determination which is to be distinguished from the question of whether a jury verdict, as a matter of law, is supported by sufficient evidence. Cohen v. Hallmark Cards, 45 N.Y.2d 493, 410 N.Y.S.2d 282, 382 N.E.2d 1145, 1147 (1978) * * *. To sustain a determination that a jury verdict is not supported by sufficient evidence, as a matter of law, there must be "no valid line of reasoning and permissible inferences which could possibly lead rational men to the conclusion reached by the jury on the basis of the evidence presented at trial." *Cohen*, 382 N.E.2d at 1148 * * *. The test is a harsh one, because a finding that a jury verdict is not supported by sufficient evidence leads to a directed verdict terminating the action without resubmission of the case to a jury * * *.

The criteria for setting aside a jury verdict as against the weight of the evidence are necessarily less stringent, for such a determination results only in a new trial and does not deprive the parties of their right to ultimately have all disputed issues of fact resolved by a jury * * *. Whether a jury verdict should be set aside as contrary to the weight of the evidence does not involve a question of law, but rather requires a discretionary balancing of many factors * * *.

The fact that determination of a motion to set aside a verdict involves judicial discretion does not imply, however, that the trial court can freely interfere with any verdict that is unsatisfactory or with which it disagrees. A preeminent principle of jurisprudence in this area is that the discretionary power to set aside a jury verdict and order a new trial must be exercised with considerable caution, for in the absence of indications that substantial justice has not been done, a successful litigant is entitled to the benefits of a favorable jury verdict. Fact-finding is the province of the jury, not the trial court, and a court must act warily lest overzealous enforcement of its duty to oversee the proper administration of justice leads it to overstep its bounds and "unnecessarily interfere with the fact-finding function of the jury to a degree that amounts to an usurpation of the jury's duty." Ellis v. Hoelzel, 57 A.D.2d 968, 394 N.Y.S.2d 91, 93 (1977) * * *. This is especially true if a verdict is contested solely on weight of the evidence grounds, and interest of justice factors have not intervened to flavor the judicial response to the motion. Absent such complications, the challenge is directed squarely at the accuracy of the jury's fact-finding and must be viewed in that light.

Analysis of the cases reveals that particular deference has traditionally been accorded to jury verdicts in favor of defendants in tort cases because the clash of factual contentions is often sharper and simpler in those matters, and the jury need not find that a defendant has prevailed by a preponderance of the evidence, but rather may simply conclude that the plaintiff has failed to meet the burden of proof requisite of establishing the defendant's culpability * * *.

Thus, it has often been stated that a jury verdict in favor of a defendant should not be set aside unless "the jury could not have reached its verdict on any fair interpretation of the evidence." Delgado

v. Board of Educ., 65 A.D.2d 547, 408 N.Y.S.2d 949 (1978), aff'd mem., 48 N.Y.2d 643, 421 N.Y.S.2d 198, 396 N.E.2d 481 (1979) * * *.

The history of the fair interpretation standard indicates that it was intended to accentuate the principle that when a jury, upon being presented with sharply conflicting evidence creating a factual dispute, resolved the controversy in favor of the defendant upon a fair interpretation of the evidence, that finding should be sustained * * * in the absence of some other reason for disturbing it in the interest of justice.

[T]he rubric that a defendant's verdict in a tort case can only be overturned if a jury could not have reached it "by any fair interpretation of the evidence" simply restates the guiding principle that in reviewing the whole trial to ascertain whether the conclusion was a fair reflection of the evidence, great deference must be given to the fact-finding function of the jury. While this approach clearly tilts the scales in favor of a verdict's survival, it leaves the court with a breadth of discretion which obviously varies with the facts and events in each case.

Clearly, that discretion is at its broadest when it appears that the unsuccessful litigant's evidentiary position was particularly strong compared to that of the victor. At that point, the question is whether the result the jury reached is so contrary to the conclusion that might fairly have been reached on the basis of the evidence that the court should exercise its power to overturn the jury's determination. Upon appellate review of the exercise of that power, the judge's presence during the trial is a significant factor. Not only has the trial court heard and seen the witnesses testify, but it also has had the opportunity to observe courtroom events that might have influenced the jury's evaluation of the evidence, while not at the same time achieving a magnitude that would warrant reversal under the interest of justice provision of N.Y.Civ.Prac.L. & R. 4404(a). What emerges, therefore, as a principle of appellate review, is that the trial court's decision to exercise its discretion and order a new trial must be accorded great respect * * *. That respect compels the appellate tribunal to view with liberality the trial court's disposition of a motion to set aside on evidentiary considerations—not only because the trial court is in the best position to properly assess the evidence presented at trial, but also because judicial independence of mind in making that determination is an essential "ingredient to the sound health of the judicial process." Mann v. Hunt, 283 App.Div. 140, 126 N.Y.S.2d 823, 825 (1953) * * *. What the appellate court reviews, after all, is the conclusion reached by the judicial participant in the trial who has attempted to balance the great deference to be accorded to the jury's conclusion against the court's own obligation to see that the jury's interpretation of the evidence was fair.

Applying these principles to the case at hand, we conclude that the record was so replete with evidence of negligence that the trial court did not abuse its discretion in setting aside the verdict and ordering a new trial. * * *

Chapter 5

CAUSATION, HARMS AND DAMAGES

INTRODUCTORY NOTE

The practice of personal injury litigation is different from taking courses in law school. In the first-year Torts class, fault is the main concern, followed by causation, with harms and damages a distant last place. In personal injury practice, causation and harms and damages take most of attorneys' preparation and trial time, and this is true of all personal injury and wrongful death cases, whether medical liability, auto accident, or product liability. This chapter therefore presents an opportunity for law students to see medical liability cases, a subset of personal injury litigation, as lawyers and trial judges see them.

The jargon that personal injury litigators use is not the same as academic usage.

The personal injury bar lumps causation with negligence as "liability"; harms and quantification are "damages." Trials can be bifurcated, or new trials limited, to liability or damages.

"Specials" are pecuniary elements of damage that are naturally expressed in money, whether out of pocket or future losses, such as lost wages, hospital and medical expenses, and lost earning capacity. "Special damages," on the other hand, are harms that must be alleged specifically if the plaintiff wants to introduce evidence to prove them.

The courts also manipulate the terms "negligence," "causation," "harms," and "damages."

"Contributory negligence" actually operates on causation. If negligence of the plaintiff caused the plaintiff's harm, the plaintiff's negligence is treated as the sole cause, cancelling the plaintiff's whole case.

"Comparative fault" actually operates on the plaintiff's damages. If both plaintiff and defendant were negligent in causing the plaintiff's harms, the plaintiff's damages are reduced to the proportion of the defendant's negligence in the harm-causing event.

"Avoidable consequences," the fancy name for "failure to mitigate damages," also operates on the plaintiff's damages. If the plaintiff's damages include harms that the plaintiff could reasonably have prevented, the defendant should not have to pay for them.

While this field could do with some clarification, for the time being, would-be litigators have some learning to do.

There is also interdisciplinary confusion, because lawyers and medical scientists do not see causation, harms, and damages in the same way. Medical negligence was different: in earlier chapters, medical experts gave their opinions on the standards of medical care and whether defendants complied with them, but neither judges nor physicians expected medical practice to be an exact science, and so conflicting opinions on negligence did not threaten cornerstones of either law or medicine.

But both courts and physicians expect that modern medicine will be scientific, and so causation will be a matter of science, and therefore testimony on causation should be "certain." How certain? Scientific theories provide theoretical certainty, but unfortunately for the legal process, a good medical scientist is rarely confident that one event in fact caused another event, let alone that it caused a legal result. Therefore, if certainty were required of scientific testimony as to causation, little expert medical testimony would get to the jury from good scientists.

What happened in courts years ago was the dilution of the test to "reasonable medical certainty." Parsing the phrase, "medical certainty" must be less demanding than "certainty," probably along the lines of the causation that would actuate a medical expert's treatment plan (clinical certainty). "Reasonable medical" certainty must be even less certain than that—less, for example, than presenting the cause of a patient's condition to one's teachers and peers on grand rounds. Under the latest and least demanding test of all, if the expert's qualifications are sufficient, the judge will let the jury hear what the expert says about causation together with whatever uncertainty the expert expresses (including "mere possibilities"), subject to the usual tests of sufficiency and weight.

After the plaintiff's action has satisfied sufficiency requirements for negligence and causation, harms and damages still must be overcome. The recognition of harms and the quantification of damages have a tendency to wash back and forth. If the court refuses to recognize a particular harm, such as fright without impact, the great extent and dazzling clarity of the plaintiff's damages are irrelevant. Likewise a court can refuse to apply unconventional ways of quantifying damages, such as economists' projections, to a conventional harm, which destroys the plaintiff's whole case just as effectively as though no such harm existed.

Finally, lawyers and doctors speak different languages in describing harms and damages, especially nonpecuniary damages. The vocabularies of physicians are full of euphemisms like "discomfort" and "resting quietly." These are not lies; they are ways of reducing emphasis on unwanted symptoms that will go away when the patient gets well. Physicians therefore resent the way that lawyers dwell on "pain and suffering" as a way of increasing verdicts: there is an element of legal hypocrisy in making money out of other people's pain. Evidently there is not only legal usage but interdisciplinary sympathy to be learned.

SECTION A. CAUSATION OF HARM BY MEDICAL NEGLIGENCE

WILLEY v. KETTERER

United States Court of Appeals for the First Circuit, 1989.
869 F.2d 648.

BAILEY ALDRICH, SENIOR CIRCUIT JUDGE.

This is a diversity action in the District Court for New Hampshire for malpractice brought on behalf of plaintiff Angela Willey * * * against John Ketterer, M.D., the delivering obstetrician, and the Mary Hitchcock Memorial Hospital, claiming that the minor plaintiff's cerebral palsy—an impairment of the nervous system's control of muscular activity—should have been anticipated and could have been avoided by a Caesarian section to shorten labor. The jury returned a verdict for defendants. Plaintiff's vehicle for asserting errors occurring during trial rests on her appeal from the denial of her motion for new trial. * * *

The prologue to this case took place in chambers when, prior to trial, plaintiff presented two motions in limine, one of which sought to preclude "reference to or introduction of evidence regarding the medical history of Angela Willey's sister, Danielle." The motion pointed to Danielle's history of seizures, and the danger that the jury might give causative weight thereto, although there would be no medical evidence forthcoming to justify any connection. * * *

Defendants' response was, inter alia, that they had evidence to support the relevancy, viz., that expert testimony would be offered tying plaintiff's condition to inheritance to rebut the claim of obstetrical causation. Thus a leading article, Antecedents of Cerebral Palsy, "mentions that a motor deficit in a sibling predisposes another sibling to a higher risk of cerebral palsy." Danielle's medical record is "clearly relevant to the predisposition genetically to cerebral palsy."

Over plaintiff's protest, assertedly based upon extensive pretrial discovery to the effect that Danielle's seizures had been febrile (fever induced) and not relevant to plaintiff, the court permitted defendants to open to the jury with extensive references to alleged family genetic tie-ins. Starting with a reference to plaintiff's counsel as "my learned Brother from Boston," after having introduced himself as "Ron" and his partner as "Bill" (translation, if the reader needs assistance, "A city slicker from Massachusetts out to take two local boys"), and four times breaking an important rule of ethical conduct, that counsel should not express his personal belief,[1] counsel went the whole hog.

> We believe that there is evidence in the genetic data which links this family to a higher predisposition towards this disease.
>
> Mrs. Willey had a daughter born in 1979, two years before Angela was born. Her name was Danielle. She suffers from a seizure disorder since 1980.[2] You'll learn that a motor deficit, that's a seizure disorder, in a sibling is a risk factor of cerebral palsy.
>
> Mr. Willey has a brother who has been diagnosed and has for many years had Down's Syndrome, which is a mental retardation disease.

At the close of the evidence plaintiff moved to strike all reference to Danielle's seizures, and to Angela's uncle's Down's syndrome. It was so obvious that no evidence had linked Down's syndrome to cerebral palsy that defendants readily conceded that that should be stricken. * * * Defendants refused, however, outright to withdraw their charge as to the relevance of Danielle's seizures, and the court agreed, albeit reluctantly. * * *

[The jury returned a verdict for defendants.]

On the basis of a full transcript, on plaintiff's post-trial motion the court stated, inter alia,

> Defendants [in opening] argued that * * * genetic flaws in both parental lines predisposed Angela to CP. * * * Late in the trial, plaintiffs' attorney * * * denied correctly that defendants' expert had equated Danielle's seizures with any type of motor deficit. * * * [D]uring the trial defendants attorney engaged in a subtle shell-game on the phrases "seizure disorder" and "motor deficit," blurring the significance of these technical words for court and jury. * * *
>
> Defendants' experts never provided the nexus.

* * *

The district court was manifestly unhappy. Referring to "the prejudicial atmosphere created by defendants' unwarranted use of genetic predisposition," it said,

> [T]he court acknowledges that defendants' irrelevant statements, which the court would not have admitted in evidence absent defendants' promise of expert testimony validating them, have at least to

---

1. E.g., "I don't believe it [plaintiff's claim] to be the truth." That a lawyer "shall not assert his personal opinion" has long appeared in the ABA Model Code of Professional Responsibility, DR 7–106(C)(4) (1980), quoted, and cited with approval, in United States v. Young, 470 U.S. 1, 7, 105 S.Ct. 1038, 84 L.Ed.2d 1 (1985). Accord, American College of Trial Lawyers, Code of Trial Conduct, 18(a)(4) (1987 Revision). Both should be known to counsel. While it is true that most judicial invocations of this principle relate to abuse by criminal prosecutors, the rule is not so limited in terms, and in Young, 470 U.S. at 8, the Court observed that it applies "on both sides of the table."

2. The evidence was uncontradicted that Danielle had been symptom-free since 1983, a significant difference from plaintiff's irreversible malady.

some extent prejudiced plaintiffs' right to a fair hearing on admissible evidence.

The question then becomes: Is that element of prejudice necessarily dispositive of plaintiffs' motion for a new trial? The court answers that question in the negative for two reasons: first, defendants' counsel, in the course of a nine-day trial, relied steadily less on genetic predisposition so that by the time of his closing summary, it scarcely entered the equation.

It is true that counsel's closing reference was brief. At the same time, when an elephant has passed through the courtroom one does not need a forceful reminder. * * *

The court, unfortunately, was confused. In spite of finding that plaintiff had been prejudiced by defendants' improper conduct, it denied a new trial, relying on a case * * * where a new trial was denied because the error was harmless. * * * In the present case the court, rather than instruct as to the improper references, had refused plaintiff's request. A new trial is clearly called for.

* * *

ALFONSO v. LUND
United States Court of Appeals for the Tenth Circuit, 1986.
783 F.2d 958.

HOLLOWAY, CHIEF JUDGE. * * *

On December 12, 1978, Robert L. Alfonso, 17 years of age, accidentally injured his right hand with a power saw in Alamogordo, New Mexico. The index and middle finger of his dominant right hand were completely severed. The ring finger was lacerated but not completely separated from the hand.

A neighbor drove Alfonso to a nearby hospital in Alamogordo, the Gerald Champion Memorial Hospital. They arrived at approximately 5:40 p.m. The emergency room physician then took the severed fingers and telephoned Dr. John Lund, who was the on-call surgeon. At Dr. Lund's instructions, the emergency room doctor administered certain antibiotics and pain medications in preparation for possible surgery.

Alfonso's mother, Elizabeth Becker, arrived a few minutes later. She called her husband and asked him to check on a helicopter to medivac her son to a different hospital. She met with Dr. Lund approximately two hours later. Dr. Lund said that too much time had elapsed for him to reattach the fingers. Instead, he recommended surgical repair of the remaining hand. When Mrs. Becker insisted that her husband was checking on a helicopter, Dr. Lund said that transfer to another hospital would be useless because too much time had elapsed since the accident. Finally, the mother consented to surgery.

* * *

Plaintiff later moved to New Jersey and consulted Dr. Gregory Rauscher, complaining of pain at the stump sites and restricted motion in his ring finger. * * * [Dr. Rauscher performed corrective surgery on Alfonso's hand.]

Plaintiff's complaint alleged negligence by Dr. Lund in failing to reimplant the severed fingers or alternatively in failing to transfer him to El Paso, Texas, or Albuquerque for reimplantation of the severed fingers and proper treatment, and in failing to treat the hand in accordance with accepted medical standards. Dr. Lund denied all such negligence at trial. The trial judge granted a directed verdict for the defendant * * *.

* * *

Dr. Rauscher testified that under the proper standard of care, Dr. Lund should have referred plaintiff Alfonso to a specialist for reimplantation of the two severed fingers. * * *

With respect to plaintiff's claim for damages for disability and disfigurement due to negligence which prevented reimplantation, we feel that a jury question on defendant's negligence was raised. However, the question remains whether plaintiff made a case sufficient for submission to the jury on the proximate cause question. This involves the problem whether the claim for damages for disfigurement and disability was made out by a showing that there was a probability that the plaintiff's fingers could have been reimplanted successfully so that he would have a functioning hand.

The plaintiff's case rested principally on the deposition testimony of Dr. Rauscher. Dr. Rauscher was Director of Reimplantation Surgery at the Hackensack Medical Center in New Jersey and was board certified as a plastic and general surgeon. * * *

Dr. Rauscher examined Dr. Lund's deposition, and reviewed medical reports concerning plaintiff Alfonso and X-rays of his injured hand taken at the Gerald Champion Memorial Hospital at the time of injury. These materials gave him information on the condition of the injured hand and the amputation. * * * Dr. Rauscher testified that reattachment surgery was possible within about 12 hours, if the detached fingers were given proper treatment and kept cool.

Dr. Rauscher testified further that there was perhaps a 15% chance that such reimplantation would not take successfully where reasonably prompt efforts to reimplant the digits were made. This was "the national average." Dr. Rauscher was asked whether they were really talking about possibilities, and he replied that "it's more than possibilities. It's the question of proper diagnosis and evaluation of a patient." Thus the argument is made that Dr. Rauscher's testimony supported the plaintiff's case sufficiently on the basis of probabilities to go to the jury, giving favorable consideration to his deposition.

We are unable to agree. With respect to the plaintiff's case in particular, Dr. Rauscher felt that Alfonso should have been transferred to Albuquerque or another facility, but "*[w]hether [his fingers] would have been successfully reattached, would have to be conjecture.*" (Emphasis added.) Dr. Rauscher said that his opinion on reattachment would not really have been changed if Dr. Lund found the tissue badly torn. When asked whether there could have been successful reimplantation, Dr. Rauscher testified that all that could be said was that reimplantation was possible. The most important consideration on reimplantation was the blood vessel damage and the "mechanism [of] injury":

> Q. So you can't really say then today what the condition of the blood vessels was at the time of amputation, can you?
>
> A. Only conjecture.
>
> Q. Would you agree with me that if the condition was poor, in other words, a lot of damage to those blood vessels, the chances of successful reimplantation would have been diminished?
>
> A. That's right.

On this state of the evidence, the plaintiff failed to make a case for the jury. Under New Mexico law the proof that the disfigurement and disability of the plaintiff was caused by the negligence of the defendant must show probabilities. Proximate cause in such cases rests on probabilities, and such facts must generally be established by expert testimony. * * * The burden of proving with reasonable certainty the causal connection between the treatment complained of and the plaintiff's loss or injury rests on the plaintiff, and a judgment in a malpractice action based on conjecture, surmise or speculation cannot be sustained. * * *

* * * When testifying as to this plaintiff's case, Dr. Rauscher conceded that whether the finger "would have been successfully reattached, would have to be conjecture." Therefore with respect to the claim based on the reimplantation theory, the directed verdict was properly granted for the defendant.

* * *

Affirmed.

SECTION B. HARMS

FERRARA v. GALLUCHIO

Court of Appeals of New York, 1958.
5 N.Y.2d 16, 176 N.Y.S.2d 996, 152 N.E.2d 249, 71 A.L.R.2d 331.[3]

CONWAY, CHIEF JUDGE.

* * * Eleanor Ferrara, who was suffering from bursitis in the right shoulder, received a series of x-ray treatments from defendants, doctors specializing in x-ray therapy. * * * Scabs formed and lasted several months, a few as long as five or six months and one lasted

---

3. Annot., Anxiety as to Future Disease, Condition, or Death Therefrom, as Element of Damages in Personal Injury Action, 71 A.L.R.2d 338 (1960); superseded by Annot., Future Disease or Condition, or Anxiety Relating Thereto, as Element of Recovery, 50 A.L.R.4th 13 (1986).

several years, leaving the shoulder with a permanently marginated area of skin approximately three by five inches exhibiting telangiectasia, hyperpigmentation, depigmentation, and a suggestion of atrophy. This condition was diagnosed as chronic radiodermatitis which was caused by the x-ray therapy. * * *

On December 3, 1951, approximately two years after the treatments, the plaintiff was referred by her attorney to a dermatologist for examination. After taking a history and making an examination, the dermatologist prescribed a substance used in the treatment of radiodermatitis and advised the plaintiff to have her shoulder checked every six months, inasmuch as the area of the burn might become cancerous.

The instant action for malpractice was predicated upon three theories: (1) that the total number of roentgens (1,400) applied to the plaintiff was excessive; (2) that the total number of roentgens was excessive when applied to a single field or portal of the shoulder area; and (3) that in any event the amount applied was excessive insofar as this particular patient was concerned * * *. [T]he plaintiff offered the testimony of a duly qualified radiologist who supported the three theories of malpractice. * * * Plaintiff also introduced, on the issue of mental anguish, the testimony of a neuropsychiatrist to the effect that she was suffering from a severe cancerophobia, that is, the phobic apprehension that she would ultimately develop cancer in the site of the radiation burn. The witness further testified that she might have permanent symptoms of anxiety.

The jury rendered a verdict in favor of Eleanor Ferrara in the sum of $25,000, and in the sum of $1,000 to her husband, plaintiff Bernard Ferrara, for the loss of her services. The appellate division unanimously affirmed [without opinion]. 3 A.D.2d 829, 161 N.Y.S.2d 832 (1957). We granted leave to appeal for the sole purpose of passing on the propriety of the award of $15,000 of the $25,000 to the plaintiff for mental anguish flowing from the cancerophobia.

* * *

In this state, as in most other states,

> The rule is now well established that a wrongdoer is liable for the ultimate result, though the mistake or even negligence of the physician who treated the injury may have increased the damage which would otherwise have followed from the original wrong. Milks v. McIver, 264 N.Y. 267, 190 N.E. 487, 488 (1934) * * *.

[T]here was a real connection between the ultimate damage and the original wrong. * * * The original wrong certainly occasioned the examination and treatment by the dermatologist. He prescribed a substance to be used by plaintiff for the burn. Had such substance aggravated plaintiff's injury no one could doubt that, under the present state of our law, the original wrongdoers would be responsible for the resulting damage to its full extent *including additional mental anguish caused plaintiff.* The only difference here is that the later treatment by the dermatologist did not aggravate the physical injury inflicted by the original wrongdoers but, rather, increased only the mental anguish attendant upon such injury. We perceive no sound reason for drawing a distinction between the two situations. The dermatologist apparently thought it essential as part of his treatment, and as a protective measure for plaintiff, to advise her to have her shoulder checked every six months because of the possibility of cancer. Under our law the risk of such advice and its effects on the plaintiff must be borne by the wrongdoers who started the chain of circumstances without which the cancerophobia would not have developed.

* * *

Freedom from mental disturbance is now a protected interest in this state. * * * It is common knowledge among laymen and even more widely among laywomen that wounds which do not heal over long periods of time frequently become cancerous. Physical culture lectures to high school and college students, radio advice from life insurance companies, newspaper daily articles by doctors, all give the same advice. Here, in addition, plaintiff was personally advised by a doctor specializing in dermatology that her wound might develop into cancer and that she should, therefore, have it checked every six months. That would appear to have been sound advice. It is entirely plausible, under such circumstances, that plaintiff would undergo exceptional mental suffering over the possibility of developing cancer. The jury, who, under our Constitution, art. I, § 2, must determine questions of fact, including credibility, observed the plaintiff's demeanor on the stand and accepted her testimony as true. Inasmuch as the circumstances of the case corroborate the plaintiff's claim, there is no warrant in law for overturning the jury's verdict.

* * *

The judgment of the appellate division should be affirmed, with costs.

FROESSEL, JUDGE, dissenting.

* * * We disagree * * * with so much of the majority opinion as sanctions the recovery of $15,000 by plaintiff for "cancerophobia," allegedly flowing from a statement *plaintiff* claims to have been made by a dermatologist to whom she was sent by her attorney two years after her injury. * * *

Whatever argument may be made to the contrary, we do not feel, on balance and as a matter of public policy, that damages based upon mental anguish, engendered by a physician's statement as to a *possible* development of another ailment, are warranted under such a rule. Physicians commonly inform patients of conceivable complications which may arise from an injury, and we do not believe that so ready a road to the multiplication of damages ensuing from physical injury should be opened to plaintiffs. The unfortunate result of the rule announced by this decision, albeit disclaimed, is that a doctor's mere statement as to a possibility is a steppingstone to an increased recovery should the patient simply claim to be concerned enough to suffer worry by reason thereof. In other words, recovery would depend upon the subjective mind of the litigating plaintiff and speculation by the physician, without even the safeguard of an opinion by the latter based on reasonable certainty.

The decision of the majority introduces into the law a new field of damages for cultivation by plaintiffs and affording countless opportunities for fraudulent unverifiable claims. In our opinion, legal responsibility for an injury may not include mental suffering in contemplation of injuries which may never develop out of those already suffered, based upon a doctor's statement as to mere possible developments.

* * * Van Voorhis and Burke, JJ., concur.

SIEMIENIEC v. LUTHERAN GEN. HOSP.
Supreme Court of Illinois, 1987.
117 Ill.2d 230, 111 Ill.Dec. 302, 512 N.E.2d 691.

Justice Ryan delivered the decision of the court.

* * * The question presented for review is not whether the plaintiffs, Janice and Thomas Siemieniec, should ultimately prevail in this litigation, but rather, more narrowly, whether the complaint states legally cognizable causes of action. * * * Accordingly, we accept, without expressing any opinion as to the defendants' liability, the allegations that the defendants failed to adequately inform Mrs. Siemieniec about various types of hemophilia, for one of which, the type with which [their son] Adam is afflicted, Christmas Disease, there is no reliable test; failed to inquire adequately into Mrs. Siemieniec's own medical and health background; and failed to obtain the death certificate of Mrs. Siemieniec's cousin, which would have disclosed that he had a factor IX clotting disorder, the same as Adam. We further accept the allegation that if Mrs. Siemieniec had been accurately advised of the chances that her already conceived child would be afflicted with hemophilia, then she would have terminated the pregnancy by abortion.

We turn now to the issues before us, whether actions for wrongful life and wrongful birth should be recognized in Illinois. * * *

"Wrongful birth" refers to the claim for relief of parents who allege they would have avoided conception or terminated the pregnancy by abortion but for the negligence of those charged with prenatal testing, genetic prognosticating, or counseling parents as to the likelihood of giving birth to a physically or mentally impaired child. The underlying premise is that prudent medical care would have detected the risk of a congenital or hereditary genetic disorder either prior to conception or during pregnancy. As a proximate result of this negligently performed or omitted genetic counseling or prenatal testing, the parents were foreclosed from making an informed decision whether to conceive a potentially handicapped child or, in the event of a pregnancy, to terminate the same. * * *

The corresponding action by or on behalf of an infant who suffers from a genetic or congenital disorder is denominated one for "wrongful life." The child claims that the physician or other health-care provider: (1) failed to accurately perform genetic screening tests prior to conception or to correctly inform the prospective parents of the hereditary nature of certain genetic disorders; (2) failed to accurately advise, counsel, or test his parents during pregnancy concerning genetic or teratogenic risks associated with childbirth suggested by maternal age, physical condition, family medical history, or other circumstances particular to the parents; or (3) failed to perform a surgical procedure intended to prevent the birth of a congenitally or genetically defective child. In a wrongful life case, the child does not assert that the negligence of the defendants caused his inherited or congenital abnormality, that the defendants could have done anything that would have decreased the possibility that he would be born with such defects, or that he ever had a chance to be normal. The essence of the child's claim is that the medical professional's breach of the applicable standard of care precluded an informed parental decision to avoid his conception or birth. But for this negligence, the child allegedly would not have been born to experience the pain and suffering attributable to his affliction. * * *

To be distinguished from the actions before us are those in which recovery is sought for what is appropriately labeled "wrongful conception or pregnancy." Liability is based either on the physician's negligence in performing a sterilization procedure or an abortion, or the pharmacist's or pharmaceutical manufacturer's negligence in preparing or dispensing a contraceptive prescription. The essence of the wrong for which compensation is sought in some cases is the birth of a healthy and normal—albeit unplanned and unwanted—child. * * *

PART I. CHILD'S CLAIM FOR "WRONGFUL LIFE"

* * * The gist of Adam's claim is that he has suffered harm or damage as a result of the defendants' negligent performance of their professional tasks, and that, as a consequence, he is entitled to recover the extraordinary expenses associated with his disability under generally applicable common law tort principles.

The overwhelming majority of jurisdictions, including Illinois, have rejected claims for relief brought by or on behalf of genetically or congenitally impaired children against medical professionals whose negligent failure to predict or to diagnose their congenital or genetic disease was allegedly the proximate cause of their birth and having to live in an impaired condition. * * *

The systematic rejection of wrongful life claims rests upon two intimately related grounds.

The first ground is the courts' unwillingness to hold that a child can recover damages for achieving life. The threshold problem has been the assertion by the infant plaintiffs not that they should not have been born without defects, but that they should not have been born at all. The essence of the infant's cause of action is that the negligent conduct of the defendants deprived the child's mother from obtaining an abortion which would have terminated its existence. Resting on the belief that human life, no matter how burdened, is, as a matter of law, always preferable to nonlife, the courts have been reluctant to find that the infant has suffered a legally cognizable injury by being born with a congenital or genetic impairment as opposed to not being born at all.

* * *

The second basis relied upon by those courts refusing to recognize a cause of action for wrongful life is the difficulty, if not impossibility, of measuring appropriate damages. The traditional tort remedy is compensatory in nature. The basic rule of tort compensation is that the plaintiff be put in the position that he would have been in absent the defendant's negligence. The damages recoverable on behalf of a child for wrongful life are limited to those necessary to restore the child to the position he would have occupied, were it not for the alleged malpractice of the physician or other health-care provider. In a wrongful life case, there is no allegation that but for the defendant's negligence the child would have had a healthy, unimpaired life. Instead, the claim is that without the defendants' negligence, the child never would have been born. Thus, the cause of action involves a calculation of damages dependent upon the relative benefits of an impaired life as opposed to no life at all, "[a] comparison the law is not equipped to make." Becker v. Schwartz, 46 N.Y.2d 401, 413 N.Y.S.2d 895, 386 N.E.2d 807, 812 (1978) * * *.

* * * In an ordinary prenatal injury case, if the defendant had not been negligent, then the child would have been born healthy. See Renslow v. Mennonite Hosp., 67 Ill.2d 348, 10 Ill.Dec. 484, 367 N.E.2d 1250 (1977) * * *. In the present case, by contrast, the indisputable tragic fact is that Adam never had a chance to be born as a whole, functional human being without hemophilia. It is alleged that if the defendants would have performed their tasks properly, then an abortion would have been procured. However, in such an event, Adam never would have come into existence. Because children with genetic disorders such as Adam are impaired from the moment of conception, it is impossible for them to have a fundamental right to be born as whole individuals. Hence, the only alternative to their suffering, and the standard against which their compensation must be determined, is nonexistence. * * * Recognition of a cause of action for wrongful life in this case would therefore require this court to find that Adam had an interest in avoiding his own birth, i.e., that there is a fundamental legal right not to be born when birth would necessarily entail a life of hardship. * * * Such a finding, however, would essentially require us to possess the divine ability to determine what defects should prevent an embryo from being allowed life so that denial of the opportunity to terminate the existence of such a defective child in embryo supports a cause of action. * * *

* * * Adam nevertheless urges us to follow the supreme courts of California, New Jersey, and Washington, which have permitted children to pursue wrongful life actions limited to the recovery of special damages attributable to the extraordinary medical expenses expected to be incurred during the child's lifetime in the management, treatment, and care of congenital or genetic ailments. See Turpin v. Sortini, 31 Cal.3d 220, 643 P.2d 954, 182 Cal.Rptr. 337 (1982) (hereditary deafness); Procanik v. Cillo, 97 N.J. 339, 478 A.2d 755 (1984) (congenital rubella syndrome); Harbeson v. Parke–Davis, Inc., 98 Wash.2d 460, 656 P.2d 483 (1983) (fetal hydantoin syndrome). We are not persuaded, however, by the reasoning of these courts.

* * *

Although the California, Washington, and New Jersey decisions allowed limited recovery while failing to establish the logical basis for the wrongful life action—the existence of harm or injury to the impaired child—this court is unwilling to discard the requirement of a legally cognizable injury in a negligent medical malpractice case.

[P]ublic policy considerations preclude this court from allowing an infant such as Adam to recover damages for the extraordinary medical expenses incurred as a result of being born with a congenital or genetic disorder. [T]he basis of Adam's claim is that the defendants failed to accurately advise his parents of the risks of his being born with hemophilia, and that their inaccurate report that his mother would give birth to a normal male child induced her to carry to term instead of aborting the fetus, resulting in his birth with a hemophilic condition that will require special treatment throughout his lifetime.

Section 1 of the Illinois Abortion Law of 1975, Ill.Rev.Stat.1985, ch. 38, par. 81–21 et seq., evinces Illinois' strong public policy of preserving the sanctity of human life, even in its imperfect state:

> [T]he General Assembly of the State of Illinois [does] solemnly declare and find[,] in reaffirmation of the *longstanding policy of this State, that the unborn child is a human being from the time of conception and is, therefore, a legal person for purposes of the unborn child's right to life and is entitled to the right to life from conception under the laws and Constitution of this State.* * * * (Emphasis added.)

To recognize that Adam has a fundamental right not to be born would thus undermine this legislatively expressed policy favoring childbirth over abortion.

* * * Accordingly, the lower courts erred in denying the defendants' motion to dismiss Adam's claim for relief for the extraordinary expenses he will incur in managing and treating his hemophilic condition after he reaches majority.

PART II. PARENTS' CLAIM FOR "WRONGFUL BIRTH"

[T]he Siemieniecs do not assert that the defendants either caused Adam's inherited genetic disorder or increased the risk that Adam, if born, would be afflicted with hemophilia. Rather, they allege that they were tortiously injured because Mrs. Siemieniec was deprived of the option of making an informed and meaningful decision either to abort the already existing and defective fetus, a decision which, at least during the first trimester of pregnancy, is not subject to state interference, or to give birth to a potentially genetically defective child. In essence, they claim that Adam's birth was wrongful. In Cockrum v. Baumgartner, 95 Ill.2d 193, 69 Ill.Dec. 168, 447 N.E.2d 385 (1983), this court held that the costs of rearing a normal, healthy child cannot be recovered as damages to the parents in wrongful pregnancy actions. Therefore, in this case only two items of damages are requested by the Siemieniecs to redress their allegedly tortious injury: (1) the extraordinary medical and related expenses that will be incurred in order to properly manage and treat Adam's hemophilic condition during his minority; and (2) compensation for the emotional anguish and suffering that has been and will continue to be experienced on account of Adam's hereditary affliction.

* * *

The courts which have considered wrongful birth claims have been almost unanimous in their recognition of a cause of action against a physician or other health care provider where it is alleged that but for the defendants' negligence, the parents would have terminated the congenitally or genetically defective fetus by abortion. * * *

Judicial acceptance of wrongful birth as a legally cognizable cause of action is premised on a number of recurrent rationales. Many courts have accepted wrongful birth as a cause of action on the theory that it is a logical and necessary extension of existing principles of tort law. E.g., Eisbrenner v. Stanley, 106 Mich.App. 357, 308 N.W.2d 209, 213 (1981) * * *. Some courts have recognized the cause of action because of the expanding ability of medical technology to accurately detect and predict genetic or other congenital abnormalities before conception or birth. Imposing liability on individual physicians or other health care providers, these courts say, vindicates the societal interest in reducing and preventing the incidence of such defects. E.g., Blake v. Cruz, 108 Idaho 253, 256, 698 P.2d 315 (1984). Other courts have expressed concern that refusing to recognize this cause of action would frustrate the fundamental policies of tort law: to compensate the victim; to deter negligence; and to encourage due care. E.g., Robak v. United States, 658 F.2d 471, 476 (7th Cir.1981) (applying Alabama law) * * *. A few courts have also stated that refusal to recognize wrongful birth claims would impermissibly burden the constitutional rights involved in conception, procreation, and other familial decisions. E.g., Speck v. Finegold, 497 Pa. 77, 439 A.2d 110, 114 (1981) * * *.

[T]he great weight of authority * * * forces us to agree with the majority of the courts and the legal commentators, and to hold that an action for the wrongful birth of a genetically or congenitally defective child may be maintained by the parents of such child.

We must next decide what elements of damages may be recovered by the parents. While the jurisdictions that have reached the merits of the wrongful birth controversy are almost unanimous in their recognition of the cause of action, they are not in agreement on how to assess damages. The complex legal, moral, philosophical, and social issues raised by wrongful birth claims have resulted in a widely divergent judicial treatment of damages. * * *

Most courts which have recognized a cause of action in the parents for wrongful birth have found a breach of duty by the physician in depriving the parents of the opportunity to accept or to reject the continuance of the pregnancy. The damages that are generally allowed are those which the courts found flow from this breach of duty, that is, only the extraordinary expenses that are attendant to the care and treatment of the afflicted child, and do not include the expenses associated with the raising of a normal, healthy child. * * * Some courts have also permitted parents to recover in their wrongful birth action the extraordinary costs incurred as a result of the child's affliction after the child has reached the age of majority. These courts reason that, under the common law, where a child is incapable of supporting himself because of physical or emotional disabilities, the parents' obligation to support continues beyond the child's age of majority. See Phillips v. United States, 575 F.Supp. 1309, 1317 (D.S.C.1983) (applying South Carolina law) * * *.

Although the question of damages has presented a difficult and troublesome problem to those courts which have considered wrongful birth claims, we align ourselves with the majority of jurisdictions which have limited the parents' recovery of damages to the extraordinary expenses—medical, hospital, institutional, educational and otherwise—which are necessary to properly manage and treat the congenital or genetic disorder. We emphasize that the plaintiffs here seek to recover only those extraordinary expenses that will be incurred *prior* to the child's reaching his majority.

PART III. PARENTS' CLAIM FOR EMOTIONAL DISTRESS

[T]he Siemieniecs ask for damages for their emotional distress, which they claim are a natural and foreseeable consequence of the injury they sustained, and hence should be included as an essential element in the calculation of damages.

This court has recently reexamined its position with regard to recovery for emotional distress. See Rickey v. Chicago Transit Auth., 98 Ill.2d 546, 75 Ill.Dec. 211, 457 N.E.2d 1 (1983). In that case, this court abandoned its previous adherence to the so-called "impact" rule and adopted what is referred to as the zone-of-danger rule. [U]nder the holding of *Rickey,* before a plaintiff can recover for negligently caused emotional distress, he must have, himself, been endangered by the negligence, and he must have suffered physical injury or illness as a result of the emotional distress caused by the defendant's negligence.

There are no allegations in the complaint from which it can be said that the defendants' alleged negligence in any way endangered the parents of the impaired child. It is also not alleged that the parents have or will suffer any physical injury or illness resulting from the emotional distress allegedly caused by defendants' negligence. * * * *Rickey* * * * brought the law of this state on the issue in question into conformity with the majority position. The Siemieniecs, however, provided us with no reason to further expand the right to recover for negligently inflicted emotional distress.

* * * The cause is remanded to the circuit court of Cook County for further proceedings consistent with the holdings of this opinion.[4]

C.S. v. NIELSON
Supreme Court of Utah, 1988.
767 P.2d 504.

HALL, CHIEF JUSTICE.

The United States District Court for the District of Utah certified two questions of law to this Court under Rule 41 of our court rules * * *:

> 1. Does a claim for "wrongful pregnancy" resulting in the birth of a normal, healthy child as a result of an unsuccessful sterilization procedure performed by a physician give rise to a tort claim for damages under the laws of the State of Utah?
>
> 2. In the event a tort claim for "wrongful pregnancy" is recognized by the laws of the State of Utah, what is the appropriate measure of damages?

The facts accompanying the certified questions indicate that defendant performed a tubal ligation procedure (a severance of the fallopian tubes for sterilization) on plaintiff. Subsequently, plaintiff became pregnant and gave birth to a normal and healthy child. Plaintiff now contends that defendant was negligent in not informing her that the procedure was not "absolute in nature," and that alternative sterilization procedures were available with varying success rates. * * *

* * * "Wrongful pregnancy," or "wrongful conception" as it is occasionally termed, refers to those cases where parents bring a claim on their own behalf for the monetary and emotional damages they suffered as a result of giving birth to a normal and healthy but unplanned and unwanted child. Such actions are usually based upon a negligently performed or counseled sterilization procedure or abortion, or negligence in preparing or dispensing a contraceptive prescription.

[T]he instant case is correctly viewed as involving a wrongful pregnancy cause of action. A vast majority of jurisdictions recognize that a cause of action for wrongful pregnancy exists in tort. See

---

4. Editors' Note: Every Part of Justice Ryan's opinion for the court drew at least one dissent, and various concurring justices distanced themselves from the court's opinion, but no justice joined any other justice's dissenting opinion.

Jackson v. Bumgardner, 318 N.C. 172, 347 S.E.2d 743, 747–748 n. 2 (1986), and cases cited therein. Courts essentially view wrongful pregnancy actions as indistinguishable from ordinary medical malpractice actions where a plaintiff alleges a physician's breach of duty and injury resulting therefrom. Indeed, much of the analytical reasoning utilized in these cases revolves around the fact that if the physician has negligently performed a sterilization operation, he or she has breached a duty to the patient, and from a proximate cause standpoint, it is foreseeable that a child will be born and the parents will incur damages as a result of this negligence. * * *

Defendant, however, argues that plaintiff's claim is barred by Utah Code Ann. §§ 78-11-23—25 (1987). We disagree. Those sections provide:

> § 78-11-23. Right to life—State policy. The Legislature finds and declares that it is the public policy of this state to encourage all persons to respect the right to life of all other persons, regardless of age, development, condition or dependency, including all handicapped persons and all unborn persons.
>
> * * *

The plain language of the legislation evidences that it seeks to address so-called wrongful life and wrongful birth actions and issues. * * *

* * * Here, plaintiff sought a means to avoid pregnancy itself. Indeed, the injury she claims resulted from the fact that she became pregnant allegedly due to her physician's negligent counseling regarding a surgical procedure designed to prevent her from being able to conceive. Clearly, "[a] person's decision *not to conceive a child* and to undergo surgical sterilization should not be confused with one's decision *to abort a child already conceived.*" Morris v. Sanchez, 746 P.2d 184, 191 (Okla.1987) (Opala, J., concurring in part and dissenting in part) (emphasis in original). In order for us to adopt defendant's view, we must ignore established and proven principles of tort law as well as the fact that in this case and others like it, it is not the birth or life of the child, but rather "the *pregnancy* [of the mother] *as a medical condition* that gives rise to compensable damages and completes the elements for a claim of negligence." Jackson v. Bumgardner, 318 N.C. 172, 347 S.E.2d 743, 748 (1986). (Some emphasis added.) This we will not do.

Furthermore, to disregard the plain language and object of the statutes and hold as defendant urges us to do would create the concerns noted by the court in Johnston v. Elkins:

> The failure to recognize a cause of action against a physician who negligently performs surgical sterilization procedures would be a grant of absolute immunity to a physician whose negligence results in injury to the patient. We decline to grant such immunity. We see no reason why a physician who performs such surgery should be held to a lesser standard of care than a physician or surgeon who performs any other surgical procedure. * * * 241 Kan. 407, 736 P.2d 935, 939 (1987).

In contrast, acknowledging the cause of action for wrongful pregnancy and permitting the plaintiffs to recover damages which they prove are the natural, probable, and direct consequences of professional negligence neither contravenes the policy of placing high value on human life nor necessarily encourages increased litigation in this area. Indeed, since such claims are generally limited to negligent and unsuccessful sterilization procedures or negligent post-operative procedures and/or counseling, it appears unlikely that there will be great proliferation of the same. At any rate, "the potential for some increase in litigation cannot justify refusal to recognize a valid cause of action." 736 P.2d at 939.

In view of the authority and rationale noted above, we conclude that an action based on wrongful pregnancy is a valid cause of action in this state and therefore answer the first certified question in the affirmative.

The remaining certified question requests that we specify the damages that are recoverable in a wrongful pregnancy action. Plaintiff seeks recovery for the medical expenses incurred during her pregnancy and the birth of the child, and in having a hysterectomy performed subsequent to the birth of the child. In addition, plaintiff seeks damages to compensate for emotional pain and suffering as well as emotional trauma during and after the pregnancy. Her final claim is for the anticipated costs of rearing and educating a healthy child.

A majority of courts that have examined the damages issue in the context of a wrongful pregnancy cause of action have ruled that most resulting damages may be recovered except child-rearing costs for a normal and health child. See, e.g., Byrd v. Wesley Medical Center, 237 Kan. 215, 699 P.2d 459, 465–67 (1985) * * *. Awarding these initial (non-child-rearing) damages is likewise congruous with our cases concerning the recovery of damages in negligent malpractice actions. Indeed, in Nixdorf v. Hicken, 612 P.2d 348 (Utah 1980), we noted that damages which may be shown to follow as a proximate cause of the negligence include reasonable charges for discovery and repair of any resultant injury and monetary compensation for mental anguish. Applying this general rule and principles involved in the majority view to the factual scenario of this case, we now conclude that the following damages are recoverable, if proven: (1) any medical and hospital expenses incurred as a result of the physician's negligence, including the costs of the initial unsuccessful sterilization operation, prenatal care, childbirth, postnatal care, and any increased costs for a second sterilization operation if obtained; (2) compensation for the physical and mental pain and damage suffered by the mother as a result of the pregnancy and subsequent childbirth, and as a result of undergoing the sterilization operation(s) and during a reasonable recovery period after the above; (3) wages necessarily lost by the mother and/or the father of the child related to the above; and (4) punitive damages, if applicable.[5]

---

5. We note parenthetically that we join with those courts which have rejected the notion that in order to obtain damages in a wrongful pregnancy cause of action, par-

A more difficult issue is whether damages may also be recovered in wrongful pregnancy actions for the ordinary costs of raising a normal and healthy child. The courts that have addressed this issue have adopted one of four theories of recovery.

No Recovery: A few cases are cited as holding that parents have no right to recover any damages or expenses for the performance of unsuccessful sterilization procedures because no damages resulted from the birth of a normal child. See, e.g., Christensen v. Thornby, 192 Minn. 123, 255 N.W. 620 (1934); Ball v. Mudge, 64 Wash.2d 247, 391 P.2d 201 (1964); * * * see also W. Prosser & W. Keaton, Torts § 55 at 372 (5th ed. 1984) (early decisions denied recovery, reasoning that benefits of having healthy child outweighed detriments as matter of law). * * *

Full Recovery: The second view is that parents have a right to recover all the damages and all the expenses, including the costs of rearing the child, resulting from a failed sterilization procedure. Courts arguably adopting this view have based their decisions in part upon the fact that the right to limit procreation through contraception is within a constitutionally protected "zone of privacy," and that to exempt the defendants from liability for the foreseeable consequences of a failed sterilization procedure would infringe upon this fundamental right. Cases recognizing this view are at best a distinct minority and are viewed by some courts as nonexistent. See, e.g., Byrd v. Wesley Medical Center, 237 Kan. 215, 699 P.2d 459, 462–63 (1985) * * *.

The Benefits Rule: A more substantial number, but still a minority of courts, recognize that an uninterrupted chain of causation is established between the failure of a sterilization procedure due to a physician's negligence and the foreseeable consequences of the conception, pregnancy, and birth of a normal child, and thus

> [I]t must be recognized that [rearing] costs are a direct financial injury to the parents, no different in immediate effect than the medical expenses resulting from the wrongful conception and birth of the child. Although public sentiment may recognize that to the vast majority of parents the long-term and enduring benefits of parenthood outweigh the economic costs of rearing a healthy child, it would seem myopic to declare today that those benefits exceed the costs as a matter of law. Sherlock v. Stillwater Clinic, 260 N.W.2d 169, 175 (Minn.1977) * * *.

Courts adopting this view, known as the "benefits rule," hold that parents have a right to recover all damages incurred and expenses resulting from the birth of an unplanned child, subject to having such amounts offset by the pecuniary and/or nonpecuniary benefits which parents will experience from their parental relationship with a normal and healthy child. Section 920 of the Restatement (Second) of Torts at 509 (1979) has been used to support this view. That section provides:

ents must have mitigated their damages by aborting or placing the child for adoption. See, e.g., University of Ariz. v. Superior Court, 136 Ariz. 579, 667 P.2d 1294, 1301 n. 5 (1983) * * *. Such alternatives are extreme and unreasonable. * * *

When the defendant's tortious conduct has caused harm to the plaintiff or to his property and in so doing has conferred a special benefit to the interest of the plaintiff that was harmed, the value of the benefit conferred is considered in mitigation of damages, to the extent that this is equitable.

One of the leading cases citing the Restatement and supporting the benefits rule is University of Arizona v. Superior Court. 136 Ariz. 579, 667 P.2d 1294 (1983) * * *.

Other courts or judges agreeing with the Arizona view have also argued that (1) the benefits rule will more fully minimize substandard medical practice in the area of sterilization, and (2) allowing recovery for the costs of rearing the child will best protect the personal and constitutionally guaranteed privacy rights of procreation. Notwithstanding all of the above arguments and rationales, jurisdictions adopting the benefits rule remain a distinct minority.

Limited Damages View—The Majority Rule: Finally, of those courts that have addressed the issue of damages recoverable in a wrongful pregnancy cause of action, a majority have held that the ordinary child-rearing expenses for a healthy child cannot be recovered. Refusal to permit recovery of child-rearing costs has been based upon various considerations.

Some of the courts adopting this rule have based their rationale upon the speculative nature of child-rearing damages. Others have expressed concern for the mental and emotional health of the child who may someday learn that he or she was not wanted, and was reared by funds forcibly obtained from another person or business. Some courts have ruled that the injury of rearing the child is too remote from the negligence caused, and allowing such recovery would place an unreasonable burden upon the defendant, while offering a windfall to the parents, who may enjoy the benefits of parenthood at the defendant's expense. Such burden, these courts indicate, is out of proportion to the culpability involved and will have a rampant and incontinent effect. Additionally, it has been noted that allowing such damages would likely impinge upon the availability and costs of sterilization surgery while creating the possibility of new and protracted litigation and fraudulent claims.

Courts and judges have also concluded that the benefits rule incorrectly applies the Restatement principle which limits the damages that can be offset to monetary benefits resulting from the birth of the unplanned child. This conclusion has been supported by the observation that the benefits rule inconsistently allows rearing costs to be recovered without requiring consideration of the parents' failure to attempt mitigation. Lastly, many courts have expressed the opinion that parents cannot be damaged by the birth and rearing of a normal, healthy child since the joy, companionship, and affection which such a child can provide are benefits that will inevitably outweigh the costs of rearing that child. * * *

[T]he court concludes that the majority rule applies in this jurisdiction, and we acknowledge it. In wrongful pregnancy actions, the projected costs of rearing a normal, healthy child may not be recovered.

* * *

STEWART, JUSTICE, concurs.

DURHAM, JUSTICE, concurring and dissenting.

In view of the authorities and rationale presented by the majority opinion, I concur that an action based on wrongful pregnancy is a valid cause of action in this state. However, I do not agree with the majority's limitation on recoverable damages. Instead, I would hold that damages should be assessed under a "benefits rule" analysis, on a case-by-case basis, to determine the extent of any substantial negative impact suffered by plaintiff and her family resulting from a subsequent childbirth. * * *

SECTION C. DAMAGE DOLLAR AMOUNTS

HERMAN v. MILWAUKEE CHILDREN'S HOSP.

Court of Appeals of Wisconsin, 1984.
121 Wis.2d 531, 361 N.W.2d 297, review denied.

SULLIVAN, JUDGE.

The Wisconsin Patients Compensation Fund (the Fund) appeals from a judgment awarding more than $3,000,000 to Regena Herman (Regena) and her parents, Gene and Nancy Herman. Milwaukee Children's Hospital co-appeals from that judgment. * * *

Regena, then age ten, underwent surgery at Milwaukee Children's Hospital on July 8, 1980, to correct idiopathic thrombocytopenic purpura, or a tendency to bleed. The surgical procedure, a splenectomy, was performed by Dr. Glicklich; it went routinely. Dr. Glicklich left the hospital at 5:15 p.m.; Regena was in the recovery room. Dr. Glicklich left an order that he should be called if Regena's blood pressure dropped below 90/60. [A ligature in the splenic artery leaked; Regena went into shock from loss of blood; the hospital staff's efforts were inadequate; and Regena suffered brain damage.]

* * *

Regena's preinjury IQ was 100 to 110; her present IQ is approximately 85, or "dull normal." Since the injury, she is deficient in general intellectual functioning, attention span, mathematical ability, three dimensional perception, memory and reconstruction, motor coordination, and judgment skills. She has epilepsy, weakness in her left arm and leg, balance problems, and reduced bone growth in her left leg, causing it to be three-eighths of an inch shorter than the right leg. The emotional quality of Regena's speech has been reduced, and she repeats statements. Regena is aware that she is now a different person than she was before the injury.

* * *

Counsel for Regena and the Hermans requested in closing argument that the jury awarded Regena $302,000 for loss of earning capacity, $25,000 for the first year of pain and suffering, and from $600,000 to $900,000 for future pain, suffering and disability. The jury found Children's Hospital, alone, causally negligent and awarded to Regena $2,609,000 for past and future pain, suffering and disability, and $281,917 for future loss of earning capacity. The jury awarded the Hermans $350,000 for loss of society, companionship, and earning capacity during the child's minority, and $30,000 for services that must be rendered to Regena because of her injuries. The court found that Regena's medical expenses amounted to $18,579.70.

* * *

[The court ordered judgment on the verdict.]

Viewing the testimony in the light most favorable to the jury's findings, we conclude that credible evidence supports the findings that Children's Hospital, acting through its employees, was negligent in the care and treatment of Regena, [and] that such negligence was a cause of her injuries * * *. Accordingly, we uphold those findings.

The Fund's second argument is that a new trial on all issues is required because of perversity or excessiveness in the jury's verdict, and because of alleged errors committed by the court during the trial.

* * *

We determine that the $2.6 million award was excessive partly on the basis that the award was greatly in excess of the amount requested in closing argument by Regena's counsel. Her counsel asked the jury to award between $625,000 and $925,000 for Regena's pain, suffering and disability. The jury awarded $2,609,000, or three times as much as the highest figure suggested by counsel. * * * We also take into consideration, although it was not before the jury, the fact that the compensation panel award for pain, suffering and disability was $260,000.

Our primary rationale for reversing this award, however, is that it is not supported by the evidence. The trial court, on motions after verdict, set forth for the record an analysis of the jury's award for pain, suffering, and disability. In the trial court's estimation the award was sustainable because Regena was aware that she was a changed person after the injury * * *.

The record reveals that Regena testified that the children in her seventh grade class called her "palsy" and threw things in her hair. She testified that she had only one friend and that, at recess, she was not invited into games, and that other children did not play with her.

We have no comment on whether there is, indeed, greater pain and suffering where there is a lesser degree of intellectual impairment as opposed to a greater degree. The pertinent point to be made is that the award is one for pain, suffering, and disability. Regena's emotional pain stemming from her poor self-concept, while undeniably worthy of generous compensation, must be considered in light of the fact that she walks, talks, reads, dresses herself, can ride a bicycle, will graduate from high school, and will be able to work in an entry-level position. In light of evidence of this nature, we deem a $2.6 million award excessive.

* * * Nevertheless, nothing in the record leads us to believe that the award, or the verdict as a whole, was perverse.

Under the * * * rule of Powers v. Allstate Ins. Co., 10 Wis.2d 78, 102 N.W.2d 393 (1960), we have the authority to reduce an excessive award and grant the plaintiff the option of accepting that sum or having a new trial on the issue of damages. * * * We determine that a reasonable and fair award for Regena's past and future pain, suffering and disability would be $925,000, the highest amount requested by her counsel.

The Fund argues that the award to Regena of $281,917 for loss of earning capacity during her majority reflects perversity in the verdict. The Fund quarrels with the fact that the figure awarded by the jury was not testified to by any witness. Dr. Karl Egge, an economist retained by the plaintiffs, testified to the effect that Regena's loss of earnings would be $302,355, assuming she would have graduated from college had she not been injured, or $192,807, assuming she would have only graduated from high school. The Fund reasons that since no defendant introduced testimony contradicting that of Dr. Egge, the award for loss of earning capacity was capable of exact computation, and the jury's award of a different figure was inconsistent with the evidence. We reject this contention summarily. The award was not clearly contrary to the evidence and was within the range of figures suggested by the evidence. * * * The Fund cites no case which holds that a jury must award, dollar for dollar, a figure suggested by an uncontradicted expert. We affirm the award to Regena for loss of earning capacity.

We also affirm the award to Regena's parents of $350,000 for their past and future loss of their daughter's society and companionship and earning capacity during minority. The Fund argues that "[w]hile there can be no doubt that the parents did sustain some loss as a result of the injury to the child, there was no specific testimony as to that point."

The jury heard testimony that Regena was permanently physically and mentally disabled; the record is replete with examples of Regena's inability to do things which her parents reasonably should have expected of her. The jury was told that Regena's personality had become flat and her expression reduced in emotional quality. The jury heard that the Hermans' marriage was a second and successful one for them and that Regena, their only child, was the center of their lives.

The court gave the standard instruction on parents' damages for loss of society and companionship from injury to a minor child, Wis. Jury Instr.—Civil 1837. The instruction illustrates the intangible nature of the loss of aid, comfort, society and companionship. It states that in evaluating the impairment of the parents' and child's relationship, the jury should consider the age of the parents and of the minor child; the love and affection and conduct of each toward the other; the society and companionship that was provided to the parents by the child; the personality, disposition, and character of the child; and the disposition and susceptibility of the parents to suffer from such loss.

The direct evidence which the jury heard and the reasonable inferences which could be drawn therefrom shed light on all of the above factors. The value which the jury placed on the Hermans' loss, though high, was not excessive. We uphold the award.

* * *

The final disputed item of damages is the award of $30,000 to the Hermans for their past and future services rendered to Regena during her minority as a result of her injury. The Fund concedes that ample testimony was presented as to the services rendered, e.g., nursing care for one month after Regena came home from the hospital, past and future supervision of Regena, Mr. Herman's playing of a video game with Regena to improve her hand-eye coordination. However, the Fund argues, and we agree, that no testimony whatsoever was presented as to the value of these services.

Wisconsin Jury Instr.—Civil 1845 instructs that the amount to be allowed for the parents' services to the child shall not exceed an amount they would have been compelled to pay others to render such or similar services. Since no testimony was presented bearing on what it might have cost the Hermans to pay others to serve and care for Regena, there was no basis for the jury to determine whether its award exceeded the amount it would have cost to pay others to render these services. Damages need not be proved with mathematical certainty, but the claimant must establish sufficient data from which the jury can properly estimate the amount. * * * Because the Hermans did not establish sufficient data from which the jury could estimate their loss for services rendered to Regena, there was a complete failure of proof such that the award could only have been based on speculation. * * * Therefore, the award must be overturned.

* * *

The Fund argues the trial court erred in striking a portion of the testimony of John Melvin, M.D., a witness retained by Children's Hospital. Dr. Melvin, medical director for Curative Rehabilitation Center, testified, over objection, concerning Regena's vocational prospects and reduction in future earning capacity. After voir dire, the trial court determined that Dr. Melvin had no expertise in economics and struck the testimony.

The admission of expert testimony is largely a matter within the trial court's discretion. * * * An expert witness may only testify within the areas in which he or she is qualified. * * * A qualified physician may give percentage-of-disability testimony from which the jury may determine impairment of earning capacity. * * *

Because Dr. Melvin practiced in the field of vocational rehabilitation and, as part of that practice, made diagnoses to determine restrictions on patients' vocational activity, we hold that he was qualified to give his opinion as to Regena's lost earning capacity. Thus, the trial court abused its discretion in striking the testimony. Nevertheless, we do not deem the error to be one affecting the substantial rights of the adverse party * * *. The testimony went only to damages, not liability; the erroneous exclusion of the testimony does not warrant ordering a new trial on all issues. We hold that the error was harmless.

The Fund charges error in the trial court's limitation on the cross-examination of economist Dr. Karl Egge so as to exclude testimony concerning the fixed cost of an annuity. The Fund contends the testimony would have been relevant to show that a much lower award than that requested, if invested in an annuity, would give the equivalent of the economist's projected figures for loss of earning capacity.

Using the cost of an annuity contract to measure the present value of future losses has never been approved in Wisconsin. A federal court has rejected the use of annuity cost evidence for that purpose:

> The cost of an annuity for the remainder of the injured person's life is not the measure of recovery for lost or diminished earning power. The measure is, as we have stated, the gross amount of the lost earnings reduced to their present cash value. Farmers Union Fed. Cooperative Shipping Ass'n v. McChesney, 251 F.2d 441, 444 (8th Cir. 1958).

There is a difference between using a mathematical annuity table to determine life expectancy * * * and using a table showing the cost of annuity contracts paying various amounts for various life expectancies to establish the present value of future losses. * * * Wisconsin Jury Instr.—Civil 1796 instructs that future losses must be reduced to present value; Wis. Jury Instr.—Civil 1797 permits consideration of inflation. Once a jury has discounted a future loss to present value, taking inflation into account, its task has been accomplished. The jury is not instructed to take into account how much can then be earned with the discounted sum. Admission of annuity evidence could have misled the jury into believing it must award a lesser sum than the present value of the future losses. Therefore, the trial court did not abuse its discretion in limiting the cross-examination of Dr. Egge so as to exclude testimony on the cost of an annuity.

* * *

The Fund contends that Regena's counsel's argument that $25,000 would be reasonable compensation for Regena's first year of pain and suffering was a per diem argument, prohibited by Affett v. Milwaukee & Suburban Transport Corp., 11 Wis.2d 604, 106 N.W.2d 274 (1960).[6] *Affett* prohibits suggesting a per diem formula for future losses because

---

6. Editors' Note: See Annot., Per Diem or Similar Mathematical Basis for Fixing Damages for Pain and Suffering, 3 A.L.R.4th 940 (1981).

it represents pure speculation about future variables. *Affett* does not prohibit a plaintiff's counsel from naming a dollar amount for either past or future pain and suffering which he or she believes the evidence would fairly and reasonably sustain. 106 N.W.2d at 280. The trial court did not err in not granting a new trial on the basis of this asserted error.

* * *

Judgment affirmed in part; reversed in part; modified in part.

BOODY v. UNITED STATES

United States District Court for the District of Kansas, 1989.
706 F.Supp. 1458.

THEIS, DISTRICT JUDGE. * * *

FINDINGS OF FACT

1. The decedent, Carol M. Boody, was born June 10, 1935. She was married to plaintiff Gordon Boody for more than 30 years. She died on December 1, 1987, at the age of 52.

* * *

5. Plaintiff alleges negligent care by the Air Force's Dr. Tuason in failing to properly read the January 1983 x-ray and catch the cancer in an early stage. Plaintiff attempted to establish negligence through the expert testimony of Dr. Bradford Reeves. Reeves is a 20–year board certified radiologist. * * * The court found Reeves a competent expert witness.

* * *

7. Reeves testified that Tuason departed from standard medical practice: "He failed to report this abnormal density we see on the lateral view of the chest at that time." Defendant United States presented no expert testimony on this question. * * *

8. Plaintiff's second expert was Dr. Dennis Moore. Moore is board certified in internal medicine, oncology, and hematology. He is a member of the American Societies of Hematology and Clinical Oncology. Moore works with the Wichita Community Clinical Oncology Program, a prominent, national cancer research center.

9. Moore testified that decedent had Stage I cancer in January 1983 and a 51% chance of surviving five years if diagnosed then. Moore based his conclusion on the research reported in several articles and his long experience with cancer patients and research. * * *

12. Decedent's tumor when discovered in 1984 was Stage III, the most serious stage * * *. By March 1984, a secondary tumor had developed in the brain (metastasis). A very slight chance for five year survival exists after brain metastasis.

13. Defendant presented expert testimony that decedent had a Stage III tumor in January 1983. Dr. Vincent Collins based his testimony on his theory of tumor growth. Collins' theory rests on two grounds: (1) the growth rate of tumors is constant and (2) primary and

secondary tumors grow at the same rate. Armed with these two assumptions, Collins can calculate a tumor's date of birth if he knows the size of a tumor at two distinct times.

14. Dr. Collins applied his theory to decedent's medical history. He first noted that in January 1983 decedent's lung tumor was one cm. in length and in March 1984, 400 days later, was two cm. Dr. Collins then calculated:

> So, in that case in this period of some 400 days some four doublings occurred, which would give us a doubling time of 100 days. If we apply the doubling of 100 days and that the tumor that was overlooked was a centimeter in diameter, then it had undergone 30 doublings. Thirty doublings of 100 days would be 3,000 days, which is approximately eight years, and this tumor has been present then for eight years before that first chest film.
>
> Q. Do you have an opinion as to whether or not that tumor in her lung had metastasized prior to 1983?
>
> A. It would have to metastasize before that time because the—if the minimal lesion in the brain was on the order of a centimeter in diameter and had undergone some 30 doublings and carrying that back, it would have to have formed back in 1976.

15. Collins concluded Dr. Tuason's failure to properly read the x-ray in January 1983 had no effect on decedent's chance of survival. Collins opined she would have died even with the proper diagnosis; the lung and brain tumors had been with her for too many years.

> Well, in view of the fact that we have shown that not only had this [the lung tumor] been present for several years, but even the brain metastasis had already been present at that time, it would not have changed the evidence for this lady.

16. Plaintiff's expert, Dr. Moore, directly contradicted Dr. Collins' explanation of tumor growth. Moore acknowledged Collins' theory once held wide support; however, he stated that over the last ten years the base assumptions of Collins' theory are no longer considered valid. Moore explained that researchers now believe a tumor has different rates of growth at different times in its life span. The tumor grows very fast up to about one cm. in size and then its growth rate begins to slow down. Second, metastases grow faster than primary tumors. Moore expressly disagreed with Collins' view that the metastasis was in the brain eight or ten years earlier. Although Moore could not say exactly when the metastasis occurred, his view was that Dr. Tuason's failure to spot the lung tumor in January 1983 significantly diminished the chance to remove the tumor before metastasis could occur.

17. The court accepts Dr. Moore's explanation of tumor growth. Dr. Collins had considerable expertise and repute. While his work in the 1950s and 1960s may have placed him at the leading edge of his field, he has not maintained that position of stature. Dr. Collins has not done research or published a paper on tumor growth rates since 1969. Collins was totally unaware of the 1985 research on tumor

growth on which Moore based his testimony. Collins currently is semi-retired. He retired from a Houston hospital in 1983 but came back to manage a department six months before testifying. He sees some patients; he also reviews case histories for litigation. Moore meanwhile is in active practice with the "primary" federally funded clinical oncology research center in this country. Moore presented the authoritative and up to date explanation of tumor growth. The court finds Dr. Moore's testimony more persuasive than Dr. Collins: decedent had a five year survival rate of 51% because of the unlikelihood her lung tumor had metastasized.

* * *

19. Both decedent and plaintiff testified concerning her past and future wages. Decedent received her LPN certificate in the late 1970's. She worked as a substance abuse counselor for two years in 1980–82. She earned less as a counselor than at her final job as the Director of Nursing at Lincoln East Nursing Home in Wichita, Kansas in 1979. Decedent worked at the nursing home for the nine months prior to July 1983. She earned just over $15,000 per year in that position: $300 per week multiplied by 52 weeks per year. Decedent quit working "[b]ecause my husband was making too much money and everything I was making was going to taxes." Plaintiff testified that decedent quit work to spend more time with the couple's two teenage children and because the bulk of her income went to taxes. He further testified that decedent would have returned to work in 1985 after the last child completed high school as a nurse or substance abuse counselor.

* * *

21. The court received significant, credible testimony from both decedent and plaintiff about her pain and suffering. Decedent went through months of chemotherapy and radiotherapy. She had several operations to remove tumors. Her struggle with cancer was long and agonizing.

22. The Boodys had a strong marriage. They enjoyed vacationing together and provided strong mutual support for each other. Decedent provided substantial care for their two children. She took time between jobs in the 1979–84 period to spend more time with the children. In particular, she wanted to work with one child to deal with school problems. The court finds decedent provided and would have continued to provide substantial assistance and affection to her family.

CONCLUSIONS OF LAW

1. The court has subject matter jurisdiction over this action pursuant to the Federal Tort Claims Act (FTCA), 28 U.S.C.A. § 1346(b).

* * *

2. * * * Kansas law controls this matter.

* * *

5. Causation is the second element of a medical malpractice claim. The standard for establishing causation in situations

involving negligent treatment of a potentially fatal condition * * * is generally a matter to be determined by the finder of fact where the evidence has established the patient had an appreciable chance to survive if given proper treatment. In making the determination, the finder of fact should take into account both the patient's chances of survival if properly treated and the extent to which the patient's chances of survival have been reduced by the claimed negligence. Roberson v. Counselman, 235 Kan. 1006, 686 P.2d 149, 159 (1984).

6. * * * *Roberson* is part of a growing number of courts to adopt this type of causation test and recognize a cause of action for a less than even chance of survival. Keir v. United States, 853 F.2d 398, 415 (6th Cir.1988) (collecting cases and quoting *Roberson* with approval).

* * *

8. * * * The court finds that decedent was deprived of "an appreciable chance to survive" by Tuason's breach of a duty of care. *Roberson*, 686 P.2d at 159. The first *Roberson* factor is "the patient's chance to survive if given proper treatment." Id. Based on Dr. Moore's testimony, the court concludes that with a proper diagnosis in January 1983 decedent would have had a Stage I tumor with a 51% chance of surviving five years. * * *

9. The other *Roberson* factor is the degree [by which] the claimed negligence reduced decedent's chance of survival. 686 P.2d at 159. A January 1983 diagnosis by Dr. Tuason would have provided decedent with a much greater chance of having the tumor removed prior to metastasizing. With Dr. Tuason's breach of care, decedent was not diagnosed until she had Stage III cancer and her five year survival rate was very slight. Thus, defendant's negligence deprived her of almost all of her chance to survive five years. The court rules that the *Roberson* causation test is satisfied.

10. Defendant's arguments against causation are completely unpersuasive. First, defendant contends Dr. Moore's testimony that the tumor had not metastasized in January 1983 and that she had a 51% chance of surviving five years is too speculative to support a verdict. Defendant is no doubt correct that Dr. Moore cannot say with ultimate certainty the state of decedent's tumor at a given moment or the number of days decedent would live. This is a problem, however, that faces all courts when trying to reconstruct events after the fact. The Kansas Supreme Court in *Roberson* relied on expert testimony in a situation remarkably like the one before the court. Plaintiff's experts in *Roberson* had to determine what chance for survival the plaintiff lost by not receiving a prompt diagnosis. 686 P.2d at 151. Defendant's argument overlooks the great reliance courts have placed on expert opinions, medical or otherwise, over the last 40 years. The court cannot accept defendant's definition of speculative; its sweep is far too wide.

11. The second contention by defendant is that a 51% chance of surviving five years is not an "appreciable chance to survive" within

Roberson, 686 P.2d at 159. The premise of defendant's point is that plaintiffs in *Roberson* type situations fall under the traditional causation rule and must show that "but for" the negligence they would have lived, or they had at least a better than 50% chance of surviving without the negligent care. The *Roberson* court explicitly rejected this rule. After reviewing numerous cases from other jurisdictions, 686 P.2d at 154, the court reversed summary judgment and remanded for trial based on expert testimony that plaintiff had only a 40% chance of survival with proper treatment. Defendant's position is exactly like that of an Ohio court the Kansas Supreme Court expressly declined to follow. The court stated:

> The reasoning of the district court herein (which is similar to the extreme position taken in Cooper v. Sisters of Charity of Cincinnati, Inc., 27 Ohio St.2d 242, 56 Ohio Op.2d 146, 272 N.E.2d 97 (1971)), in essence, declares open season on critically ill or injured persons as care providers would be free of liability for even the grossest malpractice if the patient had only a 50–50 chance of surviving the disease or injury even with proper treatment. Under such rationale a segment of society often least able to exercise independent judgment would be at the mercy of those professionals on whom it must rely for life-saving health care. 686 P.2d at 160.

* * *

13. The final issue in a medical malpractice case is damages. Plaintiff apparently premises its request for $1,364,729.25 in damages on two grounds: (1) decedent lost a 51% chance to live out a normal life, i.e., a prompt diagnosis would have cured her, and (2) plaintiff should be compensated for the entire value of decedent's life. Regarding plaintiff's first assumption, plaintiff's experts did not testify that decedent had a 51% chance of being *cured*. Instead, they testified that she had a slightly better than even chance of surviving five years. Plaintiff cannot stretch the expert testimony to encompass a cure and a normal life span. The second assumption is untested in state law. The *Roberson* court did not discuss how to calculate damages when a plaintiff loses a chance for survival. Neither party at trial or in their post-trial briefs commented on any analytical differences between the damages awarded in a typical negligence case and a lost chance of survival case.

14. Although lacking state court guidance on this question, the court is confident it can discern the sound approach the Kansas Supreme Court would likely follow. * * * Three methods of apportioning damages are possible. * * * King, Causation, Valuation, and Chance in Personal Injury Torts Involving Preexisting Conditions and Future Consequences, 90 Yale L.J. 1353, 1381–82 (1981). First, the court or jury, without explicit guidance, could arrive at a compensation figure. While simple in formulation and fully allowing a decision maker to render justice, this rule is flawed. The decision maker needs some circumscription to properly evaluate the compensation necessary for the loss of a fractional right. The damages inquiry, when possible,

should be more precise. As explained below, the loss of chance theory lends itself to precision. The first option is rejected.

15. A second method would provide full compensation for the loss of life regardless of the decedent's less than even chance of survival. Thompson v. Sun City Community Hosp., 141 Ariz. 597, 688 P.2d 605, 615 (1984) * * *. This approach is too onerous for defendants. They should not have to compensate a plaintiff for the percentage of the harm they did not cause or that would have occurred naturally. See Kan.Stat.Ann. § 60–258a (comparative negligence statute). The second method should not apply here.

16. The most logical approach is to compensate plaintiffs for what they lost: the approximate percentage chance of living or surviving for a fixed period of time. For example, if a person would have had a 30% chance to survive a heart attack with proper treatment but died because of negligent treatment, the plaintiff recovers 30% of the value placed on the decedent's life. Thus if the jury believed decedent's life was worth $2 million, plaintiff would recover $600,000. King, 90 Yale L.J. at 1382.

17. Many courts have followed Prof. King's analysis and adopted the percentage apportionment of damages method. * * *

18. The court determines the percentage allocation is the most reasonable method and the one the Kansas Supreme Court would adopt. This method is preferable because it apportions damages in direct relation to the harm caused; it neither over-compensates plaintiffs or unfairly burdens defendants with unattributable fault. Second, the percentage method gives juries and judges concrete guidelines on how to measure damages, alleviating the "pulling out of the hat" problem identified with the first method. If the decision maker believes plaintiff's expert(s) on causation, the percentage of chance lost, then it makes the usual finding on the value of a life ($X) and multiplies $X by the percentage of chance lost to arrive at the compensation for the lost chance to survive.

19. An application of the damage formula to the instant facts is straightforward. The court first calculates the total value of the decedent's life. Plaintiff's damages are defined by two state statutes, the wrongful death statute, Kan.Stat.Ann. §§ 60–1901—1905, and the survival statute, §§ 60–1801—1802. The wrongful death statute is designed to compensate the decedent's heirs for loss of companionship and support after the death; the survival statute compensates the decedent's estate for injuries suffered by the decedent between the date of injury and death. * * *

20. Plaintiff requests $1 million under the survival statute for decedent's pain and suffering from 1984 until her death in December 1987. The court has seriously considered the request. A jury applying common sense and experience and considering the commonly recognized agony of cancer treatment would probably have had no trouble with the evidence before the court showing such a prolonged period of

suffering before death. Therefore, in the absence of any contrary evidence and the fraction to be applied, the court somewhat reluctantly finds the $1 million valuation to be within reason and the evidence.

21. Under the wrongful death statute, plaintiff can recover for three amounts: nonpecuniary loss; unreimbursed medical and funeral expenses; and pecuniary loss. Kan.Stat.Ann. § 60–1903(c). Plaintiff requests the statutory maximum of $100,000 for nonpecuniary loss. § 60–1903(a). The court concludes plaintiff's testimony supports a recovery of the statutory maximum of nonpecuniary damages. The court received ample testimony of a strong marriage and extensive care of the couple's children.

22. The unreimbursed medical and funeral expenses total $29,729.25. The court agrees plaintiff should receive compensation for these expenses under the damages formula.

23. Finally, plaintiff requests a pecuniary award of $234,000 in lost wages for the rest of decedent's working life. Plaintiff's lost wages figure equals the yearly compensation at her last job prior to the illness multiplied by 15—the number of years she would have worked to age 65. Defendant did not contest this computation or any element of damages in its post-trial brief. However, after carefully reviewing the trial testimony, the court determines plaintiff lacks sufficient evidence to carry its evidentiary burden on this part of the damages inquiry.

24. Decedent's past job record and future plans do not support a lost future wages award. Recovery of lost future wages "may not be had where the alleged damages are too conjectural or speculative to form a basis for measurement." Morris v. Francisco, 238 Kan. 71, 708 P.2d 498, 503 (1985). This is the case here. The court faces too many imponderables in attempting to formulate a valid lost future wages award. First, the court would have a difficult time in determining what her wages should be for the next 15 years. A base calculation would be difficult because decedent lacked a strong earnings history prior to her illness. She did not work for almost a year prior to the time of correct diagnosis in 1984. Prior to the nursing home job, she worked in a lower paying position. Moreover, calculations for her wages in the latter years of her working life would be almost impossible. Plaintiff presented no evidence on the earnings of LPNs for 1985 and beyond; his calculation would keep her wages static for 15 years. Second, as the court found above, significant doubts exist if she would have returned to work at all. She quit working in 1983 for tax reasons and she made no claim to future employment in her deposition. In sum, the evidence is too speculative to support a claim for lost wages.

25. The total amount of recovery for decedent's loss of life is $24,377 of medical expenses + $5,353.25 of funeral expenses + $100,000 nonpecuniary loss + $1,000,000 pain and suffering award = $1,129,729.25.

26. The second step is to determine the percentage of her total life that decedent lost because of Dr. Tuason's negligence. This step is a

more complex task than in the usual case. Her lost chance was not in terms of life expectancy but in a percentage of surviving five years. The court reasons that to adhere to the percentage method described above requires the following calculations. Decedent was 48 when the negligent act occurred. Her life expectancy at that age was an additional 32.9 years. Pattern Instructions Kan. § 9.45 (2d ed. 1985 Supp.). Decedent had a significant (51%) chance of living five years. While she may have lived longer than five years, she had a 49% chance of living less than five years. The court determines that five years is the most reasonable amount of time that the negligence deprived her of living. Five years represented 15.2% of her remaining life (5 divided by 32.9). The 15.2% of her remaining life is the loss recoverable under *Roberson*.

27. The final step is to multiply the two figures: the total value of life by the percentage of life lost. Plaintiff recovers $171,718.83, or 15.2% of $1,129,729.25.

It is by the court therefore ordered that judgment in the amount of $171,718.83 plus costs is entered in favor of plaintiff.

OSTROWSKI v. AZZARA
Supreme Court of New Jersey, 1988.
111 N.J. 429, 545 A.2d 148.

O'HERN, J. * * *

On May 17, 1983, plaintiff, Eleanor Ostrowski, a heavy smoker and an insulin-dependent diabetic for 20 years, first consulted with defendant, Lynn M. Azzara, a doctor of podiatric medicine, a specialist in the care of feet. Plaintiff had been referred to Dr. Azzara by her internist whom she had last seen in November 1982. * * *

Physical examination revealed redness in the plaintiff's big toe and elongated and incurvated toenails. Incurvated toenails are not ingrown; rather, they press against the skin. Diminished pulses on her foot indicated decreased blood supply to that area, as well as decreased circulation and impaired vascular status. Dr. Azzara made a diagnosis of onychomycosis (a fungous disease of the nails) and formulated a plan of treatment to debride (trim) the incurvated nail. Since plaintiff had informed her of a high blood sugar level, Dr. Azzara ordered a fasting blood sugar test and a urinalysis; she also noted that a vascular examination should be considered for the following week if plaintiff showed no improvement.

Plaintiff next saw Dr. Azzara three days later, on May 20, 1983. The results of the fasting blood sugar test indicated plaintiff's blood sugar was high, with a reading of 306. The urinalysis results also indicated plaintiff's blood sugar was above normal. At this second visit, Dr. Azzara concluded that plaintiff had peripheral vascular disease, poor circulation, and diabetes with a very high sugar elevation. She discussed these conclusions with plaintiff and explained the importance of better sugar maintenance. She also explained that a complication of peripheral vascular disease and diabetes is an increased risk of losing a limb if the diabetes is not controlled. The lack of blood flow can lead to decaying tissue. * * *

[O]n May 31, 1983, * * * physical examination of the toe revealed redness and drainage from the distal medial (outside front) border of the nail, and the toenail was painful to the touch. Dr. Azzara's proposed course of treatment was to avulse, or remove, all or a portion of the toenail to facilitate drainage.

Dr. Azzara says that prior to performing the removal procedure she reviewed with Mrs. Ostrowski both the risks and complications of the procedure, including non-healing and loss of limb, as well as the risks involved with not treating the toe. Plaintiff executed a consent form authorizing Dr. Azzara to perform a total removal of her left big toenail. The nail was cut out. (Defendant testified that she cut out only a portion of the nail, although her records showed a total removal.)

* * *

During the time plaintiff was being treated by her internist and by Dr. Azzara, she continued to smoke despite advice to the contrary. Her internist testified at the trial that smoking accelerates and aggravates peripheral vascular disease, and that a diabetic patient with vascular disease can by smoking accelerate the severity of the vascular disease by as much as 50%. By mid-July, plaintiff's toe had become more painful and discolored.

At this point, all accord ceases. Plaintiff claims that it was the podiatrist's failure to consult with the patient's internist and defendant's failure to establish by vascular tests that the blood flow was sufficient to heal the wound, and to take less radical care, that left her with a non-healing, pre-gangrenous wound, that is, with decaying tissue. As a result, plaintiff had to undergo immediate bypass surgery to prevent the loss of the extremity. If left untreated, the pre-gangrenous toe condition resulting from the defendant's nail removal procedure would have spread, causing loss of the leg. The plaintiff's first bypass surgery did not arrest the condition, and she underwent two additional bypass surgeries which, in the opinion of her treating vascular surgeon, directly and proximately resulted from the unnecessary toenail removal procedure on May 31, 1983. In the third operation a vein from her right leg was transplanted to her left leg to increase the flow of blood to the toe.

* * * The jury found that the doctor had acted negligently in cutting out the plaintiff's toenail without adequate consideration of her condition, but found plaintiff's fault (51%) to exceed that of the physician (49%). She was therefore disallowed any recovery. On appeal the appellate division affirmed in an unreported decision. * * * We are told that since the trial, the plaintiff's left leg has been amputated above the knee. This was foreseen, but not to a reasonable degree of medical probability at the time of trial.

Several strands of doctrine are interwoven in the resolution of this matter. * * *

* * * In a fault-based system of tort reparation, the doctrine of contributory negligence served to bar any recovery to a plaintiff whose fault contributed to the accident. * * *

Comparative negligence was intended to ameliorate the harshness of contributory negligence but should not blur its clarity. It was designed only to leave the door open to those plaintiffs whose fault was not greater than the defendant's, not to create an independent gate-keeping function. * * *

* * * Avoidable consequences * * * normally comes into action when the injured party's carelessness occurs *after* the defendant's legal wrong has been committed. Contributory negligence, however, comes into action when the injured party's carelessness occurs *before* defendant's wrong has been committed or concurrently with it. * * *

A counterweight to the doctrine of avoidable consequences is the doctrine of the particularly susceptible victim. This doctrine is familiarly expressed in the maxim that "defendant 'must take plaintiff as he finds him.'" * * * It is ameliorated by the doctrine of aggravation of a preexisting condition. * * * Courts recognize that a defendant whose acts aggravate a plaintiff's preexisting condition is liable only for the amount of harm actually caused by the negligence. * * * Because it is often difficult to determine how much of the plaintiff's injury is due to the preexisting condition and how much the aggravation is caused by the defendant, some courts have relieved plaintiffs of proving with great exactitude the amount of aggravation. In New Jersey, a physician has the burden of segregating recoverable damages from those solely incident to preexisting disease. Fosgate v. Corona, 66 N.J. 268, 330 A.2d 355, 358 (1974).

Finally, underpinning all of this is that most fundamental of risk allocators in the tort reparation system, the doctrine of proximate cause. * * *

* * * Plaintiff obviously had a preexisting condition. It is alleged that she failed to minimize the damages that she might otherwise have sustained due to mistreatment. Such mistreatment may or may not have been the proximate cause of her ultimate condition.

[I]t would be the bitterest irony if the rule of comparative negligence, designed to ameliorate the harshness of contributory negligence, should serve to shut out any recovery to one who would otherwise have recovered under the law of contributory negligence. Put the other way, absent a comparative negligence act, it would have never been thought that "avoidable consequences" or "mitigation of damages" attributable to post-accident conduct of any claimant would have included a shutout of apportionable damages proximately caused by another's negligence. Negligent conduct is not "immunized by the concept of 'avoidable consequences.' This argument should more properly be addressed to the question of diminution of damages; it does not go to the existence of a cause of action." Associated Metals & Minerals Corp. v. Dixon Chem. & Research, Inc., 82 N.J.Super. 281, 197 A.2d 569, 582 (App.Div.1963), certif. denied * * *.

The confusion between the existence of a cause of action and the diminution of damages has been the result of the melding of these principles in some jurisdictions under the Uniform Comparative Fault Act. 12 U.L.A. 38. That Act includes in its definition of fault an "unreasonable failure to avoid an injury *or to mitigate damages.*" § 1(b). (Emphasis added.) * * *

[E]xpressing mitigation of damages as a percentage of fault which reduces plaintiff's damages may aid juries in their just apportionment of damages, provided that the jury understands that neither mitigation of damages nor avoidable consequences will bar the plaintiff from recovery if the defendant's conduct was a substantial factor without which the ultimate condition would not have arisen.

* * * The pre-treatment health habits of a patient are not to be considered as evidence of fault that would have otherwise been pled in bar to a claim of injury due to the professional misconduct of a health professional. This conclusion bespeaks the doctrine of the particularly susceptible victim or recognition that whatever the wisdom or folly of our life-styles, society, through its laws, has not yet imposed a normative life-style on its members; and, finally, it may reflect in part an aspect of that policy judgment that health care professionals have a special responsibility with respect to diseased patients. * * *

This does not mean, however, that the patient's poor health is irrelevant to the analysis of a claim for reparation. While the doctor may well take the patient as she found her, she cannot reverse the frames to make it appear that she was presented with a robust vascular condition; likewise, the physician cannot be expected to provide a guarantee against a cardiovascular incident. All that the law expects is that she not mistreat such a patient so as to become a proximate contributing cause to the ultimate vascular injury.

However, once the patient comes under the physician's care, the law can justly expect the patient to cooperate with the health care provider in their mutual interests. Thus, it is not unfair to expect a patient to help avoid the consequences of the condition for which the physician is treating her. * * *

[W]e approve in this context of post-treatment conduct submission to the jury of the question whether the just mitigation or apportionment of damages may be expressed in terms of the patient's fault.[7] If

---

7. In a limited number of situations, the plaintiff's unreasonable conduct may be found to have caused only a separable part of the damages. See Waterson v. General Motors Corp., 111 N.J. 238, 544 A.2d 357 (1988) (jury required to determine what damages are solely due to "second injury"). If this latter method of submitting the issue to the jury is a more pragmatic way of submitting the issue in a

used, the numerical allocation of fault should be explained to the jury as a method of achieving the just apportionment of the damages based on their relative evaluation of each actor's contribution to the end result—that the allocation is but an aspect of the doctrine of avoidable consequences or of mitigation of damages. In this context, plaintiff should not recover more than she could have reasonably avoided, but the patient's fault will not be a bar to recovery except to the extent that her fault caused the damages.

An important caveat to that statement would be the qualification that implicitly flows from the fact that health care professionals bear the burden of proving that their mistreatment did not aggravate a preexisting condition: that the health care professionals bear the burden of proving the damages that were avoidable.

Finally, before submitting the issue to the jury, a court should carefully scrutinize the evidence to see if there is a sound basis in the proofs for the assertion that the post-treatment conduct of the patient was indeed a significant cause of the increased damages. * * *

Plaintiff argues that any retrial be limited to damages, with the jury's finding of malpractice and proximate cause binding on the retrial. We believe that the interwoven facts of this case do not permit such a partial retrial.

The judgment of the appellate division is reversed and the case is remanded to the law division for a new trial.

case, court and counsel may wish not to compound the difficulty of superimposing on such apportionment the necessity of resolving percentages of fault.

Chapter 6

DEFENDING THE MEDICAL NEGLIGENCE CASE

INTRODUCTORY NOTE

In defending a medical negligence case, the result desired by the defense is to win quickly, cheaply, and finally. The defendant achieves a good result when, following full trial on the merits, the court enters final judgment for the defendant, but this involves a lot of expensive pleading, discovery, and trial—the subject of chapters already treated. An even better result occurs when the defense wins the judgment by an early motion, without trial, by invoking an immunity or by establishing an affirmative defense. The best result of all is to forestall the plaintiff's lawyer from commencing the action: one way is to settle the claim; another is to cause the plaintiff's lawyer to fear that, if the plaintiff's case is weak and the defendant wins it, the plaintiff and plaintiff's lawyer will have to pay damages to the defendant.

The defendant invokes an immunity by making a motion like Fed. R.Civ.P. 12(b)(6), asserting that the court has no capacity to grant relief against the defendant. This is a powerful weapon, because it takes the defendant completely out of the case, even if the plaintiff states a claim in all other respects. An immunity ought to function early in the proceedings, so the defendant will not have to file an answer or any other motion; an immunity that has to be established by a trial is a contradiction in functions.

Governmental immunity is in a class by itself. Whatever the justification for governmental immunity, and whatever the extent to which it has been waived by legislation, the courts treat governmental immunity deferentially and waivers of governmental immunity conservatively. Both the United States and state governments and their subdivisions possess governmental immunity, and actions based upon waivers are usually preceded by essential preliminary steps that do not apply to actions against private defendants.

The granting of immunity to a private party calls for a payback in public benefit, as was thought to be the case when the courts gave immunity to private charities. In recent years the courts have decided that the public benefit of charitable immunity is outweighed by the private need for access to compensation for negligent harm, and for the most part, charitable immunity is gone. Nowadays legislatures make the tradeoffs, whether the legislation creates an institutional immunity for the insured employer and its medical employees under a workers' compensation act, or a personal immunity under a Good Samaritan statute for the physician who performs emergency medical services.

An "affirmative defense," the term used by Fed.R.Civ.P. 8(c), operates to destroy a valid claim against a vulnerable and perhaps liable defendant. Affirmative defenses are numerous; this chapter tries to illustrate only a few of them in the medical negligence context. For example, the plaintiff may have been the cause of the harm (contributory negligence or assumption of risk); the plaintiff may have commenced the action too late (statute of limitation of actions); or the plaintiff may already have settled the action (release or satisfaction).

The "countersuit" is an action for damages, based upon a group of rare and disfavored theories of claim such as abuse of process and malicious prosecution, that the victorious doctor brings against the unsuccessful plaintiff and the plaintiff's lawyer. The countersuit operates not by defending the plaintiff's medical negligence case, but by threatening to make losing it prohibitively expensive. Doctors are more interested than lawyers in the theory and practice of countersuits, and reported cases in which doctors won them are rare. Countersuits are not counterclaims under a rule like Fed.R.Civ.P. 13(a)–(b), because the countersuit does not arise out of the transaction or occurrence (the alleged medical negligence) that is the subject of the plaintiff's action; and the joinder of a countersuit with the plaintiff's negligence action, far from being compulsory or permissive or obtainable by consolidation, is not likely to be available at all. If the states adopt the Fed.R.Civ.P. 11 sanctions procedures for the filing of frivolous pleadings and motions, they may achieve for victorious defendant doctors some of the results sought by countersuits.

SECTION A. IMMUNITIES

LILLY v. FIELDSTONE

United States Court of Appeals for the Tenth Circuit, 1989.
876 F.2d 857.

McKay, Circuit Judge.

In this malpractice diversity case, plaintiff appeals the district court's order allowing substitution of * * * the United States for defendant Dr. Paul Fieldstone. The United States is the proper party defendant in "any civil action or proceeding brought in any court against any employee of the government or his estate for * * * damage or injury." 28 U.S.C. § 2679(c). The propriety of the trial court's substitution turns on whether Dr. Fieldstone was a government employee or an independent contractor when he performed Pvt. Dean Lilly's surgery. After substitution, the trial court dismissed the complaint based upon Feres v. United States, 340 U.S. 135, 71 S.Ct. 153, 95 L.Ed. 152 (1950).[1] * * *

While a patient at Irwin Army Hospital, Pvt. Lilly needed emergency urological surgery. Because the staff urologist was absent, the hospital called Dr. Fieldstone, a civilian consultant on call at the request of the regular Army urologist, to perform the plaintiff's emergency surgery. Pvt. Lilly sued Dr. Fieldstone for medical malpractice arising out of that surgery.

* * *

The critical determination in distinguishing a federal employee from an independent contractor is the power of the federal government "to control the detailed physical performance of the contractor." Logue v. United States, 412 U.S. 521, 528, 93 S.Ct. 2215, 37 L.Ed.2d 121 (1973). In our circuit "the key inquiry under this control test is whether the Government supervises the day-to-day operations of the individual." Lurch v. United States, 719 F.2d 333, 337 (10th Cir.1983).

* * *

While the defendant urges us to adopt * * * the "modified control" test of Quilico v. Kaplan, 749 F.2d 480, 484 (7th Cir.1984), we do not find that label helpful. It is uncontroverted that a physician must have discretion to care for a patient and may not surrender control over certain medical details. Therefore, the "control" test is subject to a doctor's medical and ethical obligations. Whether we label the test "control" or "modified control" is not determinative. What we must do in the case of professionals is determine whether other evidence manifests an intent to make the professional an employee subject to other forms of control which are permissible. A myriad of doctors become employees by agreement without surrendering their professional responsibilities. The United States is equally capable of making such an arrangement by express, unambiguous agreement. Our conclusion in this case is that it simply has failed on this record to demonstrate that that was the nature of its agreement with Dr. Fieldstone.

* * * Although the defendant was a member of the Army Reserve, he was not fulfilling that obligation at Irwin Army Hospital at the time the events at issue occurred. Plaintiff argues that defendant was acting solely in his role as consultant (i.e., independent contractor) when he performed the surgery.

The trial court analyzed this case under Norton v. Murphy, 661 F.2d 882 (10th Cir.1981). The factors considered by the *Norton* court and applied by the trial court in this case are: (1) the intent of the parties; (2) whether the United States controls only the end result, or

---

1. The *Feres* doctrine grants full immunity to the Government for injuries to military personnel "which arise out of or are in the course of activity incident to service." Id. at 146.

may also control the manner and method of reaching the result; (3) whether the person uses her own equipment or that of the United States; (4) who provides liability insurance; (5) who pays Social Security tax; (6) whether federal regulations prohibit federal employees from performing such contracts; and (7) whether the individual has authority to subcontract to others. Id. at 884–85.

* * *

[W]e find that Dr. Fieldstone is an independent contractor. Although Dr. Fieldstone argues that the Provider and Pledge Agreement explicitly guaranteed him immunity from civil liability, and that he specifically relied on its language and his personal knowledge that military doctors are immune from civil liability when he agreed to substitute for a military specialist in an emergency, we believe that factors raised by the plaintiff and the defendant's own admissions more clearly manifest the parties' intent. Dr. Fieldstone did not have an arrangement with the hospital whereby he was always required to see patients there. For instance, Dr. Fieldstone could refuse to treat a military patient if he wanted to, and in fact in this case he initially requested that the Army send Pvt. Lilly to another hospital for treatment. Although the Army denied his request and Dr. Fieldstone performed Pvt. Lilly's surgery at Irwin Army Hospital, he certainly was not required to do so. In other instances he was free to see patients at his private office.

In addition, Dr. Fieldstone billed the Army separately at his standard specialty fee rates. He did not reduce his fees because he served as a National Guardsman or as a civilian consultant to the military. He maintained a private off-base office, and had exclusive control over his patients and records. The Army also did not furnish Dr. Fieldstone with permanent and private office space or secretarial help at the hospital. He only occasionally used a temporary office when he dictated his operative reports. Dr. Fieldstone did not work under a written contract with the government and was never regularly scheduled on the hospital duty roster. Nor did he maintain regular or prescribed office hours as a civilian consultant.

We find that the Army controlled little about the end result or the manner and method of reaching a result. Clearly, the end result (i.e., the outcome of surgery) was beyond the Army's control. Although Dr. Fieldstone contends he was subject to the same rules, regulations and hospital control as other military physicians, and that he had limited contact and no control over military patients he treated in emergencies after his work was completed, nothing in the record suggests that this relationship was any different than it would be for a doctor in a private hospital with staff privileges. From the record it appears that he retained all the control over the choices he made that he would have had in a private hospital. Surely, being subject to hospital's rules as a condition of staff privileges does not remotely make a private physician an employee of that hospital.

We * * * reverse the trial court's order substituting parties and remand for further proceedings consistent with this opinion.

Note on the Medical Liability of the United States and Its Employees

Lilly v. Fieldstone [2] came about because the United States is immune to intra-military medical liability actions, a doctrine perpetuated in spite of the Federal Tort Claims Act (FTCA) [3] by the Supreme Court in the *Feres* case [4] and steadfastly maintained since then [5] in spite of considerable criticism.[6] The doctrine is justified by the fact that active duty military personnel are entitled to free medical care and to disability pensions, and so, in the absence of explicit Congressional attention, those benefits are their exclusive remedies for all service-connected disabilities, whether arising from combat, accident, or medical malpractice.

Until the enactment in 1946 of the FTCA, the United States as defendant was immune to tort claims in general and to medical liability claims in particular. The FTCA's basic waiver section [7] reversed this rule, saying that the United States would respond to tort claims like a private person; but nothing in the FTCA said anything about conferring a new right to sue upon military personnel.[8] In Hohfeldian analysis terms, the incapacity of military personnel to sue was and is a legal disability; to the United States, it creates an immunity. Military personnel were and are free to sue civilian health care providers; that was the result in *Lilly*.

As for civilian recipients of health care from the United States, prior to the FTCA they could and did sue providers who were United States employees, because the providers were personally liable even though the United States as employer was immune. After 1946 the FTCA enabled civilians to sue the United States as employer for negligent patient treatment,[9] and the application of medical judgment was not a "discretionary function" that preserved the immunity of the United States.[10] The persons thus enabled to sue included military dependents, veterans, and reservists not on active or training duty.

The addition of the United States as defendant was not an unmixed blessing, however, because joinder of the United States would take away jury trial of the plaintiff's medical liability claim.[11] This led plaintiffs to

---

2. 876 F.2d 857 (10th Cir.1989), the preceding case.

3. 46 U.S.C.A. § 1346(b) (basic waiver of immunity) and §§ 2671–2680 (procedure)—especially § 2680 (exceptions from waiver of immunity).

4. Feres v. United States, 340 U.S. 135, 71 S.Ct. 153, 95 L.Ed. 152 (1950).

5. See United States v. Johnson, 481 U.S. 681, 107 S.Ct. 2063, 95 L.Ed.2d 648 (1987).

6. See Seidelson, The *Feres* Exception to the FTCA: New Insight into an Old Problem, 11 Hofstra L.Rev. 629 (1983).

7. 28 U.S.C.A. § 1346(b).

8. Within § 2680 (the list of exceptions from the waiver of United States immunity) subsection (f) excepted claims arising out of the combatant activities of the military "during time of war," but the retention of that United States immunity did not confer upon military personnel the right to sue that the FTCA accorded to civilians.

9. The theory of claim could not arise from assault, battery, false imprisonment, or some other intentional tort theories of claim. 28 U.S.C.A. § 2680(h).

10. E.g., Lather v. Beadle County, 879 F.2d 365, 368 (8th Cir.1989).

11. 28 U.S.C.A. § 2402.

bring actions against United States-employed providers alone,[12] and these actions in turn led various groups of providers to obtain relief from Congress.[13] The result today is that exclusive liability of the United States has been substituted for any liability of health care providers who were acting within the scope of their employment.

The practice of substituting the liability of the United States for the personal liability of other actors has led to other statutory immunities. In 1976, for example, the manufacturers of swine flu vaccine secured immunity from product liability claims by persuading a panicky Congress to make the liability of the United States exclusive.[14]

BING v. THUNIG
Court of Appeals of New York, 1957.
2 N.Y.2d 656, 163 N.Y.S.2d 3, 143 N.E.2d 3.

FULD, JUDGE. * * *

The plaintiff, Isabel Bing, was severely burned during the course of an operation, performed at St. John's Episcopal Hospital by her own physician, for correction of a fissure of the anus. * * * [Before the surgeon arrived, three hospital employees had spilled inflammable tincture of Zephiran on her and the three layers of sheeting under her, but they did not change the sheets.]

The surgeon was not in the operating room when the antiseptic was applied, and at least 15 minutes elapsed before he initiated the preoperative draping process. The draping completed, the doctor took a heated electric cautery and touched it to the fissure to mark it before beginning the actual searing of the tissue. There was a "smell of very hot singed linen" and, "without waiting to see a flame or smoke," he doused the area with water. Assured that the fire was out, he proceeded with the operation. Subsequent examination of the patient revealed severe burns on her body; later inspection of the linen, several holes burned through the sheet under her.

In the action thereafter brought against the hospital and the surgeon to recover for the injuries suffered, there was a verdict against both. As to the hospital, with whose liability we are alone concerned, the court charged that that defendant could be held liable only if plaintiff's injuries occurred through the negligence of one of its employees while performing an "administrative," as contrasted with a "medical," act. Upon appeal, the appellate division by a closely divided vote reversed and dismissed the complaint. 1 A.D.2d 887, 149 N.Y.S.2d 358 (1956). The majority of three, reasoning that the application of the

---

12. E.g., Henderson v. Bluemink, 511 F.2d 399 (D.C.Cir.1974).

13. The first personal immunity statute, enacted in 1965, protected medical employees of the Veterans Administration. 38 U.S.C.A. § 4116. The concept has been extended to Public Health Service medical personnel, 42 U.S.C.A. § 233 (1970), and to Department of Defense medical personnel. 10 U.S.C.A. § 1089 (1976).

14. 42 U.S.C.A. § 247b(k) (repealed in 1978; for text, see Historical Note to the citation in U.S.C.A.). See Hasler v. United States, 718 F.2d 202 (6th Cir.1983), cert. denied, 469 U.S. 817, 105 S.Ct. 84, 83 L.Ed. 2d 31 (1984).

antiseptic was in preparation for the operation and, therefore, part of the operation itself, concluded that the injury resulted from a "medical" act.

[T]he jury was thoroughly justified in concluding that the failure of the nurses to remove the contaminated vapor-producing linen constituted the plainest sort of negligence.

But, contends the hospital, such negligence occurred during the performance of a "medical" act and, accordingly, under the so-called *Schloendorff* rule, Schloendorff v. Society of New York Hosp., 211 N.Y. 125, 105 N.E. 92 (1914), the doctrine of respondeat superior may not be applied to subject it to liability. The difficulty of differentiating between the "medical" and the "administrative" in this context, highlighted as it is by the disagreement of the judges below, is thus brought into sharp focus.

That difficulty has long plagued the courts and, indeed, as consideration of a few illustrative cases reveals, a consistent and clearly defined distinction between the terms has proved to be highly elusive. Placing an improperly capped hot water bottle on a patient's body is administrative * * *, while keeping a hot water bottle too long on a patient's body is medical * * *. Administering blood, by means of a transfusion, to the wrong patient is administrative * * *, while administering the wrong blood to the right patient is medical * * *. Employing an improperly sterilized needle for a hypodermic injection is administrative * * *, while improperly administering a hypodermic injection is medical * * *. Failing to place sideboards on a bed after a nurse decided that they were necessary is administrative * * *, while failing to decide that sideboards should be used when the need does exist is medical * * *.

From distinctions such as these there is to be deduced neither guiding principle nor clear delineation of policy; they cannot help but cause confusion, cannot help but create doubt and uncertainty. And, while the failure of the nurses in the present case to inspect and remove the contaminated linen might, perhaps, be denominated an administrative default, we do not consider it either wise or necessary again to become embroiled in an overnice disputation as to whether it should be labeled administrative or medical. The distinctions, it has been noted, were the result of "a judicial policy of compromise between the doctrines of respondeat superior and total immunity for charitable institutions." Bobbé, Tort Liability of Hospitals in New York, 37 Corn. L.Q. 419, 438 (1952). The better to understand the problem presented, a brief backward glance into historical beginnings proves profitable.

The doctrine declaring charitable institutions immune from liability was first declared in this country in 1876. McDonald v. Massachusetts Gen. Hosp., 120 Mass. 432. Deciding that a charity patient, negligently operated upon by a student doctor, could not hold the hospital responsible, the court reasoned that the public and private donations that supported the charitable hospital constituted a trust fund which could not be diverted. As sole authority for its conclusion, the Massachusetts court relied on an English case * * *. [A]fter the *McDonald* case was decided, other courts in this country, though not all on the same theory or for the same reason, followed the lead of Massachusetts in exempting the charitable hospital from liability, and so in time did the courts of New York. * * *

* * * A distinction unique in the law should rest on stronger foundations than those advanced. Indeed, the first ground stated in *Schloendorff,* namely, that there is a waiver by the patient of his right to recover for negligent injury, has long been abandoned as "logically weak" and "pretty much a fiction." * * * The second ground—that professional personnel, such as doctors, nurses and interns, should be deemed independent contractors, though salaried employees—is inconsistent with what they have been held to be in every other context and, to a large extent, even in this one. * * *

Nor may the exemption be justified by the fear, the major impetus originally behind the doctrine, that the imposition of liability will do irreparable harm to the charitable hospital. At the time the rule originated, in the middle of the nineteenth century, not only was there the possibility that a substantial award in a single negligence action might destroy the hospital, but concern was felt that a ruling permitting recovery against the funds of charitable institutions might discourage generosity and "constrain * * * [them], as a measure of self-protection, to limit their activities." *Schloendorff,* 105 N.E. at 95. Whatever problems today beset the charitable hospital, and they are not to be minimized, the dangers just noted have become less acute. Quite apart from the availability of insurance to protect against possible claims and lawsuits, we are not informed that undue hardships or calamities have overtaken them in those jurisdictions where immunity is withheld and liability imposed. * * * In any event, today's hospital is quite different from its predecessor of long ago; it receives wide community support, employs a large number of people, and necessarily operates its plant in businesslike fashion.

[A] survey of recent cases—those decided since the middle 1940s—demonstrates, not only that the immunity rule has been rejected in every jurisdiction where the court was unfettered by precedent, but that the doctrine has been overruled and abandoned in a number of states where nonliability had long been the rule.

* * *

The conception that the hospital does not undertake to treat the patient, does not undertake to act through its doctors and nurses, but undertakes instead simply to procure them to act upon their own responsibility, no longer reflects the fact. Present-day hospitals, as their manner of operation plainly demonstrates, do far more than furnish facilities for treatment. They regularly employ on a salary basis a large staff of physicians, nurses and interns, as well as administrative and manual workers, and they charge patients for medical care and treatment, collecting for such services, if necessary, by legal action. Certainly, the person who avails himself of "hospital facilities" expects that the hospital will attempt to cure him, not that its nurses or other employees will act on their own responsibility.

Hospitals should, in short, shoulder the responsibilities borne by everyone else. There is no reason to continue their exemption from the universal rule of respondeat superior. The test should be, for these institutions, whether charitable or profit-making, as it is for every other employer, was the person who committed the negligent injury-producing act one of its employees and, if he was, was he acting within the scope of his employment.

The rule of nonliability is out of tune with the life about us, at variance with modern-day needs and with concepts of justice and fair dealing. It should be discarded. To the suggestion that stare decisis compels us to perpetuate it until the legislature acts, a ready answer is at hand. It was intended, not to effect a "petrifying rigidity," but to assure the justice that flows from certainty and stability. If, instead, adherence to precedent offers not justice but unfairness, not certainty but doubt and confusion, it loses its right to survive, and no principle constrains us to follow it. * * * On the contrary, as this court, speaking through Judge Desmond in Woods v. Lancet, 303 N.Y. 349, 102 N.E.2d 691, 694 (1951), declared, we would be abdicating "our own function, in a field peculiarly nonstatutory," were we to insist on legislation and "refuse to reconsider an old and unsatisfactory court-made rule."

In sum, then, the doctrine according the hospital an immunity for the negligence of its employees is such a rule, and we abandon it. The hospital's liability must be governed by the same principles of law as apply to all other employers.

The judgment of the appellate division should be reversed and a new trial granted, with costs to abide the event.

CONWAY, CHIEF JUDGE, concurring.

I concur in result.

[T]he hospital should be held to be responsible under the reasoning of the many authorities cited and collated in Judge Fuld's opinion. We should stop there and not go on to overrule the doctrine of Schloendorff v. Society of New York Hosp., 211 N.Y. 125, 105 N.E. 92 (1914).

A voluntary hospital is not conducted as a business. Very few, if any, voluntary hospitals reach the end of any year without a deficit which has to be made up by its board of directors or by other charitable gifts. This is especially so of small hospitals. In my judgment, the doctrine of the *Schloendorff* case has justified itself over the years and has enabled voluntary hospitals to survive. That is particularly so in small communities as distinguished from larger cities. We need both the large and small voluntary hospital. The alternative is public hospitals supported by county or state, or stock company hospitals operating as businesses organized for profit. * * *

PANARO v. ELECTROLUX CORP.
Supreme Court of Connecticut, 1988.
208 Conn. 589, 545 A.2d 1086.

ARTHUR H. HEALEY, ASSOCIATE JUSTICE. * * *

* * * Electrolux operated an industrial manufacturing business in Old Greenwich. The defendant Mary Ann Sheehan, a licensed, registered nurse, was hired by Electrolux in October 1962 to serve as an industrial nurse at its medical facility located at the business. Under the direction of Joel Blumberg, the company physician, and William Blois, the director of human resources, the company medical facility served over 1200 Electrolux employees. The facility was maintained solely for the benefit of its employees. Sheehan worked 40 hours a week, received a salary and fringe benefits, and her paycheck was subject to withholding for federal income tax and social security like that of any other regular full-time employee at Electrolux.

The plaintiffs' amended complaint alleged that at approximately 8:15 a.m. on May 12, 1983, Panaro bent down to lift and carry a 30-pound box of pieces to a conveyor belt. He became "dizzy, foggy, sweaty and disorganized" and then proceeded to the company medical facility. The defendant Sheehan took Panaro's blood pressure, noticed his "dizzied" and disorganized state, and had him rest for approximately one hour. Panaro was then sent back to work by Sheehan and, at approximately 3:30 p.m., was found slumped over a chair. Panaro was taken back to the medical facility and Sheehan then sent him to Stamford Hospital by company car. There he was diagnosed as having suffered a cerebrovascular accident, a stroke. Panaro alleges that he suffered various permanent injuries commonly associated with a stroke including brain damage, slurred speech, blurred vision, and muscular weaknesses throughout his body. Panaro was awarded compensation under the Workers' Compensation Act by a finding and award dated March 25, 1986.

After the institution of this action, the defendants Electrolux and Sheehan pleaded a special defense that the suit was barred by * * * the exclusivity provisions of the Workers' Compensation Act. The trial court granted the defendants' motion for summary judgment * * *.

On appeal, the plaintiffs claim that the trial court erred in rejecting the dual capacity doctrine by refusing to recognize that Sheehan, as a company nurse, could be an independent contractor as to one part of her service and an employee as to another part of her service and therefore fall outside the fellow employee rule of the Workers' Compensation Act.[15] * * *

---

15. The plaintiffs have not appealed from the [summary] judgment [for defendants] as to the first count of their complaint * * * [which] also named Electrolux as a defendant. * * *

The dual capacity * * * doctrine[16] was first announced in Duprey v. Shane, 39 Cal.2d 781, 249 P.2d 8 (1952), where the California Supreme Court permitted a nurse, who worked for a chiropractic partnership, to bring a medical malpractice claim against her employer after she had been injured in the course of her employment and allegedly had received negligent treatment from one of the partner physicians. The court found that a relationship of physician-patient had arisen in addition to that of employer-employee. This separate and distinct relationship gave rise to a duty, the breach of which permitted an action of malpractice. * * *

A number of other jurisdictions have adopted the dual capacity or independent contractor doctrine in some form. See * * * Annot., Modern Status: "Dual Capacity Doctrine" as Basis for Employee's Recovery from Employer in Tort, 23 A.L.R.4th 1151 (1983); Comment, The Dual Capacity Doctrine: Piercing the Exclusive Remedy of Workers' Compensation, 43 U.Pitt.L.Rev. 1013 (1982) (survey of case law). Not all of the decisions cited above, however, concern the fact pattern present in the instant case: a claim of negligence against a full-time company nurse employed at a company facility other than a hospital. * * * In other jurisdictions, it is the fact that hospital employees were involved that permitted liability against health care providers who employ them. See, e.g., Guy v. Thomas Co., 55 Ohio St.2d 183, 378 N.E.2d 488 (1978); Tatrai v. Presbyterian Univ. Hosp., 497 Pa. 247, 439 A.2d 1162 (1982). The logic of these decisions rests on the premise that a health care facility that is open to the public should not be shielded from liability simply because the patient it treats negligently happens to be one of its employees who is injured on the job.

The only case cited by the plaintiffs that actually holds that a company nurse at a facility other than a hospital can be sued for negligence is McDaniel v. Sage, 419 N.E.2d 1322 (Ind.App.1981). There a company nurse, who faced allegations of negligence in administering an injection, was not able to use the fellow employee rule of the Workmen's Compensation Act to preclude an action against her. * * *

A greater number of jurisdictions, however, have rejected the dual capacity or independent contractor doctrine for alleged negligence by company physicians and nurses. See, e.g., Young v. St. Elizabeth Hosp., 131 Ill.App.3d 193, 86 Ill.Dec. 389, 475 N.E.2d 603 (1985) * * *. Even before the legislature narrowed the dual capacity doctrine, courts in California limited Duprey v. Shane to its facts. * * *

16. * * * A noted authority explained the "dual capacity" doctrine as follows:

An employer may become a third person, vulnerable to tort suit by an employee if—and only if—he possesses a second persona so completely independent from and unrelated to his status as employer that by established standards the law recognizes it as a separate legal person. 2A A. Larson, Workmen's Compensation Law § 72.81 at 14–229 (1983).

* * *

Although the weight of authority therefore supports Sheehan's position, we now must look to our own Workers' Compensation Act and the cases interpreting it. General Statutes § 31–293a provides that the right to compensation "shall be the exclusive remedy of such injured employee or dependent and no action may be brought against such fellow employee." The only exceptions, specifically set out in § 31–293a, are a wilful or malicious wrong or an action based on a fellow employee's operation of a motor vehicle. An "employee," as defined in Conn.Gen.Stat. § 31–275, is "any person who has entered into or works under any contract of service or apprenticeship with an employer * * *." * * * Under the plain meaning of the statute and the cases interpreting it, there is no right to bring a direct action against the defendant Sheehan.

This court, however, has carved out a few exceptions to the exclusivity of the Workers' Compensation Act provisions. See, e.g., Blancato v. Feldspar Corp., 203 Conn. 34, 522 A.2d 1235 (1987) (exception for a minor who has been illegally employed); Jett v. Dunlap, 179 Conn. 215, 425 A.2d 1263 (1979) (exception for intentional torts committed by an employer). On the other hand, this court refused to extend the *Jett* exception to include " 'accidental injuries caused by the gross, wanton, wilful, deliberate, intentional, reckless, culpable, or malicious negligence, breach of statute, or other misconduct of the employer short of genuine intentional injury.'" Mingachos v. CBS, Inc., 196 Conn. 91, 491 A.2d 368 (1985) * * *

We decline to carve out an additional exception as the plaintiffs suggest. First, we note that both of these exceptions are for *employers*, not employees. Since one of the purposes of the statutory immunity of a fellow employee is to shield those who are usually unable to satisfy judgments involving serious injuries, exceptions to the immunity from liability at common law for employers, who are generally able to satisfy such judgments, are based on different policy considerations. * * * To this date there has not been a judicially created exception to the exclusivity provisions of the Workers' Compensation Act for fellow employees. The sole exceptions for employees are set out in Conn.Gen. Stat. § 31–293a and are applicable when the injury results from either a wilful or malicious wrong or from the operation of a motor vehicle. The legislative history indicates that the purpose of the fellow employee rule was recognized by the legislature, and the exceptions were the result of deliberate consideration of competing policy concerns.

Even if we were inclined to create an exception to the fellow employee rule, the arguments presented by the plaintiffs are not persuasive in the factual circumstances presented in this case. First, Sheehan is a nurse and not a doctor. Part of the rationale for holding a doctor or hospital liable is an ability, due "to higher income and professional liability insurance," to bear the risk of an industrial accident. * * * Although the individual defendant in this case had insurance, it is not certain that all such company nurses would have insurance sufficient to cover substantial personal injury verdicts. Second, many of the cases holding health care providers liable involve hospitals or doctors as the employer. * * * Not only are these cases an exception to *employer* immunity from liability, as opposed to an exception to fellow *employee* immunity from liability, but also those cases rested on the rationale that there is no basis for distinguishing the treatment of a hospital employee, who is a patient with a compensable injury, from the treatment of any other member of the general public who is also a hospital patient.

* * * The plaintiffs * * * argue that Sheehan, as a trained professional, had an independent relationship with her patients and therefore was not under the control of her employer. Although it is reasonable to say that nurses and other professionals, by virtue of their skill and training, are not under the direct supervision of their employers when using their expertise, the plaintiffs' argument proves too much. Under their reasoning, all employees with skills beyond the knowledge of ordinary supervisors, including those subject to licensing, such as doctors, nurses, engineers and architects, would be subject to tort actions as independent contractors. We decline to follow that reasoning and conclude that the better distinction between employees and independent contractors for workers' compensation purposes is stated in Spring v. Constantino, 168 Conn. 563, 362 A.2d 871, 877 (1975). There we adopted the following definition of independent contractor: "[O]ne who, exercising an independent employment, contracts to do a piece of work according to his own methods and without being subject to the control of his employer, except as to the result of his work." * * *. Clearly, Sheehan in this case does not fall within that definition of independent contractor.

* * * The theme of legislative preeminence in the workers' compensation area is echoed in many jurisdictions. * * * We decline to create an exception to the fellow employee rule of the Workers' Compensation Act under the circumstances of this case. Therefore, summary judgment was properly granted by the trial court.

McCAIN v. BATSON
Supreme Court of Montana, 1988.
760 P.2d 725.

HARRISON, JUSTICE. * * *

Karen McCain (McCain) and two friends, Sherry Warner (Warner) and Rosemary Checketts, spent a weekend in West Yellowstone, Montana, arriving the morning of September 25, 1982, from Ogden, Utah. They planned to stay with Warner in her condominium. That evening, after preparing and eating supper at home, the three friends decided to go into the town of West Yellowstone. The three decided to walk into town as Warner's truck battery was dead. The condominium was not far from town, so they walked to the nearby Stagecoach Inn. After spending some time at the Inn, the women became separated, and about 11:00 p.m. McCain decided to return alone to the condominium.

McCain was unfamiliar with the area, and while walking back in the dark fell into an eight-foot-deep excavation pit. The pit contained reinforcing bars set in concrete at six-inch intervals. As a result of the fall, she severely impaled her upper left leg on a piece of rebar. After extracting herself off the rebar, McCain crawled out of the pit and crawled to a lighted doorway of a nearby condominium. McCain rapped on the door of a condominium occupied by Dr. James Grindley, a Bozeman radiologist, and his wife. Mrs. Grindley answered the knock on the door. After McCain told Mrs. Grindley about her accident and injury, Dr. Grindley went to the Stagecoach Inn to retrieve her two friends. Throughout this time, Dr. Grindley did not mention that he was a physician, and McCain remained on the patio or lawn outside of the condominium. Dr. Grindley is a radiologist with extensive surgical and emergency room experience. He did not initially examine McCain's injury, and in a deposition Dr. Grindley admitted that he did not have any medical equipment at the condominium.

McCain's friends returned with Dr. Grindley and attempted to assist her. Warner, a surgical assistant, had gotten her box of medical supplies and removed McCain's pant-leg with a pair of bandage scissors. At that time Dr. Grindley informed them that he was a physician. Dr. Grindley examined the wound and advised all present that while technically he could repair the wound, he had no desire to do so without being able to "debride it and clean it."

At deposition Dr. Grindley testified he then offered to drive McCain and her friends to the nearest hospital in Ashton, Idaho. They refused his offer and informed Dr. Grindley that they believed there was a doctor staying in town who could help them, and that if they needed Dr. Grindley's services later, they would contact him.

Dr. Grindley further testified that at that time the wound may have "been bleeding a tiny bit * * * and that her panty hose seemed to be holding the tissues all in good position so that it was minimizing any bleeding." McCain testified that at that time she had little pain and the leg was "dead, numb, dead." After taking McCain back to Warner's condominium, and some three hours after the accident, Warner was able to locate where Dr. John Batson (Batson) was staying. Dr. Batson got up out of bed, left the condominium where he was staying, and agreed to come to the Warner condominium to see what could be done. Dr. Batson testified that McCain was lying on a couch and that when he examined the wound, he could see considerable dirt and mud in the wound. With the help of Warner and her surgical kit, which contained instruments, suture, IV solutions, and other items that could be used to clean the wound, Dr. Batson debrided the wound as best he could. He then loosely sutured the wound and dressed it with bandages from the medical kit. All of this was done under the light of a lamp in the Warner condominium.

Dr. Grindley testified at deposition that he informed all three women soon after the accident that the wound had to be treated at a hospital and under a general anesthesia, and that the wound needed to be treated surgically. Dr. Batson's evaluation of the injury mirrored Dr. Grindley's, that this was not an emergency situation, but that McCain should go to a hospital as soon as possible. Dr. Batson informed the women that he would call the hospital in Ashton, Idaho, and order pain and antibiotic medication and a tetanus shot to be available to McCain the next morning.

It should be noted that the reason McCain did not immediately go to a hospital was that the ambulance at West Yellowstone was not available, as it had taken someone to Bozeman, Montana, just before she was injured and would not return until the next morning. As previously noted, the truck used by the parties to travel to West Yellowstone had a dead battery but would be repaired by the next morning. As the hour was very late, the three spent the rest of the night at the Warner condominium and planned on returning to Ogden later that morning/early afternoon via Ashton, Idaho.

Dr. Batson testified that later that morning, about 11:00 a.m., he returned to check on the three women. He found them still packing and preparing to return to Ogden. Dr. Batson said he advised them again that his suturing of the wound was a first-aid type procedure and it was necessary that they go to a hospital and have the wound properly treated.

According to the deposition of Checketts, they did stop at the Ashton, Idaho, hospital where they got some pain medication and antibiotics which served as treatment until McCain returned to Ogden. They then drove on into Ogden, arriving at approximately 7:00 p.m., and took McCain to her apartment, where it was their understanding that McCain would go to the hospital and see a doctor the next morning. However, McCain did not go to the hospital or see a doctor until about one week later. By this time her wound had become infected and required considerable surgery and medical treatment.

On September 25, 1985, three years to the date of the injury, Dr. Batson was sued by McCain for suturing the wound without adequate debriding or cleansing of the contaminated wound, and for failing to inform anyone that the procedures that he followed were not final procedures. In other words, McCain claims he failed to inform her that the wound would have to be opened up, recleansed, debrided, and resutured. McCain alleges that this is a case of malpractice which has caused her serious injury.

This case was presented to the district court on depositions * * *. Based on the information contained in the depositions, the district court granted Dr. Batson's motion for summary judgment. Attached to said summary judgment was a memorandum of Judge Joseph Gary concerning the reasons for his granting of summary judgment.

* * * Did the district court improperly find that the provisions of the Montana Good Samaritan Statute,[17] Mont.Code Ann. § 27–1–714, were applicable to an instance where the negligent care rendered was remote in time and location to the scene of the accident or emergency, and was otherwise without the purpose of the act?

[T]he Montana Good Samaritan Statute * * * reads:

(1) Any person licensed as a physician and surgeon under the laws of the state of Montana, any volunteer firefighter or officer of any nonprofit volunteer fire company, or any other person who in good faith renders emergency care or assistance without compensation * * * at the scene of an emergency or accident is not liable for any civil damages for acts or omissions other than damages occasioned by gross negligence or by willful or wanton acts or omissions by such person in rendering such emergency care or assistance.

[A] physician must demonstrate that he is a member of a protected class. Dr. Batson was not a licensed physician in the state of Montana, although he is licensed to practice in Wyoming and Idaho. [H]e is, therefore, "any person" within the meaning of the statute. While she agrees with the fact that the doctor here is protected under the act, McCain alleges that immunity only attaches to malpractice which is committed at the scene of the accident or emergency.

She argues that after falling into the excavation pit, McCain crawled to Dr. Grindley's condominium and she was later carried to Warner's condominium. Therefore Dr. Batson's care, such as it was, was too remote in time and location to the scene of the accident. She alleges that with this result, Dr. Batson could not demonstrate that this was an "emergency" situation. McCain further argues that Dr. Batson's negligent care was performed when he made a "housecall" and he did not happen upon an emergency. McCain argues that because Dr. Batson's negligent care was not during an emergency situation, though her injuries were serious, they were not life-threatening, and therefore the best course of action would have been to postpone care until she reached a hospital.

* * * The central question presented to the district court, and one which is subject to our review, is whether the Good Samaritan Statute applies. We find, as the district court did, that it does. Thus, the standard of review is gross negligence and willful or wanton acts or omissions, rather than ordinary negligence—medical malpractice. We agree with the district court's finding that after reviewing all of the deposition testimony, there is no evidence whatsoever that there was such a serious level of negligence exhibited by Dr. Batson to warrant any action in this case.

* * * Dr. Grindley * * * did not and could not testify that Dr. Batson was guilty of gross negligence or willful or wanton acts or omissions. * * *

---

17. Editors' Note: See Annot., Construction and Application of "Good Samaritan" Statutes, 68 A.L.R.4th 294 (1989), superseding 39 A.L.R.3d 222 (1971).

* * * While this court generally prefers a trial on the merits of a case to dismissal by summary judgment, we affirm the district court in its findings. We are willing to look at the facts presented and not force a defendant to go through a prolonged, expensive and emotionally debilitating trial for such well intended and medically accepted deeds as Dr. Batson performed at West Yellowstone, Montana. The relevant and material facts point to this conclusion and the ultimate question is a matter of law. We further agree with the district court in this case that Dr. Batson was a good samaritan, that he acted in an emergency, and since there has been no showing of gross negligence, the decision of the district court to grant summary judgment is affirmed.

SHEEHY, JUSTICE, dissenting.

The recent penchant of this court to approve summary judgments from the district court where genuine issues of material fact exist is shown again in this case. There are two genuine issues of material fact presented here: (1) whether an emergency existed requiring, as a good samaritan, the assistance of Dr. Batson; and (2) if the answer to the first query is affirmative, whether Batson was guilty of gross negligence; and if the answer is no to the first query, whether he was guilty of ordinary negligence.

* * *

The plaintiff has lost this appeal because the facts are not appealing. The district court expressed the problem:

> The court would admit to some problems of keeping an impartial perspective in this case, but is satisfied, when all is said and done, that this is a fair decision based on thorough research, sufficient facts, and clear rules of law. Nonetheless, the court cannot help but wonder where our society is taking itself by bringing cases like this to the courtroom. We may be well on our way to making an endangered species out of good samaritans who are forced to stifle their good impulses out of fear of being taken to court. If this is the trend, it is indeed unfortunate.

The other side of that coin is that if Karen McCain has sustained serious and permanent damages to her leg because Dr. Batson, instead of rendering aid sufficient for the moment, in effect, "overtreated" her, she is entitled to have her case heard in court, even though Dr. Batson acted from the best of impulses.

The first issue here was whether an emergency existed at the time of Dr. Batson's treatment. The district court balanced those issues of fact and decided that an emergency existed. In doing so, it determined a question of fact, an improper procedure where summary judgment is concerned.

First, the district court ticked off the facts which contended for no emergency: There was no major blood loss; her life was not in danger and she was not going to die; she would not lose the limb; the leg had a numb sensation and there was an absence of pain immediately following the injury; and she was neurologically intact. Opposing that, said the court, was that the witnesses agreed the cut was extremely serious, possibly bone deep; there was no hospital in town; the Ashton hospital had no anesthesia facilities; there was no available ambulance; no police officer or other friends to provide transportation to a hospital; and reason to believe the "limb was at risk." Not mentioned by the District Court was the testimony of Dr. Grindley that a simple dressing would suffice under the circumstances, and that suturing the wound presented a case of final repair.

* * *

The second issue of fact was whether the attendance by the doctor in this case constituted either ordinary or gross negligence. The majority, without defining gross negligence in this instance, has determined that there was no gross negligence on the part of the defendant doctor. None of the witnesses defined what was meant by gross negligence. The only definition on which this court relies is the following:

> Q. Well, in your opinion, if this was a temporary suturing job by Dr. Batson, did that, in your opinion, constitute gross negligence, gross malpractice?
>
> A. Well, you see you really haven't told me what gross malpractice is yet or gross negligence.
>
> Q. Well, it's a heck of a lot worse than ordinary malpractice.

If any district court in Montana had given a jury an instruction that so defined gross negligence, we would in high dudgeon reject it as inadequate. Here, the majority, without otherwise defining gross negligence as it applies under the Good Samaritan statute, undertakes no other definition to resolve the fact issue of gross negligence.

We might entertain in ourselves a serious doubt that the plaintiff would prevail if she had been permitted to take her case to a jury to resolve the fact issues. Our personal feelings about the propriety of a case have no place in deciding questions on summary judgment. If issues of fact exist, * * * there is no discretion, in our court or in the district court, to grant summary judgment.

I would reverse and remand for further proceedings.

KEARNS v. SUPERIOR COURT

California Court of Appeal, 1988; review denied.
204 Cal.App.3d 1325, 252 Cal.Rptr. 4.

By the court. * * *

In November 1984, Malverse Martin, M.D., a codefendant in this action but not a party to this writ proceeding, performed surgery upon plaintiff Nanette Von Rader to remove a malignant ovarian tumor. During surgery, Dr. Martin determined he could not remove the tumor without additional assistance and requested the assistance of Dr. Walter Kearns in order to complete the surgery. It is undisputed that Dr. Kearns had never treated, diagnosed, consulted, or in any manner participated in the treatment and care of plaintiff prior to the request to render intraoperative assistance. Sometime during the surgery, the malignant contents of the tumor spilled into plaintiff's abdomen, seeding the abdomen with cancer cells.

Plaintiff then filed this medical malpractice action, naming Dr. Kearns as one of the defendants. By means of a motion for summary judgment and/or summary adjudication of issues, Dr. Kearns sought the protection of the Good Samaritan law codified in Business and Professions Code §§ 2395 and 2396.[18]

Section 2395 provides:

No licensee,[19] who in good faith renders emergency care at the scene of an emergency, shall be liable for any civil damages as a result of any acts or omissions by such person in rendering the emergency care.

* * *

Section 2396 provides:

No licensee, who in good faith upon the request of another person so licensed, renders emergency medical care to a person for medical complication arising from prior care by another person so licensed, shall be liable for any civil damages as a result of any acts or omissions by such licensed person in rendering such emergency medical care.[20]

The legislative purpose underlying both sections is to induce physicians to render medical assistance to persons in need of such care. Colby v. Schwartz, 78 Cal.App.3d 885, 144 Cal.Rptr. 624, 628 (1978). The legislative purpose is best effectuated by discouraging even the commencement of an action against a health care professional who has rendered emergency medical assistance. Ibid.

The Good Samaritan legislation is "directed towards physicians who, by chance and on an irregular basis, * * * are called to render emergency medical care." Ibid. An emergency exists "where the exigency is of so pressing a character that some kind of action must be taken * * *." Newhouse v. Board of Osteopathic Exam'rs, 159 Cal. App.2d 728, 324 P.2d 687, 692 (1958).

* * *

The test for determination of the existence of an emergency is objective: Whether the undisputed facts establish the existence of an exigency of "so pressing a character that some kind of action must be taken." A "stat" call is not required to identify an emergency occurring in a hospital, and is not a condition precedent for determination as to whether an emergency exists within the meaning of the Good Samaritan statutes.

18. Editors' Note: The superior court denied Dr. Kearns's motion. In California practice, this action in the court of appeal works like an interlocutory appeal.

19. Editors' Note: I.e., a holder of a license to practice medicine and surgery under § 2050.

20. Editors' Note: Both of these statutes were enacted by Stats.1980, ch. 1313, § 2. For an account of earlier California Good Samaritan legislation, see Colby v. Schwartz, 78 Cal.App.3d 885, 144 Cal.Rptr. 624 (1978).

In McKenna v. Cedars of Lebanon Hosp., 93 Cal.App.3d 282, 155 Cal.Rptr. 631 (1979), the court found that the Good Samaritan law is not limited as to the situs of an emergency, and applied the law to emergency situations arising in hospitals. 155 Cal.Rptr. at 634. The immunity offered by §§ 2395 and 2396 applies regardless of where the emergency occurs, including the surgical department of a hospital.

* * *

Because it is conceded that Dr. Kearns merely happened to be in the hospital treating his own patients and had no duty of professional care to plaintiff pre-existing the request for intraoperative assistance, Dr. Kearns had no legal duty to respond to the call for emergency surgical assistance. Clearly, under the circumstances present here, Dr. Kearns was "a medical volunteer, called to the scene of an emergency," who rendered emergency medical care to plaintiff in good faith "upon the request of another person so licensed," § 2396, at the place where the emergency occurred. § 2395.

The facts here are remarkably similar to those in Burciaga v. St. John's Hosp., 187 Cal.App.3d 710, 232 Cal.Rptr. 75 (1986), in which the court held that a staff physician who provided emergency hospital medical care within his specialty was entitled to the protection of the Good Samaritan law. 232 Cal.Rptr. at 77. Absent a duty of professional care pre-existing the emergency, the Good Samaritan law is applicable to protect a physician who renders emergency assistance in a hospital to the patient of another doctor. 232 Cal.Rptr. at 78. "The heart of the application of the Good Samaritan statutes is the inquiry whether a duty of professional care pre-existed the emergency." Ibid. The events described here fall squarely within the holding of *Burciaga*.

* * *

We conclude that the Good Samaritan statutes, which provide immunity for any acts or omissions of a medical volunteer who in good faith renders emergency medical assistance, are applicable under the circumstances present here.

* * *

Let a peremptory writ issue directing the respondent court to vacate its order denying Dr. Kearns's motion for summary judgment and/or summary adjudication of issues, and to enter instead an order in accord with the views expressed herein.

SECTION B. AFFIRMATIVE DEFENSES

WEIL v. SELTZER

United States Court of Appeals for the District of Columbia Circuit, 1989.
873 F.2d 1453.

FLOYD R. GIBSON, SENIOR CIRCUIT JUDGE.[21]

This is an appeal from a final judgment entered on a jury's verdict in a survival and wrongful death action. This case is now before us after two successive trials. The first trial resulted in a verdict for the defendant, Dr. Alvin Seltzer; however, the district court set aside the verdict and ordered a new trial * * *. On retrial before a different judge, the jury returned a verdict in favor of the plaintiff, Martin Weil.[22] The jury awarded $1,080,000 under the wrongful death claim and $3,000,000 under the survival act claim. * * *

On March 27, 1984, Martin Weil died unexpectedly at the age of 54 years. Weil's treating physicians could not explain the cause of his death nor could they account for a series of recent medical problems which he suffered from prior to his death.[23] An autopsy was performed in order to determine the cause of Weil's death. The autopsy and a subsequent investigation into the treatment that Weil received from his allergist, Dr. Seltzer, were very revealing.

Dr. Seltzer had treated Weil for more than 20 years, and over the course of this treatment Dr. Seltzer regularly prescribed medication which Weil was led to believe were antihistamines. After Weil's death, however, it was determined that Dr. Seltzer had been prescribing a drug called prednisone, which is a steroid. Suddenly, Weil's treating physicians were able to explain his bizarre medical problems that predominated the last ten years of his life. It became apparent that Weil's illnesses were attributable to his long-term ingestion of steroids prescribed by Dr. Seltzer.

The autopsy, which was consistent with long-term steroid use, determined that Weil's cause of death was a saddle block embolus (a type of blood clot), which contained several bone marrow fragments. The autopsy also revealed significant atrophy in Weil's adrenal glands and severe osteoporosis.

Medical experts testified that Weil's osteoporosis, which was linked to his steroid use, may have caused his bones to crumble, thus explain-

---

21. Of the U.S. Court of Appeals for the Eighth Circuit, sitting by designation pursuant to 28 U.S.C.A. § 294(d).

22. Editors' Note: The parties' names have been substituted throughout for other equivalents.

23. During the ten years leading up to his death, Weil suffered from: severe flu-like symptoms; cysts on his face, neck, and eye lids; a broken hip; a fractured knee; general osteoporosis; a life-threatening drop in blood pressure; an abscess in his groin; pain associated with the collapse of his vertebrae; and a severe infection in his left hand. Many of these illnesses were unusual for a man of Weil's age. Medical experts called to testify on behalf of Weil's estate linked many of these problems to long-term use of steroids.

ing the presence of bone marrow fragments in the fatal blood clot. Long-term steroid use also may have been the cause of the atrophy in Weil's adrenal glands. This condition reduces the body's ability to ward off infection.

Weil's estate filed suit against Dr. Seltzer and began discovery. Through its discovery efforts, Weil's estate learned that Dr. Seltzer prescribed steroids to Weil on his first visit in 1963 and continued to prescribe steroids over a period of more than twenty years. Indeed, Dr. Seltzer had prescribed steroids just eight days before Weil's death and on at least three other occasions during the three months immediately preceding Weil's death.

The most startling fact revealed in the discovery was the frequency with which Dr. Seltzer prescribed steroids to his patients. Dr. Seltzer's purchase orders for medication during the years 1980 thru 1984, which were produced during discovery, revealed that he purchased 10,000 tablets of the steroidal drugs. Weil's estate then contacted three of the drug companies named in the purchase orders and learned that Dr. Seltzer had purchased more than 1.7 million tablets containing steroids during the 1980–1984 period alone. Weil's estate then contacted eight of Dr. Seltzer's former patients and learned that each had been treated by Dr. Seltzer for many years, and they were prescribed pills which Dr. Seltzer represented to be antihistamines and decongestants. All of the patients later learned that the pills prescribed by Dr. Seltzer were in fact steroids. Finally, a number of boxes and bottles labeled with the names of antihistamines and other non-steroidal medications were found in the possession of Dr. Seltzer, Weil, and several of Dr. Seltzer's former patients. These boxes and bottles were mislabeled because they actually contained cortisone, another type of steroid.

* * *

The first issue raised in this appeal is whether the district court, in the initial trial, erred in granting the motion for a new trial * * * because it was persuaded that the contributory negligence instruction submitted to the jury was improper and resulted in prejudice.

* * *

The doctrine of contributory negligence operates as a defense under District of Columbia law when a party knows or by the exercise of ordinary care should have known a particular fact or circumstance and should have acted upon the fact or circumstance with reasonable care for his own safety. * * * We do not believe that the district court erred in ordering a new trial based on the submission of the contributory negligence instruction, because there were insufficient facts to support it. It does not appear to be proper to charge Weil in this case with contributory negligence when he was merely following his doctor's orders.

In Morrison v. MacNamara, 407 A.2d 555 (D.C.1979), the District of Columbia Court of Appeals noted:

>In the context of medical malpractice, the superior knowledge of the doctor with his expertise in medical matters and the generally limited ability of the patient to ascertain the existence of certain risks and dangers that inhere in certain medical treatments, negates the critical elements of the defense, i.e., knowledge and appreciation of the risk. Thus, save for exceptional circumstances, a patient cannot assume the risk of negligent treatment. Id. at 567.

While the court in *Morrison* was specifically addressing the defense of assumption of the risk, the court noted that these same principles would apply to the defense of contributory negligence in medical malpractice. Id. at 568 n. 11.

Thus, in order to submit the contributory negligence instruction, the evidence must show that Weil knew or should have known that he was taking steroids and he should have exercised reasonable care for his own safety by informing his other treating physicians accordingly. The evidence, however, clearly indicated that Weil believed that the medications prescribed by Dr. Seltzer were antihistamines rather than steroids. In fact, the evidence suggesting that Dr. Seltzer mislabeled the steroids to conceal their identity flies in the face of Dr. Seltzer's argument that Weil knew he was taking steroids.

* * *

Dr. Seltzer also contends that Weil was contributorily negligent because he should have found out what drugs he was given by Dr. Seltzer. In Stager v. Schneider, 494 A.2d 1307 (D.C.1985), however, it was held that a patient did not have a duty to call her doctor to get the results of X-rays which indicated a shadow on her lung. In *Stager* the court noted that although a patient has a duty to cooperate with her doctor,

>It is a quantum leap * * * [from requiring cooperation] to permitting a duty to be placed on a patient * * *. To do so would be, in reality, to invert the duty by transferring it from the health professional to the patient. Id. at 1312.

Stager thus places the duty to communicate information to the patient squarely on the shoulders of the physician.

* * *

Finally, we note that at the first trial the jury was instructed on both the defenses of contributory negligence and assumption of the risk. The district court, however, only discussed the propriety of the contributory negligence instruction in its order granting a new trial. Nevertheless, we note that since the contributory negligence instruction was not supported by sufficient evidence, then the same would be true of the assumption of the risk instruction. This necessarily follows because contributory negligence is determined by an objective standard (knew or should have known), whereas assumption of the risk requires evidence of a subjective nature (actually knew). * * * All of the evidence relating to Weil's actual knowledge indicated that he believed he was taking antihistamines.

In the instant case there was barely evidence presented establishing that Weil knew he was taking steroids, let alone that he knew the magnitude of the harm long-term steroidal use might cause. Thus, in the absence of evidence reflecting that Weil knew of the danger of prolonged steroid use and voluntarily accepted the risks, the assumption of risk instruction would be improper. Id. at 568. Finally, we note that the defense of assumption of the risk "has rarely been sustained in actions involving professional negligence." Id. at 567.

[T]here was no error committed by the district court in its decision not to submit the contributory negligence and assumption of the risk defenses to the jury in the second trial.

Dr. Seltzer also argues that the district court, in the second trial, erred in refusing to instruct the jury on the defense of intervening cause. Dr. Seltzer's theory underlying the requested instruction is based on the diagnosis of Weil's treating physicians made in 1977 which revealed that Weil had osteoporosis. Dr. Seltzer argues that Weil's treating physicians were negligent in not determining that his osteoporosis was caused by ingestion of steroids. The negligence of Weil's treating physicians is an intervening negligent act that insulates Dr. Seltzer from liability, Dr. Seltzer argues. * * *

We believe that the district court properly refused to submit the question of intervening cause to the jury. It was not shown that Weil knew he was taking steroids; in light of that it is easy to see why he never advised his other treating physicians that he took steroids. The physicians who treated him subsequent to Dr. Seltzer were at a great disadvantage in diagnosing Weil's deteriorating condition. There was no evidence advanced by Dr. Seltzer that Weil's physicians were in any way negligent in their dealings with Weil. Quite the contrary, it appears from the trial record that Weil was unable to tell his various physicians (all of whom asked) that he was on steroids, since Dr. Seltzer only arguably told him on only one occasion, in over twenty years of treatment, that he was receiving steroids. That one occasion is the one referred to in Dr. Seltzer's ambiguous answer to interrogatory number seven. Finally, there was no evidence that the other physicians' failure to test for steroid use, when the patient denied taking steroids, was below the standard of reasonable medical care.

* * *

[W]e reverse the district court's decision in the second trial which allowed the testimony of five of Dr. Seltzer's former patients, as it was improperly admitted as evidence of habit under Rule 406. However, we recognize that this type of testimony may be admissible and of probative value under Rule 404(b) [evidence of other wrongs or acts]. * * *

Accordingly, we vacate the judgment and remand this case to the district court for a new trial.

RAY v. WAGNER

Supreme Court of Minnesota, 1970.
286 Minn. 354, 176 N.W.2d 101, 49 A.L.R.3d 497.[24]

OTIS, JUSTICE. * * *

The plaintiff, Mrs. Mary L. Ray, first visited Dr. Robert M. Wagner on August 6, 1962, after selecting him from a telephone directory. She was examined for the purpose of obtaining a contraceptive device. As a routine matter, the doctor secured from her a so-called Pap smear to determine whether or not there was any possibility she was suffering from carcinoma of the cervix. The smear was sent to a laboratory at Northwestern Hospital and was returned within about two weeks with a report that it was "suspicious for malignancy." The doctor attempted to reach Mrs. Ray by telephone on numerous occasions to advise her of the report and to recommend further procedures. He was unsuccessful until January 1963 when she paid the bill for her medical services.

In February, Mrs. Ray was given another Pap smear test, which again was "suspicious for malignancy." The Pathology Department of the University of Minnesota Hospitals thereupon performed a biopsy which revealed an "in situ" carcinoma of the cervix about one millimeter in size. The hospital's gynecology department, however, diagnosed the carcinoma as "early invasive." As a result, Mrs. Ray underwent a series of treatments with cobalt and radium therapy which destroyed her ovaries, rendered her sterile, and precipitated symptoms of menopause.

The action was litigated on the theory that the doctor was negligent in failing to notify his patient promptly of her condition, and that as a result of her failure to undergo corrective therapy, her condition worsened to a point where drastic treatment was required to prevent further progression of the disease.

The case was submitted to the jury on the question of ordinary negligence as well as on the standard of care required of a physician. The issue of contributory negligence was also submitted. After the jury had deliberated for a time, they returned for additional instructions with respect to contributory negligence. That charge was repeated by the court in the presence of counsel.

[The jury rendered a general verdict for Dr. Wagner, and the trial judge entered an order denying Mrs. Ray's motion for a new trial.]

* * * Since the trial court seems to have felt that the decision turned on contributory negligence, it is appropriate to review the evidence bearing on that issue.

Mrs. Ray married one Jhangiani, a University student, on June 30, 1962, and moved from an apartment at 240 University Village to one at

---

24. Annot., Malpractice: Failure of Physician to Notify Patient of Unfavorable Diagnosis or Test, 49 A.L.R.3d 50 (1973).

1947 Lake St. in St. Paul. Her children by a previous marriage remained with her mother at her former address. She lived at the Lake Street residence for only a month after her examination and on September 15, 1962, moved to 1508 East 19th St. in Minneapolis. She was there until June 1963, during which time she had no telephone. Mrs. Ray represented to Dr. Wagner that she and her husband both worked at the University, she as a secretary and her husband as an accountant. The doctor testified that he tried to reach Mrs. Ray through the University, identifying her as a secretary and her husband as an accountant, but that he was unsuccessful. Mrs. Ray admitted that she was not a secretary but worked in a different capacity in the Mayo Memorial Building. Her husband actually was an accountant but was unemployed. The doctor further testified that he attempted several times to reach plaintiff at her Lake Street address without success until December, when he finally spoke to her mother and asked that Mrs. Ray call his office. Mrs. Ray testified that she gave the doctor's office her change of address and argues that she could have been reached at any time by mail.

While it seems clear that defendant had a duty to take whatever steps were reasonable to notify plaintiff of the results of the test she took in August, it was for the jury to decide whether the failure to reach plaintiff was the result of negligence on the part of the doctor, and, if so, whether such negligence proximately caused the condition which resulted from her ultimate treatment. * * * [I]t was [also] their prerogative to find that Mrs. Ray did not, in fact, advise the doctor of her change of address, nor did she apprise the receptionist of the urgency for keeping the doctor informed of her whereabouts. Ordinarily, a patient can rely on a doctor's informing her if the results of a test are positive. Here, however, plaintiff gave the doctor somewhat misleading information as to her status, she had no phone at the address where she lived, and she did not live at the address where she had a phone. We cannot say as a matter of law that under all the circumstances the evidence does not support a finding of contributory negligence.

Accordingly, the order is affirmed.

UNITED STATES v. KUBRICK

Supreme Court of the United States, 1979.
444 U.S. 111, 100 S.Ct. 352, 62 L.Ed.2d 259.

MR. JUSTICE WHITE delivered the opinion of the Court. * * *

Respondent William Kubrick, a veteran, was admitted to the Veterans' Administration (VA) hospital in Wilkes–Barre, Pa., in April 1968, for treatment of an infection of the right femur. Following surgery, the infected area was irrigated with neomycin, an antibiotic, until the infection cleared. Approximately six weeks after discharge, Kubrick noticed a ringing sensation in his ears and some loss of hearing. An ear specialist in Scranton, Pa., Dr. Soma, diagnosed the condition as bilateral nerve deafness. His diagnosis was confirmed by other specialists. One of them, Dr. Sataloff, secured Kubrick's VA hospital records and in January 1969 informed Kubrick that it was highly possible that the hearing loss was the result of the neomycin treatment administered at the hospital. Kubrick, who was already receiving disability benefits for a service-connected back injury, filed an application for an increase in benefits pursuant to 38 U.S.C.A. § 351, alleging that the neomycin treatment had caused his deafness. The VA denied the claim in September 1969, and on resubmission again denied the claim, on the grounds that no causal relationship existed between the neomycin treatment and the hearing loss, and that there was no evidence of "carelessness, accident, negligence, lack of proper skill, error in judgment or other fault on the part of the Government."

In the course of pursuing his administrative appeal, Kubrick was informed by the VA that Dr. Soma had suggested a connection between Kubrick's loss of hearing and his prior occupation as a machinist. When questioned by Kubrick on June 2, 1971, Dr. Soma not only denied making the statement attributed to him but also told respondent that the neomycin had caused his injury and should not have been administered. On Dr. Sataloff's advice, respondent then consulted an attorney and employed him to help with his appeal. In rendering its decision in August 1972, the VA Board of Appeals recognized that Kubrick's hearing loss "may have been caused by the neomycin irrigation," but rejected the appeal on the ground that the treatment was in accordance with acceptable medical practices and procedures and that the Government was therefore faultless.[25]

Kubrick then filed suit under the Federal Tort Claims Act, alleging that he had been injured by negligent treatment in the VA hospital. After trial, the district court rendered judgment for Kubrick, rejecting, among other defenses, the assertion by the United States that Kubrick's claim was barred by the two-year statute of limitations because the claim had accrued in January 1969, when he learned from Dr. Sataloff that his hearing loss had probably resulted from the neomycin. * * * 435 F.Supp. 166 (E.D.Pa.1977). * * *

Except for remanding to resolve a setoff claimed by the United States, the Court of Appeals for the Third Circuit affirmed. 581 F.2d 1092 (1978). * * *

Statutes of limitations, which "are found and approved in all systems of enlightened jurisprudence," Wood v. Carpenter, 101 U.S. 135, 139, 25 L.Ed. 807 (1879), represent a pervasive legislative judgment that it is unjust to fail to put the adversary on notice to defend within a specified period of time and that "the right to be free of stale claims in time comes to prevail over the right to prosecute them." Railroad

---

25. In 1975, upon reconsideration of its decision, the VA Board of Appeals not only found, as it had before, that Kubrick's hearing loss may have been caused by neomycin irrigation, but also concluded that there was fault on the part of the VA in administering that drug by irrigation. In the present litigation, the Government contested the allegation of malpractice despite the administrative finding of fault.

Telegraphers v. Railway Express Agency, 321 U.S. 342, 349, 64 S.Ct. 582, 88 L.Ed. 788 (1944). These enactments are statutes of repose; and although affording plaintiffs what the legislature deems a reasonable time to present their claims, they protect defendants and the courts from having to deal with cases in which the search for truth may be seriously impaired by the loss of evidence, whether by death or disappearance of witnesses, fading memories, disappearance of documents, or otherwise. * * *

Section 2401(b), the limitations provision involved here, is the balance struck by Congress in the context of tort claims against the Government; and we are not free to construe it so as to defeat its obvious purpose, which is to encourage the prompt presentation of claims. * * *

We should also have in mind that the Act waives the immunity of the United States and that in construing the statute of limitations, which is a condition of that waiver, we should not take it upon ourselves to extend the waiver beyond that which Congress intended. * * *

It is undisputed in this case that in January 1969 Kubrick was aware of his injury and its probable cause. Despite this factual predicate for a claim against the VA at that time, the court of appeals held that Kubrick's claim had not yet accrued and did not accrue until he knew or could reasonably be expected to know that in the eyes of the law, the neomycin treatment constituted medical malpractice. * * * In this case, for example, Kubrick would have been free to sue if Dr. Soma had not told him until 1975, or even 1980, instead of 1971, that the neomycin treatment had been a negligent act.

There is nothing in the language or the legislative history of the Act that provides a substantial basis for the court of appeals' construction of the accrual language of § 2401(b). Nor did the prevailing case law at the time the Act was passed lend support for the notion that tort claims in general or malpractice claims in particular do not accrue until a plaintiff learns that his injury was negligently inflicted. Indeed, the court of appeals recognized that the general rule under the Act has been that a tort claim accrues at the time of the plaintiff's injury, although it thought that in medical malpractice cases the rule had come to be that the two-year period did not begin to run until the plaintiff has discovered both his injury and its cause.[26] But even so—

---

26. * * * Restatement (Second) of Torts § 899, Comment e at 444–445 (1979), reflects these developments:

> One group of cases in which there has been extensive departure from the earlier rule that the statute of limitations runs although the plaintiff has no knowledge of the injury has involved actions for medical malpractice. Two reasons can be suggested as to why there has been a change in the rule in many jurisdictions in this area. One is the fact that in most instances the statutory period within which the action must be initiated is short—one year, or at most two, being the common time limit. This is for the purpose of protecting physicians against unjustified claims; but since many of the consequences of medical malpractice often do not become known or apparent for a period longer than that of the statute, the injured plaintiff is left

and the United States was prepared to concede as much for present purposes—the latter rule would not save Kubrick's action, since he was aware of these essential facts in January 1969. Reasoning, however, that if a claim does not accrue until a plaintiff is aware of his injury and its cause, neither should it accrue until he knows or should suspect that the doctor who caused his injury was legally blameworthy, the court of appeals went on to hold that the limitations period was not triggered until Dr. Soma indicated in June 1971 that the neomycin irrigation treatment had been improper.

We disagree. We are unconvinced that for statute of limitations purposes a plaintiff's ignorance of his legal rights and his ignorance of the fact of his injury or its cause should receive identical treatment. That he has been injured in fact may be unknown or unknowable until the injury manifests itself; and the facts about causation may be in the control of the putative defendant, unavailable to the plaintiff or at least very difficult to obtain. The prospect is not so bleak for a plaintiff in possession of the critical facts that he has been hurt and who has inflicted the injury. He is no longer at the mercy of the latter. There are others who can tell him if he has been wronged, and he need only ask. If he does ask and if the defendant has failed to live up to minimum standards of medical proficiency, the odds are that a competent doctor will so inform the plaintiff.

In this case, the trial court found, and the United States did not appeal its finding, that the treating physician at the VA hospital had failed to observe the standard of care governing doctors of his specialty in Wilkes–Barre, Pa., and that reasonably competent doctors in this branch of medicine would have known that Kubrick should not have been treated with neomycin. Crediting this finding, as we must, Kubrick need only have made inquiry among doctors with average training and experience in such matters to have discovered that he probably had a good cause of action. The difficulty is that it does not appear that Kubrick ever made any inquiry, although meanwhile he had consulted several specialists about his loss of hearing and had been in possession of all the facts about the cause of his injury since January 1969. Furthermore, there is no reason to doubt that Dr. Soma, who in 1971 volunteered his opinion that Kubrick's treatment had been im-

without a remedy. The second reason is that the nature of the tort itself and the character of the injury will frequently prevent knowledge of what is wrong, so that the plaintiff is forced to rely upon what he is told by the physician or surgeon.

There are still courts that proceed to apply the rule that the action is barred by the statute even though there has been no knowledge that it could be brought. * * *

In a wave of recent decisions these various devices have been replaced by decisions meeting the issue directly and holding that the statute must be construed as not intended to start to run until the plaintiff has in fact discovered the fact that he has suffered injury or by the exercise of reasonable diligence should have discovered it. There have also been a number of instances in which a similar rule has been applied to other professional malpractice, such as that of attorneys or accountants and the rule may thus become a general one.

proper, would have had the same opinion had the plaintiff sought his judgment in 1969.

We thus cannot hold that Congress intended that "accrual" of a claim must await awareness by the plaintiff that his injury was negligently inflicted. * * *

* * * We doubt that here we have misconceived the intent of Congress when § 2401(b) was first adopted or when it was amended to extend the limitations period to two years. But if we have, or even if we have not but Congress desires a different result, it may exercise its prerogative to amend the statute so as to effect its legislative will.

The judgment of the court of appeals is reversed.

Mr. Justice Stevens, with whom Mr. Justice Brennan and Mr. Justice Marshall join, dissenting.

Normally a tort claim accrues at the time of the plaintiff's injury. In most cases that event provides adequate notice to the plaintiff of the possibility that his legal rights have been invaded. It is well settled, however, that the normal rule does not apply to medical malpractice claims under the Federal Tort Claims Act. The reason for this exception is essentially the same as the reason for the general rule itself. The victim of medical malpractice frequently has no reason to believe that his legal rights have been invaded simply because some misfortune has followed medical treatment. Sometimes he may not even be aware of the actual injury until years have passed; at other times, he may recognize the harm but not know its cause; or, as in this case, he may have knowledge of the injury and its cause, but have no reason to suspect that a physician has been guilty of any malpractice. In such cases—until today—the rule that has been applied in the federal courts is that the statute of limitations does not begin to run until after fair notice of the invasion of the plaintiff's legal rights.

* * *

In my judgment, a fair application of this rule forecloses the Court's attempt to distinguish between a plaintiff's knowledge of the cause of his injury on the one hand and his knowledge of the doctor's failure to meet acceptable medical standards on the other. For in both situations the typical plaintiff will, and normally should, rely on his doctor's explanation of the situation.

* * *

MORGAN v. COHEN
Court of Appeals of Maryland, 1987.
309 Md. 304, 523 A.2d 1003.

Adkins, Judge.[27] * * *

On 20 July 1980, appellant Darlyn Morgan was riding as a passenger on a motorcycle operated by Frank Armetta when it overturned.

27. Editors' Note: The full opinion deals with the consolidated appeals of two slightly different cases. One appeal has been excised, and corresponding grammati-

She was taken to Franklin Square Hospital where she was treated by appellee, Dr. Edward R. Cohen, an orthopedic surgeon, for a comminuted fracture of the left femur. According to Morgan's affidavit filed in opposition to Dr. Cohen's motion for summary judgment, Dr. Cohen operated on Morgan's leg, at which time he implanted an intramedullary rod. Following surgery Dr. Cohen told Morgan that the operation had been successful and that she would be able to walk in three to six months. Morgan was not, however, able to put weight on the injured leg. Thereafter Dr. Cohen informed her that "a second operation would be necessary to heal [her] leg injury." He performed the second operation in March of 1982, again claiming success and telling Morgan not to worry about her leg as "everything would be fine."

In June of 1982 Morgan settled her claim against Armetta and in consequence thereof executed a "Release of All Claims." * * *

Approximately ten months later, Dr. Cohen informed Morgan that the operation had been unsuccessful and referred her to another physician who performed a third operation. The other physician was able to achieve union of the bone, enabling it to heal, but as a result of Dr. Cohen's negligent treatment, says the affidavit, Morgan's left leg is now two inches shorter than her right.

Morgan sued Dr. Cohen in the Circuit Court for Baltimore City. She sought to recover for harm caused by allegedly negligent treatment of the injuries she had suffered in the motor vehicle accident. The trial court granted summary judgment for Dr. Cohen * * * based solely on the release. * * *

Morgan urges us to give retrospective effect to Code, Art. 79, § 13 * * *.[28] She importunes us to adopt the "modern rule" now often applied to releases of the kind before us.[29] She claims that the harms inflicted by Dr. Cohen were separate from those inflicted by the original tortfeasor. She argues estoppel. Additionally, she asserts that the release is ambiguous, so that parol evidence is admissible to determine

---

cal changes have been made without indication.

28. Chapter 379, 1986 Md.Laws, effective 1 July 1986, added a new § 13 to art. 79. It provides:

A release executed by a person who has sustained personal injuries does not discharge a subsequent tort-feasor who is not a party to the release and:

(1) Whose responsibility for the injured person's injuries is unknown at the time of the execution of the release; or

(2) Who is not specifically identified in the release. * * *

29. At one time, the majority rule was that a release of the original tortfeasor barred an action against a subsequent negligently treating physician. See Trieschman v. Eaton, 224 Md. 111, 166 A.2d 892, 894 (1961) * * *. Since that time, many courts have adopted a "modern rule" which in general states that absent clear language to that effect, the physician is not released, as a matter of law, by release of the original tortfeasor. See * * * Annot., Release of One Responsible for Injury as Affecting Liability of Physician or Surgeon for Negligent Treatment of Injury, 39 A.L.R.3d 260, 264 (1971) [superseding 40 A.L.R.2d 1075 (1955)].

Editors' Note: On the release of the malpractice defendant first, see Annot., Release of One Negligently Treating Injury as Affecting Liability of One Originally Responsible for Injury, 64 A.L.R.3d 839 (1975) (two cases through mid-1989).

the intent of the parties. Because we view this last issue as dispositive, we need not and do not address the others. * * *

It is a general rule that a negligent actor is liable not only for harm that he directly causes, but also for any additional harm resulting from normal efforts of third persons in rendering aid, irrespective of whether such acts are done in a proper or a negligent manner. See Restatement (Second) of Torts § 457 (1964) * * *. The reasoning behind this rule is that the original tortfeasor by his actions places the plaintiff in a position of danger and should be held accountable for the risks inherent in treatment and rendering aid.

When a physician negligently treats the injuries, he also becomes liable to the plaintiff, but only for the additional harm caused by his negligence. See Restatement (Second) of Torts § 433A, comment c (1964); W. Prosser & P. Keeton, Law of Torts § 52 at 352 (5th ed. 1984). Courts in general have correctly characterized the negligent treatment as a subsequent tort for which the original tortfeasor is jointly liable. * * * This state of the law is conceptually clear enough, although it may produce difficult problems of proof because of the need of apportionment between the damages caused only by the negligent treatment and those caused by the original negligence. * * *

As Dean Prosser has noted, careless analysis and statutory change have led to the confusion of jointly liable concurrent or successive tortfeasors with true "joint tortfeasors" at common law. See Prosser, Joint Torts and Several Liability, 25 Calif.L.Rev. 413 (1937). * * *

* * * Prosser goes on to say:

> There is a genuine distinction between a satisfaction and a release. A satisfaction is an acceptance of full compensation for the injury; a release is a surrender of the cause of action, which might be gratuitous, or given for inadequate consideration. Releases at common law were under seal. A release to one of two tort-feasors who had acted in concert necessarily released the other, since there was but one cause of action, which was surrendered. But as to independent wrongdoers, not acting in concert, who were liable for the same loss, there seems to be no reason to conclude that a release of one would release the others, except in so far as it was based upon actual satisfaction of the claim.
>
> The American courts, doubtless because of the abolition of the seal, have rather hopelessly confused release with satisfaction. When, in turn, concurrent wrongdoers who have caused the same loss become "joint tort-feasors," the result is chaos. [T]here are a substantial number of jurisdictions which hold that a release of one of two concurrent tort-feasors will release the other, even though it contains an express stipulation that he is not to be released—and this without regard to the compensation actually received. Id. at 422–24.

* * *

The Maryland version of the Uniform Contribution Among Tortfeasors Act (the Act), codified as Md.Code, art. 50, §§ 16–24, * * * abrogated the common law rule that the release of one joint tortfeasor releases all.

In the case before us there are two torts. The first is the original negligence for which the original tortfeasor alone is liable. The second is the negligent treatment by the physician, for which the physician and the original tortfeasor are jointly and severally liable. In one sense, those torts may be considered concurrent wrongs—both concur in producing the additional harm. In another, they may be seen as successive. The wrongs were committed at different times and each one gives rise to a separate cause of action. If the Act applies here, however, that is, if we deem both the original tortfeasors and Dr. Cohen to be within its definition of joint tortfeasor, by the very terms of the statute, Dr. Cohen is not released. Thus, if the Act is applicable, those to be released must be determined by the scope of the release itself, a matter of bargaining and drafting, and not by a rule of law that operates in spite of what the release says.

If the Act does not apply, we hold that the release of the original wrongdoer does not, of itself, produce the legal result of releasing the injured person's claims against the subsequent negligently treating physician. * * * The parties to a release, absent legislative restriction, ordinarily are free to expand or contract the scope of the instrument in accordance with their agreement. They should not have to fear that a court will later rule that a release of the original tortfeasor also released the physician by operation of law. Compare Restatement (Second) of Torts § 885(1) (1979):

> A valid release of one tortfeasor from liability for harm, given by the injured person, does not discharge others liable for the same harm, unless it is agreed that it will discharge them.

with Restatement of Torts § 885(1) (1939):

> A valid release of one tortfeasor from liability for a harm, given by the injured person, discharges all others liable for the same harm, unless the parties to the release agree that the release shall not discharge the others * * *.

Although the release in question was broadly worded, it did not name Dr. Cohen. So far as the record reveals, he did not contribute to the amount paid in exchange for it. Indeed, he was probably unaware of its existence until after the claim had been asserted against him. Against this background, we must look at the specific language of the release, keeping in mind that the circumstances under which a contract is executed may be considered in deciding whether any of its terms are ambiguous. * * *

The Morgan document released Armetta (the original tortfeasor), his insurer

> and all other persons * * * of and from any and all claims, [and] damages which the undersigned now has * * * or which may hereafter accrue on account of or in any way growing out of any and all

known and unknown, foreseen and unforeseen bodily and personal injuries * * * and the consequences thereof, *resulting or to result from the accident*

of 20 July 1982. (Emphasis supplied.)

As a matter of syntax, one may argue that this release could be construed to extend to an unknown tortfeasor, such as Dr. Cohen, for injuries arising out of a separate but related tort. But a contrary reading is permissible. What are released are claims for injuries "resulting from" or "sustained * * * in consequence of" a specific accident caused by a specific original tortfeasor on a particular date. The damages claimed by Morgan were not so caused. Phrases like "in consequence of" and "resulting from" are not technical legal terms; they should be read in their ordinary and literal sense. * * * And they should be read in light of the circumstances that existed when the release was executed. So read, the release is ambiguous.

It is perfectly true that Dr. Cohen's alleged negligence followed, chronologically, the accident. It is also true that "but for" the accident, Morgan would not have been subjected to Dr. Cohen's ministrations. But in a very real sense the injuries purportedly inflicted by Dr. Cohen were not caused by the accident. They were caused by his asserted negligence and produced separate and additional harms for which, as we have seen, he could be held independently liable, assuming proper proof. They were in a factual way separate harms, as argued by Morgan, and this is so despite the fact that the original tortfeasor might also have been held liable for them.

In short, it is arguable that what followed from Dr. Cohen's treatment was the result or consequence of that treatment, and not of the original accident. Thus, although the release may be unambiguous as to the original tort, it is at the very least ambiguous as to the subsequent tort, and parol evidence is admissible on the issue of intent. * * * This * * * merely means that when those words in their ordinary sense under the circumstances are ambiguous, we may seek evidence of intent beyond the document. * * *

The conclusion that Morgan's release is ambiguous requires that the judgment against her in her case be reversed and that the case be remanded for further proceedings.

* * *

RODOWSKY, JUDGE, dissenting.

[I]f both tortfeasors were sued in one action, and the jury valued the bodily harm caused exclusively by the initial tort at $10,000, and valued the aggravation of that harm by medical treatment at $20,000, the original tortfeasor would be liable for $30,000 damages and the physician would be jointly and severally liable for $20,000 of that amount. Judgment would be entered against the original tortfeasor and the physician, jointly and severally, for $20,000, and against the original tortfeasor alone for $10,000.

Here the claims against the original tortfeasor and against the physician were asserted one after the other. That does not change the applicable law. It remains a matter of law that the wrong of the original tortfeasor is a proximate cause of the aggravation of the bodily harm also caused by the treating physician.

* * *

The majority's result-reaching has unfortunate effects on Maryland contract law. Consider the parol evidence rule ramifications of today's holding. The written contract of release was the product of arm's length bargaining. Morgan was represented by counsel (who was other than present appellate counsel). Morgan was paid $20,000 for her release. The subject matter of the bargaining was tort claims. The words of causation used to limit the scope of the release necessarily have the same meaning as proximate causation has in the law of torts. Indeed, Morgan, whose release contains an express integration clause, did not even present an ambiguity issue in her brief.

* * * Can anyone seriously think that there were prior or contemporaneous parol discussions about the meaning of those words in this particular release? What the majority really has sanctioned are excursions into subjective intent and individual assumptions.

I would have affirmed the circuit court judgments. CHIEF JUDGE MURPHY and JUDGE MCAULIFFE have authorized me to state that they join in this dissenting opinion.

SECTION C. COUNTERSUITS

MOROWITZ v. MARVEL

District of Columbia Court of Appeals, 1980.
423 A.2d 196.

PRYOR, ASSOCIATE JUDGE.

* * * On or about May 18, 1976, appellants, who are practicing physicians, brought a small claims suit against a patient for monies owing for medical services rendered. On June 23, 1976, counsel retained by the patient asserted a counterclaim alleging medical malpractice and professional negligence in the rendition of the services for which the doctors sought payment. The counterclaim demanded a jury trial and prayed for $30,000 in damages.

A default judgment was entered against the patient in the small claims action. The counterclaim was certified to the Civil Division of the Superior Court and thereafter was withdrawn. This action followed.[30]

It is axiomatic that the American system of jurisprudence favors free access to the courts as a medium of dispute settlement. It is the

---

30. Editors' Note: The action was brought against the patient's lawyer alone. Hereinafter "appellants" will be replaced by "the doctors," and "appellee" will be replaced by "the lawyer."

announced policy of this jurisdiction to allow unfettered access to our courts. In an effort to avoid infringing upon the right of the public to utilize our courts, we are cautious not to adopt rules which will have a chilling and inhibitory effect on would-be litigants of justiciable issues. We are likewise cognizant of our obligations to protect the innocent against frivolous litigation, and to make victims of groundless lawsuits whole where they suffer special injury as the result of the suit. Predictably, our decisions have evolved in response to these competing interests.

In Ammerman v. Newman, 384 A.2d 637 (D.C.1978), this court reviewed the law of this jurisdiction with respect to proceedings asserting malicious prosecution and, aware that the majority of the states have now rejected a special injury requirement, nonetheless opted to affirm our requirement of the same, in the belief that it best promotes this jurisdiction's policy of encouraging free access to the courts.

Thus, we reiterated that to prevail in a claim of malicious prosecution, plaintiff must plead and prove four things: (1) the underlying suit terminated in plaintiff's favor; (2) malice on the part of defendant; (3) lack of probable cause for the underlying suit; and (4) special injury occasioned by plaintiff as the result of the original action.

In the case at bar, the doctors do not allege special injury. The injuries the doctors complain of are those which "might normally be incident to the service of process on anyone involved in a legal suit." Nolan v. Allstate Home Equip. Co., 149 A.2d 426, 430 (D.C.1959). The complaint indicates that the injuries occasioned, if any, are costs incident to any litigation and "professional defamatory-type" damages. Such injury is not actionable in a malicious prosecution claim. See Martin v. Trevino, 578 S.W.2d 763 (Tex.Civ.App.1978), where on similar facts the Texas court found that the injury alleged did not constitute special injury.

We conclude that with respect to the count alleging malicious prosecution, the court did not err in finding that the doctors failed to state a claim upon which relief could be granted.

* * *

The critical concern in abuse of process cases is whether process was used to accomplish an end unintended by law, and whether the suit was instituted to achieve a result not regularly or legally obtainable. "The mere issuance of the process is not actionable, no matter what ulterior motive may have prompted it; the gist of the action lies in the improper use after issuance." Hall v. Hollywood Credit Clothing Co., 147 A.2d 866, 868 (D.C.1959).[31] Thus, in addition to ulterior motive, one must allege and prove that there has been a perversion of the judicial

---

31. We are mindful, however, that Super.Ct.Civ.R. 11 mandates that:

The signature of an attorney [on a pleading] constitutes a certificate by him that he has read the pleading; that to the best of his knowledge, information, and belief there is a good ground to support it; and that it is not interposed for delay.

process and achievement of some end not contemplated in the regular prosecution of the charge. Id. * * *

In the instant case, the lawyer merely filed a counterclaim and subsequently withdrew it. Without more, the doctors' proffer, that the lawyer filed the counterclaim with the ulterior motive of coercing settlement, is deficient. There is no showing that the process was, in fact, used to accomplish an end not regularly or legally obtainable. * * * Under these circumstances, we cannot find that the trial court erred in dismissing this count of the doctors' amended complaint.

As an alternative ground of recovery, the doctors urge that they have a cause of action against the lawyer for professional negligence. This court has not squarely addressed this issue before, but we are satisfied from a review of the cases in other jurisdictions that such an action cannot lie. Each jurisdiction which has concluded as we do, that a negligence action will not lie by a former defendant against adverse counsel, has done so primarily for the reason that there is an absence of privity of contract between counsel and an opposing party, and for public policy reasons.

Historically, there has been a strict application of the privity of contract rule. Thus, in a landmark case, National Savings Bank v. Ward, 100 U.S. 195, 25 L.Ed. 621 (1879), the Supreme Court held that the doctrine of privity of contract barred suit by a bank against adverse counsel who were professionally negligent in conducting title examinations, despite the fact that the attorneys' neglect clearly occasioned the bank's loss.

Exception was first made to this stringent requirement of privity in cases involving fraud or collusion. Later, courts began relaxing the requirement of privity in cases involving the drafting of wills and the examination of titles.[32] In these instances, the courts relaxed the requirement on the basis that the plaintiffs were direct and intended beneficiaries of the attorney's services. The mere fact that the third party was a foreseeable plaintiff was not, however, sufficient to give rise to a legal duty to the third parties.

In recent years courts which have considered whether a negligence action should lie on facts similar to those before us have overwhelmingly resolved this question in the negative. Decisions in California, Illinois, and New York are illustrative of this view. Unanimously, they have not permitted an adverse party to recover from an opposing counsel on a negligence theory.

California has declined to allow third parties to bring negligence actions against adverse counsel for at least three reasons: (1) an absence of privity of contract; (2) an adverse party is not an intended beneficiary of adverse counsel's services; and (3) policy reasons. Good-

---

32. Birnbaum, Physicians Counter Attack: Liability of Lawyers for Instituting Unjustified Medical Malpractice Actions, 45 Fordham L.Rev. 1003, 1071–72 (1977).

Editors' Note: See also Annot., Medical Malpractice Countersuits, 84 A.L.R.3d 555 (1978).

man v. Kennedy, 18 Cal.3d 335, 134 Cal.Rptr. 375, 556 P.2d 737 (1976) * * *.

Illinois rejected the notion of a negligence action by third parties against adverse counsel on the grounds that (1) it would be contrary to public policy to impose upon an attorney a duty to an intended defendant not to file seemingly frivolous lawsuits; (2) to allow the same would create an "insurmountable conflict of interest between the attorney and client," Berlin v. Nathan, 64 Ill.App.3d 940, 381 N.E.2d 1367, 1376 (1978); and (3) establishment of such a negligence cause of action would inhibit free access to the courts. Pantone v. Demos, 59 Ill.App.3d 328, 375 N.E.2d 480, 485 (1978) * * *.

New York has held fast to the traditional view that since an attorney has no privity of contract with adverse parties in a litigation, absent fraud or collusion, no negligence action will lie. * * * Further, it has declined to permit third parties to bring negligence actions against adverse counsel because it found that "to hold an attorney personally responsible for instituting a frivolous action on behalf of a client would operate to discourage free resort to the courts for the resolution of controversies, contrary to public policy." Drago v. Buonagurio, 89 Misc.2d 171, 391 N.Y.S.2d 61, 63 (Sup.Ct.1977) * * *.

For the reasons enumerated, we are satisfied that an action for professional negligence cannot lie under these circumstances.

Finding no error, we affirm.[33]

---

33. There are other avenues of redress available to physicians who are the victims of seemingly frivolous medical malpractice actions. If used properly, an administrative proceeding brought by the local bar disciplinary counsel, based on a violation of professional standards of conduct, can be an effective deterrent to instituting frivolous medical malpractice claims.

Chapter 7

TREATMENT CONSENT, INFORMATION AND REFUSAL

INTRODUCTORY NOTE

The sections of this chapter all relate to a central theme, the right of individuals to regulate the medical treatment they receive: whether, how much, from whom, and for what purposes. Patients want to be treated as subjects, not as objects, and the law supports their wishes. A failure to preserve a patient's rights may be regarded legally as negligence or as some other theory of claim.

The technological imperative, that what can be done should be done, has animated great progress in medical science, but treatment that is good for medicine is not necessarily in the best interests of the individual. The concept of individual rights, expressed in various rules of private law considered in this chapter, tries to convert the imperative into the permissive: the physician has the duty to secure the patient's consent to treatment; the patient has the power to refuse treatment, even against medical advice; the patient has the right to be informed of fairly unusual but undesirable outcomes and side-effects of medical and surgical treatment; the patient's consent must be obtained before the patient is enrolled as a subject in biomedical research.

Civil actions for damages are a clumsy and socially expensive way of adjusting the balance between providers and consumers of health care services, but they do get the providers' attention. Litigants and courts have caused hospitals to use consent forms, producing widespread compliance through what lawyers call "general deterrence" and insurance people call "risk-avoidance." Even where legislatures have acted to strengthen patients' powers, the levers of public law have to be applied to individuals through regulatory or adjudicative processes.

Persons of good will in the United States have many legal mechanisms to call upon in cooling confrontations between patients' self-determination and the logic of treatment plans. This is fortunate, because as the means are invented to cope with one problem, another problem arises. For example, the United States has recently come to require institutional review boards, so as to standardize the ways in which people give consent in human experimentation, but the states are still experimenting with mechanisms to accommodate the power of families to refuse consent to treatment on behalf of persons in a persistent vegetative state. Even as abortion becomes safer than pregnancy, the political process challenges the access of individuals to abortion as medical treatment. People in the United States expect "the law" to provide access to procedures for deciding individual cases, where no monopoly on rationality is held by political beliefs, individual rights, or scientific capabilities.

One way to challenge the health care provider is through the civil action for the tort of battery. The claim is so easy to plead (an unconsented-to touching), so difficult to defend (justification), and carries such a long train of causation that, as the courts are aware, it is a real menace in the medical context. Consequently, whether by interpretation or statute, the action for failing to obtain informed consent to medical treatment now tends to be treated as a form of negligence; and as close as the concepts of promise and consent may be, the action (and the damages) now lie in tort. Even so, consent is not unlimited, and doctors can be liable for exceeding consent with respect to who treats or what is done.

The states still have not achieved a solid majority position on the place of the patient's testimony—"If I had known, I would never have consented"—in the proceedings.[1] The "lay standard" virtually forces the patient to testify (and perhaps lie), and it seems to reward good actors. The "medical standard" seems to place the patient's legal fate in the hands of the doctors, a fundamental contradiction of the principle of individual rights. This is particularly difficult in the context of experimental procedures performed in the name of medical research, where federal law requiring institutional review boards has not preempted civil actions for damages under state law.

Last is the problem of deliberately refused treatment. The medical duty of doctors is to fight death, but individuals have the right to accept it, on the ground that there are living fates worse than death. The legal duty of doctors may be to maximize individual freedom, pressing treatment information upon patients while recognizing their right to reject it, but the doctor's duty to pay money damages for breaching that legal duty is something of a medical paradox.

1. The Model Health–Care Consent Act (1982), 9 U.L.A. 453, has been adopted only by Indiana. Pub.L. No. 205 (1987), West's Ann.Ind.Code 16–8–12–1—12.

SECTION A. TREATMENT WITHOUT CONSENT

MATTOCKS v. BELL

District of Columbia Court of Appeals, 1963.
194 A.2d 307.

HOOD, CHIEF JUDGE.

* * * The plaintiff is a female child who was 23 months old at the time in question. The defendant is a second-year medical student who at the time was serving as an extern in the emergency room of District of Columbia General Hospital. The child was taken to the hospital by her mother for treatment of a lacerated tongue. As defendant attempted to examine the child's mouth, she clamped her teeth on defendant's left middle finger and bit hard enough to cause blood to spurt from the finger, although it was enclosed in a rubber glove. Defendant shouted to the child to open her mouth but she retained her grip on the finger. He twice unsuccessfully attempted to extricate his finger by forcing a tongue depressor into her mouth. He then slapped the child on the cheek with his hand, and this caused her to open her mouth and release the finger. A doctor who immediately treated the finger testified that "the wound was deep enough to have touched the bone." The foregoing facts were not disputed, but there was a conflict of testimony regarding the severity of the slap.

The child through its mother brought this action against defendant for damages for assault and battery. The trial court denied recovery, finding that although the action of defendant may have been rash it was not malicious, that the blow was not severe, and that the child was not injured.

On this appeal it is urged that when it was established that defendant intentionally slapped the child, an assault and battery was proved, that this proof entitled the child to a recovery unless justification was established, and that there was no evidence from which the court could have found a justification.

* * * The nearest case, factually, is Burton v. Leftwich, 123 So.2d 766, 89 A.L.R.2d 980 [2] (La.Ct.App.1960), where a four-year-old child was allowed a recovery [of $250] from a doctor who slapped her leg rather severely several times in an attempt to make her lie still in order that he could remove sutures from her toe. There the trial court found that the doctor used "exceedingly bad judgment." That case is distinguishable from the present one. Here we have one slap that was not "hard" instead of several severe slaps; here we have "poor or hasty judgment" instead of exceedingly bad judgment; and here we have an emergency situation which did not exist in the other. In the other case the slaps

---

[2]. Annot., Liability of Doctor or Dentist Using Force to Restrain or Discipline Patient, 89 A.L.R.2d 983 (1963).

were in the nature of discipline. Here the single slap was more in the nature of a protective or defensive measure.

We * * * hold that the trial court could properly find that force was required, that it was not applied in an improper manner, and that a recovery should be denied.

Affirmed.[3]

MOHR v. WILLIAMS
Supreme Court of Minnesota, 1905.
95 Minn. 261, 104 N.W. 12.

BROWN, J.

Defendant is a physician and surgeon of standing and character, making disorders of the ear a specialty, and having an extensive practice in the city of St. Paul. He was consulted by plaintiff, who complained to him of trouble with her right ear, and, at her request, made an examination of that organ for the purpose of ascertaining its condition. He also at the same time examined her left ear, but, owing to foreign substances therein, was unable to make a full and complete diagnosis at that time. * * * [The plaintiff submitted to general anesthesia on the understanding that the defendant would operate on the diseased right ear. After examining both ears under anesthesia, the defendant decided that the left ear was in worse condition than the right, and so he carefully operated on the left ear only.]

It is claimed by plaintiff that the operation greatly impaired her hearing, seriously injured her person, and, not having been consented to by her, was wrongful and unlawful, constituting an assault and battery; and she brought this action to recover damages therefor.

The trial in the court below resulted in a verdict for plaintiff for $14,322.50. * * * [The trial judge decided that this amount was excessive and ordered a new trial, but he denied the doctor's motion for judgment notwithstanding the verdict. Both parties appealed. The supreme court affirmed the new trial order.]

* * * It cannot be doubted that ordinarily the patient must be consulted, and his consent given, before a physician may operate upon him. * * *

If the physician advises his patient to submit to a particular operation, and the patient weighs the dangers and risks incident to its performance, and finally consents, he thereby, in effect, enters into a contract authorizing his physician to operate to the extent of the consent given, but no further.

---

3. Editors' Note. The record does not clarify the opinion. There was no jury. The action was pleaded and tried on strongly conflicting evidence as to theories of both negligence and battery (excessive force), and the evidence on harm was also in conflict. The extern testified in his own defense. The trial judge's written statement does not itemize his conclusions of law as to the two theories of claim, but it seems that the appeal was limited to battery. See now Nichols v. Wilson, 296 Md. 154, 460 A.2d 57 (1983).

It is not, however, contended by defendant that under ordinary circumstances consent is unnecessary, but that, under the particular circumstances of this case, consent was implied; that it was an emergency case, such as to authorize the operation without express consent or permission. * * * But such is not the case at bar. The diseased condition of plaintiff's left ear was not discovered in the course of an operation on the right, which was authorized, but upon an independent examination of that organ, made after the authorized operation was found unnecessary. Nor is the evidence such as to justify the court in holding, as a matter of law, that it was such an affliction as would result immediately in the serious injury of plaintiff, or such an emergency as to justify proceeding without her consent. She had experienced no particular difficulty with that ear, and the questions as to when its diseased condition would become alarming or fatal, and whether there was an immediate necessity for an operation, were, under the evidence, questions of fact for the jury.

* * *

The last contention of defendant is that the act complained of did not amount to an assault and battery. This is based upon the theory that, as plaintiff's left ear was in fact diseased, in a condition dangerous and threatening to her health, the operation was necessary, and, having been skillfully performed at a time when plaintiff had requested a like operation on the other ear, the charge of assault and battery cannot be sustained; that, in view of these conditions, and the claim that there was no negligence on the part of defendant, and an entire absence of any evidence tending to show an evil intent, the court should say, as a matter of law, that no assault and battery was committed, even though she did not consent to the operation. * * * We are unable to reach that conclusion, though the contention is not without merit.

[T]he act of defendant amounted at least to a technical assault and battery. If the operation was performed without plaintiff's consent, and the circumstances were not such as to justify its performance without, it was wrongful; and, if it was wrongful, it was unlawful. [E]very person has a right to complete immunity of his person from physical interference of others, except in so far as contact may be necessary under the general doctrine of privilege; and any unlawful or unauthorized touching of the person of another, except it be in the spirit of pleasantry, constitutes an assault and battery.

In the case at bar, as we have already seen, the question whether defendant's act in performing the operation upon plaintiff was authorized was a question for the jury to determine. If it was unauthorized, then it was, within what we have said, unlawful. It was a violent assault, not a mere pleasantry; and, even though no negligence is shown, it was wrongful and unlawful. The case is unlike a criminal prosecution for assault and battery, for there an unlawful intent must be shown. But that rule does not apply to a civil action, to maintain which it is sufficient to show that the assault complained of was wrongful and unlawful or the result of negligence. * * *

[The supreme court affirmed denial of the doctor's motion for judgment notwithstanding the verdict.]

KENNEDY v. PARROTT

Supreme Court of North Carolina, 1956.
243 N.C. 355, 90 S.E.2d 754, 56 A.L.R.2d 686.[4]

* * * The plaintiff consulted the defendant as a surgeon. He diagnosed her ailment as appendicitis and recommended an operation to which she agreed. During the operation the doctor discovered some enlarged cysts on her left ovary, and he punctured them. After the operation the plaintiff developed phlebitis in her leg. She testified that Dr. Parrott told her "that while he was puncturing this cyst in my left ovary that he had cut a blood vessel and caused me to have phlebitis and that those blood clots were what was causing the trouble." She also testified that defendant told Dr. Tyndall, who was called in to examine her for her leg condition, "that while he was operating he punctured some cysts on my ovaries, and while puncturing the cyst on my left ovary he cut a blood vessel which caused me to bleed," to which Dr. Tyndall said, "Fountain, you have played hell."

* * *

Plaintiff had to undergo considerable pain and suffering on account of the phlebitis and still has some trouble with it.

At the conclusion of the testimony, the court, on motion of the defendant, entered judgment of involuntary nonsuit. Plaintiff excepted and appealed.

BARNHILL, CHIEF JUSTICE.

Plaintiff's action as alleged in her complaint is an action for damages for personal injury proximately resulting from the negligence of the defendant in performing an operation on her. The only allegation in the complaint which gives any indication it is an action for damages proximately resulting from an alleged technical assault or trespass upon the person of plaintiff is the allegation that the puncturing of the cysts on her ovary was unauthorized.

[I]f defendant made the statements upon which the plaintiff relies, they are so in conflict with known scientific facts that they are lacking in sufficient probative force to require their submission to a jury. Therefore, if the cause was tried in the court below on the allegation of negligence contained in the complaint, the judgment of nonsuit was well advised.

On the other hand, if her cause of action is for damages for personal injuries proximately resulting from an assault or trespass on

---

4. Annot., Liability of Physician or Surgeon for Extending Operation or Treatment Beyond That Expressly Authorized, 56 A.L.R.2d 695 (1957).

her person, as she now asserts, and such operation was neither expressly nor impliedly authorized, she is entitled at least to nominal damages.

* * *

While the law of contracts is applied as between a patient and his physician or surgeon, when a person consults a physician or surgeon, seeking treatment for a physical ailment, real or apparent, and the physician or surgeon agrees to accept him as a patient, it does not create a contract in the sense that term is ordinarily used. Usually there is no specification or particularization as to what the physician shall do. The patient selects, and commits himself to the care of, the doctor because he is confident the doctor possesses the requisite skill and ability to treat—and will treat—his physical ailment and restore him to normal good health. The physician, after diagnosing the ailment, prescribes the treatment or the medicine to be administered; but the patient is under no legal obligation to follow the physician's instructions. Thus it is apt and perhaps more exact to say it creates a status or relation rather than a contract. * * *

Prior to the advent of the modern hospital and before anesthesia had appeared on the horizon of the medical world, the courts formulated and applied a rule in respect to operations which may now be justly considered unreasonable and unrealistic. During the period when our common law was being formulated and applied, even a major operation was performed in the home of the patient, and the patient ordinarily was conscious, so that the physician could consult him in respect to conditions which required or made advisable an extension of the operation. And even if the shock of the operation rendered the patient unconscious, immediate members of his family were usually available. Hence the courts formulated the rule that any extension of the operation by the physician without the consent of the patient or someone authorized to speak for him constituted a battery or trespass upon the person of the patient for which the physician was liable in damages.

However, now that hospitals are available to most people in need of major surgery; anesthesia is in common use; operations are performed in the operating rooms of such hospitals while the patient is under the influence of an anesthetic; the surgeon is bedecked with operating gown, mask, and gloves; and the attending relatives, if any, are in some other part of the hospital, sometimes many floors away, the law is in a state of flux. More and more courts are beginning to realize that ordinarily a surgeon is employed to remedy conditions without any express limitation on his authority in respect thereto, and that in view of these conditions which make consent impractical, it is unreasonable to hold the physician to the exact operation—particularly when it is internal—that his preliminary examination indicated was necessary. We know that now complete diagnosis of an internal ailment is not effectuated until after the patient is under the influence of the anesthetic and the incision has been made.

These courts act upon the concept that the philosophy of the law is embodied in the ancient Latin maxim, *Ratio est legis anima; mutata legis ratione mutatur et lex*: Reason is the soul of the law; the reason of the law being changed, the law is also changed.

Some of the courts which realize that, in view of modern conditions, there should be some modification of the strict common law rule, still limit the right of surgeons to extend an operation without the express consent of the patient to cases where an emergency arises, calling for immediate action for the preservation of the life or health of the patient, and it is impracticable to obtain his consent or the consent of someone authorized to speak for him. Jackovach v. Yocom, 212 Iowa 914, 237 N.W. 444, 76 A.L.R. 551 [5] (1931) * * *.

Other courts, though adhering to the fetish of consent, express or implied, realize that "The law should encourage self-reliant surgeons to whom patients may safely entrust their bodies, and not men who may be tempted to shirk from duty for fear of a lawsuit." They recognize that "The law does not insist that a surgeon shall perform every operation according to plans and specifications approved in advance by the patient, and carefully tucked away in his office safe for courtroom purposes." Barnett v. Bachrach, 34 A.2d 626, 629 (D.C.1943).

This view, to which we subscribe, is fully stated in Bennan v. Parsonnet, 83 N.J.L. 20, 83 A. 948, 949 (1912) * * *.

In major internal operations, both the patient and the surgeon know that the exact condition of the patient cannot be finally and definitely diagnosed until after the patient is completely anesthetized and the incision has been made. In such case the consent—in the absence of proof to the contrary—will be construed as general in nature and the surgeon may extend the operation to remedy any abnormal or diseased condition in the area of the original incision whenever he, in the exercise of his sound professional judgment, determines that correct surgical procedure dictates and requires such an extension of the operation originally contemplated. This rule applies when the patient is at the time incapable of giving consent, and no one with authority to consent for him is immediately available. * * *

* * *

Unexpected things which arise in the course of an operation and incidental thereto must generally at least be met according to the best judgment and skill of the surgeon. * * * And ordinarily a surgeon is justified in believing that his patient has assented to such operation as approved surgery demands to relieve the affliction with which he is suffering. * * *

Here plaintiff submitted her body to the care of the defendant for an appendectomy. When the defendant made the necessary incision he discovered some enlarged follicle cysts on her ovaries. He, as a skilled surgeon, knew that when a cyst on an ovary grows beyond the normal

---

5. Annot., Consent as Condition of Right to Perform Surgical Operation, 76 A.L.R. 562 (1932), supplemented, 139 A.L.R. 1370 (1942).

size, it may continue to grow until it is large enough to hold six to eight quarts of liquid and become dangerous by reason of its size. The plaintiff does not say that the defendant exercised bad judgment or that the extended operation was not dictated by sound surgical procedure. She now asserts only that it was unauthorized, and she makes no real showing of resulting injury or damage.

* * *

What was the surgeon to do when he found abnormal cysts on the ovaries of plaintiff that were potentially dangerous? Was it his duty to leave her unconscious on the operating table, doff his operating habiliments, and go forth to find someone with authority to consent to the extended operation, and then return, go through the process of disinfecting, don again his operating habiliments, and then puncture the cysts; or was he compelled, against his best judgment, to close the incision and then, after plaintiff had fully recovered from the effects of the anesthesia, inform her as to what he had found and advise her that these cysts might cause her serious trouble in the future? The operation was simple, the incision had been made, the potential danger was evident to a skilled surgeon. Reason and sound common sense dictated that he should do just what he did do. So all the expert witnesses testified.

* * * The judgment entered in the court below is affirmed.

PERNA v. PIROZZI

Supreme Court of New Jersey, 1983.
92 N.J. 446, 457 A.2d 431, 39 A.L.R.4th 1018.[6]

POLLOCK, J. * * *

On the advice of his family physician, Thomas R. Perna entered St. Joseph's Hospital on May 8, 1977, for tests and a urological consultation. Mr. Perna consulted Dr. Michael J. Pirozzi, a specialist in urology, who examined Mr. Perna and recommended that he undergo surgery for the removal of kidney stones.

Dr. Pirozzi was associated with a medical group that also included Drs. Del Gaizo and Ciccone. The doctors testified at trial that their medical group customarily shared patients; no doctor had individual patients, and each doctor was familiar with all cases under care of the group. Further, it was not the practice of the group to inform patients which member would operate; the physicians operated as a "team," and their regular practice was to decide just prior to the operation who was to operate. If, however, a patient requested a specific member of the group as his surgeon, that surgeon would perform the operation. Nothing indicated that Mr. Perna was aware of the group's custom of sharing patients or of their methods for assigning surgical duties.

---

6. Annot., Recovery by Patient on Whom Surgery or Other Treatment Was Performed by One Other Than Physician Who Patient Believed Would Perform It, 39 A.L.R.4th 1034 (1985).

Although Mr. Perna had never consulted with Dr. Del Gaizo or Dr. Ciccone, he had been treated by Dr. Pirozzi previously in conjunction with a bladder infection. According to Mr. Perna, he specifically requested Dr. Pirozzi to perform the operation. None of the defendants directly contradicted Mr. Perna's testimony. However, Dr. Ciccone testified that he met with Mr. Perna on May 16 and, without discussing who would operate, explained that two members of the medical group would be present during the operation. The following day, in the presence of a urological resident, Mr. Perna executed a consent form that named Dr. Pirozzi as the operating surgeon and authorized him, with the aid of unnamed "assistants," to perform the surgery.[7] In this context, the term "assistants" refers to medical personnel, not necessarily doctors, who aid the operating surgeon. * * * The operation was performed on May 18 by Dr. Del Gaizo, assisted by Dr. Ciccone. Dr. Pirozzi was not present during the operation; in fact, he was not on duty that day. At the time of surgery, Dr. Del Gaizo and Dr. Ciccone were unaware that only Dr. Pirozzi's name appeared on the consent form.

Mr. Perna first learned of the identities of the operating surgeons when he was readmitted to the hospital on June 11 because of post-surgical complications. Subsequently, Mr. and Mrs. Perna filed suit for malpractice against all three doctors * * *. They further alleged that there was a failure to obtain Mr. Perna's informed consent to the operation performed by Dr. Del Gaizo. That is, plaintiffs claimed that Mr. Perna's consent to the operation was conditioned upon his belief that Dr. Pirozzi would be the surgeon.

[T]he jury subsequently returned a unanimous verdict of no cause for action in favor of defendants.[8] * * *

We now address the nature of the claim resulting from the performance of the operation by a physician other than the one named in the consent form, so-called "ghost surgery." If the claim is characterized as a failure to obtain informed consent, the operation may constitute an act of medical malpractice; if, however, it is viewed as a failure to obtain any consent, it is better classified as a battery.

* * *

In an action predicated upon a battery, a patient need not prove initially that the physician has deviated from a professional standard of

---

7. The consent form provided in relevant part:

INFORMED CONSENT TO OPERATION OR OTHER SPECIAL PROCEDURE

1. I, *Thomas Perna*, authorize *Dr. Pirozzi* and his assistants to treat the condition or conditions which are indicated by the examinations and studies already performed.

* * *

2. The procedure[s] necessary to treat my condition, as explained to me by Dr. _____ are: *remove stone from rt. kidney through flank incision.* (* * * [Italicized] portions indicate blanks on standard consent form.)

8. Editors' Note: For reasons of trial strategy, the plaintiff's attorney did not plead the battery theory, but the battery theory became entangled in all the proceedings. The supreme court ultimately ordered a new trial for evidentiary errors that are unrelated to the battery issue.

care. Under a battery theory, proof of an unauthorized invasion of the plaintiff's person, even if harmless, entitles him to nominal damages. W. Prosser, Law of Torts § 9 at 35 (4th ed. 1971) * * *. The plaintiff may further recover for all injuries proximately caused by the mere performance of the operation, whether the result of negligence or not. * * * See generally Prosser § 42. If an operation is properly performed, albeit by a surgeon operating without the consent of the patient, and the patient suffers no injuries except those which foreseeably follow from the operation, then a jury could find that the substitution of surgeons did not cause any compensable injury. Even there, however, a jury could award damages for mental anguish resulting from the belated knowledge that the operation was performed by a doctor to whom the patient had not given consent. Furthermore, because battery connotes an intentional invasion of another's rights, punitive damages may be assessed in an appropriate case. * * *

The plaintiffs here do not challenge the adequacy of the disclosure of information relating to risks inherent in the operation performed. Nor do they contend that Mr. Perna would have decided not to undergo the operation if additional facts had been provided to him. In short, they concede Perna consented to an operation by Dr. Pirozzi. However, plaintiffs contend that two other surgeons operated on him without his consent. If that contention is correct, the operating surgeons violated the patient's right to control his own body. * * *

Any non-consensual touching is a battery. See Prosser § 9. Even more private than the decision who may touch one's body is the decision who may cut it open and invade it with hands and instruments. Absent an emergency, patients have the right to determine not only whether surgery is to be performed on them, but who shall perform it. A surgeon who operates without the patient's consent engages in the unauthorized touching of another and, thus, commits a battery. * * *[9] A nonconsensual operation remains a battery even if performed skillfully and to the benefit of the patient. The medical profession itself recognizes that it is unethical to mislead a patient as to the identity of the doctor who performs the operation. American College of Surgeons, Statements on Principles, § I. A. (June 1981). Participation in such a deception is a recognized cause for discipline by the medical profession. See American College of Surgeons, Bylaws, art. VII, § 1(c) (as amended June 1976). By statute, the State Board of Medical Examiners is empowered to prevent the professional certification or future professional practice of a person who "[h]as engaged in the use or employment of dishonesty, fraud, deception, misrepresentation, false promise or false pretense * * *." N.J.Stat.Ann. § 45:1–21. Consequently, a statutory, as well as a moral, imperative compels doctors to be honest with their patients.

9. Editors' Note: The ten citations omitted here were all the authorities at the time.

A different theory applies to the claim against Dr. Pirozzi. As to him, the action follows from the alleged breach of his agreement to operate and the fiduciary duty he owed his patient. With respect to that allegation, the Judicial Council of the American Medical Association has decried the substitution of one surgeon for another without the consent of the patient, describing that practice as a "deceit." [10] A patient has the right to choose the surgeon who will operate on him and to refuse to accept a substitute. Correlative to that right is the duty of the doctor to provide his or her personal services in accordance with the agreement with the patient. Judicial Council of the American Medical Ass'n, Opinion 8.12 (1982).

* * * Sometimes circumstances will arise in which, because of an emergency, the limited capacity of the patient, or some other valid reason, the doctor cannot obtain the express consent of the patient to a surrogate surgeon. Other times, doctors who practice in a medical group may explain to a patient that any one of them may perform a medical procedure. In that situation, the patient may accept any or all the members of the group as his surgeon. In still other instances, the patient may consent to an operation performed by a resident under the supervision of the attending physician. The point is that a patient has the right to know who will operate and the consent form should reflect the patient's decision. Where a competent patient consents to surgery by a specific surgeon of his choice, the patient has every right to expect that surgeon, not another, to operate.

* * *

The judgment below is reversed and the matter remanded for trial consistent with our opinion. On remand, the court shall conduct a new pretrial conference at which all parties should have the opportunity to amend their pleadings to conform to this opinion.

SECTION B. INFORMED CONSENT

LOGAN v. GREENWICH HOSP. ASS'N
Supreme Court of Connecticut, 1983.
191 Conn. 282, 465 A.2d 294, 38 A.L.R.4th 879.[11]

SHEA, ASSOCIATE JUSTICE. * * *

[T]he defendant, Marc E. Newberg, a specialist in internal medicine, first met the plaintiff, Martha Logan, in July 1971, following the birth of her twin children at the Greenwich Hospital. After her discharge from the hospital on August 4, 1971, the plaintiff continued to consult Dr. Newberg because of continued pain, swelling and a decreased range of motion. She was hospitalized for ten days in

---

10. * * * If the patient is not informed as to the identity of the operating surgeon, the situation is "ghost surgery." Judicial Council of the American Medical Ass'n, Op. 8.12 (1982).

11. Annot., Medical Malpractice: Liability for Failure of Physician to Inform Patient of Alternative Modes of Diagnosis or Treatment, 38 A.L.R.4th 900 (1985).

February, 1972, because of pain in her neck, shoulders, arms, and legs which interfered with her sleeping.

In August 1972 Dr. Newberg advised the plaintiff that she had systemic lupus erythematosus (lupus). In October 1972 he advised her to undergo a kidney biopsy to determine the extent of lupus involvement in her kidneys. He explained that the biopsy was a simple procedure, which would be carried out under a local anesthetic, that she might suffer some bleeding and discomfort, but that she would be able to leave the hospital in a day or two if there were no complications. Dr. Newberg described the operation in a general way as consisting of the insertion of a surgical needle into her back in order to obtain a specimen of kidney tissue. He also indicated that Peter Bogdan, a urologist, would perform the operation and would describe the details more fully. The only complication which Dr. Newberg mentioned was the possibility of considerable pain and bleeding for which surgery might be necessary. He did not discuss the alternative of an open biopsy, which would require an incision and would be conducted under general anesthesia, because he did not consider that procedure advisable. He never mentioned the danger that the plaintiff's gall bladder might be punctured during the operation, an injury which did in fact occur.

As the attending physician, Dr. Newberg admitted the plaintiff to the Greenwich Hospital on October 31, 1972. On the evening of November 2, 1972, Dr. Bogdan visited the plaintiff in her room at the hospital to discuss the operation to be performed the next morning. He told her that there might be some bleeding and that there was a risk of hemorrhaging and of losing a kidney. The alternative of an open biopsy procedure under a general anesthetic was not mentioned, although Dr. Bogdan had performed such operations previously and conceded that it was a more controlled procedure in terms of visualizing the kidney. He did not consider this procedure to be a viable alternative for the plaintiff, however, because there is a greater risk of complications, especially those involving general anesthesia. After Dr. Bogdan had departed, the plaintiff, in accordance with the rules of the hospital, signed a written form consenting to the surgical procedure which had been described.

The next morning the plaintiff was taken to a room in the x-ray department of the hospital where Dr. Bogdan and a student nurse were in attendance. The defendant Forbes Delaney, the director of radiology at the hospital, was also present for the purpose of operating the fluoroscopic equipment which was necessary to provide a view of the kidney and the needle while the biopsy was being performed. * * *

After the plaintiff had been placed upon the table, Dr. Bogdan injected a local anesthetic into the kidney region by using a small gauge anesthesia needle. He then inserted the biopsy needle and, using the fluoroscopic screen between six and eight times, he located the kidney and extracted a tissue specimen. After examining the specimen he concluded that it was inadequate. He made a second attempt to obtain a piece of kidney tissue, advising the plaintiff beforehand and obtaining her consent. He adjusted the biopsy needle in order to obtain a deeper piece of kidney tissue and once again inserted it. In the course of this procedure the plaintiff suddenly felt pain far more severe than previously experienced and the needle was withdrawn before the tissue specimen could be obtained. During abdominal surgery on November 6, 1972, to determine the cause of the abdominal pain which the plaintiff continued to suffer following the biopsy procedure, it was discovered that her gall bladder had been punctured, and it was removed.

The complaint was in two counts, the first being directed against the defendant hospital and the second against the three doctors who in some manner had been connected with the biopsy procedure. One of the specifications of negligence in each count was the failure "to obtain the plaintiff's intelligent and informed consent to the performance of a percutaneous renal biopsy."

[The judge directed verdicts for the hospital and Dr. Delaney, the radiologist, and the supreme court affirmed. The jury found in favor of the internist, Dr. Newberg, and the urologist, Dr. Bogdan.]

The plaintiff's first claim of error involves the charge upon the absence of informed consent as alleged in the complaint, particularly with respect to the duty of a physician to advise a patient of feasible alternatives. The court instructed the jury that the duty to give a patient all information material to the decision to undergo an operation includes the obligation to advise of feasible alternatives. The charge continued: "Now the duty to warn of alternatives exists only when there are feasible alternatives available. *An alternative that is more hazardous is not a viable alternative.*" (Emphasis added.) The plaintiff excepted to the italicized sentence of the charge as removing from the patient the decision of which alternative procedure was the least dangerous. The same charge was repeated in response to a request of the jury, after they commenced deliberations, for a further definition of the standard of care. Again the plaintiff excepted to that part of the instructions.

We have not had previous occasion to consider substantively the doctrine of informed consent as a basis for malpractice liability of a physician. * * *

The theory of battery as a basis for recovery against a physician has generally been limited to situations where he fails to obtain any consent to the particular treatment, or performs a different procedure from the one for which consent has been given, or where he realizes that the patient does not understand what the operation entails. * * * The failure to make a sufficient disclosure, which is ordinarily the basis for claiming lack of informed consent, has been regarded by most courts as presenting the question, not whether there was an effective consent which would preclude an action for battery, but whether the physician had fulfilled his duty of informing the patient under the appropriate standard. * * *. Traditionally the standard was deemed to be one set by the medical profession in terms of customary medical practice in the community. * * *. As in other aspects of medical science, only members of the profession are ordinarily familiar with the standard and deemed qualified to testify about it. * * *

The incongruity of making the medical profession the sole arbiter of what information was necessary for an informed decision to be made by a patient concerning his own physical well-being has led to various judicial and legislative attempts within the last decade to define a standard tailored to the needs of the patient, but not unreasonably burdensome upon the physician, or wholly dispensing with the notion that "doctor knows best" in some situations. While the essential ambivalence between the right of the patient to make a knowledgeable choice and the duty of the doctor to prescribe the treatment his professional judgment deems best for the patient has not been fully resolved, the outline has begun to emerge.

In a trilogy of cases decided in 1972 the traditional standard of customary medical practice in the community was abandoned by three jurisdictions as the criterion for informed consent, in favor of a judicially imposed standard designed to provide a patient with information material to his decision upon a course of therapy. Canterbury v. Spence, 464 F.2d 772 (D.C.Cir.), cert. denied, 409 U.S. 1064, 93 S.Ct. 560, 34 L.Ed.2d 518 (1972); Cobbs v. Grant, 8 Cal.3d 229, 104 Cal.Rptr. 505, 502 P.2d 1 (1972); Wilkinson v. Vesey, 110 R.I. 606, 295 A.2d 676 (1972).

The formulations of the disclosure standard in these cases vary. "Thus the test for determining whether a particular peril must be divulged is its materiality to the patient's decision: all risks potentially affecting the decision must be unmasked." Canterbury v. Spence, 464 F.2d at 786. "The scope of the physician's communications to the patient, then, must be measured by the patient's need, and that need is whatever information is material to the decision." Cobbs v. Grant, 502 P.2d at 11. "It is our belief that, in due deference to the patient's right to self determination, a physician is bound to disclose all the known material risks peculiar to the proposed procedure." Wilkinson v. Vesey, 295 A.2d at 689.

These decisions require something less than a full disclosure of all information which may have some bearing, however remote, upon the patient's decision. * * * Although the test is phrased in terms of the "patient's need," rather than impose on the physician an obligation to disclose at his peril whatever the particular patient might deem material to his choice, most courts have attempted to frame a less subjective measure of the physician's duty. "[N]o less than any other aspect of negligence, the issue on nondisclosure must be approached from the viewpoint of the reasonableness of the physician's divulgence in terms of what he knows or should know to be the patient's informational needs." Canterbury v. Spence, 464 F.2d at 787. * * * In states which have legislated this so-called "lay" standard of disclosure vis-à-vis the orthodox professional standard, the statutes typically impose a duty to disclose such information as a "reasonable patient would consider material to the decision whether or not to undergo treatment or diagnosis." See Pa.Stat.Ann. tit. 40, § 1301.103; accord, R.I.Gen.L. § 9–19–32; Wash.Rev.Code Ann. § 7.70.050(1)(a).

The standard has been further delineated by specifying various elements which the physician's disclosure should include:

> (1) [T]he "nature" of the procedure, (2) the "risks" and "hazards" of the procedure, (3) the "alternatives" to the procedure, and (4) the anticipated "benefits" of the procedure. Meisel & Kabnick, Informed Consent to Medical Treatment: An Analysis of Recent Legislation, 41 U.Pitt.L.Rev. 407, 427 (1980) * * *.

Some limited recognition has been given also to the therapeutic privilege of a physician to withhold information where disclosure might jeopardize a course of therapy. * * *

The leading case of Canterbury v. Spence was given a generally favorable reception by the judiciary, and soon the lay standard of disclosure had been adopted in eight states,[12] obligating the physician to provide the patient with that information which a reasonable patient would have found material for making a decision whether to embark upon a contemplated course of therapy. * * * Three of these states subsequently have abandoned this standard by statutes which expressly or implicitly adopt the professional standard of disclosure in accordance with the practice of a reasonable medical practitioner under similar circumstances. See N.Y.Pub.Health L. § 2805–d(1); Ohio Rev.Code Ann. § 2317.54; Vt.Stat.Ann. tit. 12, § 1909(a)(1) * * *. Despite the possibility of legislative revision, we are persuaded that criticism of the professional standard as expounded in *Canterbury* is well-founded and we, therefore, shall follow the lay standard of disclosure.

This standard was the basis for the charge given by the trial court upon informed consent. As we have noted, the plaintiff takes issue only with the single sentence of that charge which declares "[a]n alternative that is more hazardous is not a viable alternative." During the trial there was considerable testimony about the hazards of the needle biopsy, which had resulted in puncturing the plaintiff's gall bladder, as compared to an open biopsy requiring general anesthesia and a surgical incision. Philip Roen, a urologist called by the plaintiff, testified that the alternative of an open biopsy should have been discussed with the plaintiff, with disclosure of the risks attending any surgical procedure conducted under general anesthesia. Three doctors presented by the defendants testified that an open renal biopsy was not a viable alternative to a needle biopsy. Another witness for the

---

12. California, Louisiana, New York, Ohio, Pennsylvania, Rhode Island, Vermont and Washington.

defendants, Malcolm Galen, a physician, testified that an open biopsy was more hazardous than a needle biopsy, but that he did inform his patients that the alternative of an open biopsy was available with its attendant risks, though he advised against it. It was conceded that an open biopsy alternative was never discussed with the plaintiff who, with the benefit of hindsight, testified that she would have chosen that procedure if she had known of it.

The instruction that an alternative which is more hazardous is not viable and, therefore, need not be mentioned to the patient has the effect of limiting the physician's duty to disclosure of only the least hazardous procedure available, presumably the one contemplated. The issue then becomes, not whether the patient has been informed of viable alternatives, but whether the doctor has recommended the least dangerous of them, because those which are more hazardous need not be discussed. This instruction, therefore, wholly relieves physicians of any obligation to discuss alternatives with their patients and substitutes merely a duty to recommend the safest procedure. It is incompatible, therefore, with the view which the trial court expressed in the remainder of the charge that the patient must be provided with sufficient information to allow him to make an intelligent choice.

* * * Although we are reluctant to find reversible error because of a single sentence of a lengthy charge, we are unable to avoid the conclusion that the error was probably harmful. The major focus of the testimony on the issue of informed consent was the relative hazard involved in each of the two medical procedures. In advising the jury that more hazardous alternatives were not viable and could be withheld from the patient, the trial court invited them to decide the issue of informed consent simply by comparing the risks of the two procedures. The jury could well have understood that, if they concluded that an open biopsy was more hazardous than the needle biopsy performed, there was no duty to inform the plaintiff of that alternative. Such a misunderstanding would have been wholly inconsistent with the view we have adopted requiring that all viable alternatives be disclosed even though some involve more hazard than others.

* * * With respect to the failure to discuss the open biopsy alternative, which is the single omission claimed by the plaintiff in the explanation given, it would have been presumptuous for Dr. Newberg, an internist, to suggest a surgical procedure in the field of urology other than that which Dr. Bogdan, a qualified specialist in that area of medicine, had recommended and thus possibly undermine the confidence the plaintiff should have in her surgeon. We hold that under the circumstances of this case Dr. Newberg, as the referring physician, had no obligation to inform the plaintiff of viable alternative procedures but might reasonably have relied upon Dr. Bogdan, the specialist, to provide such information. We shall not, therefore, disturb the verdict in favor of Dr. Newberg. * * *

There is error in the resolution of the claim against the defendant Dr. Bogdan for his alleged failure to obtain the informed consent of the plaintiff; that judgment is set aside and the case is remanded for a new trial of that issue * * *.

HOOK v. ROTHSTEIN

Court of Appeals of South Carolina, 1984.
281 S.C. 541, 316 S.E.2d 690, cert. denied 283 S.C. 64, 320 S.E.2d 35 (1984)
(mem. of approval).

GOOLSBY, JUDGE.

In this wrongful death action brought by Judith L. Summers Hook, as administratrix of the estate of Jack R. Summers, against Jerry C. Rothstein, M.D., the principal question on appeal concerns the test of liability in a medical malpractice case involving informed consent. Judgment was entered for the defendant physician following a jury verdict in his favor. The plaintiff administratrix appeals. * * *

On January 24, 1972, Mr. Summers reported to the x-ray department at the Lexington County Hospital for Dr. Rothstein to perform * * * [an intravenous pyelogram]. Dr. Rothstein asked Mr. Summers whether he suffered from any allergies. Although he had a long history of allergies, Mr. Summers did not tell Dr. Rothstein about it. Dr. Rothstein, however, did not inform Mr. Summers about the possibility of a fatal reaction.[13] His experience and training had convinced him that patient apprehension plays a significant role in reactions to the contrast material. Shortly after the procedure began, Mr. Summers suffered a severe reaction and died.

* * *

Neither the appellant nor Dr. Rothstein directed our attention to any case in South Carolina which expressly recognizes the doctrine of informed consent. Our own research likewise did not disclose the existence of any such case. * * *

* * * Presently, there are two major standards. One is the professional medical standard, sometimes referred to as the traditional standard; and the other is the lay standard, sometimes referred to as either the materiality of risk or prudent patient standard. * * *

Under the professional standard, the physician is required to disclose those risks which a reasonable medical practitioner of like training would disclose under the same or similar circumstances. * * * In most cases, the questions of whether and to what extent a physician has a duty to disclose a particular risk are to be determined by expert testimony which establishes the prevailing standard of practice and the physician's departure from that standard. * * *

On the other hand, under the lay standard the physician's disclosure duty is to be measured by the patient's need for information rather

---

13. Editors' Note: The frequency of fatal reactions is one in 40,000, according to the court.

than by the standards of the medical profession. * * * Unlike the professional standard, the lay standard does not ordinarily require expert testimony as to medical standards to establish the physician's duty to disclose; rather, it is for the jury to determine whether a reasonable person in the patient's position would have considered the risk significant in making his or her decision. * * * Medical testimony, however, may be required to establish the undisclosed risk as a known danger of the procedure. * * *

The greater number of the jurisdictions in this country follow the professional standard. See Annot., Modern Status of Views as to General Measure of Physician's Duty to Inform Patient of Risks of Proposed Treatment, 88 A.L.R.3d 1008, 1012 (1978) * * *. Almost as many jurisdictions adhere to the lay standard. * * * We think that the better standard is the professional standard. * * *

An informed consent action is no different from any other action for professional malpractice. Underlying every medical malpractice action is the basic principle that the physician departed from a standard of reasonable medical care. * * * Because the question of whether the physician has acted unreasonably often involves the exercise of medical judgment, we feel that, in most cases, expert medical testimony is just as necessary to establish negligence in failing adequately to disclose as it is to prove negligence in failing to treat or diagnose properly. * * *

The physician's chief concern when treating a patient should be the patient's best interests and not what a lay jury, untrained in medicine and employing perfect hindsight, might later conclude he or she should have disclosed. * * *

[T]he judgment of the circuit court is affirmed.

SECTION C. CONSENT TO RESEARCH

ESTRADA v. JAQUES
Court of Appeals of North Carolina, 1984.
70 N.C.App. 627, 321 S.E.2d 240.

BECTON, JUDGE. * * *

Plaintiff, Michael Estrada, worked in a tavern in Chapel Hill and was shot in the knee by a disruptive customer on 16 May 1979. His wound was treated at North Carolina Memorial Hospital (NCMH), with no apparent complications. Estrada developed a mass in his leg, however, and was readmitted to NCMH on 17 June 1979. The mass apparently resulted from a false aneurysm, a weakened spot in an arterial wall, which was probably caused by the passage of the bullet. Defendants Paul F. Jaques and Donald G. Detweiler (the radiologists) confirmed this diagnosis and consulted with defendants Thomas W. Powell and John R. Miles (the surgeons) as to the proper treatment.

The surgeons agreed to the radiologists' advice that the false aneurysm be treated by means of a percutaneous steel coil embolization. Basically, this procedure, still relatively new, involved insertion of a small steel coil into the weakened artery upstream from the false aneurysm, thereby cutting off the flow of blood and preventing a rupture. The radiologists were to perform the embolization. The surgeons discussed the procedure with Estrada and obtained a signed consent from him on 18 June 1979.

At 3:00 that afternoon, the radiologists performed the embolization. At 3:30 Estrada was returned to his room, complaining that his leg was giving him severe pain. Symptoms indicated that the blood supply to the lower leg was inadequate. Estrada received anticoagulants to prevent clotting in the capillaries in his leg, and was taken back to the operating room at 6:00 p.m. The surgeons operated for the next 16 hours, attempting to restore the flow of blood to Estrada's leg. By the time they were able to bypass the blocked area, the capillaries in Estrada's leg had ceased to function from the protracted lack of fresh blood and resultant clotting. Estrada's lower leg was amputated on 19 June 1979. * * *

The underlying order in question granted summary judgment to the surgeons * * * on allegations that the surgeons were negligent in failing to obtain Estrada's informed consent. Such causes of action fall under the purview of N.C.Gen.Stat. § 90–21.13, which provides in relevant part:

(a) No recovery shall be allowed against any health care provider upon the grounds that the health care treatment was rendered without the informed consent of the patient or the patient's spouse, parent, guardian, nearest relative or other person authorized to give consent for the patient where:

(1) The action of the health care provider in obtaining the consent of the patient or other person authorized to give consent for the patient was in accordance with the standards of practice among members of the same health care profession with similar training and experience situated in the same or similar communities; and

(2) A reasonable person from the information provided by the health care provider under the circumstances, would have a general understanding of the procedures or treatments and of the usual and most frequent risks and hazards inherent in the proposed procedures or treatments which are recognized and followed by other health care providers engaged in the same field of practice in the same or similar communities; or

(3) A reasonable person, under all the surrounding circumstances, would have undergone such treatment or procedure had he been advised by the health care provider in accordance with the provisions of subdivisions (1) and (2) of this subsection.

(b) A consent which is evidenced in writing and which meets the foregoing standards, and which is signed by the patient or other authorized person, shall be presumed to be a valid consent. This presumption, however, may be subject to rebuttal only upon proof that such consent was obtained by fraud, deception or misrepresentation of a material fact.

(c) A valid consent is one which is given by a person who under all the surrounding circumstances is mentally and physically competent to give consent.

* * *

In the present case, since the physicians chose to prove the adequacy of the actual consent, they had to show conclusively (1) the circumstances surrounding the consent, (2) the risks inherent in the procedures offered, (3) the standard in the community for obtaining consent, and (4) that the standard was met under the circumstances. Only then did the burden devolve upon Estrada to produce any evidence to rebut the validity of the consent. * * *

The decisions of other states which have adopted similar statutes support our interpretation of the North Carolina statute. * * *

The General Assembly of North Carolina similarly chose not to give the signed consent form conclusive weight. Compare Ga.Code Ann. § 31–9–6 and Simpson v. Dickson, 167 Ga.App. 344, 306 S.E.2d 404 (1983) (form describing treatment conclusive).[14] The form thus constitutes only some evidence of valid consent, and summary judgment may not be granted solely thereon when, as here, the adequacy of the underlying representations is disputed.

[T]he surgeons failed to satisfy the second requirement of subsec. (a)(2) conclusively. It is clear that Estrada understood the procedures offered. However, under the statute, knowledge of the procedures does not suffice; the patient must also be informed of their "usual and most frequent risks and hazards." § 90–21.13(a)(2). Obviously, Estrada could only understand what the surgeons told him. A careful reading of his whole deposition leads to the conclusion that they informed Estrada only of the risks inherent in the standard surgical procedure and the chance that the embolization might not work. The various depositions of the hospital personnel reflect at best a vague knowledge of the risks of embolization in this sort of case. This knowledge, on the present record, is traceable exclusively to a single medical article and to the ill-defined experience of one of the radiologists, apparently including only one prior operation, with little to suggest he communicated it to the surgeons. There was some evidence that steel coil embolizations had been used in other parts of the body with low risk, but nothing to

---

14. Editors' Note: Georgia Code Ann. § 31–9–6.1, effective Jan. 1, 1989, did not repeal § 31–9–6 but substantially qualified it. See also Parikh v. Cunningham, 493 So.2d 999, 1001 (Fla.1986): "[T]he presumption becomes relevant only upon a jury finding that a valid informed consent has been obtained"; otherwise the statute would be unconstitutional, as the lower court had found. 472 So.2d 746 (Fla.Dist. Ct.App.1985).

show why that knowledge should automatically apply to the peripheral arteries operated on in this case.

This omission is critical in light of the evidence that such arteries presented additional difficult problems of size and accessibility. We conclude that this evidence failed to satisfy the surgeons' burden of proof.

* * *

Since in light of our interpretation of § 90–21.13, the matter will certainly arise upon remand, we address a further feature of the case. Estrada argues that the embolization procedure was experimental and that the surgeons had a duty to so inform him. In their initial answer, all defendants admitted that the embolization procedure was experimental. Although their amended answers denied this, the original answer remained admissible against them. * * * Repeated discovery requests revealed only the one article and one operation mentioned above, and only general assertions of personal experience, none by the surgeons. This constituted substantial evidence that the procedure as used was in fact experimental.

Accepting this evidence as true, the consent obtained failed to satisfy the statutory requirements. The statute requires "a general understanding * * * * of the usual and most frequent risks and hazards inherent in the proposed procedures or treatments *which are recognized and followed by other health care providers* * * *." § 90–21.13(a)(2). (Emphasis added.) While the emphasized language is not entirely clear, it appears to require that informed consent be obtained to *established* procedure or treatments. Obviously, experimental procedures, by their very untested nature, do not fall within the category of practices described. Just as obviously, on the other hand, medical innovation must go forward, and there will also be some cases in which no recognized procedure will offer any prospect of success. We do not believe the legislature intended to preclude any valid consent to experimental procedures.

Instead, we hold that where the health care provider offers an experimental procedure or treatment to a patient, the health care provider has a duty, in exercising reasonable care under the circumstances, to inform the patient of the experimental nature of the proposed procedure. With experimental procedures the "most frequent risks and hazards" will remain unknown until the procedure becomes established. If the health care provider has a duty to inform of *known* risks for *established* procedures, common sense and the purposes of the statute equally require that the health care provider inform the patient of any *uncertainty* regarding the risks associated with *experimental* procedures. This includes the experimental nature of the procedure and the *known or projected most likely risks*. The evidence presented in this case illustrates the logic of our holding perfectly: taken in Estrada's favor, it shows that the surgeons presented a full picture of the risks of the surgical procedure and simply advised him that the embolization might not work, without informing him of its experimental nature and their consequent lack of knowledge of the risks of whether it would fail or not. Not surprisingly, Estrada chose the experimental procedure. Such actions by the surgeons do not comport with the reasonable disclosure standards established by § 90–21.13.

Our decision that health care providers must inform their patients that proposed procedures are experimental accords with the majority of courts and commentators which have considered the problem. One federal court has explicitly established such a rule, that the patient "must always be fully informed of the *experimental nature* of the treatment *and* of the foreseeable consequences of that treatment." Ahern v. Veterans Admin., 537 F.2d 1098, 1102 (10th Cir.1976). (Emphasis added.) Partially in response to *Ahern,* the Food and Drug Administration has adopted a specific requirement in its informed consent regulations that any procedures which are experimental be disclosed, 46 Fed.Reg. 8942, 8944, and 8951 (1981) * * *. The Supreme Court of Montana has recognized an informed consent cause of action where plaintiff alleged that the procedure was experimental and that the physician did not disclose this, even though plaintiff was fully informed of the nature of the operation itself. Monroe v. Harper, 164 Mont. 23, 518 P.2d 788 (1974). In a Texas case, a directed verdict for a doctor was reversed, since although he showed that his procedure was similar to previous operations, he did not inform the patient that it was the first time he employed a certain type of skin graft. Wilson v. Scott, 412 S.W.2d 299 (Tex.1967). In Karp v. Cooley, 493 F.2d 408 (5th Cir.), cert. denied, 419 U.S. 845, 95 S.Ct. 79, 42 L.Ed.2d 73 (1974), on the other hand, the court held that since the patient consented to all stages of the operation and there was no showing of concealment of material information, directed verdict for the physician was proper, despite plaintiff's contention that the procedure essentially constituted an experiment. We follow *Ahern* and *Monroe,* however.

In doing so, we also follow the great bulk of the commentators. * * * The psychology of the doctor-patient relation, and the rewards, financial and professional, attendant upon recognition of experimental success, increase the potential for abuse and strengthen the rationale for uniform disclosure. We have found little authority supporting a contrary rule. Accordingly, we reaffirm our holding that reasonable standards of informed consent to an experimental procedure require disclosure to the patient that the procedure is experimental.

* * *

Note on Institutional Review Boards

While medical practice for current patients should be based upon scientific principles and methods, including careful planning, observation, and recordkeeping, and while all this may provide benefits to future patients, consent to practice does not constitute consent to research. Here are the distinctions:

THE BELMONT REPORT [15]

A. Boundaries Between Practice and Research

[T]he term "practice" refers to interventions that are designed solely to enhance the well-being of an individual patient or client and that have a reasonable expectation of success. The purpose of medical or behavioral practice is to provide diagnosis, preventive treatment, or therapy to particular individuals.

By contrast, the term "research" designates an activity designed to test an hypothesis, permit conclusions to be drawn, and thereby to develop or contribute to generalizable knowledge (expressed, for example, in theories, principles, and statements of relationships). Research is usually described in a formal protocol that sets forth an objective and a set of procedures designed to reach that objective.

When a clinician departs in a significant way from standard or accepted practice, the innovation does not, in and of itself, constitute research. The fact that a procedure is "experimental," in the sense of new, untested, or different, does not automatically place it in the category of research. Radically new procedures of this description should, however, be made the object of formal research at an early stage in order to determine whether they are safe and effective. Thus, it is the responsibility of medical practice committees, for example, to insist that a major innovation be incorporated into a formal research project.

Research and practice may be carried on together when research is designed to evaluate the safety and efficacy of a therapy. This need not cause any confusion regarding whether or not the activity requires review; the general rule is that if there is any element of research in an activity, that activity should undergo review for the protection of human subjects.

In medical science, new drugs, surgery, and devices have to be tested empirically—that is, their safety and efficacy must be established through research by means of clinical trials on patients. While patients who have a good relationship with their physicians are remarkably willing to be the subjects of medical experimentation, they have the legal right to say "No," and this calls for informed consent.

The use of patients in the United States as guinea pigs for biomedical research received little public attention until the 1960s, when cases like Hyman v. Jewish Chronic Disease Hosp.[16] suggested that individu-

15. Ethical Principles and Guidelines for the Protection of Human Subjects of Research (Nat. Comm'n for Protection of Human Subjects of Biomedical and Behavioral Research 1979), 44 Fed.Reg. 23,192 (Apr. 18, 1979).

16. 21 A.D.2d 495, 251 N.Y.S.2d 818 (1964).

als' rights were being abused. A celebrated article by Dr. Harry Beecher broadened the inquiry and heightened the fear.[17]

But what could be done in a preventive and regulatory way to protect patients' rights from abuse by doctors? After-the-fact litigation seemed inadequate to the task of assuring good biomedical research; the states might have but did not create regulatory schemes; and the United States had no police power to create private remedies.

Two federal constitutional powers existed, though, and through the Department of Health and Human Services, the United States has applied them: the spending power, as lavished on biomedical research that is either performed at or funded by the National Institutes of Health (NIH); and the commerce power, as used by the Food and Drug Administration (FDA) to regulate investigational drugs and devices, no matter where the research is funded or performed. The mechanism chosen was to make every health care research organization police itself in matters of human research by establishing and operating an institutional review board (IRB), with the FDA supervising the self-policers. Considering the pervasiveness of the federal presence, it is hardly surprising that most medical research institutions put all of their protocols through the IRB, whether IRB approval is technically required or not.

The IRB scheme, which originated in a 1974 statute,[18] is in full force today, and it has been considerably expanded in scope and overseen by detailed federal regulation and regular inspection. Regulations of the NIH [19] and the FDA [20] require the investigator to submit for IRB approval a detailed research plan that is accompanied by a consent form. The elements of consent are listed as follows:

GENERAL REQUIREMENTS FOR INFORMED CONSENT
45 CFR § 46.116 (1988).

Except as provided elsewhere in this or other subparts, no investigator may involve a human being as a subject in research covered by these regulations unless the investigator has obtained the legally effective informed consent of the subject or the subject's legally authorized

---

17. Ethics and Clinical Research, 274 New Eng.J.Med. 1354 (1966).

18. Codified in Title 42, The Public Health and Welfare. Code § 289 was enacted as § 212(a) of the National Research Act, Pub.L. No. 93-384, Title II, 88 Stat. 352 (1974), which in turn amended the Public Health Service Act; for the skimpy legislative history, see 1974 U.S.Code Cong. & Admin.News 3648, 3565. Section 212(a) of the Act was codified as 42 U.S.C.A. § 289*l*-3 until the reenactment of §§ (a) and (b)(1) in Pub.L. No. 99-158, § 2, the Health Research Extension Act of 1985, 99 Stat. 873 (1985), which also added § (b)(2). See 1985 U.S.Code Cong. & Admin.News 710. As of 1989, no annotation reported a case under § 289 or its predecessor.

19. 45 CFR part 46, Protection of Human Subjects.

20. 21 CFR part 50, Protection of Human Subjects, and 21 CFR part 56, Institutional Review Boards.

representative. An investigator shall seek such consent only under circumstances that provide the prospective subject or the representative sufficient opportunity to consider whether or not to participate and that minimize the possibility of coercion or undue influence. The information that is given to the subject or the representative shall be in language understandable to the subject or the representative. No informed consent, whether oral or written, may include any exculpatory language through which the subject or the representative is made to waive or appear to waive any of the subject's legal rights, or releases or appears to release the investigator, the sponsor, the institution or its agents from liability for negligence.

(a) Basic elements of informed consent. Except as provided in paragraph (c) or (d) of this section [omitted], in seeking informed consent the following information shall be provided to each subject:

(1) A statement that the study involves research, an explanation of the purposes of the research and the expected duration of the subject's participation, a description of the procedures to be followed, and identification of any procedures which are experimental;

(2) A description of any reasonably foreseeable risks or discomforts to the subject;

(3) A description of any benefits to the subject or to others which may reasonably be expected from the research;

(4) A disclosure of appropriate alternative procedures or courses of treatment, if any, that might be advantageous to the subject;

(5) A statement describing the extent, if any, to which confidentiality of records identifying the subject will be maintained;

(6) For research involving more than minimal risk, an explanation as to whether any compensation and an explanation as to whether any medical treatments are available if injury occurs and, if so, what they consist of, or where further information may be obtained;

(7) An explanation of whom to contact for answers to pertinent questions about the research and research subjects' rights, and whom to contact in the event of a research-related injury to the subject; and

(8) A statement that participation is voluntary, refusal to participate will involve no penalty or loss of benefits to which the subject is otherwise entitled, and the subject may discontinue participation at any time without penalty or loss of benefits to which the subject is otherwise entitled.

(b) Additional elements of informed consent. When appropriate, one or more of the following elements of information shall also be provided to each subject:

(1) A statement that the particular treatment or procedure may involve risks to the subject (or to the embryo or fetus, if the subject is or may become pregnant) which are currently unforeseeable;

(2) Anticipated circumstances under which the subject's participation may be terminated by the investigator without regard to the subject's consent;

(3) Any additional costs to the subject that may result from participation in the research;

(4) The consequences of a subject's decision to withdraw from the research and procedures for orderly termination of participation by the subject;

(5) A statement that significant new findings developed during the course of the research which may relate to the subject's willingness to continue participation will be provided to the subject; and

(6) The approximate number of subjects involved in the study.

The object of institutional review boards is to prevent harm to patients by establishing and reviewing good informed consent practices, and so, from the standpoint of medical liability, the sanctions under federal regulations have low visibility. For regulatory failures, however, institutions can lose their NIH funding [21] and their eligibility to conduct research,[22] and researchers can lose FDA permission to test drugs and devices.[23]

While patients acquired no private rights under the federal law, it did not preempt state-law rights to damage remedies. One of the editors, having served on an IRB for many years, knows that the members are alert to the risk of damage actions from the lack of informed consent. The quoted regulation could be used as a checklist for the plaintiff's attorney. It also has a preventive function for potential defendant researchers: intelligible informed consent procedures, applied consistently, are a very good defense against damage actions.

SECTION D. REFUSED SERVICES

TRUMAN v. THOMAS

Supreme Court of California, 1980.
27 Cal.3d 285, 165 Cal.Rptr. 308, 611 P.2d 902.

BIRD, CHIEF JUSTICE. * * *

Respondent, Dr. Claude R. Thomas, is a family physician engaged in a general medical practice. He was first contacted in April 1963 by appellants' mother, Rena Truman, in connection with her second pregnancy. He continued to act as the primary physician for Mrs. Truman and her two children until March 1969. During this six-year period,

---

21. 45 CFR § 46.123, Early Termination of Research Funding; Evaluation of Subsequent Applications and Proposals.

22. 21 CFR § 56.121, Disqualification of an IRB or an Institution.

23. 21 CFR § 312.70, Disqualification of a Clinical Investigator [for misconduct that includes 21 CFR parts 50 and 56].

Mrs. Truman not only sought his medical advice, but often discussed personal matters with him.

In April 1969, Mrs. Truman consulted Dr. Casey, a urologist, about a urinary tract infection which had been treated previously by Dr. Thomas. While examining Mrs. Truman, Dr. Casey discovered that she was experiencing heavy vaginal discharges and that her cervix was extremely rough. Mrs. Truman was given a prescription for the infection and advised to see a gynecologist as soon as possible. When Mrs. Truman did not make an appointment with a gynecologist, Dr. Casey made an appointment for her with a Dr. Ritter.

In October 1969, Dr. Ritter discovered that Mrs. Truman's cervix had been largely replaced by a cancerous tumor. Too far advanced to be removed by surgery, the tumor was unsuccessfully treated by other methods. Mrs. Truman died in July 1970 at the age of 30.

Appellants are Rena Truman's two children. They brought this wrongful death action against Dr. Thomas for his failure to perform a pap smear test on their mother. At the trial, expert testimony was presented which indicated that if Mrs. Truman had undergone a pap smear at any time between 1964 and 1969, the cervical tumor probably would have been discovered in time to save her life. There was disputed expert testimony that the standard of medical practice required a physician to explain to women patients that it is important to have a pap smear each year to "pick up early lesions that are treatable rather than having to deal with [more developed] tumor[s] that very often aren't treatable." [24]

Although Dr. Thomas saw Mrs. Truman frequently between 1964 and 1969, he never performed a pap smear test on her. Dr. Thomas testified that he did not "specifically" inform Mrs. Truman of the risk involved in any failure to undergo the pap smear test. Rather,

> I said, "You should have a pap smear." We don't say, "By now it can be Stage Two [in the development of cervical cancer]," or go through all of the different lectures about cancer. I think it is a widely known and generally accepted manner of treatment and I think the patient has a high degree of responsibility. We are not enforcers, we are advisors.

However, Dr. Thomas' medical records contain no reference to any discussion or recommendation that Mrs. Truman undergo a pap smear test.

For the most part, Dr. Thomas was unable to describe specific conversations with Mrs. Truman. For example, he testified that during certain periods

---

24. Dr. Thomas conceded at the trial that it is the accepted standard of practice for physicians in his community to recommend that women of child-bearing age undergo a pap smear each year. His records indicate that during the period in which he acted as Mrs. Truman's family physician he performed between 10 and 20 pap smears per month.

I saw Rena very frequently, approximately once a week or so, and I am sure my opening remark was, "Rena, you need a pap smear." * * * I am sure we discussed it with her so often that she couldn't [have] fail[ed] to realize that we wanted her to have a complete examination, breast examination, ovaries and pap smear.

Dr. Thomas also testified that on at least two occasions when he performed pelvic examinations of Mrs. Truman, she refused him permission to perform the test, stating she could not afford the cost. Dr. Thomas offered to defer payment, but Mrs. Truman wanted to pay cash.

Appellants argue that the failure to give a pap smear test to Mrs. Truman proximately caused her death. Two instructions requested by appellants described alternative theories under which Dr. Thomas could be held liable for this failure. First, they asked that the jury be instructed that

It is the duty of a physician to disclose to his patient all relevant information to enable the patient to make an informed decision regarding the submission to or refusal to take a diagnostic test.

Failure of the physician to disclose to his patient all relevant information including the risks to the patient if the test is refused renders the physician liable for any injury legally resulting from the patient's refusal to take the test if a reasonably prudent person in the patient's position would not have refused the test if she had been adequately informed of all the significant perils.

Second, they requested that the jury be informed that

[A]s a matter of law * * * a physician who fails to perform a pap smear test on a female patient over the age of 23 and to whom the patient has entrusted her general physical care is liable for injury or death proximately caused by the failure to perform the test.

Both instructions were refused.

The jury rendered a special verdict, finding Dr. Thomas free of any negligence that proximately caused Mrs. Truman's death. This appeal followed.

The central issue for this court is whether Dr. Thomas breached his duty of care to Mrs. Truman when he failed to inform her of the potentially fatal consequences of allowing cervical cancer to develop undetected by a pap smear.

In Cobbs v. Grant, 8 Cal.3d 229, 104 Cal.Rptr. 505, 502 P.2d 1 (1972), this court considered the scope of a physician's duty to disclose medical information to his or her patients in discussing proposed medical procedures. * * *

[T]he court in *Cobbs* stated that a patient must be apprised not only of the "risks inherent in the procedure [prescribed, but also] the risks of a decision not to undergo the treatment, and the probability of a successful outcome of the treatment." 502 P.2d at 10. This rule applies whether the procedure involves treatment or a diagnostic test. On the one hand, a physician recommending a risk-free procedure may safely forego discussion beyond that necessary to conform to competent medical practice and to obtain the patient's consent. * * * If a patient indicates that he or she is going to decline the risk-free test or treatment, then the doctor has the additional duty of advising of all material risks of which a reasonable person would want to be informed before deciding not to undergo the procedure. On the other hand, if the recommended test or treatment is itself risky, then the physician should always explain the potential consequences of declining to follow the recommended course of action.

Nevertheless, Dr. Thomas contends that *Cobbs* does not apply to him because the duty to disclose applies only where the patient consents to the recommended procedure. He argues that since a physician's advice may be presumed to be founded on an expert appraisal of the patient's medical needs, no reasonable patient would fail to undertake further inquiry before rejecting such advice. Therefore, patients who reject their physician's advice should shoulder the burden of inquiry as to the possible consequences of their decision.

This argument is inconsistent with *Cobbs*. The duty to disclose was imposed in *Cobbs* so that patients might meaningfully exercise their right to make decisions about their own bodies. * * * The importance of this right should not be diminished by the manner in which it is exercised. Further, the need for disclosure is not lessened because patients reject a recommended procedure. Such a decision does not alter "what has been termed the 'fiducial qualities' of the physician-patient relationship," since patients who reject a procedure are as unskilled in the medical sciences as those who consent. 502 P.2d at 12. To now hold that patients who reject their physician's advice have the burden of inquiring as to the potential consequences of their decisions would be to contradict *Cobbs*. It must be remembered that Dr. Thomas was not engaged in an arms-length transaction with Mrs. Truman. Clearly, under *Cobbs*, he was obligated to provide her with all the information material to her decision.

Dr. Thomas next contends that, as a matter of law, he had no duty to disclose to Mrs. Truman the risk of failing to undergo a pap smear test because "the danger [is] remote and commonly appreciated to be remote." Ibid. The merit of this contention depends on whether a jury could reasonably find that knowledge of this risk was material to Mrs. Truman's decision.

The record indicates that the pap smear test is an accurate detector of cervical cancer. Although the probability that Mrs. Truman had cervical cancer was low, Dr. Thomas knew that the potential harm of failing to detect the disease at an early stage was death.[25] This situation is not analogous to one which involves, for example, "relatively minor risks inherent in [such] common procedures" as the taking of

---

25. Expert testimony established that if cervical cancer is detected in the early stages of its development, there is a very high probability that the progress of this disease can be permanently arrested.

blood samples. * * * These procedures are not central to the decision to administer or reject the procedure. In contrast, the risk which Mrs. Truman faced from cervical cancer was not only significant, it was the principal reason why Dr. Thomas recommended that she undergo a pap smear.

Little evidence was introduced on whether this risk was commonly known. Dr. Thomas testified that the risk would be known to a reasonable person. Whether such evidence is sufficient to establish that there was no general duty to disclose this risk to patients is a question of fact for the jury. Moreover, even assuming such disclosure was not generally required, the circumstances in this case may establish that Dr. Thomas did have a duty to inform Mrs. Truman of the risks she was running by not undergoing a pap smear.

Dr. Thomas testified he never specifically informed her of the purpose of a pap smear test. There was no evidence introduced that Mrs. Truman was aware of the serious danger entailed in not undergoing the test. However, there was testimony that Mrs. Truman said she would not undergo the test on certain occasions because of its cost or because "she just didn't feel like it." Under these circumstances, a jury could reasonably conclude that Dr. Thomas had a duty to inform Mrs. Truman of the danger of refusing the test because it was not reasonable for Dr. Thomas to assume that Mrs. Truman appreciated the potentially fatal consequences of her conduct. Accordingly, this court cannot decide as a matter of law that Dr. Thomas owed absolutely no duty to Mrs. Truman to make this important disclosure that affected her life.

* * *

Refusal to give the requested instruction meant that the jury was unable to consider whether Dr. Thomas breached a duty by not disclosing the danger of failing to undergo a pap smear. Since this theory finds support in the record, it was error for the court to refuse to give the requested instruction. * * * If the jury had been given this instruction and had found in favor of the appellants, such a finding would have had support in the record before us. Reversal is therefore required. * * *

CLARK, JUSTICE, dissenting. * * *

The burden of explaining the purposes of a pap smear and the potential risks in failing to submit to one may not appear to be great, but the newly imposed duty upon physicians created by today's majority opinion goes far beyond. The instruction requires disclosure of all "relevant information to enable the patient to make an informed decision regarding the submission to or refusal to take a diagnostic test." In short, it applies not only to pap smears, but to all diagnostic procedures allegedly designed to detect illness which could lead to death or serious complication if not timely treated.

* * *

Few, if any, people in our society are unaware that a general examination is designed to discover serious illness for timely treatment.

While a lengthy explanation may result in general examinations for some patients who would otherwise decline or defer them, the onerous duty placed upon doctors by today's decision will result in reduced care for others. Requiring physicians to spend a large portion of their time teaching medical science before practicing it will greatly increase the cost of medical diagnosis—a cost ultimately paid by an unwanting public. Persons desiring treatment for specific complaints will be deterred from seeking medical advice once they realize they will be charged not only for treatment but also for lengthy lectures on the merits of their examination.

The great educational program the majority embark upon, even if justifiable, is a question of public policy for the Legislature to determine: whether the cost warrants the burden, and whether the duty to educate rests with doctors, schools, or health departments. Requiring individual doctors to enlighten the public may be found through legislative hearings to be inefficient, not reaching those who need it most—the ones hesitant to consult doctors.

When a patient chooses a physician, he or she obviously has confidence in the doctor and intends to accept proffered medical advice. When the doctor prescribes diagnostic tests, the patient is aware the tests are intended to discover illness. It is therefore reasonable to assume that a patient who refuses advice is aware of potential risk.

Moreover, the physician-patient relationship is based on trust, and forcing the doctor into a hard sell approach to his services can only jeopardize that relationship.

* * *

Nothing in Cobbs v. Grant, 8 Cal.3d 229, 104 Cal.Rptr. 505, 502 P.2d 1 (1972), warrants imposition of such an onerous duty—to the contrary, that case expressly rejected any such duty. * * *

In *Cobbs*, we expressly circumscribed the duty of the doctor, holding that a "mini-course in medical science is not required," that "there is no physician's duty to discuss the relatively minor risks inherent in common procedures, when it is common knowledge that such risks inherent in the procedure are of very low incidence," that as to common procedures "no warning" is "required as to the remote possibility of death or serious bodily harm," and that recovery would be permitted only if a "prudent person in the patient's position" adequately informed of the perils would have declined treatment. 502 P.2d at 11.

Thus, *Cobbs* is not helpful to the majority because the duty of disclosure in that case was imposed to assure consent to the intrusion would be effective. When no intrusion takes place, no need for consent, effective or otherwise, arises.[26]

26. Like *Cobbs*, all other authority relied on by the majority * * * is concerned with whether consent to therapy was informed and therefore effective. The cases involved situations where there has been an intrusion to the body autonomy and it is claimed the intrusion was consensual. Thus, the question of informed con-

Furthermore, contrary to the express limitations in *Cobbs,* today's decision requires not only an explanation of the risks of a single procedure but also a "mini-course in medical science," if not a maxi-course. Similarly, because discovery of serious illness in a general examination of an apparently healthy person is remote, the doctor, contrary to *Cobbs,* is now required to disclose remote possibilities of illness. Moreover, the *Cobbs* duty to warn in cases where an adequately informed prudent person would have declined treatment shows a concern for preventing over-selling of services by physicians. By contrast, today's duty appears designed to increase selling of medical services.

* * *

Refusal to give the requested instruction does not warrant reversal. I would affirm the judgment.

RICHARDSON and MANUEL, JJ., concur.

PUBLIC HEALTH TRUST v. WONS

Supreme Court of Florida, 1989.
541 So.2d 96.

KOGAN, JUSTICE. * * *

Norma Wons entered Jackson Memorial Hospital, a medical facility operated by the Public Health Trust of Dade County, with a condition known as dysfunctional uterine bleeding. Doctors informed Mrs. Wons that she would require treatment in the form of a blood transfusion or she would, in all probability, die. Mrs. Wons, a practicing Jehovah's Witness and mother of two minor children, declined the treatment on grounds that it violated her religious principles to receive blood from outside her own body. At the time she refused consent Mrs. Wons was conscious and able to reach an informed decision concerning her treatment.

The Health Trust petitioned the circuit court to force Mrs. Wons to undergo a blood transfusion. At the hearing Mrs. Wons' husband testified that he fully supported his wife's decision to refuse the treatment and that, in the unfortunate event she were to die, their two children would be cared for by Mr. Wons and Mrs. Wons' mother and brothers. Nevertheless, the court granted the petition, ordering the hospital doctors to administer the blood transfusion, which was done while Mrs. Wons was unconscious. The trial judge reasoned that minor children have a right to be reared by two loving parents, a right which overrides the mother's rights of free religious exercise and privacy. Upon regaining consciousness, Mrs. Wons appealed to the third district, which reversed the order. After holding that the case was not moot due to the recurring nature of Mrs. Wons' condition (i.e., it was capable of repetition, yet evading review), the district court held that Mrs.

sent is crucial. None involves the situation where the patient has refused the intrusion and thus consent is immaterial.

Wons' constitutional rights of religion and privacy could not be overridden by the state's purported interests. [The third district court of appeal certified to the Florida Supreme Court the following question as one of great public importance: "Whether a competent adult has a lawful right to refuse a blood transfusion without which she may well die." Wons v. Public Health Trust, 500 So.2d 679, 680 (Fla.1987).]

An individual's right to refuse medical treatment must be analyzed in terms of our decision in Satz v. Perlmutter, 379 So.2d 359 (Fla.1980), aff'g 362 So.2d 160 (Fla.Dist.Ct.App.1978). That case, in which this court adopted the fourth district's reasoning in full, established four criteria wherein the right to refuse medical treatment may be overridden by a compelling state interest. These factors are:

(1) Preservation of life,

(2) Protection of innocent third parties,

(3) Prevention of suicide, and

(4) Maintenance of the ethical integrity of the medical profession. 362 So.2d at 162.

It is important to note that these factors are by no means a bright-line test, capable of resolving every dispute regarding the refusal of medical treatment. Rather, they are intended merely as factors to be considered while reaching the difficult decision of when a compelling state interest may override the basic constitutional rights of privacy and religious freedom.

The Health Trust asserts that the children's right to be reared by two loving parents is sufficient to trigger the second compelling state interest in the *Perlmutter* list of criteria. * * * We hold that the state's interest in maintaining a home with two parents for the minor children does not override Mrs. Wons' constitutional rights of privacy and religion.

The Health Trust expressed concern during oral argument that in future cases of this nature, the inconvenience of taking each treatment refusal case to court for an emergency judicial hearing would create problems. The Health Trust complains that this would present too heavy a burden on the hospitals to provide care between court appearances. While we understand the Health Trust's dilemma, these cases demand individual attention. No blanket rule is feasible which could sufficiently cover all occasions in which this situation will arise. Thus, it will be necessary for hospitals that wish to contest a patient's refusal of treatment to commence court proceedings and sustain the heavy burden of proof that the state's interest outweighs the patient's constitutional rights.

[W]e answer the certified question in the affirmative and approve the decision of the district court.

EHRLICH, CHIEF JUSTICE, concurring specially. * * *

* * * Absent evidence that a minor child will be abandoned, the state has no compelling interest sufficient to override the competent patient's right to refuse treatment. Sweeping claims about the need to preserve the lives of parents with minor children have an emotional appeal that facilely avoids both the constitutionally required scrutiny of the state's authority to act and the search for less restrictive alternatives.

Petitioner conceded below that the other interests enumerated in *Perlmutter* are not implicated in this case. * * * However, analysis of those other interests supports the decision in this case.

Perhaps the most important of the state interests discussed in *Perlmutter* is the interest in the preservation of life. [T]he quality of life for the patient if treatment is administered must be taken into consideration. It does not necessarily follow that where there is a favorable medical prognosis the state's interest automatically overrides the patient's right to refuse treatment. In some circumstances the cost to the individual of the life-prolonging treatment, in economic, emotional, or as in this case, spiritual terms, may be too high. * * * That "cost" must be looked at from the patient's point of view. The dissent assumes that after the blood transfusion Mrs. Wons "could return to a normal life." Is that really the case? Mrs. Wons is a Jehovah's Witness, as are the other members of her family. Receiving a blood transfusion is a serious sin for someone of her faith. After the transfusion she must live with the knowledge of that sin, and, because she has a recurring condition, she must also live with the knowledge that should she again become critically ill, she may again be forced to receive blood. Given the strength of the faith she and her family share, that knowledge must affect not only Mrs. Wons, but her family as well. From her perspective, this situation can hardly be considered "normal." Where a competent adult is involved, the best evidence of how that person views the consequences of accepting medical treatment is that person's own statements and actions. It is not for the court to second guess, or make judgments of, the reasonableness of that view. * * *

The other two state interests discussed in *Perlmutter* are the duty to prevent suicide and the maintenance of the ethical integrity of the medical profession. It is uncontested that this case does not implicate the state's interest in the prevention of suicide. Mrs. Wons does not desire to die. Rather, she has chosen not to live, if to do so would require that she receive blood. Should she die because no blood transfusion is administered, her death would be of natural causes, not suicide. * * *

The preservation of the ethical integrity of the medical profession is, in my view, the least compelling of the state interests involved. * * * Given the fundamental nature of the constitutional rights involved, protection of the ethical integrity of the medical profession alone could never override those rights.

Further, circumstances such as these are clearly distinguishable from the instances cited by the dissent where state interests have been held to override the right to act according to one's religious beliefs. Most, like snake-handling, are prohibitions against taking affirmative religiously grounded action. Only requiring compulsory medical vaccination involves a refusal to act because of religious principles, and there the state interest in preventing the widespread danger to public health is great. * * * Where the religiously grounded "action" the state is attempting to prohibit is a refusal to act rather than affirmative conduct, the state may only interfere where there is a grave and immediate public danger. In re Brown, 478 So.2d 1033, 1037 (Miss. 1985). No affirmative conduct is present in this case. By forcing Mrs. Wons to submit to a blood transfusion forbidden by her religious beliefs, the state compelled rather than prohibited affirmative conduct, and there was no immediate public danger posed by her refusal to consent to the transfusion. Therefore, cases concerning the prohibition of affirmative religiously based conduct are inapposite to this case.
* * *

OVERTON, JUSTICE, dissenting.

* * * I find that the majority misapplies our decision in Satz v. Perlmutter, 379 So.2d 359 (Fla.1980). * * *

This court specifically limited *Perlmutter* to its facts * * *. The majority opinion in this case now broadly expands the narrow *Perlmutter* holding and represents a general willingness to uphold the rights of an individual to practice a chosen religion and protect rights of privacy without regard for the effects on innocent third parties, particularly minor children.

I believe the better view has been set forth in Application of the President and Directors of Georgetown College, Inc., 331 F.2d 1000 (D.C. Cir.), cert. denied, 377 U.S. 978, 84 S.Ct. 1883, 12 L.Ed.2d 746 (1964), where the court ordered a blood transfusion to save the life of the mother of a seven-month-old child who had refused the transfusion on religious grounds. The court justified its decision in part on the following reasoning:

> The patient, 25 years old, was the mother of a seven-month-old child. *The state, as parens patriae, will not allow a parent to abandon a child, and so it should not allow this most ultimate of voluntary abandonments.* The patient had a responsibility to the community to care for her infant. Thus the people had an interest in preserving the life of this mother. Id. at 1008. (Emphasis added.)

* * *

The majority further fails to recognize the distinction between cases where the prognosis that the patient can be restored to normal life with proper medical procedures is extremely good and cases where the possibility of recovery is slight and the person is diagnosed as terminal. Here, it was unrefuted that, following medical treatment, Wons could return to a normal life, but the majority totally fails to consider this factor in applying *Perlmutter*. The patient in *Perlmutter* was a 73-year-old victim of amyotrophic lateral sclerosis (Lou Gehrig's disease), for which there is no cure, and normal life expectancy, from time of diagnosis, is two years. Mr. Perlmutter was virtually incapable of movement and unable to breathe without a mechanical respirator, and the prognosis of death was within a short time. The majority failed to distinguish the terminal nature of his condition from Mrs. Wons' condition, from which she could completely recover with treatment. This distinction based on prognosis was explained by the New Jersey Supreme Court in In re Quinlan, 70 N.J. 10, 355 A.2d 647, cert. denied, 429 U.S. 922, 97 S.Ct. 319, 50 L.Ed.2d 289 (1976). * * *

The third flaw in the majority's position is that it totally ignores the fourth factor enunciated in *Perlmutter* and necessarily places doctors and emergency medical facilities in an impossible position by leaving unresolved the issue of when and under what circumstances emergency medical personnel should treat patients who have minor children when they seek treatment but refuse blood transfusions. * * * Although the right to religious beliefs is absolute, the manner in which those beliefs are conducted may clearly be restricted by governmental action, motivated by legitimate governmental interests, such as those concerning minor children, instances involving not only blood transfusions but exposure to death from snake-handling, ingestion of poison, use of illegal drugs, and the requirement of medical vaccines. * * * To justify, as a right of the free exercise of religion, a parent's right to abandon a minor child through a death which is totally unnecessary is, in my view, neither a reasonable nor a logical interpretation of the first amendment. James Madison would not believe that his "free exercise" clause could ever be interpreted in this manner.

* * *

LEACH v. SHAPIRO

Court of Appeals of Ohio, 1984.
13 Ohio App.3d 393, 13 Ohio B.R. 477, 469 N.E.2d 1047.

BAIRD, JUDGE.

Edna Marie Leach entered Akron General Medical Center on July 27, 1980, suffering from respiratory distress. Mrs. Leach subsequently suffered a respiratory-cardiac arrest, and though her heartbeat was restored, Mrs. Leach remained in a chronic vegetative state. Mrs. Leach was placed on life support systems to sustain her breathing and circulation. On October 21, 1980, Mrs. Leach's husband, as her guardian, petitioned the Summit County Probate Court for an order to terminate the life support measures. The court issued this order on December 18, 1980. Leach v. Akron Gen. Med. Ctr., 68 Ohio Misc. 1, 22 Ohio Op.3d 48, 426 N.E.2d 809 (1980). On January 6, 1981, the respirator was disconnected, and Mrs. Leach died.

On July 9, 1982, plaintiffs filed this action seeking damages for the time Mrs. Leach was on life support systems. Defendants filed a motion in the alternative, to dismiss or for summary judgment. * * * The court * * * treated defendants' motion as one to dismiss for failure to state a claim upon which relief may be granted * * * [and] granted defendants' motion * * *.

Plaintiffs' action is generally based upon the notion that defendants acted wrongfully in placing Mrs. Leach on life-support systems and in maintaining her thereon contrary to the express wishes of Mrs. Leach and her family. A physician who treats a patient without consent commits a battery, even though the procedure is harmless or beneficial. * * * While the patient's right to refuse treatment is qualified because it may be overborne by competing state interests, we believe that, absent legislation to the contrary, the patient's right to refuse treatment is absolute until the quality of the competing interests is weighed in a court proceeding. We perceive this right as the logical extension of the consent requirement and conclude that a patient may recover for battery if his refusal is ignored.

* * * Plaintiffs do not allege that the resuscitation efforts were improper or constituted a battery. Instead, the complaint alleges that Mrs. Leach was placed on life support systems on August 1, 1980, without the consent of Mrs. Leach or her family. From the complaint it would appear that August 1, 1980, was the day Mrs. Leach was moved to a private room from intensive care. If the facts as developed prove that Mrs. Leach was in fact placed on the machines as a part of the resuscitation efforts following her cardiac arrest, we presume that plaintiffs would consider such treatment proper since they do not question the propriety of the resuscitation efforts in their complaint.

If the life support systems were first introduced as part of a properly authorized treatment, we feel that the trial court's ultimate conclusion was correct—barring significant improvement, and as long as Mrs. Leach was unconscious, these systems could only be disconnected by court order. In Ohio, at this time, the court system provides the only mechanism which can protect the interest of the doctor, the hospital, the patient, the family and the state, which can objectively weigh the competing interests in an emotionally charged situation, and which can insulate the participants from civil and criminal liability. Until such time as the legislature provides some more efficient means of protecting the rights of patients in Mrs. Leach's condition, we join those courts that require judicial authority for the termination of life-prolonging treatment of an incompetent patient. Superintendent of Belchertown State School v. Saikewicz, 373 Mass. 728, 370 N.E.2d 417 (1977); In re Eichner, 73 A.D.2d 431, 426 N.Y.2d 517 (1980), as modified by In re Storar, 52 N.Y.2d 363, 438 N.Y.S.2d 266, 420 N.E.2d 64, cert. denied, 454 U.S. 858, 102 S.Ct. 309, 70 L.Ed.2d 153 (1981). We also conclude that where the initial use of support systems was properly authorized, plaintiffs may not recover for ordinary and necessary medical expenses incurred during the time reasonably required to secure court authority for the termination of those support systems.

Plaintiffs allege, however, that Mrs. Leach was first placed on life support systems on August 1, 1980, when she was in a chronic vegetative state, and that this treatment was performed without consent of Mrs. Leach or her family. Plaintiffs allege that Mrs. Leach expressly advised defendants that she did not wish to be kept alive by machines. Absent an emergency defendants had an obligation to secure consent for Mrs. Leach's treatment from one authorized to act in her behalf, since Mrs. Leach was not capable of consenting, or by court order. If an emergency existed on August 1, 1980, when plaintiffs allege the life support systems were first employed, such an emergency would ordinarily give rise to an implied consent, but plaintiffs allege Mrs. Leach would have expressly refused to consent to such procedures in those circumstances. This court has held that where the parties contract expressly with regard to a particular procedure, an implied agreement cannot thereafter arise when the express agreement directly controverts the inclusion of any such implication. * * *

We recognize that doctors must be free to exercise their best medical judgment in treating a life-threatening emergency. * * * Carried to its extreme, however, the doctrine of implied consent could effectively nullify those privacy rights recognized in In re Quinlan, 70 N.J. 10, 355 A.2d 647, cert. denied sub nom. Garger v. New Jersey, 429 U.S. 922, 97 S.Ct. 319, 50 L.Ed.2d 289 (1976) * * *, since a physician could circumvent the express wishes of a terminal patient by waiting to act until the patient was comatose and critical. On the other hand, the prospect of refusing to act in an emergency because the patient at some time voiced vague wishes not to be kept alive on machines is equally unacceptable.

We conclude that a patient has the right to refuse treatment, and that this refusal may not be overcome by the doctrine of implied consent. Before this refusal can controvert the implied consent of a medical emergency, however, it must satisfy the same standards of knowledge and understanding required for informed consent. A terminally ill patient fully advised of an impending crisis might then be able to refuse treatments which would only prolong suffering, while a patient afflicted with a disease which would be terminal in several years and who had generally expressed the desire to die peacefully would not be denied treatment for injuries sustained in an automobile crash. Both doctor and patient would then be protected from statements not made in contemplation of the specific circumstances and the specific medical treatment required. General statements by the patient could still be considered by a court, of course, in determining the wishes of a patient in a chronic vegetative condition.

The merits of plaintiffs' claims for relief depend upon the facts that are developed in this case. The existence and nature of any consent, the existence and nature of any refusal of treatment, the nature of the treatments before August 1, 1980, Mrs. Leach's condition on August 1, 1980, and the nature of the treatment on and after August 1, 1980, are all factual questions the answers to which determine whether plaintiffs are entitled to relief. Accordingly, defendants' motion to dismiss Count 1 for failure to state a claim should not have been granted.

Plaintiffs also allege that once Mrs. Leach was placed on life-support systems, defendants failed to inform them of Mrs. Leach's true condition for a period of two months, failed to apprise the family of her course of treatments for that two-month period, and during the two-month period administered experimental drugs to Mrs. Leach without her family's consent for the purpose of observing the effects of these drugs on a person in Mrs. Leach's condition. * * * These allegations raise questions of fact on both issues, and dismissal of these claims was improper.

Plaintiffs also claim that they were not informed of Mrs. Leach's condition or prognosis for a period of two months. Failure to disclose material information concerning a patient's condition may be actionable not only as malpractice, but under the appropriate circumstances may be an actionable misrepresentation as well. * * * Because the importance of adequate disclosure increases as the patient is placed at a greater informational disadvantage, we join those courts holding that a physician's non-disclosure may give rise to an action in fraud independent of malpractice. Because the law has determined that a proper person may supply the consent for an incompetent person * * *, and since that consent must be informed to be effective and to protect the patient * * *, we also conclude that when a patient becomes incompetent the physician's fiduciary obligations of full disclosure flow to the person acting in the patient's behalf. From plaintiffs' allegations we cannot conclude beyond doubt that they can prove no set of facts which would entitle them to relief, nor can we conclude that their averments do not comply with Civ.R. 9(B). * * * We conclude that the trial court erred in granting a dismissal as to this claim.

Plaintiffs seek to recover damages for defendants' alleged conduct which invaded Mrs. Leach's right to privacy. The right to privacy is a right personal to the individual asserting it. * * * This right lapses with the death of the person who enjoys it and the decedent's heirs may not recover for the invasion. Accordingly, the dismissal of this cause of action was proper.

Plaintiffs also seek to recover for pain, suffering, and mental anguish for Mrs. Leach and for themselves. Plaintiffs allege that defendants administered treatments without proper consent and allege that some of those treatments were experimental. To the extent that plaintiffs can prove that this conduct was wrongful and caused pain and suffering beyond that which Mrs. Leach would have normally suffered from her condition, they state a claim for relief. * * *

The trial court also concluded that plaintiffs had no cause of action for the mental anguish they suffered as a result of the alleged wrongs committed against Mrs. Leach. In reaching its conclusion, the court followed the law in Ohio at that time. Since then, the Supreme Court has significantly expanded the scope of recovery in this area. Paugh v. Hanks, 6 Ohio St.3d 72, 451 N.E.2d 759 (1983). In light of that decision, we feel that the trial court's ruling is no longer a correct statement of the law in Ohio.

Plaintiffs also claim defendants caused an improper delay in effectuating the probate court order of December 18, 1980. The trial court concluded that a delay of 19 days, in light of the conditions imposed by the probate court, was not unreasonable. This requires a determination of facts which were not properly before the court, and dismissal was improper.

Finally, plaintiffs seek to recover punitive damages. Because the trial court had found no other claims upon which relief could be granted, it concluded that there was no wrongdoing upon which to base an award of punitive damages. In light of our disposition of the foregoing issues, we conclude that this claim must be reinstated as well.

The decision of the trial court is reversed and the cause is remanded for further proceedings.

Chapter 8

PRODUCT–RELATED MEDICAL LIABILITY

INTRODUCTORY NOTE

As viewed by the law, the physician's professional service consists primarily of advice to patients, the hallmark of the independent contractor, supplemented by personal services. Earlier chapters considered the attribution and allocation of medical liabilities among the providers of health care services.

Health care providers also order for patients, and use in the care of patients, substances and articles that were manufactured by others, such as pharmaceutical drugs, devices, and the tools of diagnosis and care. The product-related responsibilities of health care providers include knowing the appropriate uses and side-effects of drugs and devices, watching for unintended consequences and interactions, warning patients about risks and side-effects, and even keeping track of patients in case new risks turn up in the future. Non-physician bioscientists may be qualified to testify about the use and misuse of health care products.

Because the liabilities of goods-providers are stricter than the liabilities of service-providers, the involvement of health care providers with manufactured goods exposes the providers to theories of liability much stricter than negligence. Where a patient has been injured in the use of a product, the service providers may have to exculpate themselves from responsibility, at the risk of being held liable without proof of fault along with the goods providers.

It is hardly surprising that both providers and manufacturers have sought and are seeking legislative insulation from product-related liability doctrines, whether by statutes declaring that the furnishing of some articles (such as transfused blood) are services rather than sales, or providing outright immunity from liability as the tradeoff for producing beneficial but unavoidably dangerous articles (such as vaccines), or limiting the maximum damages that they and their insurers must pay in medical liability cases.

Note on Medical Product Manufacturers' Liability

The manufacturers of prescription drugs, articles, devices, and instruments are liable for personal injuries and death caused by defective and dangerous products. Medical product manufacturers have been in the forefront of developments in the general law of product liability—so much so, and producing judicial opinions of such great length, that to treat the liability of medical product manufacturers would call for a chapter as large as any in the casebook. Feeling that law students read these cases in other courses, the editors have devoted this chapter to liabilities of health care providers that arise in connection with medical products.

Here are abstracts of a few recent materials that have been omitted with reluctance:

MacDonald v. Ortho Pharmaceutical Corp., 394 Mass. 131, 475 N.E.2d 65, cert. denied, 474 U.S. 920, 106 S.Ct. 250, 88 L.Ed.2d 258 (1985). Where drugs (contraceptive pills) are prescribed to healthy patients who see their physicians only once a year, the manufacturers have the duty under state law to warn patients directly of serious side-effects (here stroke). The duty is neither obviated by the physician's role as learned intermediary, under state law, nor preempted by federal regulations that establish the content of manufacturers' brochures that are dispensed to the drug purchasers.

Hymowitz v. Eli Lilly & Co., 73 N.Y.2d 487, 541 N.Y.S.2d 941, 539 N.E. 2d 1069, cert. denied, ___ U.S. ___, 110 S.Ct. 350, 107 L.Ed.2d 338 (1989). In a DES case, the national market share theory is the appropriate method for determining liability and apportioning damages, but no manufacturer will be liable for damages in excess of its market share. DES cases from other jurisdictions, especially California, e.g., Brown v. Superior Court, 44 Cal.3d 1049, 245 Cal.Rptr. 412, 751 P.2d 470 (1988), are discussed and updated.

In re Richardson–Merrell, Inc., 624 F.Supp. 1212 (S.D.Ohio 1985). Chief Judge Rubin trifurcated the jury trial of an 844–case multi-district proceeding on Benectin birth defect claims. On trial of the first issue, the jury ended the case by finding that the drug did not cause the birth defects. The jury instructions are reprinted in full. Aff'd in this respect, 857 F.2d 290 (6th Cir.1988).

Richardson v. Richardson–Merrell, Inc. In another multi-district Bendectin case tried separately, District Judge Jackson bifurcated the issues and, on the issue of causation, granted judgment for the drug manufacturer notwithstanding the $1.16 million verdict for plaintiffs. 649 F.Supp. 799 (D.D.C.1986). The court of appeals affirmed. 857 F.2d 823 (D.C.Cir.1988).

Senn v. Merrell–Dow Pharmaceuticals, Inc., 305 Or. 256, 751 P.2d 215 (1988). A child received a DPT vaccination in 1977 and developed encephalopathy. Only two manufacturers could have produced the vaccine. The plaintiff argued that they were alternatively liable under Restatement (Second) of Torts § 433B (1965), but in answering questions of Oregon law certified by the Ninth Circuit, the supreme court rejected alternative liability, regardless of the number of defendants.

With respect to legal immunity for manufacturers in order to assure supplies of vaccines, the Swine Flu statute [1] has been followed by the National Childhood Vaccine Injury Act of 1986.[2]

THOMPSON v. CARTER

Supreme Court of Mississippi, 1987.
518 So.2d 609.

PRATHER, JUSTICE, for the court. * * *

* * * Dr. Robert Carter, a urologist, * * * diagnosed Lynette Inez Thompson's ailment as pyelonephritis secondary to pyelitis cystica, a form of kidney infection. * * * To treat Ms. Thompson's kidney infection, Dr. Carter prescribed Bactrim, a sulfonamide antibiotic, beginning February 10, 1976. Ms. Thompson was discharged from the hospital February 11, 1976, with instructions to continue taking two Bactrim tablets per day and to visit Dr. Carter's office February 17, 1976.

At Ms. Thompson's February 17, 1976, visit to Dr. Carter's office, a urinalysis revealed a continued presence of pus and blood in her urine but in lesser amounts. Dr. Carter advised Ms. Thompson to continue taking Bactrim and to return to his office early in March.

* * *

Ms. Thompson returned to Dr. Carter's office early in March. Ms. Thompson contends she was still experiencing a nagging cough and a mild sore throat, but no complaints were made to Dr. Carter, who determined that Ms. Thompson was well from her kidney infection. Additional Bactrim was not prescribed to Ms. Thompson.

During the evening of Friday, March 5, 1976, Ms. Thompson began to notice red marks across her back and a swelling sensation over her entire body. By the following Monday, Ms. Thompson's arms, feet, and face were swollen, her eyes were blurry, red bumps had arisen over her body, and blisters had formed in her mouth and genitals.

Ms. Thompson was hospitalized March 8, 1976, and was diagnosed as having Stevens–Johnson syndrome, a severe allergic response which causes the formation of blisters in the mouth, nose, and genitals. According to Dr. Carter's trial testimony, Stevens–Johnson syndrome is a recognized danger associated with Bactrim. Ms. Thompson remained hospitalized some 20 days and allegedly suffered severe and permanent scars.

In June of 1979, Ms. Thompson filed suit against Roche Laboratories, producer of Bactrim, and Dr. Carter. Praying for $500,000 damages, Ms. Thompson employed breach of warranty, negligence and strict liability theories against Roche Laboratories, and a negligence theory of recovery against Dr. Carter. Ms. Thompson elected a voluntary nonsuit against Roche Laboratories, but the case against Dr. Carter was

---

1. 42 U.S.C.A. § 247b(k) (repealed; see historical note in U.S.C.A.).

2. 42 U.S.C.A. §§ 300aa–1—aa–33.

tried January 14 and 15, 1985. Because Ms. Thompson was unable to provide expert medical testimony, the trial ended with a directed verdict in favor of Dr. Carter.

* * *

Did the court err in refusing to admit into evidence the package insert relative to the drug Bactrim?

* * *

Pursuant to congressional directives, the Food and Drug Administration (FDA) has developed a regulatory procedure to inform the medical profession about prescription drugs. 21 C.F.R. §§ 1, 201. The "package insert" distributed with the drug by the pharmaceutical manufacturer is the basis of this system of notification concerning composition, dosage, indications, contraindications, potential side effects, and adverse reactions of drugs. The package insert information is based upon data the manufacturer has submitted to the FDA as proof that the drug is safe and effective for the uses the manufacturer wishes to market the drug. * * * The insert advises the physician, based upon the manufacturer's testing results, of (1) the conditions under which the drug should be prescribed, (2) the disorders it is recommended to relieve, (3) the precautionary measures which should be observed, and (4) warning of adverse effects that may result. A compilation of these package inserts on drugs, referred to as the Physicians' Desk Reference, is annually distributed to the medical profession.

Under the common law scheme of hearsay exceptions, market quotations, tabulations, lists, directories and other published compilations generally used and relied upon by the public or by persons in particular occupations were excepted from the rule against hearsay. * * * Since January 1, 1986, those hearsay exceptions have been compiled in Rule 803(17) of the Miss.R.Evid., which do not significantly alter the common law scheme.

Applying this rule of evidence to the instant case, the court notes the testimony of Dr. Carter, the defendant, identifying the package insert accompanying a pharmaceutical drug as "one source of reference" and "one source of information." He relied upon this package insert for information of adverse effects, or contraindications, of the drug Bactrim.

Further, Dr. Carter identified the Physicians' Desk Reference as "a good reference with some authority" and that it represented the standard of care "in the local area" of Biloxi with respect to the administration of the drug Bactrim at the time Ms. Thompson was treated by him. Dr. Carter used and relied upon the information contained in the Bactrim package insert in his practice and particularly for the treatment of Ms. Thompson. Although Dr. Carter testified that other medical publications and information were used and relied upon by him in his practice, that testimony does not diminish the admissibility of the package insert after identification by Dr. Carter of its acceptance by him as one source of information and by the medical profession in the Biloxi area as a standard of care in the administration of drugs.

The package insert is a compilation of information concerning pharmaceutical drugs and is generally relied upon by the public as well as physicians prescribing the drug. Therefore, we hold that the package insert, properly identified, was admissible by virtue of the above described exception to the hearsay rule.

Other jurisdictions have allowed package inserts into evidence to serve a variety of purposes. See M. Dixon, Drug Product Liability, § 7.02 (1986). * * *

It is suggested by some writers in this field of pharmaceutical drugs that caution should be exercised by courts in accepting the manufacturer's test results as conclusive. Notwithstanding the government regulations in this field, the package insert is a marketing or merchandising procedure to promote sales. Drug manufacturers have had to answer for alleged dilution of warnings by over-promotion in sales programs. * * *

Likewise, independent researchers have reached contradictory results to drug manufacturers and have recommended different dosages. Updated information gained from a broader based usage of a drug is not always reflected in the original insert until a new distribution of the drug or new publication of the Physicians' Desk Reference. Text writers suggest that antibiotic drugs represent an exception to set dosages. This rationale is explained by the assertion that as bacteria become more resistant to drugs, the dosage may be increased. A doctor's experiences offers a basis for varying dosages.

[T]he package insert in the instant case should not be taken as conclusive evidence of the physician's standard of care, nor should a departure from the directions contained in the package insert be considered to establish a prima facie case of negligence. However, this court holds the package insert contains prima facie proof of the proper method of use of Bactrim and, for those purposes, was admissible at trial. * * * The package insert can be given weight as authoritative published compilation by a pharmaceutical manufacturer. It is some evidence of the standard of care, but it is not conclusive evidence. The prescribing physician can be permitted to rebut this implication and explain its deviation from the manufacturer's recommended use on dosage. The holding will shift the burden of persuasion to the physician to provide a sound reason for his deviating from the directions for its use, and will require corroborative evidence to determine whether the physician met or violated the appropriate standard.

At trial, appellant offered Michael P. Hughes as an expert witness in the fields of pharmacology and toxicology. Mr. Hughes testified that he had received a bachelor's degree from Millsaps College with major in chemistry and minor in biology and a master's degree in both pharmacology and toxicology. In the process of obtaining his degrees, he had taken five or six courses in Pharmacology and between eight and ten courses in Toxicology. After completing his graduate degree programs, Mr. Hughes became coordinator of the Regional Poison Control Center for the entire State of Mississippi. As coordinator for the Poison Control Center, which is located at the University of Mississippi Medical Center, Mr. Hughes was often consulted by physicians for suggested treatment of poisoning victims and other types of adverse reactions to various compounds or drugs. Mr. Hughes further testified he was on the teaching staff at the University of Mississippi Medical School and taught Pharmacology and Toxicology to both dental and medical students. Additionally Hughes had taken training to render emergency medical care as an "emergency medical technician."

Mr. Hughes testified that by virtue of his education and work experience, he was familiar with the drug Bactrim and its indications as well as its contraindications. Likewise, he was familiar with Stevens–Johnson syndrome and its causes.

The trial court found that Mr. Hughes was qualified to testify as an expert witness as to causation in the field of pharmacology and toxicology, but was not qualified to testify concerning the standard of care to which physicians are required to conform with respect to the use and administration of drugs.

* * *

Appellant had no other expert witness to testify concerning causation or standard of care with respect to use and administration of drugs. * * * [T]his court holds that * * * [Mr. Hughes] was qualified to deliver expert testimony, notwithstanding his lack of a medical degree, on the issue of a physician's standard of care in the use and administration of this drug.

* * *

The proffer of Mr. Hughes' testimony suggested that Mr. Hughes, had he been permitted to testify, would have opined a departure from the standard of care in the use and administration of drugs in the following respects:

> [That] the defendant departed from the standard of care as established by recognized pharmacological literature in prescribing Bactrim to the plaintiff; * * * that the defendant violated the standard of care because Bactrim was not the drug of choice to treat acute pyelonephritis and in fact that said drug was contraindicated; * * * that after prescribing Bactrim though contraindicated, the defendant should have conducted various urine tests to determine whether there were crystals of the sulfa developing in her urine, whether her kidneys were properly functioning and the level of protein and sugar in the urine; * * * that the administration of Bactrim and the failure of the defendant to properly monitor plaintiff's condition after the administration of same were proximately contributing causes of the onset of the Stevens–Johnson syndrome.

* * * Reversed and remanded for a new trial.

DAN M. LEE, PRESIDING JUSTICE, dissenting. * * *

Today's majority opinion reverses all precedent of this court and concludes, illogically, that showing causation is the same thing as showing standard of care and breach thereof. The majority confuses causation with standard of care by saying that the Bactrim drug insert, which lists Stevens–Johnson syndrome as a possible adverse reaction, is "some" evidence of the standard of care when, in fact, all the drug insert shows, by itself, is that Bactrim can cause Stevens–Johnson syndrome. No one disputes that Bactrim can cause Stevens–Johnson syndrome. But there is a question as to whether or not a urologist of ordinary skill and care in these circumstances would have prescribed Bactrim. Only another urologist can tell us that. It is just plain wrong to label evidence of causation in fact as "some" evidence of the standard of care. To do so confuses two separate theories of tort law—strict liability and negligence. A patient who reacts to a drug properly administered under the standard of care for a physician of ordinary care and skill has not made out a prima facie case of negligence. Such evidence is only enough to hold the doctor strictly liable, something neither this court nor any other has ever done before. * * *

The admissibility of the drug insert raises two troublesome issues: (1) whether it should be admitted into evidence at all, and (2) if it can be admitted, whether it must be tied to expert medical testimony to be relevant to the standard of care of physicians. Since the drug insert is hearsay, in order to be admissible it must either fit under a hearsay exception or be offered for some reason other than the truth of its statements. In other words, whether or not the drug insert is admissible is tied to the *purpose* for which it is offered.[3] * * *

[T]he drug insert as evidence of the standard of care is admissible only if it is introduced through testimony of an expert medical witness and adopted by such witness as evidence of the standard of care. But that medical expert still must articulate the proper standard of care and establish that a defendant fell below such standard. The majority opinion contemplates using the drug insert in lieu of evidence of the standard of care, again confusing strict liability with negligence. * * *

WALKER, C.J., ROY NOBLE LEE, P.J., and GRIFFIN, J., join this dissent.

---

3. The majority's analysis of the drug insert as a compilation of information concerning pharmaceutical drugs is not the most satisfactory. Our decisions * * * contemplate compilations of actuarial tables, logarithms, astronomical calculations, and market reports—standard authority for those who use them. While the drug insert probably fits within such a contemplation as to physicians, I would prefer to see us allow the Physician's Desk Reference (PDR) to serve this purpose rather than a single insert from one drug manufacturer. The PDR, a compilation of all such drugs on the market and which contains similar information to the drug inserts, is a reference that a medical expert would possibly rely on in his testimony as much as he would rely on a drug insert. My concern with allowing in the single drug insert under this hearsay exception is that it is too close to an advertising circular for comfort. To allow the insert could arguably give the impression that we consider advertising circulars to be compilations of information which could be relied on by the public for information, a result we have expressly rejected * * *.

TRESEMER v. BARKE
California Court of Appeal, 1978.
86 Cal.App.3d 656, 150 Cal.Rptr. 384, 12 A.L.R.4th 27,[4] hearing denied.

STEPHENS, ACTING PRESIDING JUSTICE.

This is an appeal by plaintiff Donna Sue Tresemer from the grant of summary judgment in favor of defendant Morton Barke, M.D. The action, filed on April 12, 1976, is for damages allegedly sustained by plaintiff from a Dalkon Shield intrauterine device. * * *

Plaintiff alleges that (1) defendant prescribed and inserted a Dalkon Shield for temporary contraceptive purposes without proper investigation to determine its safety, and (2) defendant failed to warn her that such Dalkon Shield was a health hazard when he subsequently acquired actual knowledge of the danger. * * *

Defendant's moving papers were sufficient to negate any charge that his conduct was either willfully or negligently wrongful when in 1972 he inserted the intrauterine device. He declared in his affidavit that

> In August 1972 the Dalkon Shield was one of the most popular and acceptable intrauterine devices on the market. At the time it was lauded and believed to be one of the more safe and effective intrauterine devices available. It was not until approximately two years later that serious question as to its general safety was first raised and acknowledged in the general medical community; shortly thereafter it was withdrawn from the market.

Defendant's attorney in his affidavit stated that he had been involved in numerous cases involving the Dalkon Shield and asserted, "I can certify to the court that it was not until some time in the middle of 1974 that the Dalkon Shield fell into question and shortly thereafter withdrawn from the market." Defendant in his affidavit further declared that the device had been inserted "without incident," and that he thereafter provided plaintiff with a copy of the manufacturer's "package insert" which described the Dalkon Shield and potential problems and complications. His affidavit also set forth his credentials in obstetrics and gynecology and declared that his conduct was within the standard of practice in the community.

* * * In the absence of opposing affidavits, the grant of summary judgment was proper on the issue of defendant's allegedly wrongful conduct in 1972 when he inserted the Dalkon Shield.

* * *

We turn now to plaintiff's theory of recovery, based on the proposition that defendant had a duty to warn her of the dangerous effects of the Dalkon Shield when, subsequent to its insertion, he obtained actual knowledge of its hazards, and that his failure to do so amounted to

---

4. Annot., Duty of Medical Practitioner to Warn Patient of Subsequently Discovered Danger from Treatment Previously Given, 12 A.L.R.4th 41 (1982).

negligence or willful, wanton and reckless disregard for the consequences. * * *

It has been held in numerous cases that the duty of adequate warning by the manufacturer of an ethical drug (available only upon prescription) is discharged by its warning of hazards to doctors. * * * Absent special circumstances known or foreseeable in the exercise of due care by the manufacturer, there is no duty to warn the patient, one reason being that "It would be virtually impossible for a manufacturer to comply with the duty of direct warning, as there is no sure way to reach the patient." Fogo v. Cutter Laboratories, Inc., 68 Cal.App.3d 744, 137 Cal.Rptr. 417, 423 (1977). Who then is to tell the patient of hazards newly discovered and not known at the time of the original patient-physician contact when the drug or medical appliance was prescribed?

* * *

In discussing the duty to aid a person in peril, Prosser * * * noted that

> Where the original danger is created by *innocent conduct,* involving no fault on the part of the defendant, it was formerly the rule that no * * * ["duty to make a reasonable effort to give assistance and avoid any further harm"] arose; but this appears to have given way, in recent decisions, to a recognition of the duty to take action, both where the prior innocent conduct has created an unreasonable risk of harm to the plaintiff, and where it has already injured him. * * * This process of extension has been slow, and marked with extreme caution; but there is reason to think that it may continue until it approaches a general holding that the mere knowledge of serious peril, threatening death or great bodily harm to another, which an identified defendant might avoid with little inconvenience, created a sufficient relation, recognized by every moral and social standard, to impose a duty of action.
>
> Where the duty is recognized, it is agreed that it calls for nothing more than reasonable care under the circumstances. W. Prosser, Torts § 56 at 342 (4th ed. 1971). (Italics added.)

A cause of action is stated for failure to warn plaintiff. This would arise by virtue of a confidential relationship between doctor and patient. It is not a malpractice cause of action in the commonly understood sense, but rather a malpractice action from the imposed continuing status of physician-patient where the danger arose from that relationship. It is also a cause of action for common negligence. * * * Certainly the use of summary judgment is inappropriate under such circumstance. * * *

ASHMAN v. SK & F LAB CO.
United States District Court for the Northern District of Illinois, 1988.
702 F.Supp. 1401.

HART, DISTRICT JUDGE. * * *

Tagamet is a prescription drug designed to reduce stomach acidity. It is manufactured by defendant, SK & F Lab Co. In 1984, Richard Ashman's physician, Dr. Cesar Secoquian, prescribed Tagamet for Mr. Ashman. In 1985, Dr. Secoquian prescribed Ativan for Mr. Ashman. Ativan is a sleeping pill not manufactured by defendant. The Ativan was co-administered with the Tagamet and there were no side effects. Over two years later, in April 1986, and while Mr. Ashman was still taking the Tagamet, Dr. Secoquian prescribed the drug Halcion in place of Ativan. Halcion is a sleeping pill and is not manufactured by defendant.

Prior to the Halcion prescription, Dr. Secoquian consulted both the package insert for Halcion and the 1986 version of the Physician's Desk Reference (PDR). Both of the consulted sources discuss a potential interaction between Halcion and Tagamet.[5] Nonetheless, Dr. Secoquian decided to prescribe Halcion for Mr. Ashman, even though there were other sleeping pills available. The Tagamet label does not specifically mention the interactive propensities of the drug with Halcion. While Dr. Secoquian read the Tagamet label on previous occasions, he did not read it when making the decision whether to prescribe Halcion for Mr. Ashman.

During the evening of May 3, 1986, Mr. Ashman ingested Tagamet. About four hours later, he took the Halcion. The next morning, Mr. Ashman took an overdose of Ativan tablets which he had left over from the old prescription. Mr. Ashman was then taken to the hospital in an unconscious state. Dr. Secoquian was not sure what had caused Mr. Ashman's condition but suspected cerebral hemorrhage and decided to do a lumbar puncture to confirm. Before the procedure, Mr. Ashman regained consciousness and was in a coherent state. Nonetheless, Dr. Secoquian decided to go ahead with the lumbar puncture.

5. The PDR entry for Halcion states:

Pharmacokinetic interactions [i.e., interactions without a clinically significant side effect] of benzodiazepines with other drugs have been reported. For example, the co-administration of triazolam [Halcion] and cimetidine [Tagamet] in a controlled clinical trial in normal subjects resulted in a reduction of triazolam clearance and an increase in the elimination half-life from 2.2 to 3.7 hours. The plasma concentration of triazolam approximately doubled when co-administered with cimetidine. However, this did not result in any drug accumulation.

Although it is stated that there is no clinically significant side effect, the warning is sufficient because it states the interaction that was known and because the alleged harmful effect of Mr. Ashman's use of the two drugs is the decrease in elimination that is stated in the PDR. Mr. Ashman claims that the Halcion had a stronger effect than it would otherwise have had because the concurrent use of Tagamet delayed the elimination of Halcion from his system.

As a result of alleged negligence in the performance of the lumbar puncture, Mr. Ashman was partially paralyzed.[6] Plaintiffs claim that the interaction between the Tagamet and the Halcion created the state of mind which led to confusion and the overdose which in turn set in motion the chain of events which ultimately resulted in paralysis. There is an issue over whether the interaction actually occurred. However, for present purposes, this court assumes it did occur.

The Ashmans filed a negligence claim against Dr. Secoquian which was subsequently settled. The present negligence and strict liability claims are brought by Mr. and Mrs. Ashman against the manufacturer of Tagamet, SK & F Lab Co. * * *

Defendant moves for summary judgment * * *.

The learned intermediary doctrine * * * can relieve a drug manufacturer of liability for adverse effects of its drugs. The doctrine applies to both strict liability claims and negligence claims. * * * An adequately informed physician acts as learned intermediary between the patient and the drug manufacturer, thus breaking the chain of liability. Kirk v. Michael Reese Hosp. & Med. Center, 117 Ill.2d 507, 111 Ill.Dec. 944, 513 N.E.2d 387, 393 (1987), cert. denied, 485 U.S. 905, 108 S.Ct. 1077, 99 L.Ed.2d 236 (1988) * * *.

In their brief, plaintiffs concede that Dr. Secoquian was a learned intermediary. However, they argue that the doctrine does not relieve defendant of liability because it failed to include a specific warning on the Tagamet label concerning the interactive propensities of the drug with Halcion. The warning which plaintiffs argue should have been included is essentially the same as that provided in the 1986 PDR for Halcion. Thus, plaintiffs argue that the learned intermediary doctrine does not break the chain of liability even where a learned intermediary, knowing of the dangerous propensities of the drug, prescribes it nonetheless.

This reasoning is contrary to the learned intermediary doctrine. Under the learned intermediary doctrine, "[c]ourts have consistently held that a drug manufacturer is entitled to summary judgment where the prescribing physician is aware of the risks associated with a drug." Wooten v. Johnson & Johnson Prods., Inc., 635 F.Supp. 799, 803 (N.D. Ill.1986). * * *

Plaintiffs try to create an issue by alleging that Dr. Secoquian did not know of the interactive propensities of the drugs. However, plaintiffs' allegation is not supported by the record. Standing alone, mere allegations do not establish a genuine issue of material fact. * * * The interactive propensities of Tagamet and Halcion are listed on the Halcion label and in the PDR. The PDR is an accepted method by which drug manufacturers communicate product information to the medical profession. Kirk, 513 N.E.2d at 392 * * *. Mr. Ashman was

---

6. The lumbar puncture was performed after Mr. Ashman had been given Coumadin, which the parties state should not have been done.

already on Tagamet when Dr. Secoquian decided to put him on Halcion. As Dr. Secoquian has testified, when making his decision he consulted both the Halcion label and the PDR. The PDR Halcion entry indicates that there is an interactive effect when Tagamet and Halcion are co-administered. The Halcion label also contains a similar warning of its interactive propensities with Tagamet.

The information provided by plaintiffs' own expert, Dr. James O'Donnell, supports the conclusion that Dr. Secoquian was adequately informed. Dr. O'Donnell stated that, based on the information provided both in the Halcion literature and the PDR, the interaction which occurred in Mr. Ashman was predictable. The learned intermediary doctrine applies where a physician is alerted to the dangerous propensities of a particular drug and nonetheless decides to prescribe it.

* * *

Defendant is not liable for the injuries sustained as a result of the purportedly negligent lumbar puncture because * * * Dr. Secoquian was an informed learned intermediary * * *, a sufficient basis for granting summary judgment on all counts.

* * *

ANDERSON v. SOMBERG
Supreme Court of New Jersey, 1975.
67 N.J. 291, 338 A.2d 1, cert. denied, 423 U.S. 929,
96 S.Ct. 279, 46 L.Ed.2d 258 (1975).

PASHMAN, JUSTICE.

These negligence-products liability actions had their inception in a surgery performed in 1967 on the premises of defendant St. James Hospital. Plaintiff Henry Anderson was undergoing a laminectomy, a back operation, performed by defendant Dr. Harold Somberg. During the course of the procedure, the tip or cup of an angulated pituitary rongeur, a forceps-like instrument, broke off while the tool was being manipulated in plaintiff's spinal canal. The surgeon attempted to retrieve the metal but was unable to do so. After repeated failure in that attempt, he terminated the operation. The imbedded fragment caused medical complications and further surgical interventions were required. Plaintiff has suffered significant and permanent physical injury proximately caused by the rongeur fragment which lodged in his spine.

Plaintiff sued (1) Dr. Somberg for medical malpractice, alleging that the doctor's negligent action caused the rongeur to break; (2) St. James Hospital, alleging that it negligently furnished Dr. Somberg with a defective surgical instrument; (3) Reinhold–Schumann, Inc., the medical supply distributor which furnished the defective rongeur to the hospital, on a warranty theory, and (4) Lawton Instrument Co. (Lawton), the manufacturer of the rongeur, on a strict liability in tort claim, alleging that the rongeur was a defective product. In short, plaintiff sued all who might have been liable for his injury, absent some alternative explanation such as contributory negligence.

* * *

Defendant Lawton called a metallurgist, John Carroll, as an expert witness. He testified that an examination of the broken rongeur revealed neither structural defect nor faulty workmanship. He said that the examination (conducted at an optical magnification 500 times normal size) revealed a secondary crack near the main crack, but he could not suggest how or when that crack formed. Mr. Carroll offered an opinion as to the cause of the instrument's breaking: the instrument had been strained, he said, probably because of an improper "twisting" of the tool. The strain, however, could have been cumulative, over the course of several operations, and the instrument could conceivably have been cracked when handed to Dr. Somberg and broken in its normal use.

In short, when all the evidence had been presented, no theory for the cause of the rongeur's breaking was within reasonable contemplation save for the possible negligence of Dr. Somberg in using the instrument, or the possibility that the surgeon had been given a defective instrument, which defect would be attributable to a dereliction of duty by the manufacturer, the distributor, the hospital, or all of them.

The case was submitted to a jury on special interrogatories, and the jury returned a finding of no cause as to each defendant. On appeal, the entire appellate panel concurred in an order for a new trial. 134 N.J.Super. 1, 338 A.2d 35 (1973). * * *

The position adopted by the appellate division majority seems to us substantially correct; that is, at the close of all the evidence, it was apparent that at least one of the defendants was liable for plaintiff's injury, because no alternative theory of liability was within reasonable contemplation. Since defendants had engaged in conduct which activated legal obligations by each of them to plaintiff, the jury should have been instructed that the failure of any defendant to prove his nonculpability would trigger liability; and further, that since at least one of the defendants could not sustain his burden of proof, at least one would be liable. A no cause of action verdict against all primary and third-party defendants will be unacceptable and would work a miscarriage of justice sufficient to require a new trial. * * *

In the ordinary case, the law will not assist an innocent plaintiff at the expense of an innocent defendant. However, in the type of case we consider here, where an unconscious or helpless patient suffers an admitted mishap not reasonably foreseeable and unrelated to the scope of the surgery (such as cases where foreign objects are left in the body of the patient), those who had custody of the patient, and who owed him a duty of care as to medical treatment, or not to furnish a defective instrument for use in such treatment, can be called to account for their default. They must prove their nonculpability, or else risk liability for the injuries suffered.

* * *

The rule of evidence we set forth does not represent the doctrine of res ipsa loquitur as it has been traditionally understood. Res ipsa loquitur is ordinarily impressed only where the injury more probably than not has resulted from negligence of the defendant * * *, and defendant was in exclusive control of the instrument. * * * The doctrine has been expanded to include, as in the instant matter, multiple defendants * * *, although even this expansion has been criticized * * *. It has also been expanded to embrace cases where the negligence cause was not the only or most probable theory in the case, but where the alternate theories of liability accounted for the only possible causes of injury. * * * That is the situation in this case, where we find negligence, strict liability in tort, and breach of warranty all advanced as possible theories of liability. In such cases, defendants are required to come forward and give their evidence. The latter development represents a substantial deviation from earlier conceptions of res ipsa loquitur and has more accurately been called "akin to res ipsa loquitur," NOPCO Chem. Div. v. Blaw-Knox Co., 59 N.J. 274, 281 A.2d 793 (1971), or "conditional res ipsa loquitur." Quintal v. Laurel Grove Hosp., 62 Cal.2d 154, 166, 41 Cal.Rptr. 577, 397 P.2d 161 (1965) * * *.

In *NOPCO*, the liability for damages to a delivered product could be attributed with great probability either to the negligence of any one in a series of bailees or the breach of warranty of the seller. The court stated that when several defendants individually owe plaintiff a duty, and all might have caused his loss and have superior knowledge of the occurrence, they all are bound to come forward and give an account of what happened. In that case, the application of res ipsa loquitur was thought to call for an explanatory rather than an exculpatory account, which would be sufficient to meet defendant's burden, according to the traditional rule. * * *

In *NOPCO*, however, plaintiff is still made to bear the burden of proof vis-à-vis each defendant, and it was upon such instruction that the present case was submitted to the jury. We now hold that a mere shift in the burden of going forward, as adopted in *NOPCO*, is insufficient. For this particular type of case, an equitable alignment of duties owed plaintiff requires that not only the burden of going forward shift to defendants, but the actual burden of proof as well. Since at least one primary or third-party defendant must inevitably fail to meet his burden, a verdict must be returned for the plaintiff.

* * *

Further, we note that at the close of all the evidence, no reasonable suggestion had been offered that the occurrence could have arisen because of plaintiff's contributory negligence, or some act of nature; that is, there was no explanation for the occurrence in the case save for negligence or defect on the part of someone connected with the manufacture, handling, or use of the instrument. (Any such proof would be acceptable to negative plaintiff's prima facie case.) Since all parties had been joined who could reasonably have been connected with that negligence or defect, it was clear that one of those parties was liable, and at least one could not succeed in his proofs.

In cases of this type, no defendant will be entitled to prevail on a motion for judgment until all the proofs have been presented to the court and jury. The judge may grant any motion bearing in mind that the plaintiff must recover a verdict against at least one defendant. Inferences and doubts at this stage are resolved in favor of the plaintiff. If only one defendant remains by reason of the court's action, then, in fact, the judge is directing a verdict of liability against that defendant.

* * *

The judgment of the appellate division is hereby affirmed, and the cause remanded for trial upon instructions consonant with this opinion.

JACOBS, J., concurs in the result * * *.

MOUNTAIN, J., dissenting. * * *

[T]he record is replete with testimony that other surgeons—perhaps as many as 20—have used the rongeur during the four years that it has formed part of the surgical equipment of the hospital, and that any one or more of them may perfectly well have been responsible for so injuring the instrument that it came apart while being manipulated in plaintiff's incision; or that it may have been weakened to near breaking point by cumulative misuse, entirely by persons not now before the court. In the face of this uncontroverted proof that the surgical instrument had been used upon approximately 20 earlier occasions and possibly by the same number of different surgeons, in the hands of any of whom it may have been fatally misused, how then can it be said that the wrongdoer is surely in court! There is a far greater likelihood that he is no party to this litigation at all and that his identity will never be established.

* * *

The opinion takes the view that at this point the burden of proof shifted to defendants. This, as is apparently conceded, has not hitherto been the law of this state. * * * Nevertheless this alteration in the law may be entirely reasonable and justified—at least if limited to this kind of medical malpractice case. * * * Thus far, as to the negligence claims, I might be persuaded to agree with the court.

But certainly no farther. At this point the *effect* to be given a shift in the burden of proof becomes the crucial issue. The authorities which have adopted or espoused the view that res ipsa shifts the burden of proof have, as far as I can discover, understood this to mean that upon such a shift taking place, a defendant becomes obliged to offer evidence explaining his own conduct or throwing light upon the circumstances attending plaintiff's injury, which will be of sufficient probative force to establish his lack of fault by a preponderance of the evidence. The fact finder will then be called upon to decide whether the defendant's proofs have met this test or whether they have fallen short.

The view expressed by the court in this case as to the effect of shifting the burden of proof appears to be something quite different. Under this new rule it is no longer enough that a defendant meet the standard described above. His role is no longer simply that of one who may hope to succeed if his proofs justify a verdict. Rather he now finds himself one of a band of persons from among whom one or more *must* be singled out to respond in damages to the plaintiff's claim. He is now a member of a group who must collectively, among themselves, play a game of *sauve qui peut*—and play it for rather high stakes. With all due respect I submit that at this point there has been complete departure from the rule of reason; the argument is now stripped of all rational basis.

* * *

I would vote to reverse the judgment of the appellate division and to reinstate the judgment of the trial court.

CLIFFORD, J., and JUDGE COLLESTER join in this dissenting opinion.[7]

SAMSON v. GREENVILLE HOSP. SYSTEM
Supreme Court of South Carolina, 1988.
295 S.C. 359, 368 S.E.2d 665.

PER CURIAM.

Pursuant to Sup.Ct.R. 46, we agreed to answer the following question certified by order of the Hon. Joe F. Anderson, Jr., United States District Court for the District of South Carolina:

> Whether § 44–43–10 of the South Carolina Code of Laws, 1976, as amended, is unconstitutional as being violative of the Equal Protection Clause of art. I, § 3, of the Constitution of the State of South Carolina.

Section 44–43–10 is South Carolina's "blood shield" statute; it exempts providers of blood and blood products from implied warranty-based liability:

> The implied warranties of merchantability and fitness shall not be applicable to a contract for the sale, procurement, processing, distribution or use of human tissues such as corneas, bones or organs, whole blood, plasma, blood products or blood derivatives. Such human tissues, whole blood, plasma, blood products or blood derivatives shall not be considered commodities subject to sale or barter and the transplanting, injection, transfusion or other transfer of such substances into the human body shall be considered a medical service.

Plaintiff (Mrs. Samson) was given a transfusion of blood in January 1984 while a patient at a hospital operated by defendant Greenville

---

7. Editors' Note: Three justices joined the plurality opinion, one concurred, and three dissented. The case was retried, and the jury awarded $40,000 to the plaintiff against the manufacturer (which appealed) and the distributor. Accepting the plurality opinion as the law of New Jersey, the appellate division affirmed. 158 N.J. Super. 384, 386 A.2d 413 (1978).

Hospital System (Hospital). Hospital obtained the blood from defendant Carolina–Georgia Blood Center (the Center), which had drawn the blood from volunteer donor "John Doe" in December 1983. The blood transfused into Mrs. Samson was allegedly tainted with the acquired immune deficiency syndrome (AIDS) virus. Unaware of the possibility that she may have received a tainted transfusion, Mrs. Samson became pregnant in June or July 1985 and gave birth to her son, plaintiff Camaron Joseph Samson, in March 1986.

When Doe returned to donate more blood in September 1985, a laboratory screening device to detect prior exposure to the AIDS virus was in effect. Doe's blood was tested and indicated prior exposure to the AIDS virus. Through a "lookback" program, the Center notified Hospital that Hospital had received potentially AIDS-infected blood in 1984. Mrs. Samson was notified and a laboratory analysis was conducted. Mrs. Samson allegedly tested positive for the antibody indicating prior exposure to the AIDS virus. Her son also allegedly tested positive and is now in "full-blown" AIDS.

Plaintiffs have asserted four causes of action against defendants, including a cause for breach of the implied warranties of merchantability and fitness for a particular purpose.[8] Defendants have moved for summary judgment in the district court, claiming that § 44–43–10 insulates them from the implied warranties causes of action. Plaintiffs maintain that § 44–43–10 violates the Equal Protection clause of the South Carolina Constitution.

We begin our analysis by recognizing that a statute enacted pursuant to the legislature's powers is presumptively constitutional. * * * Other courts have noted that blood shield statutes are entitled to the same presumption. * * *

Our research indicates—and plaintiffs frankly concede—that of the 48 blood shield statutes enacted nationwide, not one has been ruled unconstitutional on equal protection grounds. Numerous courts have flatly rejected equal protection-based attacks on blood shield statutes. * * *

In reviewing a statute challenged on equal protection grounds, we give great deference to a legislatively created classification, and the classification will be sustained if it is not plainly arbitrary and there is "any reasonable hypothesis" to support it. * * * The Equal Protection clause is satisfied if:

> (1) [T]he classification bears a reasonable relation to the legislative purpose sought to be effected; (2) the members of the class are treated alike under similar circumstances and conditions; and (3) the classification rests on some reasonable basis. Smith v. Smith, 291 S.C. 420, 354 S.E.2d 36, 39 (1987) * * *.

---

8. S.C.Code Ann. § 36–2–314 is the implied warranty of merchantability. S.C. Code Ann. § 36–2–315 is the implied warranty of fitness for a particular purpose.

Legislative intent is best determined by examining the language of the statute itself. * * * The language of § 44–43–10 reflects a legislative intent to exempt blood providers from liability based on implied warranties; to remove human tissues and blood from the class of "products" which are bought and sold; and to characterize the transfusion of blood as a medical service rather than a sale.

The encouragement of a readily available supply of blood and blood products has long been recognized as the legislative purpose behind enactment of blood shield statutes in other states. * * * We believe that protection of a continuing adequate blood supply also motivated the enactment of § 44–43–10 in South Carolina.

Further, we believe the classification created by § 44–43–10 bears a reasonable relation to that legislative goal. We agree with the Supreme Court of Connecticut's "reasonable relation" analysis of a blood shield statute nearly identical to South Carolina's:

> These statutes reflect a legislative judgment that to require providers to serve as insurers of the safety of these materials might impose such an overwhelming burden as to discourage the gathering and distribution of blood. To ensure that such services remain adequate and affordable, legislatures have chosen to limit liability to defects that are the result of negligence * * *. Zichichi v. Middlesex Mem. Hosp., 204 Conn. 399, 528 A.2d 805, 810 (1987).

* * *

* * * We hold that a * * * rational relationship exists here between § 44–43–10 and the legitimate legislative goal of ensuring an adequate blood supply. The statute's classification and purpose are rationally linked by the legislature's "relatively modest restriction upon the theories available to plaintiffs such as these * * *."[9]

* * *

Equal protection also requires that members of the statutory class be treated alike under similar circumstances and conditions. Equal treatment must extend to both the privileges conferred and liabilities imposed. * * *

Plaintiffs claim § 44–43–10 creates discriminatory class schemes for potential plaintiffs by irrationally distinguishing between product-related tort victims and victims of transfusion-related diseases. Plaintiffs also claim that certain potential defendants, namely hospitals and blood banks, are irrationally protected from suit on implied warranty theories while paid donors and blood components manufacturers are left exposed to warranty-based causes of action. We disagree.

First, we find nothing irrational in the legislature's decision to distinguish between individuals injured as a result of blood transfusions and individuals injured by improperly designed or manufactured man-made goods. Equally rational was the creation of a class of distributors exempt from implied warranties. We agree with the many courts and

---

9. Section 44–43–10 does not bestow complete immunity on blood providers. Nothing in the statute precludes plaintiffs from proceeding on a negligence theory.

legislatures which recognize that blood and its derivatives are rendered unique and medically vital by man's inability to produce a synthetic substitute. * * *

Next, § 44–43–10 designates the provision of blood as a service, not a product. Transfusion-related disease victims have been legislatively removed from the class of persons injured by "products" and thus eligible to bring causes of action based on breach of implied warranties. The statute applies across-the-board to individuals who are injured as a result of blood transfusions; no member of the affected class is able to pursue the warranty theories in seeking recovery from a blood provider.

Nor do we discern any unequal treatment of potential defendants. Plaintiffs' assertion that commercial blood components manufacturers and paid donors remain exposed to suits for breach of implied warranties has no basis in the statute itself. Section 44–43–10 encompasses not only blood, but also "blood products or blood derivatives." Moreover, the statute does not distinguish paid donors from voluntary donors or commercial distributors from charitable distributors. Compare § 44–43–10 with Wash.Rev.Code Ann. § 70.54.120 (exemption from implied warranties does not apply to any transaction in which donor receives compensation), and N.C.Gen.Stat. § 130A–410 (provision of blood is a service, not a sale, "whether or not any remuneration is paid").

The third requirement of equal protection is that the classification created by the statute under scrutiny rest upon some reasonable basis. * * * The initial determination of reasonableness in a classification lies with the legislature and will not be set aside by this court unless it is plainly arbitrary. Further, the party assailing the statute has the burden of showing that its classification does not rest upon any reasonable basis and is essentially arbitrary. * * *

Plaintiffs' attempt to show § 44–43–10 lacks a reasonable basis by arguing that (1) no empirical data exists indicating that protecting blood providers from liability on implied warranty theories generates a more adequate supply of safe blood, and (2) the "tremendous difference" between hepatitis victims and AIDS victims undermines the reasonableness of the statute's purpose. We disagree and hold that the classification created by the statute rests upon a reasonable basis.

First, plaintiffs, not defendants, bear the burden of showing the classification lacks a reasonable basis. Next, we believe plaintiffs' policy arguments on the efficacy of § 44–43–10 in encouraging an adequate blood supply would be better directed to the legislature, for this court will "not sit as a superlegislature to judge the wisdom or desirability of legislative policy determinations." Gary Concrete Prods., Inc. v. Riley, 285 S.C. 498, 331 S.E.2d 335, 339 (1985) (quoting City of New Orleans v. Dukes, 427 U.S. 297, 303, 96 S.Ct. 2513, 49 L.Ed. 2d 511 (1976)). Further, we do not believe that the nature of the transfusion-related disease involved here is a matter of constitutional significance. While § 44–43–10 was not passed with blood-transmitted

AIDS in mind, the rationale behind the statute's classification is as applicable to AIDS as it would be to hepatitis or malaria. * * *

Because we conclude that § 44-43-10's classification bears a reasonable relation to the legislative purpose sought to be effected, its class members are treated alike under similar circumstances, and the classification rests on a reasonable basis, we are of the opinion that the statute comports with the Equal Protection clause of the Constitution of South Carolina.

Chapter 9

NON–MEDICAL ACTS

Introductory Note

Health care providers expose themselves to medical liability by performing medical acts, such as negligently diagnosing and treating patients and failing to secure informed consent. Health care providers also incur public liability to strangers and invitees for negligent non-medical acts that arise out of life's general activities, including driving vehicles and maintaining buildings.

Lying between acts of medical negligence and acts of public liability are a miscellaneous group of theories of claim arising from non-medical acts that have their impact upon patients and significant others. Non-medical acts include promising results and methods, making misrepresentations, and otherwise engaging in tortious conduct under theories of claim that the editors in an earlier casebook called collectively "sue the bastards." The cases here have been selected to illustrate problems that are familiar to physicians in practice; the editors have exercised their policy against including medicolegal horror stories, of which there are a good many.

None of these theories of claim is used very often. The use of a particular theory testifies to the lawyer's creativity and the client's anger. Usually the theory was employed by the plaintiff's lawyer because the medical negligence claim was not available. The plaintiff usually gave up something of litigative value in order to employ it. Some of the acts alleged are not insurable. It is no accident that many of the cases that follow have not been tried to verdict—they ended at trial by dismissal or summary judgment—and by no means do plaintiffs always win, or win much money, on these theories, because they often impute implausible states of mind or intentions to the actor whose non-medical acts allegedly did the harm.

SECTION A. PROMISES AND DAMAGES

SULLIVAN v. O'CONNOR
Supreme Judicial Court of Massachusetts, 1973.
363 Mass. 579, 296 N.E.2d 183, 99 A.L.R.3d 294.[1]

KAPLAN, JUSTICE.

The plaintiff patient, Alice Sullivan, secured a jury verdict of $13,500 against the defendant surgeon, James H. O'Connor, for breach of contract in respect to an operation upon the plaintiff's nose. * * *

[T]he plaintiff alleged that she, as patient, entered into a contract with the defendant, a surgeon, wherein the defendant promised to perform plastic surgery on her nose and thereby to enhance her beauty and improve her appearance; that he performed the surgery but failed to achieve the promised result; rather the result of the surgery was to disfigure and deform her nose, to cause her pain in body and mind, and to subject her to other damage and expense. * * *

* * * The plaintiff was a professional entertainer, and this was known to the defendant. The agreement was as alleged in the declaration. More particularly, judging from exhibits, the plaintiff's nose had been straight, but long and prominent; the defendant undertook by two operations to reduce its prominence and somewhat to shorten it, thus making it more pleasing in relation to the plaintiff's other features. Actually the plaintiff was obliged to undergo three operations, and her appearance was worsened. Her nose now had a concave line to about the midpoint, at which it became bulbous; viewed frontally, the nose from bridge to midpoint was flattened and broadened, and the two sides of the tip had lost symmetry. This configuration evidently could not be improved by further surgery. The plaintiff did not demonstrate, however, that her change of appearance had resulted in loss of employment. Payments by the plaintiff covering the defendant's fee and hospital expenses were stipulated at $622.65.

The judge instructed the jury, first, that the plaintiff was entitled to recover her out-of-pocket expenses incident to the operations. Second, she could recover the damages flowing directly, naturally, proximately, and foreseeably from the defendant's breach of promise. These would comprehend damages for any disfigurement of the plaintiff's nose—that is, any change of appearance for the worse—including the effects of the consciousness of such disfigurement on the plaintiff's mind, and in this connection the jury should consider the nature of the plaintiff's profession. Also consequent upon the defendant's breach, and compensable, were the pain and suffering involved in the third operation, but not in the first two. * * *

---

1. Annot., Measure and Elements of Damages in Action Against Physician for Breach of Contract to Achieve Particular Result or Cure, 99 A.L.R.3d 303 (1980).

By his exceptions the defendant contends that the judge erred in allowing the jury to take into account anything but the plaintiff's out-of-pocket expenses (presumably at the stipulated amount). * * *

It has been suggested on occasion that agreements between patients and physicians by which the physician undertakes to effect a cure or to bring about a given result should be declared unenforceable on grounds of public policy. See Guilmet v. Campbell, 385 Mich. 57, 188 N.W.2d 601, 616 (1971) (dissenting opinion). But there are many decisions recognizing and enforcing such contracts, * * * and the law of Massachusetts has treated them as valid, although we have had no decision meeting head-on the contention that they should be denied legal sanction. * * * These causes of action are, however, considered a little suspect, and thus we find courts straining sometimes to read the pleadings as sounding only in tort for negligence, and not in contract for breach of promise, despite sedulous efforts by the pleaders to pursue the latter theory. See Gault v. Sideman, 42 Ill.App.2d 96, 191 N.E.2d 436 (1963) * * *.

It is not hard to see why the courts should be unenthusiastic or skeptical about the contract theory. Considering the uncertainties of medical science and the variations in the physical and psychological conditions of individual patients, doctors can seldom in good faith promise specific results. Therefore it is unlikely that physicians of even average integrity will in fact make such promises. Statements of opinion by the physician with some optimistic coloring are a different thing, and may indeed have therapeutic value. But patients may transform such statements into firm promises in their own minds, especially when they have been disappointed in the event, and testify in that sense to sympathetic juries.[2] If actions for breach of promise can be readily maintained, doctors, so it is said, will be frightened into practising "defensive medicine." On the other hand, if these actions were outlawed, leaving only the possibility of suits for malpractice, there is fear that the public might be exposed to the enticements of charlatans, and confidence in the profession might ultimately be shaken. See Miller, The Contractual Liability of Physicians and Surgeons, 1953 Wash.U.L.Q. 413, 416–423. The law has taken the middle of the road position of allowing actions based on alleged contract, but insisting on clear proof.[3] Instructions to the jury may well stress this requirement and point to tests of truth, such as the complexity or difficulty of

2. Judicial skepticism about whether a promise was in fact made derives also from the possibility that the truth has been tortured to give the plaintiff the advantage of the longer period of limitations sometimes available for actions on contract as distinguished from those in tort or for malpractice. See Lillich, The Malpractice Statute of Limitations in New York and Other Jurisdictions, 47 Cornell L.Q. 339 (1962) * * *.

3. Editors' Note: In Sard v. Hardy, 281 Md. 432, 379 A.2d 1014, 1027 (1977), the court wrote,

We * * * adopt the rule that although a patient may recover for breach of an express, pre-operative warranty to effect a particular result, despite the absence of a separate consideration, he may do so only upon proving by clear and convincing evidence that the physician did, in fact, make the alleged warranty.

an operation as bearing on the probability that a given result was promised. * * *

If an action on the basis of contract is allowed, we have next the question of the measure of damages to be applied where liability is found. Some cases have taken the simple view that the promise by the physician is to be treated like an ordinary commercial promise, and accordingly that the successful plaintiff is entitled to a standard measure of recovery for breach of contract—"compensatory" ("expectancy") damages, an amount intended to put the plaintiff in the position he would be in if the contract had been performed, or, presumably, at the plaintiff's election, "restitution" damages, an amount corresponding to any benefit conferred by the plaintiff upon the defendant in the performance of the contract disrupted by the defendant's breach. See Restatement of Contracts § 329 and comment a, §§ 347, 384(1).

Thus in Hawkins v. McGee, 84 N.H. 114, 146 A. 641 (1929), the defendant doctor was taken to have promised the plaintiff to convert his damaged hand by means of an operation into a good or perfect hand, but the doctor so operated as to damage the hand still further. The court, following the usual expectancy formula, would have asked the jury to estimate and award to the plaintiff the difference between the value of a good or perfect hand, as promised, and the value of the hand after the operation. (The same formula would apply, although the dollar result would be less, if the operation had neither worsened nor improved the condition of the hand.) If the plaintiff had not yet paid the doctor his fee, that amount would be deducted from the recovery. There could be no recovery for the pain and suffering of the operation, since that detriment would have been incurred even if the operation had been successful; one can say that this detriment was not "caused" by the breach. But where the plaintiff by reason of the operation was put to more pain that he would have had to endure, had the doctor performed as promised, he should be compensated for that difference as a proper part of his expectancy recovery. It may be noted that on an alternative count for malpractice the plaintiff in the *Hawkins* case had been nonsuited; but on ordinary principles this could not affect the contract claim, for it is hardly a defense to a breach of contract that the promisor acted innocently and without negligence. The New Hampshire court further refined the *Hawkins* analysis in McQuaid v. Michou, 85 N.H. 299, 157 A. 881 (1932), all in the direction of treating the patient-physician cases on the ordinary footing of expectancy. See McGee v. United States Fidelity & Guar. Co., 53 F.2d 953 (1st Cir.1931) (later development in the *Hawkins* case) * * *.

Other cases, including a number in New York, without distinctly repudiating the *Hawkins* type of analysis, have indicated that a different and generally more lenient measure of damages is to be applied in patient-physician actions based on breach of alleged special agreements to effect a cure, attain a stated result, or employ a given medical method. This measure is expressed in somewhat variant ways, but the substance is that the plaintiff is to recover any expenditures made by him and for other detriment (usually not specifically described in the opinions) following proximately and foreseeably upon the defendant's failure to carry out his promise. Robins v. Finestone, 308 N.Y. 543, 127 N.E.2d 330, 332 (1955) * * *.

This, be it noted, is not a "restitution" measure, for it is not limited to restoration of the benefit conferred on the defendant (the fee paid), but includes other expenditures, for example, amounts paid for medicine and nurses; so also it would seem according to its logic to take in damages for any worsening of the plaintiff's condition due to the breach. Nor is it an "expectancy" measure, for it does not appear to contemplate recovery of the whole difference in value between the condition as promised and the condition actually resulting from the treatment. Rather the tendency of the formulation is to put the plaintiff back in the position he occupied just before the parties entered upon the agreement, to compensate him for the detriments he suffered in reliance upon the agreement. This kind of intermediate pattern of recovery for breach of contract is discussed in the suggestive article by Fuller and Perdue, The Reliance Interest in Contract Damages, 46 Yale L.J. 52, 373 (1936), where the authors show that, although not attaining the currency of the standard measures, a "reliance" measure has for special reasons been applied by the courts in a variety of settings, including noncommercial settings. * * *

The question of recovery on a reliance basis for pain and suffering or mental distress requires further attention. We find expressions in the decisions that pain and suffering (or the like) are simply not compensable in actions for breach of contract. The defendant seemingly espouses this proposition in the present case. True, if the buyer under a contract for the purchase of a lot of merchandise, in suing for the seller's breach, should claim damages for mental anguish caused by his disappointment in the transaction, he would not succeed; he would be told, perhaps, that the asserted psychological injury was not fairly foreseeable by the defendant as a probable consequence of the breach of such a business contract. See Restatement of Contracts § 341, and comment a.

But there is no general rule barring such items of damage in actions for breach of contract. It is all a question of the subject matter and background of the contract, and when the contract calls for an operation on the person of the plaintiff, psychological as well as physical injury may be expected to figure somewhere in the recovery, depending on the particular circumstances. * * *

Again, it is said in a few of the New York cases, concerned with the classification of actions for statute of limitations purposes, that the absence of allegations demanding recovery for pain and suffering is characteristic of a contract claim by a patient against a physician, that such allegations rather belong in a claim for malpractice. See Robins v. Finestone, 308 N.Y. 543, 127 N.E.2d 330, 332 (1955) * * *. These remarks seem unduly sweeping. Suffering or distress resulting from the breach going beyond that which was envisaged by the treatment as agreed, should be compensable on the same ground as the worsening of the patient's condition because of the breach. Indeed it can be argued that the very suffering or distress "contracted for"—that which would have been incurred if the treatment achieved the promised result— should also be compensable on the theory underlying the New York cases. For that suffering is "wasted" if the treatment fails. Otherwise stated, compensation for this waste is arguably required in order to complete the restoration of the status quo ante.

In the light of the foregoing discussion, all the defendant's exceptions fail: the plaintiff was not confined to the recovery of her out-of-pocket expenditures; she was entitled to recover also for the worsening of her condition,[4] and for the pain and suffering and mental distress involved in the third operation. These items were compensable on either an expectancy or a reliance view. We might have been required to elect between the two views if the pain and suffering connected with the first two operations contemplated by the agreement, or the whole difference in value between the present and the promised conditions, were being claimed as elements of damage. But the plaintiff waives her possible claim to the former element, and to so much of the latter as represents the difference in value between the promised condition and the condition before the operations.

* * *

Defendant's exceptions overruled.

MURRAY v. UNIVERSITY OF PENNSYLVANIA HOSP.

Superior Court of Pennsylvania, 1985.
340 Pa.Super. 401, 490 A.2d 839.

WIEAND, JUDGE. * * *

A doctor and patient may, if they choose to do so, contract that a course of treatment will produce a specific result. If that result is not achieved, the patient may then have an action for breach of contract even though the doctor has exercised the highest degree of professional care. * * *

An action for breach of contract must be commenced within six years. Such an action is not controlled by the two year statute of limitations which is applicable to actions for professional negligence causing injury to another's person. It has been held, however, that the two year statute applicable to causes of action for personal injuries cannot be avoided by the expedient of pleading in contract. * * * In determining which statute will control, it is necessary to determine the nature of the damages sought to be recovered. If recovery is sought for the cost of completing performance of the contract or remedying defects

---

4. That condition involves a mental element, and appraisal of it properly called for consideration of the fact that the plaintiff was an entertainer. * * *

in performance, the applicable statute of limitations is six years. * * * If, however, the damages sought to be recovered are for personal injuries, the two year period of limitation is clearly applicable. * * *

Brenda Murray determined after the birth of her fourth child that she would have no more children. On August 12, 1970, she underwent a tubal ligation at the University of Pennsylvania Hospital to prevent further pregnancies. A jury found that Dr. Cynthia W. Cook, acting as agent for the hospital, had expressly warranted that the tubal ligation would prevent future pregnancies. However, in May, 1972, Mrs. Murray found that she was again pregnant. This pregnancy was subsequently terminated by therapeutic abortion. A second tubal ligation was performed on June 12, 1972.[5]

Mrs. Murray and Richard, her husband, commenced an action in assumpsit * * * on August 6, 1976. In a complaint thereafter filed, they alleged a breach of the agreement guaranteeing a specific result. They requested damages to compensate them for Mrs. Murray's subsequent medical and hospital expenses. However, they also sought an award of monetary damages to compensate Mrs. Murray for her personal injuries, including pain and suffering, and her husband for the loss of his wife's consortium. Both defendants filed an answer in which they pleaded the two year statute of limitations as a complete defense to the action. * * *

The jury returned a verdict in favor of the Murrays and against Dr. Cook and the hospital. Damages were awarded to Mrs. Murray in the amount of $21,000 and to Richard Murray in the sum of $5,300. * * * The trial court * * * granted a new trial * * * because "the jury was permitted to award damages for personal injuries resulting from an act which occurred two years before the plaintiff commenced the action * * *." * * *

The only argument which defendants have preserved is that plaintiffs' entire action is barred by the statute of limitations. The two year statute of limitations, they contend, is a complete defense to the plaintiff's entire cause of action. They argue, as they did in the trial court, that plaintiffs are not entitled to recover any damages in this action. This contention, as the trial court recognized, cannot be sustained. Only the claim for personal injury is subject to the two year statute of limitations. Plaintiffs' cause of action, although it requested damages for personal injuries, also sought recovery for the reasonable cost of achieving the result contracted for, i.e., prevention of conception; and the cost of remedying defendants' failure to perform their contract, i.e., the cost of the therapeutic abortion. These claims are not barred by the two year statute of limitations. They represent true contract damages intended to give the injured parties the benefit of their bargain by awarding a sum of money that would, to the extent possible,

---

5. Editors' Note: The parties' names have been simplified and made consistent.

put them in the same position as they would have been if the contract had been performed. Restatement (Second) of Contracts §§ 347–348 (1979). Such an action is controlled by the statute of limitations applicable to contracts and must be brought within six years.

* * * If the jury awarded damages not properly included in a verdict for plaintiff, it was only because of jury instructions to which the defendants did not object. * * *

Dr. Cook and the hospital have also argued that the parol evidence rule is substantively applicable to prevent recovery on an alleged oral agreement to guarantee Mrs. Murray's tubal ligation. They contend that because the authorization and release which Mrs. Murray and her husband signed prior to surgery did not contain a warranty as to the success of the procedure and, in fact, purported to release the surgeon and hospital, they could not show a warranty agreement by parol. Whether this argument is valid must depend on whether the release was intended to be the entire agreement between the parties. * * *

In the instant case, the trial court held that the authorization and release was not intended to be the entire agreement between the parties. We agree. * * * Brenda Murray testified that she consented to the operation only because she had been guaranteed that she would not become pregnant again. Neither the meaning of the release nor the fact that tubal ligations sometimes fail, she said, had been discussed with her. She was told that she had to sign the authorization before the surgical procedure could be performed. Her husband said that he had signed the form solely for the purpose of permitting his wife to have the operation. Under these circumstances, the trial court could properly conclude that the authorization for surgery was not intended to be the entire agreement between the parties. Parol evidence was admissible, therefore, to show the existence of an oral agreement to guarantee the prevention of future pregnancies.

* * *

Remanded for consideration of the remaining issues raised by Dr. Cook and the University of Pennsylvania Hospital in their motion for new trial. * * *

CAVANAUGH, JUDGE, dissenting. * * *

* * * Since I believe that the majority opinion improperly awards the Murrays an undeserved windfall, I would agree with the trial court's award of a new trial. However, since the Murrays have already successfully won the day on the liability issue, I would limit the new trial to damages only.

STEWART v. RUDNER

Supreme Court of Michigan, 1957.
349 Mich. 459, 84 N.W.2d 816.

SMITH, JUSTICE.

Mrs. Celie Lois Stewart, plaintiff herein, had conceived. Though she was a relatively young woman, at least in comparison with her husband, who was 63 (she was only 37), she was disturbed and apprehensive that she might not be able to have the child. She had had two previous stillbirths and she was convinced that she could not normally deliver. As she put it, "I know I couldn't go through normal." Yet more than anything else, she testified, she "wanted a sound, healthy baby."

A solution, however, suggested itself to the couple. They would have the baby delivered by a Caesarean section, thus avoiding what they conceived to be the hazards of a normal delivery. * * * Consequently, when she and her husband consulted the defendant, Dr. Paul Bunyan, licensed in Michigan as an osteopathic physician and surgeon, they told him that they "thought that a Caesarean operation would be absolutely necessary." (As a matter of fact the record contains language much more suitable to the urgency and the apprehension felt. "We demanded," testified Mr. Stewart, "that Dr. Bunyan perform a Caesarean operation.") The doctor replied that he was not qualified to perform it but that "Dr. Kesten was the operating physician in the hospital," and, he said, according to Mr. Stewart, "he would see to it that Dr. Kesten was available and that a Caesarean would be performed." Mrs. Stewart, plaintiff, is equally clear. "We told him," she said, "we wanted it taken; he said I would labor for a while and that the other doctor would take—Dr. Kesten would take." There can be no doubt that such a contract was made. The subject of Caesarean section was discussed not once, but "each and every time" that Mr. and Mrs. Stewart consulted with the defendant. Dr. Bunyan himself testified, "I knew Mrs. Stewart wanted a Caesarean. I knew also of the possible problems in the delivery of this child."

During the period of gestation Mrs. Stewart saw Dr. Bunyan regularly. * * *

On the morning of September 4th Mrs. Stewart's pains commenced. (She entered the hospital late that night, complaining of labor pains which had become more severe.) She and her husband again returned to Dr. Bunyan. They told him of the onset of her pains and expressed concern over her failure to deliver. They asked Dr. Bunyan why delivery was not made "at the regular period." He told them not to worry and "to go home." At this time, testified Dr. Bunyan, "the baby was alive." The fetal heart tones were audible, were normal, and sounded "quite strong." They were, however, the last heard.

Exhibit H tells the story: "White female admitted to the hospital 9–5–53 at 2:30 a.m. Fetal heart tones not heard." * * *

In the early afternoon of that same date, around one p.m., Dr. Rudner examined the plaintiff for the first time. "At that time," he testified, "I could pick up no fetal heart tones and I considered that I had a dead fetus." He left instruction for her care and about ten o'clock that night he delivered her, after performing what is described as an episiotomy, a surgical cut or incision to facilitate delivery and prevent tearing. The child was dead.

Suit was brought by plaintiff against Dr. Bunyan and Dr. Rudner. The declaration contained two counts. The first, against Dr. Bunyan alone, was for breach of contract. * * *

The jury returned a verdict of $5,000 for the plaintiff against Dr. Bunyan * * *.

* * * A doctor and his patient, of course, have the same general liberty to contract with respect to their relationship as other parties entering into consensual relationship with one another, and a breach thereof will give rise to a cause of action. It is proper to note, with respect to the contracts of physicians, that certain qualitative differences should be observed, since the doctor's therapeutic reassurance that his patient will be all right, not to worry, must not be converted into a binding promise by the disappointed or quarrelsome. * * *

* * * When we have a contract concerned not with trade and commerce but with life and death, not with profit but with elements of personality, not with pecuniary aggrandizement but with matters of mental concern and solicitude, then a breach of duty with respect to such contracts will inevitably and necessarily result in mental anguish, pain and suffering. In such cases the parties may reasonably be said to have contracted with reference to the payment of damages therefor in event of breach. Far from being outside the contemplation of the parties, they are an integral and inseparable part of it.

* * * In the case before us, can any reasonable person doubt that mental pain and suffering were within the contemplation of the parties before us in event plaintiff were damaged by breach? Is any other contemplation, in fact, within the scope of the facts established upon trial? Here we have a couple, no longer young, who are convinced (and who can say without reason?) that their only chance for life is through the Caesarean section. The demanded operation was not a trivial and subordinate aspect of their agreement. It was of the essence thereof, the sole reason for its being, the indispensable ingredient. There was not an iota of the commercial in their contract. Tragedy, they felt, would again visit them, were they not to have the safeguard of skillful surgery rather than the uncontrolled processes of nature that had proven doubly disastrous in the past. We now know that the hour of delivery having come, and gone, without the intervention of the surgeon's skill, again the plaintiff felt the exquisite cruelty of hope destroyed and life denied. It is not disputed that the suffering existed. As her doctor, defendant Dr. Bunyan, testified, "I went back to see her on September 8, 1953, but she would not talk to me. She lay there and

cried. It seemed to hit her pretty hard." If we are to avoid the jury's verdict we will have to conclude that the suffering described in the record before us was not within the reasonable contemplation of the parties when the contract for delivery of the child by Caesarean was made. This we cannot do, and the mere suggestion thereof seems somehow repellent.

* * *

The damages claimed are for pain and mental suffering, and for loss of wages (for a 13-week period following her recovery from the physical results of the episiotomy performed) due to her nervous condition and chills and fever attendant upon and arising from the circumstances hereinabove related. The jury was justified in finding that these resulted directly from defendant's failure to perform his contractual obligations. * * *

Affirmed. * * *

DETHMERS, C.J., and SHARPE, KELLY, and CARR, JJ., concurred in result.

CHEW v. PAUL D. MEYER, M.D., P.A.

Court of Special Appeals of Maryland, 1987.
72 Md.App. 132, 527 A.2d 828, cert. denied 311 Md. 286, 533 A.2d 1308 (1987).

BLOOM, JUDGE.

Appellant, Herbert Chew, filed in the Circuit Court for Baltimore City a multiple count complaint, sounding in tort and contract, against appellee, Paul D. Meyer, M.D., P.A. Appellee moved for dismissal of the complaint in its entirety, asserting that the claims were not properly before the court because the claims should have been filed with the Health Claims Arbitration Office, pursuant to Md.Cts. & Jud. Proc.Code Ann. § 3–2A–01 et seq. Dr. Meyer also moved for summary judgment as to each count. * * *

Mr. Chew was employed by Bethlehem Steel Co. The employer required all employees who missed work to produce a written explanation for the absence within 15 days of the last day worked. A medical explanation or excuse for absence from work required a writing signed by a physician, but the employer prescribed no particular form; therefore, any memorandum or insurance form signed by a physician would suffice.

On [Thursday] 8 September 1983, Chew was admitted to South Baltimore General Hospital for surgery to relieve discomfort in his left thigh. Prior to entering the hospital, Chew informed his surgeon, Dr. Meyer, that a particular insurance form entitled "Statement Claim for Sickness and Accident Weekly Benefits" had to be completed and returned to his employer promptly. It was Chew's intention that that form serve not only to enable him to collect sick pay but also to document the legitimate excuse for his absence from work.

The day following his surgery, Chew presented Dr. Meyer with the insurance form and insisted that he complete it immediately. The doctor refused, but he did accept the form for completion by his secretary. In his deposition Chew claimed that he told the doctor at that time, "make sure that you get the papers in within the next week * * * or it could cost me my job."

During the period between 10 September and 21 September Chew made several inquiries of the doctor and his secretary concerning the status of the insurance form, and on at least one occasion repeated that he could lose his job if that form was not expedited. Each time he was given assurance that the form would be mailed promptly. The form was not completed, however, until 21 September 1983 and was not received by Bethlehem Steel until 26 September 1983. As a result of the failure to supply his employer with timely documentation that his absence from work was due to an excusable cause, Chew was discharged from employment.

* * *

In ruling on appellee's motion to dismiss, the court determined that Chew's claim was essentially one for medical malpractice; accordingly, it granted that motion. At the same time, the court also ruled on appellee's motion for summary judgment, granting that motion with respect to each count except one for breach of contract.

Motion to Dismiss. * * * The critical question * * * is whether the injury sustained by appellant can be fairly characterized as having resulted from the rendering or failure to render health care. We do not think it can.

* * *

Chew's claims against Dr. Meyer do not arise out of the doctor's failure to adhere to the level of skill or expertise ordinarily expected of a neurosurgeon. As Chew acknowledged in his brief and at oral argument, he is entirely satisfied with Dr. Meyer's skill as a surgeon. Chew's complaint against Dr. Meyer lies in the doctor's failure to perform, in a proper and timely manner, a clerical task collateral to rendering "health care." We do not believe the legislature ever intended such a claim to come within the act. Cf. Nichols v. Wilson, 296 Md. 154, 460 A.2d 57 (1983) (claims for assault, battery and intentional infliction of emotional distress were not arbitrable even though striking of patient occurred during medical treatment).

Summary Judgment. * * * The court below determined that Chew's negligence claim was governed by § 323 of the Restatement (Second) of Torts (1977). * * * [6] Since Chew suffered only economic

---

6. § 323. Negligent Performance of Undertaking to Render Services. One who undertakes, gratuitously or for consideration, to render services to another which he should recognize as necessary for the protection of the other's person or things, is subject to liability to the other for physical harm resulting from his failure to exercise reasonable care to perform his undertaking, if

(a) his failure to exercise such care increases the risk of such harm, or

injury as a result of Dr. Meyer's alleged failure to complete the insurance form promptly, the court held that Chew had failed to state a cause of action for negligence.

The lower court erred by applying § 323. [T]he court of appeals has implicitly rejected that Restatement section, at least with respect to contractual undertakings.

* * * Chew has alleged that Dr. Meyer was obligated under the contract between them to complete certain insurance forms for Chew and to submit medical information concerning Chew to Chew's employer. Formerly, such a contention might well have been summarily rejected, on the basis that a physician's obligation to his patient ordinarily did not extend beyond his duty to use his best efforts to treat and cure. The traditional scope of the contractual relationship between doctor and patient, however, has expanded over the years as a result of the proliferation of health and disability insurance, sick pay, and other employment benefits.

Today, the patient commonly, and necessarily, enlists the aid of his or her physician in preparing claims forms for health and disability benefits. Such forms ordinarily require information possessed solely by the treating physician as well as the physician's signature attesting to the bona fides of that medical information. Consequently, appellant's assertion that the services Dr. Meyer contracted to perform for Mr. Chew included the completion and submission of insurance forms in addition to the surgery he performed, combined with an allegation that the doctor failed to complete and submit the document in question in a proper, i.e., timely manner, states a plausible cause of action for breach of contract.

The court, therefore, correctly denied summary judgment concerning Chew's claim of breach of contract. Should the trier of fact determine that Dr. Meyer had undertaken a contractual duty to complete and submit Chew's insurance form in a timely manner, there would be no question of contractual privity, and that privity would carry with it a concomitant tort duty. * * *

[A] combination of either a contractual obligation or a gratuitous undertaking arising from the "intimate nexus" of the doctor/patient relationship, coupled with the patient's reliance, the risk of harm, and the doctor's knowledge of both the reliance and the risk, is sufficient to give rise to a tort duty to act reasonably in fulfilling the obligation. * * * Accordingly, appellant has stated a cause of action in negligence, which he is entitled to have submitted to a jury.

Judgment reversed.

(b) the harm is suffered because of the other's reliance upon the undertaking.

SECTION B. MISREPRESENTATIONS

SIMCUSKI v. SAELI
Court of Appeals of New York, 1978.
44 N.Y.2d 442, 406 N.Y.S.2d 259, 377 N.E.2d 713.

JONES, JUDGE. * * *

On October 19, 1970, Dr. Anthony J. Saeli performed a surgical excision of a node from plaintiff's neck. Plaintiff, Eleanor Simcuski, alleges that during the operation on her neck the surgeon negligently injured a spinal accessory nerve in her neck and also injured branches of her cervical plexus. Following the operation plaintiff told her surgeon that she was experiencing numbness in the right side of her face and neck, and that it was difficult and painful for her to raise her right arm. It is alleged that the physician was aware of the negligent manner in which he had performed the surgery and aware, too, that as a result of his negligence plaintiff had suffered a potentially permanent injury. It is further alleged that the physician willfully, falsely, and fraudulently told plaintiff that her postoperative problems, pain, and difficulties were transient, and that they would disappear if she would continue a regimen of physiotherapy which he had prescribed and which was then being given by Dr. Lane. Plaintiff continued with the physiotherapy prescribed by Dr. Saeli until October 1974. In the meantime she had moved to Syracuse, New York, where she sought further medical advice.

In January 1974 she was first apprised by the Syracuse physician of the true nature of her injury and that it probably had been caused at the time of her surgery. This doctor's diagnosis was substantially confirmed in October 1974 by a professor of medicine, specializing in neurology, at Upstate Medical Center in Syracuse, who also advised that reanastomosis of the sectioned nerve four years after the surgery would not be a physiologically successful procedure. It is further alleged that Dr. Saeli had intentionally withheld information from plaintiff as to the true nature and source of her injury, in consequence of which she was deprived of the opportunity for cure of her condition.

The present action against Dr. Saeli was commenced in April 1976. Prior to service of an answer, Dr. Saeli moved to dismiss the complaint * * * on the ground that the cause or causes of action alleged were barred by the statute of limitations. Plaintiff cross-moved for leave to amend her complaint specifically to include a cause of action for malpractice. The supreme court denied defendant's motion to dismiss and granted plaintiff leave to amend her complaint as requested. On appeal, the appellate division reversed, granted defendant's motion and dismissed the complaint. 57 A.D.2d 711, 395 N.Y.S.2d 776 (1977).
* * *

The complaint sufficiently sets forth a cause of action for medical malpractice; the critical issue is whether this cause of action was barred by the then applicable three-year statute of limitations, N.Y.Civ.Prac.L. & R. [CPLR] 214(6). Normally the statute would have precluded institution in April 1976 of a claim for damages for malpractice alleged to have occurred in October 1970. This complaint, however, further alleges that defendant intentionally concealed the alleged malpractice from plaintiff and falsely assured her of effective treatment, as a result of which plaintiff did not discover the injury to the nerve until October 1974. In this circumstance principles of equitable estoppel are applicable to relieve plaintiff from the proscriptions of the statute. * * *

It is the rule that a defendant may be estopped to plead the statute of limitations where plaintiff was induced by fraud, misrepresentations or deception to refrain from filing a timely action. [S]ee Annot., Fraud, Misrepresentation, or Deception as Estopping Reliance on Statute of Limitations, 43 A.L.R.3d 429 (1972). The allegations of her complaint bring this plaintiff within the shelter of this rule. The elements of reliance by plaintiff on the alleged misrepresentations as the cause of her failure sooner to institute the action for malpractice and of justification for such reliance, both necessarily to be established by her, are sufficiently pleaded within the fair intendment of the allegations of this complaint.

* * * The doctrine [of equitable estoppel] has been applied in other states in circumstances which are legally indistinguishable from the present. * * * The quality of the relationship between physician and patient, with confidence normally reposed by the patient in the physician, and the unquestioning reliance which such relationship may be expected to engender in the patient, make application of the doctrine peculiarly appropriate in such cases.

* * * If the conduct relied on (fraud, misrepresentation, or other deception) has ceased to be operational within the otherwise applicable period of limitations (or perhaps within a reasonable time prior to the expiration of such period), many courts have denied application of the doctrine on the ground that the period during which the plaintiff was justifiably lulled into inactivity had expired prior to the termination of the statutory period, and that the plaintiff had thereafter had sufficient time to commence his action prior to the expiration of the period of limitations. [S]ee Annot., Plaintiff's Diligence as Affecting His Right to Have Defendant Estopped From Pleading the Statute of Limitations, 44 A.L.R.3d 760 (1972) * * *. That is not the present situation. Plaintiff has alleged that her discovery of the malpractice in this case (the point at which the conduct here relied on ceased to be operational) did not occur until October 1974 (or possibly in January of that year, if inference be drawn from the letter of her Syracuse doctor dated January 9, 1974, submitted in opposition to the motion). Whichever the month of discovery in 1974, the three-year statute of limitations had already expired in October 1973.

Where, as here, the conduct relied on ceases to be operational after the expiration of the period of limitations, two approaches may be discerned in the cases. By one, further delay on the part of the plaintiff in commencing his action may be held to be subject to the counterdefense of laches to be pleaded and proved by the defendant * * *. The preferable analysis, however, holds that due diligence on the part of the plaintiff in bringing his action is an essential element for the applicability of the doctrine of equitable estoppel, to be demonstrated by the plaintiff when he seeks the shelter of the doctrine * * *. Under this approach, which we endorse, the burden is on the plaintiff to establish that the action was brought within a reasonable time after the facts giving rise to the estoppel have ceased to be operational. Whether in any particular instance the plaintiff will have discharged his responsibility of due diligence in this regard must necessarily depend on all the relevant circumstances.

The length of the legislatively prescribed period of limitations is sometimes said to be relevant, and courts have held that in no event will the plaintiff be found to have exercised the required diligence if his action is deferred beyond the date which would be marked by the reapplication of the statutory period, i.e., that the length of the statutory period itself sets an outside limit on what will be regarded as due diligence. * * * In the present case such an outside limit was not exceeded; the action was brought less than three years after discovery in 1974. It is not possible or appropriate, however, on the present motion addressed to the pleading, presenting us as it must with only a skeletal record, to determine whether this plaintiff met her obligation of due diligence when she instituted the present action in April 1976. [I]t cannot now be determined as a matter of law that the reasonable time for bringing the present action had expired prior to its institution in April 1976.

[T]he other cause of action * * * asserts a claim in fraud as an intentional tort. * * *

This is more than another aspect of the malpractice or even another act of alleged negligent malpractice on the part of the treating physician; the complaint alleges an intentional fraud that Dr. Saeli, knowing it to be untrue yet expecting his patient to rely on his advice, advised her that physiotherapy would produce a cure, in consequence of which fraudulent misrepresentation the patient was deprived of the opportunity for cure of the condition initially caused by the doctor's alleged malpractice. If these allegations are proved, they will establish an intentional tort, separate from and subsequent to the malpractice claim. * * * Recovery of damages in such case is governed by the six-year statute of limitations under CPLR 213(8). The application of the three-year statute of limitations is not mandated by the circumstance that the fraud alleged arises as a sequel to an alleged malpractice.[7]

7. We observe that the alleged tortious conduct in this instance occurred prior to the adoption of CPLR 214–a (L.1975, ch. 109, § 6, eff. July 1, 1975). There is thus no basis here for any assertion that by the enactment of that statute the legislature intended to prescribe a statutory period of limitations with respect to all claims arising out of the physician-patient relation-

[W]e recognize and approve, but distinguish, cases which hold that, without more, concealment by a physician or failure to disclose his own malpractice does not give rise to a cause of action in fraud or deceit separate and different from the customary malpractice action, thereby entitling the plaintiff to bring his action within the longer period limited for such claims. * * * Such nondisclosure or concealment may affect the damages recoverable, or, conceivably in a proper case in conjunction with other factors, provide a foundation for seeking to invoke the doctrine of equitable estoppel to extend the applicable period of limitations. Standing alone such nondisclosure or concealment will not, however, serve as the basis for a distinct cause of action in fraud.

[A]s in the instance of fraud claims generally, this plaintiff, too, will be required to prove her claim by clear and convincing evidence * * *. If she succeeds in this respect, the available measure of her damages will be that applicable in fraud actions, i.e., damages caused by the fraud, as distinguished in this case from damages occasioned by the alleged malpractice.

[T]he exposure to liability we here discuss is not based on errors of professional judgment; it is predicated on proof of the commission of an intentional tort, in this instance, fraud. As to that cause of action:

First, it must be established that the physician knew (or demonstrably had reason to know) of the fact of his malpractice and of the injury suffered by his patient in consequence thereof.

Second, it must be established that, knowing it to be false at the time, the physician thereafter made material, factual misrepresentation to the patient with respect to the subject matter of the malpractice and the therapy appropriate to its cure, on which the patient justifiably relied.

Third, all elements of the intentional tort of fraud must be established by clear and convincing evidence. Recognizing, too, the hazards of proliferating litigation of baseless claims, attention is drawn to the requirements of CPLR 3016(b). While, of course, motions to dismiss under CPLR 3211 are properly addressed to the allegations set forth in the complaint, on motions for summary judgment under CPLR 3212 evidentiary proof in admissible form must be tendered in support of all the elements of the alleged cause of action.

Fourth, if there is not an available, efficacious remedy or cure which the plaintiff is diverted from undertaking in consequence of the intentional, fraudulent misrepresentation, as in many instances of medical malpractice there may not be, there will normally be only minimal damages, if any. It will be necessary to demonstrate that the condition caused by the malpractice could have been corrected or alleviated. Thus, in the present case, if it can be shown that at the time of Dr. Saeli's alleged fraudulent misrepresentations it was already

ship no matter on what legal theory predicated.

too late to undertake a reanastomosis of the severed nerve, this plaintiff will have sustained little or no damages in consequence of the alleged fraud. If only a partial cure were then possible, damages would be assessable on that basis. Recovery would be greatest, of course, if plaintiff were diverted from what could otherwise have been a complete cure.

[T]he present decision is not to be expected to open the proverbial floodgates. On the other hand, in human terms it would be unthinkable today not to hold a professional person liable for knowingly and intentionally misleading his patient in consequence of which, to the physician's foreknowledge, the patient was deprived of an opportunity for escape from a medical predicament which the physician by his own negligence had initially inflicted on his patient. With respect to the application of the doctrine of equitable estoppel to a defense of statute of limitations pleaded in a malpractice action, again we are concerned with an intentional, not merely negligent, wrong—the purposeful concealment and misrepresentation of the fact and consequences of the malpractice. It would not be tolerable to permit a physician by whose fraud, misrepresentation, or deception his patient has been induced to delay filing legal proceedings until after the time limited by statute to reap the benefits of his own misconduct.

[T]he order of the appellate division should be reversed, with costs to abide the event, and the order of the supreme court denying defendant's motion to dismiss reinstated.

COOKE, JUDGE, concurring. * * *

FUCHSBERG, JUDGE,[8] concurring.

Though I wholeheartedly join in the disposition of this case and of the questions necessary to its determination, I find aspects of the majority opinion sufficiently disturbing to compel me to comment.

For one, the court's indorsement of cases which are said to have held that mere "concealment by a physician or failure to disclose his own malpractice" does not toll the statute of limitations is both peripheral and unnecessary to today's decision. Moreover, it suffers from more than the ordinary weakness of dictum. It gratuitously renews the blessing, given at an earlier time and in a different clime, to a proposition whose soundness has, in the intervening years, been the object of widespread and increasing criticism, much of which characterizes willful nondisclosure as "constructive fraud." Morrison v. Acton, 68 Ariz. 27, 198 P.2d 590 (1948); W. Prosser, Torts § 30 at 144 (4th ed. 1971) * * *.

* * *

I also refuse to join in what I regard as the equally unnecessary and, so far as the record reveals, unfounded factual and qualitative assumptions implicit in phrases such as opening the "floodgates,"

---

8. Editors' Note: Before he was elected to the New York Court of Appeals in 1975, Judge Jacob D. Fuchsberg had been a prominent plaintiff's lawyer; he was president of the Association of Trial Lawyers of America in 1963–1964.

"ballooning malpractice recoveries," and "legitimate concern both from the standpoint of the profession and the public as to the economic import" of malpractice recoveries. Such expressions, which omit the concerns of those injured by medical negligence, are, I respectfully suggest, best avoided. All the more is that so in a situation where, as has been widely reported and openly admitted, large sums have been expended by interested parties to influence public opinion * * *.

SECTION C. TORTIOUS CONDUCT

MILLSAPS v. BANKERS LIFE CO.
Appellate Court of Illinois, 1976.
35 Ill.App.3d 735, 342 N.E.2d 329.

RECHENMACHER, JUSTICE. * * *

Plaintiff, Phillip W. Millsaps, had applied to Bankers Life Co. for major medical insurance coverage in February 1971. His suit for actual and punitive damages against the defendants [Dr. Jerry Cargill, Bankers Life, and another] was based primarily on Dr. Cargill's letter of March 26, 1971. That letter [to Bankers Life] read as follows:

> Enclosed is a summary of Mr. Millsaps recent hospitalization. Physically the man has no notable problems; emotionally, the patient is quite mercurial in his moods. He is a strong willed man obsessed with faults of others in his family, of which there has been no objective basis. He has completely resisted any constructive advice by his wife, family, minister or myself. The man needs psychiatric help for his severe obsessions and depressions some of which have suicidal tones. He is extremely poor insurance risk.

* * *

In Count 1 plaintiff alleged that Dr. Cargill's letter of March 26 "contained false, scandalous, malicious libel * * * concerning the Plaintiff," and injured his reputation. Count 3 adds that Dr. Cargill's letter caused injury to his reputation as a real estate sales and insurance broker and alleged resulting loss of confidence and esteem of Bankers Life and of friends and acquaintances.

Counts 2 and 4 are based on Cargill's two-page letter dated June 9, 1971, to one Jerry Boose and to the law firm of which Mr. Boose was a member, reciting medical history of the plaintiff and stating in part as follows:

> Mr. Millsaps is quite rigid and absolutely uncompromising in his attitude. The patient continues weight loss and severe depression alternating with spells of extreme agitation wherein he would jump up and down in a frenzied manner or weeping uncontrollably. The serious neglect of his previously successful real estate business, his paranoid thoughts against his minister and wife and I am sure certainly toward me, are all evidences of severe personality disorder. If you can persuade this man to seek psychiatric help before further loss is sustained you would do him a great service.

(That letter was written in response to an inquiry from Attorney Boose who represented plaintiff at that time.) Counts 2 and 4 alleged that the June 9 letter contained false, scandalous, malicious and defamatory libel concerning the plaintiff, injured his reputation, and resulted in a loss of business in his profession and in the loss of the confidence and esteem of the addressees and of friends and acquaintances.

* * *

[The trial court dismissed counts 1 through 4.]

First we consider the applicability to Counts 2 and 4, which are based on Dr. Cargill's letter of June 9, 1971, of the one year limitation period relating to suits for libel and defamation. * * * Inasmuch as the date of publication was more than one year prior to the date the amended complaint was filed, Counts 2 and 4 were barred by the statute of limitations. Moreover, we note in passing that the June 9 letter was directed to plaintiff's duly authorized agent, his then attorney, and written in response to the attorney's inquiry; as such, that letter is equivalent to a publication to plaintiff himself and therefore is privileged and is not actionable. * * *

[As for Counts 1 and 3, b]oth Dr. Cargill and Bankers Life rely on the defense of privilege. In support of this contention they point out that plaintiff, in connection with his insurance application to Bankers Life, signed an "authorization" to doctors and hospitals to furnish his "past medical history." Both plaintiff and Bankers Life contemplated the requirement of a complete medical report, including hospitalization. Bankers Life requested the medical report from Dr. Cargill based on plaintiff's authorization * * *.

* * * Dr. Cargill in supplying his March 26 report to Bankers Life did only what plaintiff authorized him to do and which Bankers Life had requested. It was therefore conditionally privileged. * * *

Judgment affirmed.

BUNDREN v. SUPERIOR COURT

California Court of Appeal, 1983.
145 Cal.App.3d 784, 193 Cal.Rptr. 671.

STONE, PRESIDING JUSTICE. * * *

[Elaine M. Bundren sued Los Robles Regional Medical Center for the intentional infliction of emotional distress. Los Robles moved for partial summary judgment on this claim, and in opposition Mrs. Bundren filed the following declaration:

[I was admitted to Defendant Los Robles Regional Medical Center on January 11, 1981, for elective surgery to be performed on the following day. Upon my admission I filled out all necessary forms presented to me including but not limited to required medical insurance information, financial responsibility, and general background information.

* * *

[The surgery was performed on January 12, 1981.

[The following day, January 13, 1981, during the evening dinner hour, while still under the effects of surgery, I was called by Defendant's business office. My mother, Mary Bold, was visiting me at the time. Prior to the telephone call, which was received by my mother, no one from the hospital nursing staff inquired as to my physical status or if I was to receive a telephone call from the business office.[9]

[The caller identified herself as someone from the business office and informed me that my insurance carrier had denied coverage and then proceeded to question me on how I was to pay the hospital bill. The caller continued a pattern of inquiry as to where I could obtain money, how I could apply this to the bill, and when they could expect payment. I had no response to her question as I did not know at the time how I could make the payments or where the source of funds would come from. I asked that the caller speak with my attorney. The caller did not seem to be interested in anything I said other than wanting some commitment regarding the payment of the hospital bill. Her questioning continued at least for 20 to 30 minutes. Her mannerism was abusive, rude and inconsiderate.

[As the caller continued her questioning, I became more upset and finally I was unable to continue the conversation. I believed that I would be discharged if I did not make a commitment toward payment of the medical bill.[10] I began to cry uncontrollably and my mother, who was observing my reaction to the telephone call, came to my aid, and the telephone call was terminated.

[I immediately felt sick to my stomach and could not stop crying. Although it was not the time of the month for my period, I shortly thereafter had a spontaneous menstrual flow and was required to go to the washroom to clean myself and allow the nurses to change the bedding.

[My evening meal was left uneaten, and I thereafter requested a sedative which was brought to me by the nurse.

[The superior court granted Los Robles's motion for partial summary judgment, and Mrs. Bundren immediately asked the court of appeal in effect to reverse it.]

[W]e recognize that the attempted collection of a debt, by its very nature, often causes the debtor to suffer emotional distress. Frequently, the creditor intentionally seeks to create concern and worry in the mind of the debtor in order to induce payment. However, in a society

---

9. In support of its motion for partial summary judgment, Los Robles submitted a declaration from the nurse on duty in petitioner's ward. The nurse stated that at approximately 5:00 p.m., on January 13, 1981, she

received a telephone call asking whether Mrs. Bundren was in a sufficient physical condition to receive a call. [She] * * * indicated that Mrs. Bundren's physical condition was such that she could receive a telephone call.

10. Although petitioner was never threatened with removal from Los Robles, she asserts that the effects of the prior surgery and her weakened condition caused her to fear immediate expulsion from the facility.

greatly dependent upon the extension of credit, it is important that a creditor be allowed a certain degree of freedom in demanding payment.

* * *

While it is recognized that the creditor possesses a qualified privilege to protect its economic interest, the privilege may be lost should the creditor use outrageous and unreasonable means in seeking payment. * * * The applicable test is whether or not the creditor goes beyond "all reasonable bounds of decency" in attempting to collect the debt. Restatement (Second) of Torts § 46 (1965). Under the view set forth in the Restatement, a collector who happens to demand payment in a rude and insolent manner is not liable unless other factors are present. Such "other factors" may be supplied where the creditor has knowledge that the debtor is susceptible to emotional distress by reason of some physical or mental condition.

Case law provides illustrations of the Restatement rule. * * *

Here, petitioner presented evidence raising questions of fact: that is, whether Los Robles' agent (1) acted in an unreasonable and outrageous manner; (2) acted in reckless disregard of petitioner's physical condition; (3) abused the special relationship that exists between hospital and patient.

* * *

Los Robles did not dispute assertions made by petitioner that the caller, in a "rude and offensive" manner, persisted for a 20- to 30-minute period, demanding payment; that she neglected to advise petitioner of her eligibility for alternative means of payment (i.e., state aid, in the form of Medi–Cal, although this was part of her job); and continued making demand, notwithstanding the fact that petitioner advised the caller to contact her attorney in order to arrange payment.

* * *

In short, there is a serious question as to whether the hospital's method of seeking payment, perhaps reasonable had it been attempted after petitioner had regained her health, was in fact reasonable in light of petitioner's alleged delicate physical and emotional state at the time of the call. Clearly, the resolution of this question should be through the consideration of live testimony presented to a trier of fact.

Let a peremptory writ of mandate issue commanding the respondent to * * * [deny the hospital's motion for summary judgment].

HUMPHERS v. FIRST INTERSTATE BANK
Supreme Court of Oregon, 1985.
298 Or. 706, 696 P.2d 527, 48 A.L.R.4th 651.[11]

LINDE, JUSTICE. * * *

In 1959, according to the complaint, plaintiff, then known as Ramona Elwess or by her maiden name, Ramona Jean Peek, gave birth

11. Annot., Physician's Tort Liability for Unauthorized Disclosure of Confidential Information About Patient, 48 A.L.R.4th 668 (1986).

to a daughter in St. Charles Medical Center in Bend, Oregon. She was unmarried at the time, and her physician, Dr. Harry E. Mackey, registered her in the hospital as "Mrs. Jean Smith." The next day, Ramona consented to the child's adoption by Leslie and Shirley Swarens of Bend, who named her Leslie Dawn. The hospital's medical records concerning the birth were sealed and marked to show that they were not public. Ramona subsequently remarried and raised a family. Only Ramona's mother and husband and Dr. Mackey knew about the daughter she had given up for adoption.

Twenty-one years later the daughter, now known as Dawn Kastning, wished to establish contact with her biological mother. Unable to gain access to the confidential court file of her adoption (though apparently able to locate the attending physician), Dawn sought out Dr. Mackey, and he agreed to assist in her quest. Dr. Mackey gave Dawn a letter which stated that he had registered Ramona Jean Peek at the hospital, that although he could not locate his medical records, he remembered administering diethylstilbestrol to her, and that the possible consequences of this medication made it important for Dawn to find her biological mother. The latter statements were untrue and were made only to help Dawn to breach the confidentiality of the records concerning her birth and adoption. In 1982 hospital personnel, relying on Dr. Mackey's letter, allowed Dawn to make copies of plaintiff's medical records, which enabled her to locate plaintiff, now Ramona Humphers.

Ramona Humphers was not pleased. The unexpected development upset her and caused her emotional distress, worry, sleeplessness, humiliation, embarrassment, and inability to function normally. She sought damages from the estate of Dr. Mackey, who had died, by this action against defendant First Interstate Bank as the personal representative. After alleging the facts recounted above, her complaint pleads for relief on five different theories: First, that Dr. Mackey incurred liability for "outrageous conduct"; [12] second, that his disclosure of a professional secret fell short of the care, skill, and diligence employed by other physicians in the community and commanded by statute; third, that his disclosure wrongfully breached a confidential or privileged relationship; fourth, that his disclosure of confidential information was an "invasion of privacy" in the form of an "unauthorized intrusion upon plaintiff's seclusion, solitude, and private affairs"; and fifth, that his disclosures to Dawn Kastning breached a contractual obligation of secrecy. The circuit court granted defendant's motion to dismiss the complaint on the grounds that the facts fell short of each theory of relief and ordered entry of judgment for defendant. On

---

12. This court has attempted, so far unsuccessfully, to discourage the idea that there is a general tort of "outrageous conduct," partly because the phrase misleadingly suggests potential recovery of damages whenever someone's conduct could be said to deserve this epithet. See Hall v. May Dep't Stores Co., 292 Or. 131, 637 P.2d 126, 129 (1981) * * *. Plaintiff in this case actually alleged the factual elements of intentional or reckless infliction of severe emotional distress as well as "outrageous" conduct.

appeal, the court of appeals affirmed the dismissal of the first, second, and fifth counts but reversed on the third, breach of a confidential relationship, and the fourth, invasion of privacy. Humphers v. First Interstate Bank, 68 Or.App. 573, 684 P.2d 581 (1984). * * *

A physician's liability for disclosing confidential information about a patient is not a new problem. In common law jurisdictions it has been more discussed than litigated throughout much of this century.[13] There are precedents for damage actions for unauthorized disclosure of facts conveyed in confidence, although we know of none involving the disclosure of an adoption. [T]he decisions do not always rest on a single theory.

Sometimes, defendant may have promised confidentiality expressly or by factual implication, in this case perhaps implied by registering a patient in the hospital under an assumed name. Plaintiffs were allowed to proceed on implied contract claims in Horne v. Patton, 291 Ala. 701, 287 So.2d 824 (1973), in Hammonds v. Aetna Casualty & Sur. Co., 243 F.Supp. 793 (N.D.Ohio 1965), and in Doe v. Roe, 93 Misc.2d 201, 400 N.Y.S.2d 668 (Sup.Ct.1977) (psychiatrist). * * * A contract claim may be adequate where the breach of confidence causes financial loss, and it may gain a longer period of limitations; but contract law may deny damages for psychic or emotional injury not within the contemplation of the contracting parties, see Farris v. United States Fidelity & Guar. Co., 284 Or. 453, 587 P.2d 1015 (1978), though perhaps this is no barrier when emotional security is the very object of the promised confidentiality. A contract claim is unavailable if the defendant physician was engaged by someone other than the plaintiff, see Quarles v. Sutherland, 215 Tenn. 651, 389 S.W.2d 249 (1965) (denying claim by injured customer treated by store's doctor), and it would be an awkward fiction at best if age, mental condition, or other circumstances prevent the patient from contracting; yet such a claim might be available to someone less interested than the patient, for instance her husband. Clayman v. Bernstein, 38 Pa.D. & C. 543 (1940).

Malpractice claims, based on negligence or statute, in contrast, may offer a plaintiff professional standards of conduct independent of the defendant's assent. In Furniss v. Fitchett, [1958] N.Z.L.R. 396 (Sup. Ct.), a wife was convinced that her husband was insane and was doping her, and the couple's physician gave the distraught husband a document stating that the wife's suspicions were a paranoid delusion. The New Zealand Supreme Court held the physician liable for foreseeable harm to the wife (whom he had not told of the diagnosis) under the "general conception of relations giving rise to a duty of care" stated in Donoghue v. Stevenson, [1932] A.C. 562 (H.L.). But the court found this duty in the relation between doctor and patient; a claim of negligence is unavailable against a defendant not bound to confidentiality by such

---

13. See, e.g., Hanning & Brady, Extrajudicial Truthful Disclosure of Medical Confidences: A Physician's Civil Liability, 44 Den.U.L.Rev. 463 (1967) (citing the earlier literature) * * *.

professional standards. Finally, actions for intentional infliction of severe emotional distress fail when the defendant had no such intention or, in a context of independent responsibility such as that of the physician in Rockhill v. Pollard, 259 Or. 54, 485 P.2d 28 (1971), when a defendant was not reckless or did not behave in a manner that a factfinder could find to transcend "the farthest reaches of socially tolerable behavior." Hall v. May Dep't Stores Co., 292 Or. 131, 637 P.2d 126, 130 (1981). Among these diverse precedents, we need only consider the counts of breach of confidential relationship and invasion of privacy on which the court of appeals allowed plaintiff to proceed. Plaintiff did not pursue her other theories in her response to the petition for review, Or.R.App.P. 10.15(2), and we express no view whether the dismissal of those counts was correct.

Although claims of a breach of privacy and of wrongful disclosure of confidential information may seem very similar in a case like the present, which involves the disclosure of an intimate personal secret, the two claims depend on different premises and cover different ground. Their common denominator is that both assert a right to control information, but they differ in important respects. Not every secret concerns personal or private information; commercial secrets are not personal, and governmental secrets are neither personal nor private. Secrecy involves intentional concealment. "But privacy need not hide; and secrecy hides far more than what is private." S. Bok, Secrets 11 (1983).

For our immediate purpose, the most important distinction is that only one who holds information in confidence can be charged with a breach of confidence. If an act qualifies as a tortious invasion of privacy, it theoretically could be committed by anyone. In the present case, Dr. Mackey's professional role is relevant to a claim that he breached a duty of confidentiality, but he could be charged with an invasion of plaintiff's privacy only if anyone else who told Dawn Kastning the facts of her birth without a special privilege to do so would be liable in tort for invading the privacy of her mother.

Whether "privacy" is a usable legal category has been much debated in other English-speaking jurisdictions as well as in this country, especially since its use in tort law, to claim the protection of government against intrusions by others, became entangled with its use in constitutional law, to claim protection against rather different intrusions by government.[14] No concept in modern law has unleashed a comparable flood of commentary, its defenders arguing that "privacy"

---

14. . . . Not surprisingly, elevating all interests of personality to constitutional rights has produced theories that the United States Constitution requires the states to guarantee the parent a "privacy" right not to have an adoption disclosed, see Note, Sealed Adoption Records and the Constitutional Right of Privacy of the Natural Parent, 34 Rutgers L.Rev. 451 (1982), and that the same constitution guarantees the adopted child a "privacy" right to learn his or her genealogical identity. Note, The Adult Adoptee's Constitutional Right to Know His Origins, 48 S.Cal.L.Rev. 1196 (1975). A New Jersey court confronted these competing demands in Mills v. Atlantic City Dep't of Vital Statistics, 148 N.J. Super. 302, 372 A.2d 646 (1977).

encompasses related interests of personality and autonomy, while its critics say that these interests are properly identified, evaluated, and protected below that exalted philosophical level. Indeed, at that level, a daughter's interest in her personal identity here confronts a mother's interest in guarding her own present identity by concealing their joint past. But recognition of an interest or value deserving protection states only half a case. Tort liability depends on the defendant's wrong as well as on the plaintiff's interest, or "right," unless some rule imposes strict liability. One's preferred seclusion or anonymity may be lost in many ways; the question remains who is legally bound to protect those interests at the risk of liability.

* * * Dean William L. Prosser and his successors, noting that early debate was more "preoccupied with the question whether the right of privacy existed" than "what it would amount to if it did," concluded that invasion of privacy "is not one tort but a complex of four": * * * first, appropriation of the plaintiff's name or likeness; second, unreasonable and offensive intrusion upon the seclusion of another; third, public disclosure of private facts; and fourth, publicity which places the plaintiff in a false light in the public eye. W. Prosser & R. Keeton, Torts § 117 (5th ed. 1984). The same classification is made in the Restatement (Second) of Torts §§ 652A–652E. * * *

This court has not adopted all forms of the tort wholesale. * * *

* * * The court of appeals concluded that the complaint alleges a case of tortious intrusion upon plaintiff's seclusion, not by physical means such as uninvited entry, wiretapping, photography, or the like, but in the sense of an offensive prying into personal matters that plaintiff reasonably has sought to keep private. * * * [15] We do not believe that the theory fits this case.

Doubtless plaintiff's interest qualifies as a "privacy" interest. That does not require the judgment of a court or a jury; it is established by the statutes that close adoption records to inspection without a court order. Or.Rev.Stat. §§ 7.211, 432.420. The statutes are designed to protect privacy interests of the natural parents, the adoptive parents, or the child. But as already stated, to identify an interest deserving protection does not suffice to collect damages from anyone who causes injury to that interest. Dr. Mackey helped Dawn Kastning find her biological mother, but we are not prepared to assume that Ms. Kastning became liable for invasion of privacy in seeking her out. Nor, we think, would anyone who knew the facts without an obligation of secrecy commit a tort simply by telling them to Ms. Kastning.

Dr. Mackey himself did not approach plaintiff or pry into any personal facts that he did not know; indeed, if he had written or spoken to his former patient to tell her that her daughter was eager to find her, it would be hard to describe such a communication alone as an

---

15. Hospital patients have recovered on a variety of theories for what courts recognized as an injury to privacy when the patient, without knowing consent, was exposed to nonmedical personnel * * *.

invasion of privacy. The point of the claim against Dr. Mackey is not that he pried into a confidence but that he failed to keep one. If Dr. Mackey incurred liability for that, it must result from an obligation of confidentiality beyond any general duty of people at large not to invade one another's privacy. We therefore turn to plaintiff's claim that Dr. Mackey was liable for a breach of confidence, the third count of the complaint.

* * * A number of decisions have held that unauthorized and unprivileged disclosure of confidential information obtained in a confidential relationship can give rise to tort damages. * * *

One commentator, upon analyzing the cases allowing or denying recovery on a variety of theories, concluded that the tort consists in a breach of confidence in a "nonpersonal" confidential relationship, using the word "nonpersonal" to exclude liability for failing to keep secrets among members of a family or close friends. Note, Breach of Confidence: An Emerging Tort, 82 Colum.L.Rev. 1426 (1982). The problem with this formulation of civil liability lies in identifying the confidential relationships that carry a duty of keeping secrets. The writer suggests that the duty arises in all nonpersonal relationships "customarily understood" to carry such an obligation. Id. at 1460–61. In any such relationship, a person who discloses personal information conveyed in confidence would have the burden of showing that the disclosure was justified or privileged.

We do not think the law casts so wide a net. It requires more than custom to impose legal restraints on "the right to speak, write, or print freely on any subject whatever." Or.Const., art. I, § 8. Tort liability, of course, may be a remedy for "injury to person, property, or reputation," Or.Const., art. I, § 10, even by speech. * * * But a legal duty not to speak, unless voluntarily assumed in entering the relationship, will not be imposed by courts or jurors in the name of custom or reasonable expectations. Tort liability is the consequence of a nonconsensual duty of silence, not its source.

In the case of the medical profession, courts in fact have found sources of a nonconsensual duty of confidentiality. Some have thought such a duty toward the patient implicit in the patient's statutory privilege to exclude the doctor's testimony in litigation, enacted in this state in Or.Evid.Code 504–1(2). * * * More directly in point are legal duties imposed as a condition of engaging in the professional practice of medicine or other occupations.

* * *

This strikes us as the right approach to a claim of liability outside obligations undertaken expressly or implied in fact in entering a contractual relationship. * * * The contours of the asserted duty of confidentiality are determined by a legal source external to the tort claim itself. A plaintiff asserting a breach of such a nonconsensual duty must identify its source and terms. If the tort claim asserts violation of a statute or regulation, the rule must validly apply to the facts, whether or not it actually is applied by those responsible for enforcement. When the asserted rule is one administered by a specialized agency, such as a professional board, and its scope is disputed, this may on occasion require reference to the agency's primary jurisdiction if the court does not find application of the rule to the facts clear as a matter of law. * * *

Because the duty of confidentiality is determined by standards outside the tort claim for its breach, so are the defenses of privilege or justification. Physicians, like members of many ordinarily confidential professions and occupations, also may be legally obliged to report medical information to others for the protection of the patient, of other individuals, or of the public. See, e.g., Or.Rev.Stat. § 418.750 (physician's duty to report child abuse); Or.Rev.Stat. §§ 433.003, 434.020 (duty to report certain diseases). That was true of the defendant in Simonsen v. Swenson, 104 Neb. 224, 177 N.W. 831 (1920), who reported a guest's contagious disease to a hotel. The court noted that this disclosure was legally required and affirmed a directed verdict for the defendant. Even without such a legal obligation, there may be a privilege to disclose information for the safety of individuals or important to the public in matters of public interest. * * * Some cases have found a physician privileged in disclosing information to a patient's spouse * * *, or perhaps an intended spouse * * *. In any event, defenses to a duty of confidentiality are determined in the same manner as the existence and scope of the duty itself. They necessarily will differ from one occupation to another and from time to time. A physician or other member of a regulated occupation is not to be held to a noncontractual duty of secrecy in a tort action when disclosure would not be a breach or would be privileged in direct enforcement of the underlying duty.

A physician's duty to keep medical and related information about a patient in confidence is beyond question. It is imposed by statute. Oregon Rev.Stat. § 677.190(5) provides for disqualifying or otherwise disciplining a physician for "wilfully or negligently divulging a professional secret." The court of appeals thought that breach of this statutory provision could not lead to civil liability when such liability would be quite inappropriate to provisions of Or.Rev.Stat. § 677.190, but that misses the point. The actionable wrong is the breach of duty in a confidential relationship; Or.Rev.Stat. § 677.190(5) only establishes the duty of secrecy in the medical relationship.

It is less obvious whether Dr. Mackey violated Or.Rev.Stat. § 677.190(5) when he told Dawn Kastning what he knew of her birth. She was not, after all, a stranger to that proceeding. * * * If Ms. Kastning needed information about her natural mother for medical reasons, as Dr. Mackey pretended, the State Board of Medical Examiners likely would find the disclosure privileged against a charge under Or.Rev.Stat. § 677.190(5); but the statement is alleged to have been a pretext designed to give her access to the hospital records. If only Or.

Rev.Stat. § 677.190(5) were involved, we do not know how the Board would judge a physician who assists at the birth of a child and decades later reveals to that person his or her parentage. But as already noted, other statutes specifically mandate the secrecy of adoption records. Oregon Rev.Stat. § 7.211 provides that court records in adoption cases may not be inspected or disclosed except upon court order, and Or.Rev. Stat. § 432.420 requires a court order before sealed adoption records may be opened by the state registrar. Given these clear legal constraints, there is no privilege to disregard the professional duty imposed by Or.Rev.Stat. § 677.190(5) solely in order to satisfy the curiosity of the person who was given up for adoption.

For these reasons, we agree with the court of appeals that plaintiff may proceed under her claim of breach of confidentiality in a confidential relationship. The decision of the court of appeals is reversed with respect to plaintiff's claim of invasion of privacy and affirmed with respect to her claim of breach of confidence in a confidential relationship, and the case is remanded to the circuit court for further proceedings on that claim.

ASCHER v. GUTIERREZ

United States Court of Appeals for the District of Columbia Circuit, 1976.
533 F.2d 1235, 175 U.S.App.D.C. 100.

BRYAN, DISTRICT JUDGE.[16] * * *

The plaintiff, Mrs. Bernadette Ascher, was admitted to the Columbia Hospital for Women in Washington, D.C., on July 20, 1970, for * * * [dilation and curettage of her uterus, a "d & c"]. The surgery was scheduled for July 21, 1970. The defendant-appellant, Dr. Jose E. Gutierrez, was the scheduled anesthesiologist for the procedure.[17] Following an injection by Dr. Gutierrez of sodium pentothal, Mrs. Ascher developed a condition known as a laryngospasm. This is a spasm of certain throat muscles in the vocal cord area which prevents oxygen from getting into the lungs and bloodstream. * * *

[A]t oral argument Dr. Gutierrez pressed only his contention that there was insufficient evidence of the doctor's abandonment of his patient to submit that issue to the jury. We address only that issue here * * *.

The jury was charged, correctly we think, and without objection as to its form, on the issue of abandonment as follows:

> The jury is instructed that once a physician enters into a professional relationship with a patient, he is not at liberty to terminate that relationship at will. That relationship will continue until it is ended by one of the following circumstances: (1) the patient's lack of need for further care; or (2) *the withdrawing physician being replaced by an equally qualified physician.* Withdrawal from the case under any

---

16. United States District Judge for the Eastern District of Virginia, sitting by designation * * *.

17. Editors' Note: The parties' names have been substituted for clarity.

other circumstances constitutes a wrongful abandonment of the patient and if the patient suffers any injury as a proximate result of such wrongful abandonment, the physician is liable for it. (Emphasis supplied.) [18]

It is that part of the instruction which is emphasized with which we deal here.

The evidence established that the laryngospasm began within two or three minutes of the initial injection of sodium pentothal at 12:55 p.m. [M]anual attempts to ventilate or oxygenate Mrs. Ascher failed; relaxing drugs were injected; and finally an endotracheal tube was inserted down the patient's throat so that oxygen could be forced beyond the obstruction caused by the spasm, enabling the patient to be ventilated. Improvement was noted immediately, although Mrs. Ascher continued to be cyanotic and hypotensive, and it developed that the deficiency in oxygen had been of sufficient duration to cause serious and disabling residual brain damage.

The length of time which elapsed during the efforts at resuscitation and before the intubation was effected is in dispute, but the jury could have found that the intubation was accomplished as late as 1:45 p.m., and perhaps later. If not accomplished until then, the jury could have found, based on the expert testimony before it, that Dr. Gutierrez was negligent in not providing adequate ventilation by intubation in a timely manner.

Dr. Gutierrez left the operating room at 1:30 p.m., upon request of another anesthesiologist, to attend another operation. It was Dr. Gutierrez's contention at trial that he did so only upon being replaced by an equally qualified physician. To support this contention testimony was presented that Dr. John A. O'Donnell, a qualified anesthesiologist, relieved Dr. Gutierrez at the time the latter left at 1:30, and in fact had been there since 12:55 in response to Dr. Gutierrez's call for assistance. This testimony was presented and corroborated in varying form by other witnesses. Mrs. Ascher, on the other hand, contended that Dr. O'Donnell was not in the operating room at all during the period from about 12:57 to 1:30.

The operation on Mrs. Ascher took place in Operating Room C. There was introduced in evidence, over Dr. Gutierrez's objection, a hospital record of a patient who gave birth to a baby in another room, which is referred to in the testimony as "OB," at 12:43. This record showed that anesthesia was begun at 12:30; that the baby was born at 12:43; that the patient was taken from "OB" at 2:05; *and that Dr. O'Donnell was the anesthesiologist in "OB" during this procedure.* Dr. O'Donnell testified that he was never in "OB" after 12:00, but on the contrary he was in Operating Room A from approximately 12:30 until a little before 1:00, at which time he stepped out of Operating Room A for

18. Editors' Note: The jury awarded Mrs. Ascher $1.55 million. 66 F.R.D. 548, 549 (D.D.C.1975).

another purpose and was summoned to assist Dr. Gutierrez. Another hospital record, admitted in evidence over defendant's objection, indicated that a Dr. Park was the anesthesiologist attending an operation in Operating Room A during the period 12:35 to 1:15. Dr. O'Donnell, on the other hand, as indicated, testified that for a portion of this time he was in Operating Room A, and further testified that Dr. Park was not there when he was.

This testimony and these documents, together with a prior inconsistent deposition statement by Dr. O'Donnell that Dr. Gutierrez had *not* left the operating room where Mrs. Ascher was a patient, are sufficient in our view to put in issue the credibility of Dr. O'Donnell and his statement that he was present in the operating room with Mrs. Ascher when he said he was. If Dr. O'Donnell were not present, then of course Dr. Gutierrez would not have been "replaced by an equally qualified physician" when he left the operating room at 1:30, and the jury could have concluded that he abandoned his patient.

Whether there was such an issue for the jury depends upon the admissibility of the two hospital records for their substantive content. Dr. Gutierrez concedes that one of the "record[s] * * * on its face tended to indicate that he [Dr. O'Donnell] was administering anesthesia in obstetrics on the floor below to another patient during this period of time [12:57 to 1:30]." The authenticity of the records was not questioned. The objection to the words was that their content had been thoroughly refuted by contradicting evidence, both live and documentary. But whether this was so was a matter for the fact finder, in this case the jury. It has resolved that issue in Mrs. Ascher's favor. The location of Dr. O'Donnell at the time in question, as established by the records, is not inherently incredible or contrary to human experience. Their weight, when contrasted with the weight of the defendant's evidence to the contrary, no matter how voluminous the latter, was for the jury to determine.

We conclude that the admission in evidence of the records was proper and that their substantive content warranted the jury's finding that Dr. O'Donnell was not in Operating Room C "replacing" Dr. Gutierrez when Dr. Gutierrez left at 1:30, and that consequently Dr. Gutierrez abandoned his patient.

* * *

The judgment appealed from is affirmed.

STRACHAN v. JOHN F. KENNEDY MEM. HOSP.
Supreme Court of New Jersey, 1988.
109 N.J. 523, 538 A.2d 346.

CLIFFORD, J. * * *

At approximately 4:30 p.m. on Friday, April 25, 1980, 20-year-old Jeffrey Strachan shot himself in the head in an apparent suicide attempt. He was rushed to John F. Kennedy Memorial Hospital (the Hospital) * * *. At 5:25 that afternoon Dr. Hummel, the emergency room physician, diagnosed Jeffrey as brain dead. The doctor based his conclusion on several factors, including the absence of spontaneous respiration and reflexive movement, as well as the fact that both pupils were dilated and fixed. Dr. Hummel placed Jeffrey on a respirator.

Examination later that evening by Dr. Cohen, a neurosurgeon and one of the attending physicians, confirmed that Jeffrey was brain dead. The doctor explained that painful reality to plaintiffs and informed them that nothing could be done to restore brain function.

Because the Hospital is actively involved in organ transplants through its affiliate, the Delaware Valley Transplant Program, Dr. Cohen asked plaintiffs to consider donating Jeffrey's organs. He noted on the medical chart that the staff should proceed to "harvest" Jeffrey's organs if the parents gave their permission (the obvious implication being that there was no doubt about Jeffrey's status: he was dead). Because plaintiffs were uncertain about what to do, they deferred a decision and agreed to return in the morning. Jeffrey was then transferred to the intensive care unit, where he was continued on the life support system in order that the organs would remain in a condition for harvesting should the parents' decision be in favor of donation. Jeffrey's parents were allowed to "visit" him in the intensive care unit.

Plaintiffs returned the next morning, Saturday, April 26. They informed a Dr. Pinsler * * * of their decision not to donate any of Jeffrey's organs. They also requested that he be taken off the respirator. Dr. Pinsler advised plaintiffs to "think it over some more." Plaintiffs also discussed their request with Dr. Cohen. When Mr. Strachan asked a nurse when the machine would be turned off, he was informed that the hospital administrator had not given any order for the removal of the machinery, and that the removal could not be effected without such an order.

After speaking with Mr. Strachan that evening Dr. Venkat, also a neurosurgeon and an associate of Dr. Cohen, examined Jeffrey and agreed that the young man was brain dead. He noted plaintiffs' request to turn off the respirator, and indicated on the chart that "as soon as the hospital administrator tells us the procedure, we will do so."

Assistant administrator and nursing director Jeanette Licorice communicated with defendant Augustine R. Pirolli, the hospital administrator, late that same evening. Pirolli in turn called the Hospital's general counsel, Edward Sullivan, for advice. Sullivan suggested that the Hospital obtain plaintiffs' consent for removal of the respirator. He also indicated that the Hospital should run two electroencephalograms (EEGs), twenty-four hours apart, to get a "clear understanding of what the boy's condition is." He suggested to Pirolli that a court order might be obtained as an alternative to a medical decision to turn off the respirator. Another possible solution offered by Sullivan was the convening of a prognosis committee to assist the physicians in the decision to pronounce the patient dead.

The results of the two EEGs confirmed that Jeffrey was indeed brain dead. The Hospital authorities did not convene a prognosis committee. Dr. Weinstein, also a neurosurgeon engaged in practice with Drs. Cohen and Venkat, made an entry on Jeffrey's chart for Monday, April 28, 1980, indicating: "patient officially brain dead and by hospital regulations we may discontinue respiration c̄ [with] family's permission." Plaintiffs signed a release requesting Jeffrey's removal from life-support systems. The release provided:

> We have been advised by the attending physicians of our son, Jeffrey Strachan, that he has been declared "brain dead." It is therefore requested that all life support-life-support-death devices [sic] be discontinued as soon as possible.
>
> In making this request we are fully aware of our legal responsibilities and further hold harmless John F. Kennedy Memorial Hospital and the attending physicians with regard to discontinuance of life support devices.

At 4:05 p.m., Dr. Weinstein disconnected the respirator. Dr. Santoro pronounced Jeffrey dead and executed a death certificate, after which Jeffrey's body was turned over to his family for burial.

Plaintiffs thereafter instituted this action against the Hospital, administrator Pirolli, the physicians involved, and the Delaware Valley Transplant Program and its representative Stephen Sammut. The action against the physicians, the transplant program, and Sammut was voluntarily dismissed prior to trial, and the case proceeded against the Hospital and administrator Pirolli only.

At the conclusion of trial the court instructed the jury on the bases of liability, including respondeat superior, under which the Hospital would be liable if Pirolli were found liable. The court then submitted the matter to the jury with special interrogatories, including the following:

* * *

> 2(a) Did the defendant, Augustine R. Pirolli, have a duty to have procedures in place for the removal of Jeffrey Strachan from the life support systems when requested by his parents, and negligently failed to do so, as alleged by the plaintiffs?
>
> 2(b) Was this failure a proximate cause of the infliction of additional severe emotional stress upon the plaintiffs?

* * *

> 4(a) Did the defendant, Augustine R. Pirolli, negligently hold the body of Jeffrey Strachan so as to prevent his proper burial?
>
> 4(b) Did this holding result in additional mental distress to the plaintiffs?

The jury responded affirmatively to both parts of questions 2 and 4, and awarded plaintiffs $70,000 each, for total verdicts of $140,000. [A] divided appellate division reversed. 209 N.J.Super. 300, 507 A.2d 718, 58 A.L.R.4th 181 [19] (1986).

The foregoing interrogatories, which track the trial court's charge, suggest that there were two separate causes of action, based on separate duties owed by defendants to plaintiffs, on which the jury could make separate determinations: one resting on a duty to have in place procedures for the removal of plaintiffs' son from the life-support system on plaintiffs' request, the other based on a duty to release to the parents their son's dead body. This was error. The circumstances of the case projected but one duty: to act reasonably in honoring the family's legitimate request to turn over their son's body.

* * *

We are disinclined, as a matter of sound public policy, to announce an absolute duty, henceforth to be adhered to by all affected hospitals, to have in place procedures for the removal of a dead body from a life-support mechanism on the request of the next of kin. * * * The imposition of a paperwork duty does little to advance either the mission of health-care providers or the needs of society. If "procedures" are to be viewed as more than mere "paperwork" and considered indispensable in this area—in the nature of a standard that governs the medical community—then those procedures should be designed and imposed by those most directly involved, the physicians and hospitals themselves. That is the business of the medical community itself, not of this court.

That is not to say, however, that the absence of such procedures may not be relevant on the issue of whether these defendants fulfilled the obligation that surely they had: to act reasonably in the face of plaintiffs' request to turn over the body. Plaintiffs produced an expert, Dr. Jerene Robbins, whom the trial court found to be "qualified as a medical doctor, and qualified to give opinions in regard to hospital administration." Dr. Robbins testified that in the circumstances that confronted defendant Pirolli, it was "unthinkable" that there were no forms for the parents to sign to effectuate release of the body, and that if the hospital did not have such forms, then Pirolli "should have on the instant arranged some kind of writing that he could provide for the hospital in order that releases could be signed." We take the expert's testimony to mean that if a hospital is going to insist on forms and procedures, then it should have them available and in place, or at the least improvise them on the spot, in order to fulfill its underlying obligation to take reasonable steps to release the body to the next of kin.

That there is such an underlying obligation is no longer open to question. For more than half a century this state has recognized a quasi property right in the body of a dead person. * * *

19. Editors' Note: Annot., Tortious Maintenance or Removal of Life Supports, 58 A.L.R.4th 222 (1987).

Although the appellate division recognized that cause of action as a quasi property right, the majority held that recovery could not be allowed here because Jeffrey was not legally dead until Monday, April 28, at 4:10 p.m., when he was officially pronounced dead, the respirator was turned off, and the death certificate was signed. 507 A.2d 718 at 725. It was then that Jeffrey's body was turned over to plaintiffs for burial.

Plaintiffs' right of recovery, then, depends on when Jeffrey's death occurred. Jeffrey was pronounced brain dead by the emergency room physician at 5:25 p.m. on Friday. That assessment was confirmed by a neurosurgeon that evening, and again confirmed by other doctors and by the results of additional testing throughout the weekend. The evidence is overwhelming that Jeffrey was deemed brain dead considerably earlier than Monday at 4:10 p.m., when Dr. Santoro pronounced him dead and executed a death certificate. Thus the question comes down to whether our legal definition of death should include brain death.

Traditionally, death was defined as the irreversible cessation of cardiopulmonary function. In re Quinlan, 70 N.J. 10, 355 A.2d 647, 656, cert. denied sub nom. Garger v. New Jersey, 429 U.S. 922, 97 S.Ct. 319, 50 L.Ed.2d 289 (1976). This definition, however, came under attack as failing to reflect advances in medical technology. Because cardiac and respiratory activity can be mechanically maintained for some time, definitions of "death" have increasingly focused on the cessation of brain functions. * * * Once the brain is dead, no technology exists to restore its function.

Technological advances have also made possible the performance of organ transplants on a regular basis. For organs to be preserved for transplant, the donor's cardiopulmonary system must continue functioning until the organs can be removed. Under the traditional definition of death, such a donor would be considered as still alive because the heart continues to beat and the lungs continue to perform the respiratory function. In a very real sense, then, a break from the traditional definition of death is a necessary condition to the existence of transplant programs, for otherwise the organ-removal process might be deemed to have "killed" the donor. * * *

In response to these concerns, many states have adopted new definitions of death, incorporating brain death. The Uniform Determination of Death Act (UDDA) provides:

> § 1. [Determination of Death] An individual who has sustained either (1) irreversible cessation of circulatory and respiratory functions, or (2) irreversible cessation of all functions of the entire brain, including the brain stem, is dead. A determination of death must be made in accordance with accepted medical standards. 12 U.L.A. 236. * * *

By 1985, 13 states and the District of Columbia had adopted the UDDA. [A]t least 30 states have adopted statutory definitions of death that include cessation of brain function. * * *

We therefore conclude that § 1 of the UDDA provides the appropriate legal definition of death. * * * We therefore conclude that there was ample support in the evidence for the jury's conclusion that defendants had "negligently [held] the body of Jeffrey Strachan so as to prevent his proper burial." (Answer to Interrogatory 4(a).)

Our next inquiry is whether the limitations on tort claims for emotional distress bar plaintiffs from recovering for defendant's breach of duty. * * *

The record in this case reveals particularly compelling evidence of distress. Although plaintiffs were told that their son was brain dead and nothing further could be done for him, for three days after requesting that their son be disconnected from the respirator plaintiffs continued to see him lying in bed, with tubes in his body, his eyes taped shut, and foam in his mouth. His body remained warm to the touch. Had Jeffrey's body been removed from the respirator when his parents requested, a scene fraught with grief and heartache would have been avoided, and plaintiffs would have been spared additional suffering.

* * *

Because Jeffrey was no longer alive, defendants breached no duty owed him by their failure to turn off the respirator. Jeffrey suffered no harm as a result of defendants' negligence. Plaintiffs' distress, therefore, was not the result of witnessing another's injury, but rather the result of a breach of duty owed directly to plaintiffs. Perhaps the confusion stems from the fact that the duty owed to plaintiffs related to the handling of Jeffrey's body, but that does not render this a "bystander" case. If, for example, a hospital negligently reported to a patient's parents that the patient's condition was considerably worse than in fact it was, the parents' distress would flow from the breach of a duty owed to them, not one owed to their child. * * *

The requirement of physical injury is grounded on the notion that emotional distress claims are too easily fabricated without such a limitation. Prosser & Keeton on Torts § 54 at 361 (5th ed. 1984). Finding that rationale insufficient to withhold recovery for distress claims that might prove legitimate, an increasing number of courts have abandoned the physical-injury limitation altogether. * * *

We need not decide today whether * * * [under Portee v. Jaffee, 84 N.J. 88, 417 A.2d 521 (1980), the] abandonment of the physical injury requirement for emotional distress claims should extend to all "direct" claims for emotional distress. We need look no further than the long-recognized exception for negligent handling of a corpse, see Muniz v. United Hosps. Med. Center Presbyterian Hosp., 153 N.J.Super. 79, 379 A.2d 57, 58 (1977), or the especial likelihood that this claim is genuine, see Berman v. Allan, 80 N.J. 421, 404 A.2d 8, 15 (1979), to conclude that plaintiffs need not demonstrate any physical manifestations of their emotional distress here. The result at trial was consistent with the stated principles.

* * * Under the circumstances * * * we can have no confidence in the assumption that had the jurors been properly instructed on a single cause of action rather than on two separate and distinct negligence claims, they would have concluded that the total recoverable damages amounted to $70,000. We therefore remand for a retrial on damages only on the claim for failure to have released the dead body.

O'HERN, J., concurring in part, dissenting in part. * * * I would order a retrial on all issues.

BURGESS v. PERDUE
Supreme Court of Kansas, 1986.
239 Kan. 473, 721 P.2d 239.

LOCKETT, JUSTICE. * * *

Mary A. Burgess, the plaintiff, is the mother of Stephen D. Bloomer, deceased. Stephen was a resident of Kansas Neurological Institute (KNI) from June 1970 until his death on July 17, 1983. Dr. Camille Heeb was the treating physician for Stephen while he was a resident of KNI.

On July 17, 1983, Stephen was suffering from bilateral pneumonia. Dr. Heeb was out of town at a meeting, so Dr. W. Lang Perdue, II, was called to KNI to treat Stephen. Dr. Perdue attempted to place a subclavian catheter into Stephen's vein. Because the procedure was only partially successful, Stephen was taken to Stormont–Vail Regional Medical Center for emergency treatment. Stephen died of cardiac arrest while in transit to the hospital.

After Mrs. Burgess arrived at the hospital, Dr. Perdue advised her of Stephen's death. Mrs. Burgess informed the doctor that she did not want an autopsy performed on Stephen. Dr. Perdue then called the county coroner, Dr. Kiernan O'Callaghan, and described the circumstances of the death. Dr. O'Callaghan certified the death as a coroner's case pursuant to Kan.Stat.Ann. § 19–1031 et seq. He stated that an autopsy would be required. Dr. Perdue then called Mrs. Burgess at her home. He informed her that an autopsy would be performed regardless of her granting permission. Though it was not necessary, Dr. Perdue asked for the mother's permission to perform the autopsy, mentioning that KNI would want to examine the brain. Mrs. Burgess agreed to a partial autopsy, but told Dr. Perdue that she neither wanted an autopsy done on her son's brain, nor would [she] allow KNI to examine his brain.

Dr. Perdue failed to inform the county coroner that Mrs. Burgess had consented only to a limited autopsy. Instead, Dr. Perdue furnished to the county coroner a written authorization, as if approved by the mother, allowing a complete autopsy. The assistant county coroner performed a full autopsy on the body. Stephen's brain was removed and sent to KNI by the coroner.

Three weeks after Stephen's funeral, Dr. Heeb discovered the decedent's brain among the specimens received by KNI from the county coroner's office. Dr. Heeb then called Mrs. Burgess, informed her that KNI had her son's brain, and asked her what she would like to have done with it. Later Stephen's body was exhumed and his brain buried with his body. The cost of having his body exhumed and reburied was $1,199.52.

On November 17, 1983, Mrs. Burgess filed a petition * * * [seeking] damages * * * from Dr. Perdue for negligent infliction of emotional distress.

* * * [The trial court granted Dr. Perdue's motion for summary judgment], holding that a claim for negligent infliction of emotional distress for interference with a dead body will not lie against one who does not directly mishandle a decedent's remains. * * *

* * * The court found that Mrs. Burgess had suffered no bodily injury caused by Perdue's negligence. Since her claim was based on the simple negligence of the doctor's failure to relay her wishes regarding the autopsy to the coroner, as a matter of law, the plaintiff could not recover for negligent infliction of emotional distress.

* * *

Cases in other jurisdictions have allowed suits for interference with dead bodies against other persons or agencies than those who actually performed the autopsy or in some other way directly interfered with the body. * * * See Annot., Liability for Wrongful Autopsy, 18 A.L.R.4th 858 (1982).

Kansas has recognized a cause of action for negligent infliction of emotional distress when actual physical injury is involved. In two cases, a limited exception to the rule requiring physical injury was recognized where there had been intentional mishandling of a corpse. * * * In Alderman v. Ford, 146 Kan. 698, 72 P.2d 981 (1937), the widow was suing the surgeon and his assistant who performed an unlawful autopsy on the body of her husband without her permission. The court specifically found that the right of recovery by the widow did not depend on negligence, but on her legal right to receive the body of her late husband in the condition as when he died. In Hamilton v. Individual Mausoleum Co., 149 Kan. 216, 86 P.2d 501 (1939), the children did not allege negligence but sued the mausoleum company and its employees for the willful, wrongful and malicious act of disturbing the body.

* * *

The majority rule holds that, for an individual to be liable for emotional distress for interfering with a dead body, the act must be intentional or malicious, as opposed to negligent, interference with the plaintiff's right to the body, and that interference must be the proximate cause of the mental anguish and/or physical illness of the plaintiff. *Alderman* and *Hamilton,* which establish the Kansas right of action for the mishandling of corpses, involved conduct other than negligence. Both Kansas cases follow the majority rule of liability for interference with a dead body. The district court properly granted Perdue's motion for summary judgment.

* * *

The district court [also] found that Dr. Perdue had voluntarily assumed a duty to relay the information to the coroner but had failed to carry out his promise and was therefore responsible for the reasonable cost of exhuming and reburying the body. The court entered judgment for the plaintiff in the amount of $1,199.52 and court costs.

* * *

The trial court correctly reasoned that Dr. Perdue created the situation which resulted in the alleged injury. The doctor assumed a duty which he was not required to assume. He did not follow through. Once performance was begun, Dr. Perdue owed a duty of care toward the plaintiff.

The judgment is affirmed.

Part II

TREATING THE MEDICAL LIABILITY CRISIS

Chapter 10

INSURANCE AND MEDICAL LIABILITY

INTRODUCTORY NOTE

This chapter opens a new part, Treating the Medical Liability Crisis, which begins with this chapter on insurance and medical liability.

If medical liability claims have created a crisis, every aspect of treating the medical liability crisis involves insurance: the affordability of patient care, the availability of competent doctors in all places and practices, the economic survival of health care facilities, the scope and cost of reimbursement plans, and the compensation of persons for health care accidents. Insurance also underlies the next chapter, which treats legislative efforts to slow the increase of medical liability litigation costs, and the final chapter, which takes up issues of access to and utilization of safe, high-quality health care in a time of rapidly changing patterns of management and delivery.

This chapter introduces the types of insurance and the workings of law in the context of medical liability, partly in order to sketch the configurations of conflicts between insurers and doctors, but even more to promote thinking about the role, functions, and limitations of the liability insurance mechanism. The first section takes up the availability of medical liability insurance and, assuming that it is available, its coverage and exclusions. The second section deals with conflicting interests between insurer and doctor where cooperation or coverage are at issue. The last section introduces problems of settling claims, whether the doctor does not authorize the settlement, or whether the insurer unreasonably fails to settle a claim within policy limits.

SECTION A. AVAILABILITY AND COVERAGE

Note on Medical Liability Insurance

1. The Mechanics of Liability Insurance

Accidents will happen, but in insurance language, the word "accident" is too narrow; other potentially compensable events are insurable, and so the preferred one-word insurance term is "incident." If one person sets aside money to pay for future incidents, that is a contingency fund, and the person is a self-insurer. If many persons pay someone else money now in order to be compensated for incidents in the future, the combined fund is insurance as it is commonly understood.[1] If the insuring group consists of dividend- and capital-gain-seeking investors who have no connection with the persons insured, the insurer is a stock insurance company. If a group insures only its own investors, that is mutual insurance, but membership in the group (such as automobile or home owners) may be so broad that the mutuality has little significance to the members.

A medical liability mutual insurance group may be open to all members of a class (such as licensed physicians in a particular state); this is a "reciprocal" insurer. A group of persons having common characteristics and insurance needs, such as obstetricians, can also insure the members of a subgroup as a private voluntary association that has strict membership requirements; the insurance organization then is a "captive" of the members, it may be referred to as a "club," and it has no other insurance functions.

It would be wasteful to bank the whole insurance fund until is is needed, and so some of the money is invested in income-producing assets. Some assets will need to be more liquid than others, because the insured risks are connected with the timing as well as with the amounts of funds needed. For example, at noon today the insurer knows about some incidents that have been reported but have not been evaluated; for them, the insurer sets up a loss reserve that will be easy to write checks on. Some other incidents have undoubtedly been incurred but have not yet been reported; they call for short-term investments. It is possible that very large incidents will happen at unpredictable intervals in the future; against these, insurers buy their own insurance, called reinsurance, so they can more safely put funds into long-term investments.

If the insured incident is harm to the insured person's property or person, that is casualty insurance. The loss may be total or partial; the smaller and rarer the partial losses, the lower are the insurance premiums, and vice versa.[2] If the insured incident is a compensable event such as negligence that harms the insured's property by making the insured pay

---

1. While volunteers who donate their services to repair a barn after a storm will accomplish the same result, and while a group of persons could promise one another to pay shares of a future loss, the practice of paying money in advance, so a fund of money will be available when it is needed, underlies the insurance mechanism.

2. While "life" insurance thus looks like casualty insurance, the loss by death is both total and inevitable, and so life insurance is in a class by itself and will receive no further attention.

damages to another person, that is liability insurance, with the same relationship between losses and premiums.

The two kinds of insurance produce different payouts for a compensable medical incident that causes personal injuries to a patient. If the patient has casualty insurance, it does not matter whether fault caused the accident or not: the insurer will pay (within policy limits) the pecuniary losses of the patient, but it will pay no damages such as pain and suffering. By contrast, if the patient secures a court judgment against a doctor who was at fault in causing the same medical incident, the judgment includes both the patient's economic damages and the patient's non-pecuniary damages, and so liability insurance must cover the whole judgment.

Medical liability insurance is very expensive, because the cost of insuring against the misperformance of services is related to the amount of harm the doctor can do to the patient and others, not to the size of the fee for services. If a doctor charges $50 for one office visit but negligently causes the permanent and total disability of a patient 35 years old who is earning $100,000 a year and has a spouse and three children, the insurer's loss exposure runs into the millions of dollars. While both doctors and insurers worry about the high cost of insurance, their concerns come from different directions.

In spite of the expense of medical liability insurance, few doctors are willing to risk clinical practice without it, and they are all concerned about availability, coverage, and price. If insurance is unavailable, or if coverage is inadequate, or if the price is too high, a doctor may leave the individual practice of medicine and become an employed doctor or medical administrator who is insured by the employer.

The insurer is also concerned as a business organization. Its ultimate risk exposure is the loss of profits on operations. Government regulators of insurance companies can force an insurer out of business if it is in danger of being unable to pay claims. People argue about excessive profit rates on liability insurance and how profits are to be calculated, though competition is supposed to hold profits at a sensible level of return on invested capital, but every liability insurance company first has to earn profits on operations. This is not the same as distributable net profits in a profit-making company; it has to do with not spending capital to pay claims, defense costs, and overhead. No insurer, even if it is a not-for-profit membership organization, can run indefinitely at a loss on operations.

Medical liability insurers have difficulty in determining when they have made a profit on operations. The basic unit of the insurer's income is the premium, the basic accounting period is the premium year, and the basic unit of expenditure is the lawsuit. While most businesses know how much money they have made on operations within a few months after the close of each accounting year, this is not true with medical liability insurance, because patients' claims do not have to be filed until the end of the limitation of actions period—two or three years later in most states, and with the discovery rule or continuous treatment, perhaps a decade or more. All the while, inflation is running, the interest rate is moving up and down, and juries are awarding larger verdicts.

Setting premiums at a level to assure adequate profit on operations to cover the insurer's risks has enough headaches for three heads:

In order to set premiums in 1989 for 1990, the *actuaries* had to guess how much of the premium revenue received in 1990 would be spent in defending and paying claims filed in 1990 and still being filed well into the twenty-first century. If the actuaries set premiums too low, most insurers cannot go back later and ask for more money from the doctors.[3]

In order to pay dividends, the *accountants* had to guess in mid–1991 how much net profit the insurer had earned in all premium years through 1990. Deciding when a premium year has closed for accounting purposes is quite arbitrary.

In order to regulate cash flow, the *money managers* had to guess how much of the premium income from each year to set aside to pay claims (the loss reserve, invested in short-term, low-yield assets), how much to invest in long-term, high-yield assets, how much premium income to spend on reinsurance, how the interest cycle is likely to perform, and in a stock company, how much to pay out to investors.

It may be difficult for consumer-oriented people (like law students and doctors) to sympathize with insurance companies, but unless the profitability of medical liability insurance can be assured, the insurance disappears.

2. The Availability of Medical Liability Insurance

A few doctors are unconcerned about the availability of medical liability insurance because they do not carry it.[4] For the rest, the availability of medical liability insurance requires first that an insurer be in business and willing to write a policy. In the 1970s many general insurance companies, which once had considered medical liability so small a part of their general business that they kept no statistics on profitability, decided to drop this "line" completely.[5] In order to preserve availability, many states have authorized the medical professions to set up their own medical liability underwriters, but that does not mean that the doctor-run organization must insure every licensed applicant regardless of claims experience.[6]

Another availability question involves the cost of premiums, because premiums can rise so high as to make insurance effectively unavailable. Here two insurance principles conflict. One principle says that the underwriting classes should be kept broad, so that many doctors will share the

---

3. A few non-profit joint underwriting associations have made their policies assessable. For example, the doctor paid the 1986 premium in 1985, but in 1990 the doctor can be called upon to pay an assessment on the 1986 premium—sometimes as much as the original premium or more.

4. It has been held, however, that a hospital may deny staff privileges to a physician who refuses to carry insurance. Backlund v. Board of Comm'rs, 106 Wash. 2d 632, 724 P.2d 981 (1986) (religious motivation), appeal dismissed for want of a substantial federal question, 481 U.S. 1034, 107 S.Ct. 1968, 95 L.Ed.2d 809 (1987). See Annot., Propriety of Hospital's Conditioning Physician's Staff Privileges on His Carrying Professional Liability or Malpractice Insurance, 7 A.L.R.4th 1238 (1981).

5. In one case the Maryland insurance commissioner tried to force an insurance giant either to keep writing medical liability or to pull out of Maryland altogether, but the Maryland court of appeals held that the commissioner had no such power. St. Paul Fire & Marine Ins. Co. v. Insurance Comm'r, 275 Md. 130, 339 A.2d 291 (1975).

6. A recent case raised but did not dispose of the question. Muhl v. Magan, 313 Md. 462, 545 A.2d 1321 (1988).

costs, the insurers will spread their risks, and overall rates will remain relatively low, even though some doctors will pay too much and others too little. The other principle says that the classes of high-fee, high-risk health care specialists ought to pay more, so as to keep premiums within reach of the class of low-fee, low-risk general practitioners. Evidently there is no single solution to this conflict of principles; the rates and classes change from year to year and from one state to the next.[7]

Finally, availability disappears when the insurer cancels or refuses to renew an individual doctor's insurance. Language in insurance policies tries to preserve the insurer's power to cancel upon proper notice and to refuse to renew without giving reasons, and the courts enforce these provisions if they are clearly written and fairly applied.[8]

At this writing, it is hard to imagine a place in the United States where medical liability insurance is literally unavailable to doctors with decent claims records. On the other hand, premium costs for high-risk specialties such as obstetrics are causing doctors to change the way they practice, as by ceasing to deliver babies. As for individual doctors who claim that medical liability insurance is unavailable to them, uninsurability is an deliberate instrument of health care quality assurance, and a doctor's loss of access to medical practice may be in the best interests of the patient community as well as the insurance industry.[9]

3. The Coverage of Medical Liability Insurance Policies

The medical liability insurance policy today provides two forms of protection to the doctor.[10] First, the insurer promises to pay on behalf of the doctor money owed by the doctor on account of a judgment arising out of an event covered by the insurance contract.[11] Second, the insurer promises to pay for defending the doctor from claims, including attorney,

---

7. It has been held that obstetricians and gynecologists may lawfully agree to pay higher premiums in order to keep their favorite insurer from dropping them all. Sullivan v. Commonwealth Ins. Dep't, 48 Pa.Cmwlth. 11, 408 A.2d 1174 (1979). Some states set a fairly low ceiling on individual coverage, with rates varying according to specialty, then throw all insureds into a common pool for coverage of excess amounts. E.g., Fla.Stat.Ann. § 627.6057 (individual physician coverage), § 766.105 (Patient's Compensation Fund).

8. E.g., Coira v. Florida Med. Ass'n, Inc., 429 So.2d 23 (Fla.App.1983) (companion cases, one cancellation, one refusal to renew); Pennsylvania Cas. Co. v. Chris Simopoulos, M.D., Ltd., 235 Va. 460, 369 S.E.2d 166 (1988) (declaratory judgment for insurer after claim filed; false answers on application voided the policy). See Annot., Wrongful Cancellation of Medical Malpractice Insurance, 99 A.L.R.3d 469 (1980).

9. A ten-year study completed in 1987 by the Medical Mutual Liability Insurance Society of Maryland, which insures about 85% of the doctors in Maryland, showed that 5 of 1500 insured doctors accounted for 7.5% of the insurer's payouts, and about 7% of the doctors accounted for about 94% of the payouts. Washington Post, Jan. 11, 1988, at A7.

10. "Doctor" covers all health care providers: individuals, such as physicians, dentists, and persons for whom they are liable by respondeat superior, and organizations, such as professional associations, partnerships, and corporations. Insurers are careful to require specific insurance for different configurations of business in providing health care. See Miller v. Marrocco, 28 Ohio St.3d 438, 28 Ohio B.R. 489, 504 N.E.2d 67 (1986) (4 to 3) (policy covering medical professional corporation did not cover "employee" doctor-owner).

11. This is liability insurance, not indemnity insurance, because the insurer promises to pay immediately, not after the doctor has already paid. The policy language reads like this: "The insurer will pay on behalf of the insured all sums which the insured shall become legally obligated to pay as damages because of injury to which this policy applies."

expert witness, and investigation services that arise out of covered events.[12] The duty to defend usually includes the duty to settle within policy limits if good faith indicates settlement and the doctor wants to settle.

Medical liability insurance policies vary in the scope and description of covered events and excluded events. This is not surprising; the insurance policy is a contract, and while in a particular litigation the ambiguities in the language of a particular policy will be construed against the insurer, which drafted the language, over time the bargaining between medical societies and insurers can change the language of policy coverage and exclusions back and forth—for example, the control of settlement.

As for covered events, medical professional services in patient care that cause personal injury, sickness, or death are the object of insurance coverage. Some time ago, policies covered only specified theories of claim and all other theories implicitly were excluded, so the patient's choice of a theory of claim, such as contract, could move the event out of policy coverage that was phrased as "any malpractice, error or mistake."[13] The narrow coverage may have been good law but it was bad for business, and it would have created acute problems with subsequently developed theories of claim such as informed consent and strict liability.

Today, not just the words but the balance of coverage has shifted. Policies cover all broadly enumerated events or incidents or harms, regardless of the theory of claim, using language such as "any claim or claims made against the insured arising out of the performance of professional services"; "an occurrence involving direct patient treatment provided by the insured;" "damages because of injury arising out of the performance of professional services."[14] Specific exclusions then seek to exclude coverage of particular acts and events, such as indirect and usually pecuniary harms to patients caused by such non-treatment professional activities as reviewing claims. The lists of exclusions, which often exceed a page of insurance policy text, keep growing.

Most of the exclusions today stem from intentional acts of the doctor, not from the theory of the patient's claim. This means that the theories treated in Chapter 9 need to be tested for insurability as well as exclusion. For example, criminal acts of a doctor are not insurable, so they are excluded from coverage regardless of the policy language. Battering patients without justification, and promising methods and cures, are intentional acts; since they lie within the control of the doctor, they do not fit the liability insurance model, and so they are excluded. Some policies

---

12. Some policies spell this out: "The insurer shall have the duty to defend any action against the insured seeking damages because of a professional incident, even if any of the allegations of the action are groundless, false, or fraudulent."

13. For example, the negligence statute of limitations having run, the plaintiff sued a plastic surgeon for breach of a contract to cure, and the court affirmed summary judgment for the insurer. Safian v. Aetna Life Ins. Co., 260 A.D. 765, 24 N.Y.S.2d 92, aff'd, 286 N.Y. 649, 36 N.E.2d 692 (1941). See Annot., Allegations in Third Person's Action Against Insured as Determining Insurer's Duty to Defend, 50 A.L.R.2d 458 (1956) (not confined to medical liability).

14. While the language is quoted from policies in the Editors' possession, the insurers are not identified and omissions are not indicated.

exclude intentional acts specifically: "liability arising out of any sexual,[15] fraudulent, criminal or malicious act, or slander, libel, defamation, or malicious prosecution"; "any liability which is assumed under a written or an oral contract or agreement"; "liability for punitive or exemplary damages." Allegations of intentional torts such as defamation may arise out of doctors' "professional committee activities," and a few policies explicitly cover include the activities, though they exclude defamation actions arising from "utterances in any publication or electronic medium." Other events are excluded in order to avoid overlapping coverage, such as events covered by workers' compensation and automobile insurance.

LANGLEY v. MUTUAL FIRE, MARINE & INLAND INS. CO.
Supreme Court of Alabama, 1987.
512 So.2d 752.

BEATTY, JUSTICE. * * *

From August 9, 1977, through August 8, 1978, Dr. John Langley's medical malpractice liability insurance carrier was Mutual Fire, Marine and Inland Ins. Co. ("Mutual Fire"). The policy issued to Dr. Langley by Mutual Fire was a "claims-made" insurance policy. The first sentence appearing in Dr. Langley's policy is a statement alerting the insured as to the nature of the "claims-made" type of policy; it provided as follows:

> Claims Made Policy: Except to such extent as may be provided otherwise herein, this policy is limited to liability for only those CLAIMS THAT ARE FIRST MADE AGAINST THE INSURED WHILE THE POLICY IS IN FORCE. Please review the policy carefully.

Further down on the same page of the policy, under the section entitled "The Coverage," there appears another statement explaining the claims-made character of the policy * * *.

* * * Dr. Langley did not renew his coverage with Mutual Fire, nor did he execute the optional extension of coverage offered by Mutual Fire that would have continued his coverage for three years for claims based on acts or omissions that occurred during the primary term of the Mutual Fire policy. This "optional extension period" is described at length on the second page of Dr. Langley's policy:

> 4. Optional Extension Period: In the event of the termination of this insurance by reason of non-renewal or cancellation by the Insured, or if the Company shall cancel this policy or terminate it by refusing to renew, then *the Insured upon payment of an additional premium shall have the option to extend this policy, subject otherwise to its terms, limits of coverage, exclusions and conditions, to apply to claims first made against the insured during thirty-six calendar months following*

---

15. E.g., Govar v. Chicago Ins. Co., 879 F.2d 1581 (8th Cir.1989) (exclusion upheld). See Annot., Coverage and Exclusions of Liability or Indemnity Policy on Physicians, Surgeons, and Other Healers, 33 A.L.R.4th 14 (1984).

immediately upon the effective date of such cancellation or non-renewal, but only for such malpractice committed or alleged to have been committed between the retroactive date and the effective date or such cancellation or termination. This interval shall be hereinafter referred to as the OPTIONAL EXTENSION PERIOD. (Emphasis added.)

* * *

Following Dr. Langley's non-renewal of his Mutual Fire policy, which was effective on August 9, 1978, he received the following letter from Mutual Fire concerning his option to extend his coverage in accordance with the above-quoted provision of his policy with Mutual Fire:

CERTIFIED MAIL RETURN RECEIPT REQUESTED

August 14, 1978

* * *

OPTION TO EXTEND THE CLAIMS REPORTING PERIOD

Dear Dr. Langley:

We are hereby notifying you of your right in accordance with the terms and conditions of your contract to purchase the Optional Extension Period as defined in your contract under the Section entitled THE COVERAGE.

The premium for the three year Optional Extension Period is $8,833.00, plus any applicable tax.

The right to exercise the Optional Extension Period must be exercised by you in writing no later than forty-five (45) days following August 9, 1978 or ten (10) days from the date of this letter, whichever date is later. Please return your signed and dated response in the business envelope enclosed for your use.

Sincerely,

Carolyn J. Sayre * * *

* * * Dr. Langley did not exercise his option to purchase the extended coverage with Mutual Fire. Instead, on October 20, 1978, Dr. Langley applied for coverage through Wilson & Son, the insurance to be underwritten by St. Paul Fire & Marine Ins. Co. ("St. Paul").

* * *

Dr. Langley continued his malpractice coverage through Wilson & Son until March 24, 1980, when Wilson & Son cancelled the policy for nonpayment of premiums. Dr. Langley also subsequently declined to purchase an optional "Reporting Endorsement" from St. Paul, which would have offered him the same type of benefit as the optional extension of coverage that had been offered Langley by Mutual Fire. Under the terms of the St. Paul policy and the reporting endorsement offered to Dr. Langley by St. Paul, that endorsement would have covered Dr. Langley *on a continuous basis* for injuries or deaths occurring during the policy period (October 24, 1978, through March 24, 1980) without regard to when the claim was made.

In February 1983, a medical malpractice claim was filed against Dr. Langley alleging negligence in the delivery of a child on *July 9, 1978*, which negligence resulted in the severe and permanent brain damage of the child. Dr. Langley first notified Wilson & Son of the claim, but it declined to defend, responding that Mutual Fire was Dr. Landley's insurer on the date of the alleged negligent delivery. Mutual Fire, however, also refused to defend * * *.

In the interest of clarity and convenience, the above narrative of pertinent events is set out below in chronological fashion:

August 9, 1977: Effective date of Dr. Langley's claims-made policy with Mutual Fire.

July 9, 1978: Date of alleged malpractice by Dr. Langley.

August 9, 1978: Mutual Fire policy cancelled (non-renewed).

August 14, 1978: Mutual Fire's letter to Dr. Langley notifying him of his option to purchase extension contract.

October 20, 1978: Date of Dr. Langley's application for coverage through Wilson & Son.

October 24, 1978: Effective date of Dr. Langley's claims-made policy with St. Paul.

March 24, 1982: St. Paul policy cancelled for nonpayment of premiums.

February 1983: Medical malpractice action filed against Dr. Langley for alleged negligence on July 9, 1978.

January 9, 1984: Langley's fraud, negligence, and breach of contract action filed against Mutual Fire, Pharr Hume, and Wilson & Son.

* * * The trial court granted defendants' motions for summary judgment "against plaintiff John Langley on plaintiff's amended complaint." This appeal followed.

Dr. Langley advances two arguments that he contends preclude summary judgment in favor of Mutual Fire.

First, he contends that there is some ambiguity in the wording of the Mutual Fire policy, leaving a question of fact for a jury to resolve. We disagree. The claims-made character of Dr. Langley's Mutual Fire policy is made readily apparent within the policy itself. * * *

[W]e next address Dr. Langley's second contention: that public policy dictates that this claims-made clause be declared null and void, and that, under the circumstances of this case, Mutual Fire should be required to extend coverage. * * *

[U]nder an "occurrence" policy, the time of an "occurrence" of an accident is not the time the wrongful act was committed, but rather it is when the complaining party was actually damaged. * * *

We, therefore, think that in James & Hackworth v. Continental Casualty Co., 522 F.Supp. 785 (N.D.Ala.1980), Judge Grooms correctly concluded that the claims-made type of insurance policy is not void as against the public policy of this state, thereby rejecting the argument that such policies should be treated as occurrence policies * * *.

Dr. Langley, nevertheless, argues in his brief that insurance companies should not be allowed to write contracts in such a manner so as to avoid their obligations, in situations such as the present, by including a phrase in the contract requiring that claims be *presented or made during the policy period* before such claims will be paid or defended. However, Dr. Langley cites no authority consistent with this argument regarding claims-made policies. Indeed, it appears that a decided majority of courts that have considered this argument have gone the other way. See cases discussed at Annot., Event as Occurring Within Period of Coverage of "Occurrence" and "Discovery" or "Claims Made" Liability Policies, 37 A.L.R.4th 382, 457 (1985). In most of those cases where it has been held that coverage should be provided, the decisions are based on the courts' findings that the following policy language is ambiguous because of the words "which may be made": "The company shall indemnify insured against any claim or claims for breach of professional duty *which may be made against them during the policy period.*" Ibid. As previously discussed, the policy language in question in this case is not at all like the above language, and is, in fact, quite clear and its meaning readily apparent regarding the claims-made character of the policy.

* * *

Dr. Langley, nevertheless, argues in his brief that none of the options available to him (short of renewing his policy with Mutual Fire) "would have changed the outcome of this case one iota." * * * The reference in this statement is apparently to the fact that the extended endorsement offered by Mutual Fire extended the period for making claims for only up to three years beyond the date the policy was cancelled or nonrenewed, whereas the malpractice claim made against Dr. Langley in this case was filed four and one-half years after the effective date of Dr. Langley's non-renewal of the Mutual Fire policy. * * * We hold, however, that because Dr. Langley elected not to purchase the three-year optional extension of coverage contract, he has no standing to argue that this extension of coverage contract is so inadequate as to make it invalid and violative of public policy. Moreover, Dr. Langley offered no evidence that this optional extension contract would not have been renewed.

If the optional extension contract offered to Dr. Langley by Mutual Fire could have been renewed for additional three-year periods of coverage, Dr. Langley could have so renewed in order to keep his extended coverage in effect long enough for the statute of limitations to run on all potential medical malpractice claims arising from his acts or omissions during the primary policy period, which was August 9, 1977, through August 8, 1978. Under § 6–5–482, Ala.Code, an adult patient/plaintiff has, at the outside, four years "next after the act or omission or failure giving rise to the claim" in which to bring an action thereon.

In the case of a minor patient/plaintiff "under four years of age, such minor shall have until his eighth birthday to commence such an action." Thus, Dr. Langley, whose practice included obstetrics, would have needed to extend his coverage period for making claims for at least eight years after the date, within the primary policy term, he last performed medical services injurious to a newborn child. Dr. Langley however, did not even choose to avail himself of the three-year extension contract offered by Mutual Fire, nor has he shown that that contract was nonrenewable. For these reasons, we shall not consider his contentions that the optional extension contract offered him did not afford him any protection whatsoever. We, therefore, hold that summary judgment in favor of Mutual Fire was proper.

[S]ummary judgment in favor of all defendants is * * * affirmed.

Note on Problems of Policy Construction

Cases continue to call upon the highest courts of the states to construe the language of medical liability insurance policies.[16] Two aspects of these cases deserve attention: first, what techniques of construction (including applicable statutes) do the courts use in reaching their results; and second, should the insurers change the wording of their policies in the light of the decisions?

1. Dr. Robert A. Huffaker, a psychiatrist, treated Jeffrey P. Mazza. Mr. Mazza discovered Dr. Huffaker in bed with the estranged Mrs. Mazza (who was not his patient), and ensuing litigation by Mr. Mazza for medical malpractice harms to himself resulted in a judgment for punitive damages.[17] Dr. Huffaker was insured by Medical Mutual Insurance Co. of North Carolina for "any claim made against the insured arising out of the performance of professional services." The North Carolina Supreme Court held that punitive damages were insurable under state public policy,[18] and that the insuring language was broad enough to cover them; the policy did not exclude punitive damages. The court affirmed summary judgment for Mr. Mazza in his declaratory judgment action.[19]

2. Dr. Homer House performed surgery on Shirley J. Platzer's knee October 29, 1984. Part of a needle was removed from the knee November 27, 1984. Ms. Platzer's lawyer wrote Dr. House June 21 and September 16, 1985, asserting a claim and advising Dr. House to consult his insurer, and Ms. Platzer commenced the required malpractice arbitration proceedings November 15, 1985. Dr. House's claims-made insurance expired January 1, 1986. The arbitration claim was served on Dr. House January 6, 1986, and his insurance agent received it February 14, 1986, two days after Dr. House

---

16. Occasionally a court cannot answer the call. See Pacific Indem. Co. v. Interstate Fire & Cas. Co., 302 Md. 383, 488 A.2d 486 (1985) (obstetrical delivery damaged child's brain and increased father's cost of support; in question certified from a United States court, query, whether there were two occurrences or only one).

17. See Mazza v. Huffaker, 61 N.C.App. 170, 300 S.E.2d 833 (1983) (review denied) (referred to in Chapter 2 above).

18. See Annot., Liability Insurance Coverage as Extending to Liability for Punitive or Exemplary Damages, 16 A.L.R.4th 11 at § 9 (1982).

19. Mazza v. Medical Mutual Ins. Co., 311 N.C. 621, 319 S.E.2d 217 (1984).

mailed it. The insurer declined to defend, resting on this language in its "plain English" policy:

> When is a claim made?
>
> A claim is made on the date you first report an incident or injury to us or our agent.

Four judges of the Maryland Court of Appeals thought that "claims made" in plain English could mean "a claim made by the claimant to the doctor" and affirmed declaratory judgment that Dr. House was covered; three judges thought that the policy definition unambiguously required reporting to the agent to make the coverage effective.[20]

SECTION B. DEFENSE OF CLAIMS

REA v. PARDO

New York Supreme Court, Appellate Division, 1987.
132 A.D.2d 442, 522 N.Y.S.2d 393.

DENMAN, JUSTICE. * * *

This action was instituted by Shirley Rea, as executrix of the estate of her husband, Phillip J. Rea. Defendants are Jorge M. Pardo, M.D., Phillip's former physician, and Medical Liability Mutual Insurance Co. (MLMIC), Pardo's liability insurer. * * *

Rea was treated by Dr. Pardo at St. Joseph's Intercommunity Hospital and at Pardo's office between February 1 and February 22, 1984. Several months later Rea discovered that he was suffering from cancer. He died in August 1985. Prior to his death Rea retained James Moran, an attorney, and on November 5, 1984, executed an authorization for release of his medical records to Moran. By letter dated November 9, 1984, accompanied by a copy of the authorization, Moran requested that Pardo forward copies of "all records and/or reports regarding your care and treatment" of Rea, including billings.

Dr. Pardo did not immediately comply with either the letter or Moran's repeated telephone requests for the records, but instead, at the request of MLMIC, forwarded the records to the carrier on January 10, 1985. In their affidavits Pardo and MLMIC stated that they believed that the request for release of the records to Moran indicated that a medical malpractice action against Pardo was about to commence. They also averred that Pardo was required to furnish his carrier with the records to protect his position under the notice provision of his medical malpractice liability policy. That provision states:

> Notice. As soon as practicable, after becoming aware of an event which he or she has reason to believe may lead to a claim against him or her under the statement of insurance, or after receiving information of such a claim against him or her, the insured shall give notice thereof in writing to the Company or its agent or authorized representative.

---

20. St. Paul Fire & Marine Ins. Co. v. House, 315 Md. 328, 554 A.2d 404 (1989).

According to defendants, the records were requested by MLMIC in order to evaluate the potential claim, timely investigate it, possibly avert a lawsuit, advise Pardo how to proceed, and, "if necessary, afford Dr. Pardo the best possible legal representation in the event that a malpractice suit was commenced." It is undisputed that the patient's records were used by the insurer only to investigate, evaluate, and prepare to meet the claim, and that those records were never disclosed to anyone outside MLMIC.

From discussions with Pardo and representatives of the carrier, Moran learned of Pardo's release of the records to MLMIC on January 25, 1985. Moran informed the Reas, and the insurer forwarded the records to Moran on that day. At his carrier's instruction, Dr. Pardo subsequently did the same. Although plaintiff now asserts that Moran was retained and the records sought to investigate a potential claim for medical malpractice against St. Joseph's Hospital, not Dr. Pardo, a medical malpractice action in fact was commenced against Dr. Pardo in June, 1985. That action was discontinued by plaintiff following her husband's death. This action was commenced by plaintiff in October 1985.

* * * The court * * * granted partial summary judgment for plaintiff on her first cause of action. * * * 133 Misc.2d 516, 507 N.Y.S.2d 361 (1986).

On appeal, defendants * * * argue that the doctor's disclosure of his patient's medical records to the insurer, and the insurer's solicitation of such disclosure, were justified in response to the patient's authorization of disclosure of those records to his lawyer. We agree.

In MacDonald v. Clinger, 84 A.D.2d 482, 446 N.Y.S.2d 801 (1982), we established that a physician (in that case a psychiatrist) has a duty not to make unauthorized disclosures of confidential information obtained in the course of the physician-patient relationship. However, we noted that the right of confidentiality is less than absolute * * *, and that, in order to be considered wrongful, and thus actionable, the disclosure must be without legal justification or excuse * * *.

[W]e conclude that the doctor's anticipation of a suit against him was reasonable and was not, as supreme court found, based on mere speculation and conjecture. Although the issue of reasonableness may sometimes present a question of fact, we conclude that the doctor's actions here were reasonable as a matter of law. The patient retained a lawyer to investigate the claim and authorized release of his medical records to the lawyer. That was an affirmative act from which the doctor could infer that a claim for medical malpractice was being brought against him. * * *

Since the doctor's expectation that a claim would be instituted against him was reasonable, he and his insurer were entitled to take reasonable measures to investigate and prepare to meet the anticipated claim. Although we do not attempt to delimit the permissible scope of defensive disclosure by a doctor in all circumstances, we hold that, where the case involves a precommencement authorization for disclosure of medical records to the patient's attorney, such authorization justifies the doctor's disclosure of those records to his attorney or carrier.

We emphasize that the carrier may not investigate the claim in such manner as to disclose confidential information to others. However, since it is not disputed in this case that there was no disclosure other than to the carrier, the actions of the doctor and the insurer were in all respects proper. Finally, although the issue of the doctor's conduct apart from disclosure is not before us, we do not condone the doctor's withholding of the records for several months instead of immediately forwarding them to the patient's lawyer in accordance with the medical authorization. The proper procedure would have been to forward the records to Moran immediately with copies to the carrier. Such procedure would assist in protecting the integrity of the records.

Accordingly, the order insofar as appealed from should be reversed, and summary judgment should be granted to defendants dismissing the complaint in its entirety.

Note on the Insurer's Duty to Defend

The medical liability insurance policy is a contract, and the medical liability insurer's contractual duty to defend the doctor is defined by the policy language of coverage and exclusions. Most policies promise to defend claims that are "groundless, false or fraudulent." Nowadays the patient does not have to allege a theory of claim, and the facts alleged in a notice-theory complaint may be conclusory and general, and the coverage of medical liability policies extends far beyond negligence; therefore the insurer's duty to defend continues to be broader than its duty to indemnify.[21] Even so, a doctor will occasionally notify the insurer of a claim that the insurer feels no duty to defend, and the insurer will notify the doctor that under the policy, it has no obligation to defend. The doctor may disagree and threaten to sue the insurer for breach of contract.

Whatever the outcome, doctor and insurer are no longer friends but adversaries, and the doctor must retain and pay for a lawyer.[22] How and when is this matter to be decided?

The insurer can go ahead and defend the doctor, hoping for a favorable result on the merits, and doubtless insurers have done so, but it is no

---

21. See Gray v. Zurich Ins. Co., 65 Cal. 2d 263, 54 Cal.Rptr. 104, 419 P.2d 168 (1966) (not a medical liability case, but a basic citation).

22. Another problem along the same line arises when the claim is clearly in excess of the doctor's policy limits. In Aetna Cas. & Surety Co. v. Price, 206 Va. 749, 146 S.E.2d 220 (1966), the policy limits were $70,000, the insured doctor declined to retain his own lawyer, the defense lawyer refused to settle within the policy limits on a very close causation question, and the jury found for the plaintiffs. The judgments for the plaintiffs totalled $120,000, and the doctor, who had to pay $50,000 out of his own pocket, sued the insurer. The court held that the doctor failed to show bad faith failure to settle within policy limits, and that the doctor stated no claim for negligence.

answer to all cases, because the uncontracted-for costs of a successful defense cannot later be thrown back onto the doctor.

If the insurer simply refuses to defend, the doctor retains counsel and, after the patient's lawsuit is over, sues the insurer for breaching the policy.[23] This is a bad result in economics because it maximizes transaction costs. It is also risky for the insurer, because the doctor may collect paid-out damages in excess of the policy limits if in bad faith the insurer failed to settle a covered claim within the policy limits.[24]

In years past insurers sometimes tried to perform investigations and even defend at trial under a nonwaiver agreement providing that if the patient won, the insurer would not pay the judgment against the doctor. The nonwaiver agreement was in effect a contract to settle the dispute over contract coverage, because the insurer paid the disputed costs of defense but the doctor accepted the disputed risk of judgment loss.

Insurers also had a much more risky technique, the reservation of rights letter, which sought unilaterally to impose the results of the nonwaiver agreement. If the insurer made any substantial defense, the insurer could be found to have assumed inconsistent positions and would be estopped to use the reservation of rights letter.[25]

Nowadays declaratory judgment actions[26] are widely available, enabling the parties to get an early judicial decision on the duty to defend in doubtful cases. The insurer also asks for a stay of the patient's medical liability action against the doctor while the declaratory judgment action over coverage is being litigated, but the patient may want the medical liability action to go forward anyway. While declaratory judgment actions most frequently are brought by insurers,[27] in cases already presented in

---

23. E.g., Langley v. Mutual Fire, Marine & Inland Ins. Co., 512 So.2d 752 (1987) (§ A, above). In Jaffe v. Cranford Ins. Co., 168 Cal.App.3d 930, 214 Cal.Rptr. 567 (1985), the state brought a criminal action against the insured doctor for reimbursement fraud and theft; the insurer refused to defend. The jury in the criminal action acquitted the doctor, who kept bad records but had no criminal intent, and the doctor sued the insurer for reimbursement of defense costs. The trial court dismissed the doctor's action on the ground that where there was no potential for coverage, the insurer had no duty to defend, and the appellate court affirmed.

24. See Annot., Consequences of Liability Insurer's Refusal to Assume Defense of Action Against Insured Upon Ground That Claim Upon Which Action Is Based Is Not Within Coverage of Policy, 49 A.L.R.2d 694 (1956).

25. See Annot., Liability Insurance: Insurer's Assumption of or Continuation in Defense of Action Brought Against the Assured as Waiver or Estoppel as Regards Defense of Noncoverage or Other Defense Existing at Time of Accident, 38 A.L.R.2d 1148 (1954).

26. The federal statute is 28 U.S.C.A. §§ 2201–2202, and most states have an equivalent remedy.

27. The cases go both ways. E.g., St. Paul Ins. Co. v. Armas, 173 Ill.App.3d 669, 123 Ill.Dec. 283, 527 N.E.2d 921 (1988) (policy language on how to report a claim was ambiguous, so insurer must defend); Hartford Cas. Ins. Co. v. Shehata, 427 F.Supp. 336 (N.D.Ill.1977) (event was not medical, so insurer need not defend); Public Service Mut. Ins. Co. v. Levy, 57 A.D.2d 794, 395 N.Y.S.2d 1 (1977) (dentist reasonably did not regard death of patient as reportable incident, so insurer must defend). For a basic if elderly example, see Aetna Cas. & Sur. Co. v. Yeatts, 122 F.2d 350 (4th Cir. 1941), where a doctor who had allegedly negligently performed an abortion (then a crime) got a declaratory judgment ordering the insurer to defend him in a malpractice action.

this chapter, declaratory judgment actions were brought by the doctor [28] and by the patient.[29]

SECTION C. SETTLEMENT

FELIBERTY v. DAMON
Court of Appeals of New York, 1988.
72 N.Y.2d 112, 531 N.Y.S.2d 778, 527 N.E.2d 261.

KAYE, JUDGE. * * *

On April 26, 1977, plaintiff Mario Feliberty, a Buffalo physician, for the first time was consulted by Thomas Michaels. Michaels, an ironworker, complained of recurring throat pain and lumps in his neck. Noting that Michaels had been exposed to heavy amounts of dust in his work, plaintiff examined him for about ten minutes, during which time he observed slight redness of his throat and small lumps in his neck, and then advised Michaels to have his chest x-rayed and return if the condition worsened. Michaels did not again consult plaintiff.

On October 12, 1979, plaintiff was served with a summons and complaint alleging that he had committed medical malpractice by failing to diagnose at an early, easily treatable stage what was ultimately discovered to be lymphoma. Plaintiff forwarded the papers to his insurance carrier, defendant Medical Malpractice Insurance Association, which in turn retained a Buffalo law firm to represent him in the malpractice action. The insurer also advised plaintiff that he was free to consult his own attorney, at his expense, to protect his personal interests.

After a medical malpractice panel unanimously concluded that plaintiff had committed malpractice, the case proceeded to trial, resulting in a verdict of $1,239,000. Plaintiff was assessed 60% of the fault, or $743,000 of the damages, a sum within policy limits. Plaintiff demanded of his attorneys and the insurer that they appeal this verdict, but before judgment was entered—and allegedly without plaintiff's knowledge—the insurer settled the claim for $700,000. Plaintiff then brought this action for legal malpractice against the law firm, contending that the firm's negligence and the publicity following the verdict had destroyed his practice and ultimately forced him to leave the area. He also sought compensatory and punitive damages from defendant insurer, alleging fraud and breach of contract in connection with the settlement, and liability for the legal malpractice of the attorneys it had retained to defend him.

In particular, in his complaint against the law firm plaintiff charged that his attorneys had not advised him of the meeting of the malpractice panel; had not consulted with him throughout the proceedings; and that they investigated, pleaded and prepared inadequately, failed to make obvious objections, conduct reasonable examination of

---

28. St. Paul Fire & Marine Ins. Co. v. House, 315 Md. 328, 554 A.2d 404 (1989).

29. Mazza v. Medical Mut. Ins. Co., 311 N.C. 621, 319 S.E.2d 217 (1984).

witnesses, introduce favorable evidence at trial, properly sum up, or make written submissions. Plaintiff complained that after trial, counsel had failed to move for a mistrial or reduction of the verdict, omitted to have the settlement sealed, and disregarded his requests to appeal.

Plaintiff repeated these same allegations against the insurer, contending that the malpractice of retained counsel constituted a failure on the part of the insurer to provide a proper legal defense. Additionally, he complained that the insurer neither consulted him before settling nor advised him of his rights concerning appeal.

Supreme court granted the insurer's motion to dismiss the complaint against it, holding that it had an absolute right to settle under the policy, and that it had no vicarious liability for the alleged negligence of independent counsel retained for its insured.[30] The appellate division affirmed. 129 A.D.2d 207, 517 N.Y.S.2d 632 (1987) * * *.

* * *

Both courts correctly dismissed plaintiff's claims of wrongdoing regarding the settlement. While the settlement was within policy limits and plaintiff therefore technically suffered no out-of-pocket loss, he is understandably concerned about protecting a different interest—his professional reputation. This insurance contract, however, specifies that the "company may make such investigation and such settlement of any claim or suit as it deems expedient." Unlike bargained-for, and presumably costlier, policy provisions contemplating the insured's consent to settlement * * *, here the parties' contract unambiguously gave the insurer the unconditioned right to settle any claim or suit without plaintiff's consent.

Nor, on this record, can plaintiff succeed in his contention that, in settling, the insurer violated any implied obligation or acted in bad faith. [P]laintiff has alleged no failure to respond accurately to requests regarding settlement offers. His discontent centers instead on the insurer's settlement without his knowledge or consent, as it had the right to do under the policy, instead of taking an appeal.

[P]laintiff's request that an appeal be taken did not put the insurer on notice that he wished to be informed of any contemplated settlement so that he could protect against personal exposure,[31] and the settlement the insurer negotiated was well within policy limits. Thus, we agree with supreme court and the appellate division that, in the present circumstances, no fraud or breach of contract claim was stated against the insurer in connection with its settlement of the medical malpractice action.

30. This appeal concerns only the case against the insurer. The record does not disclose the status of plaintiff's action against the law firm.

31. Plaintiff's request that an appeal be taken did not even foreclose the possibility that he would have been satisfied by a settlement on more favorable terms than the $1,239,000 verdict. There is no suggestion in the record that plaintiff at the time expressed fear of injury to his reputation and wished to assume personal responsibility for the appeal.

Similarly, the complaint fails to state a cause of action against the insurer for the second, independent basis of liability—the alleged malpractice of retained counsel.

When an insured has been sued, the insurer does not satisfy its duty to defend merely by designating independent counsel to defend the litigation. * * * This appeal, however, does not call upon us to set out all the parameters of the insurer's duty to defend in litigation because it presents a limited issue. Plaintiff does not allege that the insurer designated incompetent or conflicted counsel * * *, and he does not allege that the insurer ignored complaints regarding counsel's incompetence, or indeed that he expressed any dissatisfaction to the insurer about counsel's services. His sole contention is that, in its day-to-day conduct of his defense, the law firm performed inadequately, and that, for this malpractice, the insurer stands vicariously liable.

* * *

Plaintiff does not seriously dispute that the law firm retained by defendant to represent him was an independent contractor; he does not claim that, in the conduct of his defense, the law firm was subject to defendant's actual direction and control. The question is simply whether the facts of this case fall within one of the recognized exceptions to the general rule that an employer is not liable for the acts of an independent contractor, and if not, whether a new exception should be recognized.

Plaintiff urges that the insurance company's contractual duty to defend him was a nondelegable duty, thus bringing his claim within an exception to the general rule of nonliability. A nondelegable duty has been described as one that the employer is not free to delegate to a contractor and "requires the person upon whom it is imposed to answer for it that care is exercised by anyone, even though he be an independent contractor, to whom the performance of the duty is entrusted." Restatement (Second) of Torts, Introductory Note at 394 (1965). In large part, whether a duty—or, perhaps more accurately, whether liability—is "nondelegable" turns on policy considerations. A duty is nondelegable when "the responsibility is so important to the community that the employer should not be permitted to transfer it to another." Prosser & Keeton, Torts § 71 at 512 (5th ed. 1984).

* * *

We have not previously recognized an insurer's obligation to defend its insured in the conduct of a litigation as a "nondelegable duty," and we decline to do so in this case.

[T]he remedy for negligence of trial counsel in the actual conduct of an insured's defense in a litigation should lie in an action against counsel for malpractice and not a suit against the insurer based solely on vicarious liability [f]or the following reasons * * *.

First, the duty to defend an insured is by its very nature delegable, as * * * an insurance company is in fact prohibited from the practice of law. * * * Accordingly, the insurer necessarily must rely on independent counsel to conduct the litigation. Second, the paramount interest independent counsel represents is that of the insured, not the insurer. The insurer is precluded from interference with counsel's independent professional judgments in the conduct of the litigation on behalf of its client. * * * Vicarious liability thus produces an untenable situation here: on the one hand an insurer is prohibited from itself conducting the litigation or controlling the decisions of the insured's lawyer, yet on the other hand it is charged with responsibility for the lawyer's day-to-day independent professional judgments in the "nuts and bolts" of representing its client. Finally, in determining whether a new exception should be recognized, we note that an insured is not otherwise left without a remedy for a law firm's claimed incompetence, and a law firm is not insulated from liability for wrongdoing; indeed, in the case before us, plaintiff has sought full recovery for his damages in a legal malpractice claim against the firm.

* * *

Accordingly, the order of the appellate division should be affirmed, with costs.

ARANA v. KOERNER, 735 S.W.2d 729 (Mo.App.1987). Mary Elam sued Dr. Victor A. Arana for medical malpractice. Dr. Arana's medical liability insurance company, Medical Protective Co., retained Brown, Douglas & Brown to defend Dr. Arana, and Wendell E. Koerner was a member of the firm. The Medical Protective policy provided that claims would not be settled without Dr. Arana's consent, but the attorneys settled the Elam case without informing Dr. Arana, who alleged that they did so in order to further their relations with Medical Protective.

Dr. Arana sued Medical Protective in the Western District of Missouri in 1983, and in 1985, they settled the action for $250,000. The release contained paragraphs reserving Dr. Arana's right to pursue the attorneys for further damages in this action, which was pending in a Missouri state court.

In 1986 the attorneys were granted summary judgment in the Missouri state court action on the grounds of release and res judicata. The Missouri Court of Appeals reversed and declined to rehear or transfer the action to the Missouri Supreme Court. Two of Dr. Arana's theories of claim remained open, breach of contract and negligence, and the court of appeals granted leave to substitute breach of fiduciary duty or constructive fraud for willful tort.

INSURANCE CO. OF NORTH AMERICA v. MEDICAL PROTECTIVE CO.

United States Court of Appeals for the Tenth Circuit, 1985.
768 F.2d 315.

TIMBERS, CIRCUIT JUDGE.[32]

* * *

In April 1969, Lois Laptad, a married, 37-year-old mother of two, entered the Wesley Medical Center in Wichita, Kansas, for diagnostic tests[33] to be performed by Dr. Peter Torbey, a radiologist. Dr. E.J. Fieldman was to administer a general anesthetic. On the day of the procedure, Dr. Fieldman supervised William Mohan, a certified registered nurse anesthetist, and Ms. Reese, a student anesthetist, in the administration of the anesthetic Innovar, manufactured by McNeil Laboratories. Once the anesthetic was administered, Dr. Fieldman left the room. While Dr. Torbey was out of the room preparing for the radiological procedure he was to perform, Mohan noticed that Laptad had fallen into an unusually deep state of anesthesia. He left the room to find Dr. Fieldman. Laptad was left alone with the student anesthetist. Dr. Torbey re-entered the room and began the radiological procedure. Subsequently he noticed that Laptad had no pulse. Both Dr. Torbey and the student anesthetist became alarmed. The student attempted various emergency measures in an effort to revive Laptad. Dr. Torbey did nothing. Even though Dr. Torbey was the only physician in the room at the time, he was of the opinion that, as a radiologist, he should not involve himself in what appeared to be an anesthesiological problem. Laptad sustained severe brain damage as a result of these actions and inactions. She remained in a semicomatose state in a nursing home for the next seven years—until she died.

The administrator of Laptad's estate commenced a negligence action in the district court against Dr. Fieldman; his assistants, Drs. Glenn Martin and M.M. Tinterow; Dr. Torbey; William Mohan; Laptad's referring general physician, Dr. J.T. Stewart; Wesley Medical Center; and McNeil Laboratories. Prior to trial, the Laptad estate settled with Drs. Fieldman, Martin, and Tinterow for $300,000, and with the Wesley Medical Center for $75,000. The case against Mohan and Dr. Stewart was dismissed. The remaining defendants at the time of trial were Dr. Torbey and McNeil Laboratories.

The first trial in November 1974 ended with the jury unable to reach a verdict. A second trial in July 1975 ended with a verdict in favor of the Laptad estate against Dr. Torbey. McNeil was found not liable. The jury awarded the Laptad estate $750,000, which was reduced by the $375,000 settlement reached with the other defendants. The judgment entered on the jury verdict was affirmed by our court.

---

32. Honorable William H. Timbers of the Second Circuit, sitting by designation.

33. Editors' Note: Apparently studies of the celiac artery, which supplies blood to the stomach, liver, and spleen.

Lupton v. Torbey, 548 F.2d 316 (10th Cir.1977). Medical Protective Co., as the primary insurer of Dr. Torbey, had a policy limit of $100,000. Insurance Co. of North America (INA), as the excess insurer of Dr. Torbey, had a policy limit of $1,000,000. As a result of the judgment, INA was required to pay $323,121.90, representing the balance remaining due on the judgment after exhaustion of the Medical Protective policy.

INA subsequently commenced the instant action in the District of Kansas, claiming that Medical Protective acted negligently and in bad faith in pursuing settlement negotiations in the action between the Laptad estate and Dr. Torbey, and in failing to settle that claim within the limits of the Medical Protective policy. The court found the following facts with regard to the settlement negotiations in the *Laptad* action, all events being in 1971 unless otherwise stated.

Medical Protective was obligated to defend Dr. Torbey. For that purpose it retained Emmet Blaes, Esq., of Wichita, Kansas. Nearly all of Medical Protective's contacts with Dr. Torbey concerning the *Laptad* action were through Blaes. Counsel for the Laptad estate, Gerald Michaud, Esq., stated in December 1970 at a pre-trial conference with counsel for all the defendants that Dr. Torbey would be sued for negligence as the "captain of the ship." Dr. Torbey had been the only doctor present in the room when the crisis occurred but had done nothing except stand by while Laptad suffered irreversible brain damage.

On January 4, Michaud, an experienced attorney in medical malpractice cases, offered to settle with all defendants for $500,000. Blaes and counsel for the other defendants considered the offer to be a reasonable one. On January 11, Blaes informed Medical Protective that the case against Dr. Torbey was strong enough to go to a jury and that, on the basis of sympathy alone, a jury might well return a verdict in favor of the Laptad estate. Blaes, however, recommended that Dr. Torbey's contribution to any joint settlement fund be minimal. On February 1, Blaes requested authorization to offer $25,000 as Dr. Torbey's contribution to such a fund. On February 3, Medical Protective agreed to this request.

On January 29, at a meeting of all defense counsel, William Tinker, Esq.—an attorney retained by INA to defend its insured, Dr. Fieldman—stated that experts consulted by him were critical of everyone involved, and especially Dr. Torbey because of his inaction at the critical time.

In February, Medical Protective indicated that it would rather take its chances on winning a jury verdict than offer a very high figure to the Laptad estate to settle the case. Medical Protective told Blaes that they would be willing to increase the $25,000 settlement offer only slowly and reluctantly.

On February 12, Tinker offered Michaud $325,000 to settle the case on behalf of all defendants. Dr. Torbey was never informed of the offer. Michaud rejected the offer. On February 15, defense counsel made an offer of $400,000. Michaud rejected this offer. This latest offer would have included a $50,000 contribution for Drs. Torbey and Stewart, the latter still being a codefendant. Dr. Torbey was never informed of this offer.

On February 17, Wesley Medical Center settled with the Laptad estate for $75,000. During the negotiations of January and February, INA received personal reports from Blaes concerning some aspects of the negotiations, as well as some of the correspondence between Blaes and Medical Protective.

In April, Dr. Fieldman settled with the Laptad estate for $300,000. During discovery proceedings, Tinker represented to Michaud and the district court that this was the total amount of Dr. Fieldman's insurance coverage. Dr. Fieldman, in fact, actually was insured to the extent of $1.1 million.

On June 9, Michaud offered to settle with Drs. Torbey and Stewart for $75,000—$50,000 of which would be Dr. Torbey's contribution. Medical Protective refused to negotiate on the basis of this offer. The offer was never communicated to Dr. Torbey. On July 12, without authority from Medical Protective, Blaes offered Michaud $37,500. Medical Protective eventually did authorize this amount in November. It never authorized a higher amount.

The court found that, under all the circumstances, Michaud's offer to settle with Drs. Torbey and Stewart for $75,000 was reasonable. Blaes himself testified that he would have been comfortable settling the case for $50,000–$60,000. In August 1972, Michaud received a report highly critical of Dr. Torbey's conduct and withdrew his $75,000 offer. In September 1972, Blaes informed Medical Protective of this report and of his belief that the Laptad estate's damages might be greater than previously had been expected. Medical Protective did not reevaluate its position. In September 1974, INA informed Medical Protective that it expected Medical Protective to settle the case for an amount within its $100,000 policy limit. On September 23, 1974, Blaes suggested to Medical Protective that it raise its $37,500 offer by $5,000. Medical Protective rejected this suggestion. It stated that it would rather pay Blaes to try the case than pay the Laptad estate any amount. On October 11, 1974, Michaud told Blaes that he would be willing to accept something less than $75,000 to settle the case against Dr. Torbey—the case against Dr. Stewart having been dismissed—but that this offer, and all prospects for settlement, would terminate on October 15 when Michaud made his opening statement to the jury. Medical Protective never responded to this offer.

The court found that Dr. Torbey was not informed or advised of any settlement offers, demands or negotiations prior to October 17, 1974. On that date he was informed that the Laptad estate had offered to settle for around $75,000. He was not told that Medical Protective had determined not to settle for a figure higher than $37,500. He was not told that he could protect his professional reputation by settling while denying liability. He was not told that he might be exposed to liability above Medical Protective's policy limits. He was not told that he should consider retaining private counsel to protect his own interests. On October 17, Blaes dictated a letter for Dr. Torbey's signature in which he had Dr. Torbey state that he never wanted any settlement which would recognize fault or liability on his part. He also stated that, since all settlement negotiations had failed, he wished to proceed to trial.

[The trial court awarded INA $323,121.90 and refused to order INA to contribute to Medical Protective's expenses in defending Dr. Torbey.]

* * *

We turn first to Medical Protective's primary contention on appeal—that it cannot be held liable for failing to effect a settlement since Dr. Torbey did not approve and, so it claims, would not have approved any settlement in the *Laptad* action. Medical Protective places massive reliance on Paragraph D of its policy with Dr. Torbey which states that the "company shall not compromise any claim hereunder without the consent of the insured," and on Dr. Torbey's deposition testimony, portions of which tend to indicate that Dr. Torbey was opposed to the idea of settling the *Laptad* action and was aware of the consequences of that decision. We find that Medical Protective's claim ignores critical facts and does not ring true. We reject it.

First, we agree with the district court that the consent clause quoted above is immaterial to the question of whether Medical Protective acted in bad faith in pursuing settlement negotiations with Michaud. It is common practice for an insurer to conduct settlement negotiations in advance of obtaining the insured's final consent to the agreement. These negotiations must be conducted in good faith and without negligence * * *, regardless of whether or not the insured eventually will consent.

Second, although Dr. Torbey testified in his deposition that, because he believed he was innocent of any wrongdoing, he never wanted to settle the *Laptad* action, he also testified that he would not have prevented Medical Protective from settling the case and would have relied on the advice of his attorney, Blaes, in determining whether or not to settle. Also, Medical Protective's claim that Dr. Torbey steadfastly had refused from the beginning to permit a settlement is plainly inconsistent with its efforts on his behalf to effect such a settlement— albeit halfhearted efforts undertaken in bad faith. * * * This claim is further contradicted by Dr. Torbey's October 17, 1974, letter wherein he states only that he never wanted a settlement which would have recognized fault or liability on his part, and that since settlement negotiations had not succeeded, he wished to proceed to trial.

Third, the court held that any lack of consent by Dr. Torbey was immaterial since he had not been informed of any settlement negotiations until after Michaud's October 15, 1974, deadline for completing such negotiations. The court also found that Dr. Torbey had never been informed of the strong possibility that the Laptad estate might recover a judgment against him in excess of the Medical Protective policy limit. Dr. Torbey's testimony as to knowledge of settlement negotiations is vague, contradictory, and marked by significant lapses of memory.

Based on all the evidence on this point, we hold that the district court's finding that Dr. Torbey was not kept informed concerning settlement negotiations was not clearly erroneous. Fed.R.Civ.P. 52(a).

Furthermore, we reject Medical Protective's suggestion that the court did not properly consider Dr. Torbey's after-the-fact statements contained in his deposition testimony to the effect that his position would not have been different even if he had been completely informed. Once something no longer exists, it is very easy for a person to say that he did not want it anyway. We cannot be sure what course Dr. Torbey might have taken had he been aware of all the circumstances. Medical Protective had a duty to keep Dr. Torbey informed of all settlement negotiations. * * * It cannot escape the consequences of a breach of that duty by saying that it would not have made any difference even had it fulfilled its obligation.

The district court held that INA was entitled to be subrogated to the rights of Dr. Torbey under the Medical Protective policy in order to assert the claim that the latter acted in bad faith in failing to effect a settlement.

* * * Dr. Torbey's policy with INA clearly states that INA "shall be subrogated to the extent of any payment hereunder to all of insured's rights of recovery therefore." To the extent that any of Dr. Torbey's deposition testimony might be construed as exculpating Medical Protective from any liability for its conduct of settlement negotiations, such testimony does not affect any of INA's rights under its contract with Torbey.

Medical Protective, however, argues that, since Dr. Torbey refused to consent to a settlement, he would have been precluded from bringing an action against Medical Protective for bad faith. Its argument continues that, since INA—as subrogee—could have no greater rights than the subrogor, INA's action also must be barred. This argument fails * * * [because] any refusal by Dr. Torbey to consent to a settlement was immaterial, since Medical Protective breached its duty to Dr. Torbey by failing to keep him adequately informed of the settlement negotiations or of his exposure to risk beyond the limit of the Medical Protective policy. * * *

Medical Protective also argues that INA's action should be barred because INA failed to take any steps of its own to effect a settlement between the Laptad estate and Dr. Torbey. Medical Protective ignores Section II of INA's policy with Dr. Torbey which gives INA the right to defend or settle any claim against one of its insureds only where the occurrence is not covered by an underlying policy of insurance such as the Medical Protective policy here. Under Kansas law, INA—as an excess insurer—was under no duty to defend Dr. Torbey. * * *

Medical Protective further claims that INA should be estopped from claiming "legal" or "equitable" subrogation because it lacks the "clean hands" necessary to invoke equity. Medical Protective bases this claim on the alleged misrepresentation by Tinker—the attorney hired by INA to represent Dr. Fieldman—to Michaud and the district court in the *Laptad* action, that Dr. Fieldman's policy with INA had a coverage limit of $300,000 when, in fact, the policy provided for coverage up to $1,100,000. First, as the district court observed, this allegation has yet to be proven. Second, the court was correct in concluding that, in spite of the fact that INA paid Tinker's bill, any misconduct of which Tinker may have been guilty could be attributed only to his client, Dr. Fieldman. ABA Code of Professional Responsibility DR 5–107(B). Third, any misrepresentation which may have occurred could have injured only Michaud and Laptad. Since Medical Protective is unable to show that it relied to its detriment on any misrepresentation by Tinker, it may not claim estoppel. * * *

We hold that the district court correctly concluded that INA was entitled to be subrogated to the rights of Dr. Torbey under the Medical Protective policy for the purpose of asserting the claim that the latter acted in bad faith in failing to settle within its policy limits.

Turning to the district court's finding that Medical Protective acted in bad faith in failing to settle within its policy limits, it is axiomatic that, in defending and settling claims against its insured, an insurer owes to its insured a duty to act in good faith and without negligence. * * * In Bollinger v. Nuss, 202 Kan. 326, 449 P.2d 502 (1969), the Supreme Court of Kansas stated that the question of liability depends upon the circumstances of the particular case and must be determined by taking into account the various factors present, rather than on the basis of any general statement or definition. 449 P.2d at 512.

The court went on to set forth eight factors which had been indicated by the California Court of Appeals in Brown v. Guaranty Ins. Co., 155 Cal.App.2d 679, 319 P.2d 69, 75 (1957), as bearing upon the question of liability for acting in bad faith. These factors are: (1) the strength of the insured claimant's case on the issue of liability and damages; (2) attempts by the insurer to induce the insured to contribute to a settlement; (3) failure of the insurer to properly investigate the circumstances so as to ascertain the evidence against the insured; (4) the insurer's rejection of advice of its own attorney or agent; (5) failure of the insurer to inform the insured of a compromise offer; (6) the amount of financial risk to which each party is exposed in the event of a refusal to settle; (7) the fault of the insured in inducing the insurer's rejection of a compromise offer by misleading it as to the facts; and (8) any other factors tending to establish or negate bad faith on the part of the insurer. * * *

With regard to the two factors which the court explicitly considered in determining bad faith, we hold that the court's findings are not clearly erroneous. A young, gainfully employed mother of two had suffered catastrophic injury. At the critical time, Dr. Torbey was the only physician in the room and yet he stood by and did nothing. There were expert reports which were highly critical of Dr. Torbey's conduct. Michaud, an experienced attorney in the medical malpractice field, was aware of the tactical significance of these reports. In view of these facts, together with probable jury sympathy for Laptad, the case against Torbey was strong. The court also was correct in concluding that Dr. Torbey was exposed to financial risk beyond the coverage provided by the Medical Protective policy. Blaes had suggested to Medical Protective that a jury verdict against Dr. Torbey in excess of $500,000 was not improbable. Michaud had expressed his belief to Blaes that the Laptad estate might recover as much as $1 million.

A finding of bad faith is further supported by two other factors discussed by the court in its opinion but not expressly relied upon by the court in determining bad faith. First, Medical Protective failed to keep Dr. Torbey adequately informed concerning settlement negotiations. We are not persuaded by Medical Protective's attempt to exculpate itself from liability by claiming that it reasonably could believe that Blaes—Dr. Torbey's attorney—would keep Dr. Torbey adequately informed of negotiations. The duty to inform was squarely that of Medical Protective. Second, there was evidence that Medical Protective rejected the advice of Blaes. Whether or not Blaes ever informed Medical Protective of his personal belief that the case against Dr. Torbey was worth about $50,000 to $60,000, he did inform Medical Protective on several occasions that Dr. Torbey might be in serious trouble. On at least one occasion he suggested raising the $37,500 offer. Medical Protective did not adjust its settlement position in response to this information; rather, it maintained its position that it would rather go to trial than pay the Laptad estate any amount over $37,500.

In light of all of the facts disclosed by this record, we hold that the district court was correct in concluding that there was no justification for Medical Protective's intransigence and that it acted in bad faith.

Medical Protective's final contention is that the district court erred in not requiring INA to contribute a pro rata share of the cost of defending Dr. Torbey. Medical Protective relies principally on American Fidelity Ins. Co. v. Employers Mut. Cas. Co., 3 Kan.App.2d 245, 593 P.2d 14, 23 (1979) * * *. We agree with the district court that the Kansas court's statement regarding contribution was dictum since it went beyond the issues properly before the court.

* * * Medical Protective had the primary obligation to defend and protect both its insured and, by subrogation, INA from excess liability. Dr. Torbey was entitled to an unlimited defense under his contract with Medical Protective, in contrast to his contract with INA,

which obligated the latter to provide a defense only where primary coverage did not exist or had been exhausted. We find no equitable considerations justifying a departure from the express obligations embodied in these policies. Indeed, under all the circumstances of this case, we do not believe that Medical Protective is in any position to invoke equity in order to obtain contribution to Dr. Torbey's defense costs.

* * *

Affirmed.

Chapter 11

CHANGING THE LITIGATION SYSTEM

INTRODUCTORY NOTE

The states have treated the medical liability crisis by changing various aspects of their litigation systems, but they have not adopted a uniform list of aspects changed. Even as to the same change, state courts have responded in different ways to the charge that the change is unconstitutional; and state legislatures keep enacting further changes and amendments to changes. For a national casebook, this is a picture of chaos. In a particular state, however, a fairly clear picture can be had, and it is worth working for.

What follows is an attempt to arrange some of the changes in chronological order, from claims through actions to recoveries; to illustrate them by cases drawn from various states; and to show how the changes have been attacked on constitutional and public policy grounds.

The chapter is short, because it will take a lot of supplementation to match it with the law of a particular state. For readers who want rules of law, it will be tempting to omit the chapter, or to treat it only as background reading. For readers who are interested in legal process, the chapter shows how legislators and judges have analyzed the medical liability crisis and changed the litigation system, and what limitations of public policy and constitutionality confine the changes.

SECTION A. THE MECHANISMS OF CHANGE

Note on the Mechanisms of Change

By the mid-1970s it was widely perceived that the United States litigation system was not handling medical liability claims in a satisfactory manner, and most of the state legislatures enacted either individual statutes, treating one or two perceived problems, or packages that sought to deal with a wide array of problems.¹ The original statutes have been tested by experience and litigation, some have been modified, and further litigation carries forward the testing. Comprehensive packages have been proposed recently.²

This Note arranges litigation system problems and solutions from various states in the sequence in which litigation progresses. The cases that follow the Note emphasize the challenges to validity of the changes, not the ways in which the statutes operate, though even when a statute has been declared valid, it is fair to ask whether it is a good idea.

Claims

The first stage in medical liability litigation is the formulation and filing of the patient's claim against the health care provider. The sheer number of medical liability claims is a significant cost factor in the litigation system, because for every claim, the provider and the insurer incur expenses in setting up files and conducting investigations, no matter what becomes of the claim.

The best way to cut down on claims is to provide safe and successful medical services. Risk management and quality assurance programs in health care institutions seek to prevent medical liability claims.

In spite of preventive measures, claims do arise. Hospital ombudsmen try to reduce confrontations between patients and health care providers, and regardless of blame, patients will accept a lot of bad results if they feel listened-to. Insurers have also experimented with advanced payments to cover patients' out-of-pocket expenses arising from medical incidents that may involve liability, without going through the mechanics of taking a release from liability, but with the hope of keeping claim-creating medical incidents from maturing into litigation.

Incident prevention and claim amelioration can go only so far. It became apparent in the 1970s that lawyer-designed paperwork containing claim-arresting clauses, furnished by providers, and signed by patients in advance of claims, could not prevent future claims: the instruments were adhesive or otherwise contrary to public policy, and the courts refused to

1. Probably the best known package was California's "MICRA," the Medical Injury Compensation Reform Act of 1975. 1975 Cal.Stat. ch. 1–2, codified in various parts of the California Code of Civil Procedure. Another comprehensive approach was enacted in Indiana. Acts 1975, Pub.L. No. 146, codified as Ind.Code 1976, title 16, art. 9.5; for a survey of causes and a favorable report on experience, see Bowen, Medical Malpractice in Indiana, 11 J.Legis. 15 (1984) (Dr. Bowen was Secretary of Health and Human Services from 1985 to 1989). Some packages were struck down in their entirety, e.g., Wright v. Central DuPage Hosp. Ass'n, 63 Ill.2d 313, 347 N.E.2d 736, 80 A.L.R.3d 566 (1976); Carson v. Maurer, 120 N.H. 925, 424 A.2d 825, 12 A.L.R.4th 1 (1980), but have been replaced with different statutes.

2. See A Proposed Alternative to the Civil Justice System for Resolving Medical Liability Disputes: A Fault–Based, Administrative System (American Medical Association–Specialty Society Medical Liability Project, January 1988) (proposal to replace litigation altogether by a new state administrative agency).

The Model Health Care Provider Liability Reform Act was circulated to state governors in late 1987 by the Secretary of the United States Department of Health and Human Services. The Model Act was prepared by the Secretary's Task Force on Medical Liability and Malpractice; it does not seem to have been published as a government document. A source in HHS said in early 1990 that the Model Act had produced reactions (but no full-scale adoption) in about 15 states.

enforce them. The entry of some medical liability claims into the litigation system seems therefore to be inevitable, especially under state constitutions that guarantee claimants' access to the courts.

Actions

Once a patient has hired a lawyer to pursue a claim, it is easy for the lawyer to commence an action by filing a complaint in court, but filing the complaint does not establish that the claim has any merit. Doctors describe as "spurious" the complaints that lawyers call "frivolous." Some medical liability complaints are indeed frivolous; others are simply weak. The challenge that these complaints bring to the litigation system is to identify and dispose of, cheaply and quickly, the frivolous actions that should never have been filed and the congenitally weak actions that will never go to trial.

Since 1983, if the plaintiff's attorney files a frivolous complaint in federal court without adequately investigating the patient's angry or greedy assertions, the judge must impose a sanction of one kind or another upon the attorney under Fed.R.Civ.P. 11. Rule 11 is being used a lot in the federal courts, but it is controversial. It remains to be seen whether the states will adopt widely the 1983 sanctions provisions of Rule 11, and if they do, whether the threat of sanctions will shrink the number of medical liability actions that are dismissed on summary judgment for their intrinsic futility.

Some states have raised the threshold to the courthouse door. One technique is to require that the plaintiff's attorney notify the defendant of the intent to sue 90 days before filing the complaint, with the objective of enabling well-informed settlement negotiations to precede filing.[3] Another technique is to require that the plaintiff's lawyer file, along with the complaint, a "certificate of merit" in which the attorney certifies that a medical expert thinks there is a claim, and the expert must also certify to that effect.[4] Without the certificate of merit, the judge will dismiss the complaint, and the certificate of merit therefore may be invalid under a state constitution that provides for access to the courts.

Another way of inducing plaintiffs' attorneys to screen out weak cases before filing the complaint would be to make the ultimately losing plaintiff pay the winning defendant's legal expenses, contrary to the usual "American Rule" under which the parties pay their own lawyers, but this idea has not caught on.[5]

Plaintiffs' lawyers commence some actions as "nuisance" actions, filed on adequate grounds but in the hope of a small settlement rather than full litigation. For each nuisance action, the insurer incurs file-opening expenses, and each settlement shows on the provider's claims record, as well

---

3. E.g., West's Fla.Stat.Ann. § 766–106.

4. E.g., Ill.Rev.Stat. § 2–622; Md.Ann. Code § 3–2A–04(b).

5. Florida tried it. The statute had to be phrased neutrally, so the winner would pay the loser's expenses, West's Fla.Stat. Ann. § 768.56, enacted by L.1980, ch. 80–67, §§ 1, 3, and sometimes the plaintiffs did lose and had to pay; but it soon became apparent that most of the payments were moving from losing defendants to winning plaintiffs, and so the legislature repealed the statute. L.1985, ch. 85–75, § 43. See Spence & Roth, Closing the Courthouse Door: Florida's Spurious Claims Statute, 10 Stetson L.Rev. 397 (1981).

as leaving a permanent scar on the provider's ego. State laws provide for pre-testing the sufficiency of both nuisance and substantial actions by applying either of two basic alternatives to litigation.[6]

Under the first alternative, every medical liability action, before it reaches the courtroom, must detour through a claim-screening system. The states use and misuse various terms, such as "mediation" and "arbitration," but all of the screening systems are designed to pre-test the sufficiency of the evidence supporting the patient's case in chief, the function later performed by a judge on the doctor's motion for summary judgment or directed verdict. The states vary as to what persons comprise the screening panels, what kinds of findings the panels report, and what use can be made in a subsequent trial of the panels' findings—for example, whether the jury can be told about it; but in all of the screening systems, the objective is to force the plaintiff's lawyer to persuade a group of legal and medical experts that substantial evidence is available to litigate negligence, causation, and damages. If the panel finds against the plaintiff, the plaintiff can still go to court, but the plaintiff may have to post a bond for the defendant's legal expenses if the defendant wins. If there is a fatal gap in the plaintiff's case in chief, then the plaintiff's lawyer may withdraw from the case even if the plaintiff wants to fight on. If the plaintiff's case is sound, the defendant's insurer may decide to settle without further litigation. If there is sufficient evidence but genuine controversy, the case may well have to be tried.

The second alternative is to litigate through the out-of-court arbitration process instead of the in-court adjudication process. Three basic formats exist, along with numerous variations, but only where the parties' participation is voluntary can the result be binding.

First, the parties to an *existing dispute* over medical liability may agree to arbitrate it to a binding award. The laws of most states and certainly the federal law encourage the arbitration to proceed to award, and the award can then be entered as a judgment of court. Existing dispute arbitration is not a controversial idea, it rarely produces litigation, and it is being used in medical liability cases.

Second, the provider may supply and the patient may sign a form agreement to arbitrate *future disputes* before any services are performed. When a dispute arises, the enforceability of the agreement is hard to predict, because of the inequality of bargaining positions and the unforeseeability of specific disputes. Some states have enacted statutes that make future disputes arbitration agreements enforceable as long as they meet detailed requirements of language and circumstances.

Third, a state may require parties who want to litigate to enter *compulsory arbitration*. This leads either to a final award, as in existing disputes voluntary arbitration, or to a non-binding result that has some use in subsequent litigation, much like a screening panel report.

6. Federal judges have to follow the state law. In Feinstein v. Massachusetts Gen. Hosp., 489 F.Supp. 419 (D.Mass.1979), the district judge referred the claim to a state arbitration panel, which gave the plaintiff an unfavorable report. The plaintiff did not follow subsequent state procedural requirements, so the district judge dismissed the action, and the First Circuit affirmed. 643 F.2d 880 (1981).

In spite of detours on the road to the courthouse, medical liability cases are still litigated, and changes continue to be made in the litigation system itself. Statutes of limitations are a prominent target of change. To the plaintiffs' bar, judicial glosses on the statutes wisely extended the limitation periods in three kinds of cases: where the doctor continued to treat the patient's problem and allayed suspicions about the negligence that caused the problem; where a patient's injuries were undiscoverable until after the statute had run; and where a minor could not sue until reaching majority. To medical liability insurers, these glosses created the "long-tail claims" problem that made it difficult to set premiums. Many legislatures have enacted specialized statutes of limitations that refine statutes of limitations in medical liability actions.

Another problem in litigation has been securing the attendance of treating doctors at trial. Courts, bar associations, and medical societies have created on-call systems to alert doctors when they are about to be needed, instead of keeping them waiting in court for days. But if a busy doctor will not come to court when called, a subpoena will issue, and the judge can then demand obedience regardless of the doctor's inconvenience.[7]

Jury trials pose a number of problems and proposed solutions. For example, evidence can be in hopeless conflict: it may be impossible for the patient to establish satisfactorily that the doctor was negligent, or for the doctor to establish satisfactorily that the patient consented to an unintended consequence. As a matter of social policy rather than truth-finding, the medical liability system lets the jury decide contests over fault, and there is not much that changing the litigation system can do to change the jury system in this respect. As for damages, though, the broader use of special interrogatories can restrain the jury from letting an oversupply of horrible damages overcome weakness in the plaintiff's expert testimony on fault.

For another example, defense-oriented lawyers think that it is in their interests to keep twelve-person juries and unanimous verdicts in medical liability cases, though many states use smaller juries and do not insist upon unanimity.

As the final example, medical scientists think that scientific questions should not be decided by juries. They concede that there is nothing scientific about allocating a dollar value to pain and suffering; the judges have other tools, such as remittitur and new trial, for bringing down extravagant verdicts. But medical scientists are indignant at letting lay juries decide lopsided arguments about medicolegal causation, and they take no comfort from the power of judges to decide that a verdict for a plaintiff is against the clear weight of the evidence. So far, though, no change to the litigation system has tried to cope with this problem; expert juries on scientific questions do not exist, though it is possible that scientific expertise carries more weight before arbitrators than jurors.

Recoveries

Doctors and their insurers have found that they do not necessarily share the payment of large damage verdicts in proportion to their shares of

---

7. See In re Tarpley, 293 Ala. 137, 300 So.2d 409 (1974), where the physician narrowly escaped jail for criminal contempt of court.

fault. If a jury specifies three doctors' shares of fault in a patient's damages, and if insurance does not cover fully the damage share of Doctor A, the doctrine of several tort liability says that Doctor B or Doctor C or both of them must make up the balance of Doctor A's share of damages. A few states have modified the rule of several liability for medical liability defendants, so no doctor has to pay a share of damages greater than the share of fault.

The aspect of medical liability litigation that gets the most attention is the enormous size of some verdicts. Undoubtedly a multi-million-dollar verdict can have an impact on the insurance premiums paid by insured doctors.[8] Working from the perception that plaintiffs are being awarded too much money by judges and juries, state legislatures have enacted three basic methods to reduce recoveries.

The first method is to place a cap on the total amount of the patient's damages, regardless of the type of damages and the number of doctors.

The second method is to place a cap only on the amount of the patient's non-pecuniary damages. Pecuniary damage amounts rest upon documents and financial projections, and they can be reviewed by trial judges for excessiveness. Non-pecuniary damages, usually called "non-economic," are extremely difficult for judges to review at any level, and so some statutes have "capped" non-economic damages at sums in the hundreds of thousands of dollars.[9]

The third method is to reduce the amount of total recovery that will *not* go to the patient. For example, in most cases the patient's lawyer will have contracted with the patient to receive a contingent fee of 30% to 50% that comes out of the patient's recovery, and many states have imposed ceilings or sliding scales on the percentages that the victorious patient's lawyer may recover.

In a few cases, a horribly injured patient will have a short life expectancy but no close and deserving kin, so most of a lump sum payment will go as a windfall to remote recipients, or it may be wasted by the patient or those who were supposed to provide care. Here a few legislatures have sought to guarantee *periodic payments* of funds for care while the patient lives, but to shut off the payments when the patient dies.[10] The

---

8. For example, New Jersey had about 20,000 doctors in 1988. 1989 World Almanac 845. In theory, a $2 million case (judgment and defense costs) thus would cost each doctor $100. However, less dramatic forces also operate on premiums. For example, if only 1% of those doctors (200) had a claim in any one year, and if the insurers spent $10,000 per claim to open files and investigate, the total expense would be $2 million.

9. See Fein v. Permanente Medical Group, 38 Cal.3d 137, 211 Cal.Rptr. 368, 695 P.2d 665, appeal dismissed for want of a substantial federal question, 478 U.S. 892, 106 S.Ct. 214, 88 L.Ed.2d 215 (1985) (Justice White dissented with opinion). The cap is another part of MICRA. It withstood federal constitutional attack in Hoffman v. United States, 767 F.2d 1431 (9th Cir.1985).

10. See American Bank & Trust Co. v. Community Hosp., 36 Cal.3d 359, 204 Cal. Rptr. 671, 683 P.2d 670, 41 A.L.R.4th 233 (1984) (a MICRA case); the annotation is Validity of State Statute Providing for Periodic Payment of Future Damages in Medical Malpractice Action, 41 A.L.R.4th 275 (1985). The court held that the statute, West's Ann.Cal.Code Civ.P. § 667.7, was constitutional, but three justices dissented in two long opinions that give all the earlier background. In a later case, Kansas declared unconstitutional a second-generation package that included both a damage cap and an annuity provision. Kansas

concept has its merits, but design and administrability problems have shown up in the small number of cases.

Structured settlements are a familiar mechanism for getting money to patients as long as they need it, but not thereafter. Stretching out the payment of money to patients has two objectives, long-term availability and avoidance of windfalls, that seem to be easier to achieve by contract than by statute.[11]

Many of the forces that push the costs of medical liability claims upward, such as the increasing use of medical care and the expanding expectations for what it can accomplish, are beyond the control of state legislatures and even the Congress of the United States. It seems doubtful that the dollar cost of claims will actually turn downward from any cause, least of all because of changing the litigation system. The rate of increase in medical liability claims costs may be slowed by changing the litigation system, but none of the changes discussed in this chapter have been in place long enough to show this effect clearly.

SECTION B. FORESTALLING CLAIMS

TATHAM v. HOKE, 469 F.Supp. 914 (W.D.N.C.1979), affirmed, 622 F.2d 587 (4th Cir.1980) (mem.). The patient signed the following document before the doctor performed an abortion on her:

INFORMED CONSENT TO TREATMENT, ANESTHETIC, AND OTHER MEDICAL SERVICES

* * *

13. In the event of any dispute between me and Hallmark Clinic, my physician, or other personnel, I agree to make a written claim within thirty (30) days of this date. If such a claim is not timely made, I waive any and all rights of recovery. If such a claim is made, be it for professional liability, personal injury, contract, warranty, or other breach of duty, I agree to submit the claim to binding arbitration. In the event of such arbitration, I understand and agree that Hallmark shall choose one physician arbitrator; I shall choose a second physician arbitrator; a third such arbitrator shall be designated by the American Arbitration Association office in Washington, D.C. The decision of the arbitrators shall be binding upon me without recourse to any other judicial or other tribunal. I further agree that liability shall in no case exceed $15,000, and that I shall post in advance a bond to cover the costs of arbitration and the counsel fees of Hallmark Clinic, its physician(s), or other personnel.

The patient sued the doctor for negligence, and the doctor moved to dismiss or for a stay pending arbitration.

Denying both motions, District Judge McMillan found that the exculpatory provisions were unenforceably adhesive under the law of

---

Malpractice Victims Coalition v. Bell, 243 Kan. 333, 757 P.2d 251 (1988); again, there were dissents.

11. See D. Hindert, J. Dehner & P. Hindert, Structured Settlements and Periodic Payment Judgments (1986).

North Carolina. He found that the arbitration provisions were not severable, so he did not consider their validity.[12]

EMORY UNIV. v. PORUBIANSKY
Supreme Court of Georgia, 1981.
248 Ga. 391, 282 S.E.2d 903.

CLARKE, JUSTICE. * * *

Diane Porubiansky became a patient at the Emory University School of Dentistry Clinic in 1976. Prior to treatment she was required to execute an "Information–Consent" form. The clinic * * * offers dental services to the public at fees that, on the average, are less than the average price of those of private practitioners. The form explains that patients are accepted based upon the training needs of the school and that treatment will proceed more slowly than in a private office. There is also a statement that complete dental treatment cannot be assured. The last paragraph of this form provides:

> In consideration of Emory University School of Dentistry performing dental treatment, I do hereby expressly waive and relinquish any and all claims of every nature I or my minor child or ward may have against Emory University, its officers, agents, employees, or students, their successors, assignees, administrators, or executors; and further agree to hold them harmless as the result of any claims by such minor child or ward, arising out of any dental treatment rendered, regardless of its nature or extent.

In April of 1977 Mrs. Porubiansky had an impacted tooth removed by Dr. Haddad, an employee of the dental clinic. She alleged that as a result of negligent treatment her jaw was broken during the surgical procedure and filed suit against Emory University and Dr. Haddad. The defendants denied any negligent treatment and further asserted that the signing of the information-consent form was a complete bar to the action. The trial court granted summary judgment to the defendants based upon the exculpatory clause in the form. The court of appeals held the clause in question to be void as against public policy. 156 Ga.App. 602, 275 S.E.2d 163 (1980).

* * * Emory University and Dr. Haddad contend that the form is a valid covenant not to sue which would prohibit recovery for negligent dental treatment. They argue that a doctor and patient may bargain for a shifting of liability without offending any policy of this state, and further contend that the Emory University School of Dentistry occupies a unique position in that it services the public need by training dental professionals and offering dental services to the general public.

We agree that through the dental clinic Emory provides a worthwhile service of lower cost professional care and in the training of dental professionals. We also agree that because the clinic is part of a

---

12. See Annot., Validity and Construction of Contract Exempting Hospital or Doctor from Liability for Negligence to Patient, 6 A.L.R.3d 704 (1966).

teaching facility it may require that prospective patients waive the right to insist on complete treatment. However, the attempt to relieve the clinic, its employees and students from the statutory duty of care for licensed professional medical services conflicts with and frustrates the policies of the state as expressed through our General Assembly.

* * * The legislature has established a minimum standard of care for the medical profession. * * * Ga.Code Ann. § 84–924. This standard also governs the duties and responsibilities of a dentist. * * *

We find that it is against the public policy of this state to allow one who procures a license to practice dentistry to relieve himself by contract of the duty to exercise reasonable care. * * *

The status of the Emory University School of Dentistry as primarily a training institution does not allow for an exemption from the duty to exercise reasonable care. The clinic in offering services to the public is engaged in the practice of dentistry. The legislature while allowing such clinics to operate has not exempted them from the standard of care necessary for the protection of the public. * * *

* * * The court of appeals was correct in reversing the summary judgment and allowing Mrs. Porubiansky to proceed on her allegations * * *.

Judgment affirmed.

JORDAN, C.J., and MARSHALL, J., dissent.

SECTION C. LITIGATION ALTERNATIVES AND HURDLES

Note on Agreements to Arbitrate Future Disputes

Most states enforce contract clauses in which the parties agree to arbitrate future disputes, as long as the contracts are otherwise valid. In routine commercial contracts between parties of approximately equal bargaining power, if one party goes to court, the court normally will stay the action and may order arbitration under the contract.

But the forms that patients sign in entering medical service relationships with health care providers are not routine commercial contracts. For example, when a patient goes to a hospital for acute care, and the hospital presents an admitting form that contains a future disputes arbitration clause, and the patient later wants to sue the hospital for medical negligence, the agreement to arbitrate is vulnerable to the charge that the patient never read it or never agreed to it, and so it may be held unenforceable as a contract of adhesion.[13] If arbitration is to function in

---

13. This was the result in California in a 1976 case testing a form signed in 1971. Wheeler v. St. Joseph Hosp., 63 Cal.App.3d 345, 133 Cal.Rptr. 775, 84 A.L.R.3d 343 (arbitration ordered and award confirmed; judgment reversed); see Annot., Arbitration of Medical Malpractice Claims, 84 A.L.R.3d 375 (1978).

this context, legislation is the answer, and a few states have enacted this kind of law.[14]

For example, in 1975, the California legislature included in the Medical Injury Compensation Reform Act (MICRA) two statutory texts for health care provider intake forms:

ARBITRATION OF MEDICAL MALPRACTICE
Cal.Code Civ.P. § 1295.

(a) Any contract for medical services which contains a provision for arbitration of any dispute as to professional negligence of a health care provider shall have such provision as the first article of the contract and shall be expressed in the following language:

> It is understood that any dispute as to medical malpractice, that is as to whether any medical services rendered under this contract were unnecessary or unauthorized or were improperly, negligently or incompetently rendered, will be determined by submission to arbitration as provided by California law, and not by a lawsuit or resort to court process except as California law provides for judicial review of arbitration proceedings. Both parties to this contract, by entering into it, are giving up their constitutional right to have any such dispute decided in a court of law before a jury, and instead are accepting the use of arbitration.

(b) Immediately before the signature line provided for the individual contracting for the medical services must appear the following in at least 10-point bold red type:

> NOTICE: BY SIGNING THIS CONTRACT YOU ARE AGREEING TO HAVE ANY ISSUE OF MEDICAL MALPRACTICE DECIDED BY NEUTRAL ARBITRATION AND YOU ARE GIVING UP YOUR RIGHT TO A JURY OR COURT TRIAL. SEE ARTICLE 1 OF THIS CONTRACT.

(c) Once signed, such a contract governs all subsequent open-book account transactions for medical services for which the contract was signed until or unless rescinded by written notice within 30 days of signature. Written notice of such rescission may be given by a guardian or conservator of the patient if the patient is incapacitated or a minor.

(d) Where the contract is one for medical services to a minor, it shall not be subject to disaffirmance if signed by the minor's parent or legal guardian.

(e) Such a contract is not a contract of adhesion, nor unconscionable nor otherwise improper, where it complies with subdivisions (a), (b) and (c) of this section.

* * *

---

[14]. The bulk of decisions nationwide come from California and Michigan. See McKinstry v. Valley Obstetrics–Gynecology Clinic, P.C., 428 Mich. 167, 405 N.W.2d 88 (1987) (validity of arbitration statute upheld with little discussion; text reprinted).

The California Supreme Court has not passed on the validity of § 1295, but a number of lower court cases have explored the coverage as to claims and persons,[15] and arbitration awards are not always received gladly by the doctors.[16]

KEYES v. HUMANA HOSP. ALASKA, INC.
Supreme Court of Alaska, 1988.
750 P.2d 343.

RABINOWITZ, CHIEF JUSTICE. * * *

Petitioner Melanie Keyes filed suit in superior court for personal injuries arising from an automobile accident against the driver of the vehicle in which she was a passenger, and against the hospitals and physicians involved in treating her injuries. Her complaint alleged, inter alia, negligent diagnosis and treatment by each of the defendant physicians. Most of the acts complained of were allegedly committed in the emergency rooms of the hospital defendants, by physicians who were employees or agents of the hospitals.

On September 17, 1986, Keyes filed a motion for a protective order requesting the superior court not to present her case to an expert advisory panel as required by Alaska Stat. § 09.55.536,[17] based on alleged constitutional defects of the statute. The medical defendants opposed. The superior court denied the motion and thereafter ap-

---

15. E.g., Gross v. James A. Recabaren, M.D., Inc., 206 Cal.App.3d 771, 253 Cal. Rptr. 820 (1988) (arbitration agreement held to cover both a series of unrelated procedures performed on the patient and his wife's claim for loss of consortium).

16. See Baker v. Sadick, 162 Cal.App.3d 618, 208 Cal.Rptr. 676 (1984) ($300,000 punitive damages affirmed), hearing denied.

17. Alaska Stat. § 09.55.536 provides in relevant part:

(a) In an action for damages due to personal injury or death based upon the provision of professional services by a health care provider when the parties have not agreed to arbitration of the claim under AS 09.55.535, the court shall appoint within 20 days after filing of answer to a summons and complaint a three-person expert advisory panel unless the court decides that an expert advisory opinion is not necessary for a decision in the case. * * *

(b) The expert advisory panel may compel the attendance of witnesses, interview the parties, physically examine the injured person if alive, consult with the specialists or learned works they consider appropriate, and compel the production of and examine all relevant hospital, medical, or other records or materials relating to the health care in issue. The panel may meet in camera, but shall maintain a record of any testimony or oral statements of witnesses, and shall keep copies of all written statements it receives.

(c) Not more than 30 days after selection of the panel, it shall make a written report to the parties and to the court * * *.

(e) The report of the panel with any dissenting or concurring opinion is admissible in evidence to the same extent as though its contents were orally testified to by the person or persons preparing it. The court shall delete any portion that would not be admissible because of lack of foundation for opinion testimony, or otherwise. Either party may submit testimony to support or refute the report. The jury shall be instructed in general terms that the report shall be considered and evaluated in the same manner as any other expert testimony. Any member of the panel may be called by any party and may be cross-examined as to the contents of the report or of that member's dissenting or concurring opinion.

pointed three physicians to serve as the expert advisory panel in Keyes' case. Subsequently Keyes filed the instant petition.

A. RIGHT TO JURY TRIAL

Keyes claims that § 09.55.536 substantially impairs her right to a jury trial as guaranteed by art. I, § 16 of the Alaska Constitution. She appears to argue that introduction of the medical expert panel's report into evidence at trial will undercut the jury's role as the trier of fact, based on her belief that the jury will give undue deference to the panel's opinion.

Similar charges have been leveled in nearly all of the cases which have addressed the constitutionality of statutes providing for some form of non-binding review of medical malpractice claims prior to trial. The vast majority have rejected the charge on the ground that the jury remains the ultimate arbiter of factual questions and upon the belief that the jury weighs the panel's opinion in the same manner as it weighs all of the other evidence presented. * * * [18] We join these jurisdictions in rejecting Keyes' jury trial attack on § 09.55.536 on this ground, and note in particular our agreement with the view expressed by the court in Comiskey v. Arlen:

> The panel's recommendation is, in effect, an expert opinion which is to be evaluated by the jury in the same manner as it would evaluate any other expert opinion, as directed by the instructions of the trial justice. 55 A.D.2d 304, 390 N.Y.S.2d 122, 126 (1976), aff'd mem., 43 N.Y.2d 696, 401 N.Y.S.2d 200, 372 N.E.2d 34 (1977). * * *

Finally, we also reject Keyes' contention that the admissibility of a panel report adverse to the malpractice claimant violates his or her right to a jury trial by impermissibly increasing the burden of persuasion. * * *

We find distinguishable from the case at bar those cases which have invalidated statutes allowing the admission of panel reports as depriving litigants of their right to a jury trial. * * *

* * * We therefore adhere to the view which has emerged from the remaining jurisdictions which have considered the point and hold that the statute does not impermissibly infringe on the constitutional right to a jury trial by requiring pre-trial review of medical malpractice claims by an expert advisory panel.[19]

---

18. Each of these cases involved a state statute authorizing the admissibility of the panel recommendation or opinion but leaving the jury free to determine the weight of that opinion. * * *

In a similar vein, some courts have characterized provisions authorizing the admissibility of medical review panel findings as simply evidentiary rules allowing a specialized form of expert opinion. * * * Thus viewed, such provisions have been found constitutionally unobjectionable on the ground that litigants have no vested right in particular rules of evidence. * * *

19. Keyes does not make the argument that pre-trial screening by a medical review panel violates the constitutional jury trial guarantee because it obstructs a litigant's access to a jury. We observe that those courts faced with this claim have held that requiring a medical malpractice plaintiff to begin the process of obtaining a final determination of his claim by submit-

B. DUE PROCESS

Keyes claims that § 09.55.536 denies her due process of law as guaranteed by art. I, § 7 of the Alaska Constitution. * * *

1. Substantive Due Process

Keyes' claim that due process is violated because there is no justification for the requirement that only medical malpractice cases and not other tort cases are subject to pre-trial screening essentially alleges deprivation of substantive due process. * * * The constitutional guarantee of substantive due process assures that a legislative body's decision is not arbitrary but instead based on some rational policy. * * *

Courts in other jurisdictions have uniformly rejected substantive due process attacks on statutes authorizing medical review panels. Each of them has found the review procedure to be a reasonable legislative response to a perceived crisis in medical malpractice insurance rates, a means of assuring the availability of malpractice insurance coverage at reasonable rates and of improving the availability and reducing the cost of medical care in general, by attempting to eliminate frivolous malpractice claims and encourage settlement of meritorious ones. [W]e see no reason to depart from the result reached in other jurisdictions and accordingly hold that the statute does not deny medical malpractice plaintiffs substantive due process.

2. Procedural Due Process

Keyes' remaining claims under Alaska Const. art. I, § 7 concern alleged violations of procedural due process. * * * Identification of the specific dictates of due process generally involves consideration of three distinct factors: the private interest affected by the official action; the risk of an erroneous deprivation of such interest through the procedures used and the probable value, if any, of additional or substitute procedural safeguards; and finally, the government's interest, including the fiscal and administrative burdens that additional or substitute procedural requirements would entail. * * *

* * * Keyes in essence argues that the procedural safeguards which inhere in an adversarial trial proceeding must also attend the review panel's evaluation of a claim because the panel's determination carries such great weight when admitted at the subsequent trial. We disagree. * * *

We also find meritless Keyes' specific claim that a panel composed of physicians offends notions of due process because it does not constitute an impartial decisionmaker. She does not assert that actual bias exists in this case or that a particular procedure for selecting panel members creates a probability of systematic bias, but instead bases her claim on the status of the panel members, who, like the defendants, are

ting it to the panel is a permissible interference with the jury trial right. * * *

local health care providers. Essentially identical contentions have been summarily dismissed in other jurisdictions. * * *

Keyes ignores the fact that, given the complex medical issues involved in malpractice cases, the goal of an expert panel review statute would be completely thwarted without the specialized expertise or medically-trained panel members, * * * and that for the same reason professionals are often permitted to sit on administrative boards dealing with disciplinary proceedings for members of their own professions. * * * Finally, § 09.55.536 itself contains explicit safeguards against such bias in that it affords the parties an opportunity to object or make suggestions regarding the court's determination of the professions or specialties to be represented on the panel, § .536(a); prohibits parties and their counsel from initiating ex parte communications with the panel members concerning the case, § .536(h); provides for compensation of panel members by the court in accordance with established fee schedules, § .536(g); and requires the court to delete from the panel report any portion that would not otherwise be admissible. § 536(e).

In conclusion, Keyes has failed to show that the panel review procedures of § 09.55.536 create any risk of an erroneous deprivation of her interest in litigating her malpractice claim. Keyes would have the panel mirror the adversarial adjudicatory procedures employed in judicial proceedings, but the probable value of such safeguards seems insignificant given the probability that the panel report carries no greater evidentiary weight than any other expert opinion, and the parties can cross-examine the panel members about the foundation for their opinion. * * * Thus, the protections of procedural due process do not require us to declare § 09.55.536 unconstitutional.

C. Delegation of Judicial Power

Keyes argues that § 09.55.536 contravenes the separation of powers principles inherent in art. IV, § 1 of the Alaska Constitution by vesting judicial power in nonjudicial personnel. Keyes contends that the statute confers judicial authority on the members of the review panel in that they can compel the appearance of witnesses and production of documents, interview the parties, examine the plaintiff's physical condition, § 09.55.536(b), and ultimately make factual findings and draw legal conclusions concerning issues of liability and damages.[20]

20. § 09.55.536(c) directs the panel to make a written report answering the following questions and other questions submitted to it by the court:

(1) What was the disorder for which the plaintiff came to medical care?

(2) What would have been the probable outcome without medical care?

(3) Was the treatment selected appropriate for the case?

(4) Did an injury arise from the medical care?

(5) What is the nature and extent of the medical injury?

(6) What specifically caused the medical injury?

(7) Was the medical injury caused by unskillful care?

(8) If a medical injury had not occurred, how would the plaintiff's condition differ from the plaintiff's present condition?

* * *

We are aware of only one appellate court that has accepted an argument like Keyes' and held a system of screening panels for medical malpractice cases unconstitutional based on its improper delegation of judicial function. * * *

Having found no apposite judicial authority, and no independent basis, for Keyes' claim that the panel review procedure of § 09.55.536 authorizes an invasion of judicial function by the panel, we decline to invalidate the statute on this ground.

D. Equal Protection

A further contention is that § 09.55.536 violates equal protection guarantees of the Alaska Constitution by creating an impermissible classification, treating medical malpractice litigants differently from those involved in other kinds of tort cases. Courts in every jurisdiction which have addressed such contentions have sustained their review panel statutes, the overwhelming majority doing so on the ground that the statutes are rationally related to effectuating a legitimate governmental purpose.[21] * * * They have uniformly declined to apply a "strict scrutiny" standard of review, most finding explicitly that the statute's classification neither implicates a suspect class nor impinges upon any fundamental right which would justify this higher standard. * * *

Our approach to evaluating challenges brought under Alaska's equal protection clause involves a sliding scale of review ranging from relaxed to strict scrutiny. * * * The higher the level of scrutiny applied, the more compelling the governmental purpose and the closer the means-to-end fit must be. * * *

[A]pplying a relatively low level of scrutiny on our "sliding scale," a conclusion that § 09.55.536 bears a fair and substantial relation to its purposes is unavoidable absent some showing by Keyes that the statute is unlikely to encourage settlement and reduce litigation over malpractice claims. Keyes has made no such showing, and the present record therefore furnishes no basis for finding § 09.55.536 contrary to Alaska's constitutional guarantee of equal protection.

E. Right of Access to the Courts

The final potential challenge to § 09.55.536 is that the statute unconstitutionally denies malpractice plaintiffs access to the courts by forcing them to wait to proceed to trial until after the expert panel has rendered its opinion. As noted above, application of the statute mandates a delay of at most 80 days before discovery may commence.

Most courts have rejected contentions that the added delay and expense caused by their panel review statutes impermissibly obstructs a malpractice claimant's access to the courts. * * * Access to the courts is not an independent right; it enjoys special protection only

---

21. * * * The commentators are in agreement that medical panel review statutes present no equal protection problems. * * *

when the right to be asserted through such access is entitled to special protection, and no alternative forum exists to enforce that right. * * * In cases such as this which involve rights not accorded special constitutional protection, access may be hindered if there is a rational basis for the restraint imposed. * * * Thus, the courts upholding their panel review statutes have, either expressly or impliedly, found a rational basis for the alleged delays and/or expense. * * *

Consistency with the due process and equal protection analysis undertaken herein requires us now to reaffirm that a rational basis for the § 09.55.536 panel review requirement exists.[22] We therefore hold that § 09.55.536 does not unconstitutionally deprive medical malpractice plaintiffs of their right of access to the courts.

* * *

Affirmed.

BURKE, JUSTICE, dissenting. * * *

* * * What the majority fails to recognize about the jury trial guarantee is that it is as much the right of an individual to *keep the court out* of the fact-finding process as it is to *bring jurors into* it. * * *

I believe that there is a significant danger that the jury will associate the opinion of the court-appointed panel with the opinion of the court itself and will, accordingly, afford the panel's opinion undue weight, simply because the panel will be presented to the jury as "impartial." This, of course, would be a serious mistake. * * *

It is true that * * * the jury is to be "instructed in general terms that the report shall be considered and evaluated in the same manner as any other expert testimony." § 09.55.536(e). However, given the grave danger that the jury will accord the panel's decision undue weight under the circumstances, I am not persuaded that the curative instruction in the statute renders it constitutionally acceptable. *Neither the panel nor its report may be cross-examined* by the party against whom the report is offered. All that the party may do is question members of the panel, individually. The notion that this is equivalent to cross-examination of an ordinary expert witness is pure nonsense, and anyone who believes otherwise has spent entirely too little time in the trial arena. Absent the tempering influence of such cross-examination, it is difficult to imagine how the jury can evaluate the panel's report "in the same manner as * * * other expert testimony," and my belief is that it will not in most cases.

Originally, statutes such as § 09.55.536 were designed to address the so-called "battle of the experts"; it was perceived that juries, being unschooled in medical science, were confounded by the conflicting views of the parties' paid experts and were, hence, unable to reach a just result. * * * The answer to this problem, according to some, was to

---

22. The courts which have invalidated panel review statutes as unconstitutional denials of access have done so for reasons inapplicable to this case. * * *

require expert juries or to abolish the right to jury trial in complex cases. Most legal scholars, however, recognized that both of these solutions would almost certainly be held unconstitutional. * * * Some of these scholars concluded that a similar effect could be achieved by the use of expert witnesses chosen and paid for by the court. * * *

With due respect for the views expressed by these venerable scholars, I believe that our duty under the Alaska Constitution is to protect against such eventualities, not to encourage them. *If juries are incapable of making rational decisions in medical malpractice cases based upon the evidence placed before them by the parties, then the flaw is in the jury system itself, and it is the Constitution, not the rules of civil procedure, which must be changed.* In the meantime, we are sworn to protect the constitutionally guaranteed right to trial by jury against any scheme designed to frustrate its utilization or undermine its purposes. * * *[23]

Note on Certificate of Merit Legislation

In its 1985 medical liability package, the Illinois legislature enacted a "certificate of merit" hurdle to the plaintiff's action:

Ill.Rev.Stat. Ch. 110. Practice

§ 2–622. Healing Art Malpractice

(a) In any action, whether in tort, contract or otherwise, in which the plaintiff seeks damages for injuries or death by reason of medical, hospital, or other healing art malpractice, the plaintiff's attorney * * * shall file an affidavit, attached to the original and all copies of the complaint, declaring one of the following:

1. That the affiant has consulted and reviewed the facts of the case with a health professional who the affiant reasonably believes is knowledgeable in the relevant issues involved in the particular action and who practices in the same specialty as the defendant if the defendant is a specialist; that the reviewing health professional has determined in a written report, after a review of the medical record and other relevant material involved in the particular action that there is a reasonable and meritorious cause for the filing of such action; and that the affiant has concluded on the basis of the reviewing health professional's review and consultation that there is a reasonable and meritorious cause for filing of such action. * * * A copy of the written report, clearly identifying the plaintiff and the reasons for the reviewing health professional's determination that a reasonable and meritorious cause for the filing of the action exists, must be attached to the affidavit, but information which would

---

23. Editors' Note: Compare Hoem v. State, 756 P.2d 780 (Wyo.1988), where a split supreme court found a milder system unconstitutional. See also Annot., Validity and Construction of State Statutory Provisions Relating to Limitations on Amount of Recovery in Medical Malpractice Claim and Submission of Such Claim to Pretrial Panel, 80 A.L.R.3d 583 (1977).

identify the reviewing health professional may be deleted from the copy so attached.

* * *

(g) The failure to file a certificate required by this section shall be grounds for dismissal under section 2–619.

Since the law was enacted, three districts of the appellate court of Illinois have declared it constitutional, but the district that includes Chicago has declared that it unconstitutionally delegates the judicial power to persons outside the court system, in violation of the separation of powers clause of Ill.–S.H.A. Const. art. II, § 1, and art. VI, § 1. DeLuna v. St. Elizabeth's Hosp., 184 Ill.App.3d 802, 132 Ill.Dec. 925, 540 N.E.2d 847 (1989).

SECTION D. ACTIONS

Note on Limitation of Medical Liability Actions

Most personal injury torts manifest themselves immediately, and so plaintiffs can make claims within days or weeks. If the plaintiff makes no claim within the period set by the statute of limitations, defendants and their insurers may assume that the plaintiff will not make a claim and can plan accordingly. This is not true of some medical liability claims, and the uncertainty of claims and the lateness of defenses undoubtedly combine to increase defense costs.

For example, Dr. J. Wesley Osborne, a general practitioner, had an elderly patient, Mrs. Effie Frazor, who fell and broke a hip in December 1951. Dr. Don Eyler, an orthopedic surgeon, performed three operations on the hip, and Dr. Osborne assisted only at the first two. At the last operation December 16, 1952, a gauze surgical sponge was left in the incision. Dr. Osborne continued to treat Mrs. Frazor at her home, but the incision failed to heal. On May 2, 1961, Mrs. Frazor's family saw threads in the incision and called Dr. Osborne, who was out of town; his associate came out and removed the sponge. The physician-patient relationship terminated that day at the latest.

The plaintiff filed an action against Dr. Osborne on March 19, 1962, alleging that he negligently failed to refer Mrs. Frazor back to Dr. Eyler. At the time, there was some doubt, but it seemed likely that until February 4, 1954, Hartford Accident & Indemnity Co. (Hartford) had insured Dr. Osborne for $5000, and so Hartford provided defense counsel under a non-waiver notice that reserved its right to decline to pay any judgment. While the plaintiff alleged treatment under a continuous physician-patient relationship, which would have tolled the start of the Tennessee one-year limitation of actions period until discovery of the sponge on May 2, 1961, the trial judge held that the relationship ended and the limitations period began with Dr. Osborne's final visit to Mrs. Frazor November 14, 1960; therefore he directed a verdict for Dr. Osborne. The appellate court reversed and remanded for a new trial, holding in a case of first impression that under the continuous treatment doctrine, there was sufficient evidence for a jury to find that the period began with discovery of the sponge.[24] The second trial ended in 1967 with a hung jury.

At the third trial, the jury awarded the plaintiff $8000 in compensatory damages and $1000 in punitive damages. Dr. Osborne appealed but lost.[25] Dr. Osborne borrowed money and paid the judgment and interest.

Dr. Osborne then sued the three insurance companies that had covered him on occurrence policies between 1952 and 1962: Hartford through February 3, 1954 ($5000 in coverage), Insurance Co. of North America from 1954 to 1958 ($20,000), and Shelby Mutual Ins. Co. from 1958 to 1962 ($50,000 or more). The trial court dismissed INA and Shelby. The only evidence that Dr. Osborne had negligently treated Mrs. Frazor during the Hartford policy period was Hartford's 1968 answer, alleging a series of house calls that commenced January 15, 1954. The court treated Hartford's answer as an admission of coverage and awarded Dr. Osborne the Hartford policy limits plus interest and costs, $6281. Hartford had previously furnished counsel and apparently had defended three actions and two appeals. The appellate court affirmed,[26] and the Supreme Court of Tennessee denied certiorari January 3, 1972.

The period from the date of Dr. Osborne's relevant negligence in premium year 1954 (which was determined late in the proceedings) to the final denial of further appeal in 1972 constituted a "tail" nearly 18 years long.

Consider an even longer tail. Neil Schack was born in January 1954. His action against his mother's attending physician gave rise to an opinion by the New York trial judge on November 24, 1976,[27] 22 years thereafter, and the defense made no motion to dismiss his action on the ground that it should have been commenced sooner.

Could legislatures respond to the long-tail problem by cutting off medical liability claims filed far after the normal limitation of actions period? The legislatures have come up with different statutes and the courts with different answers.[28]

A limitation of actions statute directed at the entire medical liability subset of tort claims may violate a state constitutional prohibition against class legislation.[29]

A statute of limitations that purports absolutely to cut off medical liability claims may also run afoul of state constitutional provisions. For example, Ohio's statute used to read, "In no event shall any medical claim

24. Frazor v. Osborne, 57 Tenn.App. 10, 414 S.W.2d 118 (1966), cert. denied.

25. Osborne v. Frazor, 58 Tenn.App. 15, 425 S.W.2d 768, 35 A.L.R.3d 338 (1968), cert. denied. See Annot., Malpractice: Physician's Failure to Advise Patient to Consult Specialist or One Qualified in a Method of Treatment Which Physician Is Not Qualified to Give, 35 A.L.R.3d 349 (1971).

26. Osborne v. Hartford Acc. & Indem. Co., 63 Tenn.App. 518, 476 S.W.2d 256 (1971).

27. Schack v. Holland, 89 Misc.2d 78, 389 N.Y.S.2d 988 (1976).

28. See Annot., When Statute of Limitations Commences to Run Against Malpractice Action Against Physician, Surgeon, Dentist, or Similar Practitioner, 80 A.L.R.2d 368 (1961).

29. See Reynolds v. Porter, 760 P.2d 816 (Okl.1988).

against a physician, podiatrist, or hospital be brought more than four years after the act or omission constituting the alleged malpractice occurred," and it made only a limited exception for minors.[30] Ohio's constitution has provisions guaranteeing access to courts and equal protection, and under them, the exception for minors is invalid,[31] unknown claims cannot not be cut off,[32] and persons who discover their claims late within the last year of the four-year period cannot be cut off at the end of it.[33] Evidently the statute had problems that the Ohio legislature could not cure. But a similar statute in Illinois was held to be constitutional.[34]

SECTION E. RECOVERIES

ETHERIDGE v. MEDICAL CENTER HOSPITALS
Supreme Court of Virginia, 1989.
237 Va. 87, 376 S.E.2d 525.

STEPHENSON, JUSTICE. * * *

Louise Etheridge * * * sued Medical Center Hospitals and * * * the estate of Clarence B. Trower, Jr. * * *, alleging that the hospital and Trower were liable, jointly and severally, for damages Richie Lee Wilson sustained as a result of their medical malpractice. Evidence at trial revealed that, prior to her injuries, Wilson, a 35–year–old mother of three children, was a normal, healthy woman. On May 6, 1980, however, Wilson underwent surgery at the hospital to restore a deteriorating jaw bone. The surgery consisted of the removal of five-inch-long portions of two ribs by Trower, a general surgeon, and the grafting of the reshaped rib bone to Wilson's jaw by an oral surgeon. The jury found that both Trower and the hospital were negligent and that their negligence proximately caused Wilson's injuries.

Wilson's injuries are severe and permanent. She is brain damaged with limited memory and intelligence. She is paralyzed on her left side, confined to a wheelchair, and unable to care for herself or her children.

* * *

The jury returned a verdict for $2,750,000 against both defendants. The trial court, applying the recovery limit prescribed in Va.Code Ann.

---

30. Ohio Rev.Code § 2305.11(B) (1981). In a similar case, the Missouri supreme court held that if its new statute were construed to cut off the actions of minors (who cannot sue in their own right) when they achieved majority, it would violate the state constitutional right of access to the courts. Strahler v. St. Luke's Hosp., 706 S.W.2d 7, 62 A.L.R.4th 735 (Mo.1986). See Annot., Medical Malpractice Statutes of Limitation Minority Provisions, 62 A.L.R.4th 758 (1988).

31. Mominee v. Scherbarth, 28 Ohio St. 3d 270, 28 Ohio Bar R. 346, 503 N.E.2d 717 (1986).

32. Hardy v. VerMeulen, 32 Ohio St.3d 45, 512 N.E.2d 626 (1987).

33. Gaines v. Preterm–Cleveland, Inc., 33 Ohio St.3d 54, 514 N.E.2d 709 (1987).

34. See Anderson v. Wagner, 79 Ill.2d 295, 37 Ill.Dec. 558, 402 N.E.2d 560 (1979). See also Douglas v. Hugh A. Stallings, M.D., Inc., 870 F.2d 1242 (7th Cir.1989), upholding against federal constitutional attack the complex Indiana statute of limitations for minors.

§ 8.01-581.15, reduced the verdict to $750,000 and entered judgment in that amount. Wilson appeals.

* * * Section 8.01-581.15, * * * as originally enacted and in effect at all times pertinent to the present case, provided as follows:

> In any verdict returned against a health care provider in an action for malpractice where the act or acts of malpractice occurred on or after April one, nineteen hundred seventy-seven, which is tried by a jury or in any judgment entered against a health care provider in such an action which is tried without a jury, the total amount recoverable for any injury to, or death of, a patient shall not exceed seven hundred fifty thousand dollars.

It is firmly established that all actions of the General Assembly are presumed to be constitutional. * * * Therefore, the party assailing the legislation has the burden of proving that it is unconstitutional * * *, and if a reasonable doubt exists as to a statute's constitutionality, the doubt must be resolved in favor of its validity * * *.

One of Wilson's primary contentions is that § 8.01-581.15 violates her right under the Virginia Constitution to a trial by jury. * * *

Without question, the jury's fact-finding function extends to the assessment of damages. * * * Once the jury has ascertained the facts and assessed the damages, however, the constitutional mandate is satisfied. * * * Thereafter, it is the duty of the court to apply the law to the facts. * * *

The limitation on medical malpractice recoveries contained in § 8.01-581.15 does nothing more than establish the outer limits of a remedy provided by the General Assembly. A remedy is a matter of law, not a matter of fact. * * * A trial court applies the remedy's limitation only after the jury has fulfilled its fact-finding function. Thus, § 8.01-581.15 does not infringe upon the right to a jury trial because the section does not apply until after a jury has completed its assigned function in the judicial process.

* * *

Wilson also contends that § 8.01-581.15 violates the constitutional guarantee of due process. The due process clauses of the federal and Virginia Constitutions provide that no person shall be deprived of life, liberty, or property without due process of law. U.S. Const. amend. XIV, § 1; Va. Const. art. I, § 11. Both procedural and substantive rights are protected by the due process clauses.

* * * Wilson bases her claim of a due process violation solely upon the irrebuttable presumption rationale. She contends that she has been "deprived of an effective opportunity to be heard, since [§ 8.01-581.15] purports to preordain the result of the hearing." Thus, she asserts, the statute "creates a conclusive presumption that no plaintiff's damages exceed $750,000." * * *

* * * Wilson has not been denied reasonable notice and a meaningful opportunity to be heard. Section 8.01-581.15 has no effect upon

Wilson's right to have a jury or court render an individual decision based upon the merits of her case. * * * The section merely affects the parameters of the remedy available to Wilson after the merits of her claim have been decided. We hold, therefore, that Wilson's constitutional guarantee of procedural due process has not been violated.

The effect of § 8.01–581.15 on the remedy available to Wilson likewise is not violative of any substantive due process right. [A] party has no fundamental right to a particular remedy or a full recovery in tort. A statutory limitation on recovery is simply an economic regulation, which is entitled to wide judicial deference. * * * Because § 8.01–581.15 is such a regulation and infringes upon no fundamental right, the section must be upheld if it is reasonably related to a legitimate governmental purpose.

* * * The purpose of § 8.01–581.15—to maintain adequate health care services in this Commonwealth—bears a reasonable relation to the legislative cap—ensuring that health care providers can obtain affordable medical malpractice insurance. We hold, therefore, that substantive due process has not been violated.

Wilson further contends that § 8.01–581.15 violates the doctrine of separation of powers set forth in Article III, § 1 of the Virginia Constitution. That constitutional provision states, inter alia, that "[t]he legislative, executive, and judicial departments shall be separate and distinct, so that none exercise the powers properly belonging to the others." * * *

[W]hether the remedy prescribed in § 8.01–581.15 is viewed as a modification of the common law or as establishing the jurisdiction of the courts in specific cases, clearly it was a proper exercise of legislative power. Indeed, were a court to ignore the legislatively determined remedy and enter an award in excess of the permitted amount, the court would invade the province of the legislature. Accordingly, we hold that § 8.01–581.15 does not violate the separation of powers doctrine.

* * *

Wilson also claims that § 8.01–581.15 violates Article IV, § 14, which provides, in pertinent part, that "[t]he General Assembly shall not enact any local, special, or private law * * * [g]ranting to any private corporation, association, or individual any special or exclusive right, privilege, or immunity." Wilson argues that § 8.01–581.15 "purports to confer special privileges and immunities upon a small segment of the population—physicians and their insurers—while at the same time arbitrarily distinguishing between severely injured victims of medical malpractice and less severely injured malpractice claimants as well as all other tort plaintiffs." We do not agree.

* * *

According the legislation the presumption of validity to which it is entitled, we conclude that the classification is not arbitrary and bears a reasonable and substantial relation to the object sought to be accomplished by the legislation. We further conclude that the legislation applies to all persons belonging to the class without distinction and, therefore, is not special in effect. Accordingly, we hold that § 8.01–581.15 does not violate the prohibition against special legislation.

In Wilson's final constitutional attack upon § 8.01–581.15, she contends that it violates the Equal Protection Clause in the Fourteenth Amendment to the federal Constitution. That clause provides in pertinent part that no state shall "deny to any person * * * the equal protection of the laws." U.S. Const. amend. XIV, § 1.

To withstand an equal protection challenge, a classification that neither infringes upon a fundamental right nor creates a suspect class must satisfy the "rational basis" test. * * *

* * * Section 8.01–581.15 was enacted only after a thorough study had been made of the problem. The General Assembly made specific findings and a legislative judgment as to how the problem could be best addressed. Bearing in mind that the General Assembly is presumed to have acted within its constitutional powers and according its action the presumption of validity to which it is entitled, we cannot say that the means the General Assembly chose to promote a legitimate state purpose are unreasonable or arbitrary. Accordingly, we hold that the classification does not violate the Equal Protection Clause.

* * * Wilson contends that the limit of $750,000 imposed by § 8.01–581.15 "applied as to each health care provider"; therefore, Wilson says she is entitled to recover $1,500,000. * * *

The statute provides that "[i]n any verdict returned against a health care provider in an action for malpractice * * * *the total amount recoverable for any injury to * * * a patient* shall not exceed seven hundred fifty thousand dollars." (Emphasis added.) Wilson's claim was for an indivisible injury * * * caused by the concurring negligence of each defendant. Giving § 8.01–581.15 its plain meaning, we hold that Wilson's damages are limited to a total of $750,000.

[W]e will affirm the trial court's judgment.

RUSSELL, JUSTICE, dissenting. * * *

The General Assembly enacted § 8.01–581.15 with the salutary legislative purpose of providing a remedy for a perceived social problem, the unavailability of medical malpractice insurance at affordable rates. Yet the unintended consequence of the Act was the creation of a class, described as "health care providers," clothed with a special privilege in the courts. Alone among the multitudes of corporations, associations, groups, and individuals who are daily subjected to tort actions in the courts, the members of this privileged elite (and those who insure them) are granted a special immunity from all damages exceeding $750,000 (now $1,000,000). All defendants not falling within the favored class lack that shield and must pay the full amount a jury may decide to award.

The other side of this unhappy equation is that § 8.01–581.15 creates a corresponding disfavored class—those who are so unfortunate as to suffer injury as a result of the negligence of a "health care provider." Their right to recover damages is limited by the Act while those injured by the torts of accountants, airlines, architects, barbers, bandits, banks, bus drivers, cooks, dog owners, engineers, financial advisors, horse trainers, golfers, hotel keepers, inebriates, jailors, kidnappers, lawyers, etc., retain an unlimited right of redress in the courts. This is precisely the kind of economic favoritism at which the special-laws prohibitions were aimed. * * *

It may be argued that the legislature, perceiving a problem, need not attempt its resolution at one stroke, but may move against it piecemeal. Thus, it would be constitutionally permissible to legislate with respect to the "liability crisis" within the field of health care at one session, to turn to the plight of municipalities at the next, and to other professions, businesses, and occupations at another. Fair enough. But the General Assembly enacted the Medical Malpractice Act in 1976, and has made no other discernible approach to the problem as it might affect others subject to the "liability crisis" in the courts during the ensuing twelve years. The special protection granted to the narrowly defined class of "health care providers" stands alone: a unique monument to the effectiveness of a particularly vocal group which sought and found a privileged position in the courts.

* * *

THOMAS, J., and POFF, SENIOR JUSTICE, join in dissent.[35]

Note on Collateral Sources

The general judge-made rule in personal injury litigation is that the plaintiff can "keep" the money that comes in from accident and disability insurance paid for by the plaintiff; outside sources of funds like insurance are "collateral" to money that the defendant owes to the plaintiff, and so collateral source funds are not deducted from the defendant's judgment. These outside funds indemnify the insured plaintiff for economic damages. It has occurred to persons who are interested in changing the medical liability litigation system that there is an aspect of double recovery where both insurers and the defendant health care provider pay some of the same economic damages, and some states have enacted statutes that try to abolish the overlap.

Two cases decided the same year tested two collateral source statutes, applying both the federal and state requirements for constitutional validity, and the two courts came out with opposite conclusions on rather different statutes.

35. Editors' Note: In Boyd v. Bulala, 877 F.2d 1191 (4th Cir.1989), the court of appeals held that the Virginia cap did not violate the Seventh Amendment right to jury trial or federal separation of powers or due process and equal protection rights. The cap has been raised to $1 million as to claims arising after Oct. 1, 1983. 1983 Va. Acts ch. 496.

In Baker v. Vanderbilt Univ.,[36] the Tennessee statute read as follows:

> Tenn.Code Ann. § 29-26-119. In a malpractice action in which liability is admitted or established, the damages awarded may include (in addition to other elements of damages authorized by law) actual economic losses suffered by the claimant by reason of the personal injury, including, but not limited to cost of reasonable and necessary medical care, rehabilitation services, and custodial care, loss of services and loss of earned income, but only to the extent that such costs are not paid or payable and such losses are not replaced, or indemnified in whole or in part, by insurance provided by an employer either governmental or private, by social security benefits, service benefit programs, unemployment benefits, or any other source except the assets of the claimants or of the members of the claimants' immediate family and insurance purchased in whole or in part, privately and individually.

The federal judge responded to the plaintiffs' challenge on federal equal protection grounds by applying the least-demanding "rational basis" test, finding the statute constitutional as economic and social legislation. He held that the same test also validated the statute under the Tennessee constitution, under the reasoning of a recent Tennessee supreme court decision on another statute in the state's medical liability package.

In Wentling v. Medical Anesthesia Services, P.A.,[37] the statute as follows:

> Kan.Stat.Ann. § 60-471(a). In any action for damages for personal injuries or death arising out of the rendering of or the failure to render professional services by any health care provider, evidence of any reimbursement or indemnification received by a party for damages sustained from such injury or death, excluding payments from insurance paid for in whole or in part by such party or his or her employer, and services provided by a health maintenance organization to treat any such injury, excluding services paid for in whole or in part by such party or his or her employer, shall be admissible for consideration by the trier of fact * * *. Such evidence shall be accorded such weight as the trier of fact shall choose to ascribe to that evidence in determining the amount of damages to be awarded to such party.

Kansas comprises a single federal district. Two District of Kansas judges in three prior cases had tested this statute, dividing on its validity under the equal protection clauses of the United States and Kansas constitutions. A majority of the Kansas supreme court sided with the reasoning of the federal judge who found the act unconstitutional,[38] illustrating its reasoning in this paragraph;

> Assume a married couple is injured in the same catastrophe. They are both treated by the same health care provider with disastrous results. The husband is employed and his employer provides health insurance. The wife is not gainfully employed. In separate actions for similar treatment provided by the same health care provider as a

---

36. 616 F.Supp. 330 (M.D.Tenn.1985).

37. 237 Kan. 503, 701 P.2d 939 (1985) (5 to 2).

38. Doran v. Priddy, 534 F.Supp. 30 (D.Kan.1981).

result of the same catastrophe, the fact that the wife's medical expenses were paid by insurance is proper evidence to submit to the jury but the same evidence as it applies to the husband is not. Such a distinction makes no sense whatsoever.[39]

In 1985 the Kansas legislature repealed § 60–471 and replaced it with a new act.

JACKSON v. UNITED STATES
United States Court of Appeals for the Ninth Circuit, 1989.
881 F.2d 707.

WIGGINS, CIRCUIT JUDGE. * * *

Appellants retained attorney Wesley H. Harris to represent them in a suit arising from alleged medical malpractice in the care and treatment of appellant Richard Jackson at the San Diego Naval Hospital. The initial contract between appellants and their attorney provided for fees of 25% of any recovery, the maximum allowed for any judgments rendered under the Federal Tort Claims Act (FTCA). See 28 U.S.C.A. § 2678. After a bench trial on the issue of liability alone, the district court ruled in favor of appellants and requested that the parties hold a settlement conference to determine the amount of damages. The parties agreed to settle the case for $1,300,000. The attorney fees under the original contract would have been $325,000 (25% percent of $1,300,000), but appellants and their attorney agreed to a lower fee of $248,000, which represented a compromise between the maximum allowed by federal law and the maximum allowed by California law. See Cal.Bus. & Prof.Code § 6146.[40]

The government disputed the attorney's entitlement to fees exceeding that allowed by California law.[41] Rather than allow the settlement

---

39. Wentling v. Medical Anesthesia Services, P.A., 701 P.2d at 950.

40. Editors' Note: In Roa v. Lodi Medical Group, Inc., 37 Cal.3d 920, 211 Cal. Rptr. 77, 695 P.2d 164 (1985) (4 to 3), the court found this part of MICRA constitutional against attacks based on due process, equal protection, and separation of powers. The dissenters saw federal First Amendment and state constitutional problems with inhibiting plaintiffs' access to the courts through the contingent fee system, a system that the opinion discussed at length. The Supreme Court dismissed the plaintiffs' appeal for want of a substantial federal question. 474 U.S. 990, 106 S.Ct. 421, 88 L.Ed.2d 352 (1985) (Justices Brennan and White dissented). See Annot., Validity of Statute Establishing Contingent Fee Scale for Attorneys Representing Parties in Medical Malpractice Actions, 12 A.L.R.4th 23 (1982).

41. The allowable attorney fee under the state statute based on the settlement amount of $1,300,000 is calculated as follows:

40% of the first $50,000 =	$ 20,000
33⅓% of the next $50,000 =	16,667
25% of the next $100,000 =	25,000
10% of any amount exceeding 200,000 (here, $1,100,000) =	110,000
	$171,667.

* * *

The California legislature amended § 6146 in 1987 by increasing allowable fees in medical malpractice cases so that attorneys are entitled to collect up to 25% of any amount recovered between $100,000 and $600,000 and 15% of any amount recovered exceeding $600,000. Appellants' attorney would be entitled to $266,666.66 under the terms of the revised statute, but the revisions did not become effective until January 1, 1988.

agreement to collapse, however, the parties stipulated to a judicial resolution of the attorney fees dispute. The government then sought a ruling from the district court that would restrict appellants' attorney from collecting more than the maximum fee allowed under California law. * * * The court * * * granted the government's motion and entered an order preventing appellants' attorney from collecting more than $171,667. * * *

Issues arising from actions brought under the FTCA are, obviously, governed by federal law. But federal law specifically makes state law controlling to the extent needed to fix the government's substantive liability. See 28 U.S.C.A. §§ 2674 * * * [and] 1346(b) * * *. At the same time, issues not affecting the government's substantive liability are determined solely by federal law; at most, state law provides only an interpretive guide to the outcome of these issues. * * * The government asserts that these provisions require application of the California statute. To agree with this proposition we must conclude that a limitation on attorney fees somehow relates to the government's substantive liability. We do not find any of the government's arguments for reaching this conclusion persuasive.

* * *

The government asserts alternatively that California has the power to regulate attorney fees generally, and that its statute applies notwithstanding the fact that attorney fees are not part of the government's substantive liability. Appellants counter that the state statute is preempted by its federal counterpart. * * *

Section 2678 unambiguously permits an attorney to collect on a contingency fee basis up to 25% of the recovery. The legislative history to this provision indicates that anything less than 25% is deemed to be a matter of private negotiation between the attorney and his client. * * * We believe that permitting states to regulate within this private sphere is contrary to the intent of Congress. * * * We therefore hold that California's statute is preempted to the extent that it purports to limit the amount of attorney fees that can be collected from a client who recovers in an action brought under the FTCA.

Accordingly, the judgment of the district court is reversed. Both parties are to bear their own costs on appeal.

Chapter 12

ACCESS TO HIGH-QUALITY HEALTH SERVICES

INTRODUCTORY NOTE

Within the memory of doctors still in practice, family doctors treated their patients in homes and offices, referred them to friendly specialists, and got the patients back again when the specialists were through. Hospitals were hotels where physicians practiced medicine and surgeons practiced surgery. Access to medical services was primarily the private responsibility of medical practitioners, who provided a lot of professional services for reduced fees or for nothing. The quality of doctors' services rested upon the opinions of other doctors, who controlled membership in private organizations such as county medical societies and voluntary hospital staffs. State boards of medical examiners conferred but rarely took away licenses to practice medicine and surgery. "Lay intermediaries" of various kinds paid some of the patients' bills, ran the hospitals, and raised the tax funds for the care of indigents.

Times have changed, mainly in the direction of organized review of patients' care and doctors' performance by organizations that are not controlled by peers whom the doctors know well. Licensure agencies now have disciplinary functions; accreditation of facilities now involves a wide array of medical care activities; certification of specialized knowledge and skills takes up where licensure left off.

Nothing illustrates the changes better than the rise since 1951 of a private accreditation agency, the Joint Commission on Accreditation of Healthcare Organizations.[1] The Commission is "joint" because it was created by the American College of Surgeons, the American College of Physicians, the American Hospital Association, and (with reluctance) the American Medical Association.

---

1. See Jost, The Joint Commission on Accreditation of Hospitals: Private Regulation of Health Care and the Public Interest, 24 B.C.L.Rev. 835 (1983). The commission changed its name slightly in 1988.

The Joint Commission was and is a not-for-profit corporation rather than a government agency. From its initial concern with hospital facilities and non-physician staffing, the Joint Commission expanded into medical staff membership and organization, and now it also looks at mechanisms for the prevention of claims, the assessment of patient care outcomes, and the appropriateness of care provided. The expansion of interests has coincided with enlarged public financing for health care services and with the greatly enhanced powers of institutions over the way doctors practice. The Joint Commission performs essential accrediting functions for federal and state funding agencies, and had it not existed already, governments would have had to create it. Its key document, the Accreditation Manual for Hospitals, is the basic checklist for accreditation surveys, but inevitably it also serves as the skeleton for organizing hospitals,[2] and incidentally it is a valuable checklist for attorneys in medical liability practice.

The practice of medicine and surgery today is full of new occupations and organizations, and new terms, acronyms, and abbreviations. For example, the doctor is one of many "health care providers." Three other terms of recent coinage express both the central place of institutions in health care and the ways in which institutions respond to problems of business management in the health care setting. All have implications for medical liability, and all have been impelled to some extent by legal considerations.

First, "risk management," which originated in the insurance context, is intended to prevent legal claims against health care providers, including not only medical liability claims of patients, but also premises liability claims of patients and visitors, and workers' compensation claims of employees. Incident reports are intended to flag dangerous conditions and practices for correction, whether a claim arose or not.

Second, "quality assurance" establishes organizational structures, operational processes, and individual assessments of outcomes that address the patient care delivered by all health care providers—physicians, technicians, nurses, and other physician extenders. The objectives are to set performance standards, to detect persons who do not meet the standards, and to sanction persons who cannot perform satisfactorily.

Third, "utilization review" introduces the concept of managed care, which is intended to reduce the capacity of the patient's attending doctor to order medically unnecessary services (including defensive medicine) or services provided in an overly expensive setting. The

---

2. The 1989 Manual listed Standards for these units of health care organizations: alcoholism and other drug dependence services, diagnostic radiology services, dietetic services, emergency services, governing body, hospital-sponsored ambulatory care services, infection control, management and administrative services, medical record services, medical staff, nuclear medicine services, nursing services, pathology and medical laboratory services, pharmaceutical services, physical rehabilitation services, plant, technology, and safety management, professional library services, quality assurance, radiation oncology services, respiratory care services, social work services, special care units, surgical and anesthesia services, and utilization review.

primary objective is to hold down costs, but it is accompanied by the risk that economic considerations will reduce the quality and timeliness of clinical judgments.

The three phrases characterize an entire course that is very timely but quite different from medical liability, the course in health care delivery. This chapter looks at the health care delivery from the viewpoint of medical liability, sampling the liability-producing aspects of contemporary health care delivery systems.

SECTION A. ACCESS TO SERVICES

RITTER v. WAYNE COUNTY GEN. HOSP.
Court of Appeals of Michigan, 1988.
174 Mich.App. 490, 436 N.W.2d 673, leave to appeal denied.

PER CURIAM.

Plaintiff appeals as of right from separate orders entered granting summary disposition to defendants Wayne County General Hospital (WCG) and Detroit Osteopathic Hospital Corporation (DOH) and dismissing defendants as party defendants.

On March 17, 1984, plaintiff's decedent, Melvin Ritter, presented himself to the emergency room of Northwest General Hospital. In her complaint, plaintiff alleges that on March 17, 1984, WCG had "refused to accept Melvin Ritter because of 'no beds' available." According to the discharge summary from Northwest General Hospital, Ritter complained of fever and chills, diminished appetite, weakness, and diarrhea. Ritter was an intravenous drug user and underwent aortic valve replacement surgery in 1982. A series of tests were performed on Ritter and he was treated for probable infective endocarditis. A decision was made to transfer Ritter to defendant DOH "for more vigorous treatment." Ritter, who had no medical insurance at the time, was refused admittance by DOH and Henry Ford Hospital. Ritter underwent further treatment at Northwest General.

On March 28, a physician at Henry Ford Hospital again refused to accept Ritter, but stated he would accept him as a transfer through the emergency room at Henry Ford. Ritter was transferred that day, underwent open heart surgery, never regained consciousness, and died on April 6, 1984.

Plaintiff sought damages for defendants' alleged wrongful refusal to admit Ritter as a patient. * * * In granting defendants' respective motions for summary disposition, the trial court found there was no duty on the part of defendants to provide services to Ritter. On appeal plaintiff argues that the trial court erred in determining that, as a matter of law, defendants had no duty to admit Ritter.

Where there is no legal duty, there can be no actionable negligence.
* * *

Plaintiff first contends that the trial court erred in failing to find that the Hill–Burton Act, 42 U.S.C.A. §§ 291 et seq., obliged defendants to admit Ritter.

The Hill–Burton Act was enacted in 1946. The stated purpose of the Act was to assist the several states to survey the need for construction of hospitals and develop programs for the construction of public and nonprofit hospitals as will, with existing facilities, "afford the necessary physical facilities for furnishing adequate hospital, clinic, and similar services to all their people" and "to construct public and other nonprofit hospitals in accordance with such programs." Hospital Survey and Construction Act of 1946, Pub.L. No. 725, § 601, 60 Stat. 1040, 1041. Newsom v. Vanderbilt Univ., 653 F.2d 1100, 1104 (6th Cir. 1981).

Under the Hill–Burton Act, as amended, and federal regulations promulgated pursuant to the act, hospitals which accept federal funds under the act are required in exchange to guarantee that the facility will be available to all persons residing in the area and that a "reasonable volume of uncompensated services" will be provided to persons unable to pay for them. 42 U.S.C.A. § 291c(e)(1). Once a reasonable volume of uncompensated services is provided to local residents, the hospital may deny uncompensated care to future patients, except in the case of emergency services. 42 C.F.R. §§ 124.603(a)(1) and (b)(1). The term "emergency services" is not defined by the subchapter which includes 42 C.F.R. § 124.603, and research discloses no case law construing the provision in this context. A related definition, however, is set forth in a different part of the federal regulations dealing with grants for training and emergency medical services. 42 C.F.R. § 57.2103 defines "emergency medical services" as "services used in responding to the perceived individual need for immediate medical care in order to prevent loss of life or aggravation of physiological or psychological illness or injury."

According to plaintiff's complaint, defendant WCG refused to accept Ritter on March 17, 1984, because there were no beds available. A facility is not in violation of its community service assurance under the Hill–Burton Act where it refuses service on account of the unavailability of the needed service in the facility. 42 C.F.R. § 124.603(a)(1). Summary disposition in favor of defendant WCG was appropriate under Mich.Civ.R. 2.116(C)(8). * * *

Nor do we believe that plaintiff has created a genuine issue of material fact as to the issue of defendant DOH's refusal to provide emergency services to Ritter. The cases cited by amicus curiae are inapposite because they all concern hospitals' refusals to render emergency services to individuals who first appeared in their alleged emergency condition at the defendant hospital. None of the cited cases involve the liability of an attempted transferee hospital.

* * *

The remaining federal regulations and Michigan statutes cited by plaintiff do not give rise to a duty to treat Ritter. The federal regulations concern standards for hospital certification for Medicaid reimbursement while the Michigan statutes generally provide the scope of rule-making authority at the Department of Public Health. The cited provisions are inapplicable to this case.

In the second count of her complaint, plaintiff asserted a right to relief under 42 U.S.C.A. § 1983.

> To establish a right to relief under § 1983, a plaintiff must plead and prove two elements: (1) that he has been deprived of a right secured by the Constitution and laws of the United States; and (2) that defendant, deprived him of this right while acting under color of law. * * * Moore v. City of Detroit, 128 Mich.App. 491, 340 N.W.2d 640, 644 (1983).

The actions of a private entity do not become state action merely because the government provides substantial funding to the private party or because the entity is subject to extensive state regulation. *Newsom* at 1113–1116. In order to invoke the state action doctrine, a complaining party must demonstrate a sufficient nexus between the challenged action and the regulatory scheme alleged to be the impetus behind the private action. Crowder v. Conlan, 740 F.2d 447, 451 (6th Cir.1984). We seriously question whether plaintiff could satisfy the state action requirement of a § 1983 cause of action. *Newsom, Crowder.* However, we find it unnecessary to consider this issue because plaintiff's claim fails to satisfy even the first element of a cause of action under § 1983. Where defendants had no obligation to admit Ritter as a patient for treatment, defendants' refusal to do so cannot constitute a deprivation of rights secured by the United States Constitution and federal law.

Accordingly, because we agree with the trial court that the defendants had no duty to admit Ritter, we hold that summary disposition was properly granted to defendants.

REID v. INDIANAPOLIS OSTEOPATHIC MEDICAL HOSP., INC.

United States District Court for the Southern District of Indiana, 1989.
709 F.Supp. 853.

BARKER, DISTRICT JUDGE.

This case presents an issue of apparent first impression. On September 5, 1986, Ralph and Lillian Reid were involved in a serious accident and Mrs. Reid was brought to the emergency room of the defendant, [Indianapolis Osteopathic Medical Hosp., Inc., doing business as] Westview Hospital. After being examined and treated by certain physicians at the hospital, arrangements were made to transfer Mrs. Reid to Methodist Hospital in Indianapolis. Sometime after Mrs. Reid was admitted to Methodist Hospital, she died.

The plaintiff brought this action claiming that Westview had failed to provide Mrs. Reid appropriate medical care, had failed to provide her the necessary stabilizing treatment, and had transferred her to Methodist Hospital before her condition had properly stabilized. The complaint was filed under a relatively new federal statute designed to deter "patient dumping." 42 U.S.C.A. § 1395dd (hereinafter "§ 1395dd").[3] The term "patient dumping" is used to refer to the practice of those hospitals which, despite being capable of providing the needed medical care, send patients to other facilities or turn patients away because those patients are unable to pay.

As an enforcement mechanism, § 1395dd creates, inter alia, a private cause of action against a hospital that improperly transfers a patient. The language of this federal statute, however, incorporates state standards to delineate the damages that would be available through such a civil action:

> Any individual who suffers personal harm as a direct result of a participating hospital's violation of * * * [this statute] may, in a civil action against the * * * hospital, *obtain those damages available for personal injury under the law of the state in which the hospital is located,* and such equitable relief as is appropriate. 42 U.S.C.A. § 1395dd(d)(3)(A). (Emphasis added.)

In Indiana, medical malpractice actions are statutorily limited in two different ways: they are limited procedurally, see Ind.Code § 16–9.5–9–2 (stating that "[n]o action against a health care provider may be commenced in any court of this state before the claimant's proposed complaint has been presented to a medical review panel established pursuant to this chapter and an opinion is rendered by the panel"), and they are limited in the amount of damages they may seek, see Ind.Code § 16–9.5–2–2(b) (stating that a "health care provider qualified under this article is not liable for an amount in excess of one hundred thousand dollars [$100,000] for an occurrence of malpractice").

The defendant has moved to dismiss Mr. Reid's complaint * * *. Westview argues that the complaint fails to state a claim upon which relief can be granted because the plaintiff's allegations fall within the scope of the Indiana Medical Malpractice Act, and the plaintiff has admittedly not filed his proposed complaint with the medical review panel as Indiana Code § 16–9.5–9–2 would require. * * *

[T]he court finds that even if § 1395dd(d)(3)(A) could reasonably be read as calling for the general incorporation of state procedural restrictions, such incorporation of Indiana's statute would be barred by the preemption clause of § 1395dd(f). The Indiana Code's provision that no cause of action against a health care provider arises until an opinion has been rendered by the state medical review panel "directly conflicts" with § 1395dd's provision that such a cause of action arises whenever "[a]ny individual * * * suffers personal harm as a direct result of a

---

3. Editors' Note: The statute was enacted in 1986. See Note, Preventing Patient Dumping: Sharpening the COBRA's Fangs, 61 N.Y.U.L.Rev. 1186 (1986).

participating hospital's violation of a requirement of this section." 42 U.S.C.A. § 1395dd(d)(3)(A).

Furthermore, at oral argument the defendant conceded that the Indiana Medical Malpractice Act was based on a negligence standard, whereas the federal anti-dumping statute was based on a strict liability standard. Thus, if the Indiana medical review panel were permitted to screen Mr. Reid's complaint before it could be properly presented to this court, the panel's determination of whether or not Mr. Reid stated a valid claim under the state's negligence standard would, at best, be totally irrelevant to this court's determination of whether Westview violated § 1395dd. At worst, the panel's opinion that Mr. Reid failed to state a valid claim could "directly conflict" with the strict liability standards of the federal statute—further justifying preemption under § 1395dd(f).

On the other hand, the court finds equally untenable the plaintiff's position that § 1395dd(d)(3)(A) should be read as not incorporating any of the provisions of the Indiana medical malpractice statute. According to the plaintiff, § 1395dd(d)(3)(A) expressly incorporates the state's measure of damages for "personal injury"—and this general term should not be read as meaning "personal injury due to medical malpractice."

* * *

[I]t is entirely reasonable to read the language of § 1395dd(d)(3)(A) as incorporating state law caps on medical malpractice damages: the federal statute states that individual plaintiffs can only "obtain those damages available for personal injury under the law of the state," and in those states (such as Indiana) with restrictive medical malpractice statutes, the amount of damages that would be "available" for a personal injury claim against a health care provider would be only those damages available under that medical malpractice statute itself.

* * *

In light of the above analysis, the court hereby denies the defendant's motion to dismiss Mr. Reid's complaint made on the grounds that the plaintiff failed, pursuant to Indiana Code § 16–9.5–9–2, to present his proposed complaint to Indiana's medical review panel prior to commencing the present action. In addition, all future action in this case relating to the measure of plaintiff's damages under the Act, if any, shall be subject to the analysis and holding in this entry.

SECTION B. UTILIZATION REVIEW

CASSIM v. BOWEN

United States Court of Appeals for the Ninth Circuit, 1987.
824 F.2d 791.

SKOPIL, CIRCUIT JUDGE. * * *

M.M. Cassim is a licensed and practicing surgeon in Dallas, Oregon. Forty percent of the income from his practice comes from Medicare patients. In early 1985 the Oregon Medical Professional Review Organization (OMPRO) initiated a routine review of the quality of Cassim's surgical care. OMPRO has a contract with the [United States] Department of Health and Human Services (HHS)[4] to operate as the Medicare peer review organization for the State of Oregon.

After its initial review OMPRO decided to examine all surgery performed by Cassim during a prior six-month period. In April 1985 OMPRO informed Cassim and the hospital where he practiced of its review. OMPRO checked the medical records of 80 of Cassim's patients and identified 13 "gross and flagrant" violations of Cassim's obligation under the Social Security Act to adhere to professionally recognized standards.

In making its investigation, OMPRO did not discuss the cases with Cassim. Nor did it contact any of the patients, the attending nurses, the other physicians involved in the care of the patients, or the hospital's quality assurance committee. Finally, OMPRO did not seek a complete copy of all medical records related to the care of the patients. It lacked some x-rays, scans, and other lab data.

On October 30, 1985, OMPRO informed Cassim of its findings. It listed the patient records it had examined and provided Cassim with its analysis and conclusions. OMPRO gave Cassim 30 days to submit information to "rebut or mitigate" its findings and allowed him to make a "written request to meet with representatives of OMPRO to discuss case specifics." OMPRO warned him that its preliminary recommendation was exclusion from the Medicare program.

Cassim then met with OMPRO's surgical review panel and medical director. OMPRO did not allow Cassim to present witnesses or to confront adverse witnesses. Cassim was, however, represented by counsel. A transcript was made of the meeting. Cassim presented his side of the story and introduced exculpatory documentation, including lab data missing from OMPRO's records. The OMPRO panel questioned him on the techniques he had used in caring for his patients. After the meeting, "based on the additional information * * * [Cassim] provided," OMPRO dropped 5 of the 13 alleged violations.

OMPRO recommended to the Office of Inspector General (OIG) of HHS that Cassim be suspended from the Medicare program for a minimum of one year and informed Cassim of its recommendation. It told him that he had 30 days to submit to OIG "any additional material which affects the recommendation to exclude you from participation in the Medicare program." Cassim, through his attorney, took advantage of this opportunity to defend himself and submitted additional material.

Notwithstanding Cassim's efforts, OIG affirmed OMPRO's findings. * * * It excluded Cassim from Medicare for one year and informed

---

4. Editors' Note: Defendant Otis Bowen was then Secretary of Health & Human Services.

him it would publish "a notice in a local newspaper to advise the community of the effective date, the duration, and the reason for this exclusion." See 42 U.S.C.A. § 1320c–5(b)(2); 42 C.F.R. § 1004.100. Finally, OIG told Cassim of his right to appeal the ruling to an administrative law judge (ALJ). See 42 U.S.C.A. § 1320c–5(b)(4); 42 C.F.R. § 1004.130. Neither the Social Security Act nor its regulations guarantee the timeliness of the hearing on appeal.

Cassim then sought a preliminary injunction in district court. He argued that the Act and its regulations violated due process (1) in not providing for a full-blown pre-exclusion and pre-publication (pre-deprivation) ALJ hearing, and (2) in not guaranteeing the promptness of a post-exclusion and post-publication (post-deprivation) hearing. The district court held that it had jurisdiction over Cassim's action but denied the preliminary injunction. Cassim timely appealed. We granted a stay pending the appeal.

Title 42 U.S.C.A. § 405(g) provides a claimant who has exhausted an agency's administrative process with the right to obtain judicial review. * * *

* * * We conclude that Cassim fulfilled the jurisdictional requirements of § 405(g).

A party seeking a preliminary injunction must fulfill one of two standards * * *. Under the traditional standard, a court may issue preliminary relief if it finds that (1) the moving party will suffer irreparable injury if the relief is denied; (2) the moving party will probably prevail on the merits; (3) the balance of potential harm favors the moving party; and (4) the public interest favors granting relief. * * *. Under the alternative standard, the moving party may meet its burden by demonstrating either (1) a combination of probable success and the possibility of irreparable injury, or (2) that serious questions are raised and the balance of hardships tips sharply in its favor. * * *

The district court held that Cassim failed to satisfy either standard. Under the traditional standard, the court found that Cassim had neither established that he would probably prevail on the merits, nor that the balance of potential harm favored him. Under the alternative standard, it ruled that (1) Cassim raised serious questions, but the balance of hardships did not tip sharply in his favor; and (2) Cassim demonstrated the possibility of irreparable injury, but not the probability of success on the merits.

Cassim challenges the district court's analysis under the alternative standard. * * *

Cassim argues that the district court improperly balanced the hardships. First, he emphasizes that his livelihood, reputation, and professional career will be irreparably harmed. He contends the stigma of exclusion and publication could not be removed even if the ALJ completely exonerated him. Second, he asserts that the district court mistakenly believed he threatened the lives or health of his patients. Instead, he claims, OIG accused him of skillfully performing excessive surgery.

We reject Cassim's argument even though we recognize the possibility of irreparable harm created by the Secretary's sanctions. Cassim is simply mistaken in asserting that HHS did not believe he threatened the health of his patients. OIG charged Cassim with doing unnecessary surgery in eight cases culled from a six-month period. In those eight cases, Cassim's patients ranged in age from 66 to 86. In each case, OIG concluded that Cassim had placed his patients in "high risk" situations or in "imminent danger." The Secretary persuasively argues that unnecessary surgery on elderly patients endangers their health.

Against the harm Cassim might suffer we must balance the harm his patients might suffer. We affirm the district court's finding that the balance of hardships neither tips sharply in Cassim's favor nor favors him. Cassim fails under one prong of the alternative standard.

Under the other prong, he must demonstrate a combination of probable success and the possibility of irreparable injury. Cassim has shown the possibility of irreparable injury. * * *

Cassim alleges that as a matter of due process he is entitled to a full-blown pre-deprivation hearing. He also contends that the Social Security Act and its regulations violate due process because they fail to guarantee the promptness of the post-deprivation hearing. * * *[5]

We assume, arguendo, that Cassim has implicated either a property right or a liberty interest. * * *

Cassim's interests are substantial. * * * On the one hand, only 40% percent of Cassim's income comes from Medicare. * * * Cassim may still treat Medicare patients. If he prevails in his administrative appeal, he must be reimbursed. A successful appeal would also help restore his reputation and practice. The Secretary would have to reinstate Cassim as a Medicare participating physician, 42 C.F.R. § 1004.120(b), and give notice of his reinstatement to the public. 42 C.F.R. § 1001.134(a)(2). On the other hand, even that vindication may not remove all of the stigma associated with the Secretary's sanctions. Some damage might remain. Cassim's patients and members of the public may distrust him.

The Government's interests, however, are compelling. In the judgment of OMPRO and OIG, Cassim performed unnecessary surgery. Such surgery wastes public resources and, even more important, threatens the patient's health. OIG found that Cassim placed his patients in situations with the "potential for * * * harm." In enacting 42 U.S.C.A. § 1320c–5, Congress sought to protect Medicare beneficiaries from questionable medical practices. As an indication of the extent of

---

5. As part of his argument on the probability of success on the merits, Cassim asserts that the ALJ will probably reduce or reverse OIG's sanction. This argument misses the point. The "merits" at issue involve the due process claim, not whether OIG properly sanctioned Cassim.

Congress' concern, if the Secretary fails to act within 120 days of a peer review organization's recommendation, then the physician being investigated is automatically excluded from Medicare. 42 U.S.C.A. § 1320c–5(b)(1). Requiring full-blown pre-deprivation hearings would frustrate Congress' intent and impede the Secretary's ability to act quickly.[6] It would also impose significant administrative costs.

* * * Cassim * * * contends * * * that the statute and its regulations violate due process in failing to guarantee a timely post-deprivation hearing. The Secretary has represented that an ALJ decision could be reached four or five months after Cassim requests a hearing. Cassim does not challenge the constitutionality of the four or five month time period. Instead, he launches a facial attack on the statute and its regulations.

* * * Cassim's suspension from Medicare is for one year. He could receive an ALJ decision four or five months after he requests a hearing. Thus, he will put HHS to its proof before he suffers the full penalty imposed. Cassim may even be able to receive an expedited hearing. Moreover, the ALJ is not authorized to delay issuing an order after a hearing. * * *

* * * We vacate the temporary stay. The district court's denial of the motion for preliminary injunction is affirmed.

WICKLINE v. STATE

California Court of Appeal, 1986.
192 Cal.App.3d 1630, 239 Cal.Rptr. 810, review dismissed.[7]

ROWEN, ASSOCIATE JUSTICE. * * *

[Lois J. Wickline sued the State of California as administrator of the Medi–Cal Act, Cal.Welf. & Inst.Code §§ 14000 et seq., for causing her to be discharged prematurely from a hospital.]

Responding to concerns about the escalating cost of health care, public and private payors have in recent years experimented with a variety of cost containment mechanisms. * * *

Early cost containment programs utilized the retrospective utilization review process. In that system the third party payor reviewed the patient's chart after the fact to determine whether the treatment provided was medically necessary. If, in the judgment of the utilization reviewer, it was not, the health care provider's claim for payment was denied.

In the cost containment program in issue in this case, prospective utilization review, authority for the rendering of health care services must be obtained before medical care is rendered. * * *

---

6. A long-established principle of due process jurisprudence is that Government must sometimes be allowed to act promptly to avoid public harm. * * *

7. Editors' Note: The citation has been simplified, the parties' names have been used throughout, and a few short paragraphs have been run together.

A mistaken conclusion about medical necessity following retrospective review will result in the wrongful withholding of payment. An erroneous decision in a prospective review process, on the other hand, in practical consequences, results in the withholding of necessary care, potentially leading to a patient's permanent disability or death.

* * * In 1976 Mrs. Wickline, a married woman in her mid-40s, with a limited education, was being treated by Dr. Stanley Z. Daniels, a physician engaged in a general family practice, for problems associated with her back and legs. Failing to respond to the physical therapy type of treatment he prescribed, Dr. Daniels had Mrs. Wickline admitted to Van Nuys Community Hospital in October 1976 and brought in another physician, Dr. Gerald E. Polonsky, a specialist in peripheral vascular surgery. * * *

Dr. Polonsky examined Mrs. Wickline and diagnosed her condition as arteriosclerosis obliterans with occlusion of the abdominal aorta, more generally referred to as Leriche's Syndrome. Leriche's Syndrome is a condition caused by the obstruction of the terminal aorta. * * * Dr. Polonsky concluded that it was necessary to remove a part of Mrs. Wickline's artery and insert a synthetic (Teflon) graft in its place. After agreeing to the operation, Mrs. Wickline was discharged home to await approval of her doctor's diagnosis and authorization from Medi–Cal for the recommended surgical procedure and attendant acute care hospitalization. * * * In response to Dr. Daniels' request, Medi–Cal authorized the surgical procedure and ten days of hospitalization for that treatment.

On January 6, 1977, Mrs. Wickline was admitted to Van Nuys by Dr. Daniels. On January 7, 1977, Dr. Polonsky performed a surgical procedure in which a part of Mrs. Wickline's artery was removed and a synthetic artery was inserted to replace it. Dr. Polonsky characterized that procedure as "a very major surgery." [The same day Dr. Polonsky reopened the incision and removed a clot from the graft, and five days later he performed a lumbar sympathectomy in order to stop arterial spasms.]

* * *

Mrs. Wickline was scheduled to be discharged on January 16, 1977, which would mean that she would actually leave the hospital sometime before 1 p.m. on January 17, 1977. On or about January 16, 1977, Dr. Polonsky concluded that "it was medically necessary" that Mrs. Wickline remain in the hospital * * *.

Dr. Polonsky cited many reasons for his feeling that it was medically necessary for Mrs. Wickline to remain in an acute care hospital for an additional eight days, such as the danger of infection and/or clotting. His principal reason, however, was that he felt that he was going to be able to save both of Mrs. Wickline's legs and wanted her to remain in the hospital where he could observe her and be immediately available, along with the hospital staff, to treat her if an emergency should occur.

In order to secure an extension of Mrs. Wickline's hospital stay, it was necessary to complete and present to Medi–Cal a form called "Request for Extension of Stay in Hospital," commonly referred to as * * * [a "180 form"]. * * *

The physician's responsibility in the preparation of the 180 form is to furnish (to the hospital's representative) the patient's diagnosis, significant history, clinical status, and treatment plan in sufficient detail to permit a reasonable, professional evaluation by Medi–Cal's representative, either the "on-site nurse" or/and the Medi–Cal consultant, a doctor employed by the state for just such purpose.

* * *

Doris A. Futerman, a registered nurse, was, at that time, employed by Medi–Cal as a Health Care Service Nurse, commonly referred to as an "on-site nurse." * * * Futerman had the authority, after reviewing a 180 form, to approve the requested extension of time without calling a Medi–Cal consultant. She could not, however, either reject the request outright or authorize a lesser number of days than requested. If, for any reason, she felt she could not approve the extension of time in the hospital as requested, she was required to contact a Medi–Cal consultant and that physician would make the ultimate decision on the request.

Futerman, after reviewing Mrs. Wickline's 180 form, felt that she could not approve the requested eight-day extension of acute care hospitalization. While conceding that the information provided might justify some additional time beyond the scheduled discharge date, nothing in Mrs. Wickline's case, in Futerman's opinion, would have warranted the entire eight additional days requested and, for those reasons, she telephoned the Medi–Cal consultant. She reached Dr. William S. Glassman, one of the Medi–Cal consultants on duty at the time in Medi–Cal's Los Angeles office. The Medi–Cal consultant selection occurred randomly. As was the practice, whichever Medi–Cal consultant was available at the moment took the next call that came into the office.

Dr. Glassman was board certified in general surgery and had practiced in that field until 1975 when he became employed by the Department of Health of the State of California as a Medi–Cal Consultant I. * * *

After speaking with Futerman on the telephone, Dr. Glassman rejected Mrs. Wickline's treating physician's request for an eight-day hospital extension and, instead, authorized an additional four days of hospital stay beyond the originally scheduled discharge date.

* * *

After review of Mrs. Wickline's 180 form, Dr. Glassman testified that the factors that led him to authorize four days, rather than the requested eight days, was that there was no information about the patient's temperature which he, thereupon, assumed was normal; nothing was mentioned about the patient's diet, which he then presumed was not a problem; nor was there any information about Mrs. Wickline's bowel function, which Dr. Glassman then presumed was functioning satisfactorily. Further, the fact that the 180 form noted that Mrs. Wickline was able to ambulate with help and that whirlpool treatments were to begin that day caused Dr. Glassman to presume that the patient was progressing satisfactorily and was not seriously or critically ill.

* * *

Complying with the limited extension of time authorized by Medi-Cal, Mrs. Wickline was discharged from Van Nuys on January 21, 1977. Drs. Polonsky and Daniels each wrote discharge orders. At the time of her discharge, each of Mrs. Wickline's three treating physicians were aware that the Medi-Cal consultant had approved only four of the requested eight-day hospital stay extension. While all three doctors were aware that they could attempt to obtain a further extension of Mrs. Wickline's hospital stay by telephoning the Medi-Cal consultant to request such an extension, none of them did so.

* * *

Dr. Polonsky testified that at the time in issue he felt that Medi-Cal consultants had the state's interest more in mind than the patient's welfare and that that belief influenced his decision not to request a second extension of Mrs. Wickline's hospital stay. In addition, he felt that Medi-Cal had the power to tell him, as a treating doctor, when a patient must be discharged from the hospital. Therefore, while still of the subjective, non-communicated, opinion that Mrs. Wickline was seriously ill and that the danger to her was not over, Dr. Polonsky discharged her from the hospital on January 21, 1977. He testified that had Mrs. Wickline's condition, in his medical judgment, been critical or in a deteriorating condition on January 21, he would have made some effort to keep her in the hospital beyond that day even if denied authority by Medi-Cal and even if he had to pay her hospital bill himself.

* * *

All of the medical witnesses who testified at trial agreed that Dr. Polonsky was acting within the standards of practice of the medical community in discharging Mrs. Wickline on January 21, 1977.

* * *

Mrs. Wickline testified that in the first few days after she arrived home she started feeling pain in her right leg and the leg started to lose color. In the next few days the pain got worse and the right leg took on a whitish, statue-like marble appearance. * * * Thereafter, gradually over the next few days, the Mrs. Wickline's leg "kept getting grayer and then it got bluish." * * * Mrs. Wickline returned to Van Nuys * * * January 30, 1977, nine days after her last discharge therefrom.

* * * Dr. Polonsky concluded that Mrs. Wickline had developed clotting in the right leg, that there was no circulation to that leg, and that she had developed an infection at the graft site.

* * *

Attempts to save Mrs. Wickline's leg through the utilization of anticoagulants, antibiotics, strict bed rest, pain medication and warm water whirlpool baths to the lower extremity proved unsuccessful. On February 8, 1977, Dr. Polonsky amputated Mrs. Wickline's leg below the knee because had he not done so "she would have died." The condition did not, however, heal after the first operation and on February 17, 1977, the doctors went back and amputated Mrs. Wickline's leg above the knee.

Had the eight-day extension requested on Mrs. Wickline's behalf been granted by Medi–Cal, she would have remained in the hospital through the morning hours of January 25, 1977. In Dr. Polonsky's medical opinion, based upon hypothetical questions derived from Mrs. Wickline's recollection of her course subsequent to her discharge from the hospital, had she been at Van Nuys on January 22, 23 or 24, he would have observed her leg change color, would have formed the opinion that she had clotted, and would have taken her back into surgery and reopened the graft to remove the clot again, not an uncommon procedure in this type of case. * * * Dr. Polonsky testified that had Mrs. Wickline developed an infection while she was in the hospital, it could have been controlled with the vigorous use of antibiotics.

In Dr. Polonsky's opinion, to a reasonable medical certainty, had Mrs. Wickline remained in the hospital for the eight additional days, as originally requested by him and her other treating doctors, she would not have suffered the loss of her leg.

* * *

Dr. Polonsky testified that in his medical opinion, the Medi–Cal consultant's rejection of the requested eight-day extension of acute care hospitalization and his authorization of a four-day extension in its place did not conform to the usual medical standards as they existed in 1977. He stated that, in accordance with those standards, a physician would not be permitted to make decisions regarding the care of a patient without either first seeing the patient, reviewing the patient's chart or discussing the patient's condition with her treating physician or physicians.

[The judge entered judgment on the verdict for Mrs. Wickline.]

From the facts thus presented, Medi–Cal takes the position that it was not negligent as a matter of law. Medi–Cal contends that the decision to discharge was made by each of Mrs. Wickline's three doctors, was based upon the prevailing standards of practice, and was justified by her condition at the time of her discharge. It argues that Medi–Cal had no part in Mrs. Wickline's hospital discharge and therefore was not liable, even if the decision to do so was erroneously made by her doctors.

* * *

As to the principal issue before this court, i.e., who bears responsibility for allowing a patient to be discharged from the hospital, her treating physicians or the health care payor, each side's medical expert witnesses agreed that, in accordance with the standards of medical practice as it existed in January 1977, it was for the patient's treating physician to decide the course of treatment that was medically necessary to treat the ailment. It was also that physician's responsibility to determine whether or not acute care hospitalization was required and for how long. Finally, it was agreed that the patient's physician is in a better position than the Medi–Cal consultant to determine the number of days medically necessary for any required hospital care. The decision to discharge is, therefore, the responsibility of the patient's own treating doctor.

Dr. Harry Kaufman [chief consultant at the Los Angeles field office] testified that if, on January 21, the date of Mrs. Wickline's discharge from Van Nuys, any one of her three treating doctors had decided that in his medical judgment it was necessary to keep Mrs. Wickline in the hospital for a longer period of time, they, or any of them, should have filed another request for extension of stay in the hospital, that Medi–Cal would expect those physicians to make such a request if they felt it was indicated, and upon receipt of such a request further consideration of an additional extension of hospital time would have been given.

* * *

The patient who requires treatment and who is harmed when care which should have been provided is not provided should recover for the injuries suffered from all those responsible for the deprivation of such care, including, when appropriate, health care payors. Third party payors of health care services can be held legally accountable when medically inappropriate decisions result from defects in the design or implementation of cost containment mechanisms as, for example, when appeals made on a patient's behalf for medical or hospital care are arbitrarily ignored or unreasonably disregarded or overridden. However, the physician who complies without protest with the limitations imposed by a third party payor, when his medical judgment dictates otherwise, cannot avoid his ultimate responsibility for his patient's care. He cannot point to the health care payor as the liability scapegoat when the consequences of his own determinative medical decisions go sour.

There is little doubt that Dr. Polonsky was intimidated by the Medi–Cal program, but he was not paralyzed by Dr. Glassman's response nor rendered powerless to act appropriately if other action was required under the circumstances. If, in his medical judgment, it was in his patient's best interest that she remain in the acute care hospital setting for an additional four days beyond the extended time period originally authorized by Medi–Cal, Dr. Polonsky should have made some effort to keep Mrs. Wickline there. He himself acknowledged that responsibility to his patient. It was his medical judgment, however, that Mrs. Wickline could be discharged when she was. All Mrs.

Wickline's treating physicians concurred and all the doctors who testified at trial, for either Mrs. Wickline or Medi–Cal, agreed that Dr. Polonsky's medical decision to discharge Mrs. Wickline met the standard of care applicable at the time. Medi–Cal was not a party to that medical decision and therefore cannot be held to share in the harm resulting if such decision was negligently made.

In addition thereto, while Medi–Cal played a part in the scenario before us in that it was the resource for the funds to pay for the treatment sought, and its input regarding the nature and length of hospital care to be provided was of paramount importance, Medi–Cal did not override the medical judgment of Mrs. Wickline's treating physicians at the time of her discharge. It was given no opportunity to do so. Therefore, there can be no viable cause of action against it for the consequences of that discharge decision.

* * *

This court appreciates that what is at issue here is the effect of cost containment programs upon the professional judgment of physicians to prescribe hospital treatment for patients requiring the same. While we recognize, realistically, that cost consciousness has become a permanent feature of the health care system, it is essential that cost limitation programs not be permitted to corrupt medical judgment. We have concluded, from the facts in issue here, that in this case it did not.

* * *

The judgment is reversed.

SECTION C. PEER REVIEW

DE LEON v. ST. JOSEPH HOSPITAL, INC.

United States Court of Appeals for the Fourth Circuit, 1989.
871 F.2d 1229.

MURNAGHAN, CIRCUIT JUDGE. * * *

I. Jose S. De Leon, a Filipino national, received his medical degree from the University of the Philippines in 1970. He performed a general surgical residency at the Philippines General Hospital Medical Center from 1970 until 1975. In 1976 he emigrated to the United States. De Leon underwent a one-year fellowship at the Texas Heart Institute and an internship and residency at the Brooklyn–Cumberland Medical Center from 1977 to 1979. De Leon then transferred to the Pennsylvania College of Medicine for his second year of residency. Due to poor performance, he was not reappointed to a third year residency and was forced to apply elsewhere.

Although De Leon submitted numerous applications, St. Joseph Hospital (the Hospital) was the only institution willing to accept him at a third year level (the others required him to repeat his second year). De Leon completed his third, fourth and fifth (final) years of residency at St. Joseph. He was then hired by St. Joseph on a contractual basis as a "house surgeon" for the period of July 1, 1983, to June 30, 1984. A "house surgeon" could not admit patients to the hospital and was required to treat patients only under the supervision of another physician.

In January of 1984 De Leon applied for medical privileges that would allow him to admit patients to the Hospital. * * *

Pursuant to the Hospital's bylaws, De Leon's application was forwarded to the Credentials Committee, consisting of seven appointed and elected members. Appraisal forms were sent out to De Leon's references and his previous employers. Dr. William L. Macon, the head of surgery, was required to assess De Leon's qualifications. Macon supervised the house surgeons and was in a position to evaluate De Leon's medical skills.

Macon submitted a letter concerning De Leon's qualifications to the Credentials Committee. Macon concluded De Leon's qualifications were unsatisfactory and recommended that his application be denied. The district court summarized De Leon's credentials as follows:

> [S]ubjective impressions were confirmed by Dr. De Leon's performance on objective tests. During his residency at the Brooklyn–Cumberland Medical Center, he scored in the 21st percentile on the In-Training Examination. During his residency at the Hospital, he scored in the 11th percentile in a similar test. Moreover, he failed the American Board of Surgery's examination for Board certification in 1983, scoring in the 17.6 percentile. [The trial court's footnote 2 followed:]
>
> 2. In subsequent attempts, Dr. De Leon had repeatedly failed the examination for Board certification. In 1984, he scored in the 9th percentile; in 1985, he scored in the 7th percentile; and, in 1986, he again scored in the 7th percentile. A doctor designated as an expert by plaintiff has stated that even if De Leon took a full year or more off to study, it is highly doubtful that he would ever pass the examination for board certification.

On July 16, 1984, the Credentials Committee met and considered De Leon's application. The Committee found De Leon's credentials to be unsatisfactory. Pursuant to the Hospital Bylaws, the negative recommendation was forwarded to the Hospital's Medical Executive Committee, to the Board of Trustees Medical Staff Privileging Committee, and finally to the full Board of Trustees of St. Joseph Hospital (the Board). Each body reviewed the record and independently determined De Leon's credentials were unsatisfactory. On September 27, 1984, the Board voted to deny De Leon's application.

De Leon appealed the Board's decision. An ad hoc committee of the Board was formed to hear De Leon's appeal. * * * At the hearings, the district judge found:

> De Leon was accorded the full panoply of due process rights. His counsel was given De Leon's credentials file; the testimony of witnesses was presented, and his attorney cross-examined witnesses on De

Leon's behalf. Following the hearings, the ad hoc committee allowed De Leon to submit supplemental written argument.

On February 12, 1986, the ad hoc committee issued an 11-page report recommending De Leon's application be denied. De Leon's counsel was permitted to submit written supplemental and rebuttal argument to the full Board. On May 22, 1986, the full Board met, considered De Leon's appeal, and voted to deny the application.

That day, De Leon filed suit in the United States District Court for the District of Maryland. De Leon sued the Hospital for breach of contract, defamation, and interference with economic advantage. De Leon also sued Macon for interference with economic relations and defamation. The complaint also contained a derivative claim for loss of consortium on behalf of De Leon's wife. De Leon sought injunctive relief, compensatory and punitive damages.

Ample discovery was conducted by both sides, including over twenty depositions. * * * Judge Harvey granted summary judgment for the defendants on all counts. * * *

II. The district court based its grant of summary judgment on four major points * * *. If even one of the * * * [court's] contentions is correct, the grant of summary judgment is proper. * * *

A. In connection with his application for admitting privileges, De Leon executed a release agreement providing:

> I hereby authorize Saint Joseph Hospital, Inc., to consult with administrators and members of the medical staff of other hospitals or institutions with which I have been associated and with others, including past and present malpractice carriers, who may have information bearing on my professional competence, character and ethical qualifications. I consent to the inspection of all documents and data, including medical records at other hospitals and other sources of available data, that may be material to any evaluation of my professional qualifications and competence to carry out the clinical privileges requested, my pattern of practice, as well as my physical and mental health status and moral and ethical qualifications for medical staff membership.
>
> I release Saint Joseph Hospital, Inc., its agents, servants, employees and staff members from liability for all acts performed in connection with evaluating my application and my credentials, qualifications and practices, and I release from liability any and all individuals and organizations who provided information to Saint Joseph Hospital, Inc., concerning my professional competence, medical practice patterns, ethics, character, and other qualifications for staff appointment and clinical privileges. I consent to the release of such information, including otherwise privileged or confidential information to Saint Joseph Hospital, Inc.

The district court found the release a bar to all of De Leon's claims. The court correctly recognized that, "[u]nder Maryland law, absent circumstances not present here, parties may validly exculpate themselves from liability for anything short of 'willful, wanton, reckless, or gross conduct,'" quoting Boucher v. Riner, 68 Md.App. 539, 514 A.2d 485, 488 (1986). The court found De Leon failed to point to specific facts that would establish "extreme or wanton conduct" on the part of the defendants.

De Leon argues that Macon, by making allegedly malicious and intentionally false statements to the Board and Committees considering De Leon's application, and the Hospital, by intentionally denying De Leon's application on the basis of such statements, are each guilty of such willful and wanton conduct that the release is no longer effective. * * * The district court correctly refused to review the "correctness" of the hospital's decision.[8] Thus, the sole task for this court is to determine if De Leon has established a factual or legal basis for reviewing the Hospital's decision at trial. The district court concluded that De Leon "failed to establish a triable issue of fact under any of the legal theories advanced." The legal theories advanced on appeal are no more meritorious.

As a prime example, De Leon alleged that Macon made * * * seven false statements, and also alleged facts from which he claimed the jury could have inferred that Macon had known of their falsity and that further reflected his bad faith and intent to harm.

* * * A mere scintilla of evidence does not suffice to provide factual support for De Leon's claims of wanton behavior and bad faith. De Leon's "facts" are nothing more than conclusory allegations. Of the above "falsities," only one is supported *at all*, and with its accompanying qualification, is hardly dispositive. De Leon has not even approached a showing of the extreme, wanton behavior needed to disregard the release.

Aside from the lack of false statements, De Leon has failed to demonstrate any basis for a claim of bad faith or intent. * * *

* * * Without support as to intent or wantonness, the release precluded recovery on every claim De Leon has alleged.

B. Turning to the issue of whether there was publication, to state a viable claim for defamation De Leon must establish:

(a) A false and defamatory statement concerning another;

(b) An unprivileged publication to a third party;

(c) Fault amounting to at least negligence on the part of the publisher; and

(d) Either actionability of the statement irrespective of special harm or the existence of special harm caused by the publication. Restatement (Second) of Torts, § 588 at 155 (1977). * * *

---

8. Courts have been reluctant, and with good reason, to intervene in any hospital credentialing process. Public policy concerns obviously weigh heavily towards leaving such determinations to the hospitals themselves. * * *

The district court found De Leon's defamation claims insufficient, inter alia, because there had been no publication of defamatory statements to a third party. The Hospital has not published its decision denying De Leon privileges. De Leon argues that he will be forced to reveal the fact of denial when applying for other positions, resulting in a compelled "self-publication." See Lewis v. Equitable Life Ins. Soc., 389 N.W.2d 876, 886 (Minn.1986). The theory of self-publication has not gained widespread acceptance and De Leon could cite no Maryland authority for his proposition. On the other hand, *Lewis* has been subjected to some criticism. * * * See Restatement (Second) of Torts § 577 at 206 (rejecting self-publication). The district court concluded that the Maryland Court of Appeals, at least on the facts presented here, would not adopt self-publication. We do also, bearing in mind that, otherwise, the theory of self-publication might visit liability for defamation on every Maryland employer each time a job applicant is rejected.

The district court also found that during the application process Macon acted solely in his capacity as a Hospital official, and all the allegedly defamatory statements were made to other Hospital officials. Thus, the district court reasoned, there was no publication to a "legally distinct third party."

* * *

C. The district court held that, "assuming such intracorporate communication could constitute a publication," Macon's statements were privileged under Maryland law. A conditional privilege protecting this type of communication exists under both statute, Md. Health Occ.Code Ann. §§ 14–601, 14–603, and the common law. Section 14–601 provides, in pertinent part:

> (f) Immunity from civil liability. A person who acts in good faith and within the scope of jurisdiction of a medical review committee is not civilly liable for any action as a member of the medical review committee or for giving information to, participating in, or contributing to the function of the medical review committee.

Section 14–603 provides, in pertinent part:

> (c) Immunity from civil liability. A person described in subsection (b) of this section is not civilly liable for giving information to any hospital, hospital medical staff, related institution, or other health care facility, professional society, medical school, or professional licensing board, if the person:
>
> (1) Gives the information in good faith and with the intention of aiding in the evaluation of the qualifications, fitness, or character of a physician; and
>
> (2) Does not represent as true any matter that the person does not reasonably believe to be true.

Macon clearly is protected by the two statutory sections. Furthermore, although the court did not address it, Macon also enjoyed the benefit of a conditional privilege at common law. Maryland recognizes that communications arising in an employment context or by common interest in the subject matter are privileged. * * * The privilege is particularly apt in the present context, since the privilege, along with others, arose by way of recognition of the desirable public benefit of encouraging uninhibited communication where a public or private duty may lie. * * * As Macon had a reasonably perceived duty to communicate the information he possessed to the Credentials Committee, his communications were privileged.

Once, by statute or common law, a conditional privilege has been established, it must be overcome by a showing of *New York Times* malice. Marchesi v. Franchino, 283 Md. 131, 387 A.2d 1129, 1133 (1978). See New York Times Co. v. Sullivan, 376 U.S. 254, 84 S.Ct. 710, 11 L.Ed.2d 686 (1964). Thus, De Leon had to show Macon knew his statements were false or acted with reckless disregard as to their truth to escape the privilege bar. *New York Times,* 376 U.S. at 279. He has, as indicated earlier in this opinion, clearly failed to do so.

D. Finally, the district court found, in the context of the entire record, that none of the statements were defamatory. The court was correct. Many of the statements were indeed Macon's opinion, labelled as such. * * * And, as the district court noted, where Macon reported factual incidents that De Leon denied, he consistently noted De Leon's denial or explanation.

* * *

The judgment is affirmed.

HUMANA HOSPITAL DESERT VALLEY v. SUPERIOR COURT

Court of Appeals of Arizona, 1987.
154 Ariz. 396, 742 P.2d 1382, review denied.

CORCORAN, JUDGE.

These * * * special actions arise from the same medical malpractice case against petitioner Paul Blumberg, D.O., and petitioner Humana Hospital. The other petitioners [9] * * * are not parties to the underlying action. These hospitals were served with subpoenas duces tecum by real party in interest, Marilyn Darice Edison, plaintiff in the trial court. Petitioners allege that the trial court improperly denied their motions to quash the subpoenas duces tecum.

Arizona's Peer Review Act (the Act) governs the discoverability of peer review material. The Act states:

9. Editors' Note: The other petitioners were Samaritan Health Service, Phoenix General Hospital, Chandler Community Hospital, John C. Lincoln Hospital, Mesa Lutheran Hospital, and Phoenix Community Medical Center.

§ 36–445. Review of certain medical practices. The governing body of each licensed hospital * * * shall require that physicians admitted to practice in the hospital * * * organize into committees or other organizational structures to review the professional practices within the hospital or center for the purposes of reducing morbidity and mortality and for the improvement of the care of patients provided in the institution. Such review shall include the nature, quality and necessity of the care provided and the preventability of complications and deaths occurring in the hospital * * *.

§ 36–445.01. Confidentiality of information; conditions of disclosure. A. All proceedings, records and materials prepared in connection with the reviews provided for in § 36–445, *including all peer reviews of individual health care providers practicing in and applying to practice in hospitals or outpatient surgical centers and the records of such reviews, shall be confidential and shall not be subject to discovery except in proceedings before the board of medical examiners, or the board of osteopathic examiners,* or in actions by an individual health care provider against a hospital * * *. No member of a committee established under the provisions of § 36–445 or officer or other member of a hospital's or center's medical, administrative or nursing staff engaged in assisting the hospital or center to carry out functions in accordance with that section or any person furnishing information to a committee performing peer review may be subpoenaed to testify in any judicial or quasi-judicial proceeding if such subpoena is based solely on such activities.

B. This article shall not be construed to affect any patient's claim to privilege or privacy or to prevent the subpoena of a patient's medical records if they are otherwise subject to discovery * * *. In any legal action brought against a hospital or outpatient surgical center * * * claiming negligence for failure to adequately do peer review, representatives of the hospital or center are permitted to testify as to whether there was peer review as to the subject matter being litigated. *The contents and records of the peer review proceedings are fully confidential and inadmissible as evidence in any court of law.* (Emphasis added.)

The subpoenas duces tecum requested the following documents from the hospitals' credentials files on Dr. Blumberg:

1. Any and all records in your possession relative to Paul Blumberg, D.O., including, but not limited to:

(a) application for staff privileges;

(b) application for any training program;

(c) any records reflecting hospital investigation into the application for staff privileges, including, although not limited to, the physician's background, experience and work before becoming associated with your organization * * *.

Petitioners either objected to the subpoenas pursuant to Rule 45(e), Ariz.R.Civ.P., or filed motions for protective orders, claiming that the requested materials were absolutely privileged under the Act.

The trial court held that applications for staff privileges or training program positions, and any investigations made by the reviewing committees into those applications, are not subject to the Act. * * *

THE ANTI–ABROGATION CLAUSE

Edison claims Humana is liable for negligently supervising Dr. Blumberg * * *.

Arizona Const. art. 18, § 6 (the anti-abrogation clause) provides: "[T]he right of action to recover damages for injury shall never be abrogated, and the amount recovered shall not be subject to any statutory limitation." * * * We * * * hold that the anti-abrogation clause applies to negligent supervision actions.

* * * Edison is left with ample alternatives to prove her negligent supervision theory against Humana without obtaining access to privileged information. Information which originated outside the peer review process is not subject to the privilege and, if otherwise admissible, could be used to prove Edison's case. * * * Such original sources include court records about previous malpractice claims and administrative records or testimony about a physician's education and training.

A plaintiff can also discover a hospital's general credentialing or review procedure policies. Arizona Rev.Stat. § 36–445.01(B) provides that representatives of a hospital may testify whether peer review was conducted with regard to the subject matter being litigated. A plaintiff also has access to medical records available pursuant to a patient's consent. Finally, a plaintiff can retain experts to give opinions regarding all of the above matters. Edison apparently found an expert who has expressed opinions in support of her claims. Therefore, neither the Act nor our holding today bars a malpractice plaintiff from proving a negligent supervision claim against a hospital.

Moreover, if this court were to eliminate the peer review privilege, it would negate an important state interest. * * * Arizona courts have recognized that the confidentiality of peer review committee proceedings is essential to achieve complete investigation and review of medical care. These deliberations would terminate if they were subject to the discovery process. * * *

These important policy considerations mandate our protection of the peer review privilege. Because plaintiff is not deprived of her ability to bring a negligent supervision action, and because of the overriding public interest in candid professional peer review, we hold that the peer review act merely regulates a plaintiff's claim against a hospital for negligent supervision, and does not violate Ariz. Const. art. 18, § 6.

Peer Review Act and the Supreme Court's Rule-making Power

Arizona Const. art. 6, § 5(5), empowers our supreme court to make rules regarding all procedural matters in our courts. Pursuant to that rule-making power, the supreme court promulgated both the Rules of Civil Procedure and the Rules of Evidence.

Statutes which deal with rules of procedure are not per se unconstitutional as infringements upon this power. * * *

In some instances, the legislature may create a substantive privilege. * * *

Rule 26(b), Ariz.R.Civ.P., provides for general discoverability of information, subject to an exception for privileged matters. Likewise, the Arizona Rules of Evidence exempt privileged material from admission, including material granted a privilege by statute. Rule 402. Additionally, Rule 501 expressly recognizes that privileges may be established by statute:

> Except as otherwise required by the Constitution of the United States, the Constitution of Arizona, *or by applicable statute or rule*, privilege shall be governed by the principles of the common law as they may be interpreted in light of reason. (Emphasis added.)

The Act is a "reasonable and workable" statute consistent with the supreme court's rules. It protects the peer review process itself—the discussions, exchanges, and opinions found in the committee minutes. It does not protect otherwise discoverable factual information obtained from alternative sources.

The legislature has determined that a peer review privilege is necessary to encourage the free flow of information essential for effective peer review. Like other statutory privileges, the hospital peer review privilege meets the four traditional criteria for privileged communications:

> 1. It originates in confidence that it will not be disclosed;
>
> 2. This element of confidentiality is essential to the full maintenance of the relationship between the parties;
>
> 3. The relationship is one which the community thinks ought to be fostered; and
>
> 4. The injury to the relationship that would occur from the disclosing would be greater than the benefit gained by the aid given to the litigation. 8 H. Wigmore, Evidence § 2285 at 527 (McNaughton rev. 1961) * * *.

Due to the overwhelming public policy supporting the hospital peer review privilege, and because the statute does not conflict with any rule, it remains valid. * * * We hold that the hospital peer review privilege does not invade the rule-making power of the supreme court.

* * *

The Information Sought in the Subpoenas Duces Tecum is Privileged

The trial court ordered production of Dr. Blumberg's applications for staff privileges at the hospitals, as well as records relating to investigations into those applications. The hospitals claim that the trial court erred when it ordered production of credentials committee documents because the Act precludes discovery of the review of medical staff privilege applications by credentials committees. * * *

A court should look to the words, context, subject matter, consequences, reason, and spirit of the law to garner legislative intent. * * * Examination of these factors mandates that credentials committee files be protected by the peer review privilege.

First, the express language of the statute protects the credentials file. Arizona Rev.Stat. § 36–445.01(A) and (B) * * *.

Specific reference to the application process is also found in § 36–445.02, which provides immunity to individuals involved in the peer review process:

> B. No hospital * * * and no individual involved in carrying out review or disciplinary duties or functions of a hospital * * * pursuant to § 36–445 may be liable in damages *to any person who is denied the privilege to practice in a hospital* * * * or whose privileges are suspended, limited or revoked. (Emphasis added.)

Despite these express references to the application process, Edison urges this court to hold that peer review refers only to retrospective review of care provided by physicians already practicing in hospitals.

We cannot accept such a narrow construction. Section 36–445 does not include such limiting language. The rules of statutory construction require that statutes be read so that no portion of a statute is rendered superfluous or void. * * *

The statute speaks of review of the "nature, quality and necessity of the care provided and the *preventability of complications and deaths occurring in the hospital.*" (Emphasis added.) This type of review includes investigation of the qualifications of physicians seeking to provide medical services at a hospital as well as review of medical services already provided. * * *

Edison's untenable position would encourage full candor when peer review committees evaluate care already provided, but would discourage full candor when credentials committees review the qualifications of physicians seeking to provide medical care. The narrow interpretation urged by Edison has been specifically rejected in California. * * *

Therefore, because the statutes expressly refer to the confidentiality of peer review of applications for staff privileges, and because of the public interest in such confidentiality, we hold that the peer review privilege protects the credentialing process.

We note, though, that evidence possessed by the credentials committee which is not otherwise privileged may be discovered; the mere fact that a committee has obtained evidence does not render that evidence privileged if it was not previously privileged. * * * To hold otherwise would result in such evidence being more protected than it was before being obtained by the committee. * * * Personnel, administrative, and other hospital records regarding Dr. Blumberg which do not contain references to proceedings before medical investigative committees are not immune from discovery. * * *

While the internal workings and deliberative processes of regularly constituted committees are immune from discovery, the effect of the proceedings is not * * *.

Therefore, Edison can obtain information she needs to prove Humana's actual or constructive knowledge of Dr. Blumberg's shortcomings from other sources without compromising the privilege. The investigations regarding Dr. Blumberg's applications for staff privileges at various hospitals, as well as the applications, are privileged under the Act.

STANDING OF DR. BLUMBERG AND HUMANA

* * * Dr. Blumberg and Humana have a personal right to a privilege concerning the subpoenaing of Dr. Blumberg's credentials file. The entire peer review process would be crippled if production were required, and the underlying purpose of the privilege would be defeated if the privilege could not be asserted by those subpoenaed. Furthermore, the legislature has not stated that the privilege can be invoked only by the person holding the records. Therefore, Dr. Blumberg and Humana have standing to object to the subpoenaing of information from the nonparty hospitals.

* * *

We therefore grant special action relief and reverse the trial court's order compelling production. We order the court to deny discovery of all otherwise privileged documents which would be subject to discovery under the trial court's order, including Dr. Blumberg's applications for staff privileges at Humana and the nonparty hospitals.

SALAYMEH v. ST. VINCENT MEMORIAL HOSP. CORP.

United States District Court for the Central District of Illinois, 1989.
706 F.Supp. 643.

RICHARD MILLS, DISTRICT JUDGE. * * *

* * * Plaintiff M.T. Salaymeh [10] is a physician and a former member of the Hospital's medical staff. From 1971 through August of 1984, Dr. Salaymeh had staff privileges at the Hospital as a general surgeon with a subspecialty of thoracic surgery. In April of 1984, the

---

10. Editors' Note: The parties' names have been substituted throughout.

Hospital commissioned InterQual, an independent medical review entity, to evaluate 100 operative procedures conducted during a one year period at the Hospital. The report of InterQual "identified substandard and unacceptable practice related to [Dr. Salaymeh's] performance." It concluded that "the community would be better served if [Dr. Salaymeh's] private privileges to perform major intra-abdominal and gastrointestinal surgical procedures were completely withheld."

The Hospital's administrator provided Dr. Salaymeh with a copy of the pertinent part of the InterQual report on August 27, 1984. On August 28, 1984, the Hospital's administrator delivered a letter to Dr. Salaymeh which outlined three options (which had been discussed with Dr. Salaymeh on the 27th) which Dr. Salaymeh could pursue. First, Dr. Salaymeh could voluntarily terminate his surgical privileges. Second, he could receive a summary suspension pending a hearing pursuant to the Hospital's by-laws. Finally, Dr. Salaymeh could voluntarily refrain from performing surgery at the Hospital pending review of the InterQual report by the Hospital's Medical Staff pursuant to the by-laws. On August 29, 1984, Dr. Salaymeh tendered his resignation of his surgical privileges, thereby avoiding by-law procedures.

Upon receiving Dr. Salaymeh's resignation on behalf of the Hospital, the administrator sent a letter to Dr. Salaymeh accepting the resignation and stated: "In accordance with this withdrawal of all surgical privileges, the hospital agrees that the review of the hospital's surgical practice (InterQual Study) will be maintained by the hospital in a confidential manner and will not be released to anyone except pursuant to a court order." Dr. Salaymeh alleges that a contract of confidentiality arose as a result of these two letters * * *.

On November 16, 1984, the Hospital held a public meeting and invited prominent members of the Taylorville community and the press. Dr. Salaymeh alleges that certain statements were made at this meeting by agents of the Hospital which breached Dr. Salaymeh's contract of confidentiality.

* * * The Hospital asserts that no legally binding consideration was exchanged because the Hospital was obligated by Illinois statute to keep the InterQual report confidential. The pertinent statute, in effect when the contract was made (having become effective July 1, 1984), stated that all information and reports used by hospitals for internal quality control must remain privileged and confidential. Such information or reports may be used only for medical research, improving quality of care, or granting, limiting, or revoking staff privileges.[11]

---

11. The pertinent part of the statute states:

All information, interviews, reports, statements, memoranda or other data of * * * accredited hospitals or their medical staffs, including Patient Care Audit Committees, Medical Care Evaluation Committees, Utilization Review Committees, Credential Committees and Executive Committees (but not the medical records pertaining to the patient), used in the course of internal quality control or of medical study for the purpose of reducing morbidity or mortality, or for improving patient care, shall be privileged, strictly confidential and shall

Improper disclosure of such information or report is a criminal offense and is classified as a misdemeanor. Ill.Ann.Stat. ch. 110, § 8–2105.

The Hospital argues that because it was legally obligated to keep the report confidential, the promise to keep it confidential cannot serve as consideration to form a binding contract. As a general rule, this proposition is correct. * * *

Dr. Salaymeh puts forth two arguments in opposition to this line of defense. First, Dr. Salaymeh argues that the confidentiality statute (§ 8–2101) does not apply to the InterQual report because the original intent in procuring the report was not for the purpose of internal quality control. Second, Dr. Salaymeh argues that if the confidentiality statute does apply, the Hospital should be estopped from asserting it. Dr. Salaymeh argues that the Hospital used the confidentiality promise to induce him to voluntarily resign his surgical privileges, and he has performed his part of the agreement.

* * *

Clearly, the intent of commissioning the report was for the purpose of internal quality control to improve patient care. The study was commissioned to evaluate surgical procedures of the Hospital's physicians. This is just the type of report to which § 8–2101 applies.

Dr. Salaymeh's second argument, that the Hospital should be estopped from asserting the statute as a basis for negating consideration for the alleged contract, is facially appealing. On one side, we have a physician allegedly given less than 24 hours to make a decision which will directly affect his career. He is given three choices for a course of action—none of them very appealing from his perspective. Finally, he is told, and subsequently receives a letter to the effect that, if he voluntarily resigns his privileges, the damaging report will be kept confidential.

On the other side, we have a hospital administrator who, it is alleged, was attempting to short-circuit hospital by-law procedure. And it is argued that he pressures Dr. Salaymeh into a corner from which Dr. Salaymeh must choose from among three unappealing choices which will effectively end his career as a surgeon at the Hospital. The administrator offers to keep the report confidential if Dr. Salaymeh will voluntarily resign his privileges.

But—as we have said—this argument is only *facially* appealing.

* * * The Hospital's offer to keep the report confidential may have induced Dr. Salaymeh to voluntarily resign his privileges. Resigning his privileges was certainly a "detriment" to Dr. Salaymeh. However, whether the report was to be kept confidential solely based on a hospital administrator's promise to do so or because Illinois law required it was apparently immaterial to Dr. Salaymeh. Dr. Salaymeh provides us with no evidence that the hospital administrator's failure to

be used only for medical research, the evaluation and improvement of quality care, or granting, limiting or revoking staff privileges * * *. Ill.Ann.Stat. ch. 110, § 8–2101.

tell him that the law required the Hospital to keep the report confidential had the effect of inducing Dr. Salaymeh to follow a course of action that he would not have otherwise followed. Dr. Salaymeh's objective was to avoid the Hospital's by-law procedure which would have subjected him to the peer review process, which, in Dr. Salaymeh's opinion, may well have damaged his professional record.

Explaining why he selected the option of resigning his privileges and bypassing by-law procedure, which the other two options would have mandated, he stated: "So I took the voluntary action which will save my privileges from any damaging record, which is the voluntary withdrawal of all my privileges." Dr. Salaymeh does not argue that he would have chosen a different option (which would have included review under by-law procedure) had he known the report was to be kept confidential pursuant to state law. Further, Dr. Salaymeh resigned his privileges *before* the confidentiality promise was put in writing by the Hospital's administrator. We find, considering all the circumstances of this cause, that equitable estoppel does not apply.

* * *

Ergo, the Hospital's motion for summary judgment is allowed.

PATRICK v. BURGET

Supreme Court of the United States, 1988.
486 U.S. 94, 108 S.Ct. 1658, 100 L.Ed.2d 83.

JUSTICE MARSHALL delivered the opinion of the Court. * * *

I. Astoria, Oregon, where the events giving rise to this lawsuit took place, is a city of approximately 10,000 people located in the northwest corner of the state. The only hospital in Astoria is the Columbia Memorial Hospital (CMH). Astoria also is the home of a private group-medical practice called the Astoria Clinic. At all times relevant to this case, a majority of the staff members at the CMH were employees or partners of the Astoria Clinic.

Petitioner Timothy Patrick is a general and vascular surgeon. He became an employee of the Astoria Clinic and a member of the CMH's medical staff in 1972. One year later, the partners of the Clinic, who are the respondents in this case, invited petitioner to become a partner of the Clinic. Petitioner declined this offer and instead began an independent practice in competition with the surgical practice of the Clinic. Petitioner continued to serve on the medical staff of the CMH.

After petitioner established his independent practice, the physicians associated with the Astoria Clinic consistently refused to have professional dealings with him. Petitioner received virtually no referrals from physicians at the Clinic, even though the Clinic at times did not have a general surgeon on its staff. Rather than refer surgery patients to petitioner, Clinic doctors referred them to surgeons located as far as 50 miles from Astoria. In addition, Clinic physicians showed reluctance to assist petitioner with his own patients. Clinic doctors often declined to give consultations, and Clinic surgeons refused to provide back-up coverage for patients under petitioner's care. At the same time, Clinic physicians repeatedly criticized petitioner for failing to obtain outside consultations and adequate back-up coverage.

In 1979, respondent Gary Boelling, a partner at the Clinic, complained to the executive committee of the CMH's medical staff about an incident in which petitioner had left a patient in the care of a recently hired associate, who then left the patient unattended. The executive committee decided to refer this complaint, along with information about other cases handled by petitioner, to the state Board of Medical Examiners (BOME). Respondent Franklin Russell, another partner at the Clinic, chaired the committee of the BOME that investigated these matters. The members of the BOME committee criticized petitioner's medical practices to the full BOME, which then issued a letter of reprimand that had been drafted by Russell. The BOME retracted this letter in its entirety after petitioner sought judicial review of the BOME proceedings.

Two years later, at the request of respondent Richard Harris, a Clinic surgeon, the executive committee of the CMH's medical staff initiated a review of petitioner's hospital privileges. The committee voted to recommend the termination of petitioner's privileges on the ground that petitioner's care of his patients was below the standards of the hospital. Petitioner demanded a hearing, as provided by hospital bylaws, and a five-member ad hoc committee, chaired by respondent Boelling, heard the charges and defense. Petitioner requested that the members of the committee testify as to their personal bias against him, but they refused to accommodate this request. Before the committee rendered its decision, petitioner resigned from the hospital staff rather than risk termination.[12]

During the course of the hospital peer-review proceedings, petitioner filed this lawsuit in the United States District Court for the District of Oregon. Petitioner alleged that the partners of the Astoria Clinic had violated §§ 1 and 2 of the Sherman Act. Act of July 2, 1890, ch. 647, 26 Stat. 209, 15 U.S.C.A. §§ 1–2. Specifically, petitioner contended that the Clinic partners had initiated and participated in the hospital peer-review proceedings to reduce competition from petitioner rather than to improve patient care. Respondents denied this assertion, and the district court submitted the dispute to the jury with instructions that it could rule in favor of petitioner only if it found that respondents' conduct was the result of a specific intent to injure or destroy competition.

The jury returned a verdict against respondents Russell, Boelling, and Harris on the § 1 claim and against all of the respondents on the § 2 claim. It awarded damages of $650,000 on the two antitrust claims

---

12. The court below did not address any issues arising from petitioner's decision to resign from the hospital staff prior to the ad hoc committee's determination, and respondents did not raise this matter in their response to the petition for certiorari. Accordingly, we do not address the significance, if any, of petitioner's resignation.

taken together. The district court, as required by law, 15 U.S.C. § 15(a), trebled the antitrust damages.

The Court of Appeals for the Ninth Circuit reversed. 800 F.2d 1498 (1986). It found that there was substantial evidence that respondents had acted in bad faith in the peer-review process.[13] The court held, however, that even if respondents had used the peer-review process to disadvantage a competitor rather than to improve patient care, their conduct in the peer-review proceedings was immune from antitrust scrutiny. * * *

II. In Parker v. Brown, 317 U.S. 341, 63 S.Ct. 307, 87 L.Ed. 315 (1943), this Court considered whether the Sherman Act prohibits anticompetitive actions of a state. * * * Relying on principles of federalism and state sovereignty, this Court refused to find in the Sherman Act "an unexpressed purpose to nullify a state's control over its officers and agents." 317 U.S. at 351. The Sherman Act, the Court held, was not intended "to restrain state action or official action directed by a state." Ibid.

Although *Parker* involved a suit against a state official, the Court subsequently recognized that *Parker's* federalism rationale demanded that the state action exemption also apply in certain suits against private parties. * * *

We accordingly established a rigorous two-pronged test to determine whether anticompetitive conduct engaged in by private parties should be deemed state action and thus shielded from the antitrust laws. See California Retail Liquor Dealers Ass'n v. Midcal Aluminum, Inc., 445 U.S. 97, 100 S.Ct. 937, 63 L.Ed.2d 233 (1980). First, "the challenged restraint must be 'one clearly articulated and affirmatively expressed as state policy.'" 445 U.S. at 105 * * *. Second, the anticompetitive conduct "must be 'actively supervised' by the State itself." Ibid. Only if an anticompetitive act of a private party meets both of these requirements is it fairly attributable to the state.

In this case, we need not consider the "clear articulation" prong of the *Midcal* test, because the "active supervision" requirement is not satisfied. * * * The active supervision prong of the *Midcal* test requires that state officials have and exercise power to review particular anticompetitive acts of private parties and disapprove those that fail to accord with state policy. Absent such a program of supervision, there is no realistic assurance that a private party's anticompetitive conduct promotes state policy, rather than merely the party's individual interests.

Respondents in this case contend that the State of Oregon actively supervises the peer-review process through the state Health Division, the BOME, and the state judicial system. * * *

---

13. Viewing the evidence in the light most favorable to petitioner, as appropriate in light of the verdicts rendered by the jury, the court of appeals characterized respondents' conduct as "shabby, unprincipled and unprofessional." 800 F.2d at 1509.

* * * The Health Division's statutory authority over peer review relates only to a hospital's procedures;[14] that authority does not encompass the actual decisions made by hospital peer-review committees. The restraint challenged in this case (and in most cases of its kind) consists not in the procedures used to terminate hospital privileges, but in the termination of privileges itself. The state does not actively supervise this restraint unless a state official has and exercises ultimate authority over private privilege determinations. Oregon law does not give the Health Division this authority: under the statutory scheme, the Health Division has no power to review private peer-review decisions and overturn a decision that fails to accord with state policy. Thus, the activities of the Health Division under Oregon law cannot satisfy the active supervision requirement of the state action doctrine.

Similarly, the BOME does not engage in active supervision over private peer-review decisions. The principal function of the BOME is to regulate the licensing of physicians in the State. As respondents note, Oregon hospitals are required by statute to notify the BOME promptly of a decision to terminate or restrict privileges. See Or.Rev. Stat. § 441.820(1) (1987). Neither this statutory provision nor any other, however, indicates that the BOME has the power to disapprove private privilege decisions. The apparent purpose of the reporting requirement is to give the BOME an opportunity to determine whether additional action on its part, such as revocation of a physician's license, is warranted. Certainly, respondents have not shown that the BOME in practice reviews privilege decisions or that it ever has asserted the authority to reverse them.

The only remaining alleged supervisory authority in this case is the state judiciary. * * * This case, however, does not require us to decide the broad question whether judicial review of private conduct ever can constitute active supervision, because judicial review of privilege-termination decisions in Oregon, if such review exists at all, falls far short of satisfying the active supervision requirement.

* * *

Because we conclude that no state actor in Oregon actively supervises hospital peer-review decisions, we hold that the state action doctrine does not protect the peer-review activities challenged in this case from application of the federal antitrust laws. In so holding, we are not unmindful of the policy argument that respondents and their amici have advanced for reaching the opposite conclusion. They contend that effective peer review is essential to the provision of quality medical care and that any threat of antitrust liability will prevent physicians from participating openly and actively in peer-review proceedings. This argument, however, essentially challenges the wisdom

---

14. Indeed, the statutory scheme indicates that the Health Division has only limited power over even a hospital's peer-review procedures. The statute authorizes the Health Division to force a hospital to comply with its obligation to establish and regularly review peer-review procedures, but the statute does not empower the Health Division to review the quality of the procedures that the hospital adopts.

of applying the antitrust laws to the sphere of medical care, and as such is properly directed to the legislative branch. To the extent that Congress has declined to exempt medical peer review from the reach of the antitrust laws,[15] peer review is immune from antitrust scrutiny only if the state effectively has made this conduct its own. The State of Oregon has not done so. Accordingly, we reverse the judgment of the court of appeals.

JUSTICE BLACKMUN took no part in the consideration or decision of this case.

SECTION D. EXTRA–PROFESSIONAL FORCES

GILBERT v. MEDICAL ECONOMICS CO.

United States Court of Appeals for the Tenth Circuit, 1981.
665 F.2d 305.

McKAY, CIRCUIT JUDGE.

* * * On April 3, 1978, defendants published in the periodical Medical Economics an article entitled "Who Let This Doctor In The O.R.? The Story Of A Fatal Breakdown In Medical Policing." The article, a copy of which is contained in the record before us, outlines two incidents of alleged medical malpractice in which patients of plaintiff, an anesthesiologist, suffered fatal or severely disabling injuries in the operating room as a result of plaintiff's acts of alleged malpractice. The article indicates that in the case of the disabling injuries, plaintiff's insurer settled the ensuing malpractice action for $900,000. It notes further that in the case of the fatal injury, the patient's family was attempting to reach a settlement. Following a description of these incidents, the article suggests that they occurred because of "a collapse of self-policing by physicians and of disciplinary action by hospitals and regulatory agencies." To show the substantiality of this inadequate policing of medical personnel, the article discusses plaintiff's history of psychiatric and related personal problems. The article suggests (1) that there was a causal relationship between plaintiff's personal problems and the acts of alleged malpractice, (2) that plaintiff's lack of capacity to engage responsibly in the practice of medicine was or should have been known to the policing agents of the medical profession, and (3) that more intensive policing of medical

---

15. Congress in fact insulated certain medical peer-review activities from antitrust liability in the Health Care Quality Improvement Act of 1986, 42 U.S.C.A. §§ 11101–11152. The Act, which was enacted well after the events at issue in this case and is not retroactive, essentially immunizes peer-review action from liability if the action was taken "in the reasonable belief that [it] was in the furtherance of quality health care." § 11112(a). The Act expressly provides that it does not change other "immunities under law," § 11115(a), including the state action immunity, thus allowing states to immunize peer-review action that does not meet the federal standard. In enacting this measure, Congress clearly noted and responded to the concern that the possibility of antitrust liability will discourage effective peer review. If physicians believe that the Act provides insufficient immunity to protect the peer-review process fully, they must take that matter up with Congress.

personnel is needed. The article identified plaintiff by name and included her photograph.

On the basis of the pleadings and a copy of the article, the district court held a hearing on cross-motions for summary judgment. Defendants moved for summary judgment on the ground that the article contained only truthful factual statements or opinions relating to newsworthy matters and therefore was protected by the First Amendment. Plaintiff conceded that no issues of fact were involved. She urged summary judgment on the theory that although the general theme of the article was newsworthy and therefore privileged, the defendants nevertheless had tortiously invaded her privacy by including in the article her name, photograph, and certain private facts about her life that were not privileged.

In granting summary judgment for the defendants, the trial court agreed that the general subject of the article was indeed newsworthy insofar as it dealt with the competency of licensed professionals. * * * To question whether defendants should have omitted certain details from this particular article, the court believed, would amount to "editorial second-guessing" rather than legal analysis. The court therefore held that the entire article was protected by the First Amendment.

On appeal, plaintiff's first contention is that defendants tortiously invaded her privacy by publicly disclosing embarrassing private facts about her personal life. Colorado has recognized a common-law right to privacy. * * * Defendants, however, raised the defense of First Amendment privilege, and thus, we must turn to federal substantive law in this diversity case to determine the extent of defendants' federal constitutional defense.

* * *

This privilege is not absolute, however, and as in other areas involving the media, the right of the individual to keep information private must be balanced against the right of the press to disseminate newsworthy information to the public. In attempting to strike an acceptable balance between these competing interests, liability may be imposed for publicizing matters concerning the private life of another "if the matter publicized is of a kind that (a) would be highly offensive to a reasonable person, and (b) is not of legitimate concern to the public." Restatement (Second) of Torts § 652D (1977). As comment h points out, not all matters are of legitimate public interest:

> The line is to be drawn when the publicity ceases to be the giving of information to which the public is entitled, and becomes a morbid and sensational prying into private lives for its own sake with which a reasonable member of the public, with decent standards, would say that he had no concern.

Thus, dissemination of non-newsworthy private facts is not protected by the First Amendment.

The privilege does immunize the reporting of private facts, however, when discussed in connection with "matters of the kind customarily regarded as 'news.'" Comment g. Any information disseminated "for purposes of education, amusement or enlightenment, when the public may reasonably be expected to have a legitimate interest in what is published," is also protected by the privilege. Comment j. * * *

Even where certain matters are clearly within the protected sphere of legitimate public interest, some private facts about an individual may lie outside that sphere. * * * Therefore, to properly balance freedom of the press against the right of privacy, every private fact disclosed in an otherwise truthful, newsworthy publication must have some substantial relevance to a matter of legitimate public interest. When these conditions are satisfied, the facts in the publication and inferences reasonably drawn therefrom fall within the ambit of First Amendment protection and are privileged.

* * *

With respect to the publication of plaintiff's photograph and name, we find that these truthful representations are substantially relevant to a newsworthy topic because they strengthen the impact and credibility of the article. They obviate any impression that the problems raised in the article are remote or hypothetical, thus providing an aura of immediacy and even urgency that might not exist had plaintiff's name and photograph been suppressed. Similarly, we find the publication of plaintiff's psychiatric and marital problems to be substantially relevant to the newsworthy topic. While it is true that these subjects would fall outside the First Amendment privilege in the absence of either independent newsworthiness or any substantial nexus with a newsworthy topic, here they are connected to the newsworthy topic by the rational inference that plaintiff's personal problems were the underlying cause of the acts of alleged malpractice.

Plaintiff claims that the drawing of such inferences is not within the protected scope of editorial discretion unless a public tribunal first declares such an inference to be legally established. We conclude, however, that a rule forbidding editors from drawing inferences from truthful newsworthy facts would result in a far too restrictive and wholly unjustifiable construction of the First Amendment privilege. If the press is to have the generous breathing space that courts have accorded it thus far, editors must have freedom to make reasonable judgments and to draw one inference where others also reasonably could be drawn. This is precisely the editorial discretion contemplated by the privilege. Because the inferences of causation drawn in this case are not, as a matter of law, so purely conjectural that no reasonable editor could draw them other than through guesswork and speculation, we hold that defendants did not abuse their editorial discretion in this case.

* * *

Accordingly, the court did not abuse its discretion in finding that defendants are entitled to summary judgment as to every issue in this case.

Affirmed.

UNITED STATES v. ZWICK

United States District Court for the Northern District of Ohio, 1976.
413 F.Supp. 113.

CONTIE, DISTRICT JUDGE.

The plaintiff, United States of America * * * filed its complaint against the defendants, Dr. Louis S. Zwick and Louis S. Zwick, M.D., Inc., for violations under 21 U.S.C.A. §§ 828(e) and 353 * * *.

This court * * * finds that the defendants consent to the entry of this declaratory judgment and order of permanent injunction personally, and by and through their counsel.

The court further finds that the defendant, by means of order forms issued under 21 U.S.C.A. § 828, obtained anorectic controlled substances through interstate commerce in the amount of 3,886,634 dosage units from October 1972 through October 1975 for the purpose of dispensing in the conduct of his medical bariatric practice, which involved a substantial number of patients who were being treated for obesity. Further, that the aforesaid medication was in fact dispensed to the defendant's patients in unlabeled packets, each containing 30 anorectic dosage units of controlled substances, pursuant to his bariatric practice from October 1972 through October 1975, which practice continues to the present time.

The court finds that a legal issue exists as to the circumstances under which it may become unlawful for a physician under 21 U.S.C.A. § 828 to dispense or prescribe anorectic controlled drugs described therein in the treatment of obesity to a large number of patients, whereby the cumulative and accrued effect is that large quantities of controlled anorectic substances are thereby prescribed or dispensed, in that under some circumstances such dispensing or prescribing may be outside the practice of medicine in the treatment of obesity.

To resolve this legal issue it is necessary for the court to declare the minimum medical diagnostic requirements, tests, and procedures and the medically accepted standards that must be met and performed by any physician involved in treating patients for obesity and dispensing of scheduled anorectic drugs which are controlled substances regulated by 21 U.S.C.A. and 21 C.F.R.

It is therefore ordered, adjudged, decreed and declared:

For the physician, the obese patient poses one of the most complex problems he is likely to confront. Obesity itself presents as a spectrum ranging from mildly inconvenient and/or unattractive "overweight" to massive and often life-threatening excess poundage. Its treatment likewise involves measures ranging from relatively modest dietary restriction to intestinal surgery. Above all, obesity almost invariably involves a complex interplay between physiology and behavior, so that the physician must perforce combine purely physiologic and medical measures with the skills of the psychologist and educator. Largely for this reason there is no "standard" treatment that will serve to manage most obese patients or even a large fraction of them. In each case, treatment must be geared to the specific problems, habits, personality, and life-style of the patient. Therefore, the treatment of obesity requires an eclectic approach by the physician.

It is further declared that the minimum medical standards of practice for physicians treating obesity by dispensing and prescribing large quantities of controlled anorectic drugs is not met where they are dispensed and prescribed to a large number of patients as a standard treatment, nor are they met by only taking the pulse, blood pressure, weight, stethoscopic examination of the patient, a five minute personal interview with the physician, a casual concern as to possible dependency or addiction of the patient to anorectic drugs, and the delivery of a recommended diet to the patient on any office visit.

The decision to use an anorectic drug in any patient can only be made after evaluation of the patient's needs and the risks which such drugs pose to the patient, and a determination as to whether the benefit from the use of such drugs outweighs those risks.

Since no medical authority disagrees over the need to individualize the treatment of obesity, it follows that in a practice where a large number of patients are treated for obesity, there will be significant variations in the approach to treatment. It is prima facie improper for a single approach to be used. It is improper that the prescribing and dispensing of anorectic drugs be included as a routine part of the treatment of obesity. In other words, it is not proper for the physician dispensing and prescribing anorectic controlled drugs to adopt a unitary approach to the treatment of obesity in that no standard approach to treatment exists.

The court declares that the standards of medical practice and other modalities of care and treatment of obesity and the use of anorectic drugs * * * [were set forth in five listed authorities on obesity found in collected essays, medical journals, and textbooks].

[T]he Food and Drug Administration regulations as set forth in 21 C.F.R. § 310.504 * * * [are] incorporated by reference as though fully rewritten herein.

It is further ordered, adjudged and decreed that the defendant, Dr. Louis S. Zwick, and the defendant, Louis S. Zwick, M.D., Inc., its agents, officers, employees and all persons under its control, are hereby restrained and enjoined from violating the within orders of this court.

[An appendix reprinted the Standards of Bariatric Practice of the American Society of Bariatric Physicians, and 21 C.F.R. § 310.504, Amphetamines.]

Appendix

CASE RECORD IN REMINGTON v. AVERY

§ A. Introduction

Introductory Note	388
Factual Summary of Remington v. Avery	391
Initial Interview With Susan Remington	392

§ B. Pre-Surgery Documents

Exhibit A:	Office Records of Dr. Avery	395
Exhibit B:	Office Records of Dr. Marshall	396
Exhibit C:	Breasts Before Surgery	396

§ C. First Hospitalization: Subcutaneous Mastectomy and Insertion of Implants

Exhibit D:	Admission Summary	397
Exhibit E:	Physician's Orders	398
Exhibit F:	Operative Consent Form	399
Exhibit G:	Operative Notes	400
Exhibit H:	Anatomy of the Normal Breast	401
Exhibit I:	Subcutaneous Implantation	402
Exhibit J:	Prosthesis of the Type Implanted in Susan Remington's Breasts	403
Exhibit K:	Anesthesia Record	404
Exhibit L:	Recovery Room Record	405
Exhibit M:	Physician Progress Record	406
Exhibit N:	Nursing Progress Record	407
Exhibit O:	Computerized Medication Record Summary	410
Exhibit P:	Laboratory Reports	411
Exhibit Q:	Breast Hematoma	412
Exhibit R:	Pathology Report	413
Exhibit S:	Discharge Summary	413

§ D. Documentation of Medical Care Between Hospitalizations

Exhibit T:	Office Records of Dr. Reeves	414

§ E. Second Hospitalization: Removal of Implants

Exhibit U:	Admission Summary	415
Exhibit V:	Mrs. Remington With Breast Skin Necrosis	416
Exhibit W:	Operative Notes	417
Exhibit X:	Pathology Report	418
Exhibit Y:	Discharge Summary	418

§ F. Third Hospitalization: Submuscular Insertion of Implants

Exhibit Z:	Admission Summary	419
Exhibit AA:	Breasts Before Submuscular Insertion of Implants	420
Exhibit BB:	Operative Notes	421
Exhibit CC:	Submuscular Implantation	422

§ G. Pre-filing Documents

Exhibit DD:	Breasts After Submuscular Insertion of Implants	423
Exhibit EE:	Dr. Avery's Letter to Plaintiff's Lawyer	424
Exhibit FF:	Report of Dr. Bergan to Mr. Brown	425
Exhibit GG:	Report of Dr. Sears to Mr. Brown	426
Exhibit HH:	Report of Dr. Shumacher to Mr. Brown	427
Exhibit II:	Report of Dr. Burns to Mr. Brown	429
Exhibit JJ:	Report of Dr. Hickman to Mr. Brown	430

§ H. The Complaint

§ I. Discovery Documents

Document 1:	Dr. Avery's Interrogatories to Mrs. Remington	433
Document 2:	Dr. Avery's Deposition of Mrs. Remington	439
Document 3:	Mrs. Remington's Deposition of Dr. Avery	446
Document 4:	Mrs. Remington's Deposition of Dr. Reeves	453
Document 5:	Dr. Avery's Deposition of Dr. Sears	455
Document 6:	Dr. Avery's Deposition of Dr. Shumacher	461
Document 7:	Dr. Avery's Deposition of Dr. Bryant	465
Document 8:	Dr. Avery's Deposition of Claire Garvey	468
Document 9:	Dr. Avery's Deposition of Sheila Elliott	469
Document 10:	Dr. Avery's Supplemental Interrogatories to Mrs. Remington	470
Document 11:	Mrs. Remington's Request for Admissions to Dr. Avery	471

§ J. Pretrial Hearing Documents

Document 12:	Pretrial Stipulation Rules	473
Document 13:	Concise Statement of Fact	473
Document 14:	Plaintiff's Proposed Pretrial Stipulations of Issues of Law for Determination at Trial	474
Document 15:	Plaintiff's Proposed Pretrial Stipulations of Issues of Fact for Determination at Trial	475

§ K. GLOSSARY

Glossary of Medical Terms Relating to Breast Surgery 477

§ A. Introduction

INTRODUCTORY NOTE

The Appendix consists of litigation documents generated in the course of a medical malpractice case, Remington v. Avery, showing how a medical liability case may be persuasively prepared for trial using various sources of data.

In this case the allegation that the surgeon was negligent could be expected to be contested vigorously. The specific surgical procedure, while going out of fashion, was not obsolete; and an unsatisfactory result could occur without negligence. In addition, the patient sought and generally consented to the procedure. Post-surgery attendance of the surgeon may have been within the outer limits of due care.

Causation of the harm was likewise disputed. Even if the surgeon was negligent in some respect, the kinds of harms that occurred could have been caused by factors and circumstances outside the control of a competent surgeon.

The physical harms themselves were to some extent expected consequences of the surgical procedure itself. While the untoward consequences may have been magnified by the surgeon's negligence, that could be difficult to establish. The plaintiff's mental and emotional harms, and her disappointed expectations, were subjective and might not persuade a jury.

Finally, the damages would be difficult to demonstrate since the female patient probably would not disrobe in court; and the photographs showing various stages of treatment may have been too gory along the way, yet too bland at the conclusion.

These documents represent the case data—some consistent, some conflicting. Turning the data into evidence requires thoughtful interplay between the patient, the advocate and medical experts. In effective litigation, evidence is the masonry and advocacy is the architecture. Attorneys need to depict carefully and draw attention to the evidence in order to persuade in the courtroom. Evidence attracts the attention of both judge and jury, engaging their interest, sympathies, and finally convincing them to accept the position of the advocate. The fact-finders resolve conflicts in the evidence by believing or disbelieving witnesses, thereby turning the evidence into "the facts in the case." [1]

Students study the law by reading appellate cases, in which the "facts" are no longer in doubt. Variations on the facts are called "hypotheticals," yet any lawyer who knew a case before reading the appellate opinion knows how hypothetical the facts in the opinion are—like a newspaper account of an event that the reader observed in person.

---

1. Highlights in the following page and a half were drawn from an article by then-professorial lecturer in law Mark Foster, Advocate's Great Moment: Picking, Choosing Facts, Legal Times of Washington, April 1982, at 1.

Unfortunately, many attorneys neglect the evidence, relegating the "statement of facts" to a minor role in the case and glossing over the proposed findings of fact at the beginning of the opening statement. Although these attorneys produce subtle treatises on the law, they give little attention to the factual targets that make the law apply.

The appellate opinion approach used in the casebook method misrepresents the dynamic aspect of evidence and depreciates the role that evidence plays in advocacy. By the time a case reaches an appellate court, the evidence has been massaged and manipulated by several attorneys. By performing their assigned tasks of reconciling conflicts in the evidence, the judge and jury have decided authoritatively what happened. Finally, the appellate court neatly sets in cement the "facts" in its written opinion. Thus, the law student gains the impression that the facts are an immutable feature of the case's legal landscape. They naturally infer that the creative attorney manipulates the law around the facts to create a successful legal theory—and when law is being extended, that happens; but the great bulk of negligence cases turn on the selection and presentation of evidence to fit the law and to achieve the favorable conclusion.

Some attorneys neglect evidence because it requires a different type of effort. The law is nearby and accessible in books and computers, but the evidence is in hospital records and physicians' offices. Thus, someone has to go out where the evidence is, take it in hand, and bring it back. Many advocates are content to interview the client, send out interrogatories, take a few depositions, and feel comfortable that they know the case inside out. A competent attorney knows what to look for, where to look, how to modify the search, and when to keep looking. When a client walks into the advocate's office, the account given by the client contains a lot of leads to usable evidence in the hands of other people. The attorney must prepare a plan for collecting evidence, and then the plan must be executed, gathering quantities of usable and unusable evidence.

The attorney who can present a plaintiff as a patient who was neglected, ignored, or lied to, or who can present the defendant as an upstanding professional person who has been lied about, put upon, and stigmatized, will win more cases than the attorney who presents abstract and impersonal "plaintiffs" and "defendants." For example, the attorney may go through a detailed clinical recitation of the various complications that a post-surgery patient endured while his or her surgeon neglected to come to the hospital. This is not purely sentimental; these facts are relevant to proving damages for pain and suffering. In showing why a client deserves to win, one or two key pieces of evidence can tip the balance of a case in favor of one party.

To accomplish this, the attorney must sort through the collection of evidence, selecting the items that fit the ultimate theory of the case. Next the attorney must shape and highlight the evidence that helps the client's position. The attorney's most creative and productive time is spent assembling the bits of evidence into a presentation that seems to lead irresistibly to the conclusion that favors the client. The attorney does not invent evidence, but imagining what evidence would be helpful may lead to discovering it. The attorney does not need to suppress evidence, but the qualities that make it uncomfortable may also make it inadmissible. The organization and presentation of evidence, then, leaves the attorney latitude that must be used to be appreciated.

Unlike scientists and journalists, attorneys do not observe and describe events; the written and oral presentations of events that attorneys deal with were prepared long after the events described. The differences between events and descriptions have enormous practical consequences. The attorney who collects, selects, and presents evidence passively will be outmaneuvered by the attorney who practices the arts of selection and emphasis.

In addition to oral testimony, medical liability cases use large quantities of demonstrative evidence. Demonstrative evidence is addressed directly to the senses without the intervention of testimony from witnesses. Demonstrative evidence includes medical charts, anatomical drawings and photographs of various tissues, structures and devices. For the trial lawyer, documents and illustrations create an image in the minds of the jury which helps them to understand and appreciate the lawyer's arguments. The following types of demonstrative evidence should be organized to support the appropriate central theme of a medical malpractice case:

Medical Charts: To create a forceful concept in the minds of the jury, hospital and physician office records must be assembled which give a clear picture of the patient's treatment and the course of the illness or injury.

Anatomical Drawings: To demonstrate evidence during formal discovery and at trial by expert witnesses, attorneys conceive of and arrange for drawings of various aspects of anatomy. Such drawings may also be a useful reference for the attorney during opening and closing statements. To withstand objection by the opposing party, anatomical drawings should be reasonably understandable in appearance and layout, and they should fairly and accurately reflect the anatomical tissue or structure that they represent.

Photographs: To emphasize evidential physical conditions and to make anatomical landmarks recognizable by laymen, the attorney should present appropriate photographs. The trial attorney should determine how graphic photographs should be based on the persuasive effect these photographs may have in the litigation.

Data derived from depositions serves primarily as a source of persuasive evidence relating to the proof of the case. Documents in Section I have been condensed by eliminating most of the inconsistencies and many of the jumbled responses often occurring in depositions. In addition, no objections or arguments between attorneys have been included.

FACTUAL SUMMARY OF REMINGTON v. AVERY

After watching a TV talk show about a surgical procedure that involved removing breast tissue and inserting silicone gel implants, Susan Remington, a 34-year-old widow, consulted Dr. Douglas Avery, a plastic surgeon. Dr. Avery told her that he felt she was at "high risk" because of her strong family history of breast cancer. Dr. Avery recorded in the chart that he told her infection, hemorrhage, and numbness of the skin and nipples were complications of the procedure.

Mrs. Remington then consulted a general surgeon who told her that he thought surgery advisable, but that he recommended delayed insertion of the breast implants. Although she was concerned that she might develop breast cancer, Mrs. Remington was also hopeful that the operation would improve the sagging appearance of her breasts, similar to results obtained by her friends who had undergone breast augmentation.

Dr. Avery performed a bilateral subcutaneous mastectomy and inserted breast prostheses in the subcutaneous space. At the conclusion of the surgery he applied a bulky compression dressing. Later, a nurse notified Dr. Avery by telephone that Mrs. Remington's blood count and blood pressure dropped in the Recovery Room, but Dr. Avery did not go to the hospital. Several hours later, while attempting to go to the bathroom, Mrs. Remington fainted. Dr. Avery was notified, but again did not go to the hospital. As soon as the effects of the anesthesia wore off, Mrs. Remington complained of severe bilateral breast pain, for which she received analgesics.

Dr. Avery's first postoperative examination of Mrs. Remington was 24 hours after surgery. He noted that her surgical dressing remained clean and dry and he reassured her that breast pain was to be expected. Later that day, when a nurse notified Dr. Avery that bloody drainage was noted on the back of Mrs. Remington's surgical dressing and bed, he gave the nurse telephone orders to reinforce the dressing.

On the second postoperative day, when Dr. Avery removed the breast drains, blood came out of the drain incision sites. Dr. Avery then compressed each breast, expressing even more blood. Thereafter, Mrs. Remington's breasts appeared and felt swollen. Mrs. Remington cradled her arms under her breasts for support when she was sitting.

Mrs. Remington's breast pain persisted and parts of her breasts became discolored, although the swelling reduced slightly.

On the seventh postoperative day, the slight discoloration and swelling of Mrs. Remington's breasts persisted. She continued to ask for and receive medication for pain. She was discharged from the hospital on the eighth postoperative day. Her breasts, especially around the nipple, had become blackened with surrounding redness.

Three days after her discharge from the hospital she went to Dr. Avery's office and asked him if she was "rejecting" the implants. He replied, "No, but there may be some infection," and said that she might need to have the implants removed. He told her that she would be given an appointment three days later with a plastic surgeon whom Dr. Avery had asked to "cover" for him because Dr. Avery was going on vacation. Dr. Avery told the covering surgeon that Mrs. Remington had developed complications from a subcutaneous mastectomy, but that Mrs. Remington was reluctant to have the implants removed.

When Mrs. Remington saw the covering surgeon, he observed that the blood supply to the breast skin was compromised. He debrided the wound and requested Mrs. Remington to return in three days, at which time he observed continued evidence of vascular compromise.

Seventeen days after he had seen her on his first postoperative visit, Dr. Avery re-examined Mrs. Remington and noted that she still had evidence of necrosis. Ten days later, he examined Mrs. Remington's breasts and diagnosed bilateral areas of dead skin overlying the nipple with exposure of one implant. He hospitalized her, removed the implants, and performed extensive debridement of necrotic breast tissue.

Fourteen months later, Dr. Avery inserted new breast implants under Mrs. Remington's chest muscles. Nevertheless, Mrs. Remington's breasts had residual scarring and indentations.

INITIAL INTERVIEW WITH SUSAN REMINGTON

Dictated by Gordon Brown, Esquire
May 14, 1985

Medical Appointments Prior To First Breast Surgery:

May 31, 1983—Because Remington felt a lump in her breast, her gynecologist referred her for a mammogram which showed fibrocystic disease.

June 22, 1983—Remington went to Dr. Avery to discuss a treatment utilizing breast surgery which she had learned about on a TV talk show. Dr. Avery said that she could possibly experience a loss of a lot of blood in the hospital, and that she would be in the hospital for 5 or 6 days.

July 8, 1983—Remington went to Dr. Marshall, a general surgeon, who explained that she needed the surgery because she was a "time bomb." He told her to go ahead with the operation and that Dr. Avery was qualified to do it. However, he told her to wait 6 months for her breasts to heal before having the implants put in. He also said that the implants were usually inserted under the chest muscles.

(Attorney's Note: Initial breast implants were under the skin.)

July 21, 1983—When Remington went back to Dr. Avery to discuss the surgery, he told her he always put the implants in right away to save money and another operation. Remington thinks he said he would put them under the muscles if necessary; however he didn't think there would be such a need.

August 5, 1983—Dr. Avery made arrangements for Remington to go into the hospital.

First Hospitalization:

August 9, 1983—Dr. Avery operated on Remington. On the day after the operation, Remington's breasts seemed fine except for black and blue areas around and under them. On the next day the two drains were removed. A lot of blood squirted out and she thought she was going to bleed to death. Dr. Avery pushed her breasts, and more blood came out. He said he didn't think the drains worked. Remington had a lot of pain and could not eat. The IV was in longer than expected after the operation and she was kept on high doses of antibiotics.

August 17, 1983—Remington left the hospital early in the morning.

Followup:

After the surgery, Dr. Avery told Remington to replace the gauze pads every day and put Mercurochrome on her breasts.

August 22, 1983—When Remington saw Dr. Reeves (Dr. Avery's vacation replacement) she told him she was not feeling good. He prescribed Percodan and told her to stay on the antibiotic. He also gave her another prescription. He did not tell Remington anything, although she had asked him if anything was wrong.

August 23, 1983—Remington went to see the general surgeon she had seen prior to surgery, Dr. Marshall, because she was getting worse and her skin was peeling off around her breasts. The surgeon told her to do what the other doctors had told her, and to see if the implants had broken through the skin. He prescribed a pain killer.

August 25, 1983—Remington saw Dr. Reeves again and received the same treatment.

August 29, 1983 Remington saw Dr. Reeves again.

(Attorney's Note: Dr. Reeves, on all these visits basically gave Remington the same treatment as reflected in above notes for August 22, 1983, and would occasionally use tweezers to remove some of the dead skin around her breasts.)

September 2, 1983—When Remington saw Dr. Reeves she told him that she was most concerned about her nipples because the skin was peeling off, as if they had been badly burned. He did not respond to her inquiry.

September 6, September 9 and September 13, 1983, Remington saw Dr. Avery and got the same treatment.

Second Hospitalization:

September 16, 1983—While changing the pads that she had been given to place between bra and skin Remington noticed that the left breast had opened up with a small hole on the right center. She called Dr. Avery. She met Dr. Avery at the office and he took her to check in the hospital, where he operated on Remington the same day to remove the implants, which he stated had broken through.

September 20, 1983—Remington asked Dr. Avery if she had rejected the implant. He said "No." He also said she would have to wait 6 months for further corrective surgery, and implants would have to be placed under the muscle. Additionally he stated that he had to cut very close to the surface of the skin on the first surgery because of the reason for the surgery.

After the emergency surgery Remington never experienced any of the pain, swelling or other problems that she had experienced the previous five weeks.

Followup:

October 1983—Remington went back to Dr. Avery to consult about the corrective surgery.

Third Hospitalization:

November 16, 1984—Dr. Avery put the implants in under the muscles.

(Attorney's Note: Obtain further notes about doctors' visits after the corrective surgery)

Between the second and third operations, she believed that after the corrective surgery she would look normal, even though in one of the last visits before the third surgery, Dr. Avery commented that she would "not be perfect." Remington presumed he meant that she would look as good as most normal people, with the exception that her nipples would need later surgery.

February 28, 1985—Remington again asked Dr. Avery about reconstructing her nipples, which he said he could do, but they would never look normal. He then said that her breasts, as far as the scarring and indentations were concerned, would never be improved.

Remington has never let her daughter see her breasts through the whole thing because she didn't want her to think that this could happen to her.

Remington was afraid to date or begin any kind of relationship with a man, as she could not bear the thought of exposing herself to the kind of rejection she might experience.

During the time between the first operation and the third operation, Remington had never thought of the surgery as a "mastectomy," until she was in the hospital for the third operation, and one of the nurses referred to her as a patient who had had a "double mastectomy."

§ B. Pre-Surgery Documents
Exhibit A.
OFFICE RECORDS OF DR. AVERY

Douglas Avery, M.D.
Plastic & Reconstructive Surgery
6688 Euclid Drive
Middletown, U.S.A.

DATE	
6/22/83	34 y.o ♀ – strong family hx of breast cancer – No bx Plan: Subcut. mastectomy w/ reconstruction Complications explained – infection, hemorrhage & sensory changes D. Avery md
7/21/83	Mammogram discussed D. Avery md.
8/5/83	Surgery scheduled – see dictated admission summary D. Avery md
8/9/83	Surgery – Subcutaneous Mastectomy w/ reconstruction D. Avery md
8/20/83	Skin viable? Explained may need graft Schedule appointment w/ Dr. Reeves D. Avery md
9/6/83	Still has evidence of necrosis – needs demarcation Explained nature Rx Reflex & Percodan D. Avery md
9/9/83	Skin necrotic! – awaiting separation. Explained tx D. Avery md
9/13/83	Still separating – D. Avery md
9/16/83	Has necrosis – To O.R. D. Avery md

Exhibit B.

OFFICE RECORDS OF DR. MARSHALL

Donald Marshall, M.D.
General Surgery

July 8, 1983 — Mrs. Remington has dominant fibrocystic changes, several small axillary nodes, an inverted left nipple. Advised bilateral subcutaneous mastectomy.

August 23, 1983 — Had surgery two weeks ago with immediate implants above the muscle. Edema subsiding. Breasts tender both sides. Areas of superficial skin desquamation. No obvious hematoma. Incisions clean. Advise seeing plastic surgeon for opinion regarding why skin condition is not improving. Would advise removal of implants.

Exhibit C.

BREASTS BEFORE SURGERY

Photographs taken by Dr. Avery on August 5, 1983, of Susan Remington's breasts before subcutaneous mastectomy and implantation of prostheses

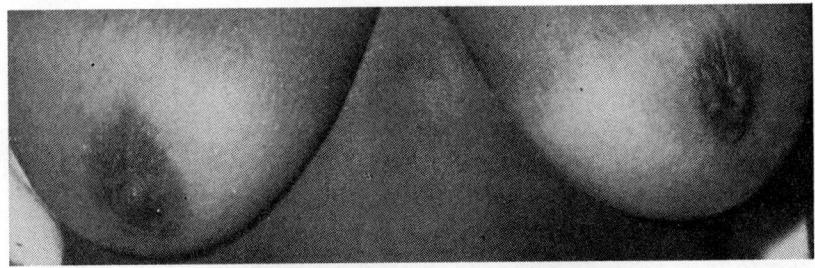

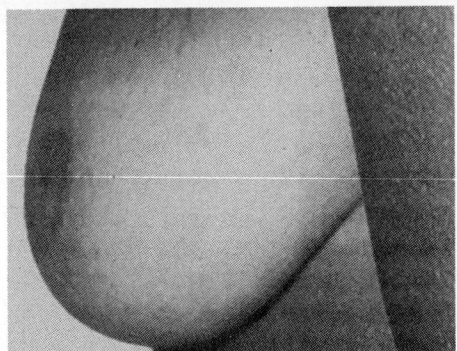

Photographs depict slight ptosis (sagging) of breasts secondary to natural relaxation of supportive tissues due to childbirth and aging. The inverted left nipple is congenital.

§ C. First Hospitalization: Subcutaneous Mastectomy and Insertion of Implants

Exhibit D.

ADMISSION SUMMARY

COMMUNITY HOSPITAL

ADMISSION SUMMARY   PATIENT: Susan Remington

DATE OF ADMISSION: August 8, 1983.

CHIEF COMPLAINT: Breast tumor, right breast.

HISTORY OF PRESENT ILLNESS: This 34-year-old widowed female has a lesion or tumor of the right upper outer quadrant of the right breast.

PAST MEDICAL HISTORY: History is significant in that her mother, grandmother and aunt have had breast cancer. She has had no previous biopsies, no history of any breast pain.

PHYSICAL EXAMINATION: Reveals a healthy-looking female, with a 24 centimeter nipple-sternal distance bilaterally, a lumpy consistency to both breasts, with a 3 centimeter mass in the right upper outer quadrant, which appears to be benign. She has had a mammogram which was negative. These areas of the breasts are not tender.

Head and neck: Within normal limits.

Chest: Clear.

Heart: Regular sinus rhythm.

Abdomen: Soft.

Extremities: Within normal limits.

Admitting Diagnosis: Bilateral Cystic Dysplasia.

Exhibit E.
PHYSICIAN'S ORDERS
COMMUNITY HOSPITAL

PHYSICIAN'S ORDERS

ORDER DATE & TIME	ORDER NO.		NURSE'S SIGNATURE & TIME
8-8-83		Type and cross match for 2 units Morphine 10 mg. ✓ IM Vistaril 75 mg. Telephone Order Dr. Avery / F. Miller RN	
8/9/83	(1) (2) (3) (4) (5) (6)	Reg diet as tolerated D5W @ 75 cc / hr. - + gm Keflex q 6h Demerol 75 mg. IM QHS Nembutal 100 mg. po HS Compazine 100 mg po HS Hemovac to suction q 8h D. Avery MD	

		Give 2 units of blood
		                    Verbal order
		              /f Dr Avery / L. Boies, RN.	

		H & H @ 1800 - Call doctor if Hct ↓ 30 Telephone Orders Dr. Avery / F. Miller RN	
	1 2	Demerol 50 mg q 3h pr pain HCT @ 0600 tomorrow Telephone order Dr. Avery / L. Boies RN.	
		Out of bed & Walking TID D. Avery MD	
8-9-83		May reinforce dressing Telephone Order Dr. Avery / F. Miller RN	
8/10/83		Hematocrit today — Change drainage site dressing prn D. Avery MD	
8/11/83		D/C IV Keflex 500 mg po QD D. Avery MD	
8-12-83		D/C Demerol Tylenol gr X q4h po pro pain Telephone order Dr. Avery / L. Boies RN.	
8/14/83		Demerol 50 mg p.o. or IM q 3-4 h Verbal Order Dr. Avery / F. Miller RN	
8/15/83		Discharge in Am To Office in 3 days D. Avery, MD	

Exhibit F.

OPERATIVE CONSENT FORM

COMMUNITY HOSPITAL

CONSENT FOR OPERATION(S) AND SPECIAL PROCEDURES

Patient's Name __Susan Remington__ Date __Aug. 8, 1983__ Time __3:00__ ~~a.m.~~/p.m.

1. I hereby authorize Dr. __Avery__ Date __Aug 9, 1983__ Time __8__ a.m/~~p.m.~~ to perform upon the above patient the operation and/or procedure known as __Bilateral Subcutaneous Mastectomy__

2. If any unforseen conditions arise during the course of the operation, I do hereby authorize and request him and his assistants to take whatever steps, and to perform whatever procedures they deem advisable, which may be in addition to or different from those now planned.

3. The Doctor has explained to me that the procedure is __Removal of tissues in both breasts__ . If any unforseen condition arises in the course of the diagnostic procedure and/or operation calling, in his judgment, for procedures in addition to or different from those now contemplated, I authorize him to do whatever he deems advisable.

4. The Doctor also explained to me, and I understand, the medically acceptable alternative procedures or treatments and the substantial risks and hazards inherent in the proposed treatment or procedure, I was told that one of the alternatives is that I would refuse the operation or procedure.

5. I acknowledge that no guarantee or assurance has been made to me as to any of the results or risks, and I assume such risks, and that the practice of medicine is not an exact science and I understand.

6. I hereby consent to and authorize the transfusion or administration of blood or blood components and drugs to me during my surgery and hospitalization at the Hospital, whenever deemed necessary by those physicians attending my care, with no warranties made in connection with such blood or blood components.

7. I consent to the disposal by the Hospital of any tissue or parts which may be removed from me.

8. I consent to the taking of photographs in the course of this operation for the purpose of advancing medical education, as may be authorized by my doctor, and to the admittance of qualified observers to the operating room, as determined by the Hospital.

9. I (~~do~~/do not) _____ want to have further explanation, discussion or description of the operation or risks involved in all of these procedures.

I HAVE READ THE ABOVE AND ALL BLANKS ARE FILLED IN AND I UNDERSTAND THE WORDS

__Susan Remington__ __Claire Harvey__
Patient (Signature)   Witness to Signature of Patient or Responsible Party, (Signature)

_____   __Friend__
Relative Responsible for Patient   Relationship to Patient

I have provided the patient and/or the relative indicated with the information necessary to have a general understanding of the procedure, medically acceptable alternative procedures or treatments, and the substantial risks and hazards inherehnt in the proposes treatment or procedures.

__D. Avery, MD.__
Physician (Signature)

Exhibit G.

OPERATIVE NOTES

COMMUNITY HOSPITAL

OPERATIVE NOTES   PATIENT: Susan Remington

DATE: August 9, 1983

SURGEON: Douglas Avery, M.D.

PREOPERATIVE DIAGNOSIS: Bilateral breast dysplasia.

OPERATION: Bilateral subcutaneous mastectomy with immediate implantation. The implants are 240 cc. round, backless Surgitek implants.

POSTOPERATIVE DIAGNOSIS: Same.

HISTORY:

This is a 34-year-old female with a strong family history of breast cancer. The mother, aunt and grandmother have died from breast cancer. The patient has multiple cystic masses on both breasts.

PROCEDURE:

The patient was placed in the supine position and general anesthesia administered. The chest is prepped and draped in the usual fashion. A 6 cm incision is made 9 cm from the midline, 6 cm beneath the areolae bilaterally. Starting on the right breast the breast is separated from the pectoralis major by means of blunt and sharp dissection. Hemostasis is secured. The entire breast is separated in this fashion. In a level in the subcutaneous plane using a Metzenbaum scissor the skin is then separated from the breast in a complete circle. The area beneath the nipple is similarly cut sharply. The breast is removed. The inferior margin is marked with # 000 nylon along with the nipple site with a # 000 nylon suture. Hemostasis again secured and the breast is packed. Next, attention is turned to the left side and in a similar fashion dissection is carried out. Then attention is again turned to the right side. Hemostasis is secured in the superior pole and along the axilla. A large hemovac drain is brought out through a separate stab wound in the axilla. It is sutured in place by means of # 000 nylon. The breast is then implanted with the 240 cc round Surgitek implant. Delayed closure is carried out with # 000 Vicryl on the deep layer of the incision and a running # 000 nylon on the skin. Steristrips are applied. In a similar fashion the left breast is operated on. Then a bulky compression dressing is used to bind the patient into position. There appeared to be no bleeding from the hemovac drains at the completion of the procedure.

Exhibit H.
ANATOMY OF THE NORMAL BREAST

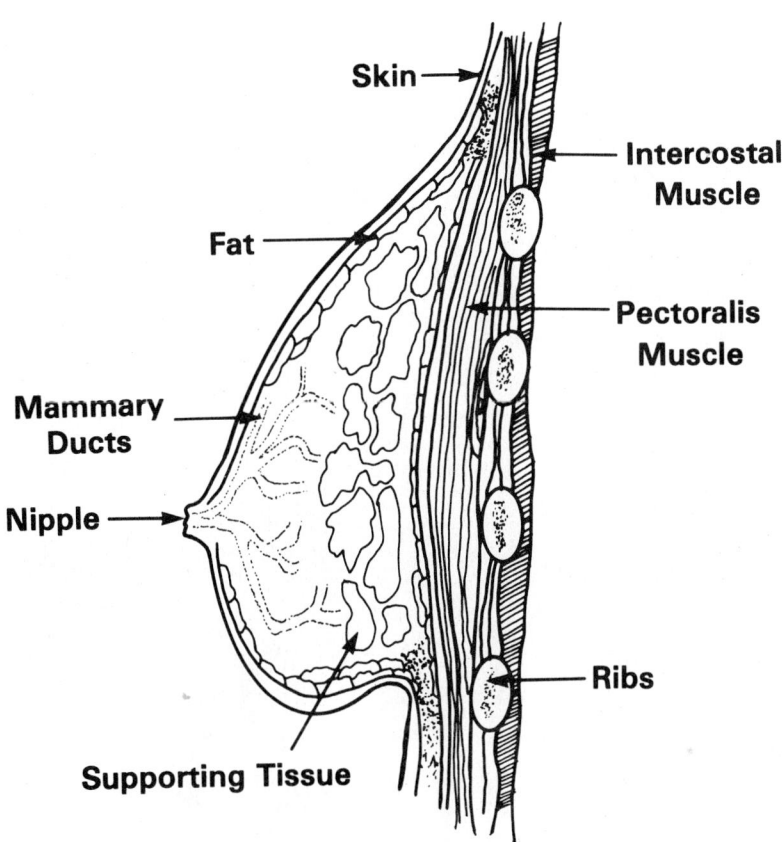

Exhibit I.
SUBCUTANEOUS IMPLANTATION
BREAST WITH SUBCUTANEOUS IMPLANTATION OF PROSTHESIS
AFTER MASTECTOMY

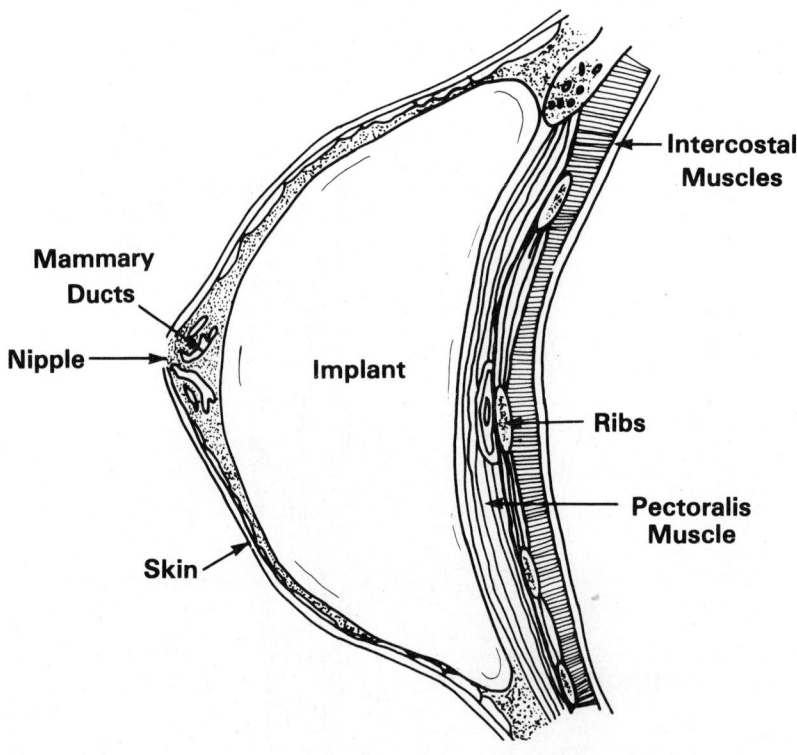

Cross-sectional drawing of the breast depicting the replacement of subcutaneous breast tissue (mammary ducts, fat and connective tissue) with a silicone-filled vinyl prosthesis. Note that the shape and configuration of the breast are altered, and that there is not a space-occupying source of internal pressure within the breast. Remember that the skin envelope has been surgically undermined.

Exhibit J.
PROSTHESIS OF THE TYPE IMPLANTED IN SUSAN REMINGTON'S BREASTS

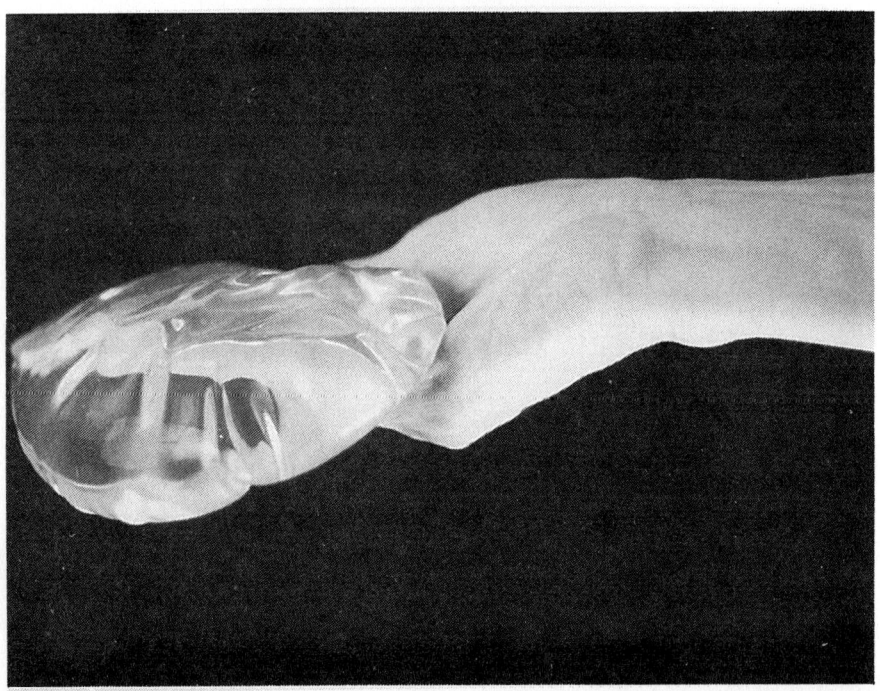

Photograph depicts the configuration and malleability of a gel-filled prosthesis which can be inserted into a surgically created space either on top of or underneath the chest muscle.

Exhibit K.

ANESTHESIA RECORD

COMMUNITY HOSPITAL
ANESTHESIA RECORD

SURGEON: Avery 8/9/83 ASSISTANT: None 97.8/84/29/122/70
PHYSICAL STATUS: _____ CARDIOVASCULAR: No Sx. EKG - WNL.
PULMONARY: Heavy Smoker HGB: 14.5 HCT: 43 BP 100/70
OTHER: _____ PREMED: morph. 10 / Vist. 75 0630 EFFECT: Apprehensive

[Anesthesia chart with vital signs plotted from 0730 to 1000]

FLUIDS: 5% D/LR 1L, 2000 + 300 → R.L.
ANESTHETIC AGENTS: Pent., Anec., Flua, N2O, O2
AIRWAY (CIRCLE): ORAL ENDOTRACH 7.0, CUFF INFLATED 2 ml.
MEDICATION DURING SURGERY: morphine, Flaxity

OPERATION: Bilateral subcutaneous mastectomy with reconstruction
IV 18 Jelco - Antecub.
CONDITION AT CLOSE: Satisfactory
POST ANES. STATE: To R.R. - asleep

ANESTHESIA BEGAN: 0725 ENDED: 1010
SURGERY BEGAN: 0750 ENDED: 1000

RECOVERY ROOM (CIRCLE): (O2) IPPB OTHER
64- P 88 R-20
FLUIDS: H/H Give 1 unit WBC

ANESTHETIST: Tapley

Exhibit L.

RECOVERY ROOM RECORD

COMMUNITY HOSPITAL
RECOVERY ROOM RECORD

DATE: 8/9/83

ROOM # 421 PRE-OP B/P 120/80 P 68 R 18

CONDITION ON ON ADMISSION BY [signature] RN TIME 1010
1) ARTIFICIAL AIRWAY: ORAL___ ENDO ✓ NASAL___
2) SUCTIONED: YES___ NO___ EXTUBATED___
3) COLOR: GOOD ✓ CYANOTIC___ JAUNDICE___ PALE___
4) LEVEL OF CONSCIOUSNESS: ALERT___ DROWSY___
   PARTLY REACTED ✓ NOT REACTED___

REMARKS:
Asleep, OA out @ 1030
O₂ @ 10 L/min. via mask
Chest dressing dry & intact
Hemovac compressed & draining well.
H & H drawn @ 1040 — results given
to Anesthesiologist.
Pt. c/o pain @ 1100.
Surgeon notified of H & H
VSS — 1300. Awake, oriented
Chest dressing dry & intact. Hemovac
compressed & patent. Report called to floor.

DRAINS: Hemovac

I.V.: # 18 j L AC.
Post-op D5W ↑ @ 1220

BLOOD: #1 unit WRC # 8216 @ 1115-1145
#2 unit whole blood # 8713 @ 1145
   ↓ @ 1220

Time:					
Urine Output:					

CONDITION DISCHARGE: ALERT ✓ DROWSY___
   INTUBATED:___

PAD CONDITION ON DISCHARGE: DRY ✓ REINFORCED___
   CHANGED___

TIME	RX. AND MEDS.
1100	Demerol 25 mg IM # 1

	TOTAL INTAKE	OR AND RR	TOTAL OUTPUT
BLOOD	WRC 1 unit		
I.V.	2,000 + 400		
PLASMA	Whole blood 1 unit		

DISCHARGED BY ANESTHESIOLOGIST

TIME 1300   SIGNATURE B. Jones, RN

Exhibit M.
PHYSICIAN PROGRESS RECORD
COMMUNITY HOSPITAL
PHYSICIAN PROGRESS RECORD

DATE	TIME	
8/9/83		BP dropped in R.R. — probably change in position. Dropped again after Demerol — OK now. Blood count down in R.R. — partly due to dilution from IVs. Condition stable at present. D. Avery MD
8/10/83		Hct 33. Skin looks viable. Afebrile. Will leave drains in. Dressing dry. D. Avery MD
8/10/83		Feels a little better post transfusion. Condition OK. D. Avery MD
8/11/83		Hemovac removed — large amt. of drainage removed from (R) breast. Placed in bra — somes areas of erythema. Path noted to pt. D. Avery, MD
8/12/83		No bleeding — Skin appears viable. Hct 31 D/C IV. D. Avery, MD
8/14/83		Skin viable — recovering. Pain bilateral — Skin OK. D. Avery MD
8/16/83		Afebrile doing well. Pain bilateral — Skin viable. Hopefully home in AM. D. Avery, MD
8/17/83		Can manage at home. Discharge in AM. D. Avery MD

Exhibit N.

NURSING PROGRESS RECORD

COMMUNITY HOSPITAL

NURSING PROGRESS RECORD

DATE	TIME	TREATMENT/MEDICATION	DOCTOR'S REMARKS	SIGNATURE & TITLE
8/8/83	1700		OR prep done. Watching TV. No complaints.	L. Miller, R.N.
8/9/83			Pt. sleeping at intervals	
	0630		Pre-op med. Ready for O.R.	L. Miller, R.N.
	0705		To O.R.	
	1315		Returned to room. I.V. running 75 cc/hr. BP 112/66 P 72 Hemovac in place	
	1525		Demerol 25 mg IM given for pain. No staining through dressing.	
	1600		Awake & alert. No c/o pain. Hemovac intact. Pt. req. to go to BR. Felt dizzy & weak c voiding. Pt. fainted. Pt. assisted to bed by me & chest dsg dry & intact. BP 100/60. No physical complaint. Watching TV. No complaint.	L. Miller, R.N.
	2200	75 cc bloody drainage from Hemovac	Chest dsg dry & intact. C/o pain.	N. Siu, R.N.
8/10/83		Demerol 50 mg IM	Awake, watching TV. Hemovac in place. Dressing dry and intact. Medicated for complaint of pain.	C. Thomas, R.N.
	0300		Sleeping on and off. No further complaints.	
	0415	Demerol 50 mg IM	Medicated for complaint of pain. Made comfortable in bed.	C. Thomas, R.N.
	0600	D5W 1000 cc	Hemovac emptied. 'c 10cc of bloody drainage. In no distress. Dressing dry & intact. Doctor attending.	C. Thomas, R.N.
	1125		Doctor notified of Hct 33.5. Friend visiting.	
	1200		Ate better for lunch. Encouraged to take more. But c/o slight nausea. Hemovac intact. Red drainage noted. Bloody drainage noted under dsg on back.	L. Bowler, R.N.
	1500		Hemovac patent - emptied of 40 cc red drainage. Doctor notified. Instructed to reinforce dressing. 5x9 applied & secured c Kling. Dsg D & I. Appetite poor for dinner c/o nausea. Medicated c Compazine 10 mgm IM. Relief noted. Dsg remains D & I to breast. Hemovac patent. Medicated for pain c Demerol 50 mgm IM - relief noted. BP 112/8. Resting comfortably in bed. Assisted OOB to chair at bedside. No c/o dizziness noted.	
	1950		Remains awake - watching TV. Hemovac emptied of 15 cc red drainage.	T. M.

NURSING PROGRESS RECORD

COMMUNITY HOSPITAL
NURSING PROGRESS RECORD

DATE	TIME	TREATMENT/MEDICATION	DOCTOR'S REMARKS	SIGNATURE & TITLE
8/11/83	0300	Demerol 50 mg	Given for c/o pain. Sleeping comfortably c̄ no further complaint of pain. Dsg dry & intact.	
	0510		Resting in bed quietly.	C Thomas RN
		Demerol 50mg IM	Given for c/o pain. Poor appetite.	J Thomas R.N
	0830		Removed and dressing removed by doctor. Complaining of pain.	L Bowle
		Demerol 50mg	Given for pain. Poor appetite. Not steady on her feet.	
	1450	Demerol 50mg	Given for pain. Bra out, dressing D+I	L Bowe RN
	1820	Med for pain c̄	Up in chair for dinner - appetite poor. No c/o noted	
	2100	Demerol 50 IM	Dsg remains D+I	L Mill RN
8/12/83	0001		Color good. Dressing dry and intact. No complaints of pain.	
	0800		Appetite poor.	
		Medicated c̄	Medicated with 50mg Demerol IM for	
	0940	Demerol 50mg IM for incisional pain	breast pain c̄ good relief. Friends visiting c/o incisional pain. Medicated.	
	1500		Resting - no complaints.	C Thomas RN
			Dsg dry + intact. Relief obtained from Demerol.	
		Demerol 50 mg IM for pain		
		Compazine 10 mg	for nausea	
		Pentobarbital 100 mg	P.O. given for HS	L Mill RN
8/13/83	0001		Dsg dry + intact c̄ bra on. Rested quietly remainder of night. c̄ no c/o's offered.	
		Demerol 50mg IM	Pain. Dsg dry & intact. Pt. has bra on at doctor's request.	
	1300		Resting in bed. Relief from meds. Dsg dry + intact c̄ bra on. Apt tol. poor. Pt. states she has no appetite.	L Mill RN
8/14/83	0001		Appears to be in no distress. Dressing checked by Doctor. Assisted c̄ bath.	C Thomas RN
	0530		Visiting... No voiced complaints. Dsg D+I c̄ bra on	L Bowe RN
	1500	Tylenol tabs #1	pc given for pain.	
		Tylenol tabs #1	pc given for pain	
			Pt c/o of pain	
		Tylenol tabs #1	pc given for pain	L Mill RN

NURSING PROGRESS RECORD

COMMUNITY HOSPITAL
NURSING PROGRESS RECORD

DATE	TIME	TREATMENT/MEDICATION	DOCTOR'S REMARKS	SIGNATURE & TITLE
8/15/83		Tylenol ii tabs	Resting quietly. Dressing intact. Tylenol required for pain in breast area. Has been unable to sleep. Still having breast pain.	C. Thomas RN
	1030	Demerol 50 mg p.o.	Up & about. Enjoyed breakfast. Assisted c̄ bath. Complaining of pain in operative site. Relief from medication.	
	1450	Demerol 50 mg p.o.	for pain in operative area. Relief from sedative. Friends visiting. Complaining of pain & Requested pain med. Dressing dry & intact.	L. Crue RN
	1710	Demerol 50 mg.	given for pain. Pt. complaining of nausea and headache. Would like Compazine.	
		Compazine	given for nausea. Pt. wants something for pain.	
	2100	Demerol 50 mg.	given for pain.	
8/16/83		Nembutal	Medicated for c/o incisional pain c̄ relief. Doctor in to check patient. Breasts remain ecchymotic & slightly edematous. Bra on for support. Medicated for pain c̄ relief.	L. Crue RN
	1300	Demerol 50 mg	given p.o. for incision discomfort. Good relief from Demerol. Medicated again c̄ tylenol gr x p.o.	
8/17/83			Drain around site in armpit open to air. Ambulatory down the hall. Up about. Assisted to dress. Discharged in wheelchair.	C. Thomas RN

Exhibit O.

Computerized Medication Record Summary

COMMUNITY HOSPITAL

MEDICATION RECORD SUMMARY

PATIENT: Susan Remington

DRUG ALLERGIES: **NO KNOWN ALLERGIES**

AUGUST 9
MORPHINE 10 MG.
VISTARIL 75 MG., I.M.
PENTOBARBITAL
100 MG. ORAL CAPSULE
GIVE 1 CAP Q HS
DEMEROL 25 MG. I.M.
KEFLIN 1 GM
DEMEROL 75 MG Q 3H
COMPAZINE 10 MG Q 3–4H PRN
DEMEROL 50 MG I.M. Q 3 PRN PAIN

AUGUST 10
PENTOBARBITAL
100 MG. ORAL CAPSULE
GIVE 1 CAP Q HS
PROCHLORPERAZINE
10 MG./2 ML. I.M.
GIVE Q 3–4H
DEMEROL
50 MG/ML. I.M.
GIVE I.M. Q 3H PRN PAIN

AUGUST 11
PENTOBARBITAL
100 MG. ORAL CAPSULE
GIVE 1 CAP Q HS
DEMEROL
50 MG./ML I.M.
GIVE I.M. Q 3H PRN PAIN

AUGUST 12
PENTOBARBITAL
100 MG. ORAL CAPSULE
GIVE 1 CAP Q HS
PROCHLORPERAZINE
10 MG./2 ML. I.M.
GIVE Q 3–4H PRN
DEMEROL
50 MG./ML. I.M.
GIVE I.M. Q 3H PRN PAIN

AUGUST 13
PENTOBARBITAL
100 MG. ORAL CAPSULE
GIVE 1 CAP Q HS
PROCHLORPERAZINE
10 MG. I.M.
GIVE Q 3–4H PRN
DEMEROL
50 MG. I.M.
GIVE I.M. Q 3H PRN PAIN

AUGUST 14
PENTOBARBITAL
100 MG. ORAL CAPSULE
GIVE 1 CAP Q HS
PROCHLORPERAZINE
10 MG. I.M.
GIVE Q 3–4H PRN
ACETAMINOPHEN
325 MG. ORAL TABLET
GIVE 2 TABS Q 3–4H PRN PAIN

AUGUST 15
PROCHLORPERAZINE
10 MG. I.M.
GIVE Q 3–4H PRN
ACETAMINOPHEN
325 MG. ORAL TABLET
GIVE 2 TABS Q 3–4H PRN PAIN
DEMEROL
50 MG. I.M. Q 3–4 PRN

AUGUST 16
ACETAMINOPHEN
325 MG. ORAL TABLET
GIVE 2 TABS Q 3–4H PRN PAIN

AUGUST 17
ACETAMINOPHEN
325 MG. ORAL TABLET
GIVE 2 TABS Q 3–4H PRN PAIN
DEMEROL
50 MG. ORAL TABLET
GIVE 1 CAP–S Q 3–4H PRN PAIN

Exhibit P.
LABORATORY REPORTS
COMMUNITY HOSPITAL
LABORATORY REPORTS

INTAKE & OUTPUT PARENTERAL FLUID RECORD

DATE	TOUR	INTAKE ORAL	IV	OTHER	TOTAL	URINE	EMESIS	OUTPUT GASTRIC	OTHER	TOTAL
8/9/83	7-3	OR				1200			Hemovac	
	3-11	30	800		830	1500			75	
	11-7	50	500			600			10	
	TOTAL	80	1300			2100			85	2185
8/10/83	7-3	280	750		280	625			40	625
	3-11	420	500		1170	1000			15	1000
	11-7	—			500	700			5	700
	TOTAL				1950					2325
8/11/83	7-3	350			350	BR(3)				
	3-11	240	800		1040	250+BR X3				
	11-7	—	450			400				
	TOTAL		1250							

HEMATOLOGY REPORT

	WBC	RBC	HGB	HCT	MCV	MCH
NORMAL	5.0-10.8	4.00-5.00	12-16	37-47	81-99	27-31
AUG 8	9.8	4.33	14.5	43.0	99.3	33.4
AUG 9	10.2		7.4	21.9		
AUG 9			10.5	30.7		
AUG 10				33.5		

Exhibit Q.
BREAST HEMATOMA
Hematoma formation in implanted breast

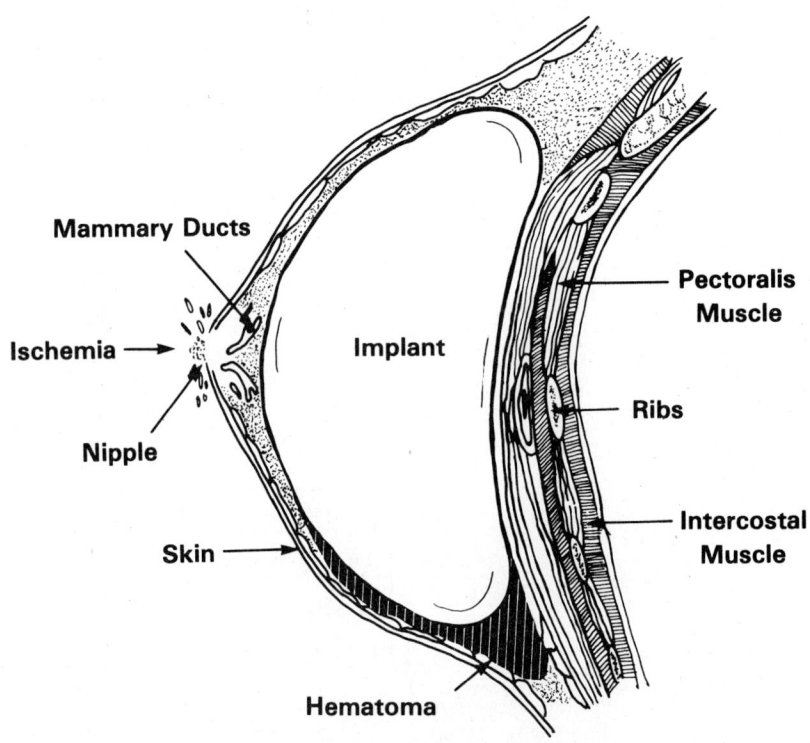

Cross-sectional drawing of the breast depicting the formation of a hematoma (a space-occupying accumulation of blood) within the breast skin envelope. At some point progressive accumulation of such fluid may significantly increase the pressure within the breast cavity enough to embarrass the already surgically compromised circulation to the breast skin, especially the nipple/areolar complex.

Exhibit R.

PATHOLOGY REPORT

COMMUNITY HOSPITAL

PATHOLOGY REPORT   PATIENT: Susan Remington
August 12, 1983

SPECIMEN: 1. Right Breast Tissue
                    2. Left Breast Tissue

MACROSCOPIC: The first specimen consists of an oval 380 gram mass of breast tissue which on cut surface demonstrates severe fibrocystic change, with numerous ducts plugged with mucoid and tenacious debris. The second specimen is a 360 gram oval mass of breast tissue with firm, gray fibrocystic change on cut surface, and numerous punctate areas of inspissated mucoid debris.

MICROSCOPIC DIAGNOSIS: Severe Fibrocystic Mastopathy with Intraductal Papillomatosis and mild chronic periductal mastitis.

Exhibit S.

DISCHARGE SUMMARY

COMMUNITY HOSPITAL

DISCHARGE SUMMARY   PATIENT: Susan Remington

Date of Admission: August 8, 1983

Date of Discharge: August 17, 1983

This is a 34-year-old female with strong family history of breast cancer. Both the mother, the aunt and grandmother have a history of dying from breast cancer. The patient has bilateral breast cysts. Preoperative evaluation was within normal limits. She was taken to the operating room and had a bilateral subcutaneous mastectomy. Postoperatively she did well but did require a total of two units in the immediate postoperative stage. Drains were removed on the second day with evacuation of large amount of blood from the right breast. The skin viability appeared to be intact. She was discharged on the 8th postoperative day.

FINAL DIAGNOSIS: Bilateral breast dysplasia.

§ D. Documentation of Medical Care Between Hospitalizations

Exhibit T.

OFFICE RECORDS OF DR. REEVES

Oscar Reeves, M.D.
Plastic & Reconstructive Surgery

Name of Patient: Susan Remington

August 22, 1983

Patient appears to have some compromised skin on both sides. Minimally debrided. Will start dressings and see her on Thursday.

August 25, 1983

Areas on the right continue to show evidence of skin compromise. It appears to be split-thickness; however, there is an area over the left breast which may be full-thickness. Overall, however, breasts look much better and are clean. There is no cellulitis.

August 29, 1983

Essentially unchanged. Portions of the right side look better as well as the left, but there is still an area of probable full-thickness eschar on the left side. Continue to treat conservatively and see her on Thursday.

September 2, 1983

Debrided minimally again. More or less unchanged. To see Dr. Avery on Tuesday.

[Cross reference: Look back at Exhibits A and B.]

§ E. Second Hospitalization: Removal of Implants

Exhibit U.

ADMISSION SUMMARY

COMMUNITY HOSPITAL

ADMISSION SUMMARY   PATIENT: Susan Remington

Date of Admission: September 16, 1983.

CHIEF COMPLAINT: Necrosis of the breasts.

HISTORY OF PRESENT ILLNESS: This is a 34-year-old female who has bilateral necrosis of the anterior portion of both breasts subsequent to a subcutaneous mastectomy which was performed approximately six weeks ago. At that time 360 grams and 380 grams of tissue were removed which showed multiple cysts with no evidence of any cancer. After the procedure there was a hematoma in the right breast which was evacuated by means of a drain. She subsequently went on to necrose the anterior portion of both breasts but has been reluctant to have both prostheses removed until the indication has been clear. This afternoon she developed a small leak around the area of one of the necroses on the left breast. She is admitted at this time for debridement and removal of the implants bilaterally.

PAST MEDICAL HISTORY: Mother, grandmother and aunt had breast cancer.

REVIEW OF SYSTEMS: Within normal limits.

SOCIAL HISTORY: She is widowed, has two children.

PHYSICAL EXAMINATION: General: Reveals a nervous, upset female.

Head & Eyes: React normally to light.
Neck: Supple.
Chest: Clear.
Heart: Regular sinus rhythm.
Breasts: Bilaterally there is an area of necrosis approximately 3 × 4 cm. overlying the nipple on both sides. There is a pinhole opening, left breast.

Exhibit V.

MRS. REMINGTON WITH BREAST SKIN NECROSIS

Photograph taken by Dr. Avery on September 16, 1983, of Susan Remington's breasts the day that he removed the implanted breast prostheses and debrided devitalized breast tissue.

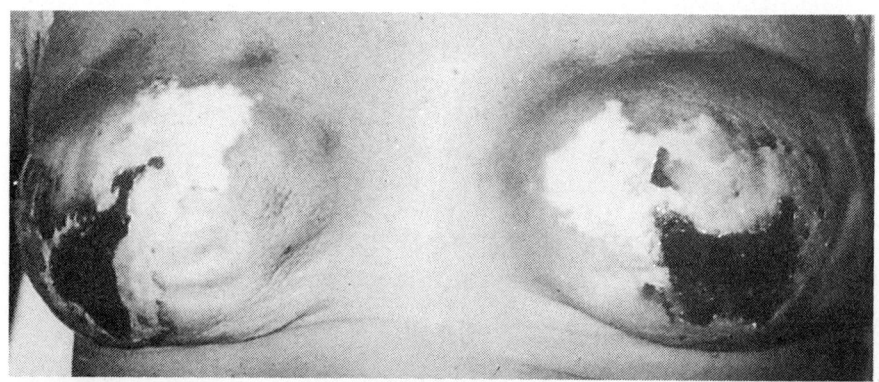

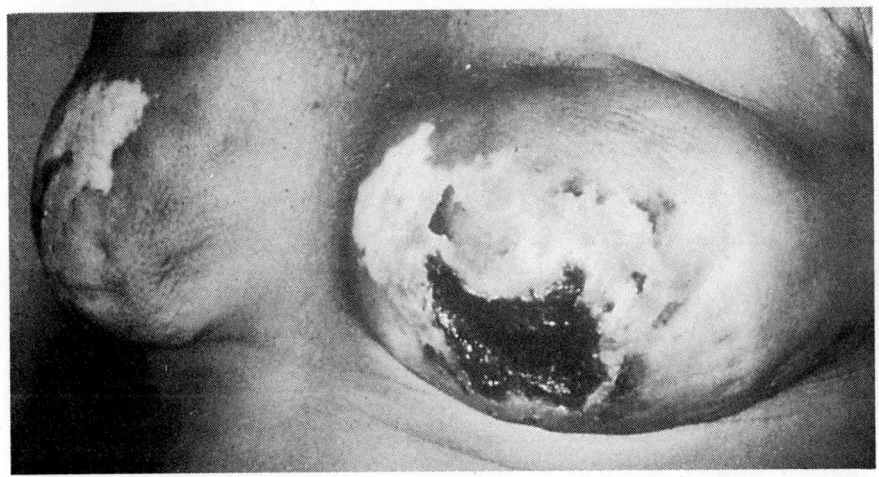

Photographs depict symmetrical skin changes to the breasts. The nipple/areolar complex shows full-thickness necrosis which is represented by the dark areas.

Exhibit W.
OPERATIVE NOTES
COMMUNITY HOSPITAL

OPERATIVE NOTES PATIENT: Susan Remington

DATE: September 16, 1983

SURGEON: Douglas Avery, M.D.

PRE–OPERATIVE DIAGNOSIS: Breast necrosis with exposure of implant.

OPERATION: Excision of necrotic tissue and removal of implant bilaterally with closure over drains.

POST–OPERATIVE DIAGNOSIS: Same

HISTORY: The patient is a 34-year-old female who underwent a subcutaneous mastectomy for strong family history of breast cancer. She had cystic breast disease. At the present time she has a pinhole exposure of the implant on the left breast with a necrotic area measuring 3×4 cm. There is a similar necrotic area of the same size on the right breast.

PROCEDURE: The patient is placed in the supine position, general anesthesia administered, the chest is prepped and draped in the usual fashion. Starting on the left breast the necrotic tissue was excised and the wound edges freshened. The implant is removed. A culture is taken. The wound inside is cleaned and the transverse closure was planned with a double Penrose placed in the wound secured with a safety pin and a suture of 0000 nylon suture. Interrupted averting sutures of 0000 nylon are used along a transverse closure. In a similar fashion the necrotic tissue is excised from the right breast, however, the closure that is carried out after the debridement of the necrotic tissue and removal of the implant is in a stellate shape to preserve as much tissue as possible. From the dependent portion of the stellate wound two Penrose drains are similarly secured with a safety pin and suture. The wound is closed and interrupted 0000 nylon sutures. A light compression dressing is applied. The patient tolerated the procedures well and left the operating room in good condition.

Exhibit X.

PATHOLOGY REPORT

COMMUNITY HOSPITAL

PATHOLOGY REPORT PATIENT: Susan Remington
September 19, 1983

SPECIMEN: 1. Right Breast Implant and Tissue
2. Left Breast Implant and Tissue

MACROSCOPIC: The first specimen consists of a prosthetic breast implant along with a triangularly shaped portion of apparent skin measuring $4 \times 3 \times .5$ cm. in greatest dimensions. Representative sections of the tissue submitted.

The second specimen is a prosthetic breast implant along with a flattened, dark purple indurated apparent skin measuring 6 cm. in greatest dimensions.

MICROSCOPIC DIAGNOSIS: Severe acute inflammation with fibrosis, scar and necrosis

Exhibit Y.

DISCHARGE SUMMARY

COMMUNITY HOSPITAL

DISCHARGE SUMMARY PATIENT: Susan Remington

ADMITTED: September 16, 1983.

DISCHARGED: September 19, 1983.

DISCHARGE SUMMARY; This is a 34–year–old female who was admitted with bilateral breast necrosis over implants after having subcutaneous mastectomy for strong family history of carcinoma of the breast. On examination she had bilateral breast necrosis with a pinhole opening on the left breast. She was taken to the operating room where she underwent excision of the necrotic tissue, removal of the implants bilaterally, and a closure over drain. Postoperatively she was comfortable. The drains were removed on the 2nd postoperative day and she was discharged to be followed as an outpatient.

FINAL DIAGNOSIS: Breast necrosis bilaterally with exposed left implant.

§ F. Third Hospitalization: Submuscular Insertion of Implants

Exhibit Z.

ADMISSION SUMMARY

COMMUNITY HOSPITAL

ADMISSION SUMMARY   PATIENT: Susan Remington

DATE OF ADMISSION: November 15, 1984.

CHIEF COMPLAINT: Fibrocystic disease of both breasts.

HISTORY OF PRESENT ILLNESS: This is a 35-year-old female who underwent a subcutaneous mastectomy in August 1983. She had a strong family history of breast cancer. At the time of the initial operation she had multiple cystic diseases bilaterally and had resection of 360 and 380 grams from the breasts with no evidence of any cancer. Immediately postoperatively she developed large hematomas in spite of drainage and developed exposure of the implants with loss of the implants. The implants were removed at a subsequent procedure six weeks after their insertion and the breast tissue slowly healed. At this time she has some loss in nipple substance, has no breast substance but the breast tissue is pliable for reconstruction.

PAST MEDICAL HISTORY: Unremarkable.

REVIEW OF SYSTEMS: Within normal limits.

SOCIAL HISTORY: She is widowed, has 2 children.

PHYSICAL EXAMINATION:

General: Reveals a female in no distress.

Eyes: React normally to light.

Neck: Supple.

Chest: Clear.

Heart: Regular sinus rhythm.

Breasts: Bilaterally large amounts of skin overlying the breast area with good pliable area. No evidence of infection or tenderness. The previous mastectomy incisions and the infra-areolar area are well healed.

Abdomen: Soft.

Extremities: Within normal limits.

Neuro: Within normal limits.

DIAGNOSIS: Bilateral fibrocystic disease
             Post subcutaneous mastectomy.

Exhibit AA.

BREASTS BEFORE SUBMUSCULAR INSERTION OF IMPLANTS

PHOTOGRAPHS TAKEN BY DR. AVERY ON NOVEMBER 15, 1984, OF SUSAN REMINGTON'S BREASTS FOURTEEN MONTHS AFTER HE HAD REMOVED THE IMPLANTED PROSTHESES AND DEBRIDED DEVITALIZED BREAST TISSUE

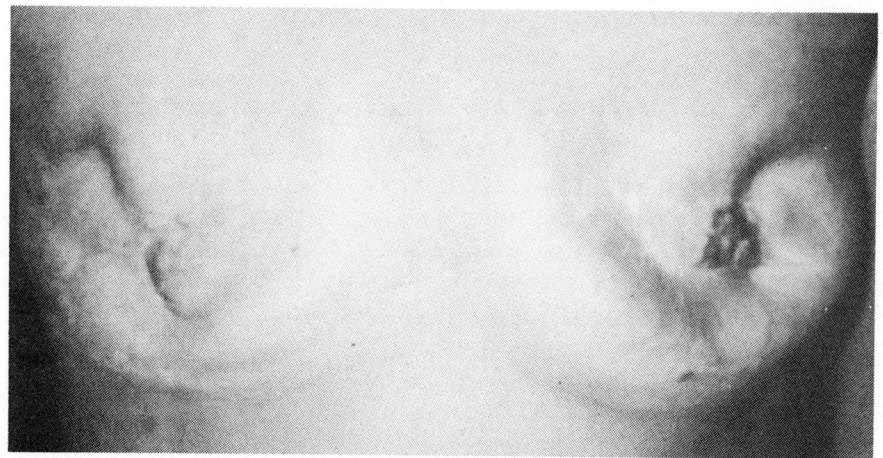

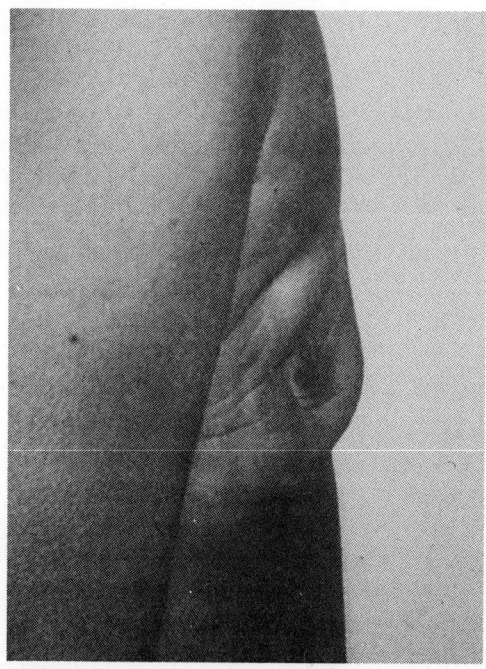

Photographs depict the appearance of necrotic breast tissue which has healed with scarring and irregularities making it difficult to expand the breasts for reimplantation and reconstruction.

Exhibit BB.

OPERATIVE NOTES

COMMUNITY HOSPITAL

OPERATIVE NOTES PATIENT: Susan Remington
November 16, 1984

SURGEON: Douglas Avery, M.D.

PRE-OPERATIVE DIAGNOSIS: Bilateral fibrocystic disease with familial carcinomatosis.

OPERATION: Bilateral breast reconstruction with subpectoral implant.

POST-OPERATIVE DIAGNOSIS: Same.

HISTORY: This is a 35-year-old female who underwent bilateral subcutaneous mastectomy, the major indication being a strong family history of carcinoma. Postoperatively, the patient developed severe difficulty and the implants had to be removed. The breast was left in a scarred contracted area with loss of nipple substance. After an appropriate wait of approximately 14 months, the skin of the breasts is pliable enough to be reconstructed.

PROCEDURE: Patient was placed in supine position. The chest was prepared and draped in the usual fashion after general anesthesia was administered. An outline of the proposed incision is made bilaterally in the inframamillary fold with Methylene Blue. A five cm incision excising the previous scar is marked in Methylene Blue and the scar is excised. The incision is carried down to the pectoralis fascia. Both the minor and major pectoral muscles are split, enabling entrance into the subpectoral area. By means of dissection a large pocket is elevated and packed with gauze. In similar fashion, the opposite side is operated on. Going back to the right side, hemostasis is satisfactorily secured and a round backless 240 cc Surgitek implant is inserted. The wound was closed in layers with # 0000 Vicryl and running suture of # 000 Nylon. Steristrips also support the wound. In a similar fashion, the left side is operated on, and same size implant is inserted. Then a bulky light compression dressing is applied after the # 000 Nylon is tied over a bolster. The patient tolerated the procedure well and left the operating room in good condition.

Exhibit CC.
SUBMUSCULAR IMPLANTATION
Breast with submuscular implantation of prosthesis

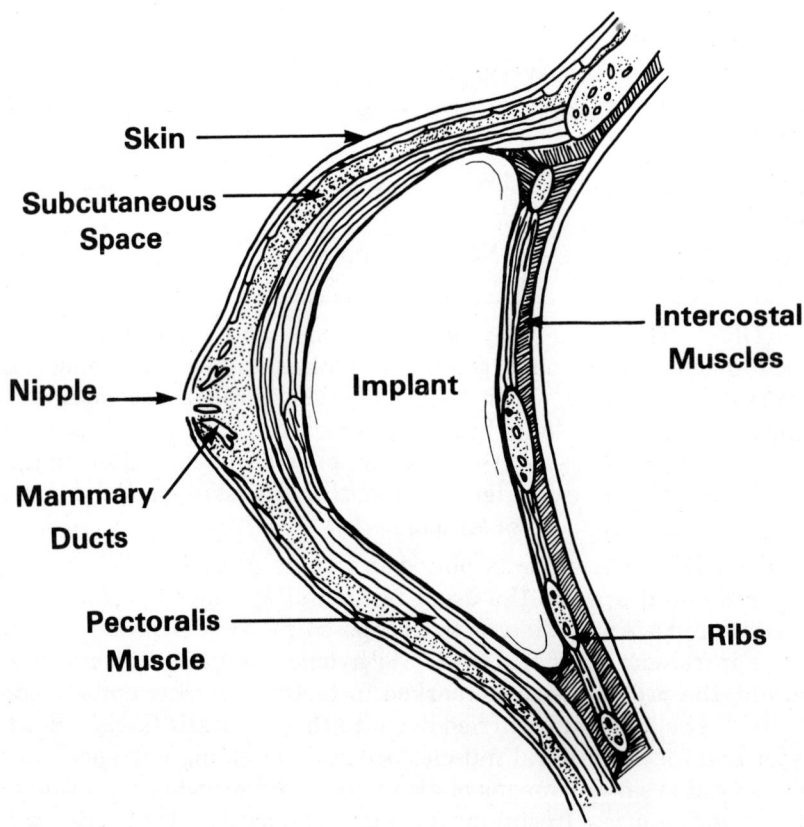

Cross-sectional drawing of the breast depicting the placement of a silicone implant under the pectoralis (chest) muscle. This places a pad of muscle between the prosthesis and the breast skin. In addition, the muscle can serve to provide a cushioning effect on the expansion of the prosthesis.

§ G. Pre-filing Documents

Exhibit DD.

BREASTS AFTER SUBMUSCULAR INSERTION OF IMPLANTS

Photographs taken by Dr. Avery on February 28, 1985 of Susan Remington's breasts seven months after he had implanted breast prostheses underneath the chest muscle

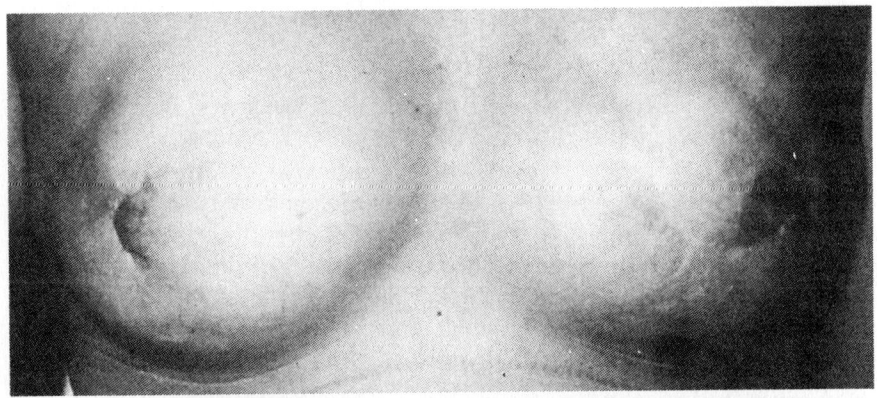

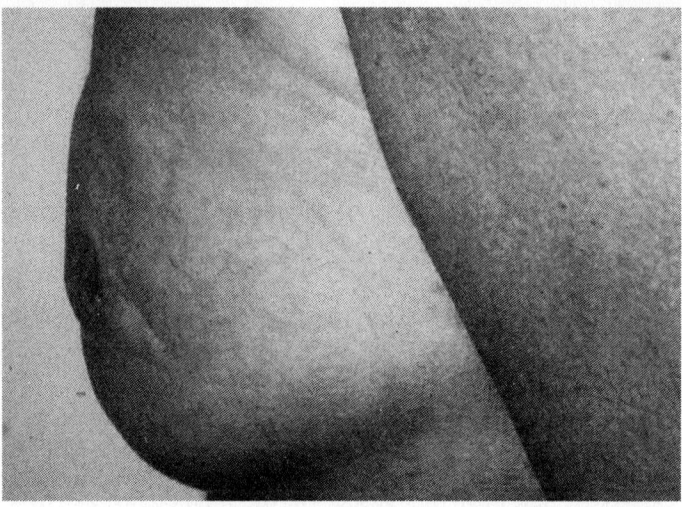

Photographs depict the appearance, shape and residual deformity of the breasts after submuscular implantation.

Exhibit EE.

Dr. Avery's Letter to Plaintiff's Lawyer

DOUGLAS AVERY, M.D.
6688 Euclid Drive
Middletown, U.S.A.

May 20, 1985

Gordon Brown, Atty.
987 Elm Street
Middletown, U.S.A.

Dear Mr. Brown:

When I saw Mrs. Remington on June 22, 1983 concerning the possibility of a subcutaneous mastectomy, she related that several relatives had developed breast cancer. She wanted information about replacing breast tissue with an implant. She was informed at that time and at subsequent times about the high rate of complication associated with this procedure, including infection, hemorrhage, numbness, sensory loss and loss of prostheses. She returned on July 21, 1983 and indicated that another surgeon had confirmed that she was a good candidate for subcutaneous mastectomy.

On August 9, 1983, the patient underwent a subcutaneous mastectomy. She did have some hemorrhaging from both breasts while in the hospital, but the skin appeared viable at her discharge. At an office visit August 20, 1983, there was a question of skin viability. The patient was seen several times up to September 16, 1983 when the prostheses became exposed. The necrotic skin and the prostheses were removed. After that procedure the patient was followed conservatively to enable the area to heal and the skin to become more pliable. On November 16, 1984, she underwent bilateral submuscular prosthetic implantation. This made a significant improvement in her appearance.

Subsequent to the surgery, the areas continued to improve in appearance with remodeling of the breast tissue. The patient has complained repeatedly about the appearance of her nipples, some portions of which were lost due to skin loss and infection. At the time of her visit on February 28, 1985, it was felt that a decision concerning the nipples should be put off until the area further settles and softens down. It has been explained to her multiple times that a normal breast is not to be expected after a subcutaneous mastectomy, and that this type of surgery is a cancer preventive treatment which has not been statistically proven to prolong life. However, on a logical basis it has been implied that this will prevent cancer. Pursuant to your request, copies of all photographs and records will be sent to you.

Yours truly,

Douglas Avery, M.D.

Exhibit FF.

Report of Dr. Bergan (Reviewing Expert Pathologist) to Mr. Brown

HOWARD BERGAN, M.D.
Pathology
2001 Greenpeace Boulevard
Middletown, U.S.A.
June 28, 1985

Dear Mr. Brown:

I have reviewed the material on Susan Remington that you referred to me, including the pathology protocol and histologic slides marked as being from her right and left breasts; the deposition and office records of Dr. Avery; color photographs of Susan Remington labeled "before" and "after"; and hospital records.

Susan Remington underwent a subcutaneous mastectomy as a prophylactic measure to prevent cancer. Reconstruction was performed at the same time using silicone gel implants placed in subcutaneous pockets. Two days later drains which had been placed at the time of the operation were removed. She was transferred temporarily to the care of another plastic surgeon while the primary surgeon was out of town for 17 days. On his return, necrosis of the skin overlying the prostheses was apparent; and 24 days later the implants were removed. It was thought that a hematoma might have developed after the drains had been removed, possibly being a causative factor in skin necrosis. Fourteen months later implants were inserted in the submuscular plane. This time the wounds healed satisfactorily. Photographs reveal that her breasts were deformed bilaterally due to irregularity of the contour, with scarring around the nipple/areolar complex, which had partly been lost due to the necrotic process.

The histologic material contains severe epithelial hyperplastic changes with focal atypia, intraductal papillomatosis, papillary apocrine metaplasia, and cystic duct dilation. The extent as well as the degree of change would certainly dictate close subcutaneous dissection of breast tissue. In conjunction with the described clinical findings, the subcutaneous mastectomy was reasonable.

Issues regarding technique and handling of complications are best left to specialists who deal with these clinical problems. There does not seem to be any deviation from standard of care. The unfortunate aesthetic result shown in the photographs is within the realm of complications of surgery performed for reasonable indications.

Sincerely yours,

Howard Bergan, M.D.

Exhibit GG.

Report of Dr. Sears (Reviewing Expert Plastic Surgeon) to Mr. Brown

GEORGE SEARS, M.D.
Plastic and Reconstructive Surgery
2443 Anderson Medical Center
Midtown, USA

July 9, 1985

REPORT ON REMINGTON vs. AVERY

Mrs. Remington had approximately 380 grams of tissue removed from one breast and 360 grams of tissue removed from the other breast. From the records, it does not appear that Dr. Avery discussed with the patient the complete nature of the procedure that he would carry out nor that there was a probability that she might have some loss of skin. There was no discussion as to the options of the procedure as to whether her prosthesis could be placed under the pectoralis muscle. He did not discuss with her the fact that if the prosthesis were placed in the subpectoral position, the eventuality of skin necrosis was markedly lessened as well as decreasing the possibility of postoperative deformity. He did not adequately discuss with the patient the other hazards including hematoma formation. The most difficult thing to comprehend is that he did not see the patient postoperatively when according to the records, she was out of bed a few hours after the surgery and fell. She was continuously complaining of chest pain, but no attempt was made to remove the dressing and actually examine the breast tissue itself as to firmness, discoloration or any abnormal appearance, although the patient complained of tightness in the chest and swelling and enlargement of her breast areas. The patient had considerable bloody drainage on her dressings, but no physical examination was carried out, although instructions were given to the nurse to re-enforce her dressings. When she was dressed on the second postoperative day, blood was expressed from the breasts, but no suggestion was made that the operative sites should be re-explored and any hematoma present should be evacuated. By the time the patient was seen on the tenth postoperative day, it was obvious that the patient had necrosis of the tissue of both breasts and that it was probably too late to do anything to try to prevent this from occurring.

It is my impression that Dr. Avery did not follow or use accepted standards of care in explaining and carrying out the procedure of a subcutaneous mastectomy, and that the patient's poor final result was directly related to this fact.

George Sears, M.D.

Exhibit HH.

Report of Dr. Shumacher (Reviewing Expert General Surgeon) to Mr. Brown

IVAN SHUMACHER, M.D.
General Surgery
1313 Medical Center Parkway
University Heights, USA

July 10, 1985

Gordon Brown, Esq.
Miller, Brown & McGraw
987 Elm Street
Middletown, U.S.A.

Dear Mr. Brown:

Any surgeon counseling a patient about subcutaneous mastectomy with implant reconstruction must inform her that the breasts' nipple/areolar complex will never be normal. Most surgeons do not even bother to preserve the nipple/areolar complex because the objective of the procedure is to have a patient look nearly normal in clothes. Dr. Avery was responsible for providing her with an enlightened, realistic explanation and clinical approach. A bilateral mastectomy should have been employed only if the indication was the presence of cancer, or a phobia for it. The technique employed by Dr. Avery was inappropriate. If Dr. Avery referred to the procedure as a "scooping out," it was not the type of careful, bilateral mastectomy which the indication of severe risk of cancer or its immediate development would demand.

Dr. Avery noted that he detected a mass in the upper outer quadrant of Mrs. Remington's right breast. This is not an incidental finding but a major indication for careful examination and follow-up tests, including excisional biopsy. If these tests had been performed and had detected malignancy, a modified radical mastectomy or subtotal mastectomy with immediate radiation therapy, not a subcutaneous mastectomy, would be clinically indicated. There was no frozen section examination by the pathologist of the breast mass palpated by Dr. Avery, nor is there further mention of it in the records. I see no indication that this ominous finding disturbed him, or that he provided any follow-up care of it. The final Pathology diagnosis reports merely mild, chronic, periductal mastitis, something that any woman of Mrs. Remington's age can be shown to have.

Dr. Avery's admission diagnosis was "Mastodynia," an archaic term referring to constant, continual pain in the breast requiring medication for swelling and tenderness. There is no evidence in the record that a complaint of this nature was ever made by Mrs. Remington. Dr. Avery's preoperative diagnosis was "Bilateral Breast Dysplasia." Neither "diagnosis" seems to square with the preoperative finding of a breast mass. Nonetheless, Dr. Avery performed a bilateral subcutaneous mastectomy (an error in judgment) by "scooping out" breast tissue (an error in technique). Bilateral subcutaneous mastectomy is indicated for a severe fear of cancer. The decision to perform it should be based on much harder clinical evidence than presented by Mrs. Remington. However, if Dr. Avery labels this as the operation he performed, he erroneously performed it by employing a technique which can accurately be described as "scooping out" breast tissue.

It was also an error in judgment to perform this "outmoded" procedure. To minimize the recognized complications of a subcutaneous mastectomy with immediate subcutaneous implant and reconstruction, the prostheses are frequently placed beneath the muscles. Failure to perform such a procedure probably reflects Dr. Avery's failure to keep abreast of surgical advances and developments.

It is not necessarily a culpable result that Mrs. Remington bled underneath the skin flaps, since this operation may have that as an immediate sequel. However, placing a surgical drain does not relieve the surgeon of responsibility to monitor for problems that may require surgical action. The drain alone does not prevent or treat hemorrhage under the skin flaps. At best, it only indicates hemorrhage is occurring. That information was not even needed in this case, since there was other clinical evidence of hemorrhaging. In the Recovery Room, Mrs. Remington was already hypotensive. Her postoperative hematocrit and hemoglobin were one-half the concentrations of her preoperative values. A mastectomy patient may lose a unit of blood routinely in the excision of a breast on one side. However, when Mrs. Remington had lost several units, Dr. Avery's first priority should have been the physiology of her altered circulation. He should have become concerned about where that blood had gone. The anesthesiologist was concerned enough to start two units of blood transfusion in the Recovery Room. Mrs. Remington probably lost 4–5 units of blood into the breast reconstruction site, since her post-transfusion hematocrit did not return close to normal. Orthostatic hypotension, manifested by her fainting upon getting out of bed, reflects that she was at least two units of blood short in her transfusion. However, Dr. Avery did not make an effort to assess or treat Mrs. Remington's condition. He did not make rounds during the immediate postoperative period, a signal that he has no reason to be checking the patient, or that he does not care there may be a serious problem. From the moment of her awakening from anesthesia, Mrs. Remington had pain so severe that it required excessive narcotics. This is atypical for a superficial (subcutaneous) plastic procedure. At the first postoperative visit 24 hours later, Dr. Avery falsely reassured Mrs. Remington that the intensity of her breast pain was normal with this type of operation. No direct inspection of the wound or attention to the area of the patient's complaint was made until after the 48th postoperative hour. Dr. Avery instructed the nursing staff to "reinforce" the dressing, thereby obscuring the offending clinical findings. A saturated dressing is the indication for its removal, if for no other reason than it would form a crusted "cuirass," a stiff unyielding shell around the chest that inhibits respiration and can contribute to external pressure.

When Dr. Avery examined Mrs. Remington's breasts 48 hours post surgery, he removed the drains and blood gushed out from the site of the drain punctures in the skin. The volume which remained, however, was large enough to make Mrs. Remington continue to complain of pain and swelling of her breasts.

Sincerely yours,

Ivan Shumacher, M.D.

Exhibit II.

Report of Dr. Burns (Examining Expert Plastic Surgeon) to Mr. Brown

GILBERT BURNS, M.D.
Plastic and Reconstructive Surgery
1519 Nicholson Lane, Suite B
Midtown, U.S.A.

October 2, 1985

Dear Mr. Brown:

Mrs. Remington's breasts are deformed bilaterally due to irregularity of the contour of the breast shape, with significant scarring around the nipple/areolar complex, which had partly been lost due to the previous necrotic process. She is dissatisfied with the overall shape of the breasts, with the scarring, and with the appearance of her nipples. She informed me that it had been suggested by another plastic surgeon, whom she had gone to for a further opinion, that an inflatable type implant might be inserted instead of the present implant to smooth out the irregularity of contour.

In my opinion the only way a satisfactory result can be obtained would be to use a bilateral transverse abdominal flap, which would be brought up on each side based on the superior epigastric artery and the rectus muscle. This flap could be used to reconstruct the breasts after the scarred areas had been excised. It would necessitate transverse scars running across the breasts on each side, but hopefully the resulting shape would be symmetrical, and it would be possible to reconstruct a more normal looking nipple on the reconstructed breast mound. This would be a rather radical procedure, but I felt that she had a severe problem which could not be corrected satisfactorily by any other means. Because of the complexity of the surgery, I would only recommend somebody to do it who was very familiar with this operation.

Very truly yours,

Gilbert Burns, M.D.

Exhibit JJ.

Report of Dr. Hickman (Treating Psychiatrist) to Mr. Brown

John Hickman, M.D.
Psychiatry
1234 Hoyt Avenue
Hometown, USA

October 18, 1985

Gordon Brown, Esq.
2128 McKinley Street
Hometown, USA

Dear Mr. Brown: Re: Susan Remington

I saw Mrs. Remington in September 1984. At this time she discussed the complications of her mastectomy, and how she had dealt with the children. She returned several times thereafter. She was feeling depressed and disfigured. Her image of herself was poor. She feared establishing relationships, anticipating rejection. She was not satisfied with concentrating on rearing the children and doing organizational work, but yearned for a loving relationship. She felt too vulnerable and handicapped to pursue such a relationship. When I saw her on February 6, 1985 she was very depressed, wondering what was ahead for her. She felt immobilized and unable to deal with her disfigurement emotionally. She felt very alone, with little prospect for change in her life. She expressed a need for more intensive therapy, but an inability to afford it.

Very truly yours,

John Hickman, M.D.

§ H. The Complaint

SUPERIOR COURT
CIVIL DIVISION

SUSAN REMINGTON
              Plaintiff

v.

DOUGLAS AVERY
              Defendant

[CLERK STAMP]
Civ. A. No. 85–2516

COMPLAINT FOR DAMAGE

(Physician Negligence)

Comes now the Plaintiff, Susan Remington, by and through her Attorney, Gordon Brown, complaining of the defendant above named.

1. On or about June 22, 1983, Mrs. Remington consulted Dr. Douglas Avery, a plastic surgeon, about a breast operation. Dr. Avery said he thought surgery was a good idea. On August 9, 1983, Dr. Avery performed a prophylactic bilateral subcutaneous mastectomy on Mrs. Remington and inserted prosthetic implants into the subcutaneous space of her breasts. During the postoperative period Mrs. Remington developed large bilateral breast hematomas which threatened the viability of her breast skin.

2. On August 17, 1983, without providing the necessary treatment for the hematomas that had formed in Mrs. Remington's breasts, Dr. Avery discharged her from the hospital.

3. On August 20, 1983, when Mrs. Remington saw Dr. Avery in his office, he told her she may need a skin graft on her breasts, but did not remove the implants.

4. On September 6, 1983, and September 13, 1983, she again was checked by Dr. Avery, who again took no definitive action, nor did he explain the development of complications to Mrs. Remington.

5. On September 16, 1983, Dr. Avery admitted Mrs. Remington to the hospital, removed the prosthetic implants, and excised necrotic breast tissue. On November 16, 1984, Mrs. Remington underwent bilateral breast reconstruction, and the insertion of implants under the chest muscles.

6. In late March 1985, Mrs. Remington consulted Dr. Bryant, another plastic surgeon, to find out what could be done to improve the appearance of her breasts. He indicated that her only possibility even for slight improvement was to undergo an innovative "molding procedure, the results of which were yet unknown."

7. The permanently deformed appearance of her breasts has caused Mrs. Remington to be depressed and to experience great mental anguish which will continue for her lifetime.

COUNT I. Negligent Failure to Obtain Informed Consent for the Operation

Dr. Avery negligently failed to properly and adequately disclose to Mrs. Remington the nature of and the necessary clinical indications for a bilateral prophylactic subcutaneous mastectomy, and therefore the consent he obtained from her was not informed consent.

COUNT II. Negligent Performance of the Operation

Dr. Avery chose to perform a subcutaneous mastectomy and then negligently inserted prosthetic implants immediately.

COUNT III. Negligent Postoperative Monitoring

Dr. Avery negligently failed to monitor Mrs. Remington for early warning signs of postoperative complications, and therefore he did not remove the implants at the first sign of complications and resultant scarring.

COUNT IV. Negligent Management of Surgical Complications

Dr. Avery negligently ignored the clinical warnings of surgical complications, causing unnecessary destruction of breast tissue.

The aforementioned acts of negligence of Dr. Avery have caused the disfigurement of Mrs. Remington's breasts, and resulted in attendant medical costs from additional surgery. It has also caused Mrs. Remington great mental anguish, pain and suffering in the past and will continue to cause such anguish throughout her lifetime.

Wherefore, Plaintiff demands judgment against defendant for the sum of One Million Dollars ($1,000,000) with interest thereon from August 9, 1983, together with the costs and disbursements of this action.

Gordon Brown, Esq.
Miller, Brown & McGraw
987 Elm Street
Middletown, U.S.A.
426/976-0412

and state why you were unable to work those days: <u>Answer</u> At least $500/month for 2 months—I was very sick the whole time.

7. State the names and addresses of any persons believed by you or known by you or your attorney to have any knowledge pertaining to the occurrence of the incident in question: <u>Answer</u> Claire Garvey, Sheila Elliott.

8. Do you or your attorneys possess any photographs of the subject incident or the objects involved therein or of the parties, or do you know of any other person in possession of any such photographs? <u>Answer</u> Yes.

   a. If so, state when, where and by whom the photographs were taken, the subject matter of the photographs, the number of photographs taken, and give the name and address of the photographer: <u>Answer</u> Taken by Dr. Avery.

9. State whether any written, recorded or oral statements were made by any <u>witnesses</u> (not expert) or by the <u>defendant</u>, and, if so, state as to each:

   a. Was said statement oral or written or recorded?

   b. The name and address of the person giving the statement.

   c. The name and address of the person to whom said statement was made or given.

   d. The date the statement was obtained.

   e. The present custodian of such statement.

   f. If the statement was oral and was made by the Defendant(s) or a representative or agent of the Defendant(s) and is res gestae in nature, or so alleged to be, state the contents of such statement.

   BY PLAINTIFF'S ATTORNEY: Plaintiff objects to this interrogatory because the question is overbroad and calls for the disclosure of opinions received in preparation for litigation which are not subject to discovery, unless the persons giving these opinions have been selected as witnesses for trial.

10. Please state the name, address and qualification of every expert witness known to you, your agents, employees, investigators or attorneys whom you expect to call as an expert witness at the trial of the subject cause:

   BY PLAINTIFF'S ATTORNEY: Since the factual legal discovery is not yet complete, expert witnesses, who will testify at trial, have not yet been selected and the decision to call has not been made as yet. After factual and legal discovery are complete, expert witnesses will be selected to evaluate these elements. Since factual and legal discovery are not complete, such expert witnesses who will testify at trial cannot be answered at this time. When

§ I. Discovery Documents

Document 1.

DR. AVERY'S INTERROGATORIES TO MRS. REMINGTON

Issued September 6, 1985

1. **State in detail, each injury you claim to have received in the incident sued upon in this case:** <u>Answer</u> Permanent disfigurement of my breasts, causing embarrassment, psychological and mental anguish; pain and suffering as a result of negligent surgery and postoperative care. The probable necessity for extensive, future breast surgery to improve my breasts' appearance. Loss of income because of disability related to surgery, loss of enjoyment and activities of life. Expected costs for future surgery. Hospital and medical expenses. Loss of consortium with my family.

2. **List in detail, any permanent scars, disfigurements, disabilities or discomfort growing out of the within incident:** <u>Answer</u> I have multiple obvious permanent scars and disfigurements of my breasts. Emotionally disabled from engaging in the degree of social intercourse and activities that I was accustomed to prior to surgery. Socially isolated, making prospects for future meaningful relationship poor.

3. **Set forth in detail the exact nature of all present physical complaints which you allege are attributable to the injuries you received in the within incident:** <u>Answer</u> Discomfort and sensitivity of breasts. Nausea when I think about the condition of my breasts.

4. **If you have been hospitalized by reason of the incident here sued upon, list the name and address of all such hospitals, clinics, or other medical institutions in which you were a patient as a result of this incident, the dates of confinement, and the sums of money paid by you or on your behalf or owing to each for their services to you:** <u>Answer</u> Community Hospital, September 16, 1983: approx $1200; Community Hospital, November 14, 1984: approx. $5,000.

5. **Will it be necessary for you to have any future medical treatment by reason of the within incident? If the answer is in the affirmative, state, from your own knowledge and what your doctors have told you, what future medical treatment you will need:** <u>Answer</u> I may have to undergo additional breast surgery for cosmetic purposes in an attempt to improve the appearance of my disfigured breasts.

6. **Exactly how much income, if any, do you claim to have lost to date as a result of the within incident? If you have lost time from work, itemize the number of days, and give the exact date, month, and year of each day lost, or each partial day lost**

such experts are selected and this information is available, it will be disseminated to all Defendants.

11. State the name, address and qualification of every expert witness with whom you, your agents, employees, investigators or attorneys have conferred pertaining to the facts and/or allegations of your Complaint in this cause or who have been retained or who have been specially employed by you, your agents, employees, investigators or attorneys and who are not expected to be called as a witness at trial either in person or by deposition:

BY PLAINTIFF'S ATTORNEY: Plaintiff objects to this question because the answer calls for work product of Plaintiff's attorney, and the question calls for disclosure of opinions of experts who have not been selected as yet because discovery is not complete. See 37.

12. Do you claim to have a permanent injury? Answer Yes.

a. If so, describe the injury in detail: Answer Permanent scarring and disfigurement of breast. Emotional scarring, psychological depression, interference with enjoyment of life.

b. If so, give the name and address and specialty of each physician who will state that you have a permanent injury within reasonable medical certainty or probability: Answer Undetermined at the present time.

c. For each physician listed in section "b" of this question, who has given you a disability rating, give the percent of disability and the date the rating was first given, indicating if it was given in writing: Answer See above.

13. Do you claim that this Defendant caused you to sustain, or was responsible for your injury because

a. He was not qualified to undertake the type of treatment he gave you? Answer Plaintiff has not yet undertaken formal factual and legal discovery. It is Plaintiff's belief that discovery will demonstrate evidence that Defendant lacked the requisite knowledge and skill to perform a prophylactic bilateral subcutaneous mastectomy with immediate reconstruction in accordance with prevailing standards of care.

b. He failed to diagnose your illness correctly? Answer Yes, he failed to detect and diagnose the occurrence of complications of the surgery he performed. Under the circumstances, he should have been duly, diligent and careful.

c. He did not obtain consent or authorization to operate? Answer He failed to obtain informed consent for the surgery he performed because he failed to fully inform Plaintiff of the nature and risks of the procedure. This contention is based on a review of defendant's office records and Plaintiff's observations and experience and the law relating to a surgeon's duty to his patient.

d. He did not maintain reasonable standards of hygiene or sterilization? Answer Plaintiff has not yet undertaken formal factual and legal discovery and therefore cannot answer this question.

e. He failed to use modern techniques and procedures? Answer See (d) above.

f. He did not give the correct treatment? Answer Yes, he improperly performed the procedure, and improperly managed the complications that ensued. He excessively undermined the circulation to the breast skin during the surgery, through a lack of knowledge, skill, diligence, care, and he did not treat the circulatory compromise in a timely or proper manner. He should have been more knowledgeable, skillful, diligent and careful in performing the surgery and more attentive in the postoperative period.

g. He inflicted physical or mental injury on you during the course of treatment? Answer Yes, by not removing the breast implants earlier than he did, he subjected Plaintiff to persistent unrelenting severe pain which affected her entire body. In addition, the patient was made very anxious because of the development of complications. More importantly, Plaintiff's psychological well-being has been permanently impaired because of the scarring and disfigurement of her breasts. The Defendant was insensitive to the Plaintiff's concern at times when she desperately required medical attention. The Defendant should have taken action to prevent or minimize the occurrence of serious complications of surgery.

h. He failed to observe proper operative or postoperative procedures? Answer Yes, Defendant negligently cared for Plaintiff during the postoperative period and did not remove the breast implants in timely manner. As a result, Plaintiff suffered pain and mental anguish, and sustained breast tissue injury, leaving her breasts in a permanently scarred and disfigured state. Defendant should have closely and carefully monitored Plaintiff for evidence of vascular compromise and impending breast injury, and then taken appropriate steps when such evidence became evident.

i. Of other specified negligence or inadequacy? Answer Plaintiff has not yet undertaken formal factual and legal discovery, and therefore cannot complete answer this question at this time.

14. Did this Defendant on any occasion refuse to attend you?

BY PLAINTIFF'S ATTORNEY: It is not known to Plaintiff whether Defendant refused to attend on any occasion because Plaintiff has not yet undertaken formal factual and legal discovery.

15. On what date was the physician-patient relationship between you and this Defendant terminated?

BY PLAINTIFF'S ATTORNEY: Plaintiff objects to interrogatory because the answer may be derived or ascertained from the examination of the medical records of Plaintiff, the burden of which is substantially the same for the party propounding the interrogatories, and Plaintiff has not already fully derived or ascertained the requested information; and, interrogatory calls for a legal conclusion.

16. Was the relationship terminated by you or by this Defendant? Answer By Plaintiff.

17. If terminated by you, state

a. The reason you terminated the relationship: Answer When Defendant announced that he could do no more to improve the appearance of Plaintiff's breast, Plaintiff sought another opinion of a specialist in plastic surgery.

b. Whether you gave this Defendant notice of termination and if so, what notice and on what date: Answer Plaintiff did not give express or specific notice of termination of relationship.

18. Were you suffering from any illness or injury when you consulted this Defendant? Answer None that were known to or experienced by Plaintiff.

19. Prior to treating you, did this Defendant explain what treatment he proposed to give you? Answer Defendant did not properly or fully disclose, inform or explain the proposed treatment to Plaintiff. Please refer to Defendant's office records.

20. If so, for each such occasion, state

a. The date and place: Answer June 22, 1983.

b. A description of the explanation given to you by this Defendant: Answer A "scooping out" and implants being put in.

c. Whether you understood what this Defendant explained and if not, what action you took in order to understand what he explained: Answer Saw the Defendant three times prior to surgery—June 22, 1983, July 21, 1983, August 5, 1983. I did not ask questions as I put my trust in the Defendant.

21. Did you ever fail to observe any medical instruction or advice given to you by this Defendant? Answer No.

22. Do you contend that this Defendant neglected to inform, instruct or warn you as to any matter relating to your condition, care or treatment? Answer Yes.

23. Were you aware that any risk was involved in the treatment given you by this Defendant? Answer Yes.

24. If so, for each risk of which you were aware, state

a. The type of risk: Answer Hemorrhage, infection, sensory change of breasts.

b. The extent of danger involved in the risk: Answer Slight and controllable.

c. **The date you first became aware of the risk:** <u>Answer</u> June 22, 1983.

d. **A description of how you became aware of the risk:** <u>Answer</u> Disclosed by Defendant.

25. Did this Defendant warn or advise you concerning the possible risk or result of the treatment? <u>Answer</u> Partially, incompletely and improperly warned of some risks.

26. Did this Defendant make any representation as to his ability to cure any of the complaints from which you suffered? <u>Answer</u> No, he did not specifically represent that he would cure my complaints, but he reassured me that he would properly manage any complications of the treatment he had proposed.

27. On what date did you receive notice of each of the injuries complained of in this action? <u>Answer</u> In late February or early March 1985, early January 1985, Plaintiff learned that injury to breasts was likely to be permanent.

28. Describe the circumstances under which you received notice of each of the injuries complained of in this action: <u>Answer</u> Disclosure by Defendant; subsequently confirmed by another plastic surgeon.

29. Have you received information from anyone that this Defendant was negligent or failed to exercise requisite skill in attending and treating you?

BY PLAINTIFF'S ATTORNEY: Plaintiff objects to this interrogatory because this question calls for the disclosure of opinions received in preparation for litigation which are not subject to discovery, unless the persons giving these opinions have been selected as witnesses for trial.

30. State specifically and in detail why a two-step procedure would be more likely to lead to a medically acceptable result than the procedure done by Defendant: <u>Answer</u> There would be less probability of significant hemorrhage which causes tissue destruction necessitating corrective surgery with resultant breast injury. Unless performed by a highly qualified surgeon, a one-step procedure increases the risk of complications of hemorrhage and vascular compromise. Until Plaintiff has undertaken factual and legal discovery, a determination cannot be made whether or not Defendant lacked such requisite skill to perform this procedure.

Document 2.

DR. AVERY'S DEPOSITION OF MRS. REMINGTON

August 14, 1985

* * *

Q. Why did you go to see Dr. Avery? Answer. To ask him if he did the type of surgery which scooped out breast tissue and put in implants as a preventive measure.

Q. What did Dr. Avery say? Answer. He said it would just be a simple type of thing to remove most of the tissue and put in implants.

Q. Did Dr. Avery mention to you any other procedures that could be done other than this scooping out procedure? Answer. No.

Q. Did you ask him if any other procedures could be done? Answer. No.

Q. Was anything discussed about the potential complications of the procedure? Answer. Not much was discussed about that.

Q. But he did not describe to you where the incision would be or anything? Answer. I don't recall exactly where it would be.

Q. Did he tell you whether the implant would be under the skin or under the muscle? Answer. Most likely it would be under the skin unless when he looked at it he wanted to put it under the muscle.

Q. Did he explain what factors he would take into consideration in making that decision? Answer. No.

Q. Did you ask him? Answer. No.

Q. Did he discuss with you the complications of the procedure itself? Answer. He explained that there could be bleeding, but not to worry about it because it is normal to lose a lot of blood, and he would have blood ready for me.

Q. Anything else? Answer. He said I might lose a little sensation in my breasts.

Q. Did he tell you that the surgery was the type of procedure where a surgeon cannot see real well, and that is why sometimes there is bleeding? Answer. No.

Q. What else did he mention besides bleeding and loss of sensation? Answer. He mentioned infection.

Q. Other than those three, was there a discussion of any other possible complication? Answer. No.

Q. Was there any discussion concerning the possible loss of skin tissue, the fact that tissue could die? Answer. No.

Q. Necrosis? Answer. No.

Q. If he had told you that there is a possibility that you could have skin necrosis and your skin could just die, would you have gone ahead with the procedure? Answer. I'm not sure.

Q. Why not, because of hindsight? Answer. No, I would have probably asked more questions at that point.

Q. What questions would you have asked? Answer. I would have asked, "What do you mean by necrosis of the skin?"

Q. If it had been explained to you that necrosis was a possibility, would you have declined the surgery? Answer. I might have thought about it a little more.

Q. If I am not mistaken, you did think about it a little bit more anyway and went to see another surgeon, Dr. Marshall, about it. Right? Answer. Yes.

Q. What did Dr. Marshall tell you? Answer. The only thing he had said to me was to heal six months before putting in the implants.

Q. Did that surgeon tell you why he thought that would be best? Answer. No.

Q. Didn't you ask him? Answer. No.

Q. Had Dr. Avery ever mentioned that you were a high risk for breast cancer? Answer. He said I fit in the high risk category.

Q. Did that mean to you that you were a good candidate for a mastectomy? Answer. I was never told or used the word mastectomy through all that.

Q. Neither the other surgeon you consulted nor Dr. Avery ever called the procedure "subcutaneous mastectomy?" Answer. No.

Q. Did that bother or affect you? Answer. Well, it bothered me because two years later when I saw it in writing in a record, I was totally surprised. I didn't think that is what I had.

Q. Did you speak with Dr. Avery in his office after that visit with the surgeon who gave you a second opinion? Answer. Yes.

Q. Was this a pre-arranged appointment preparing you for the operation or was this something that you specially made? Answer. I made it specially.

Q. For what purpose? Answer. To question him about putting the implants in right away because Dr. Marshall recommended against it.

Q. What did Dr. Avery say? Answer. He said, "That's the way I do the procedure. I do it immediately." And, not to worry about it.

Q. Did you ask him why there is a split of opinion between physicians in doing this procedure? Answer. No, I didn't.

Q. Did you ask him whether there could be any complications that might arise when you do it all in one as opposed to doing it in two steps? Answer. No.

Q. Was there any further discussion about doing it in one step? Answer. Well, he said he didn't want to put me in the hospital twice and he wanted to save me money. That's why he preferred doing it in one procedure.

Q. Was there any mention that if at the time of this procedure he felt that it wasn't appropriate to put the implants in, that he might not put them in and actually put you back in the hospital at some time later and put them in? Answer. I don't recall him ever saying that.

Q. When is the first time you remember seeing Dr. Avery after you were taken back to your hospital bed? Answer. I think the following morning.

Q. Can you recall that conversation? Answer. He just came in, asked me how I was. I think I said I was in a lot of pain. I was afraid to move. I probably mentioned to him that I had fainted the day before. He just checked my bandages that everything was dry and said I was doing fine.

Q. When had you fainted? Answer. A few hours after the surgery.

Q. This was after you were in your room? Answer. Yes.

Q. Had you gotten up to do something? Answer. I had to go to the bathroom, and the nurse came in and said I could get up and go.

Q. Was the nurse assisting you when you fainted? Answer. I think she helped me out of bed, but that was it.

Q. Were any doctors called in at that time? Answer. No.

Q. How were you bandaged? Answer. These big pads were on me. I only know that from when they took them off.

Q. Do you mean these pads were underneath? Answer. Yes, and then I had some kind of gauze going all the way around (indicating).

Q. Are you talking about going around your back as well? Answer. Yes. The whole thing was—I was like bound up, and there were two drains with these packs coming out of my breasts.

Q. Did you see Dr. Avery the afternoon or evening of surgery? Answer. No.

Q. At any time during that day were your bandages changed so you were able to observe your breasts? Answer. No.

Q. Did you have breast pain? Answer. A lot of pain.

Q. Were you being given pain medication? Answer. Yes.

Q. Did it help at all? Answer. Not really.

Q. Did you have any other sensations in or around your breasts? Answer. I felt very full and tight. I was afraid to move. I thought everything would fall out.

Q. That first morning when you saw Dr. Avery after surgery, did you say anything to him about this sensation of fullness or tightness? Answer. I'm pretty sure I did.

Q. You do not know? Answer. I don't recall. I told him the pain that I was in. He said it was normal.

Q. Did you mention this feeling of fullness or tightness to any of the nurses that were attending to you during that first full day after surgery? Answer. Not that I recall.

Q. Why not? Answer. I thought it was normal.

Q. The second full day after surgery, did you see Dr. Avery? Answer. Yes.

Q. What conversation did you have that day? Answer. Very little because he came in to remove the bandages and take the packs out.

Q. He did that himself? Answer. Yes. There wasn't much of a conversation. I was in too much pain.

Q. When he took the bandages off, what did you see? Answer. I saw that I was very large and I just saw the stitches underneath, and—

Q. You were able to see the stitches underneath your breasts? Answer. Yes, and they also had some white tape over them. I was black and blue underneath.

Q. Tell me exactly where you remember seeing black and blue or discoloration. Answer. Right under the breast.

Q. Where the stitches and the tape were? Answer. Yes.

Q. The center portion, but below that particular suture line? Answer. Yes.

Q. On both breasts or just one? Answer. Both.

Q. What was the size of the discoloration that you saw? Answer. Large.

Q. You saw it also on the inside of your breast? Answer. Maybe a day or two later it started to be visible on the inside.

Q. You said that your breasts were large? Answer. Yes, very swollen up here (indicating).

Q. Up top close to your neck? Answer. Yes.

Q. Anything else about their appearance that you remember thinking was unusual or abnormal? Answer. I didn't think they were unusual or abnormal.

Q. Was there any comment made by Dr. Avery after he took the drains out? Answer. When he pulled the drains out, they hurt a lot and some blood started coming out, and then he pressed on them to get more blood out.

Q. Dr. Avery pressed on your breasts? Answer. Yes. He said that he didn't think the drains were working because more blood came out at that point. I felt very faint.

Q. Was there any discussion about whether the pain medications were helping you as far as keeping down the pain? Answer. I kept telling him I was in pain.

Q. During the whole time that you were in there did you make any mention to any of the nurses about the swelling? Answer. No. I thought it was normal.

Q. How did the size of your breasts go from that day? Answer. I think they stayed pretty much the same.

Q. What about the discoloration? Answer. It just seemed to keep going up around the whole breast and under the sides and under the armpit (indicating).

Q. Do you remember when that discoloration first came up in conversation with any doctor? Answer. The only time it came up that I remember is March 1985 when I found out what happened.

Q. No one had mentioned up to that point that you either had a compromised blood supply or something else that caused skin necrosis? Answer. No.

Q. Did Dr. Avery tell you on August 20, 1983 that the implants might come out? Answer. I think that was the date he said something.

Q. The first office visit after you got out of the hospital? Answer. Right, because it was so black and skin was peeling off me.

Q. Where were they black? Answer. The front of the breasts started to look very crusty, black, blistery.

Q. Was there any discussion about what was happening? Answer. I asked him if I was rejecting the implants and he said, "No."

Q. Nothing was mentioned about doing a graft, possibly? Answer. No.

Q. But you believe he said that the implants might come out and then you would have to be re-hospitalized? Answer. Right.

Q. Had there been any change in the appearance of your breasts between the time you saw Dr. Reeves, and the time you saw Dr. Marshall? Answer. There were no changes.

Q. Did Dr. Marshall tell you to go back to Dr. Avery or Dr. Reeves and ask either of them any particular questions? Answer. No.

Q. Did Dr. Marshall recommend that if your breasts weren't getting any better, to have the implants taken out? Answer. No.

Q. When you returned to Dr. Reeves after seeing Dr. Marshall, did you have any further concerns or questions for Dr. Reeves that might have been raised by Dr. Marshall? Answer. No.

Q. When you saw Dr. Avery on September 6, 1983, what did he do? Answer. He repeated again that the implants might come through, and at some point when I was more concerned about the nipples—I can't say if it was on that day or a little bit later on—he said we can always do a grafting for nipples.

Q. So, you seem to remember the grafting was mentioned, but not any sooner than September 6, 1983 and it might have even been later than that? Answer. Right, because I was just concerned about the nipples.

Q. Just for the nipples? We are not talking about any other part of the breast? Answer. No, I didn't know anything else was going to happen tissue-wise.

Q. Again, you were not advised at that time to go into the hospital and have your implants removed? Answer. Right.

Q. When you were in the hospital the second time, was there any mention made of necrosis or compromise of blood supply or anything like that? Answer. No.

Q. No? Answer. No. I really didn't understand what was happening.

Q. Did Dr. Avery explain why the implant would have to be placed under the muscle this time, as opposed to under the skin like it was before? Answer. It just didn't hold under the skin.

Q. Did he offer any explanation as to why the implants did not hold under the skin? Answer. No.

Q. Did you ask if that may have been the reason the skin died? Answer. No.

Q. Did that thought ever cross your mind? Answer. No, I didn't know my skin died.

Q. You had never even heard or seen the word necrosis in relation to yourself? Answer. Right.

Q. Until when? Answer. March 1985.

Q. Is that when you saw Dr. Bryant? Answer. Yes.

Q. Is that the day that everything became known to you? Answer. Yes.

Q. What did he tell you? Answer. He told me exactly what had gone wrong.

Q. What did he say? Answer. He used the word "necrosis," and I said, "What are you talking about?" He explained that it was probably lack of oxygen getting to the tissues.

Q. Did he express any opinion that he would have done anything differently than Dr. Avery? Answer. He said he would have removed the implants within 24–48 hours of seeing these signs.

Q. What signs? Answer. The fullness and the discoloration that appeared.

Q. Did he say that would have made any difference in saving your breast tissue? Answer. He said I probably would not have lost my breast skin.

Q. Would he have done anything else different? Answer. He also did not recommend putting the implants under the skin.

Q. Did Dr. Bryant render an opinion to you that initially Dr. Avery should have just done the mastectomy part and not put the implants in? <u>Answer.</u> Yes.

Q. Did Dr. Bryant explain to you why? <u>Answer.</u> He told me the circulation to the breasts is poor and it's best to let everything heal and then put the implants in.

Q. Why are you seeing Dr. Hickman? <u>Answer.</u> Well, emotionally because it's been very hard on me to date and do things. He's trying to convince me it doesn't matter, but it does in my mind.

Q. Why is it that you cannot date? <u>Answer.</u> Because I'm afraid of what it will lead to. I find it very difficult to want to get undressed in front of anyone and to explain anything.

Q. You are afraid that it may lead to a more permanent relationship which would necessitate—<u>Answer.</u> I just don't want to explain anything.

Q. So, you don't bother to go out on dates? <u>Answer.</u> I have, but I see a man only once. I don't want to continue seeing anyone and have to go into details.

* * *

Q. Did the physical pain basically end after the implants were removed? <u>Answer.</u> I still have some discomfort, but different than when the implants were first put in.

Q. Have the doctors indicated to you that such pain is unusual? <u>Answer.</u> No.

Q. Pain is expected with an implant under the muscle, correct? <u>Answer.</u> Yes.

Q. Have any of the doctors you have spoken with indicated to you that they would have placed the implants under the muscle the first time? <u>Answer.</u> No.

* * *

Q. Do you intend to have any further surgery? <u>Answer.</u> Yes, I have looked at pamphlets, literature describing how more tissue should be removed and especially around the nipples because that's where cancer will start.

Q. The result could be the possibility that you could get cancer? <u>Answer.</u> Right.

Document 3.

MRS. REMINGTON'S DEPOSITION OF DR. AVERY

November 18, 1985

* * *

Q. Do you recognize any standards of care in reconstructive breast surgery? <u>Answer.</u> I am concerned about the body of knowledge of plastic surgery and the standards I have been taught in my residency.

Q. How many prophylactic subcutaneous mastectomies have you performed? <u>Answer.</u> One or two a year.

Q. Have you had any special training in breast surgery? <u>Answer.</u> No.

Q. Did Mrs. Remington express any concerns regarding her breasts? <u>Answer.</u> She was concerned that several relatives had breast cancer.

Q. Did you suggest or propose any treatment? <u>Answer.</u> I suggested two courses of treatment: doing nothing, or having a subcutaneous mastectomy.

Q. What did you tell her about a subcutaneous mastectomy? <u>Answer.</u> I told her that the operation is not a cosmetic operation. It involves removing the breast substance from an incision underneath the breast by scooping out all of the material, and then reconstructing her with an implant.

Q. Did you indicate to her that you were aware of controversy involving this procedure? <u>Answer.</u> I did not suggest that she proceed without thought.

Q. What was the objective of a subcutaneous mastectomy? <u>Answer.</u> To remove as much as possible of the breast substance, thereby decreasing the possibility of developing breast cancer.

Q. Did you discuss the high complication rate associated with this surgery? <u>Answer.</u> The complications that I listed in my medical chart are not the only ones that we discussed. Other complications are rejection of the implant and skin necrosis.

Q. You discussed skin necrosis? <u>Answer.</u> I told her that the operation could lead to loss of the skin and exposure of the implant.

Q. How high a complication rate do you believe this surgery carried with it? <u>Answer.</u> Twenty to twenty-five percent.

Q. Did you explain or disclose to her what the consequences of these complications might be? <u>Answer.</u> Not in detail.

Q. Did she ask you any questions about the procedure? <u>Answer.</u> I do not have any specific recollection of any questions. I am sure there were lots asked.

Q. Did you have any discussion with her regarding disfigurement? <u>Answer.</u> I emphasized to her that this is not a cosmetic operation, and that other patients that I have done do not have normal appearing breasts.

Q. What do you mean, "normal appearing breasts"? Answer. Breasts are not the same afterwards as before.

Q. Did you ever discuss with her doing a "staged" procedure, i.e., implanting the prostheses later? Answer. I told her I would assess the situation at the operating table after removing the breast tissue.

Q. Are there any advantages to performing a two-stage procedure? Answer. With a two-stage procedure you are most assured of the blood supply to the skin because you do not have an implant in to give a possible problem.

Q. At the time you proposed a subcutaneous mastectomy, were you aware of any technical advances that made this procedure have less complications? Answer. Not that I am aware.

Q. How much breast tissue did you plan to remove under the nipple-areolar complex? Answer. You want to clean out as much as possible underneath the nipple because this area is more prone to cancer.

Q. Are you aware of any inherent risk associated with this procedure? Answer. The closer you cut to the skin to remove more breast tissue, the more you make the skin flap thin. You are trying to remove as much breast tissue as possible to do the best prophylactic procedure, versus trying to preserve the skin envelope.

Q. What percentage of breast tissue did you remove? Answer. I have no idea. I removed all of the breast tissue that I visibly saw.

Q. What are principal concerns or complications associated with this operation? Answer. Vascular compromise, hemorrhage and loss of implant.

Q. In disclosing the nature and the risk of the procedure, did you indicate that as an alternative, the implant may be placed underneath the muscle rather than in the subcutaneous space? Answer. I may have very well discussed that.

Q. Are there recognized disadvantages to this approach? Answer. You might lose use of the muscle, and you may develop a deformity of the implant.

Q. Are there recognized advantages in terms of better protection or less likelihood of exposure? Answer. Submuscular insertion decreases the incidence of exposure of the implant.

* * *

Q. Is there a tendency for surgeons to perform fewer subcutaneous mastectomies? Answer. People are getting away from doing subcutaneous mastectomies. The suggestion now in the literature is for total mastectomies, which I think are unacceptable except in a high risk patient.

Q. Are you familiar with the dermal plexus? Answer. It is the blood supply to the breast skin tissue, the subdermal vessels.

Q. Did the blood pressure drop during the surgery? Answer. I have no independent recollection.

Q. Did you consider that Mrs. Remington might have required a blood transfusion? Answer. No, because her hematocrit of 33 did not dictate that she receive a transfusion.

Q. What was the hematocrit during the postoperative period? Answer. On the fourth postoperative day it was 31.

Q. How much drainage had been recorded from the Hemovac? Answer. The Hemovac removed 75 cc. on the first postoperative day, and 60 cc. on the following day.

* * *

Q. Is a hematoma a recognized complication of a subcutaneous mastectomy? Answer. Yes, as a result of hemorrhage.

Q. What is the significance of a hematoma? Answer. A large breast hematoma may cause skin compromise.

Q. What is the treatment for a hematoma? Answer. If you have a tight breast, i.e., a breast where the vascular supply is compromised, the right procedure is to return the patient to the operating room.

Q. Did a hematoma form in Mrs. Remington's case? Answer. The condition that I just outlined with the tight breasts did not exist.

Q. How would you determine whether she had tight breasts? Answer. By looking at them.

Q. How would they appear? Answer. They would give the impression of bursting at the seams.

Q. Anything else? Answer. Rock hard to touch. They would be shiny.

Q. When did you first examine Mrs. Remington's breasts postoperatively? Answer. The second post-op day, I placed her in a bra and examined her breasts. At that time I noted that there was no pressure on skin.

Q. Was there any drainage when you removed the Hemovac on the second post-op day? Answer. A large amount of drainage was removed.

Q. If it was bloody drainage, would that not be indicative of a hematoma? Answer. By definition it would be, but it is also being removed.

Q. Do you have any way of knowing how long that hematoma was present? Answer. No. I can say that when I examined her after surgery, I noted that her skin looked viable.

Q. Do you know whether she was experiencing pain? Answer. I do not think that the discomfort that she was experiencing was out of the ordinary.

Q. How do you account for Mrs. Remington's breasts swelling? Answer. You expect to have swelling after operating on breasts.

Q. At what point would you return a patient to the operating room who had developed a hematoma? Answer. When I thought that the skin would be compromised and that the bleeding continued underneath the area of surgery.

Q. How would you recognize continued bleeding into the breast pocket? Answer. The breast would continually get larger, and look tense and swollen.

Q. What would you do? Answer. Remove the source of excessive pressure.

Q. If you have a full thickness necrotic skin loss, would you remove both the skin and the implant? Answer. Yes.

Q. But you have no way of knowing which way it is going to turn out when you first detect vascular compromise, do you? Answer. No.

Q. And if the vascular compromise goes on to cause a full thickness skin loss, that skin is dead and must be excised? Answer. That's correct.

Q. And if it is excised, you're likely to have unwanted scarring where it is removed? Answer. Yes.

Q. Is there any way to anticipate that development or occurrence of a full thickness skin loss? Answer. By monitoring for skin viability.

Q. What does "viability" mean to you? Answer. That the skin is alive, not necrotic.

Q. Could it be ischemic and still be viable? Answer. Yes.

Q. What does "ischemic" mean to you? Answer. Less than a perfect blood supply to it. The skin may or may not remain viable.

Q. What factors might cause ischemic process? Answer. Extremely tight dressings; excessively large implants.

Q. Do those factors compromise oxygen to the skin? Answer. Sometimes.

Q. May ischemia be a precursor to necrosis of skin tissue? Answer. Yes.

Q. So is it important to intervene at a time when ischemia is likely to be present? Answer. There was no indication that ischemia was present in Mrs. Remington's case.

Q. In your opinion, what caused necrosis in her case? Answer. I performed a complete surgical procedure. Trying to do the best possible removal of breast tissue is a factor that adds to the development of necrosis.

Q. Why did you perform such a complete procedure? Answer. I think that is the duty of the surgeon who performs this procedure to try to do the best job possible in preventing the patient from getting breast cancer.

Q. Could internal and/or external pressure factors contribute to or cause ischemia? Answer. I still do not see any attributes of the hematoma causing this problem, because the breasts were not tense, but the implant under the skin in and of itself also may contribute to vascular compromise.

Q. Were there any other factors that contributed to the ultimate skin loss? Answer. I think if she would have allowed me to operate on her prior to when I went away, although she still probably would have ended up with the same result, but she would have been spared a lot of discomfort.

Q. When was the first time that you detected or recognized a problem with skin viability? Answer. I would say on August 20, 1983. That was the first time that skin viability was not assured, that the skin may not be alive. Although I had looked for this problem before, it was not evident.

Q. Was her skin viable on August 20, 1983? Answer. I was not sure of the skin viability at that point.

Q. Did you recommend removal of the implant at that time? Answer. I discussed that she needed an operation, but she did not want to have it at that time.

Q. On what basis did you conclude that? Answer. Even after I returned from vacation, she was still reluctant to have surgery. Only when the necrotic area separated and exposed the implant did she permit herself to be put in the hospital.

Q. Did she outright refuse to have surgery that was proposed? Answer. In essence, yes. I explained to her what was necessary. I believe she was hopeful that the skin loss would be only partial rather than full thickness and that the area would heal or improve by itself. And it was quite evident it was not going to happen.

Q. Did you indicate to her that some skin areas were necrotic? Answer. Yes.

Q. Did she understand what "necrotic" meant? Answer. I don't have any opinion on that.

Q. And you are saying that you proposed this to her, and she declined to have this procedure? Answer. That's correct.

Q. If she had agreed to surgery on August 20, 1983, when did you propose to perform the operation? Answer. I would have put her in the hospital and done the procedure that evening.

Q. Were you not planning to go out of town on vacation soon after that? Answer. Yes.

Q. Are you suggesting now that you would have cancelled the vacation to operate on her that evening? Answer. No. I would have operated on her that evening. And if I could not operate on her, I would make sure that somebody would operate on her. I have left patients in mid-treatment to go on a vacation for the fortuitousness of the way that the time schedule works out. That is when my cross coverage surgeon would take care of whatever problem I have with the patient.

Q. At this point, you had diagnosed a complication of the initial surgical procedure, correct? Answer. That's correct.

Q. Ordinarily would you leave a patient that was having a complication of a surgical procedure that you had performed in the hands of another surgeon? Answer. If I made arrangements, yes. I don't see anything wrong with that, to leave her in competent hands with a board certified surgeon.

Q. Even if that surgeon might not have known anything about the patient's condition or problems? Answer. There is nothing wrong with talking to the surgeon and explaining what the problem is and having the covering surgeon provide the postoperative care from that point on.

Q. Did you talk to the covering surgeon about your patient's condition? Answer. I believe so.

Q. Did you explain to him the problem that your patient was having? Answer. I would imagine that I did. I don't have any record of that specifically.

Q. Did you send a copy of your records and notes to the covering surgeon prior to your going away on vacation? Answer. I do not recall anything specific about that.

Q. She was still your patient that he was seeing, right? Answer. Yes.

Q. Do you recall telling him that she refused to have surgery to have the implant removed? Answer. I have a vague recollection of that, yes.

Q. On August 22, 1983, the covering surgeon recorded that the skin did not look like it was totally lost. Do you agree? Answer. Maybe.

* * *

Q. Could you describe what you see on the September 16, 1983 photographs which you took of her breasts, which have been marked Exhibit V? Answer. There are darkened black to brown tissue areas beneath and including a portion of the nipples bilaterally, with a discoloration extending out on the side of more pinkish tissue over a larger area.

Q. In your opinion, are these photographs representative of a skin necrosis of her breasts? Answer. Yes.

Q. Could you describe the condition of her breasts since the reconstruction in November 1984 by referring to the photographs marked Exhibit DD? Answer. Her breasts have multiple surface scars, with loss of the nipple area and loss of substance due to necrosis.

Q. Will future surgery likely improve the appearance of her breasts? <u>Answer</u>. It is doubtful because breasts that have a subcutaneous mastectomy are never normal looking breasts; they are not equal to the pre-operative condition.

Q. What do you mean by "never normal." <u>Answer</u>. I don't think you get the same shape, touch or appearance. On her last office visit February 28, 1984, she was unhappy with her nipples. I expressed my reluctance to operate on her.

Q. In your opinion did she obtain a satisfactory result to breast surgery? <u>Answer</u>. Considering the problems she had, I think the final result is respectable.

Q. Would you say that her breasts are disfigured? <u>Answer</u>. They are not the same as before, and I think that was made clear to her prior to the operation.

Q. Is Mrs. Remington presently still at risk for developing breast cancer? <u>Answer</u>. Yes.

* * *

Q. What type of dressing did you use postoperatively? <u>Answer</u>. Cotton four by fours and a wrap-around cling dressing.

Q. Wrapped all the way around Mrs. Remington's chest? <u>Answer</u>. That's correct.

Q. With such a dressing, how were you able to observe her breasts? <u>Answer</u>. It is easy to see the breasts underneath the dressing, and if there would be a hematoma it would be quite evident through the dressing.

Q. Through the dressing? <u>Answer</u>. Yes.

Q. You don't recall splitting the dressing to expose the entire breasts do you? <u>Answer</u>. No. The second postoperative day I took her out of a dressing.

Document 4.

MRS. REMINGTON'S DEPOSITION OF DR. REEVES

(Dr. Avery's "Covering Plastic Surgeon")
December 1985

Q. Do you specifically recall seeing Mrs. Remington in August, 1983? Answer: I don't remember the specifics. All I can remember is what I have recorded as interim notes in Dr. Avery's absence.

Q. After reviewing those notes, is your memory refreshed? Answer: Yes, somewhat.

Q. Do you have any independent recollection, without the notes? Answer: I have vague recollections of what went on.

Q. Do you recall Dr. Avery telling you about Mrs. Remington's condition prior to your seeing her? Answer: I remember that she had undergone a subcutaneous mastectomy with immediate reconstruction and had some compromised skin. He was worried about it and wanted to take the implants out, but the patient did not want them removed. He wanted me to more or less try to carry her through his absence.

Q. What did it mean to "carry her through?" Answer: Debride necrotic breast tissue if absolutely necessary.

Q. Did it imply removing the implants, if indicated? Answer: She did not want them removed. So I didn't really delve into it. My job was to act as a stopgap and prevent her from having any real trouble. If she extruded a prosthesis, of course, I would have taken care of her.

Q. Did you feel that she was your patient? Answer: I felt she was Dr. Avery's patient.

Q. Was the information you've just recited given to you by Dr. Avery prior to your seeing Mrs. Remington? Answer: Yes.

Q. Did he provide you with any written information? Answer: I don't recall whether he sent the patient's chart with her.

Q. In your opinion, would it be good medical practice to provide such records of a prior treating physician? Answer: Sure.

Q. Did Dr. Avery provide any means by which you could communicate with him if you needed to talk to him? Answer: If I'm not mistaken, he went out of the country.

Q. At that time, were you familiar with a subcutaneous mastectomy with immediate reconstruction? Answer: I had some books on it, yes, sir.

Q. Do you consider those books authoritative on the subject? Answer: Not really. It's a rather controversial subject.

Q. In what way is it "controversial?" Answer: The "old" subcutaneous mastectomy left the nipple and ducts. The "new" operation is called "total mastectomy." The surgeon takes the nipples off, cores out the ductal system underneath and reapplies the nipple as a full thickness graft.

Q. Why is this "new" procedure being performed? <u>Answer</u>: Because it greatly reduces the ductal structure within the nipple itself, which is the source of most breast cancers.

Q. Are there any other controversial aspects of this procedure? <u>Answer</u>: There is the issue of whether you should insert the implant above the muscle in the subcutaneous space or below the muscle. I think it has been shown that delayed reconstruction leaves a poor aesthetic result.

Q. Are the aesthetics an important consideration in this operation? <u>Answer</u>: Well, it's not really a cosmetic operation.

Q. Have you personally performed subcutaneous mastectomies? <u>Answer</u>: I have done some subcutaneous mastectomies in the past. At the present time I do "total" mastectomies.

Q. But you have in the past performed prophylactic subcutaneous mastectomies with immediate reconstruction? <u>Answer</u>: Only in residency, never in private practice.

* * *

Document 5.

DR. AVERY'S DEPOSITION OF DR. SEARS

(Plaintiff's Expert Plastic Surgery Witness)
February 1986

Q. Do you have an opinion as to whether Dr. Avery properly informed Mrs. Remington of the risks of the surgery Dr. Avery was going to perform? Answer: Yes.

Q. What is that opinion? Answer: Dr. Avery did not fully inform Mrs. Remington of the inherent risks and complications of procedure, namely skin loss and breast deformity.

Q. Now, doctor, if all the information is disclosed to a patient and the patient still wants the procedure, would it be okay for the surgeon to operate? Answer: If the patient knew what she was getting into, yes.

Q. Under circumstances where the patient has been given this information, is the patient making a knowledgeable choice? Answer: I think the legal people can argue that. That is a question beyond me.

Q. In your opinion doctor, is Mrs. Remington's outcome with the operation she underwent totally unexpected? Answer: One of the sad facts about this particular operation is that the way her breasts now appear is not that far from others who have undergone similar surgery.

Q. Without complication, you mean? Answer: What I am saying, the nipple, areola and dermal scarring represent a special problem, but the form and shape of her breast is expected.

Q. Do I understand you to say if there had been no complications, you would not have expected the appearance of her breasts to be significantly different, other than the scarring and the nipple/areola complex changes? Answer: Right. After subcutaneous mastectomy reconstruction the breasts will not look as good as the natural breasts. It is the exception for the breasts to look good, compared to breast augmentations for cosmetic reasons where it is the exception for the breasts to look bad.

Q. Was this high complication rate generally known at the time the surgery was proposed? Answer: Plastic surgeons should have been aware of it at that time.

* * *

Q. In what way, if any, could Dr. Avery have reduced the risks of the surgery he performed on Mrs. Remington? Answer: By performing a two-stage procedure delaying implantation; and by using a submuscular implantation rather than a subcutaneous implantation.

Q. Doctor, are you saying that simply performing a subcutaneous mastectomy and implantation in one-stage was below standard of care? Answer: No.

Q. You are not saying that just doing a subcutaneous mastectomy was below the standard of care? Answer: I would not say that was necessarily a deviation from the standard of care.

Q. Do you know plastic surgeons that prefer to do implants either submuscularly or subcutaneously? Answer: Yes, but less with this particular operation, because the serious complication rate with subcutaneous implantation at the time of the ablative procedure is so much higher.

Q. Specifically, what complications are you referring to? Answer: Subcutaneous implantation has a significantly higher rate of exposure of the implant than a submuscular implantation.

Q. What source can you site that says it would be below the standard of care to place the implants in the subcutaneous space? Answer: There is no written material that says this is the standard of care. Plastic surgeons are taught that this is what you should do.

Q. If somebody has been practicing for many years and they may not have been taught the particular procedure, is it that surgeon's standard of care to do it this way? Answer: It is incumbent upon a specialist to keep up with newer techniques by attending courses, reading literature and conversing with each other.

Q. Are there any articles which you would consider to be authoritative as far as what the knowledge in plastic surgery that now reveal complications and risks of a subcutaneous mastectomy? Answer: The standard of care is based on what we are taught. I was taught that such procedure was fraught with hazards even though such procedures were still being performed.

Q. Did you have any criticisms of the surgical technique employed by Dr. Avery in carrying out the surgery? Answer: I don't think so. Whenever you do surgery you will get problems at times. Although the approach he chose is controversial, it is sometimes utilized by good people.

Q. Is there something that you would criticize about Dr. Avery's postoperative care as being below the standard of care? Answer: There were several pieces of information that required personal evaluation by Dr. Avery. One, Mrs. Remington was having a lot of breast pain. Two, she had experienced significant enough blood loss to require a transfusion. Three, she fainted when getting up.

Q. What is the clinical significance of that information? Answer: Pain, blood loss, and fainting made it incumbent upon Dr. Avery to investigate the reasons for these occurrences.

Q. It is your impression from your review of the records and depositions that Dr. Avery did not investigate these matters? Answer: It is my understanding that he did not remove the dressing until 48 hours after surgery.

Q. How would the ultimate status of Mrs. Remington's breasts have been changed if Dr. Avery had taken the dressings off 24 hours earlier? Answer: If indeed her skin at the time was in a non-compromised situation, the only problem that it presented was that Mrs. Remington had a significant period of discomfort.

Q. If Dr. Avery had come in to personally evaluate Mrs. Remington, what would he have found? Answer: I am not certain I can answer that question.

Q. Then do you have a definite opinion whether failure to come at that time caused or contributed to her subsequent complications. Answer: No.

Q. Do you feel Dr. Avery was remiss in any other ways in Mrs. Remington's postoperative followup? Answer: Yes. He failed to see the patient after he was contacted by nurses regarding excessive drainage on Mrs. Remington's surgical dressing.

Q. If he did in fact fail to do that, how did it cause or contribute to cause Mrs. Remington's ultimate problem? Answer: That occurrence may have been a manifestation of a hematoma, which could have caused compromised circulation to the skin.

Q. What should Dr. Avery have done after being called by the nurse? Answer: He should have examined her breasts to determine whether there was indeed a hematoma formation.

Q. Anything else? Answer: If the skin was taut and shiny as a result of being under tension from accumulation of blood, he should have drained the breast cavity.

Q. Why should he have done that? Answer: Not only do you relieve the tension, but you ligate any bleeding vessels.

Q. Did you find anything in the records at the point when those drains were removed to cause you to feel that Dr. Avery deviated from the standard of care in not evacuating the breasts? Answer: The fact that he mentions hematoma in the record, and that ultimately Mrs. Remington had a problem with skin necrosis.

Q. Are there any other causes for the skin necrosis? Answer: Ordinarily, there are no events eight, nine, ten days, after such a procedure, other than infection, that will cause such necrosis.

Q. Are you assuming something would have been observable at that time that should have keyed him to evacuate the breasts? Answer: Yes.

Q. What if it wasn't there? Answer: Then it is a question of clinical judgment.

Q. Don't you routinely see some swelling as a result of this procedure? Answer: Yes.

Q. You are not suggesting that all the swelling has gone down within 48 hours on a patient who has undergone breast surgery, are you? Answer: I am referring to the swelling associated with a shiny skin appearance and pain that seems out of proportion to what is expected with that particular procedure.

Q. Would you expect to see any discoloration in 48 hours? Answer: Yes, some bluish discoloration.

Q. Wouldn't you expect those findings in a breast that didn't have any compromise as well? Answer: Yes.

Q. At what point should Dr. Avery have removed the implants? Answer: That depends on clinical judgment.

Q. Was it a deviation in the standard of care in not removing them then 48 hours postoperatively? Answer: It is a judgment question again.

Q. If the implants had been removed when you believe that there may have been something to indicate a need to evacuate a hematoma, would Mrs. Remington have suffered any breast damage? Answer: If the breast skin was viable at that particular time, and was under tension because of accumulation of blood, removing the implant and evacuating the hematoma would have gotten rid of an additional pressure. Then it is possible that the subsequent problems could have been alleviated.

Q. At what point could she have had the implants removed and no damage would have occurred to her breasts? Answer: I could not answer that question on the basis of what was written in the records. It is not clear when the skin was so totally involved that injury was irreversible.

Q. Wouldn't you agree that a hematoma which has been compromising the blood supply to the breast for 48 hours would have caused some irreversible damage? Answer: You could still have ischemia and have viable tissue. If the focus of pressure is removed then you can go on to have healing and not lose tissue. But if the focus of pressure that is contributing to ischemia is allowed to persist, then instead of the ischemia reversing itself, you get further vascular compromise, necrosis of skin, and subsequent loss of tissue.

Q. But in your review of the records you can't give a point when you feel that ischemia had reached a level where you weren't going to reverse at least some of the injury no matter what was done at that point? Answer: The only time I could say that is on September 16, 1983.

Q. Again by way of clarification, is it your opinion that both internal and external pressure factors contributed to the ultimate skin loss and disfiguration? Answer: Yes. An external dressing applying pressure over an implanted object can add to the problem where ischemia is occurring.

Q. Are you suggesting that the application of a wrap-around dressing contributed to the breast injury sustained by Mrs. Remington? Answer: Applying a compressive wrap-around dressing for a subcutaneous implantation may impair the vascularity of the breast and nipple.

Q. Are you aware that many plastic surgeons use a circumferential dressing? Answer: Yes.

Q. Then you don't find its use was below the standard of care? Answer: Not necessarily.

Q. Are there any other factors that may have contributed to the failure of Mrs. Remington's breast tissue to heal? Answer: Inadequate replacement for the blood lost may have impeded wound healing because less circulating red blood cells may cause decreased oxygenation to tissue already compromised by surgical dissection and pressure.

Q. What evidence is there that the postoperative loss of breast skin was caused by circulatory compromise? Answer: Primarily, the symmetrical area of full thickness skin and nipple and areolar loss associated with a surrounding area of superficial dermal compromise.

Q. Do you believe that the dissection was also a basis for the loss of breast skin? Answer: I believe skin flaps may have been overzealously thinned in the areas where skin loss eventually occurred.

Q. Are you saying that simply performing the subcutaneous mastectomy resulted in vascular and dermal compromise? Answer: Yes, if Dr. Avery removed too much breast tissue underlying the skin.

Q. Is excessive thinning of breast tissue an expected result of a subcutaneous mastectomy? Answer: Not necessarily. A surgeon adequately trained in creating skin flaps during a subcutaneous mastectomy should be aware when the flaps are being made too thin.

Q. Are there corrections a surgeon can make intraoperatively if it is discovered the skin flaps are being made too thin? Answer: The surgeon should avoid putting a subcutaneous implant into that area of compromised skin.

Q. Does the standard of care allow latitude in surgical creation of skin flaps? Answer: Yes.

Q. Are there anatomical landmarks which should guide a surgeon during the thinning procedure? Answer: A surgeon must be aware of and take precautions not to interfere with the dermal plexus, that is, the blood supply of the breast skin.

Q. But isn't some such interference an inherent complication of subcutaneous mastectomy? Answer: Yes, but it may also be an avoidable hazard.

Q. Is there an indication in Mrs. Remington's medical chart of the primary cause of the loss of breast tissue? Answer: In my opinion, the breast tissue loss was primarily due to the bilateral hematomas which increased internal pressure.

Q. What did you observe in the medical record that would have indicated hematoma formation? Answer: Thirty hours after surgery she had bloody drainage on the bedsheets. At 48 hours, a large amount of blood was removed from her breasts despite existence of drains.

Q. Were there any other sources that led you to this conclusion? Answer: Her breasts were swollen. Swelling is not expected from this procedure unless there is accumulation of fluid in the breast envelope, because there is not significant amount of tissue left in breast to swell.

Q. Are you saying that you would not expect swelling after a subcutaneous mastectomy? Answer: Significant swelling is not to be expected as a normal postoperative finding, with this procedure, especially when associated with pain.

Q. Isn't pain an anticipated aspect of the postoperative course with this kind of surgery? Answer: A significant degree of pain over a prolonged period is not expected in a normal postoperative finding.

Q. What characterizes "significant" pain? Answer: Pain that requires protracted use of narcotics for control.

Q. In your opinion what was the cause of Mrs. Remington's breast pain? Answer: The collection of blood in the breast cavity resulting in distention of skin tissues and compromise of skin circulation.

Q. What could Dr. Avery have done to minimize the effects of the vascular compromise? Answer: When vascular compromise became obvious, he should have attempted to salvage some breast skin to minimize scarring and disfigurement which was likely to result if necrosis occurred.

Q. Does the medical record reflect a time frame for the progress of Mrs. Remington's complication? Answer: It is difficult for me to believe that there was not evidence of compromised circulation earlier than September 16, 1983. That is the latest date that I would have removed the implants.

Q. To what degree is Mrs. Remington's breast disfigurement irreversible? Answer: Additional surgery to improve appearance would only result in a 10% improvement.

Q. What would you say if another plastic surgeon indicated that the scars could be revised? Answer: Any surgeon who indicates that he or she can bring about a significant improvement with additional surgery doesn't understand the nature of the problem. There may or may not be improvement by revising the scars.

Document 6.

DR. AVERY'S DEPOSITION OF DR. SHUMACHER

(Plaintiff's General Surgeon Expert Witness)
March 5, 1986

Q. What fault do you find with what Dr. Avery did? Answer. The clinical indications for a prophylactic subcutaneous mastectomy were insufficient.

Q. Do you hold that opinion even if the surgery was for "mastodynia"? Answer. Mastodynia is severe breast pain, a diagnosis not supported by the medical chart.

Q. Are you saying that the decision to do a subcutaneous implantation was below the standard of care? Answer. It would not comport with the standard of care that I am familiar with.

* * *

Q. You seem to find fault with Dr. Avery's description of the procedure as "scooping out" of tissue? Answer. Yes. It implies a simple procedure, when in reality a surgeon must expertly remove breast tissue as near to totally as possible without sacrificing the skin vascularity.

Q. Are you suggesting that it is a hazardous procedure? Answer. Yes, it is a compromise between the threat of cancer and an unsatisfactory cosmetic outcome.

Q. Would not the threat of cancer be a sufficient indication for the surgery? Answer. Mrs. Remington's admitting diagnosis is "cystic dysplasia," but she had never had a breast biopsy, nor a history of any breast pain. There was nothing to clearly suggest breast cancer.

Q. What are the clinical indications for subcutaneous mastectomy? Answer. Cancer on the opposite side, multiple biopsies for suspicious lesions, and untreatable fibrocystic disease.

Q. If there are multiple instances of breast cancer in the family, isn't it more likely than the standard population area that the person may get breast cancer? Answer. Yes.

Q. What if you have a history such as Mrs. Remington's family history, how high is that rate now? Answer. About one in ten instead of one in eleven.

* * *

Q. What should Mrs. Remington have been told about the expected appearance of her breasts after surgery? Answer. That the surgery was a destructive procedure, always leaving less than a normal breast. The best she could expect was for the surgery to make her look normal in clothes.

Q. What if Dr. Avery says he told Mrs. Remington about what you have just mentioned? Answer. If this information was transmitted by

Dr. Avery, it does not appear to have been understood by Mrs. Remington.

Q. And if a patient doesn't understand it, you never know it until the complications arise? Answer. Yes.

Q. If there had been any vascular compromise during the 48-hour postoperative period, did Dr. Avery affect the ultimate result? Answer. Yes. One of the consequences, bleeding into the pocket containing the prosthesis, adds further tension on the skin causing it to become ischemic. This is the reason she lost the skin there, having had it turn from viable to non-viable.

Q. Based on his clinical observations, his talking with the patient, and his review of the chart, Dr. Avery could have made just as good an evaluation as to the status of Mrs. Remington at 48 hours as he could have if he had seen her every four hours, can he not? Answer. Had he seen her regularly, recognized the problem and decompressed her breasts, he might have salvaged more skin. Hemorrhage after the operation added to the tension from the dressing. The hematoma further compromised the circulation to the skin. If he had recognized and treated this, there would have been less loss than subsequently occurred.

Q. Clinically what indication was there of any bleeding problem at all? Answer. Mrs. Remington was hypotensive, and the most obvious place for loss of blood is in the site of operation.

Q. Are you critical of the manner in which Dr. Avery placed the surgical dressing on Mrs. Remington? Answer. If a patient shows indications of blood loss from somewhere, I would closely examine the most obvious place, the incision site. I would not reinforce dressings to cover that up.

Q. After checking and making a judgment that it doesn't require any further change, putting on a new dressing would not be inappropriate, would it? Answer. Because the patient lost that much blood, I would still be curious and concerned as to where all that blood went, even if on the surface there does not appear to be anything abnormal.

Q. What type of investigation should have been conducted? Answer. One designed to find out what is causing the blood loss, especially after having been transfused with two units of blood. She has saturated both dressings, fainted due to hypotension, and her hematocrit is low. Dr. Avery should have taken down the dressing to see if there was evidence of a hematoma.

Q. What evidence was there of a hematoma? Answer. She had swelling, dissection of blood going up toward her neck, into arms, and down the chest. She was in pain due to tension in the breasts.

Q. When surgery is done, swelling occurs, does it not? Answer. Yes.

Q. So it would be the physician making the clinical determination whether such swelling is normal or abnormal? Answer. Correct.

Q. Discoloration of skin is a normal sequela of such surgery, is it not? Answer. Not if the skin is being filled with blood under tension; then the blood may dissect into tissue planes not operated on in the neck, arm, and other areas, moving from one point to another.

* * *

Q. Do you have an opinion whether the prostheses should have been removed before Mrs. Remington was discharged? Answer. Whatever it is that caused the devitalization of skin, if it were possible to detect, should have also been corrected before discharge.

Q. Do you have an opinion that Dr. Avery deviated from the standard of care in failing to do something that would have corrected this problem during the hospitalization? Answer. If there was any clinical evidence, and there should be on the basis of those physiologic changes that we have discussed, that she had significant blood loss in the breasts, then Dr. Avery should have made some attempt to find the lost blood, or the sites where it would most likely accumulate.

Q. At what time did whatever damage that resulted to the skin become irreversible? Answer. That is asking when ischemia has become necrosis. That is when the vascularity of the skin doesn't improve over time.

Q. When should something have been done? Answer. As soon as there was evidence that there was vascular compromise to the circulation, something should have been done in order to prevent that from progressing further.

Q. Do you have an opinion as to what caused necrosis of the skin? Answer. Tension from a large hematoma caused by bleeding under the skin flaps, combined with the space-occupying prostheses, which caused circulatory embarrassment and the subsequent tissue loss.

Q. Is it is your opinion, then, that the compromise did not occur during surgery? Answer. I don't think it was caused at the time of the operation; that is, that the road to necrosis of the skin was inexorably set in motion at the time of operation. It was the hematomas, thereafter, along with the prostheses which further stretched and devitalized the skin.

Q. What indications are there in the medical chart that there was a large hematoma in each breast that caused this necrosis? Answer. Her lost blood. The transfused units still did not bring the hematocrit up to the normal level it was preoperatively. She was complaining of severe breast pain. Typically this operation is not attended by an awful lot of pain.

Q. How else would that be reflected? Answer. By abnormal swelling and discoloration.

Q. Is there any other evidence of bilateral hematomas? Answer. Ordinarily when the drain is pulled out from the breast pocket, a gush does not come out unless there is an accumulation of blood under pressure.

Q. Which was evacuated at the time by Dr. Avery? Answer. Which presumably was evacuated at the time, but certainly was not entirely evacuated. There would still be pockets of blood clots in the breast pocket somewhere that were not evacuated.

Q. But isn't that what a drain is supposed to do? Answer. Drainage is an indicator of bleeding, but not the treatment of bleeding. A drain is not there simply to conduct blood away and thereby affect the treatment, but to tell us there is bleeding going on.

Q. You indicated that Dr. Avery inappropriately responded to Mrs. Remington's complaint of breast pain. What was inappropriate about his response? Answer. He just increased the pain medication in response to her persistent complaints of pain. With progressing pain, he should have found out the reason for that pain.

Q. Why did you feel her pain was unusual or indicative of a problem? Answer. From the time she awakened from anesthesia she had had pain. This is unusual.

Q. Was there a change in the frequency or the dosage of medication for pain? Answer. Getting Demerol regularly would be unusual for this sort of operation. It wasn't discontinued, even several days after the procedure.

Q. Are you critical of what Dr. Avery did after August 20, 1983? Answer. I don't think you can do anything at this point that would have changed her course or outcome. The prosthesis was doomed. However, had she been operated on August 20, 1983 rather than later, she might have had less skin loss.

Q. Can you say within reasonable medical probability that there would have been a different result as far as the loss of breast skin? Answer. Dr. Avery's statement in Mrs. Remington's medical chart that "skin viability is not assured," means that some part of her skin was still viable and, by implication, that the skin losses seem to be progressive. At this time there is some clinical evidence that the ischemia might reverse itself, so that an early operation would probably would have salvaged some skin.

Document 7.

DR. AVERY'S DEPOSITION OF DR. BRYANT

(Plastic Surgeon Whom Mrs. Remington Consulted after She Terminated Her Relationship with Dr. Avery)
April 1986

Q. Doctor, do you have any criticism of Dr. Avery doing a subcutaneous mastectomy and reconstruction on Mrs. Remington all in one procedure? Answer: No, some reputable surgeons do it that way.

Q. Are there disadvantages in doing the procedure in one stage? Answer: The problem with doing it in one stage is the possibility of skin compromise.

Q. Are there any disadvantages in doing it in two stages? Answer: Yes. The likelihood of getting contracted and irregular breasts.

Q. And was it a deviation from the recognized standard of care to do the procedure all in one stage? Answer: Not in and of itself.

* * *

Q. Do you feel that Dr. Avery deviated from the recognized standard of care in his care and treatment of Mrs. Remington postoperatively? Answer: I see nothing in the records to suggest that.

Q. Is swelling something that you might expect to find after surgery of this type? Answer: Yes.

Q. Would you expect to find some discoloration of the skin after surgery of this type? Answer: Bruising can occur after any surgery.

Q. When you first examined Mrs. Remington in March 1985, was anything discussed in regard to Dr. Avery's treatment of Mrs. Remington? Answer: If it was, it was in a superficial manner.

Q. Have you ever expressed an opinion with reasonable medical probability that Dr. Avery deviated from the standard of care in his treatment of Mrs. Remington? Answer: No, I have not.

Q. Do you have such an opinion? Answer: I have no such opinion.

Q. Can the complications that occurred to Mrs. Remington happen without anyone deviating from the standard of care? Answer: Yes.

Q. Do you have any criticism of Dr. Avery initially placing the implants subcutaneously as opposed to submuscularly? Answer: That is a personal choice of the surgeon. I personally place the implants in the submuscular space, but I think there are surgeons who may still do it the other way.

Q. Do you have any criticism of Dr. Avery performing a prophylactic subcutaneous mastectomy on Mrs. Remington? Answer: She had a family history of breast cancer and cystic disease. The incidence of cancer in such a patient is high.

Q. Do you have any opinions that Dr. Avery fell below the standard of care in his care and treatment of Mrs. Remington? Answer: As I understand it Mrs. Remington underwent a subcutaneous mastectomy with immediate implantation. Subsequently she developed some necrosis of skin. The implants were then removed. A period of time elapsed for the tissue to heal. Then she had reaugmentation by placing the implants under the muscle. I don't have criticism of that sequence.

Q. Based upon the history given to you by Mrs. Remington, have you ever rendered an opinion that the implants should have been removed within 24 to 48 hours after initial surgery? Answer: I don't recall having said that.

Q. Do you have any criticism of the fact that she received two units of blood postoperatively and, while in the recovery room, she had a drop in blood pressure? Answer: No, I seem to recall that the drop in blood pressure was thought to be due to a change of Mrs. Remington's position.

Q. Do you have any criticism of the fact that the Hemovac drains were removed two days later and a fair amount of blood was removed at that time? Answer: No, that sometimes happens.

Q. Dr. Avery noted in Mrs. Remington's medical chart that "skin viability appeared to be intact." Does this indicate anything to you? Answer: That it was his clinical judgment that her skin was okay.

Q. Do you have an opinion based on giving you those additional facts as to whether the implant should have been removed at that time? Answer: Just from what you told me there, I don't have an opinion.

Q. What further things would you be looking for to decide whether to remove the implants? Answer: I would like to know how much blood still remained in the breasts. If the breast pocket is full of blood, I would remove them. If skin viability is intact, however, I would tend not to have me remove them.

Q. Are there any other factors that you would be considering to decide whether the implants should be removed? Answer: If the implant were to show through the incision site, I would remove it. Sometimes it can be saved, but usually if the implant shows through it means it became contaminated and closing it back up may lead to an infection.

Q. What about a situation where you see some sloughing of skin. Is it appropriate to debride and wait until the skin has demarcated before making a decision to remove the implant? Answer: If you have "embarrassed skin" that results in a blistering type of superficial loss of the outer layers of skin but not extending all the way through the layer of skin down to the implant, you might allow the area to heal by itself. By doing this you can avoid two operations: removing the implants and putting them back in.

Q. Now, this is something that only the plastic surgeon that is seeing the patient can really determine; is that not right? **Answer:** Right. It is a difficult decision. I have myself had situations where I have thought about taking out the implant because I felt I was going to lose some skin, but I have waited and it has turned out okay.

Q. Is it your opinion then that unless you are certain there is a full skin thickness to the implant, it is appropriate to leave the implant in place, assuming there is no infection? **Answer:** If there appears to be an area of embarrassed skin, it needs close watching. If it appears to be progressing you might act quicker. So, how long to wait is a clinical judgment call, and it is hard to give you a definite answer without having seen the situation.

Q. From a physiological standpoint, do you have an opinion why Mrs. Remington developed the scarring and disfigurement? **Answer:** I believe it was primarily due to the vascular embarrassment of the skin, assuming she had no infection.

Q. Did you recall making any statement to Mrs. Remington in your office meeting regarding the cause of her breast skin loss and scarring? **Answer:** I think I probably told her that with this procedure there are complications of skin loss with skin slough because the vascular supply is tenuous.

* * *

Q. Is hematoma formation a recognized complication of subcutaneous mastectomy? **Answer:** Yes, because you are prophylactically taking out as much breast tissue as possible, and in doing so you are developing large skin flaps with raw surfaces that ooze blood. In addition, a blood vessel can occasionally bleed after surgery. That is when you develop blood in the breast pocket, or a hematoma.

Q. What is the proper clinical management of a suspected hematoma? **Answer:** It depends on the size of the hematoma. If it is small it can be watched and will eventually dissolve and be reabsorbed. If it continues to get larger, then it would probably be necessary to open the breast, remove the hematoma, stop the bleeding and clean the area out of any remaining blood clot.

* * *

Q. And you have told me that these complications could happen without a surgeon deviating from the required standard of care? **Answer:** Correct.

Document 8.

DR. AVERY'S DEPOSITION OF CLAIRE GARVEY

(Close Personal Friend of Mrs. Remington)
April 1986

Q. Do you remember any conversations with Mrs. Remington in the hospital after she had undergone surgery? <u>Answer:</u> Yes. She kept complaining of a lot of pain. She kept saying she can't lift her arms because it hurts.

Q. When did she start her complaining, three, four, five days after the surgery? <u>Answer:</u> Four or five days after, I would say.

Q. Did you see any black and blue later on in the hospitalization? <u>Answer:</u> Yes.

Q. Did she say anything about the discoloration? <u>Answer:</u> Yes. She said that's the way it's supposed to be after the operation.

Q. Did you ever observe her entire breasts after the operation? <u>Answer:</u> Only when I brought her home from the hospital. She said she wanted her back washed and she took off her bra.

Q. What did you observe? <u>Answer:</u> Blotches of skin were coming off. The red areas right around the nipple didn't really look like much of a nipple, but like a dark mark.

Q. What do you mean? <u>Answer:</u> It just looked bad.

Q. During that second week do you remember discussing anything about what her doctors were recommending her to do? <u>Answer:</u> I remember her saying she should have the transplants taken out.

Q. Did she say that the doctor said that maybe they should be removed? <u>Answer:</u> She said, maybe they should be removed, not that the doctor said that they be removed.

Document 9.

DR. AVERY'S DEPOSITION OF SHEILA ELLIOTT

(Close Personal Friend of Mrs. Remington)
April 1986

Q. Did you see Mrs. Remington while she was in the hospital? Answer: I must have been there daily.

Q. Did you recall anything unusual? Answer: She seemed uncomfortable when she tried to move about.

Q. Do you remember seeing her skin from her waist to her neck while she was in the hospital? Answer: She wore nightgowns which partially exposed the upper part of her breasts.

Q. What could you see? Answer: I could see cleavage.

Q. Did you notice any unusual skin color or texture above her breasts? Answer: They were discolored.

Q. After she went home did she discuss anything with you? Answer: She said her doctors had told her to watch for silver from the implants to show through.

Q. When did she tell you that? Answer: I think it was fairly soon after she was released from the hospital.

Q. Is she any different then when you knew her before the surgery? Answer: Before surgery she was active in the community. After surgery, she became increasingly withdrawn. She became very distressed about her social life. She was less inclined to hear of anyone's romantic lives.

Document 10.

DR. AVERY'S SUPPLEMENTAL INTERROGATORIES TO MRS. REMINGTON
May 1986

1. State the substance of the facts to which each expert listed is expected to testify.

    Because of Mrs. Remington's family history of breast cancer, Dr. Avery did not inform Mrs. Remington of the nature and risks of a bilateral subcutaneous prophylactic mastectomy. Dr. Avery performed an immediate reconstruction of the breasts by inserting the prostheses into the subcutaneous space. During the immediate postoperative period, Mrs. Remington formed hematomas which Dr. Avery simply treated by pulling out the hemovac drains. Eleven days after surgery, Dr. Avery first expressed concern about the skin viability of Mrs. Remington's breasts, but did not treat this impending problem. Shortly thereafter, he went on vacation and was unavailable for two and one-half weeks. He turned the care of Mrs. Remington over to Dr. Reeves who had not seen the patient previously. On the first visit, Dr. Reeves felt that the skin was compromised, but he did not feel that he had a right to surgically treat Mrs. Remington's problem unless the prostheses eroded through the breast skin. Approximately five weeks after surgery, a prosthesis did erode through the skin. Dr. Avery removed the prostheses and, more than a year later, inserted other prostheses. As a result of the foregoing facts and circumstances, Mrs. Remington's breasts became markedly and irreversibly disfigured.

2. State the opinion to which the experts aforementioned are expected to testify.

    — Inadequate disclosure for prophylactic mastectomy.

    — Incorrect ablative technique and approach.

    — Inadequate postoperative monitoring.

3. Give a summary of the grounds or bases of each opinion stated.

    Dr. Avery did not adequately disclose to Mrs. Remington that subcutaneous mastectomy carries a high rate of serious complications.

    Dr. Avery ignored signs and symptoms of increased pressure endangering skin viability.

    Dr. Avery failed to remove the implants when viability of the breast skin was in serious question.

    Dr. Avery did not properly manage the hematomas that formed in Mrs. Remington's breasts.

    Dr. Avery used an outmoded technique in inserting the implant in the subcutaneous rather than the submuscular space.

Document 11.

MRS. REMINGTON'S REQUEST FOR ADMISSIONS TO DR. AVERY
May 1986

SUPERIOR COURT

CIVIL DIVISION

Susan Remington,
               Plaintiff

v.   Civ. A. No. 85–2516

Douglas Avery,
               Defendant

REQUEST FOR ADMISSIONS TO DEFENDANT

The Plaintiff hereby submits the following Request for Admissions pursuant to Rule of Civil Procedure 36(2), which provides:

> The answer shall specifically deny the matter or set forth in detail the reasons why the answering party cannot truthfully admit or deny the matter. A denial shall fairly meet the substance of the requested admission, and when good faith requires that a party qualify the answer or deny only a part of the matter of which an admission is requested, the party shall specify so much of it as is true and qualify or deny the remainder. An answering party may not give lack of information or knowledge as a reason for failure to admit or deny unless the party states that the party has made reasonable inquiry and that the information known or readily obtainable by the party is insufficient to enable the party to admit or deny. All admissions must be responded to within thirty (30) days after service.

1. Skill and diligence in performing breast plastic surgery is governed by a nationwide standard of care. <u>Answer</u>: Admitted.

2. Defendant did not limit the scope of his preoperative disclosure because he expected that it would adversely and substantially affect Mrs. Remington's condition or the outcome of the surgery. <u>Answer</u>: Admitted.

3. Defendant did not set forth the known risk of disfiguring scars which is associated with a subcutaneous mastectomy with immediate subcutaneous insertion of prostheses. <u>Answer</u>: Denied.

4. Defendant's sole treatment for Mrs. Remington's postoperative hematoma formation was removal of the drains and manually squeezing the breasts. <u>Answer</u>: Admitted.

5. The Hemovac drain inserted on August 9, 1983, and removed on August 11, 1983, did not function properly. <u>Answer:</u> Admitted.

6. Defendant was informed by the Hospital personnel that Mrs. Remington had fainted several hours after being returned to her room from the Recovery Room. <u>Answer:</u> Admitted.

7. Defendant undertook no formal training or courses on subcutaneous mastectomies since completion of his Plastic Surgery residency. <u>Answer:</u> Admitted.

8. Defendant was unavailable for advice or consultation to Dr. Reeves between August 21, 1983, and September 6, 1983. <u>Answer:</u> Admitted.

9. Defendant was aware of necrotic changes in Mrs. Remington's breasts August 20, 1983. <u>Answer:</u> Denied.

10. Mrs. Remington did not assure Defendant that she would undergo the surgery proposed by him regardless of the risk involved. <u>Answer:</u> Cannot be admitted or denied.

11. Vascular compromise is a recognized complication of a subcutaneous mastectomy with immediate insertion of a subcutaneous breast implant. <u>Answer:</u> Admitted.

12. Defendant did not unwrap Mrs. Remington's surgical dressing during the first 48 postoperative hours. <u>Answer:</u> Admitted.

13. Skin necrosis and hematoma formation are less likely to occur with a <u>two-stage</u> subcutaneous mastectomy than with a <u>one-stage</u> procedure involving immediate insertion of breast prostheses. <u>Answer:</u> Admitted in part, but other considerations may override this risk.

14. Defendant put an elastic compression dressing on Mrs. Remington's breast wound at the completion of the initial surgery. <u>Answer:</u> Admitted.

15. Preoperatively, Defendant did not precisely discuss advantages and consequences of <u>submuscular,</u> rather than <u>subcutaneous,</u> implantation of the breast prostheses. <u>Answer:</u> Denied.

16. Preoperatively, Defendant did not specifically discuss with Mrs. Remington the consequential differences and effects of <u>delayed,</u> rather than <u>immediate,</u> reconstruction of her breasts. <u>Answer:</u> Admitted.

17. Defendant diagnosed postoperative hematoma between August 11–20, 1983. <u>Answer:</u> Admitted.

§ J. Pretrial Hearing Preparation

Document 12.

PRETRIAL STIPULATION RULES

[Editors' Note: Under general rules like Federal Rule 16, the trial court has adopted local rules that contain the following requirement:]

PRETRIAL STIPULATION. It shall be the duty of counsel for plaintiff to see that the Pretrial Stipulation is drawn, executed by counsel for all parties, and filed with the Clerk prior to the date set for trial. Counsel for all parties are charged with good faith cooperation in this regard. The Pretrial Stipulation shall contain the following in separate numbered paragraphs:

1. A concise statement describing the facts of the case in an impartial, easily understandable manner.

2. A list of all pending motions requiring action by the Court and the dates on which those motions were heard or are set for hearing.

3. A statement of rules of law on which there is agreement, and stipulated facts which require no proof at trial and which may be read to the trier of fact.

4. A statement of all issues of law and fact for determination at trial.

* * *

Document 13.

CONCISE STATEMENT OF FACT

Susan Remington consulted Dr. Avery, a plastic surgeon, about replacing her breast tissue with prosthetic implants because she was concerned about developing breast cancer. Dr. Avery told her that the operation might be complicated by infection, hemorrhage, numbness and sensory changes of the skin and nipples. Dr. Avery performed a bilateral subcutaneous mastectomy with immediate insertion of prostheses into the subcutaneous space of the breast. Eleven days after surgery Dr. Avery told Mrs. Remington that she might need to have the implants removed. Seventeen days later, Dr. Avery noted that Mrs. Remington had evidence bilateral breast skin and nipple necrosis. Ten days after that, Dr. Avery noted there was exposure of one of Mrs. Remington's breast implants. He removed both implants and performed extensive debridement of necrotic breast tissue. Mrs. Remington now has multiple, irregular disfiguring scars over her breasts despite the fact that Dr. Avery has subsequently implanted prostheses under Mrs. Remington's chest muscles.

Document 14.

PLAINTIFF'S PROPOSED PRETRIAL STIPULATIONS OF ISSUES OF LAW FOR DETERMINATION AT TRIAL

1. Did Dr. Avery have a duty to disclose inherent and material risks of surgery in obtaining informed consent from Mrs. Remington for the procedure?

2. Did Dr. Avery have a duty to disclose to Mrs. Remington alternative approaches to dealing with the risk of developing breast cancer?

3. Did Dr. Avery have a duty to disclose to Mrs. Remington that the more breast tissue removed, the less attractive would be the appearance of her breasts?

4. Did Dr. Avery have a duty to provide Mrs. Remington sufficient information concerning advantages and disadvantages of "immediate" versus "delayed" breast implantation?

5. Did Dr. Avery have a duty to provide Mrs. Remington with sufficient information concerning the advantages and disadvantages of "subcutaneous" versus "submuscular" prosthetic implantation?

6. Did Dr. Avery have a duty to adequately monitor Mrs. Remington for well-recognized complications of a subcutaneous mastectomy with immediate implantation reconstruction?

7. Did Dr. Avery have a duty to assess Mrs. Remington's breast viability for specific evidence of breast viability, such as vascular compromise and ischemia?

8. Did Dr. Avery have a duty to perform a specific and focused investigation into the cause of Mrs. Remington's persistent and severe breast pain?

9. Did Dr. Avery have a duty to properly and adequately manage the complication of hematoma formation?

10. If, in fact, Mrs. Remington was "reluctant" to have the implants removed, did Dr. Avery have a duty to explain to her the possible consequences of her reluctance?

11. Did Dr. Avery have a duty, after he determined that there may be problems with skin viability, either to make himself reasonably available, or to provide a qualified substitute experienced in treating Mrs. Remington's problems or condition and who was familiar with Mrs. Remington's surgery and case?

Document 15.

PLAINTIFF'S PROPOSED PRETRIAL STIPULATIONS OF ISSUES OF FACT FOR DETERMINATION AT TRIAL

1. Did Dr. Avery disclose the following information to Mrs. Remington in obtaining her consent to a bilateral prophylactic subcutaneous mastectomy with immediate subcutaneous implantation:

(a) The operation was a "mastectomy" rather than a "scooping-out" of tissues and putting in implants;

(b) The consequence of a hemorrhagic complication may be hematoma formation which might compromise vascularity;

(c) Breasts would not be normal-appearing after the operation;

(d) Vascular compromise was a serious complication of the operation which could devitalize the skin and nipples, ultimately causing scarring and disfigurement;

(e) The risk of vascular compromise would be increased with immediate insertion of the implant;

(f) The risk of vascular compromise would be increased with *subcutaneous*, rather than *submuscular*, insertion of the implant?

2. Did Dr. Avery use the standard approach and technique in caring for Mrs. Remington by:

(a) Inserting the implant into the submuscular space when he knew or should have known that the viability of the skin flap was threatened;

(b) Applying a wrap-around surgical dressing which might have caused excessive external pressure on the breasts, further compromising vascularity?

3. Did Dr. Avery adequately monitor and manage the postoperative complications of a subcutaneous mastectomy by:

(a) not observing Mrs. Remington's breasts during the first 48 hours postoperatively to detect sentinel signs of vascular compromise which would have alerted him to the need to take corrective action before serious irreversible tissue injury resulted;

(b) not fully exposing Mrs. Remington's breasts for examination when she complained of persistent, severe breast pain;

(c) not acting to reasonably assure himself that Mrs. Remington's breast pain was not a premonitory sign of vascular compromise;

(d) not removing the implants at the point he should have detected evidence of hematoma formation, to immediately relieve internal pressure and to reasonably assure himself that the bleeding which caused the hematoma was not continuing;

(e) not investigating the cause and source of bleeding when a nurse made him aware of bloody drainage on the bedsheets;

(f) not replacing blood lost during surgery and the early post-operative period;

(g) not conveying to Mrs. Remington the significance of his opinion that there was threatened loss of viability of breast tissue on the first post-discharge visit?

§ K. Glossary

GLOSSARY OF MEDICAL TERMS RELATING TO BREAST SURGERY

Ablate: To remove a body part, e.g., breast tissue.

Areola: The pigmented area on the breast surrounding the nipple.

Benign: Not cancerous; favorable for recovery.

Bilateral: Pertaining to both sides.

Biopsy: The removal and microscopic examination of tissue for diagnosis. If cancer is evident, the biopsy is referred to as "positive"; if no cancer exists, the biopsy is referred to as "negative."

Breast Augmentation: A procedure to increase the size of the breast.

Cyst: A closed cavity or sac that contains liquid or semi-solid material.

Dermal Integrity: Adequate blood circulation to provide oxygenation necessary for continued viability of skin tissue.

Edema: The presence of abnormally large amounts of fluid in a tissue or organ, characterized by swelling or puffiness.

Fat: Adipose tissue that helps give shape and substance to tissue such as the breast.

Fibrocystic Disease: A benign breast condition consisting of an overgrowth of fibrous tissue often combined with formation of cysts.

Hypoxia: Insufficient oxygenation of tissue.

Implant: A special type of plastic bag filled with silicone gel or saline that is placed under the skin or under the muscle to replace a natural breast.

Ischemia: Insufficient circulation to tissue.

Lump: Any kind of mass in the breast.

Malignant: Cancerous.

Mammography: Low-dose X-ray examination of the breast to detect breast disease.

Mastectomy: Surgical removal of the breast. (See Radical and Subcutaneous Mastectomy.)

Mastodynia: Painful breasts.

Necrosis: An irreversible condition in which tissue dies.

Nipple: The pigmented projection on the breast which is surrounded by, but does not include, the areola.

Pectoralis Muscles: Muscles attached to the chest wall and to the upper arms, divided into a larger group called pectoralis major, and a smaller group called pectoralis minor.

Prognosis: A forecast as to the probable outcome, of a disease or the prospect as to recovery from a disease as indicated by the nature and symptoms of the case.

Prosthesis: An artificial substitute for a missing body part. In the case of a breast prosthesis, the term is often used interchangeably with the term breast implant.

Radical Mastectomy: Surgical removal of the breast, and most of the axillary lymph nodes, leaving the chest muscles intact.

Reconstructive Mammaplasty: Rebuilding of the breast by surgery.

Subcutaneous Mastectomy: Surgical removal of internal breast tissue, leaving the skin, and preserving the nipple, if possible. A prophylactic treatment for breast cancer.

Subpectoral Insertion: Implant inserted below the pectoralis muscle.

Supporting Tissue: Connective tissue which helps give structure to tissue such as the breast.

Total Mastectomy: Surgical removal of internal breast tissue, leaving the skin, but sacrificing the functional use of the nipple/areolar complex.

Vascular Compromise: Insufficient circulation to prevent tissue injury.

Index

The object of the Index is to narrow the area of the reader's search more than the Table of Contents can do. The quickest search uses the narrowest word or phrase, and in the Index, legal terms and medicolegal jargon are listed narrowly—for example, there is no heading for "constitutional law," but "procedural due process of law" and "equal protection of law" are listed. The Index also attempts to list medical specialties, procedures, injuries, and diseases, but on a more general level—for example, "Fuch's dystrophy" is not listed, but "eye disease" is.

Within a case or note, the Index lists only the first occurrence of the topic; it is not a concordance. Where a whole chapter or section deals with an indexed topic, the caption may or may not include the word or phrase indexed, and so the Index entry refers to the entire chapter or section; it is then advisable to consult the Table of Contents in order to refine the search. This is particularly true with respect to the Appendix, which has not been indexed exhaustively.

A

Abandonment of patient, 282
Abbreviations, 82
Abortion, 127, 129, 131, 133, 327
Abuse of process, 156, 190
Access: to courts, 189, 323, 335, 340; to jury, 332; to medical services, 348, Ch. 12 § A
Accident defined, 295
Accreditation of: facilities, 348; specialists, 365
Accreditation Manual for Hospitals, 348, 349
Accrual of negligence claim, 184
Adhesive contract, see Contract of adhesion
Administrative act, 160
Admission of negligence, 99, 100, 108
Admission summary, 397, 415, 419
Admissions, request for, 471
Admitting privileges, see Staff privileges
Adoption records, 276
Advanced payments on claims, 322
Adversary medical examination, 15
Adverse: drug reaction, 236; witness examination, 73
Affirmative defenses, 155, 156, Ch. 6 § B
Aftercare duties, 6
Agency by estoppel, 11
Aggravation: of condition, 152; of harm, 71, 125
AIDS, 250
Allergies and allergic reactions, 175, 210, 236
Alternative: liability, 235; methods of treatment, 206, 218
Ambiguous release, 184

American Board of Medical Legal Consultants, 93
Amphetamines, 384
Amputation of: finger, 122; leg, 151, 212, 358
Anaphylaxis, 210
Anatomical drawings: of breast, 401, 402, 412, 422; use of, 390
Anesthesia and anesthesiologists, 282, 313, 381
Anesthesia record, 404
Aneurysm, 211
Annuity: payment of judgments, 326; value of verdict, 142
Anorectic drugs, 384
Anti-trust law, 377
Antibiotics, 236
Antihistamines, 175
Anxiety, 125; damages, see Mental anguish damages
Apparent agency, 11
Apparent authority, 10
Appendectomy, 198
Apportionment of damages: among tortfeasors, 68; between plaintiff and defendant, 153
Arbitration, 324, 327, 329; statutes, 264, 330
Arm paralysis, 109
Artery graft, 358
Assault and battery, see Battery of patient
Assistant to surgeon, 202
Assumption of risk, 156, 177
Authorization to release records, 84, 85, 305, 366
Autopsy, see Post-mortem examination
Availability of liability insurance, 297

Average qualified practitioner, 29
Avoidable consequences, 118, 152

B

Babies, 195; *see also* Newborn
Back surgery, 15
Bactrim, 236
Bad faith failure to settle case, 307, 310, 316, 318
Bad result, 22
Balance of hardships, 356
Bariatric medicine, 384
Battery of patient, 194, 195, 196, 198, 203, 206, 265, 299
Battle of experts, 79, 144, 336
Belmont Report, 216
Bendectin, 235
Benefit: of bargain damages, *see* Expectancy damages; to patient of research, 281
Benefits rule, 136
Best efforts, 22
Bias of medical experts, 94
Bifurcated trial, 118, 235
Bill collection, 274
Biological mother, 276
Biomedical research, 193, 216
Biopsy, 80, 179, 205
Birth defects, 235
Blindness from treatment, 38
Blood: shield statutes, 249; transfusion, 225, 234, 249
Borrowed servant, 56
Brain damage, 25, 120, 138, 282, 313, 340
Brain death, 285
Breast: anatomy, 401; cancer, Appendix; implants, 402, 403, 412, 423; surgery, Appendix; surgery terms glossary, 477
Burden of proof shifted to defendant, 247
Burns: heat, 160; radiation, 124
Business records exception to hearsay rule, 81

C

Caesarean section, 262
Cancer, 80, 143, 172, 179, 220, 305, Appendix; *see also* particular types of cancer
Cancerophobia, 125
Cap on damages, 234, 326, 327, 340, 354
Captain of the ship, 56, 314
Captive insurer, 295
Cardiac arrest, 230, 290
Casualty insurance, 295
Catheter, 67
Causation: in general, Ch. 5; in release, 189; intentional torts, 194, 203; patient awareness of, 181; medicolegal, 119, 240, 325
Cautery, 160
Cerebral palsy, 120
Certainty of causation, 119, 126

Certificate of merit, 323, 337
Certification of medical specialists, 348, 365
Cervical cancer, 179, 220
Champerty, 74
Chance of: cure, 147; survival, 144, 146, 147
Changing standards of care, 37
Charitable immunity, 57, 156, 160
Charts of patients, 390
Child abuse, 17
Childbirth, 25
Children, *see* Babies, Minors, and Newborn
Chronic vegetative state, 194, 229
Circumstantial evidence defined, 109
Civil Rights Act action, 352
Claim-screening, 324
Claims: experience, 297; reduction, 322, 349
Claims-made insurance, 300, 304
Club insurance, 295
Collateral source, 344
Common knowledge: of jury, 108; of patients, 223
Company nurse, 164
Comparative fault or negligence, 118, 152
Compelling state interest, 226
Compilation of information hearsay exception, 237, 240
Complaint for negligence, 431
Compulsory arbitration, 324
Concealment of malpractice, 268
Concert of action, 68, 71, 186
Concurrent torts, 69, 71, 186
Conditional privilege, *see* Qualified privilege
Conditional res ipsa loquitur, 247
Confidentiality: contract of, 276, 374; defenses to claim for breach, 281; of patient records 51, 88, 218, 275, 306; of peer review proceedings, 368, 369
Conjecture as to causation, 123
Consent: by necessity, 196, 198; in emergency, 197, 200; to human research, Ch. 7 § C; to particular surgeon, 201; and *see* Informed consent
Consent forms, 193, 261, 322, 327, 328, 399
Consortium, 260
Conspiracy of silence, 27, 97
Constructive fraud, 271
Consultation duty, 8, 63, 339
Contingency fund, 295
Contingent fee, 326, 346
Continuous treatment, 296, 325, 338
Contraception, 128, 133, 179, 235, 241
Contract: breach as negligence, 256, 258, 259; of adhesion, 322, 327, 329, 330; theory of informed consent, 196, 198; to cure, 256, 299; to fill out forms, 265; to obtain result, 24, 254, 256, 259; to use method, 254, 262; unenforceable, 256, *see also* Contract of adhesion
Contraindications, 237

Contribution: among tortfeasors, 56, 69, 70, 186; to defense costs, 319
Contributory negligence, 118, 152, 156, 176, 179
Control of: doctors, 157; medical acts, 54; nurses, 57; settlement, 299, 310, 317
Cooperation with insurer, 305
Corneal transplant, 101
Coroner, 290
Corporate: negligence, 62, 65; practice of medicine, 61
Cost containment mechanisms, 358
Counterclaims, 156, 189
Countersuits, 156, 189
Covenant not to sue, 328
Coverage of liability insurance, 298
Credentials review, 365, 369
Criminal acts exclusion, 299

D

Dalkon Shield, 241
Damage sharing and shifting, 55
Damages: defined, 118; details, Ch. 5 § C; for breach of promised result, 255
Dangerousness, 48
Data: defined, 79; discussed, 388
Dead body rights, 287, 291
Deafness, 180
Death defined, 288
Debt collection, 274
Deceit, 270
Declaratory judgment, 308, 384
Defamation, 18, 190, 272, 300, 367
Defective products, Ch. 8
Defense: costs, 298, 319; of medical liability cases, Ch. 6, 219
Defensive medicine, 256, 349
Delegation of: judicial power, 334; sponge count, 106
Demonstrative evidence, 390
Dentistry and dentists, 107, 328, 340
Depositions: discussed, 390; examples, Appendix
Dermatology and dermatologists, 125
DES cases, 235, 276
Devices, 6, 234
Diabetes, 3, 150
Diagnosis error, 17, 60, 70, 80, 113
Diagnostic tests, 219, 234; see also Screening tests
Dilation and curettage, 282
Direct evidence defined, 109
Directed verdict, 79, 115
Disability to: sue, 159; work, 141
Discharge from hospital: order to, 361; summary upon, 413, 418
Discipline: of patient, 195; of professional, 98, 192, 203; see also Legal ethics, and Medical ethics
Disclosure standards for informed consent, Ch. 7 § B
Discomfort euphemism, 120, 218

Discount of damages to present value, 142
Discovery: before complaint, 84; document examples, Appendix; of malpractice, 182, 268, 296, 325, 339; procedures, 78, 369; protective orders, 85
Discretionary function, 159
Disfigurement damages, 255
Disqualification to engage in research, 219
Distributor's liability, 245
DPT cases, 235
Drug effects and interactions, 234, 243
Dual capacity doctrine, 164
Due care standards, 22, Ch. 2 § A
Due process, see Procedural due process of law, and Substantive due process of law
Dumping patients, 352
Duty to: admit patient, 350; assist doctor in emergency, 174; avoid consequences, 119; change address, 180; consult next of kin, 232; consult other doctors, 6, 63; cooperate with doctor, 177; cooperate with insurer, 305; defend insured, 299, 307, 311; fill out benefits form, 264; follow up patient, 179, 241; have emergency room, 5, 14; indemnify insured, 307; inform insured of settlement negotiations, 309, 312, 313; inform patient of risks, Ch. 7—of treatment, § B, and of refusing tests, § D; inquire about treatment, 6; instruct patient, 6, 177, 339; keep confidences, 275; mitigate damages, 119; notify insurer, 305; obtain consent, Ch. 7; provide medical care, Ch. 1; relay information to coroner, 292; release body to next of kin, 289; report diseases and injuries, 281; review treatment, 63, 65; settle within policy limits, 299; treat patient, 3, 174; turn off life-support equipment, 229, 289

E

Ear surgery, 196
Earning capacity loss, 140, 145, 149
Economists' projections, 119, 140
Embolization, 212
Emergency: consent implied, 197, 200, 204; defined, 170, 173; in hospital, 172
Emergency room: duty to maintain, 10; services, 3, 10, 65, 72, 331, 351, 352
Emotional damages, see Mental anguish damages
Emotional distress: intentional infliction of, 265, 273, 276; negligent infliction of, 44, 132, 286, 291
Employee: doctor, 60, 157; immunity, 156, 164; nurse, 164; relationship, 156, 164
Enterprise liability, 10
Equal protection of law, 250, 335, 343, 345
Equitable estoppel, 268, 376

Estoppel: agency by, 11; contract by, 376; to invoke statute of limitations, 268
Ethical drug, 242
Ethics: see Legal ethics, and Medical ethics; see also Discipline
Event defined, 295
Evidence of medical negligence, Ch. 4, Appendix; process of gathering, 388
Excess insurance, 315
Excess liability, 308, 313
Excessive damages in verdict, 139
Excessive surgery, 354
Exclusions from insurance coverage, 299
Exclusive remedy: of military, 159; of workers, 164, 166
Exculpatory clause, 328
Exemplary damages, see Punitive damages
Existing dispute arbitration, 324
Expectancy damages, 257, 260
Expenses of raising: defective child, 128, 132; healthy child, 132, 133, 136
Experimental: defined, 216; treatment, Ch. 7 § C, 232
Expert: advisory panel, 331; jury, 337
Expert medical testimony: admission of defendant, 100; causation, 121; defendant as plaintiff's expert, 102; intimidation of experts, 96; not required, 10; qualifications of witnesses, 25, 90, 92; textbook as, 102, 105; use of, 79
Exploratory surgery, 35
Extension of operation, 199
Eye: disease, 101; lid injury, 79

F

Face injury, 107
Facts: defined, 79; discussed, 388
Fair interpretation of evidence by jury, 115
Federal Tort Claims Act (FTCA), 145, 159, 181, 346
Fellow employee rule, 164
Fiduciary: duty, 312; relation of doctor and patient, 199, 222
Financial interest of medical experts, 94
Finger: amputation, 122; bite, 195
First Amendment privileges, 381
Fishing expedition, 78
Fluid intake and output record, 411
Food and Drug Administration, 217
Foreign medical graduates, 364
Foreign object left in body, 106, 112, 246; see also Sponge
Foreseeability of person, 20, 132, 191
Form completion duty, 264
Fractures: femur, 185; hip, 6; jaw, 328; knee, 23; spine, 72
Fraud, 232, 269, 312
Free exercise of religion, 225
Frivolous: actions, 190, 323; pleadings and motions, 156
Funeral expenses, 149
Future dispute arbitration, 324, 327, 329

Future wages, see Earning capacity loss

G

Gall bladder, 35, 206
General: deterrence, 193; verdict, 37
Genetic: counseling, 127; defects, 120, 127
Ghost surgery, 201
Glaucoma, 30, 33
Glossary of breast surgery terms, 477
Going bare, 297
Good result promised, 24
Good Samaritan statutes, 47, 156, 167, 172
Governmental immunity, 155, 156, 159, 182
Gross negligence, 170, 172
Group practice, 201
Guinea pigs for research, 216
Gunshot wounds, 211
Gynecology and gynecologists, 105, 108, 133, 179, 241; see also Obstetrics and obstetricians

H

Halcion, 243
Harms from medical liability, Ch. 5 § B
Health care: delivery course, 350; provider defined, 349
Health maintenance organization (HMO), 60
Hearing loss, 180
Heart: arrest, 230; disease, 113, 350; surgery, 99
Hematology report, 411
Hematoma in breast, 412
Hemophilia, 127
Hepatitis, 253
Hill–Burton Act, 351
Hindsight in informed consent, 209
Hold-harmless agreement, 328
Homosexuality, 17
Hospital: bill collection, 274; bylaws, 5, 14; organization, 349; staff privileges, 54, 62, 364, 369, 374, 377; records admissibility, 81; treating patients, Ch. 3 § B, 162
Hospitalization: discharge, 361; insurance, 273; utilization review, 358
Human research, 194, Ch. 7 § C
Hysterectomy, 105, 108

I

Identity of operating surgeon, 210
Immunity, 155, Ch. 6 § A, 234, 236; of United States employee, 156; personal, 160; and see type, such as Charitable immunity; see also Confidentiality, and see Privileged communications
Impact rule, 132
Impeachment of expert witnesses, 90, 93
Implanted: device, 6, 241; prosthesis, 403

Implied consent, 231; and see Emergency
In limine motion, 120
Incident: defined, 295; expenses of, 322; report, 308, 349
Incompetent patients, 229
Indemnification among defendants, 55, 70
Indemnity insurance, 298
Independent contractor, 10, 61, 63, 157, 162, 164, 167
Indigent patients, 351, 352
Individual rights, 193
Indivisible injury, 68
Infants, see Minors, and see Newborns
Infection, 169, 180
Inference of medical negligence, 110
Inflation and verdict amount, 142
Informed consent, Ch. 7, especially § B; 327; statutes, 208, 212; see also Lay standard of disclosure, and see Medical standard of disclosure, 327
Inherent function of hospital, 64
Injunction, see Permanent injunction, and see Preliminary injunction
Inquiry duty, 7
Institutional review boards, 194, 215
Insurance, Ch. 10; construction of policy, 304; benefits form, 264; of charitable hospitals, 162; terms defined, 295
Insurer influence on trial, 72, 313
Insuring clauses, 299
Intent: to harm in battery, 197; to sue notice, 323
Intentional: acts exclusion, 299; infliction of emotional distress, see Emotional distress
Interaction of drugs, 234, 243
Interrogatory examples, Appendix
Intervening cause, 178
Intimidation of witness, 96
Intrauterine device, 241
Invasion of privacy, 382
Irrebuttable presumption, 213, 341

J

JCAH Manual, 14
Jehovah's Witnesses, 225
Jewett nail, 6
Joinder of defendants, 55
Joint: liability, 235; tortfeasors, Ch. 3 § C, 186; see also Contribution among tortfeasors
Joint Committee on Accreditation of Hospitals, 14, 348, 349
Joint underwriting associations, 297
Judge's discretion in weighing verdict, 115
Judgment notwithstanding the verdict, 79, 235
Judicial decisions for incompetent patients, 230
Jury discretion, 115
Jury trial: problems, 325; right to, 159, 332, 337, 341

Justification defense, 194, 195, 281

K

Keloid scar, 107
Kidney: biopsy, 205; damage, 10; infection, 236; stones, 201
Knee injury, 23, 211

L

Label warning, 244
Laboratory reports, 411
Laches defense, 269
Lahey technique, 41
Laminectomy, 245
Laparotomy sponge, 56, 105
Lay: intermediary, 348; standard of disclosure, 194, 207, 210; see also Medical standard of disclosure
Learned intermediary, 235, 244
Leg injury, 70, 168, 358
Legal: ethics, 121; expense shifting, 323, 324; malpractice, see Malpractice
Letters by doctors, 18, 272
Liability: defined, 118; insurance, 296, 298; see also Insurance
Liability without fault, see Strict liability
Libel, 272; see also Defamation
Life-support equipment, 229, 286
Limitation of actions, see Statute of limitations
Limited new trial, 118, 154
Litigation system changes, Ch. 11
Liver injury, 36
Locality rules, 25
Long-tail problems, 325, 338
Lookback program, 250
Loss: exposure, 296; of society damages, 140; reserve, 295
Lost wages, see Wage loss damages
Lou Gehrig's disease, 229
Lumbar puncture, 243
Lung cancer, 143
Lupus erythematosus, 205
Lymphoma, 309

M

Maintenance, 74
Malice, 369
Malicious prosecution, 156, 190
Malpractice: defined, Ch. 1, esp. 19; insurance, Ch. 10, and see Insurance; legal, 191, 309; reform legislation, 322
Mammogram, 392
Managed care, 349
Manufacturers' liability, 235, 243
Market share apportionment of damages, 235
Mary Carter agreement, 56, 72, 76
Mastectomy, Appendix
Master and servant, 54

Maximum damages, 234; see also Cap on damages
Mediation, 324
Medi–Cal Act, 358
Medical: act, 160; certainty, 119; charts, 390; discipline, 98, 348, 378; ethics 5, 203, 226; evidence of negligence, Ch. 4, especially § A; examination, 15; examiner boards, 348, 378; examiners, see Post mortem examination; excuse for absence from work, 264; expenses of raising child, 130, 132, 135; expert locators, 92; expert witnesses, Ch. 4 § B; liability insurance, Ch. 10, and see Insurance; locality, 28; malpractice, see Malpractice; negligence, Ch. 2; professional relationship, Ch. 1; research, Ch. 7 § C; scientific evidence, 79; societies, 348; standard of disclosure, 194, 208, 210; testimony, see Expert medical testimony; tests, see Diagnostic tests, and see Screening tests; textbooks as evidence, 102
Medical Injury Compensation Reform Act, see MICRA
Medical liability: claim costs, 327; crisis, 294, 321, 333, 344; of United States, 159
Medical records: patient's right to see, 84, 305; see also Confidentiality
Medicare reimbursement, 354
Medication record, 410
Medicolegal consultants, 93
Meningitis, 53
Mental anguish damages, 131, 132, 203, 232, 258, 263
Metastasis, 143
Method of treatment promised, see Contract
MICRA, 322, 326, 330, 346
Military medical liability claims, 156, 159
Minors: expenses of medical care to, 132; parent's refusal of blood transfusion, 225; statutes of limitation for, 325, 339, 340
Misrepresentation, 254, Ch. 9 § B
Missing witness charge, 81
Mitigation of damages, 119, 152
Model Health–Care Consent Act, 194
Model Health Care Provider Liability Reform Act, 322
Modified control test, 157
Mootness, 225
Murder by patient, 48
Mutual insurance company, 295

N

National Childhood Vaccine Injury Act of 1986, p. 236
National Institutes of Health, 217
National standard of care, 25
Necrosis of tissue, 416

Needle: biopsy, 208; break, 99
Negligence: defined, 22; medical negligence in general, Ch. 2; per se, 106
Negligent: diagnosis, 23, 30; failure to examine others, 53; failure to warn others, 48; infliction of emotional distress, see Emotional distress; prognosis, 48; psychotherapy, 43; staff selection, 476; supervision by hospital, 11, 371; treatment, 23, 25, 35; use of obsolete treatment, 37, 40
Neomycin side-effects, 180
Nerve damage, 267
Neurosurgeons and neurosurgery, 97, 245, 264
New trial, 79, 114, 325; limited to damages, 118, 140, 154, 261, 290
Newborn, 25, 37, 262, 276
Next of kin rights in dead body, 287
Nominal damages, 199
Non-delegable duty, 10, 63, 311
Non-disclosure, 232, 268
Non-economic damages, 326
Non-medical acts, Ch. 9
Non-pecuniary damages, 119, 120, 149, 277, 326
Non-waiver agreement, 308
Nose surgery, 255
Nuisance actions, 323
Nurses, 56, 164
Nursing progress record, 407

O

Obesity, 384
Obsolete treatment, 37, 40
Obstetrics and obstetricians, 25, 37, 120, 262, 300, 327; see also Gynecology and gynecologists
Occurrence insurance policy, 302
Office records: admissibility, 81; examples, 395, 396, 414
Offsetting benefits of healthy child, 136
Ombudsmen, 322
On-call physician: emergency room, 3; witness, 325
Open biopsy, 208
Operative notes, 400, 417, 421
Ophthalmologists and ophthalmology, 30, 33, 79, 101
Opinion of expert defined, 79
Organ transplantation, 285
Orthopedics and orthopedic surgeons, 7, 44, 96, 185, 338
Ostensible agency, 11, 64
Osteopathy and osteopaths, 90
Osteoporosis, 175
Outrageous conduct, 275, 276
Ovarian: cyst, 198; tumor, 172
Overpromotion of drugs, 238
Oxygen treatment for premature newborns, 37

P

Package insert, 7, 237, 241, 243
Pain and suffering damages, 120, 135, 142, 145, 232, 255, 257, 260, 263
Pap test, 179, 220
Paralysis, 109, 244, 267
Paranoia, 48
Parens patriae, 228
Parents' services damages, 141
Parol evidence rule, 189, 261
Partial disability damages, 140
Particularly susceptible victim, 152
Partisanship of medical experts, 94
Pathology and pathologists' reports, 413, 418, 425
Patient dumping, 352; medical records, 79, 305
Pecuniary damages, 118, 149, 326
Pediatricians and pediatrics, 37
Peer review, 44, 355, Ch. 12 § C
Per diem pain and suffering argument, 142
Performance standards, 349
Periodic payment of judgment, 326
Permanent injunction, 384
Persistent vegetative state, 194, 229
Personal: belief of counsel, 121; immunity, 160
Pharmacology and pharmacologists, 238
Phlebitis, 198
Photographs as evidence, 390
Physical examination, 15
Physician: progress record, 406; reports admissibility, 81
Physician-patient relationship, Ch. 1, 199, 242, 268
Physician's Desk Reference (PDR), 237, 243
Physician's orders, Appendix
Pituitary rongeur, 245
Plastic surgery and surgeons, 79, 122, 255, Appendix
Pleading negligence in multiple counts, 35
Podiatry and podiatrists, 150
Policy limits, 307, 308
Possibility of harm, 119, 126
Post mortem examination, 175, 290
Power to refuse treatment, Ch. 7
Practice defined, 216
Pre-litigation discovery, 84
Preemption of state law, 219, 235, 347, 353
Preexisting condition, 152
Preliminary injunction, 356
Premature: discharge from hospital, 358; infant, 37
Premium for insurance, 296
Prenatal: injuries, 129; testing, 127
Prepaid health care plan, 60
Pressure test for glaucoma, 30
Pretrial: rules, 473; statement of facts, 473; issues of law, 474; issues of fact, 476
Privacy right: common law, 232, 276, 382; constitutional, 90, 225, 278
Privilege: to report patient information, 281; to touch, 197; to withhold information from patient, 208; *see also* Qualified privilege, and *see* Confidentiality
Privileged communications: patient confidences, 78, 87; peer review, 368, 369
Privileges, *see* Staff privileges
Privity of contract, 191
Probability of causation, 124
Procedural due process of law, 333, 341, 356
Proctor of surgeons, 44
Product liability, Ch. 8
Professional: relationship, Ch. 1; service corporation, 62; witness, 92
Proffer of excluded evidence, 239
Prognosis, 48
Promise of result or method, *see* Contract
Proprietary hospital, 164
Prospective utilization review, 358
Protection of human subjects, 216
Protective order, 85
Protocol for research, 216
Proximate cause, *see* Causation
Psychiatrists and psychiatry, 43, 48, 85, 304, 430
Psychologists, 17, 85
Psychotherapist-patient privileged communications, 87, 90
Public: hospitals, 164, 350; liability, 254
Publication of defamation, 273, 367
Punitive damages, 44, 135, 203, 233, 272, 300, 304, 331, 339
Pyelogram, 210

Q

Qualifications of expert witnesses, 25
Qualified privilege: to defame, 273, 364; to invade privacy, 382
Quality: assurance, 322, 349, 375; of care, 348

R

Radiodermatitis, 125
Radiology and radiologists, 72, 124, 143, 168, 212
Reasonable medical certainty, 119
Reasonably competent practitioner standard, 29
Reattachment of fingers, 122
Reciprocal insurer, 295
Recovery room record, 405
Refusal: evidence of 231; of harvest of organs, 285; of treatment, Ch. 7, especially § D; to treat, 4
Reinsurance, 295
Relationships of: physician and patient, Ch. 1; primary care physician and specialist, 6

Release of: claim, 66, 156, 185, 312; records, 366; rights, 218, 322
Reliance: damages, 257; on misrepresentations, 268
Religious beliefs, 225
Remittitur, 92, 140, 325
Renal artery damage, 10
Request for admissions, 472
Res ipsa loquitur, 100, 110, 247
Res judicata, 312
Research: defined, 216; on humans, Ch. 7 § C
Reservation of insurer's rights, 308
Resident doctor, 204
Respondeat superior, 10, 54, Ch. 3 § A, 161, 312
Resting comfortably euphemism, 120
Restitution damages, 257
Restraint of trade, 377
Result promised, see Contract
Resuscitation, 230
Retroactive date of insurance, 301
Retrolental fibroplasia (RLF), 37
Retrospective utilization review, 354, 358
Right: not to be born, 129; to be informed, Ch. 7; to know who operates, 201; -to-life statutes, 130, 134; to refuse or regulate treatment, Ch. 7; to remain silent, 103
Risk: avoidance, 193; exposure, 296; management, 322, 349; of research, Ch. 7 § C; treatment, Ch. 7
Rule 11 sanctions, 156, 190, 323

S

Same injury requirement, 71
Sanctions under Rule 11, pp. 156, 323
Satisfaction of judgment, 156
Schizophrenia, 48
Schools of practice, 90
Screening: panels, 139, 264, 324, 331, 353; tests, 30, 219, and see Diagnostic tests
Second injury damages, 153
Seizure disorder, 121
Self-defense, 195
Self-insurer, 295
Self-publication of defamation, 368
Separation of powers, 342
Settlement of cases, 56, 66, 72, 156, 191, 299, 309, 312, 313, 323
Several tort liability, 69, 187, 235, 326
Sexual relations and treatment, 4
Sherman Act, 378
Side-effects, Ch. 8, 235, 236
Silicone gel prosthesis, 403; implanted, 402, 412, 422
Similar locality standard of care, 26
Slander, 18; see also Defamation
Slap, 195
Social workers, 44
Society loss damages, 140
Sole cause, 118

Special: damages defined, 118; injury in malicious prosecution, 190; interrogatories, 246, 286, 325; legislation, 342; relationship, 47, 53; verdict, 37, 114
Specialists' standard of care, 28
Specials defined, 118
Speculative causation, 146
Spine injury, 15
Splenectomy, 138
Sponge: count, 56, 105; in incision, 338
Spurious claims, 323
Stabilizing treatment, 353
Staff privileges, 54, 62, 158, 364, 369, 374, 377
Standards of care, 25, 104; changes in, 37
State action: under Civil Rights Act, 352; under Sherman Anti-trust Act, 378
State boards of medical examiners, 348, 379
State interest, 226
Status of doctor and patient, 199, 242
Statute of limitations, 156, 181, 256, 259, 267, 273, 303, 325, 338
Sterilization as contraception, 128, 133, 260
Steroids, 175
Stillbirth, 262
Stock insurance company, 295
Strict liability, 32, 55, 59, 234, 240, 244, 245, 299, 354
Stroke, 164, 235
Structured settlements, 327
Subpoena, 83, 325, 369
Subrogation, 317
Substantive due process of law, 333, 342
Successive torts, 71, 186
Sufficiency of evidence, 115
Suicide, 226, 284
Summary judgment, 79, 171
Surgeons and surgery, see names of surgical specialists, specialties, and procedures
Surgeon's identity, 201
Surgical: encore, 199; sponge, 105, 338
Survival: actions for death, 148; rates for cancer, 145
Swine flu vaccine, 160, 236

T

Tagamet, 243
Technological imperative, 193
Terminal illness, 229, 231
Termination of research, 219
Textbook as expert medical evidence, 102, 105
Therapeutic reassurance, 256, 263
Thoracic surgery, 374
Thyroidectomy, 40
Tiger lily, 91
Time of death, 288
Tooth extraction, 107
Tort reform, Ch. 11; legislation, 322
Transfer of patients, 352

Transfusion of blood, 225, 234
Transplantation of organs, 285
Trial preparation: materials, 78, Appendix; process, 388
Tubal ligation, 260

U

Unconscionable contract, 330
Undertaking to: fill out benefits form, 266; inform coroner, 292
Uniform Determination of Death Act, 288
Unit of time pain and suffering argument, 142
United States: medical employees, 157; immunity, 156, 159
Urology and urologists, 156, 201, 205, 236
Utilization review, 349, Ch. 12 § B

V

Vaccination, 228
Vaccine manufacturers' liability, 234, 235
Vascular surgeons and surgery, 358, 377
Vegetative state, 194, 229
Venue, 19
Verdict against clear weight of evidence, 79, 114
Verdicts, 325, 326
Viable alternative methods, 206
Vicarious liability, 10, 54, Ch. 3 § A, 312
Videotape, 84
Voluntary: hospitals, 163; participation in research, 218

W

Wage loss damages, 135, 145, 264; *see also* Earning capacity loss
Waiver of: governmental immunity, 155, 159, 182; patients' rights, 78, 87, 162, 218, 322, 327, 328; physicians' rights, 366
Warranty of: merchantability or fitness, 245, 249; result, 256, 260
Weight of evidence, 79, 114, 325
Willful or wanton acts or omissions, 170
Withdrawal from: research, 219; treating patient, 282
Withholding information from patient, 208
Work product, 78
Workers' compensation, 15, 156, 164, 349
Wrongful autopsy, 291
Wrongful birth: defined, 127; applied, 130
Wrongful conception: 128, 133
Wrongful death and survival, 143, 148, 175
Wrongful life: damages, 128; defined, 128
Wrongful pregnancy, *see* Wrongful conception

X

X-ray treatment, 124

Z

Zone of danger rule, 132